Software product lines and generative programming offer the potential for breathtaking improvements in software cost, time to market, and flexibility. *Software Factories* is the definitive source for applying these technologies in a real business context.

—*Paul C. Clements*
Senior Technical Staff Member at the Software Engineering Institute, Co-author of Software Product Lines: Practices and Patterns

Software Factories integrates the best of the emerging approaches to software development, including patterns, frameworks, components, and generative development. Although the book is visionary, it is also firmly grounded in reality. Focusing on the combination of software product lines and domain-specific languages, *Software Factories* gives the reader both a very deep understanding of the technologies underlying software factories and practical insights about their application. This book is a true landmark in the field of generative software development!

—*Krzysztof Czarnecki*
Assistant Professor of Electrical & Computer Engineering, University of Waterloo, Co-author of Generative Programming: Methods, Tools, and Applications

Software Factories: Assembling Applications with Patterns, Models, Frameworks, and Tools

Jack Greenfield
Keith Short

Wiley Publishing, Inc.

Software Factories: Assembling Applications with Patterns, Models, Frameworks, and Tools

Published by
Wiley Publishing, Inc.
10475 Crosspoint Boulevard
Indianapolis, IN 46256
www.wiley.com

For general information on our other products and services please contact our Customer Care Department within the United States at (800) 762-2974, outside the United States at (317) 572-3993 or fax (317) 572-4002.

Wiley also publishes its books in a variety of electronic formats. Some content that appears in print may not be available in electronic books.

Library of Congress Cataloging-in-Publication Data:

ISBN: 0-471-20284-3

Printed in the United States of America

10 9 8 7 6 5 4 3

To Julie, Leigh Ann, Emily and Meg, for supporting my work on this book so graciously, and for being so patient through all the weekends, evenings and days at the beach without Dad. Thank you. I love you all very much.

—JG

To Rebecca, Hannah and Matthew who have cheered from the sidelines, offering encouragement when it was needed, and selflessly supported a husband and father working on a book in addition to a demanding day job.

—KS

Credits

Vice President and Executive Group Publisher
Richard Swadley

Vice President and Publisher
Joseph B. Wikert

Executive Editor
Robert Elliott

Editorial Manager
Kathryn A. Malm

Development Editor
Kenyon Brown

Senior Production Editor
Angela Smith

Text Design & Composition
TechBooks

Contents

Preface

Marx had a vision of the pianist as a performer who produced something that couldn't be commoditized. Then along came the recording, a commoditization of the pianist's art.

John Markoff

This book is about the industrialization of software development. A quick review of the scorecard for the last decade shows only marginal improvements in the productivity of software development or the quality of software products. Most software today is still developed by hand from scratch using labor-intensive methods. As a result, software development is slow and expensive, and yields products containing serious defects that cause problems of usability, reliability, performance, and security. These problems are symptoms of success, created by growing customer demand. As the industry matures, however, it must grow beyond the methods that brought it to this point, and adopt the patterns of industrialization demonstrated by neighboring industries. These include assembling products from components, automating rote or menial tasks, forming product lines and supply chains, and standardizing processes, architectures, and packaging formats. In this book, we offer a road map for a transition from craftsmanship to manufacturing in the software industry, and we describe the critical innovations that make it possible today.

Software Factories in a Nutshell

Business applications are the new frontier.

For most of the past two decades, the software industry has focused on system and personal productivity software. Now, it is turning its attention to the applications that automate business processes. This change in focus is manifested by increasing levels of investment in tools for business application development and in platforms for their execution.

Higher levels of automation are making architectural complexity increase, and requirements and platforms change more rapidly.

As businesses seek higher levels of automation, they are demanding much richer functionality, and imposing more stringent quality of service requirements to ensure the integrity and availability of business critical data and operations. This is creating increasing architectural complexity. With the migration now under way from multitier architectures to service-oriented architectures, applications must now provide secure programmatic access to partners and customers to support business integration. At the same time, requirements are changing more rapidly, as global connectivity breaks down traditional barriers to competition, and lets customers and partners participate more directly in internal business processes. Applications must get to market faster, and change more often than in the past. Platform technology is also moving rapidly to support these new requirements, replacing the traditional notion of development with continuous incremental maintenance and enhancement.

The fundamental forces in software development are complexity and change.

Perhaps not surprisingly, the industry is having trouble meeting expectations. One of the most visible manifestations is the acute shortage of qualified developers. The skilled labor bottleneck has led to rapidly escalating costs, time to market delays, and widespread problems with reliability, security, and performance. Of course, software development has always been a challenging endeavor, and the fundamental forces that make it so remain the same. Indeed, the history of software development can be seen as an ongoing assault against complexity and change, with gains countered by losses, as customers respond to innovation with increasing demands. As happens from time to time in this struggle, we are now at a point where current methods and practices are no longer adequate to sustain forward momentum, and new ones are needed.

The exhaustion of current methods and practices is demonstrated by chronic problems.

As on such occasions in the past, the exhaustion of current methods and practices is demonstrated by a growing sense of urgency and frustration regarding a number of chronic problems that have stubbornly resisted solution. This time, the problems are the difficulty of finding and closing security holes, the difficulty of making components that worked in the lab do the same in production, the inability to achieve commercially significant levels of reuse despite the pervasive adoption of object technology, and the difficulty of striking the right balance between preserving the agility of individual teams and providing enough process to support cross-team collaboration. Of course, these problems are merely symptoms of deeper ones that reflect fundamental flaws in the way we build software. As we will show in this book, the root causes fall into four major categories: monolithic construction, excessive generality, one-off development, and process immaturity.

Of course, we wrote this book not only to document problems with current methods and practices, but also to propose a way to solve them. Clearly, great progress has been made in reducing the time and effort required to build software, and improving the usability, reliability, performance, and supportability of the resulting products. Some tasks are now much easier than they once were. For example, fetching data from storage to satisfy certain criteria is now much easier than it was before the advent of database management systems and declarative query languages. Similarly, constructing a graphical user interface is now much easier than it was before the advent of user interface widget frameworks and WYSIWYG editors. Looking closely at how this progress was realized, we find a recurring pattern that integrates four practices to automate software development tasks. A framework is developed to enable the development of products based on a common architectural style by adapting, configuring and assembling framework components. A language is then defined to support the assembly process and automated by tools. The tools then help developers engage customers and respond rapidly to changes in requirements by building software incrementally, keeping it building and running as changes are made, and capturing design decisions in a form that directly produces executables.

A recurring pattern that yields significant productivity gains is automating software development tasks by integrating languages, patterns, frameworks and tools.

Currently, providing this kind of automation is extremely expensive, and only makes economic sense in broad horizontal domains, such as user interface construction and data access. We intend to show how new technologies can be used to dramatically reduce the cost of providing this kind of automation, making it economically feasible to realize the resulting

New technologies make automation cheaper.

productivity gains in narrow vertical domains, such as health care and financial services.

A Software Factory produces unique variants of an archetypical product.

Our approach is based on a concept called Software Factories. A Software Factory, as we define the term, is a configuration of languages, patterns, frameworks, and tools that can be used to rapidly and cheaply produce an open-ended set of unique variants of an archetypical product. Software Factories are not just about automating software development within an individual organization, however. Broad adoption of Software Factories will promote the formation of supply chains, distributing cost and risk across networks of specialized, and interdependent suppliers. It will also promote software mass customization by increasing value chain integration within each supplier.

Embracing Change as an Industry

Further productivity gains require a different economic model.

One of the most difficult challenges on an industrial scale is a significant discontinuity between old and new ways of doing things. The languages, patterns, frameworks, and tools that provide automation today are produced by platform vendors and consumed by the rest of the industry. We are now at a point where this economic model will no longer work. In order to realize further productivity gains, these assets must become more vertically focused, providing much more value for solving much smaller classes of problems. This presents two problems: 1) markets for vertically focused assets are much smaller than markets for horizontally focused ones, and 2) domain knowledge is housed mainly in end user organizations, not in traditional software suppliers.

The industry is at the threshold of a major transition.

As a rule, industries resist change. The software industry, being no exception, has long resisted industrialization. Like the last row house on a block of skyscrapers, it remains a cottage industry, reliant on the craftsmanship of skilled individuals engaged in labor-intensive manual tasks, while its neighbors have moved on to more modern methods. We think the time for industrialization has finally come, however, and that the industry is at the threshold of a transition that will reshape it radically over the next 10 years.

The ideal project is the exception not the rule.

Some of our peers see things differently. Some say software development cannot be industrialized because of its creative character. Others say that we understate the potential for further gains using current methods and practices. We understand these perspectives. Skilled developers can indeed build high quality software by hand from scratch on time and within budget. The problem, however, is that these experiences are the exception, not the rule.

We therefore challenge our colleagues to consider our message carefully, and not to dismiss it quickly as a misguided attempt to reduce an inherently creative discipline into a purely mechanical and deterministic one. On the contrary, we propose to make software development even more creative by promoting the use of methods that will bring it closer to the real-world problems it is intended to solve, and by leaving more of the mechanical and deterministic aspects of the process to tools. To that end, we have tried to identify the problems that are keeping the industry from moving forward, and solutions that will enable it to meet the demands of an increasingly computerized society.

We challenge our colleagues to consider our message carefully.

The changes we propose are similar to the changes that replaced the methods and practices of earlier generations, giving us the ones we now have. Those who are old enough to remember may recall that object orientation was seen as quite threatening by the industry when it initially appeared, and that its adoption was agonizingly slow. Objects are now mainstream, of course, a sure sign that the time is ripe for change. Now, as then, most of the industry will balk at strange sounding ideas that threaten established practices. But now, as then, ideas that make software development faster, easier, and cheaper will ultimately change the industry.

Ideas that make software development faster, easier and cheaper change the industry.

Road Map to the Rest of the Book

The road map shown in Figure FM.1 explains how each chapter of this book fits into its overall structure. As indicated by the illustration, this book has three parts.

Part I introduces Software Factories. Chapter 1 presents an example used throughout the book and looks at challenges facing software developers. Chapter 2 describes the problem of complexity and looks at current methods and practices for dealing with it. Chapter 3 describes the problem of change and looks at current methods and practices for dealing with it. Chapter 4 describes chronic problems that object orientation

Part I introduces Software Factories.

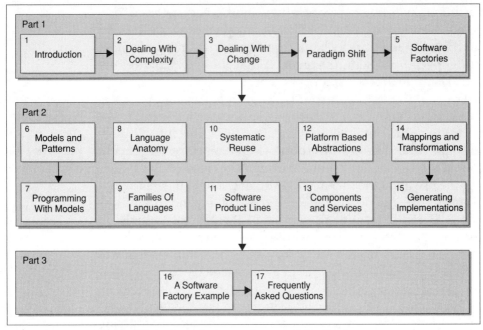

Figure FM.1   A road map to the rest of the book

has not been able to overcome, and introduces critical innovations that form the basis of Software Factories. Chapter 5
describes Software Factories in detail and presents a vision of
industrialization.

Part II describes the critical innovations introduced in Part I, and contains threads that can be read in parallel.

Part II consists of several threads, each describing one of the
critical innovations introduced in Part I. While the threads can
easily be read in parallel, the chapters in each thread should be
read sequentially.

- Chapters 6 through 9 discuss model driven
  development. Chapters 6 and 7 describe models,
  patterns, and programming with models. Chapters 8
  and 9 explore language anatomy and tools for building
  families of languages.

- Chapters 10 and 11 discuss family-based development.
  Chapter 10 lays the groundwork by describing
  systematic reuse. Chapter 11 describes software product
  lines, one of the most important innovations.

- Chapters 12 and 13 discuss development by assembly.
  Chapter 12 looks at platform-based abstractions,
  including classes, libraries, and frameworks, and

Chapter 13 discusses components and services, and introduces the concept of assembly by orchestration.

■ Chapters 14 and 15 discuss generative programming. Chapter 14 talks about mappings and transformations. Chapter 15 then looks at how code and other implementation artifacts can be generated from models.

Part III reviews concepts introduced in Part I, drawing on material presented in Part II, and brings the book to its conclusion. Chapter 16 presents an example of a Software Factory, and Chapter 17 answers Frequently Asked Questions. There are also two appendices following Chapter 17. Appendix A describes forms of abstraction and refinement, and Appendix B discusses the strengths and weaknesses of the Unified Modeling Language.

Part III brings the book to its conclusion

For a quick overview of Software Factories, read the beginning of Chapter 1, Chapter 5, Chapter 16, and Chapter 17. For an overview of the critical innovations that make them possible, read Chapter 4. For insights regarding problems with current methods and practices addressed by Software Factories, read the rest of Chapter 1, Chapter 2, and Chapter 3. For detailed discussions of the critical innovations, read Chapters 6 through 15.

How to read the book.

For More Information

For more information on Software Factories, visit the Software Factories web site, at http://www.softwarefactories.com.

Acknowledgments

Special thanks go to several people. Steve Cook and Stuart Kent, our guest authors and coworkers, have contributed in every possible way, publishing papers that influenced our thinking, engaging us in discussion, reviewing drafts and providing constructive criticism, and, of course, contributing two chapters and an appendix to the book on one of its most important topics.

Thanks to Steve Cook and Stuart Kent.

John Crupi is a long-time friend and supporter, contributing to our grasp of this subject through many productive discussions, reviewing many chapters, providing valuable criticism, and of course, writing the foreword, for which we are truly grateful.

Thanks to John Crupi.

Doug Schmidt was a major source of motivation and encouragement. In addition to providing particularly insightful comments, as a leading authority on patterns, models and generative systems, he was always ready to help, and was always encouraging, even when pointing out things that needed improvement. His enthusiastic support will be remembered and appreciated.

Thanks to Doug Schmidt.

Krzysztof Czarnecki was a key collaborator, first by writing the book *Generative Programming* and several other papers that have greatly influenced our thinking, then by getting involved, maintaining an ongoing discussion by phone, e-mail and visits, reviewing drafts and providing critical commentary, and finally by promoting the book and its spin-off papers and talks at GPCE, OOPSLA, and other venues.

Thanks to Krzysztof Czarnecki.

Thanks to Ralph Johnson.

Ralph Johnson was a major supporter, reviewing the manuscript and giving us detailed comments, reviewing excerpts with his students, sending us recordings of the discussion, meeting us for discussion at conferences, and supporting us in many other ways.

Thanks to Paul Clements.

Paul Clements played a pivotal role, helping us with material on software product lines, promoting our books and its spin-off papers and talks at SPLC and other venues, and generally coaching us on many points and on many occasions.

Thanks to key reviewers and helpers.

DL Parnas graciously reviewed some of the early material and gave us key insights on abstraction. Randy Stafford gave us a deeper appreciation of craftsmanship, and showed us how it dovetails with automation. Martin Fowler and Gregor Hohpe from ThoughtWorks have been companions in thought, sharpening our ideas through many discussions. Grady Booch gave us critical direction early on. Bruce Eckel, Philippe Kruchten, Ivar Jacobson, Erik Mavrinac, Jimmy Nilsson, Ed Pinto, Craig Randall, Jim Rumbaugh, Bran Selic, Pete Sheill and Dave Weiss reviewed drafts and provided valuable criticism. David Frankel helped us crystallize our vision, and produced some of the diagrams in the book from hand drawings. Julie Greenfield devoted many hours to proofreading, copy editing, and formatting.

Thanks to our coworkers at Microsoft.

Also, many people at Microsoft were both helpful and influential. Bill Gates reviewed some of our early papers and encouraged us to keep going. Craig Symonds reviewed the manuscript and promoted it within the company. Rick La-Plante and Julia Liuson, led the development of products that embody many of the ideas described in this book, and gave us feedback that honed our thinking. Also, many of the architects, developers, program managers, and marketing managers with whom we work gave us key insights and encouragement on many occasions. They include Steve Anonsen, Steve Antoch, Anthony Bloesch, Tim Brookins, Christian Hiede Damm, Dan Dosen, Bill Gibson, Jim Green, Bindia Hallauer, Lars Hammer, Jakob Steen Hansen, Anders Hejlsberg, Thomas Hejlsberg, Kate Hughes, Gareth Jones, Norm Judah, Wojtek Kozaczynski, Mike Kropp, Darren Laybourn, Gary MacDonald, Niall McDonnell, Dennis Minium, William Parkhurst, Michael Platt, Ramesh Rajagopal, Beny Rubinstein, Jochen Seemann, Peter Borring Sørensen, John Stallo, Blake Stone, Michael Thomsen, Alex Torone, David Trowbridge, David Vaskevitch, Alan Wills, and Kevin Wittkopf. Special thanks go to Prashant Sridharan, Harry Pierson, and Arvindra Sehmi for their help in promoting the book.

Supporters and influencers are too numerous to mention, but we would like to thank the following people for their direct or indirect contributions to this book: John Abbey, Don Baisely, Steve Brodsky, Alan Brown, Murray Cantor, Cory Casanave, John Cheesman, Jim Coplien, Magnus Christerson, Jim Conallen, Carolin Dhaens, Desmond D'Souza, Keith Duddy, Bill Dudney, Larry Fitzpatrick, Peter Herzum, Sridhar Iyengar, Simon Johnston, Kevin Kelly, Cris Kobryn, Grant Larsen, Dan Leroux, Fred Mannby, Trey Matteson, Jim McGee, Brand Niemann, Dmitri Plotnikov, Andy Roberts, Mike Sanford, Darryl Schaffer, Ed Seidewitz, Bertrand Serlet, Andy Simmons, Van Simmons, Oliver Sims, David Sprott, Jim Thario, Jim Tremlett, and Lawrence Wilkes.

Finally, but most importantly, Bob Elliott and Terri Hudson, our editors at John Wiley & Sons, Inc., were instrumental in bringing this book to the market. Their vision, commitment, and support made it possible. We also appreciate Kathryn Malm, Kenyon Brown, Angela Smith, and the rest of the editorial staff at John Wiley & Sons, Inc., for their help in the practical aspects of getting it published.

Thanks to many others.

Thanks to John Wiley & Sons, Inc.

Foreword

Software languages have become more abstract. Frameworks, like J2EE and .NET, are providing greater and greater functionality and dramatically enhancing productivity. IDEs are becoming more intelligent and acting as background compilers. Patterns and best practices are everywhere. So with all that going for us, why is software development still so complex? Sure, I can create a simple web app in an hour, but that's not what I'm talking about. I'm talking about the enterprise applications made up of thousands of classes and running companies like eBay, Amazon.com, Saleforce.com and any other company with hundreds of thousands, even millions of customers.

I think the problem is simple to understand but the solution is extremely difficult to implement. Interestingly, they are both the same—"tooling". Let me explain. I've been using emacs for fifteen years and just recently switched to an IDE. Ask any emacs user why they use it, and most likely they'll state similar reasons; speed, power, and flexibility. But, it wasn't until a few years ago when I began using IDEs (which had emacs bindings, of course) that I realized they only slowed me down a little, and they added more contextual understanding and assistance to what I was developing. In other words, when programming in Java, they knew about Java and offered code completion, class imports and best of all, syntax error detection without having to compile. But, the real coup was refactoring. Since, we're always refactoring, what a blessing it was to have an IDE do all the grunt work of something as simple as "Rename Method". And that's just the development part. IDEs also helped in the packaging and deployment process since so much of J2EE and .NET is about packaging and deploying a bunch of things. Finally, all these features really made me feel like the IDE was not-so-stupid (maybe even a little intelligent) after all, and had some clue as to what I was doing.

But, just like many things, the more you get, the more you want. And, since I'm an architect and co-author of *Core J2EE Patterns*, I got more and more frustrated with the fact that all these so-called intelligent features were really just aimed at the code, and not the architecture, design and patterns. Now there are a bunch of tools out there that prescriptively do things for you. In the J2EE space, there are tools that let you say you want to create a Front Controller which talks to a Business Delegate pattern and generate the skeleton for you. But, there's no tool that I know of that lets an architect say, "I want my developers to use Front Controllers, Business Delegates and Session Facade patterns," and offers the right patterns to the developer in the right part of the project, detects changes that break the pattern, and suggests possible corrections. As far as I can tell, the reason is that some tools are good at the designing and some are good at the coding, but none meld the two together. And that is exactly where Software Factories come in.

When you first see the term "Software Factories" you may initially be skeptical, assuming that the underlying message is that software development will become so commoditized that it will no longer be creative, and that developers will be reduced to laborers doing rote tasks. But, that's not it. Today's factories create an environment that automates the menial tasks, and frees you up to focus on the creative ones. A primitive physical factory may have nothing more than tables, chairs, raw materials, tools, and of course laborers. But, look inside a highly sophisticated factory, such as an automobile factory, and you'll see autonomous robots picking parts from highly automated materials distribution systems, and assembling them into finished products at incredible speeds. They were designed by engineers to automate many things that were previously mind-numbing grunt work. Everything in the sophisticated automobile factory is built around optimized assembly processes to ensure the highest quality product at the lowest cost. The automobile factory is optimized to build cars, not semiconductors or shoes—so it is specialized. While the factory is most likely optimized to build a specific car class, it can build a wide variety of related models, each containing many different combinations of features. So what's the point? The point is that factories are environments optimized around the context of what is being built. And this is what Software Factories is about. It is about providing assets and tooling that create an environment optimized around a specific type of application, with a specific architecture, making it easy to build them faster and more efficiently.

And, the nice thing about this book is that since the authors are practitioners, they speak from experience. So, this isn't just a good idea, it's a well-thought out approach which is currently being applied in many different settings. The reason I am excited about this is because Software Factories isn't about wizards and property sheets. It's about architectural and design specifications that are core to the development process. Whether they act prescriptively or provide guidance and validation, it doesn't matter; they are there and live throughout the development and deployment process. This means that architects can define patterns, frameworks, DSLs (Domain Specific Languages) and what the authors call "Software Factory Schemas" to drive the development process and enable the tooling. This changes the game completely. No longer will IDEs just be general purpose software tools that understand little beyond basic syntax, but rather architecturally driven and contextually aware power tools designed for specific application domains, helping developers understand and rapidly build complex systems using proven patterns with well-known properties.

I see Software Factories becoming the next big thing, not just another software development fad. With knowledge of architecture and design at the core of any new paradigm, Software Factories is bound to catalyze radical software development productivity gains.

Read this book and apply its lessons to participate in the future of software development.

—John Crupi
Sun Distinguished Engineer
*Co-author, Core J2EE Patterns: Best Practices
and Design Strategies, Second Edition*

Introduction to Software Factories

This is a continuation of what started well before the Industrial Revolution. Genghis Khan was one of the first to grasp the necessity of quick transmittal of information. Now we can do everything instantly, worldwide. It's frightening.

John C. Dvorak

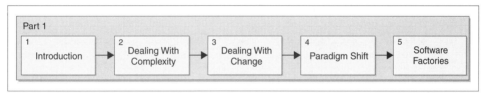

Figure P1.1 A road map to Part I

The road map shown in Figure P1.1 describes Part I. Part I introduces Software Factories. Chapter 1 presents an example used throughout the book and looks at challenges facing software developers. Chapter 2 describes the problem of complexity and looks at current methods and practices for dealing with it. Chapter 3 describes the problem of change and looks at current methods and practices for dealing with it. Chapter 4 describes chronic problems that object orientation has not been able to overcome, and introduces critical innovations that form the basis of Software Factories. Chapter 5 describes Software Factories in detail and presents a vision of industrialization.

Introduction

If this industry doesn't deliver, it will lose the hearts and minds of business leaders, and they will look elsewhere to make their gains.
Michael Fleisher

According to the Standish Group, businesses in the United States spend about $250 billion annually on software development, with the cost of the average project ranging from $430,000 to $2,300,000, depending on company size. Only 16% of these projects are completed on schedule and within budget. Another 31% are canceled, primarily because of quality problems, creating losses of about $81 billion annually. Another 53% cost more than planned, exceeding their budgets by an average of 189%, creating losses of about $59 billion annually. Projects that reach completion deliver an average of only 42% of the originally planned features.

Most software projects fail to deliver what they promised on time and within budget.

In any other industry, results like these would generate a quick response aimed at restoring the bottom line. For at least the last 10 years, however, stakeholders have looked the other way, letting corporate earnings generated by the strong economy absorb the costs of these failures. In these less certain economic times, they are now calling the industry to account for underperforming technology.

Stakeholders are focusing on underperforming technology.

Are these problems of interest only when the economy is weak? Will they recede into the background again, as the

Progress appears to have slowed significantly.

3

market rebounds, or are there more pervasive and fundamental forces at work? For quite some time, they were cast against a backdrop of rapid innovation. No one seemed to mind if we struck out twice for every three times at bat, as long as we hit it out of the park the third time. Recently, however, progress seems to have slowed significantly. Is the engine of innovation running dry, or is something holding it back?

Tools Lag Platforms

Development methods and tools have not kept pace with rapid advances in platform technology...

We think the problem is that software development methods and tools have not kept pace with the rapid advances in platform technology of the last few years. Using the latest wave of Web service platform technology, for example, we can now integrate heterogeneous systems across multiple businesses located anywhere on the planet, but we still hand-stitch every application deployed on this technology, as if it were the first of its kind. We automate large abstract concepts like insurance claims and security trades using small concrete concepts like loops, strings, and integers. If the hardware industry took the same approach, they would build the massively complex processors that power these applications by hand soldering transistors. Instead, they assemble Application Specific Integrated Circuits (ASICS) using software and generate the implementations. Why can't we do something similar?

...and the ensuing raised expectations of stakeholders.

The problem is that stakeholder expectations tend to grow as platform technology advances. We have met increasing expectations for some time by finding ways to hone the skills of developers. Or, to put it differently, we have met the expectations of an increasingly computerized society in much the same way that artisans in the first few years of the industrial revolution met the expectations of an increasingly industrialized society by honing the skills of craftsmen. Up to a point, craftsmanship works well enough. Beyond that point, however, the means of production are quickly overwhelmed, since the capacity of an industry based on craftsmanship is limited by its methods and tools, and by the size of the skilled labor pool. We think the software industry will soon face massive demand on a scale beyond anything we have seen before, driven by a blistering pace of platform technology innovation, not only in the business application market, but also in the markets for mobile devices, embedded systems, digital media, smart appliances, and biomedical informatics, among others.

Currently, the most popular way to hone the skills of developers is to harvest and disseminate the practices of the most productive developers, as exemplified by the agile development movement [Coc01]. The value of this approach has been amply demonstrated. We question the assumption, however, that we can solve current problems, much less prepare to meet the demands of the next decade, by honing developer skills. Apprenticeship is a proven model for industries based on craftsmanship, but it does not scale up well. Observers have noted that the most productive developers produce as much as a thousand times the output of the least productive ones, while the least productive developers generally outnumber the most productive ones by a similar ratio [Boe81]. This means that there will never be more than a few extreme programmers, no matter how much we hone the skills of developers. Moreover, the practices of the most productive developers cannot be applied on an industrial scale because they are optimized for people with uncommon talents. We need a better way to leverage the talents of the best developers, one that can scale up beyond what that they can collectively deliver today.

Apprenticeship is a proven model for industries based on craftsmanship, but it does not scale up well.

Other industries solved problems like the ones we are now facing by learning how to rapidly customize and assemble standard components to produce similar but distinct products, by standardizing, integrating, and automating their production processes, by developing extensible tools and configuring them to automate repetitive tasks, and by managing customer and supplier relationships to reduce cost and risk. From there, they developed product lines to automate the production of product variants, and formed supply chains to distribute cost and risk across networks of specialized and interdependent suppliers, enabling the production of a wide variety of products to satisfy a broad range of customer demands. This is what we call *industrialization*. It is also the vision espoused by the pioneers of object orientation.

Other industries embraced industrialization to solve problems like the ones we now face.

We are not suggesting, simplistically, that software development can be reduced to a highly mechanical process tended by unskilled workers. On the contrary, the key to meeting demand on an industrial scale is to stop wasting the talents of skilled developers on rote and menial tasks, so that they can spend more time thinking and less time doing housekeeping chores. Also,

We propose to replace apprenticeship with automation that exploits best practices.

we must make better use of these few but valuable resources than expending them on the construction of end products that will require maintenance or even replacement when the next major platform release appears, or when changing market conditions make business requirements change, which ever comes first. We need a way to leverage their skills and talents by asking them to encapsulate their knowledge as reusable assets that others can apply. Does this sound far fetched? Patterns have already demonstrated limited knowledge reuse in software design [GHJV94]. The next steps are to move from the manual application of patterns expressed as documentation to the codification of patterns in frameworks, then to the assisted application of patterns by developers using tools, then to the encapsulation of patterns by languages, and then finally to the fully automatic application of patterns by language compilers. By encapsulating knowledge in languages, patterns, frameworks, and tools, and by reusing these assets systematically, we can automate more of the software life cycle.

Reuse has been an elusive goal.

Software components will not be as easy to snap together as ASICs soon, since ASICs are the highly evolved products of two decades of innovation and standardization in component packaging and interface technology. Software components are moving in the same direction, however. The Web service technology that we mentioned earlier represents significant progress in packaging and interface technology for software components. There is much more to be done, of course, as we will demonstrate in Chapter 13. Building reusable software components is challenging, and assembling them generally requires adaptation or changes in the components themselves.

There are innovations to exploit.

We think there is room for significant innovation in these areas, however, such as using models and patterns to automate many aspects of component assembly, and using aspect-oriented methods [KLM97] to weave contextual features into functional ones, instead of rewriting the functional features repeatedly by hand for every new context that we encounter. We think the software industry can climb the innovation curve faster than the hardware industry did by using specialized languages, patterns, frameworks, and tools in software product lines. Of course, the hardware industry has the added burden of engineering the physical materials used for component implementation, while we have the luxury of building with bits. At the same time, the ephemeral nature of bits creates challenges like those faced by the music industry, such as the protection of digital property rights.

The Software Development Landscape

In this chapter, we want to set the scene for the discussion of critical innovations in software development methods and practices in later chapters. To justify our call for a new approach to software development, we must demonstrate our understanding of the challenges that software developers face today. Their world, indeed our world, consists of rapidly evolving platform technologies, increasing customer expectations, a seemingly endless need to acquire new skills quickly, and intense pressure to extract value from older applications while realizing strong returns on investments in new technology. At the same time, few developers are fortunate enough to build green field applications. Most developers must also deal with challenges presented by existing application portfolios and platform technologies. To keep the story simple and easy to follow, we tackle these two sets of challenges separately.

First, we explore the changes in platform technology and stakeholder expectations that created new kinds of applications and produced the portfolios that businesses hold today. To support this study, we introduce a fictitious company, and show how it might have grown over the last 30 years, describing the evolution of its application portfolio and platform technologies. We will follow this fictitious company throughout the book as it adopts the Software Factory approach.

We explore changes in platform technology and stakeholder expectations.

Second, we analyze new platform technologies that are now emerging, identifying the new challenges they create and the existing ones they exacerbate. Here, again, we use our fictitious company. We walk through a skeletal set of requirements for an application that must be developed to support its relationships with customers and suppliers. We then describe the architecture of this application in just enough detail to expose some of the challenges that the company encounters using the emerging platform technologies. At the end of this book, we will rebuild this application using the Software Factory approach to show how it compares with current methods and practices.

We analyze new platform technologies and the challenges they create or exacerbate.

Platform Technology Evolution

We introduce our fictitious companies.

Our fictitious company manufactures tools and equipment used in the construction industry. Its name is Construction Tools, Inc., or CTI. We will also need a fictitious software company to illustrate some of the ideas described in the book. It will be hired by CTI from time to time to help design and implement business applications. Its name is Greenfield & Short Software, Inc., or GSS. Neither the companies nor the applications intentionally resemble any actual companies or applications.

We will use the timeline shown in Figure 1.1 to help us keep our bearings as we tell this story.

Platform technology evolution has pushed the scope of automation outward.

As we shall see, earlier generations of platform technology supported applications that served users inside the business and the transaction volumes they generated, while the current generation, by contrast, supports distributed applications that serve large numbers of users outside the business, such as customers and partners, and the transaction volumes they generate. Each wave of platform technology pushed the scope of automation outward, from inward facing processes at the heart of the business, such as accounting and materials management, to outward facing ones on its periphery, such as supplier management and warranty maintenance.

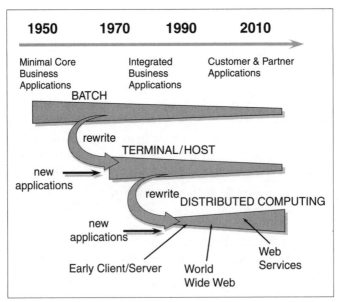

Figure 1.1   Application types and technology trends

The Batch Era

In 1968, CTI employed about 500 people, and had annual revenues of $250m. It was a typical medium-sized manufacturing business. Structured along conventional lines for the period, the organization chart for CTI is shown in Figure 1.2. The company employed a full-time data processing staff of 30 people, including 10 in operations who managed equipment and job scheduling for their small IBM® mainframe running OS/360. Notice that Data Processing reported to Accounting. This was common in the Batch Era. Expenses for computer equipment, development, and operations did not fall into well-defined categories, and were often buried as accounting expenses.

CTI's organization structure.

Batch applications of the 1960s and early 1970s were used by only a few people within the business. Clerks captured data on paper forms that were sent to data entry staff who keyed the data onto machine-readable media, such as punched cards or tape. Most batch applications automated existing manual business procedures. The goal was to gain productivity by exploiting the calculating power of the computer to reduce processing time.

Batch applications computerized existing practices.

The Materials Management and Shop Floor Operations applications at CTI were typical Batch Era applications. As

Few people actually used computers.

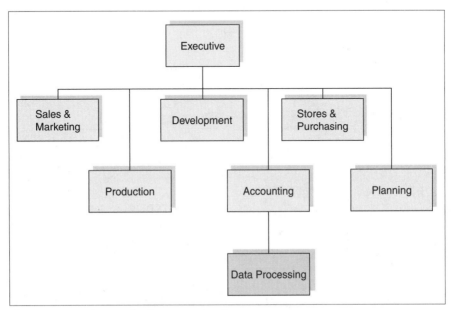

Figure 1.2 CTI's organization structure circa 1968

machine operators milled parts for Hand Drills and Jack Hammers, they reported time and material usage to a clerk who compiled the information and sent daily summaries to the data entry staff. The data was fed into a daily run of each application. At the start of each day, the Shop Foreman received a report from which he could determine the status of each order and allocate work to machine operators. The Stores Manager also received a daily report identifying the materials to be trucked from the warehouse to the various shop floors around the factory.

Dependencies between applications made maintenance a nightmare.

Because they automated existing manual business procedures, most applications were associated with a single department. The resulting application portfolios looked like Figure 1.3. They contained multiple islands of data, each used by a small number of applications, or sometimes by just a single application. Data was often duplicated across applications and stored in a different file structure by each application, making it difficult to retrieve and process. In the early part of the era, data was stored mostly on tape, making it difficult to keep the islands consistent. For example, in addition to entering daily data

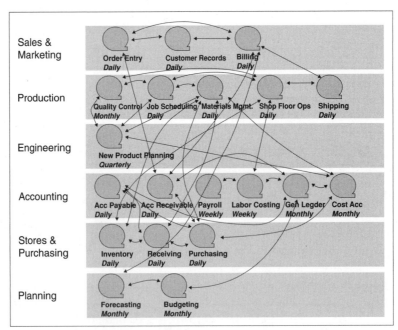

Figure 1.3 CTI's application portfolio in the batch era

for Materials Management, the clerks had to record operator job times on a separate form for the weekly run of the Labor Costing application. The overall effectiveness of Shop Floor operations could be reported only by sorting and merging the files maintained by both of these applications. Figure 1.3 illustrates the kinds of interdependencies between applications created by affinities between data items or by data duplication. For example, data describing parts and assemblies in inventory was spread across applications managed by Accounting, Production and Stores, since some of the items were purchased and some were produced in-house. Maintaining consistency became increasingly difficult as the business grew, requiring more complex sorts and updates over larger numbers of files.

This portfolio of complex interdependent applications eventually became fragile, as overnight processing approached the limits of the time window. During the sixties, CTI twice upgraded its IBM mainframe. By the end of the decade, however, the portfolio was so complex that new applications took unreasonable amounts of time to develop. When the Director of Sales and Marketing was told that his campaign effectiveness report would take two years to implement, it became clear that something would have to change, if CTI was to remain competitive. Obviously, hardware upgrades would not solve the problem. Application architectures and development methods would have to change.

Developers could not keep up with demands for new applications.

The Terminal/Host Era

The innovations that made the necessary changes possible were transaction processing systems, database management systems, terminals, fast random access disks, and networking hardware. Introduced in the early 1970s, they collectively created the Terminal/Host Era illustrated previously in Figure 1.1. *Data integration* was needed to solve the data duplication and dependency problems, and *data independence* was needed to solve the application fragility problems. These were the two siren calls of this era. Database management technology provided a way to integrate the islands of data and to isolate programs from physical data storage structures. Data communications and transaction processing technology provided the means to serve many types of clerical and managerial users across the business.

Database, transaction processing and network technology heralds a new era.

The industry has a vision of widespread online access to information.

A vision of online access to enterprise-wide data was established. Everyone's job would be made easier by the new technology. Shop floor staff, order entry clerks, and storekeepers could directly enter operational data without going through data entry staff. Some of the data entry and clerical staff would be displaced, but they could be reassigned to do more productive work using the new green-screen 3270 terminals. Once the data had been integrated into the new database, managers would be able to use report generators to define new reports, eliminating the need to wait for the Data Processing staff to produce one-off programs.

The new technology gives rise to new application types that offer huge efficiencies.

New kinds of applications that exploited the new platform technology, inconceivable in the Batch Era, were now possible. CTI upgraded their mainframe and installed IMS DB/DC. A database was built to manage customer order information. Using a simple linking technique (starting a new transaction using the same customer key), sales staff using the new online order entry application could see while a customer was on the telephone whether there were any bills outstanding for the customer, and could take action depending on the severity of the problem, ranging from a reminder to order denial. Using this real time information saved CTI hundreds of thousands of dollars per year in bad receivables.

Batch applications were rewritten.

The batch applications that once supported Production were rewritten. Their data was extracted and placed into the new database, and their functionality was recast as the Materials Requirements Planning (MRP) application. The new programs could be used via online terminal by shop floor workers, storekeepers, and planners, enabling the real time entry of time and material data. Up-to-the-minute status reports allowed managers to respond to factory events, load balancing, and changing job schedules in real time. The MRP application saved millions of dollars by raising operator efficiency and reducing material waste, and enabled CTI to outstrip competitors slower to adopt these technologies. Data independence created huge savings during the maintenance phase of an application. New data items could be added to the database with minimal disturbance to running applications, and physical database designs could be changed to accommodate new usage patterns without breaking applications in production.

Information technology as competitive advantage.

Budget for data processing grew enormously in the mid-1970s, as online access to integrated data became a major competitive advantage. At CTI, it reached 10% of net revenue, a typical figure for the period. The Data Processing group, now called the Information Systems Department, became a top-level organization with a direct report to executive management.

Of course, there were downsides to the new technology. Developers had to learn new programming skills. Administrators had to learn new servers, operating systems, and communications infrastructure. Whole new disciplines appeared to support the new technology. Database administrators, network architects, and data modelers were in demand by the early 1980s.

The new technology created new disciplines with significant learning curves.

Despite the hopes of the data modeling evangelists of the early 1980s, widespread data integration across multiple business departments proved a tantalizing vision that was extremely difficult to realize. Many ambitious attempts to produce enterprise-wide data models for enterprise-wide databases foundered due to *analysis-paralysis*, a term that summarized the difficulty of achieving enterprise-wide consensus on the design of shared resources, and the resulting delays in starting the actual coding of applications. Data integration was ultimately achieved, but it was often reduced to a more localized scope than originally envisioned, such as a department or perhaps a division, leading to the "application stovepipe" problem that we see today, where applications in different parts of the organization have different architectures, making them difficult to integrate. Integration across databases was often rudimentary, and most often implemented by "swivel-chair integration"[1] or redirection from common data elements on the screen. This can be seen in a snapshot of CTI's application portfolio circa 1980, shown in Figure 1.4.

Enterprise Data Modeling was mostly a failure.

This era produced a net increase in skills required, since, of course, many batch applications did not disappear. Some online applications were older batch programs with CICS or IMS/DC facades, added to allow broader access. For example, it was common to build an online application to allow clerical staff to enter data for the original batch application. This was the case at CTI with respect to Payroll. The original batch application had become expensive to maintain, but was lower in priority for rewrite than the MRP application. Consequently, an online time-reporting application was created by batching data and sending it to the weekly run of the original Payroll application that was still maintained by IS staff.

Some older applications remained in service, causing maintenance headaches.

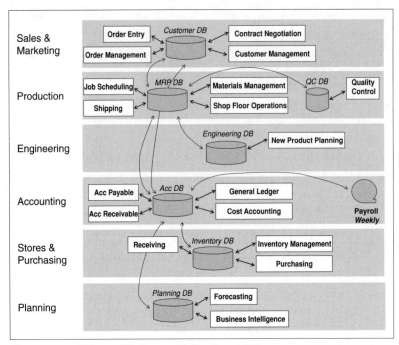

Figure 1.4 CTI's application portfolio circa 1982

And all the backlogs and frustrations reappeared.

In some ways, IS was too successful for its own good. The terminal/host era brought unprecedented growth in business efficiencies, and propelled IS executives to key positions in major organizations, creating the role of the Chief Information Officer (CIO). As IS budgets for new hardware and software grew, however, dissatisfaction set in, again. Application backlogs increased, and eventually became worse than they had been in the early 1970s. By the 1980s something had to change to allow IS to meet the increasing stakeholder expectations. The stage was now set for another major change in platform technology.

The Personal Computing Era

The PC had a profound effect on business applications and IS staff.

That change was provided initially by innovations that led to widespread availability of the Personal Computer and local area networks. In 1985, CTI employed more than 1,000 people and had annual revenues of $700 million, pushing it into the lower end of the large corporations category in the USA. The IS department now employed more than 150 people. By the end of 1986, the CIO estimated that there were more than 250 PCs in use throughout the company. Most of them had been bought on departmental budgets and most of the traditional users of green-screen terminals had either moved to PCs for their connection to the mainframe, or were hankering to do so. What caused such a significant change in user practices?

Much has been written about the effects of the PC revolution on businesses and information technology. For example, Vaskevitch [Vas93] presents the perspective of a Microsoft® executive on this phenomenon in his book *Client/Server Strategies*. He identifies two key issues that led to a dramatic change in platform technology and the application portfolio, creating serious challenges for IS developers:

The PC revolution created serious challenges for IS developers.

- Proliferation of departmental applications written by individuals or small teams of people outside IS.
- Changes in common perceptions about user interfaces to computers, creating demands for PC capabilities in mainframe and server-based enterprise applications.

With the availability of PC applications like MultiMate, Lotus 1-2-3, dBASE and WordStar, staff outside the shop floor, who became known as knowledge workers, had enjoyed the ease with which they could describe and manage budgets, design and run multiformula forecasts, write memos, manage project staff, and organize databases relevant to their work. They effectively became *custom application developers*. As Vaskevitch asks,

Knowledge workers became application developers...

> *Why wait for IS to develop a sales forecasting system when your local hacker can build the same system in three days?*
>
> *Why wait, particularly when the system developed in three days will be easier to use, more flexible, and run on cheaper hardware?*
>
> *And most of all, why wait when the IS [solution] will take two years, cost tens of thousands of dollars, and then be too expensive to run anyway?*

Of course, these applications were simple. They rarely had to deal with shared data, multiple users, or backup and restore. They added to the concerns of IS staff, however, since their users required helpdesk support and assistance with upgrading to new versions of PC applications and operating systems. By the end of the 1980s, these concerns had become serious. Information technology bifurcated into two streams, one for

...But still required support from IS.

personal computing, and one for "serious" enterprise applications. The software industry bifurcated too, along similar lines. Despite these changes, most IS departments still struggled to keep up with the demand for new applications and for the maintenance of older ones. The only difference was that now they also had to satisfy the demands of a growing population of PC users. This illustrates the phenomenon described by Christensen, who notes that newer, cheaper products are constantly cutting into the low end of the market. While they may not initially pose serious threats to established products, they often improve over time and ultimately displace the market leaders [Chr97].

Users demanded integration between their enterprise applications and their PCs.

Added to this problem was another consequence of the proliferation of business PCs. Attracted to the PC by the rich user experience, graphical user interfaces and local personal storage, knowledge workers demanded that corporate applications be updated to exploit these benefits. They demanded not just connectivity to other PCs via local area networks, but also connectivity to enterprise applications above and beyond running IMS DC transactions in a window. This is not to belittle the use of PCs as replacements for 3270 terminals. Many knowledge workers wanted better integration of data across separate departmentally oriented host applications. Copy-paste integration was far better than swivel-chair integration or transaction linking. Beyond these simple, but real, productivity gains was the desire to make the PC part of the enterprise application. For example, at CTI, managers in the Accounting department not only wanted to use their PCs as replacements for their 3270 terminals, they wanted to make their Lotus 1-2-3 forecasting spreadsheet part of the Accounting application suite. They wanted to extract information from the database, perform local analysis, and then write the results back to the database.

The Client/Server Era

The PC raised the expectations of business users and heralded the start of the distributed computing era.

With the main focus on data integration, and each database mostly managed by a large server or mainframe, there was little real demand for developers to build features that required connectivity. Connectivity protocols were arcane and were generally used only in system code. But the widespread use of the business PC again raised stakeholder expectations. To achieve the level of integration mentioned earlier, developers had to view applications not as a monoliths, but as distributed entities composed of connected parts. In the early days of the client/server era, part of the application, called the client, ran on the PC, and part, called the server, remained on the mainframe, or ran on a departmental computer. For client/server architecture to become mainstream, connectivity protocols had to become simpler, so that developers with ordinary skills could use them. This was achieved by standard and proprietary remote procedure calls (RPC).

The first client/server application at CTI was an adjunct to the Order Entry application. In 1988, the Sales Manager defined a set of discounting rules and built them into a dBASE application. The dBASE application extracted information from the Customer Database and applied the discounting rules to support the completion of order forms when customers telephoned or faxed orders. Completed orders were posted as IMS DC messages using terminal emulation software installed on the PC. This example reveals the features of early client/server applications, which used the local processing power of the PC to create a "thick client" for mainframe-based applications, as illustrated in Figure 1.5.

Early client/server systems matched the power of the PC to 3270 terminal emulation.

More complex client/server applications that had to be written by the professional developers in the IS group included quality control applications, which used the PC to perform statistical analysis on data extracted from the MRP database, and business analysis applications, which used spreadsheet programs like Excel to drill down into sales data sliced by region, by customer type, and so on, and to display the results

New higher level programming languages made complex applications much easier to write.

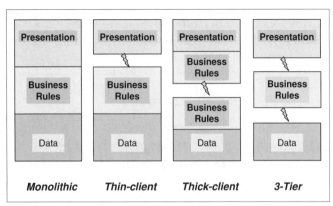

Figure 1.5 Common application architectures

graphically. Until the early 1990s, these were challenging applications to build, since RPC programming was too difficult for all but the top 10% of developers. New higher level programming languages like dBase from Ashton and Visual Basic from Microsoft made client/server programming much easier by introducing event-based user interface programming abstractions like Form and Control, letting almost any developer write efficient client/server applications.

Client/Server had downsides too—like deployment problems...

While the first generation of client/server applications brought improvements in usability, local processing and the disconnected use of mainframe-based data, it also compounded software deployment problems. Many client/server applications were no more flexible than the mainframe applications they replaced. While they were physically partitioned into client and server components, they were logically monolithic, hard wiring every client to a specific server in a fixed location. This lack of flexibility played havoc when programs moved from development to test, and from test to production. Also, when the client had to be upgraded, tracking which PCs had which version of the client software was a major headache. What would happen if a key PC was turned off when a major upgrade occurred?

...data duplication and data staleness.

Problems that were solved in the terminal/host era began to resurface. If data was moved from mainframe systems to PCs, how could IS avoid the problems of data duplication and data disintegration that were overcome by moving from batch to terminal/host? Making data read-only at the PC was one answer, but then how could it be as fresh as the business demanded? This problem surfaced in the order entry application at CTI. The customer data snapshot was downloaded to the order entry clerk PCs only once a day. Bad discounting decisions could be made if a receivables problem was found after the snapshot was taken.

The Growth of Packaged Applications

The 1990s was an era of rapid sales growth for packaged application vendors.

By the end of the 1980s, demand for both new applications and updates to existing ones far outstripped the capability of most corporate IS groups to supply them. And the bifurcation into Personal Computing and Enterprise Computing pressured IS budgets. Together these effects created a huge growth in the packaged application industry, especially in the early 1990s, as IS groups turned to packaged software vendors, who offered to meet their needs with ready-built software. Packages did a good job at providing well-structured databases that served the business needs of functional business areas like payroll and financial control, and packages such as R/3 from SAP dominated the market for the broader Enterprise Resource Planning (ERP) applications. No matter that often it was easier to change business practices than to change the package, important functionality and high degrees of data integration could be had without waiting for customized applications to be developed internally. Yet despite providing broader data integration, packaged applications used limited and proprietary mechanisms for accessing data, making it very difficult to integrate them to support cross-function business processes.

CTI succumbed to this temptation in 1991. They started with the old payroll application, which was still essentially a much-modified variant of the original batch application from 1968. It had become brittle, making it hard to change without breaking it, and only a few developers who could maintain it were still at the company (it was written in COBOL and RPG). Faced with yet another change in employment law, the CIO declared that the existing application could no longer be altered and a search was made to purchase a ready-built package. People-Soft's package was selected and installed in a six-month project, and the old payroll application was taken out of service at the end of 1991. The other employee applications were converted to work with the PeopleSoft application since they provided functionality not present in the package.

CTI buys a package to replace its ancient payroll application ...

After 10 years of service, the CTI home-built MRP system was also showing signs of age. Faced with the task of adding client/server functionality to the old application, the CIO elected to replace it, along with parts of the accounting application, with an integrated package that was already based on client/server architecture. The main Accounting Database remained, since many of the business rules for accounting at CTI resided there. In 1994, after a lengthy installation project, CTI joined thousands of other US companies switching to the R/3 ERP system from SAP, as illustrated in Figure 1.6. In the process of selecting R/3, CTI also took a major decision to move away from IBM mainframes. Along with the installation of People-Soft and R/3, the company purchased several large server machines running UNIX from Hewlett Packard, became the proud owner of relational database technology, and entered forever the wonderful world of heterogeneous platform technologies.

... and then another to replace and upgrade its old MRP application.

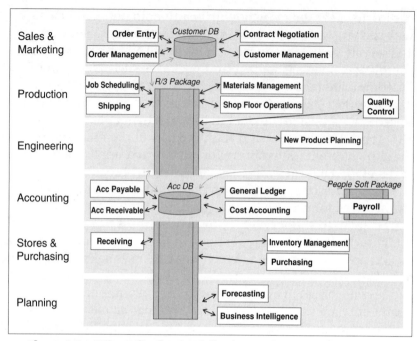

Figure 1.6 CTI's application portfolio circa 1994

The Rise of Outsourcing

Outsourcing is a reaction to rising data center costs and application backlogs.

Another phenomenon that arose in the 1990s in response to the application backlog at in-house IS groups, and the rising cost of datacenter operations, was outsourcing. In its extreme form, outsourcing can mean handing over all responsibility for datacenter management to a third party—eliminating a large part of the in-house IS staff, and most of its hardware. Another trend that continues to grow in popularity is outsourcing application or component development to offshore programming teams, who command lower salaries than their peers in the U.S. do. There is much political controversy about this activity, and what it means for the home market in Information Technology (IT) jobs. Such issues aside, there is still some doubt about the effectiveness of outsourcing, due to mixed results.

It can be successful if managed well, but requires a disciplined approach to development.

Having heard about outsourcing in 1997 from a CIO at another manufacturing company, CTI's CIO thought he would try outsourcing a project to a company based in the Philippines that specialized in extending R/3 for manufacturing business intelligence reports. The results were mixed. While the code had few defects, and was delivered on time and within budget, deployment in the production data center did not go well. This was primarily the fault of the CTI business users and IT staff who wrote the requirements for the project given to the offshore company. They were not used to writing precise specifications with well thought out scenarios, exception handling, and acceptance criteria. They had also failed to communicate information about CTI's custom extensions to R/3. The result was several costly debugging exercises, and protracted negotiation with the offshore company over the changes required to correct the software. The project was finally completed, but at three times the original cost, eradicating all of the anticipated savings. The CIO decided not to risk another outsourced project until his own organization had much better development discipline.

Stitching Applications Together

By the late 1990s and beyond, businesses were realizing that data integration, though important, was not enough, and that it was also necessary to identify, manage, and integrate business processes. Business processes usually span several organization units, and therefore had to be automated by stitching together multiple applications. Since these applications and packages often ran on different servers, simplifying server-to-server connectivity was an essential prerequisite. But viewing them as components from which cross-function business process applications could be assembled raised a number of issues. Restricted access to data within the packages was a key challenge, as was data transformation between them, which was usually unable to preserve all of the information. A category of software known as Enterprise Application Integration (EAI) software was created to solve these problems and to manage the flow of data between packages, creating the illusion of an integrated process-oriented application.

Distributed computing is driven by the need for business process integration.

At CTI, as we've seen, heterogeneous platforms are the order of the day. Writing cross-functional code therefore forces developers to also cope with server-to-server code that jumps between different platform technologies, requiring bridges and special adapters. Figure 1.7 illustrates this with some common cross-functional business processes that became the subject of industry discussions and *Harvard Business Review* articles. Brokering technologies that addressed a few of these connectivity

DCOM and CORBA were partially successful but were too closely tied to component implementation technologies.

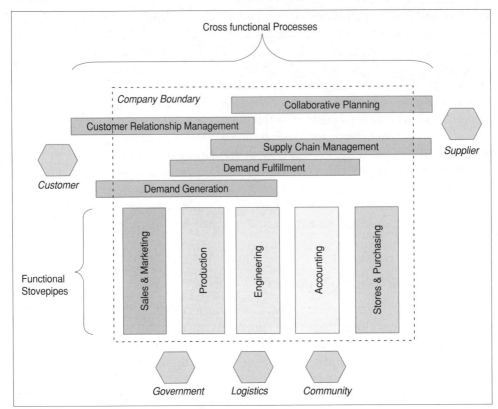

Figure 1.7 Application stovepipes and business processes

issues were available from several vendors as implementations of the OMG™ CORBA® specification, and as a technology called Microsoft DCOM® for the Microsoft Windows® operating system. While these technologies were successful within their domains, problems with cross-platform scenarios, and their close coupling to specific component implementation technologies kept them from becoming more widely adopted.

To support business process integration we need a process perspective and multiplatform technology.

The application stovepipes that most companies found in their data centers by the late 1990s created inertia against the construction of cross-functional applications to support reengineered business processes. Technology resisted the early adopters of process-oriented applications, and while that is changing with modern Web service technology, this is more than just a technology issue. In some respects, Hammer's classic "stop paving the cow paths" paper on business process reengineering was ahead of its time [Ham90]. To avoid integration problems, applications should be built from a process perspective, using widely accepted technologies that work on multiple platforms and that adhere to industry standards. We address these two issues in the next section.

Opening Up the Enterprise

The arrival of the World Wide Web technologies in the early 1990s had a profound effect on us all. We do not need to go into that effect here. But keeping our focus on technology change and its effect on stakeholder expectations and corporate application portfolios, we can observe how the Internet technologies were adopted by businesses. Early use of Internet technologies was for the most part the creation of static content at a web site with public access. Soon, however, it was recognized that the real power of the web for business was in driving electronic commerce—interactions between organizations participating in potentially complex *value chains* offering rich, rewarding business relationships to their participants. Using the Internet, even small companies now handle millions of transactions per business day from thousands, tens of thousands or even millions of concurrent users. The ability to include customers and partners in the scope of an information system makes reengineered business solutions possible.

The World Wide Web for business is about electronic commerce.

By promoting near-universal adoption of location-independent protocols, especially *http* and *https*, the web allows distributed applications to include data and services outside the businesses that host them. At the same time, however, these protocols do not yet provide some of the features required to distribute business and mission critical applications, such as transactions, security, routing and referral, and reliable asynchronous messaging. Distributed middleware platforms, such as DCOM and CORBA, provided these features. Because they were tightly coupled to specific component implementation technologies, however, they were difficult to use across business boundaries.

The web extends applications to include data and services outside the business.

As a standard format for data exchange, eXtensible Markup Language (XML) has been one of the primary catalysts of electronic commerce. XML technologies at either end of an interaction can eliminate many problems related to data transformation between applications. XML documents adhering to well-formed and discoverable rules, described in XML using XML Schema Definitions (XSD), are becoming the standard medium of interaction between connected applications wherever they are located.

XML enable a standard format for data exchange.

Internet technology is also used within companies.

As the nascent Distributed Computing Era progressed, a less visible but equally important development was increasing server-to-server connectivity. While PC-to-PC connectivity had been around since the early days of the local area networks, and PC-to-server connectivity was commonplace, by the early 1990s server-to-server connectivity was still unusual in applications. In this guise, the web has done more to push application boundaries than anyone could have predicted. Many companies have found it easier to set up internal Internet servers using the same protocols and standards—the so-called Intranets. This is the basis for a new approach to process implementation that can supercede early EAI technology.

Building Applications with Services

Web service technology enables application connectivity on an unprecedented scale.

New Web service technologies, such as those being standardized by the World Wide Web Consortium (W3C) and the Web Services Interoperability Organization (WS-I), illustrated in Figure 1.8, promise to provide the necessary features by supporting service-oriented architectures (SOAs), where loosely coupled, coarse grained components interact by exchanging messages. These technologies are also breathing new life into component-based development (CBD) methods, as we shall see later in this book.

It crosses platform and business boundaries.

For most organizations, heterogeneous technology platforms are the norm, so the role of Web service technology as a platform for distributed applications is a lifeline. With Web services, distributed business processes have become a reality, since a software component residing within a partner's business data center can legitimately be regarded as part of a larger application that spans the boundaries of both enterprises. Similarly, software components locked within proprietary packages or

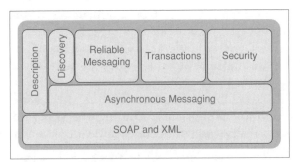

Figure 1.8   Layered web service protocols

buried in older, more monolithic applications can be wrapped with Web services and easily integrated to better support business processes. As Web service technology matures to better support security, cross service transactions, and other key features, so does its suitability as a platform for connected applications and distributed computing, both between businesses and within them.

The application of Web service technology creates service-oriented architectures, where loosely coupled coarse grained components interact by exchanging messages containing documents according to sequencing protocols defined by well-formed contracts subject to negotiated constraints called service level agreements. We will revisit this definition in Chapter 13. Examples of service-oriented architecture can be seen today in the edge systems that provide facades for back end systems to expose business processes to the Internet. Of course, this is just an early example of service-oriented architecture. As Web service technology matures, we expect to see service-oriented architectures become much more pervasive and eventually ubiquitous.

Web services have popularized service-oriented architectures.

Inevitably, platform technology evolution has once again come with a price. Building distributed applications using principles of service-oriented architecture is a challenge. Technical issues such as security, versioning, caching, deployment and management, which were tough enough in the client-server era, become even harder with service oriented architectures. Problems created or exacerbated by service orientation are described in the following sections of this chapter.

But service orientation does not solve all problems.

Many observers believe that the next step in platform technology evolution will be the emergence of Business Process Management Systems (BPMS). These are logical analogs of Database Management Systems (DBMS). DBMS applied structure to corporate data, offered data independence to programs that used the data, and provided a wide range of support utilities, such as common backup and restore, transactions, ad hoc query and business intelligence. BPMS, on the other hand, will apply structure to corporate business processes, and allow them to change independently of functional programs, while providing useful features like process state management, process composition, process tracking and process monitoring. Strong theoretical underpinnings exist for both technologies—relational calculus in one case, pi-calculus (and other formal algebras of cooperating processes) in the other. As BPMS technology matures, process-oriented applications will form the

Business Process Management Systems are the next step in platform technology.

backbone of application portfolios over the next decade. Let's look at how SOA and BPMS would be used by CTI.

An eCommerce Application

CTI builds an eCommerce app.

CTI has once again found its stakeholders raising pressing requirements for new kinds of applications already in use by their competitors and partners based on the new Web service technology. Three main business drivers are the following:

- CTI has produced a new line of power tools and accessories specifically oriented towards the consumer. Their existing channels have mostly been dealers who sell to large contracting firms, with large volume orders at predictable intervals. The CTI Marketing Director decides that the consumer products will be sold through two new channels. First, via an online web-based catalog that would potentially reach millions of consumers. Second, via a small number of tight collaborative deals with major out-of-town discount retail outlets like Target and Wal-Mart.

- CTI needs to improve its relationships with both its customers and its partners. It has determined that its customer loyalty is lower than the industry average, and that its purchasing activities could be optimized by reducing the number of suppliers and sharing demand forecasts with those that remain, resulting in better terms and faster delivery of goods.

- CTI needs to better track its existing sales force and combine their leads with those generated from online marketing campaigns.

CTI gets help from GSS.

Clearly over its head in facing these challenges, CTI has decided to contract out to Greenfield and Short Software, Inc. (GSS), a systems integrator with a track record of helping its clients integrate their value chains. GSS works with CTI to describe its business processes and the flows of information among them. The result of this effort is a model of the CTI value chain, illustrated in Figure 1.9. The key to helping CTI will be to facilitate the exchange of information among the processes that comprise the value chain. Figure 1.9 shows groups of business processes that GSS has identified for CTI. While

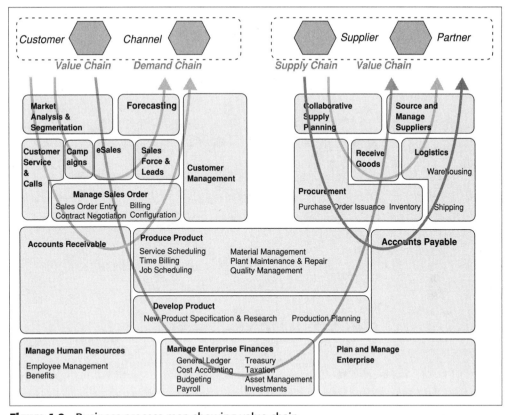

Figure 1.9 Business process map showing value chain

this kind of chart is useful as a summary for executive feedback sessions, more detailed business process definitions are drawn up by GSS consultants working with key CTI people. This analysis of the way CTI does business, combined with the process models to meet the new requirements, is a critical prerequisite used by the GSS systems staff in designing software components that will wrap existing CTI applications, or implement new functionality. The new business processes are summarized next.

Business Processes

The Web Site Management process will provide a business web presence and the basic web-based storefront for CTI, as illustrated in Figure 1.10. It defines how CTI will setup e-mail accounts, and how it will design and manage the layout and content of its web site. Other activities supported by the process

Web Site Management Process

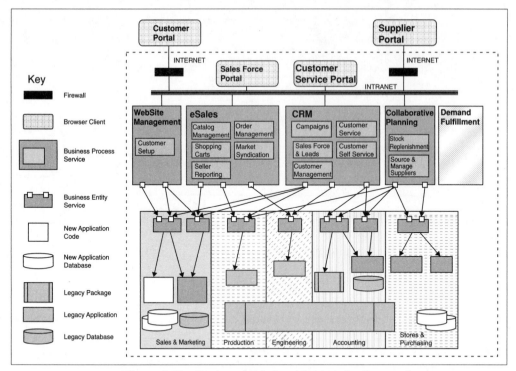

Figure 1.10   Service-oriented architecture for the new business processes

include registration of the site with search engines and submission to banner exchange networks.

Customer Relationship Management Process

The Customer Relationship Management (CRM) process will provide a complete suite of tools to automate and improve customer acquisition, conversion, service, retention and feedback gathering. It contains the following sub processes:

- Campaigns: the process used to create, execute, and track direct marketing campaigns, initially focusing on e-mail direct marketing.

- Sales Force and Leads: the process that defines how sales people and sales managers track and manage their leads, prospects and current customers, including automated prospecting, sales processes, task management, customer acquisition, team selling, goal setting, and commission tracking.

- Customer Management: the process that defines how customer information is recorded and used, what happens when a new customer is acquired, and what happens when customers ask to be unregistered.

- Customer Service: the process that defines how customers are provided with self-help (knowledge base access, natural language search, solution rating), how incidents are tracked and escalated, how service representative effectiveness is tracked, and how chat/e-mail/phone routing and queue management, and Service Level Agreements (SLA) are managed.

- Customer Self-Service: the process that defines how a customer "logged in" on the web site is managed, and how they perform self service, how they check order status, and how they obtain incident or opportunity/sales status, or customized quotes and configurations.

The eSales process contains five primary sub processes:

eSales—the eCommerce Selling Processes

- *Catalog Management:* the process that enables CTI to enter products and services into their catalog, manage merchandising rules, configuration rules, and create custom catalogs and pricing.

- *Order Management:* the process that defines how CTI manages orders received from any marketplace or partner. It's also the process by which CTI will configure rules (e.g., discounts) and identify service providers (e.g., credit card processors) required in processing orders

- *Shopping Cart Processing:* the process that defines how orders from customers are handled, and that defines order self-service activities allowing customers to check on the status of their orders and retrieve their order history.

- *Market Syndication:* the process that defines how CTI submits catalog data to marketplaces, such as eBay.

- *Seller Reporting:* the process that gives Sales Management a snapshot of sales activity across all their partners and marketplaces.

The Collaborative Supply Planning process contains two primary subprocesses:

Supply Chain Management Process

- *Stock Replenishment:* the process that defines how stock from inventory is replenished by placing restocking orders to suppliers, and forecasts are shared with suppliers to enable automatic restocking and goods receipt.

- *Source and Manage Suppliers:* the process that defines how suppliers are vetted and selected for close collaboration.

Implementation Strategy

An overview of the implementation of the new processes.

CTI and GSS decide to implement the new set of business processes using a service-oriented architecture. The user interaction scenarios will be encapsulated in portals—easy to use and personalized web pages that provide access to business processes. Each business process will be implemented as a Web service, with its lower level activities performed by a new type of service—a business entity service—which takes responsibility for reusable business logic and access to underlying data stores. Since these data stores and their accompanying business logic still reside in older databases and packaged applications, the architecture must define the new services as facades that wrap those assets. These services will manage implementation of the newly defined service by working with older databases and packages. This is a complex undertaking for CTI and GSS. We'll return to see how this was finally accomplished using a software factory in Chapter 17.

Software Development Challenges

We summarize the landscape as a list of development challenges.

This concludes our overview of the landscape that provides the backdrop in which the development of new applications must take place. We have highlighted many serious challenges. To summarize, software developers must:

Some are created by new business requirements.

- Support reengineered business processes and an increasing focus on process-oriented applications

- Expose existing systems to massive user loads created by web-based front ends

- Design protocols (valid message sequences) and enforceable service level agreements to support processes that span multiple enterprises

- Determine strategies for versioned data and snapshots, such as price lists, that are widely distributed yet have limited lifetimes

- Cope with the complexity created by transformed business models from business leaders such as Wal-Mart, who insist on deep integration with their partners

- Integrate heterogeneous application stovepipes and avoiding lossy transformations between them

- Avoid reintroducing the batch era problem of multiple file layouts and lack of data format consistency in the rush to describe XML schemas for every software service

- Determine strategies for wrapping older applications executing on heterogeneous platforms

- Customize packaged software to satisfy proprietary requirements

- Address the special needs of data warehousing and business intelligence

- Demonstrate return on investment in custom software in the face of rising software development costs

- Protect corporate data from hackers and viruses, while giving customers and partners direct access to the same resources

  Some arise from an increasing focus on security.

- Mitigate the increasing risk of legal liability from the improper use of corporate data

- Satisfy operational requirements, such as security, reliability, performance and supportability, in rapidly changing applications

  Some are caused by increasing deployment complexity.

- Integrate new and existing systems using a wide range of architectures and implementation technologies

- Understand the effects of partitioning and distribution on aggregate qualities of service

- Design multitiered applications that deploy correctly to server farms on segmented networks partitioned by firewalls, with each server running a mixture of widely varying host software configurations

- Support applications developed by end users (for example, spreadsheets to 4GLs) while enforcing corporate policy and maintaining the integrity of corporate data

  Some are created by decentralized software development.

- Integrate personal productivity applications, such as word processors and spreadsheets, with back end systems

- Work with applications or components that are increasingly outsourced to development centers in remote locations forcing a discipline on requirements designs and acceptance tests that was often neglected in the past

- Make departmental applications integrate effectively and scale to satisfy enterprise requirements

Discontinuous Innovation

The industry will not solve all of these problems through business as usual.

Now that we know the challenges we face, we can ask what methods and practices are at our disposal, how effective they are, and whether or not they can be improved upon. The remainder of this book seeks to answer these questions. Solving software development challenges is a major focus of the industry, and tremendous progress has been made in a mere 50 years. Historically, however, this progress has not been steady. Instead, it has followed the pattern of innovation curves, illustrated in Figure 1.11.

Software development technology evolves primarily through disruptive changes called paradigm shifts.

A discontinuous innovation establishes a foundation for a new generation of technologies. Progress is initially rapid, but gradually slows down, as the foundation becomes stable and mature. Eventually, the foundation loses the ability to sustain innovation, and a plateau is reached. At that point, another discontinuous innovation establishes another foundation for another generation of new technologies, and the pattern repeats. Kuhn calls the foundations paradigms, and the transitions between them paradigm shifts [Kuh70]. According to

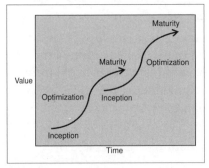

Figure 1.11 Innovation curves

Cox, each new paradigm is launched to correct the failures of its predecessors, and to explore new thinking that breaks away from established practice [Cox90]. Because they are produced by discontinuous innovation, paradigm shifts are by nature disruptive, and often interfere with existing social and economic structures. According to Shaw, engineering-based industries, like software development, are prone to paradigm shifts because they are driven by underlying currents in science and mathematics [Sha97].

Object orientation has changed much since its inception, but remains the current paradigm. It improved on structured programming by providing a way to encapsulate state in behavioral wrappers. A good overview of the paradigm is provided by Taylor [Tay97]. Like most new paradigms, it initially had many problems could only be corrected by gaining experience. One problem was the assumption that object-oriented solutions would be resemble the problems they solved, allowing functional requirements to map rather directly onto classes. Another problem was that inheritance, as initially implemented, violated encapsulation by allowing subclasses to depend on private features of their base classes. A third problem was that during early adoption, many object-oriented programming practices resembled practices established by the structured programming paradigm. These and many other problems were solved, some completely, some partially, by incremental but significant adaptations, such as interfaces, patterns, and agile methods.

Object orientation is the current paradigm.

Sadly, despite this tremendous progress, the vision espoused by the pioneers of object orientation, with its emphasis on industrialization, has not been realized. Many problems remain unsolved. Some have resisted solution since the inception of the paradigm, while others have simply been overlooked. According to Kuhn, this should be expected. A paradigm provides focus that accelerates the solution of problems at the center of its concerns, while distracting attention from those on its periphery. As the problems at the center are gradually solved, attention begins to move to the ones on the periphery, which then begin to loom large as impediments to progress. The focus that enabled the paradigm to accelerate the solution of the problems it chose to emphasize now prevents it from offering assistance in solving the problems it chose to deemphasize.

Many parts of its original vision have been realized, but many have not.

Object orientation has reached a plateau—a new paradigm is needed.

We think innovation based on object orientation has reached a plateau. Indeed, with a few notable exceptions, such as patterns and byte code languages, most of the innovations of recent memory represent only incremental progress. We still build software in basically the same way we did when early object-oriented languages like Smalltalk arrived on the scene. Perhaps the biggest change is that now these practices have been adopted much more widely, though imperfectly. In other words, there is evidence that we are near the end of the current paradigm, and that a new paradigm is needed to support the next leap forward in software development technology. If this is true, then we should be able to identify chronic problems with the current paradigm, problems that have stubbornly refused solution for a long time despite the best efforts of the industry to solve them. We should also be able to identify critical innovations that solve those problems at the cost of changes in accepted methods and practices. According to Kuhn, the new paradigms will build on the strengths of their predecessors while addressing some of the weaknesses that gave rise to their chronic problems. They will also create technical, social, and financial dislocations by disenfranchising entrenched constituencies.

On to the rest of Part 1.

In Chapters 2 and 3, we study complexity and change, the two fundamental forces responsible for the failures of object orientation and every other paradigm invented in pursuit of developer productivity. We also look at methods and practices that have been added to the foundation of object orientation, since they show us where to look to find the chronic problems that it cannot solve, and the critical innovations that will launch the next offensive in the assault on complexity and change. In Chapter 4, we describe those chronic problems and critical innovations. In Chapter 5, we explain how those critical innovations could be applied to form a new software development paradigm called Software Factories.

Notes

1. It was not uncommon for clerks to have more than one green screen terminal on their desk for this purpose—hence swivel-chair integration. Thanks to Pat Helland for this insightful terminology.

Dealing with Complexity

Complexity tends to increase until it reaches a point where it can no longer be managed, creating an uncomfortable equilibrium.

Peter Principle of Programming

In this chapter, we look at complexity, one of the two fundamental forces that make software development challenging. We also look at methods and practices for dealing with complexity based on object orientation.

The Problem of Complexity

Complexity and its reduction by reorganization are central ideas in both mathematics and software development. While complexity is not easy to define precisely, we can think of it as a measure of the difficulty of solving a given problem. Complexity was recognized as a significant challenge in software development more than 25 years ago. This is still true, because advances in methods and technologies since then have been offset by demand for more complex systems, as predicted by the Peter Principle of Programming (epigraph). To understand the causes and effects of complexity, we need to distinguish between essential and accidental complexity, as described by Brooks [Bro87].

Complexity is a principal bottleneck in software development.

Essential complexity is inherent in the problem.

Essential complexity is inherent in the problem being solved. Intuitively, it is a function of the number of features and the number of relationships among them that must be considered simultaneously to decompose the problem. For example, the problem of automating online commerce—where the product catalog, the order entry process, the order fulfillment process, the invoicing process, and the payment process are all managed by different companies—contains much more essential complexity than the problem of automating online commerce where all of these processes are managed by a single company. Since essential complexity is inherent in the problem being solved, it cannot be reduced or eliminated. Software products generally exhibit higher levels of essential complexity than other kinds of products because they generally support more features and more variability in the way the features can be combined, according to Wegner [Weg78].

Accidental complexity is an artifact of the solution.

Accidental complexity is an artifact of the solution, i.e., the software written to solve the problem. Intuitively, it is a function of the number of features and the number of relationships among them that must be considered simultaneously to compose the solution. For example, an online commerce application written in assembly language using system calls contains more accidental complexity than the same application written in the Microsoft Visual C#® language using an online commerce framework. As we will show later, accidental complexity is created when fine grained, general purpose abstractions like integers and strings are used to implement coarse grained, problem-specific concepts like Customers and Products, and can be reduced or eliminated by using more coarse grained, problem-specific abstractions like Customer and Product classes.

Solutions to even simple problems can have enormous accidental complexity.

Solutions to even simple problems can contain enormous accidental complexity. Consider the implementation of an Order Entry process using current technology, such as the Java 2 Software Development Kit, Enterprise Edition (J2EE™).

- Processes are typically implemented by distributed components.
- The components use interfaces to expose remote and local methods, such as accessor, relationship, and business methods, as well as methods for managing identity, finding factories and instances, accessing metadata and handling errors

- They use classes, such as factory, proxy, facade, adapter, delegate, event, exception, command, connection, metadata, and value classes to implement the interfaces

- They use system services to initialize and register component instances, and to manage their state, distribution, concurrency, transactions, naming, security, and resources

- They use web client and server pages, forms, scripts, tag libraries, and servlets to present information to the user

- They use data access objects, object relational mappings, queries, schemas, connection factories, connections, and adapters to manage data

- They use Web service descriptions, resource locators, class wrappers, protocols, document schemas and documents to interact with other processes

- They use connection factories, connections, and adapters to interact with external information systems, such as legacy systems and packaged applications

- These objects are spread across multiple development artifacts, including Java^{TM} source code and class files, HTML files, XML files, SQL DDL and DML files, resource files and archives, including JARs, EJB-JARs, WARs, and EARs

- Changes must be synchronized when the members of a development team modify the same artifacts concurrently

- Many of the artifacts must be processed by tools, such as compilers, interface generators, and archive generators to produce deployment artifacts

- To make the software operational, the results must be assembled, configured, and packaged to produce executables, which must then be replicated, installed, and registered on target platforms, such as web servers, application servers, database servers, transaction monitors, messaging systems, and enterprise information systems.

   Now, all of this may seem to be par for the course to a typical Java developer, but we can see how much of this complexity is accidental by observing that none of the things in this list are specifically about Order Entry.

None of the things in this list are specifically about Order Entry.

FEATURES

In this book, we use the term *feature* as defined by Bosch
[Bos00]. A feature is a logical unit of behavior specified by a set
of functional and non-functional requirements. A feature usually
represents many requirements, and aggregates them for scoping
purposes. Features are generally not independent, and can be
related in a variety of ways. For example, one feature may require
or exclude another. Features can be modular. For example, a
credit card authorization feature can be packaged as an
individual service that can be called by other services. They can
also cut across modular units. For example, a security feature
may cut across many operating system and application objects.
Features will play a prominent role in this book.

Feature Delocalization

*Feature
delocalization is
one of the
primary sources
of accidental
complexity.*

As noted by Coplien [Cop99], early object-oriented methods
incorrectly assumed that each object in the problem would be
represented by an object in the solution. In other words, they
assumed that problem features would map directly to solution
features. In practice, problem features are usually scattered and
interwoven across multiple solution features. For example, the
implementations of Product, Order, and Customer in Figure 2.1
are scattered and interwoven across the Web Server Pages, Distributed Component and Database Connectivity assemblies.
To change the implementation of Product, we might have to
change all three assemblies, affecting the implementations of
Order and Customer. This phenomenon, called feature delocalization, is one of the primary sources of accidental complexity.

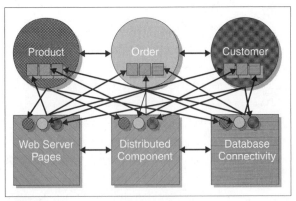

Figure 2.1   Feature delocalization

It occurs when multiple solution features such as Web Server Pages, Distributed Component, and Database Connectivity, in the example, implement a single problem feature, such as Product, or when a single solution feature, Web Server Pages, implements multiple problem features, such as Product, Order, and Customer.

We can make some additional observations by noting that the problem features are defined by requirements, while the solution features are defined by implementations. (We will define requirements and implementations precisely later in this chapter.)

Problem features are most localized in requirements. Solution features are most localized in executables.

- Problem features are most localized and solution features are most delocalized in the requirements. For example, Order is defined by single analysis class, but Web Server Pages is implied by multiple analysis classes, along with Security, Distributed Component, and Database Connectivity.

- Solution features are most localized and problem features are most delocalized in implementations. For example, Web Server Pages is defined by a single assembly, but Order is scattered across multiple assemblies, along with Customer and Product.

The delocalization of solution features can often be seen in the way requirements are expressed. For example, the requirements for Figure 2.1 might have one section each for Product, Order, and Customer, and each section might say what information will be retrieved from the database and displayed on a web page for authorized users. The delocalization of problem features can often be seen in the way implementations are expressed. The implementation for Figure 2.1, for example, might include web pages for Product, Order, and Customer, distributed Product, Order, and Customer components, and a SQL DDL file describing the Product, Order, and Customer tables.

Feature delocalization is apparent in the way the requirements and the executables are expressed.

Of course, if the problem is not well defined, or well modeled by the requirements, we might find that problem features are not well localized even in the requirements. For example, we might find that information about Product, Order, and Customer are scattered across the descriptions of the Order Fulfillment and Order Entry processes and interwoven with each other in the requirements, because that is how they are

Features may be poorly localized for other reasons.

defined by the business. Similarly, if the solution is not well designed, we might find that solution features are not well localized, even in the implementation. For example, we might find that Security and Database Connectivity are interwoven and scattered across the implementations of Web Server Pages and Distributed Components, because that is how they were designed by the developers.

Feature delocalization causes two well-known programming problems: the traceability problem and the reconstruction problem, described below.

The Traceability Problem

The traceability problem makes it hard to know what should be modified when requirements change.

The traceability problem occurs when the solution features that implement a problem feature cannot be easily identified. This makes it hard to identify all of the things that need to change in the implementation, and to ensure that all of the changes are made consistently, when the requirements change, as illustrated in Figure 2.2. For example, a property of Order, such as Order Status, may be implemented by a field on a web page, a tag in a Java Server Pages™ (JSP) file that generates the web page, a property of a JavaBeans™ component used by the JSP, a method on an Enterprise JavaBean (EJB™) that generates the JavaBean, a method on a data access object used by the EJB, and a column in a database table mapped to the data access

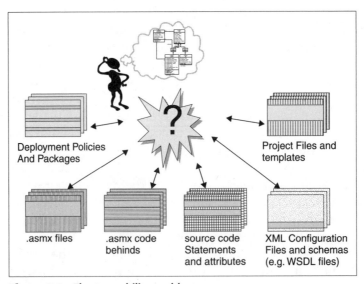

Figure 2.2   The traceability problem

object. It may be difficult to identify all of these things, or to ensure that they are changed consistently, when the name or type of the property changes.

The Reconstruction Problem

The reconstruction problem arises when design information is lost and cannot be easily reconstructed, making maintenance and enhancement difficult. As we saw earlier, solutions are organized by making design decisions according to some rationale. This information is usually understood during development, but when the development is finished, it is rarely preserved, except in the minds of the participants. People are mobile, and forget details with the passage of time, so the information is easily lost. Both maintenance and enhancement involve modifying existing software to correct defects or to accommodate changes in requirements, as we have seen. If the original design decisions and rationale have been lost, then developers responsible for maintenance and enhancement may not be able to reconstruct them. Without this information, they may not know how to make the required modifications, or when they can remove parts of the software that are no longer needed. It is quite difficult to modify poorly documented software with confidence, and it is quite common to discover that a feature has been maintained long after it was no longer required, because no one knew why it was added, or whether it could be safely removed.

The reconstruction problem makes it hard to know how to make changes to the software.

Working at the Wrong Level of Abstraction

Software development involves implementing requirements. Feature delocalization is caused by the conceptual gap between requirements and executables that implement them, illustrated

Feature delocalization is caused by the abstraction gap.

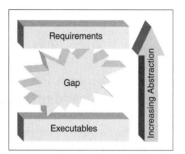

Figure 2.3 The abstraction gap

in Figure 2.3. We call it the abstraction gap because it is created by the difference in level of abstraction between the requirements and the executables. This gap is revealed by the way it is bridged during the software development process using abstraction and its inverse, refinement. Before we look more closely at the abstraction gap, let's define abstraction and refinement, and look at the roles they play in software development.

What Is Abstraction?

Abstraction selectively removes details from a description to simplify it for some purpose.

Abstraction is a process that selectively removes some information from a description to focus on the information that remains. (Appendix A describes several common forms of abstraction and refinement.) The less information a description contains, the more abstract it is. The term abstraction can also refer to a description created by the process of abstraction. A map, for example, is an abstraction of an area, such as a part of a city. In the UK, London Transport publishes bus route maps, called spider maps, which describe the city of London [Lon03]. One of them is shown in Figure 2.4. Obviously, spider maps remove a lot of detail. They do not show the streets, for example. A spider map is therefore more abstract than a street map. A more abstract description is generally more useful for its intended purpose than a more detailed description. By removing irrelevant details, it helps its user focus on the relevant ones. For example, navigating London by bus is much easier with spider maps than with a street map, because the spider maps remove details that are not relevant for bus travel. In the same way, a business application expressed in C# is much easier to understand than a business application expressed using the processor instruction set of the target platform.

We can separate the concerns of different parties by creating more than one abstraction for the same subject.

Of course, we can devise more than one abstraction for a given subject, each removing different details for a different purpose. By abstracting away streets and applying a topological transformation, London Transport produces another map, the ubiquitous London Underground Map, shown in Figure 2.5, which helps travelers navigate their way around London by the Tube. Multiple abstractions can be used to separate the concerns of different parties. For example, the spider maps address the concerns of bus riders, while the Underground map addresses the concerns of Tube riders. The concern

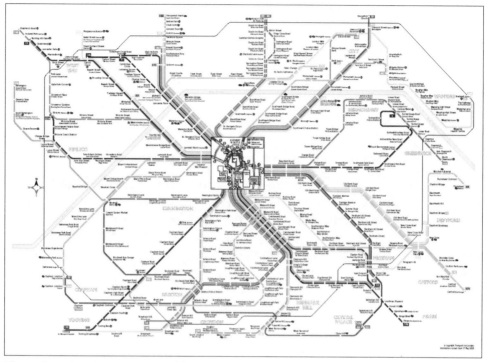

Figure 2.4 London transport spider map

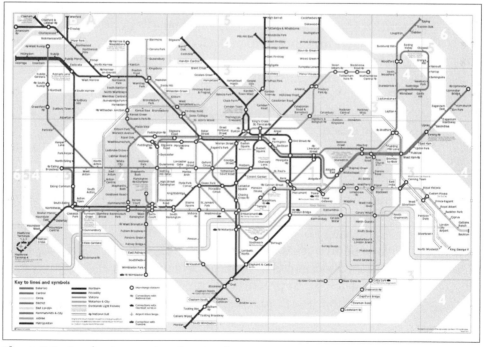

Figure 2.5 London transport underground map

addressed by an abstraction is called a viewpoint or aspect. Bus travel and Tube travel are aspects of the city of London. We can relate abstractions addressing different aspects using cross-references. On a spider map, for example, some bus stops reference Tube stations, helping bus riders transfer to the Tube and vice versa.

Refinement in Software Development

Requirements are seen as the starting point for software development.

Refinement is the opposite of abstraction. It makes a description more complex by adding information, and is used in software development to produce executables from requirements. Requirements are seen as the starting point for software development. We start with requirements and progressively produce more concrete descriptions of the software, such as analyses, designs, implementations and ultimately executables, by adding information. This process is called progressive refinement. For example, we might add information to a description of Order, to indicate that it will be implemented as a distributed component, to identify properties and behaviors that will be accessed remotely.

Design decisions select solutions.

When we add information, we must usually choose among alternative solutions. For example, we added information about distribution because we chose to make Order remotely accessible. If we had chosen to make it only locally accessible, instead, we would have added different information to the description. These choices are called design decisions.

Refinements are applied progressively until the executables are produced.

Each time we add information to a description, we produce a new one that is more concrete than its predecessor. If the new description is executable, and satisfies non-functional or operational requirements (see the sidebar for more information about these requirements), then the process is complete. No additional refinement is required. If not, then additional refinement is required to produce an executable. For example, the description of the distributed Order component might be further refined by defining it to be an EJB entity bean, by adding Java source code that implements its behaviors, by mapping its persistent fields to columns in a database, and by tuning its performance. In practice, we produce a series of descriptions, each refining its predecessors. The process of producing the executables can be seen as a sequence of successive refinements.

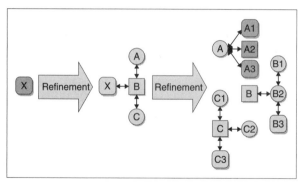

Figure 2.6   Producing executables by progressive refinement

We can think of each step in this process as a transformation that maps a problem to a solution. The outputs of each transformation become inputs to others. Each step except the last one produces new problems to be solved, and each step except the first one produces solutions to those problems. For example, the requirements are problems to be solved by analysis, the analyses are problems to be solved by design, the designs are problems to be solved by implementation, and the implementation is a problem to be solved by compilation. The executables are the ultimate solution. The requirements are the ultimate problem. Progressive refinement is effective because the mappings at each step are smaller and easier to find than one large mapping that bridges the entire abstraction gap. This is illustrated in Figure 2.6, where a coarse grained feature is decomposed into fine grained features in two steps, rather than one.

Progressive refinement is effective because the mappings at each step are smaller and easier to find than one large mapping.

We can now see that each of the descriptions produced by progressive refinement is a solution when seen from above, but a problem when seen from below. In other words, problem and solution are relative concepts. Their meaning depends on our perspective. We can think of the objects that comprise each description as residing in some domain, as illustrated in Figure 2.7. All of these domains, except the execution domain, are abstract. The most abstract is the domain where the requirements reside. The most concrete is the domain where the executables reside. These two domains are the starting and ending points for progressive refinement. We will call them the requirements domain and the execution domain, respectively, to distinguish them from the others, which we will call intermediate

Each of the descriptions produced by progressive refinement is a solution when seen from above, but a problem when seen from below.

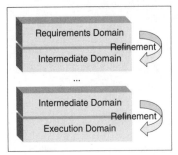

Figure 2.7 Progressive refinement from requirements to executables

domains. Of course, we can think of the intermediate domains as either problem domains or solution domains, depending on our perspective. What about the requirements domain and the executable domain? Clearly, we can think of the executable domain only as a solution domain. For now, we can also think of the requirements domain as only a problem domain, since it is the most abstract. We shall see later, however, that we can think of the requirements domain as a solution domain by changing our perspective.

Refinement implies subsequent abstraction.

Implicit in the strategy of progressive refinement is the assumption that breaking a large problem into smaller ones makes it easier to solve. For this strategy to be effective, the smaller problems must be easier to solve than the large one, and we must be able to recombine the solutions to the smaller problems to form a solution to the large one.

We do not have enough information to work strictly top-down.

In theory, we could use refinement to decompose problems all the way from the requirements domain to the execution domain, render the solutions defined at the bottom, and then work all the way back up again, progressively composing solutions to produce the executables. For example, we might start with a system specification, break it into subsystem specifications, break those into component specifications, break those into class specifications, and break those into method and variable specifications. We might then implement the specified methods and variables, combine those to implement the specified classes, combine those to implement the specified components, combine those to implement the specified subsystems, and combine those to implement the specified system, as illustrated in Figure 2.6. In practice, however, we cannot work strictly top-down because we do not have enough information at each step to ensure that the solutions we choose will yield executables that satisfy the non-functional requirements.

NON-FUNCTIONAL REQUIREMENTS [GRA92, POSA1]

USABILITY

Usability is a measure of how well the software supports the execution of user tasks. Key factors contributing to usability are the presentation of information and the management of user interaction. Usability includes two other measures, affordance and accessibility.

- ◆ Affordance is a measure of the cost of learning to be productive with a user interface [Nor]. A user interface may be highly usable once it has been learned, but difficult to learn. The well-known EMACS text editor is an example of such an interface. A user interface that is highly intuitive, and therefore easy to learn, is said to have high affordance.

- ◆ Accessibility is a measure of how broad a pool of users can interact effectively with the user interface. A highly accessible user interface can accommodate the needs of users with a wide variety of requirements, for example by providing interface mechanisms to help users with physical impairments, or by providing localized versions of the user interface.

RELIABILITY

Reliability is a measure of the frequency and severity of defects encountered during normal operation of the software. The more severe the defects and the more frequently they are encountered, the less reliable the software. Three related measures are fault tolerance, robustness and security.

- ◆ Fault tolerance is a measure of how well the system can maintain normal operation when defects are encountered. Examples of fault tolerance in distributed business applications include recovering from failed transactions and routing tasks to other resources when the original resources are incapacitated.

- ◆ Robustness is a measure of how well the system avoids failures when confronted with invalid data or incorrect usage.

- ◆ Security is a measure of how well the system avoids a specific type of failure, namely the unauthorized exposure of the processes and entities manipulated by the system.

(continued)

NON-FUNCTIONAL REQUIREMENTS *(continued)*

PERFORMANCE

Performance is a measure of how quickly the system responds to stimuli, and how well it utilizes resources in providing that response. Performance is often defined in terms of latency, throughput, efficiency and scalability.

- ◆ Latency is a measure of the amount of time that elapses in performing a given operation under a given operating load.

- ◆ Throughput is a measure of how many operations can be performed in a given amount of time under a given operating load.

- ◆ Efficiency is a measure of how many resources must be consumed by the software to provide acceptable latency and throughput under a given operating load.

- ◆ Scalability is a measure of how many additional resources must be consumed by the software to maintain acceptable latency and throughput with increasing load.

SUPPORTABILITY

Supportability is a measure of the cost of supporting the software after it has been delivered to the customer. Measures that contribute to supportability include maintainability, malleability, extensibility, portability, interoperability and testability.

- ◆ Maintainability is a measure of how easy it is to correct defects in the software. This is determined by the degree of cohesion within the components, and by how well features are localized within the software.

- ◆ Malleability is a measure of how easy is to modify the software to accommodate changes in requirements. This is determined by the degree of encapsulation of the components, and by how well they can vary independently of one another.

- ◆ Extensibility is a measure of how easy it is to replace existing parts of the software, and how easy it is to add new functionality. This is determined by the degree of coupling among the components. When components are highly coupled, it is difficult to replace one without affecting the others.

- ◆ Portability is a measure of how easy it is to adapt the software to run on different platforms. This is determined by how well platform dependencies are localized and encapsulated within the software.

◆ **Interoperability is a measure of how easy it is to compose the software with other systems. This is determined by how well the software exposes its functionality through programmatic interfaces and how much context must be maintained by the other systems to use those interfaces.**

◆ **Testability is a measure of how easy it is to design tests that exercise the features of the software to expose defects. This is related to the level of factoring of the features. When features are highly factored, they are easier to access in isolation, and therefore to test independently, and defects are easier to isolate.**

Abstraction in Software Development

An alternative approach is to use abstraction to compose new solutions from existing ones to solve the problems that we expect to encounter during refinement. These solutions are called abstractions because they are created by abstraction. For example, assume that we have operations for reading and writing bytes on an external device in the execution domain. If we thought we would frequently manage groups of bytes, we might compose these operations to create a new abstraction called a file. We could then use the file abstraction during progressive refinement, whenever we wanted to create, destroy, name or copy groups of bytes. Abstractions make problems easier to solve by removing details from the solution. The file abstraction, for example, defines an interface that hides the details of managing groups of bytes using device operations. In other words, using an abstraction hides the details of its implementation from the solution. Since an abstraction can be implemented in many ways, it is like a one-to-many mapping in the process of progressive refinement [WL99]. Many design decisions that would have to be taken to implement a solution are replaced by one design decision taken to apply the abstraction.

By building new abstractions from existing ones, we progressively produce more abstract solutions. As we might expect, this process is called progressive abstraction. We can think of each step in this process as an inverse transformation that maps a solution to a problem. The output of each inverse transformation becomes the input to others. Progressive abstraction is effective because the mappings at each step are smaller and

Abstraction can be used to compose new solutions from existing ones to solve problems that we expect to encounter during refinement.

Progressive abstraction is effective because the mappings at each step are smaller and easier to find than one large mapping.

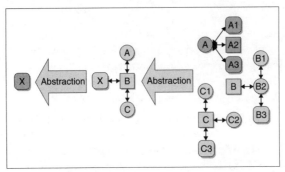

Figure 2.8   Producing solutions by progressive abstraction

easier to find than one large mapping that bridges the entire abstraction gap. This is illustrated in Figure 2.8, where a coarse-grained feature is composed from fine-grained features in two steps, rather than one.

We do not have enough information to work strictly bottom up.

In theory, we could use progressive abstraction to compose solutions all the way from the execution domain to the requirements domain, until we had implemented the requirements. The result would be a tree[2] of nested abstractions, where each node in the tree would be an abstraction consisting of lower level abstractions or objects in the execution domain [Gar95]. In practice, however, we cannot work strictly bottom-up, because we do not have enough information at each step to choose problems that must be solved to satisfy the functional requirements.

Top-Down and Bottom-Up

Abstractions are easier to develop, but harder to apply bottom-up, and easier to apply, but harder to develop top-down.

We can now observe the following conundrum:

Working top-down, we cannot produce an acceptable decomposition of a given problem in terms of available abstractions, but working bottom-up, we cannot produce an acceptable composition of available abstractions to solve a given problem.

Working bottom-up makes abstractions easier to develop, but more difficult to apply [Bus00a]. For example, we might develop two class libraries, one for persisting objects and another for managing user interfaces. Later, we might find it hard to develop a complete application using the libraries, since they were not designed to work together. On the other hand, working top-down makes abstractions easier to apply, but harder to develop, since they must satisfy requirements imposed by the top-down structure [Ale79, Bus00a]. For example, we might

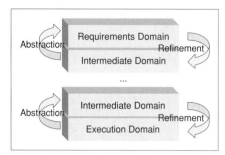

Figure 2.9 Working top-down and bottom–up

start by requiring all class libraries to register the services they offer and to locate other services by checking the registry. This would make the complete application easier to develop by defining how the front and back ends work together. However, the two class libraries would now be harder to develop, since they would now have to provide call backs, and perform other tasks to satisfy the requirements imposed by the registry.

To resolve this conundrum, we must work in both directions at the same time, using abstraction and refinement, iteratively, to make ends meet, as illustrated in Figure 2.9.

We must use abstraction and refinement, iteratively, to make ends meet.

We compose abstractions to solve problems that we expect to encounter during refinement. For example, we build object relational mapping technology to facilitate the storage and retrieval of data using objects. We also decompose problems in terms of existing solutions by refinement. For example, we break up large concepts that appear in the requirements into graphs of smaller objects that can be mapped to a database. We then iterate to improve both sets of decisions to produce executables that satisfy the requirements. Decisions made when decomposing problems are influenced by our knowledge of existing solutions, and decisions made when composing solutions are influenced by our knowledge of commonly occurring problems. With each iteration, we learn more about both the problems and the solutions. In other words, we iteratively develop abstractions and refine requirements, until we can bind the requirements to the abstractions, as shown in Figure 2.10.

Decisions made during refinement are influenced by knowledge of existing solutions, and decisions made when developing abstractions are influenced by knowledge of recurring problems.

Satisfying Constraints

Of course, it is not enough to merely solve these problems in the course of developing the software. We must solve them in

Non-functional requirements must be satisfied by design.

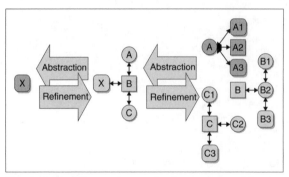

Figure 2.10 Abstraction and refinement combined

a way that satisfies non-functional requirements to ensure that the solution has acceptable performance, usability, reliability, and supportability. Since this will not happen by chance, we must impart these qualities to the solution by design. Since all possible solutions to any problem are configurations of the same solution domain objects, the only thing that differentiates one solution from another is the selection and arrangement of solution domain objects. All network file systems, for example, manipulate the same underlying networking hardware, but some are much faster than others because they use better algorithms.

Design decisions determine solution structure.

Design decisions partition the solution, and allocate responsibility among its components.[3] They define component properties and behaviors, and determine how components are related and interact. They also define aspects of the solution that are not well localized, such as how security is enforced, how transactions propagate, how resources are shared among concurrent threads of control, and how persistent state is stored and retrieved [Cop99, Gar00, KLM97. MR97, POSA1]. In other words, design decisions determine solution structure.

Design decisions navigate a decision tree.

There are many ways to decompose problems, and to compose solutions, as we have seen, so there are many ways to implement functional requirements. Assuming no coding errors,[4] the solution we produce to solve a given problem is determined by design decisions. As Parnas suggests, we can think of the set of all possible design decisions as forming a decision tree[5] that leads from a problem to the set of all possible solutions, as illustrated in Figure 2.11 [Par76]. When we make a design decision, we select a branch at a node in the tree. This narrows the set of branches that remain to be selected. To select a solution,

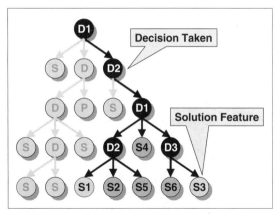

Figure 2.11   Navigating a decision tree

we start at the problem and make design decisions until we have selected a path that spans the entire tree. At times, we work top-down, at times we work bottom-up, and we iterate until we make ends meet. We select a specific solution from the set of possible solutions by making design decisions. The sequence of design decisions taken determines the structure of the solution by selecting one solution from the set of possible solutions that appear at the leaves of the tree.

Clearly, it would not be practical to wait until all of the design decisions had been made and the executables had been produced to measure their success or failure in satisfying the non-functional requirements. This means that we must be able to predict the qualities imparted to the software by a given design decision. How can we do this? One way is to reuse design patterns with known properties. We will return to this topic in Chapter 6.

We can predict the qualities imparted to the software by specific design decisions using patterns with known properties.

Raising the Level of Abstraction

Raising the level of abstraction is one of the most fundamental techniques in software development. In fact, most developers do it daily, but often without thinking about it in these terms. Raising the level of abstraction is a way of reusing knowledge about how to solve frequently recurring problems in a given domain by developing abstractions in advance and then applying those abstractions to solve the problems when they are encountered. Let's look more closely at applying abstractions,

Raising the level of abstraction lets us solve frequently recurring problems in advance and reuse the solutions.

and then at developing abstractions, to see how knowledge is reused.

Applying Abstractions

We must combine the same abstractions in different ways to solve different problems.

Remember that we can develop solutions, called abstractions, and apply them to solve problems that we encounter during refinement. Of course, since the problems in a domain are similar but not identical, their solutions are similar but not identical, also. So, although we can use the same abstractions to solve these problems, we must use them in different ways. For example, we can use files and directories in many different ways to solve many different problems. Also, we may not be able to solve any given problem completely using only the abstractions defined in advance. Parts of the solution may therefore have to be developed specifically for each problem. We can now define an abstraction more precisely as a partial solution developed in advance to the problems in a given domain, which can be used, along with other abstractions, to partially or completely solve multiple problems in the domain.

The cost of developing abstractions is amortized across the problems in the domain.

Developing abstractions effectively migrates effort from decomposing problems to composing solutions. This migration is important because it reduces the total effort required to solve multiple problems. The level of cost reduction depends on the number of times we can apply the abstraction. In other words, it depends on the number of problems that contain the subproblem solved by the abstraction. This suggests that we should develop abstractions for closely related families of problems. In Chapter 4, we will describe software product lines and show that this is exactly what they do.

When we encounter a problem repeatedly, we can reuse knowledge gained from previous encounters.

Developing Abstractions

According to Van Vliet, the value of an abstraction is not merely that it eliminates effort, but also that it captures knowledge that can only be acquired by experience, and that it makes the knowledge available for reuse in later efforts [Vli93]. Recall that we develop abstractions to solve problems that we expect to encounter during refinement. This means that the decisions made when developing abstractions are based on knowledge of commonly occurring problems. Where did that knowledge come from? It came from experience, gained either directly (e.g., in the school of hard knocks) or indirectly (e.g., by studying experience gained and documented by others). When we encounter a problem that we have already seen, we remember how we solved it before, and we solve it the same way again. Solving it again is easier than solving it the first time, since we can reuse some of the analysis we did before to decompose the problem and some of the synthesis we did before to compose the solution. We may also learn from mistakes we made before, and improve our strategy accordingly.

Abstractions capture knowledge that can only be gained by experience.

If we encounter a problem often enough, we may find that the savings justify a more systematic approach to reuse that lets us recognize and solve the problem more quickly, or that captures this knowledge more formally, so that other people can achieve similar results. One way to be more systematic is to define a pattern. A pattern describes a recurring problem encountered in a specific context, and a proven strategy for solving the problem. Another way to be more systematic is to make an implementation of the solution available as a framework. Patterns and frameworks are mechanisms for packaging abstractions. We will look at patterns and frameworks more closely, and at other abstraction packaging mechanisms, such as languages and tools, in Chapters 6 through 15.

The savings may justify a more systematic approach to reuse for frequently encountered problems.

Of course, in practice, a problem rarely occurs in exactly the same way twice. Instead, it looks slightly different each time we encounter it. Instead of thinking of it as one problem that varies, we can think of it as multiple similar but distinct problems that comprise a family. To solve more than one member of the family, we must now develop either a new abstraction for each member, or some smaller number of abstractions that solve multiple members, either individually or in combination, by supporting variation. Since the whole point of developing abstractions is to reuse knowledge, the first alternative adds no value. It simply puts us back where we started, solving every problem from scratch. In other words, to add value, an abstraction must solve more than one problem by supporting variation. The file abstraction, for example, supports variation in the name, type, length, content, nesting, and location of files. We might conclude that the more variation, the better. We will see later in this chapter, however, that there is an important trade-off between the number and size of problems solved by an abstraction. We can now define an abstraction more precisely as a solution developed in advance to solve a family

An abstraction is a solution developed in advance to solve a family of related problems.

of related subproblems that are common to the problems in a given domain, which can be used, along with other abstractions, to partially or completely solve multiple problems in the domain.

We can solve multiple problems in a domain by composing abstractions that solve its subproblems.

We have just seen that we can think of a single variable problem as a family of related problems. Conversely, we can think of a family of related problems as a single variable problem. We can think of the family of problems solved by the file abstraction as the single variable problem of file management, for example. If we often encounter the members of one problem family when decomposing the members of another, then we can think of the first problem family as a subproblem of the second problem family. If we often encounter file management problems when decomposing applications, for example, then we can think of file management as a subproblem of application development. This is an important result because it means that we can solve multiple problems in a given domain by composing the abstractions that solve their common subproblems. Since file and user interface management are common subproblems of application development, for example, we can solve multiple application development problems by composing file and user interface abstractions.

Reusing Knowledge

Abstractions let us reuse knowledge.

At this point in the discussion, we can see that the value of an abstraction depends on how completely it solves a given problem. Let's consider a scale that ranges from none at one end to completely at the other end. The more knowledge the abstraction provides, the less knowledge its user must provide to solve the problem. Conversely, however, the more knowledge the abstraction provides, the narrower its scope of application. This is illustrated in Figure 2.12.

A black-box abstraction implements a solution.

At the high end of the scale, an abstraction provides a fully implemented solution that is completely opaque to the user. This is called a black-box abstraction. The user does not need to understand how the abstraction solves the problem, only what problem is solved and how the solution is applied. Of course, an abstraction that provides a completely fixed solution is inflexible, because it can only be applied to problems that require exactly that solution. For this reason, black-box abstractions generally allow the user to customize the implementation, e.g., by setting parameter values or by

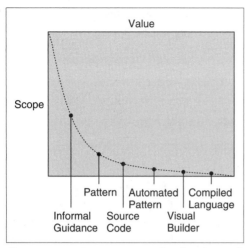

Figure 2.12 Scope versus value for abstractions

combining multiple abstractions in different ways. Features supplied by libraries or compiled languages, such as user interface widgets or method dispatch, are generally black-box abstractions. Black-box abstractions answer questions like these [ACM00]:

- What technologies should be used to solve a given problem?
- How can the technologies be applied and configured?
- What defaults should be supplied when information is missing?
- How should the solution be optimized?

At the low end of the scale, an abstraction provides no value. The user must provide all of the knowledge required to solve the problem, including the design and implementation of the solution. Of course, an abstraction that provides no value is uninteresting. For this reason, let's to move a little farther up the scale to consider an abstraction that provides a description of the solution, but not an implementation. This is called a white-box abstraction. The user of a white-box abstraction studies the solution description, and then applies that knowledge when called upon to solve a problem. A white-box abstraction is essentially a form of documentation. It can therefore be applied in many contexts. The user supplies its implementation, and can tailor it in any way necessary for the problem at hand. Patterns

A white-box abstraction describes a solution, but does not provide an implementation.

are familiar examples of white-box abstractions. White-box abstractions answer questions like these [ACM00]:

- What practices should be repeated or avoided?
- What problems are frequently encountered in a given domain?
- How can frequently encountered problems be solved?
- How can solutions be refactored to improve their qualities?

A gray-box abstraction helps the user solve the problem.

It is interesting to consider abstractions that fall between these two extremes, or gray-box abstractions, as they are called. A gray-box abstraction might supply the source code for a partial or complete implementation of the solution, which the user can complete or modify as necessary. Alternatively, it might provide a tool, such as a visual builder, where the user can configure a visual representation of the solution, and then generate source code that instantiates and configures library classes according to the configuration.

The Effect of Granularity

Granularity is a measure of the size of an abstraction.

Granularity is a measure of the size of an abstraction. A coarse-grained abstraction encapsulates more functionality than a fine-grained abstraction. A credit authorization service, for example, is more coarse grained than a String class. Behaviors required and offered by coarse-grained abstractions are frequently too complex to understand by experimentation. They must therefore offer richer descriptions of their behaviors than simple interfaces like those provided, for example, by the Web Service Definition Language (WSDL). These descriptions should define valid sequences of interaction supported by the component, the policies it uses to handle exceptions, and the levels of service it requires and guarantees, as we shall see in Chapters 12 and 13.

The size of abstractions has increased over time, with the power of programming languages.

The size of abstractions has increased over time, with the power of programming languages. Early programs were assembled from individual processor instructions representing basic arithmetic and memory access. Programs written in languages like FORTRAN and COBOL contained statements representing arithmetic expressions, input/output operations, and simple data structures. Programs written in languages like C were able to describe more complex data structures through pointer arithmetic and structure types, and enjoyed the benefits of structured control flow constructs representing case logic, alternative decisions, and conditional loops. Continuing this trend, classes represent fine-grained objects like collections, local components represent moderately fine-grained objects like user interface widgets, distributed components represent moderately coarse-grained objects like business entities, and Web services represent coarse-grained objects like credit authorization services.

The Effect of Specificity

Specificity defines the scope of an abstraction. To paraphrase Jackson, the value of an abstraction increases with its level of specificity to the problem domain. A more specific abstraction holds more knowledge about the problem domain than a more general one because it encapsulates more knowledge about the problem domain. In other words, it is more powerful for solving problems in the domain [Jac00]. This increase in power has two major consequences:

Increasing the specificity of an abstraction increases its power but reduces its scope and the amount of control it provides.

- *Reduced Scope.* A more specific abstraction solves a smaller number of problems. For example, J2EE provides abstractions for business applications from more general ones provided by Java 2, Standard Edition (J2SE™). J2EE abstractions are more powerful than J2SE abstractions for building business applications, but less powerful for building for other types of applications, such as personal productivity applications.

- *Reduced Control.* By encapsulating part of the solution, an abstraction removes opportunity to change that part of the solution. In other words, it binds design decisions. A more specific abstraction binds more design decisions, leaving fewer to the developer. For example, J2EE binds decisions about the security, life cycle, persistence, distribution, and deployment of a component, which J2SE leaves to the developer. As we saw earlier in this chapter, design decisions are the primary mechanism available to the developer to control the structure and operational qualities of the solution. This loss of control is acceptable because the abstraction helps to solve the problem. We give up control to reuse the knowledge supplied by the abstraction. The control we lose is gratuitous. It is not needed to solve the problem. For example, while assembly language provides more control, most developers would rather use a language like C# or Java to solve a business problem, since they are easier to use, and will almost certainly yield a more usable, more reliable, more supportable solution. We can now see that raising the level of abstraction reduces complexity by reducing the number of possible solutions that can be considered. At the same time, it increases the learning curve for developers by introducing new abstractions that developers must learn to be productive.

Narrowing the Abstraction Gap

Abstractions create a new solution domain.

An interesting phenomenon occurs when we apply abstractions systematically. We start to think in terms of the abstractions, rather than in terms of the original solution domain. The abstractions essentially create a new solution domain that replaces the original one. This is raises the level of abstraction because the new solution domain is closer to the problem domain than the original one.

Raising the level of abstraction reduces the number of abstractions required.

Raising the level of abstraction gives developers larger solution features that are more specific to the problem domain. Because each solution feature solves more of a given problem than the features in the original solution domain, fewer are required to solve the problem and there are fewer ways to combine them. In other words, raising the level of abstraction makes solutions easier to find by making it easier to compose solution features to solve the problem.

Raising the level of abstraction narrows the abstraction gap.

We can now see that raising the level of abstraction narrows the abstraction gap by bringing the solution domain closer to the problem domain. The new solution domain appears to be a new platform, as illustrated in Figure 2.13. Programs based on the abstractions defined by the new solution domain appear to run on the new platform. When the new platform includes an interpreter, such as LISP, they actually do run on it. In most cases, however, they actually run on a lower level platform, and must be compiled, linked, deployed, or processed in other ways before they can run. Programs based on Java, for example, are first compiled into byte code programs, which run on an interpreter called the Java Virtual Machine (JVM). Programs based on .NET are first compiled into an Intermediate Language

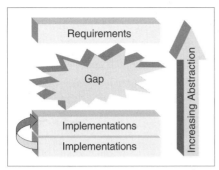

Figure 2.13 Narrowing the abstraction gap

(IL), and then compiled into binary form just prior to execution by a Just-In-Time (JIT) compiler.

At this point, it is appropriate to consider who does the work of bridging the abstraction gap. We said earlier that it is the developer who does the work by making design decisions and coding the artifacts that capture them. In practice, however, the developer bridges only part of the abstraction gap, namely the part between the requirements and hand-coded artifacts, such as source code and configuration files. We think of these hand-coded artifacts as the implementation of the requirements. We think this way because we rarely see what happens later, as hand-coded artifacts are further refined to produce executables. That work is done by compilers, assemblers, and interpreters. To a compiler developer, hand-coded artifacts are specifications, not implementations. The artifacts produced by the compiler are the real implementations.

The developer spans only part of the abstraction gap.

We can now see that part of the abstraction gap, namely the part between the hand-coded artifacts and the executables, is bridged by tools. This is a key observation because it means that refinement can be performed automatically. Indeed, it happens every day during compilation. We can now ask whether or not more of the abstraction gap could be bridged automatically. We will show in later chapters that this is indeed possible. This possibly surprising conclusion suggests that we may be working at the wrong level of abstraction. We could be using more powerful abstractions and letting tools do more of the work.

We could be using more powerful abstractions and letting tools do more of the work.

Packaging Abstractions

Abstractions are generally delivered using either platforms or languages.

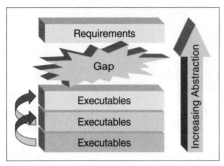

Figure 2.14 The effect of platform-based abstractions

Platform-Based Abstractions

Platform-based abstractions make the execution platform more abstract.

Platform-based abstractions make the solution domain more abstract by making the execution platform more abstract. The abstractions supplied by an execution platform form an execution domain, as we have seen. For example, the execution domain supplied by the .NET Framework contains abstractions for exposing classes as Web services. A given execution domain may be based on a lower level one. For example, the .NET Framework is based on the Common Language Runtime (CLR), which in turn is based on the primitive execution domain supplied by hardware and privileged software components, such as operating systems and device drivers. For example, the primitive execution domain might contain Microsoft Windows Server™ running on Intel® hardware. These concepts are illustrated in Figure 2.14.

Client programs call implementations supplied by the platforms.

Client programs use platform-based abstractions by calling procedures, classes, or components that implement them. For example, client programs call .NET Framework classes to expose components as Web services. Since they supply implementations that are opaque to the user, platform-based abstractions are black-box abstractions. The computational cost of platform-based abstractions is incurred at runtime, when the implementations they supply are called by client programs.

Some design decisions are bound at runtime and some at platform development time.

Platform-based abstractions may bind some design decisions, such as policies and algorithms, using dynamic composition mechanisms, such as strategy objects and abstract factories [GHJV95]. Other decisions, such as trade-offs among operational qualities, may be statically bound at platform development time. Since the statically bound decisions may not satisfy all users, this can lead to multiple implementations of the same abstractions, each binding a different set of assumptions. For

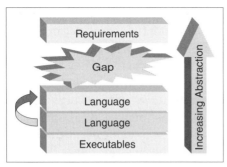

Figure 2.15   The effect of language-based abstractions

example, it is not unusual to have multiple implementations of the same collection abstraction, each optimized for a different usage pattern. New implementations may also be required as technology evolves. For example, Java and the Java Development Kit (JDK) changed significantly on several occasions, requiring existing implementations based on earlier versions to change significantly, as well.

Language-Based Abstractions

Language-based abstractions make the solution domain more abstract, without changing the execution domain by forming new solution domains above the platform, as illustrated in Figure 2.15. For example, the C# compiler generates Web service wrappers for C# classes flagged with language attributes.

Language-based abstractions make the development vocabulary more abstract. They are often supported by tools.

Formal language-based abstractions are defined by language constructs, and are often supported by tools, such as editors, compilers, and debuggers. They are usually black-box abstractions, and their implementations are usually assembled, compiled or interpreted. Informal language based abstractions, such as patterns, are defined by documentation. They are usually white-box abstractions, and while they are based on experience with implementations, they usually do not supply implementations. The computational cost of language-based abstractions may be incurred at development time, when their implementations are generated by tools, or at runtime, when their implementations are executed.

Some design decisions are bound at run time, some at application development time, and some at tool development time.

Formal language-based abstractions bind some design decisions statically at tool development time. For example, marshalling routines for remote procedure calls may be statically bound when a CORBA IDL compiler is developed. They bind others statically at application development time through parameterization. For example, a CORBA IDL compiler may use configuration options or compiler directives to decide which of the statically bound marshalling routines to use. They also bind some design decisions at runtime. Some argument types for remote procedure calls, for example, may not be known until runtime. Informal language-based abstractions bind some design decisions statically at application development time. An algorithm and the strategy object interface are defined when the Strategy pattern is implemented. They also bind some decisions at runtime. Using the Strategy pattern, for example, specific strategy objects can be supplied at runtime.

Relative Levels of Abstraction

Abstraction delivery can be mixed.

Language and platform-based abstractions can be mixed, as illustrated by well-known combinations, such as Java and the JDK, C# and the .NET Framework, or ATL and COM. Let's look at the relationship between these two forms of delivery. Three general scenarios can be identified.

When the language is more abstract, language based abstractions must be maintained by tools.

- When the language is more abstract than the platform, the language-based abstractions must be maintained by tools. For example, abstractions defined by C++, such as classes and methods, are not supported by the underlying platforms, and must be maintained by C++ specific tools, such as compilers, debuggers, test generators, and measurement and analysis tools. To debug a C++ program in terms of classes and methods, rather than in terms of machine instructions, instruction level trace information must be mapped to class and method definitions in the source code using symbol tables. In this case, each of the tools must implement the language-based abstractions. Differences between these implementations can create subtle errors. Worse, some tools may not fully support the abstractions, forcing developers to use a lower level domain. For example, if we don't have a language specific debugger, we may have to trace execution using an assembly language debugger.

When the platform is more abstract, complexity is exposed.

- When the platform is more abstract than the language, the platform-based abstractions expose complexity because they are not encapsulated by language constructs. They have the same level of encapsulation as the abstractions defined by the application. For example, because JavaBeans are not encapsulated by the Java language, the mechanisms they use to implement abstractions like properties and events are exposed to the developer.

- When the language and the platform are matched, platform-based abstractions are encapsulated by the language and language-based abstractions are supported by the platform. For example, CLR-based languages like C# and Visual Basic encapsulate abstractions defined by .NET similar to those defined by JavaBeans.

Language and platform-based abstractions can be matched.

Solution Domain Evolution

Of course, the solution domains currently used by most developers are not the most primitive. They were created using combinations of platform and language based abstractions. Historically, the level of abstraction for developers has been gradually raised through both platforms and languages. Most of these advances have been made possible by new ways to define and use abstractions. For example:

Platforms and languages have become more abstract over time.

- On the platform side, we have progressed from hardware, through operating systems, network operating systems, message oriented middleware, distributed object and distributed component middleware, to asynchronous, loosely coupled Web services. Platform-based abstractions have been packaged as programs, as libraries of procedures, classes or components, as application frameworks, and as component assemblies.

- On the language side, we have progressed from numerical encoding, through assembly languages and structured languages, to object-oriented languages for general purpose programming, plus special purpose languages for functional programming, logic programming, graphics programming, device programming, virtual reality programming, music generation, data definition and manipulation, user interface definition, printing and many other applications. These include assembled languages, macro languages, compiled languages, template languages, scripting languages, interpreted languages, semi-compiled languages and pattern languages.

The history of programming is an exercise in hierarchical abstraction.

Smith and Stotts summarize this eloquently [SS02]:

The history of programming is an exercise in hierarchical abstraction. In each generation, language designers produce constructs for lessons learned in the previous generation, and then architects use them to build more complex and powerful abstractions.

New abstractions tend to appear first in platforms, and then migrate to languages.

They also point out an important relationship in this progression, namely that new abstractions tend to appear first in platforms, and then migrate to languages. As we shall see in Chapter 6, these abstractions tend to appear first as isolated practices, then as recognized patterns, and then in tools and frameworks, before they are finally codified by languages. This is precisely what happened with the property and event abstractions described earlier. They first appeared as isolated practices in programs based on C++ and Smalltalk, then as documented patterns [GHJV95], then in tools like Symantec Visual Café™ and frameworks like JavaBeans, before they were finally codified by the CLR based languages.

Languages have lagged behind platforms for a long time.

We are now at a point in this progression where language-based abstractions have lagged behind platform-based abstractions for a long time. In other words, tool technology has lagged behind platform technology for a long time. One of the themes of Software Factories is accelerating the migration of abstractions from platforms to languages by advancing tool technology.

Current Methods and Practices

How does object orientation deal with complexity?

We said earlier that complexity is a fundamental force in software development, and that every software development paradigm has been motivated at least in part by the need to attack complexity. How does object orientation deal with complexity? The answer to this question will help identify some of the chronic problems that it cannot solve, and some of the critical innovations needed to overcome them. Dealing with complexity was the primary motivation for most of the features that collectively form the paradigm of object orientation.

While dealing with change has become the primary focus of innovation in recent years, dealing with complexity is still the foundation on which the paradigm rests. One indication that innovation based on object orientation is reaching a plateau is that not much progress has been made in recent years in finding new ways of dealing with complexity using the principles of object orientation.

Encapsulation

The primary means of attacking complexity in object orientation is its basic metaphor, encapsulation. Encapsulation raises the level of abstraction by wrapping one or more related data elements in a software construct like a class or a component that defines their collective behavior, creating a locus of identity and responsibility. This improves feature localization and limits interactions among features.

OO attacks complexity through encapsulation.

Improving Feature Localization

Traceability and reconstruction problems are caused by feature delocalization, as we have seen. Encapsulation attacks them by improving feature localization. As shown in Figure 2.16, we make the solution features that implement each problem feature easier to identify, and the design decisions and rationale

Encapsulation improves feature localization.

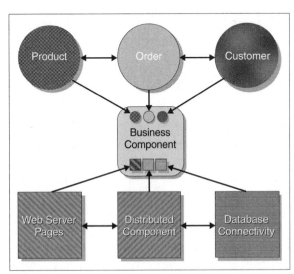

Figure 2.16 Reducing feature delocalization

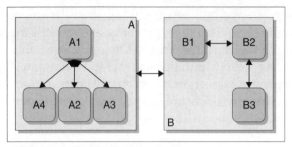

Figure 2.17 Reducing complexity

used to develop the solution easier to reconstruct by introducing an abstraction, Business Component, that wraps data elements comprising a Product, Order or Customer, and defines their collective behaviors [HS00]. As we shall see, patterns are often used to improve encapsulation in some way. For example, the Business Component abstraction used in Figure 2.16 is based on the Façade pattern [GHJV95].

Limiting Feature Interactions

Encapsulation limits feature interactions.

When the implementation of an abstraction is encapsulated, its complexity is hidden behind an interface. By hiding implementation, encapsulation keeps complexity from growing as smaller solutions are composed to form larger solutions. In other words, it reduces the number of features and the number of relationships between them that must be considered simultaneously. The developer using abstractions A and B shown in Figure 2.17 does not see abstractions A1 through A4 or B1 through B3 since they are encapsulated by A and B.

Partitioning Responsibility

The primary concern of OO methods is partitioning responsibility to define encapsulation boundaries.

Since encapsulation is the primary means of attacking complexity in object orientation, the primary concern is partitioning responsibility. This involves defining encapsulation boundaries by defining the behaviors offered by each class, and therefore the set of all possible class interactions and the operational qualities of the software. Object-oriented methods and practices therefore focus on capturing requirements and mapping them to software structure. Several methods for capturing requirements are widely understood, including use cases, user stories, and tables, which are described by Jacobson, Beck, and

TeleLogic, respectively [Bec00, JCJ+92]. Quite ironically, methods for mapping requirements to software structure are less well understood. The term Object-Oriented Analysis and Design (OOA& D) is often used to describe this activity. Originally coined by Booch as the name of a formal methodology, it has long since come to refer to a broad range of formal and informal methods for partitioning responsibility [Boo95]. We will look at four: Design By Contract, role composition, Aspect Oriented Programming, and pattern application.

ANALYSIS AND DESIGN

Despite their apparent significance, the terms analysis and design are not well defined. Both are concerned with the decomposition of the requirements and the composition of the executables, but there is no widespread agreement regarding their exact meaning, or regarding the distinction between them. Some argue that analysis is concerned with refinement, while design is concerned with abstraction, but this begs the question of what to call the parts of the process where refinement and abstraction meet and are totally intertwined. Some try to draw the distinction by suggesting that design depends on implementation technology, while analysis does not. This distinction is not compelling, however, since requirements contain many assumptions about implementation technology, though most are quite abstract, such as what kinds of behaviors are possible within the bounds of the operational requirements. As development involves iterative abstraction and refinement, we see no value in trying to isolate analysis and design as discrete activities. The primary concern is partitioning responsibility among classes by making design decisions. Depending on level of formality, this may take place before, during and/or even after the actual development of the implementation, as described in Chapter 4.

Design by Contract

Design By Contract (DBC) has been widely used since the mid-1990s. The basic idea is that classes should interact on the basis of published contracts, not on the basis of implementation. Building on the established concept of an *interface*, DBC makes a hard distinction between the interface and implementation of a class. The interface describes the behavior of the class, including its operations, parameters, and pre- and

Design By Contract requires classes to interact only on the basis of published contracts.

post-conditions, in terms of relationships between specification types. No hint of any underlying implementation may surface through the interface, and yet the interface must be rigorous enough to support tool-based assembly and analysis. It serves as a contract to clients of the class.

Its most visible applications are the Eiffel programming language and Component-Based Development (CBD).

The effects of DBC can be seen in modern programming languages like C# and Java that use interface rather than implementation inheritance as the primary basis for polymorphism. They can also be seen in the widespread use of assertions in source code that document and enforce pre- and post-conditions. Perhaps the most visible applications, however, are the Eiffel programming language, which offers explicit DBC mechanisms, such as precondition, postcondition and invariant declarations for every method, and Component-Based Development (CBD), which arrived on the scene in the late 1990s, focusing on the assembly of independently developed coarse grained components, especially commercial off-the-shelf (COTS) components. In addition to requiring the use of interfaces rather than implementations as the basis for assembly, CBD provides stronger encapsulation mechanisms to minimize interdependencies, formalizing dependencies not only among interacting components, but also between each component and the execution environment, making it possible to deploy them independently.

Role Composition

With role composition, we design collaborations among roles, then compose groups of related roles to form component specifications.

CBD goes beyond encapsulation by building on the idea that structure and behavior can be formalized and analyzed in terms of component interactions. Using a concept called role composition, it partitions responsibility among components by designing collaborations among roles played by arbitrary components, without any knowledge of implementation, and then composing groups of related roles to form component specifications. For example, given the four roles Officer, Gentleman, Scoundrel, and Thief, we might compose Officer and Gentleman to form one component specification, then Scoundrel and Thief to form another. Using a different strategy, we might compose Officer and Scoundrel, then Gentleman and Thief. Collaborations can be parameterized and systematically reused as patterns. The implementations of component-based designs can also be generated in part and sometimes in whole by progressively refining compositions of collaborations using

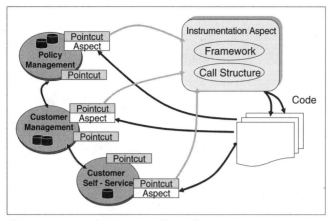

Figure 2.18 An instrumentation aspect crosscuts many components

model-driven development techniques, as described in Chapters 6 and 7.

Aspect-Oriented Programming

Aspect-Oriented Programming (AOP) is a method developed at the Xerox Palo Alto Research Center (PARC) that uses aspectual decomposition and composition to separate and then recombine, respectively, different aspects of a system [KLM97]. Aspects, such as security and logging, are generally operational features that must be distributed across functional features. Because of this cross cutting, the implementations of aspects become tangled with the implementations of the functional features, making maintenance difficult. With AOP, an operational feature can be developed independently, and then merged automatically with functional features prior to compilation. An operational feature handled in this way is called an aspect and the merge process is called aspect weaving. Figure 2.18 shows an instrumentation aspect developed independently of its potential usages being woven into marked positions, called pointcuts, in multiple components. Here, the pointcuts are the first and last lines in each method of each class. The aspect adds a call to an instrumentation framework, so that all calls to the methods of each class can be logged. AOP is not only a method for partitioning responsibility, but also a method for automating development by automatically recombining the results of the partitioning. We will look much more closely at AOP in Chapter 7.

Operational features called aspects can be developed independently and then woven into functional features.

Applying Patterns

Patterns are one of the most widely used partitioning techniques. They provide reusable strategies for partitioning responsibility.

Patterns have been widely used since the publication of the book, *Design Patterns* [GHJV95]. Quite a lot has been written about patterns since they were adapted from the work of Christopher Alexander to the realm of software development, most of it being the definitions of specific patterns. Much less has been written about how to discover and write patterns, or about how, when, and why to apply them. See Schmidt for an overview of this work [POSA2].

According to Alexander, a pattern is a relationship between a context, forces often encountered in that context, and a strategy for resolving the forces [Ale79] [AIS77]. Buschmann gives the following definition (paraphrased) [POSA1].

> *A pattern describes a particular design problem that is frequently encountered in specific contexts, and presents a proven, generalized approach to solving it. The approach specifies the roles and responsibilities of components that will be used in providing the solution, and describes how forces that gave rise to the problem are resolved by collaborations among the components.*

In other words, a pattern provides a strategy for solving a recurring problem in a specific context by partitioning responsibility among components.

They capture design knowledge in a reusable form.

Patterns provide value because they capture design knowledge. Developers rarely design from scratch. Instead, they usually copy and adapt existing designs. In other words, design reuse is one of the most common activities in software development. Unfortunately, design knowledge is often stored only accidentally, not systematically, and in places that make it difficult to find, understand or apply, such as source code or expert opinion. Schmidt notes that recovering knowledge opportunistically from source code is expensive because it is difficult to separate essential design decisions from inconsequential implementation details [POSA2]. It can also be difficult to find experts with the knowledge required to solve a given problem when the problem is encountered. If the knowledge we need cannot be recovered, then it must be rediscovered. Of course, rediscovery is expensive. Most software development projects involve large amounts of trial and error, as issues are rediscovered and resolved in ad hoc ways. Applying patterns suitable to the target problem domain can significantly reduce the amount of rediscovery involved. Finding patterns suitable to a given target problem domain may not be easy, however. We will return to this issue in Chapter 4, and we will have much more to say about applying patterns in Chapters 6 through 9.

Documenting Design

Documenting design provides a way to capture design decisions and the rationale behind them. It can help to provide traceability and to facilitate reconstruction. Given the significance of design decisions in determining the operational qualities of the software, documenting design has long been considered a critically important activity. It took on much more significance under object orientation, however, and many new methods and practices were developed. In practice, of course, design documents are difficult to keep current. Because they are not source artifacts, they are not forced to change as the software changes, and can therefore become obsolete very quickly. Architecture documentation is easier to maintain than detailed design documentation, since it describes more coarse grained aspects of the design that change less rapidly, but even these documents are prone to obsolescence. Models developed during the early stages of OOA& D, for example, are abandoned when source code becomes the focus of development activity because the cost of keeping them synchronized with the source code outweighs the benefits they provide. This problem is exacerbated by iterative development, because the frequent introduction of new requirements makes the source code and the models diverge more rapidly. This is a manifestation of the tension between dealing with complexity and dealing with change. We look at three approaches to documenting design: pattern authoring, visual modeling, and code visualization. All of them are widely used, but one of them, pattern authoring, has been much more successful than the others. As we shall see in Chapter 4, serious problems with visual modeling and code generation technologies have contributed to their failure. In Chapters 6 through 9, we will describe new technologies that correct these problems.

Design is documented to capture design decisions and rationale.

Pattern Authoring

Pattern authoring is an important form of documenting design. Indeed, it is a way of documenting the architecture of a family of software products, as we shall see later. A pattern is

There are two aspects to developing patterns: a creative one and a mechanical one.

written by a pattern author, typically a developer with experience in solving the recurring problem addressed by the pattern. As with developing software, there are two aspects to pattern authoring, a creative one and a mechanical one. Both are described in the pattern literature. See the *Pattern Languages of Program Design* books for patterns that describe the creative aspect, such as patterns for discovering patterns, for prioritizing forces, for team-based design, and for holding pattern writing workshops. See the *Pattern-Oriented Software Architecture* books for insights on the mechanical aspect, which involves writing a pattern specification. We will focus on the mechanical aspect in this chapter. The creative aspect is discussed in Chapters 6 and 7. While there is no standard form for specifying patterns, there are some well-known parts that often appear in pattern specifications. We will have much more to say about writing patterns in Chapters 6 through 9.

The context helps narrow the search for patterns that address a specific problem.

The *context* is generally some domain in which the recurring problem is frequently encountered. This could be a domain defined by requirements, such as the domain of health care applications, a domain defined by architecture, such as the domain of Web service applications, or a domain defined by technology, such as the domain of C# applications. The context helps narrow the search for patterns that address a specific problem. It also provides a way to collect knowledge about domains, and helps solve problems that span individual patterns by exposing relationships between patterns.

The pattern describes the problem to be solved...

The *problem description* defines the recurring problem to be solved. The general problem statement is supported by a description of the forces that give rise to the problem. These can include requirements that must be fulfilled, constraints that must be satisfied, or properties that the solution must exhibit.

...and shows how it is solved by partitioning responsibilities among components.

The *solution strategy* shows how the problem is solved by a configuration of components, and how the forces are balanced by the partitioning of responsibilities among them. Typically, the components are defined as roles played by components, not as whole components. A role describes a part that a component plays in an interaction, and defines specific features, such as properties or methods, required of components that play the part. The roles and the relationships between them define the structural aspects of the solution strategy, and the interactions that occur between them define the behavioral aspects.

The pattern may describe solution variants and selection guidelines.

If there is more than one way to apply a solution strategy, the pattern specification may also include *solution variants*, and *guidelines* for selecting the appropriate variant for various situations. It may also describe one or more *implementation strategies*, which suggest ways to implement the solution or its variants. Buschmann calls them micro methods, and shows how they complement general development methods by providing more specific and more detailed direction [Bus00b].

The strategies describe alternative solutions or implementations.

The *consequences* describe the anticipated effects of applying the pattern, such as expected costs and benefits, providing additional guidance regarding how and when to apply the pattern. Some of these effects may change the way the software satisfies non-functional requirements, such as security or performance. The consequences may also identify trade-offs among solution variants or implementation strategies.

The consequences describe the expected effects of application.

In addition to these abstract elements, a pattern specification typically includes at least one concrete *example*, or scenarios that illustrate the application of the pattern.

Examples are important.

Visual Modeling

A model of anything (e.g., a plastic model of a naval vessel, a set of parameterized B-Spline equations for a solid object, an entity-relationship diagram of some part of an application, etc.) is a representation of that thing which hides certain characteristics of it that are irrelevant for some purpose, while emphasizing others. In other words, it is an abstraction. A model of a set of interacting software components, for example, might describe only the interfaces of the components, ignoring the details of their implementation, to help architects focus on what the components do and how they collaborate.

A model is an abstraction.

We will show later that the key characteristic of a software model is its structure. It is a graph, in the mathematical sense, meaning that it consists of nodes and edges. Unlike tree-structured artifacts, such as source code, models are not hierarchical. As we shall see in Chapters 8 and 9, this means that they provide a richer medium for describing relationships between abstractions, giving them greater efficiency and power than source code. We will also show later that models can be rendered using non-graphical notations, including textual notations and user interface controls, such as trees, forms and wizards.

Models can be more efficient and powerful than source code.

Visual modeling refers to the development of graphical design documentation for the purpose of visualizing software structure or behavior. Visual models can capture high-level

They reveal information that is hard to see from the implementation artifacts alone.

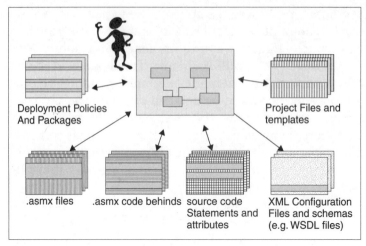

Figure 2.19   Capturing relationships among features

information, addressing concerns that span implementation artifacts and revealing information about relationships between components in a way that is hard to see when looking at the implementation artifacts alone, as illustrated in Figure 2.19. Visual models can be used to discover key abstractions and relationships, which would otherwise have to be discovered by examining multiple implementation artifacts. In the diagram, a set of collaborating Web services, each implemented by multiple artifacts, is visualized in a single diagram.

Code Visualization

Code visualization uses reverse engineering to work around the problem of currency.

Code visualization uses reverse engineering to work around the problem of currency, described earlier, by generating models from the source code, so that its structure and behavior can be visualized graphically. Figure 2.20 shows a visualization of Java® language source code. Code visualization requires more formal relationships between models and source code than visual modeling. Code visualization using general purpose modeling languages can actually be less appealing than working directly with the source code, since it does not use the terminology of the programming language, and does not capture all of the features expressible in source code. UML® class diagrams, for example, use terms like attribute and operation instead of field and method, and do not capture features of C# class files, such as properties, events or delegates. This kind of code visualization is neither abstract enough to capture high-level design concerns, nor concrete enough to capture low-level

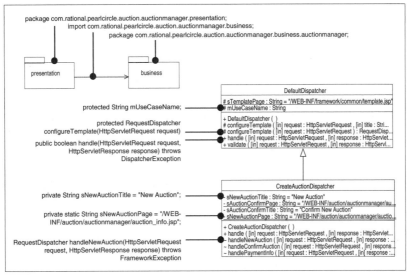

Figure 2.20 Visualizing java source code

design and implementation concerns. To be genuinely useful, code visualization must be a high-fidelity representation of the source code.

Automating Development

A key theme of the vision espoused by the pioneers of object orientation, with its emphasis on industrialization, was automating the rote or menial aspects of software development. Most developers acknowledge that tools are better at housekeeping chores than humans, and the best developers build custom tools to perform repetitive housekeeping chores, so that they can focus on the parts of the software development process that involve abstract reasoning, which cannot be performed by tools. Widely used methods for automating development include code generation, visual assembly, Rapid Application Development, and round trip engineering.

Automating rote or menial tasks was part of the vision of the pioneers of object orientation.

Code Generation

One of the most important forms of automation is code generation. We said earlier that part of the abstraction gap can be bridged automatically by automatic refinement, and that this happens every day in compilers. Compilation is one of the very earliest innovations in the industry. Indeed, most developers simply take it for granted without stopping to think about what

Almost all software is written by tools from specifications written by developers.

is actually happening, and see themselves as writing the actual software, when in fact, they are writing specifications used by tools that write the actual software. Code can be generated in other ways, as well, using similar methods. Two common practices are generating code from metadata captured by models and generating code from other forms of metadata. In both cases, code generation tools must understand the architecture, the platform and the development process, to generate meaningful code. The Windows Form Editor, for example, generates code based on the Windows runtime from properties of individual user interface widgets, which are set by the user within the editor. The generated code configures runtime variability points, such as widget coordinates, visual characteristics and event handling, using a set of simple design patterns and programming language idioms. One of the hardest problems to solve is maintaining the integrity of the relationship between the metadata, the generated code, and the handwritten code that customizes or interacts with the generated code. We will look at this issue and many other code generation issues in Chapter 4, and again in Chapters 14 and 15.

Generating code from higher level abstractions provides the most value.

Visual modeling tools often support the generation of source code from models. Code generation can use patterns, code templates, and other mechanisms to produce a range of implementations from a given model. Generating source code from graphical visualizations provides marginal value above working directly with the source code, unless the visualizations contain higher-level abstractions, such as business entities constructed from multiple classes, or call processing protocols for telecommunication systems.

Code can be generated from other sources of metadata.

Code can also be generated from other sources of metadata, including source code, attributes or structure comments embedded in source code, and metadata files that are not derived from visual models. For example, code can be generated to marshal remote procedure call arguments from the method signatures of a general purpose programming language, as in both .NET Remoting and Java Remote Objects.

Visual assembly is a way of generating code and metadata by manipulating graphical shapes in a tool.

Visual Assembly

Visual assembly is a way of generating code and metadata by manipulating graphical shapes in a tool. When Microsoft Windows was introduced, only expert programmers could build graphical user interfaces. When Microsoft Visual Basic defined the Form and Control abstractions, a much larger number of

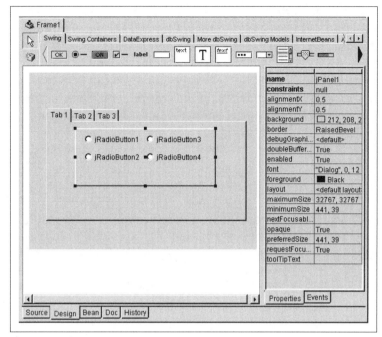

Figure 2.21   A visual assembly tool

developers were suddenly able to build these applications by visually assembling user interface widgets and writing small amounts of code to provide custom behavior. Forms and Controls are part of a graphical language for user interface design on Microsoft Windows. Visual assembly can be used to automate other software development tasks if suitable abstractions can be found for the components involved. The primary distinction between visual assembly and visual modeling is that in visual assembly, the shapes manipulated in the tool are visualizations generated by the components being assembled, while in visual modeling, they are defined by a visual modeling language. Figure 2.21 shows an example of a Java-based user interface design developed using visual assembly in the Borland JBuilder visual development tool.

Rapid Application Development

Rapid Application Development (RAD) is a logical extension of visual assembly. In addition to manipulating graphical shapes, the user manipulates other user interface constructs, such as forms, wizards, and dialogs, to automate various development activities. For example, a RAD tool might capture information about project types and dependencies between projects, to

RAD is an extension of visual assembly that automates many other development activities.

generate build scripts. It might also parse source code files to find all defined types, to support automatic name completion as the developer types, or to provide abstract visualizations of the source code, such as a class-oriented view that reveals inheritance relationships. Similarly, it might provide a view that exposes major constructs in the source code, such as class, method, and variable declarations, enabling the developer to navigate rapidly to those constructs by clicking in the view. Popular RAD tools include Microsoft Visual Basic and Borland Delphi[TM].

RAD is also an approach to managing development.

In addition to emphasizing automation, RAD differs from other approaches in the way it manages development [Man97]. It relies heavily on prototyping, where a demonstrable result is created as early as possible, and then iteratively refined based on feedback from users. It also uses time or cash boxing, where the project scope or requirements may change, but the time or cost of delivery may not. Because RAD emphasizes time or cost reduction over other factors, such as satisfying requirements, it may not be appropriate for some projects, such as building mission critical systems. Gantthead suggests the criteria shown in Table 2.1 for determining the suitability of a RAD for a project [Gan04].

Table 2.1   Suitability for rapid application development

CRITERION	SUITABLE	NOT SUITABLE
SCOPE	Focused scope where the business objectives are well-defined and narrow.	Broad scope where the business objectives are obscure or unfocused.
DATA	Complete or partial data already exists. The project largely comprises analysis or reporting of the data.	Complex and voluminous data must be analyzed, designed, and created.
DECISIONS	Decisions can be made by a small number of available people who are preferably co-located.	Many people must be involved in the decisions on the project, the decision makers are not available on a timely basis or they are geographically dispersed.

Table 2.1 (*continued*)

CRITERION	SUITABLE	NOT SUITABLE
TEAM	The project team is small (preferably six people or less).	The project team is large or there are multiple teams whose work needs to be coordinated.
ARCHITECTURE	The architecture is defined and clear and the key technology components are in place and tested.	The architecture is unclear and much of the technology will be used for the first time within the project.
REQUIREMENTS	Operational requirements are reasonable and well within the capabilities of the technology being used. Targeted performance should be less than 70% of the published limits of the technologies.	Operational requirements are tight for the equipment to be used, and/or there are stringent requirements, such as safety certification or mission-critical availability.

Round Trip Engineering

Round Trip Engineering (RTE) combines code visualization and code generation, and reconciles changes between the models and the source code, to keep them synchronized. For example, if a developer used a code editor to change the name of a class, RTE would cause the change to be reflected in any models used to visualize the class. Similarly, if a developer used a model editor to change the name of a class, RTE would cause the change to be reflected in the generated source code. There are two major concerns with RTE:

RTE combines code visualization and code generation.

- It may not be possible to reliably reconcile every change automatically, especially when changes can be made outside the tool that implements RTE. For example, it may not be possible to tell whether a class was renamed, or whether the original one was deleted and another one was added. The difference is significant because renaming an existing class would preserve all of the code added to it by the developer, while deleting it and adding a new one destroys all of the added code.

It may not be possible to reliably reconcile every change automatically.

Complex synchronization issues can arise in team development scenarios.

- Complex synchronization issues can arise in team development scenarios, where models and source code are edited independently by multiple developers. For example, if three developers made overlapping changes to the same model and source code file in their local workspaces, and then tried to check in their changes, a nine-way merge problem would arise, since it would be necessary to reconcile the changes among the three versions of the model and among the three versions of the source code, while keeping all three model and source code versions synchronized.

Humans should not edit generated artifacts.

In general, it is a bad idea to let humans edit generated source code files or other generated artifacts, since this causes confusion about which artifact is considered the master when conflicting changes are found. There is one exception to this rule, which arises when only certain parts of an artifact are generated, such that both the humans and the tools can easily and unequivocally determine which parts are generated and which parts are supplied by hand, such as when a source code model captures only the structure declarations like class, field, method, event, and property declarations, and leaves the method bodies to be supplied by hand. Unfortunately, modeling only the structure declarations is rarely satisfying. To provide real value, tools need to generate significant amounts of implementation, including method bodies. We will look at several ways to solve this problem in Chapter 15.

Organizing Development

Formal processes are optimized for dealing with complexity, while agile development methods are optimized for dealing with change.

One of the most visible aspects of object-oriented software development is what is known as the development process. We can think of a development process as a way of describing what is being developed, how the project is organized, what tools are being used and how they must be configured to interoperate effectively. Having this information readily at hand can be quite important, since without it a project can easily founder under the weight of these concerns. An exhaustive survey of object-oriented development processes would fill another book, so we will not attempt one here. We can make some general observations, however, such as identifying the spectrum of available approaches, and the relative strengths and weaknesses of approaches at each end of the spectrum. Formal processes like the Unified Process (UP) define one end of the spectrum. They are optimized primarily for dealing with complexity. Agile development methods like XP, SCRUM, and DSDM, define the other end. They are optimized primarily for dealing with change. Since we are concerned with complexity in this chapter, we will discuss formal processes here, and leave the discussion of agile development methods to Chapter 3.

According to Booch, a formal process prescribes activities generally performed in the course of developing software, the skills generally required to perform them, the order in which they must generally be performed, the artifacts they consume and produce, and the criteria for measuring and evaluating the way they are performed [Boo94]. It may also prescribe the roles played during software development, such as architect, developer, administrator or database designer, the artifacts to which people playing these roles contribute, and the communication that should take place between them. A formal process may also prescribe a specific workflow strategy. For example, it may require software development to proceed in a top-down or bottom-up manner; or by analogy to a waterfall or a spiral; by writing specifications before code and code before test cases, or test cases before code and code before specifications; or to develop the artifacts in full or incrementally.

A formal process may prescribe activities, skills, artifacts, roles, communication patterns and workflow strategies.

Most formal processes cover the front end of the life cycle, including requirements capture, analysis, design, and implementation. At this point, we start to encounter the bleeding edge of current methods and practices. There are few established methods or practices for the back end of the life cycle, starting with the packaging and organization of executable artifacts, and including

Most formal processes cover the front end of the life cycle, but there are few established methods or practices for the back end, which harbors massive complexity.

- The specification of constraints on the deployment environment
- The mapping of executable artifacts to the deployment environment
- The validation of the constraints at deployment time
- The provisioning and configuration of resources
- The installation and configuration of the executable artifacts
- The derivation of test cases from the executables or the requirements
- The development or generation of test harnesses and data sets

- The capture and analysis of test results

- The instrumentation of executables for measurements like elapsed time, resource usage, or code coverage

- The computation of static complexity metrics

- The execution of load, feature, and integration tests

- The monitoring and management of the software and the resources it uses during execution

- The maintenance and enhancement of the software to correct defects, improve operational qualities, or support changes in requirements.

The back end of the life cycle harbors massive complexity, most of which is attacked using proprietary tools and processes. As we shall see starting in Chapter 5, a key theme of Software Factories is capturing more information in the front end of the life cycle to make the back end more tractable.

The UP is a formal and highly prescriptive software development process.

While the UP is by no means the only method in use today, nor the most popular by any means, we focus on it for the purposes of this section, since it is widely used, and illustrates the characteristics of formal processes. The UP and its derivatives like the Rational Unified Process® (RUP®) [Kru00, RUP02] are based on the original OOA& D methodology by Booch, Object Modeling Technique (OMT) by Rumbaugh [RBP+91] and the Objectory Method by Jacobson [JCJ+92]. The UP is a formal software development process, meaning that it prescribes specific workflows, such as Analyze Behavior, Refine Architecture and Detail Design, in the context of disciplines, such as Requirements, Analysis and Design, and Implementation. Each workflow prescribes specific activities, such as Describe Distribution and Identify Design Mechanisms, to be performed by people in specific prescribed roles, such as Software Architect and Implementer.

It uses visual modeling extensively, but does not emphasize code visualization or generation.

The UP uses visual modeling extensively, but does not focus on code visualization or generation. In other words, it uses models as documents, not as source artifacts. It prescribes a fixed set of eight general purpose models for all systems (i.e., Business, Use Case, Analysis, Design, Implementation, Deployment, Data and Test), each using one or more of the general purpose sublanguages of the UML, and playing a specific role in the process. In addition, the UP defines relationships among models, allowing requirements to be traced through various stages of development. The relationships are informal, and therefore cannot be reliably used to support automation, such as code generation, transformation or validation, but they do provide constraints that can be implemented manually. For example, when a noun is changed in the requirements, the names of derived or related objects in the analysis, design, implementation and deployment models can theoretically be identified and changed accordingly.

The UP also uses projections of models called views. It prescribes five general purpose views for all systems (i.e., Use Case, Logical, Deployment, Implementation, and Process). They are used to describe the architecturally significant elements of the models. In other words, they provide a summary description. The views were not part of the original process definition, and are not well integrated.

UP prescribes generic views and models.

Notes

1. Coplien notes that hierarchy is merely an approximation of the structure of real world problems and solutions. Most systems would be better described as forests of overlapping hierarchies, but we think of them as hierarchies for the sake of convenience [Cop99].
2. Here, we use the term component to refer to a discretely identifiable piece of software, and not to a construct defined by a specific component architecture.
3. Of course, perfect coding is highly improbable. If coding flaws affect all designs more or less uniformly, however, we can think of them as a form of noise, and ignore them for the purposes of this discussion.
4. We should actually think of it as a directed acyclic graph (DAG), since there may be more than one way to reach the same solution. For the sake of simplicity, we will think of it as a tree.

CHAPTER 3

Dealing with Change

Software is called upon to bear the brunt of change because,
being as it is made of bits, it can change.

B. Foote and J. Yoder

In this chapter, we look at change, the other fundamental force that makes software development challenging. We also look at the role of requirements as a mechanism for dealing with change, and at methods and practices for dealing with change based on object orientation.

The Problem of Change

The ability to change is an essential property of software as a medium, as noted by Foote and Yoder (epigraph). We should expect software to change in response to changes in its environment and its requirements. Paradoxically, software is quite expensive to change in practice. Let's consider how software responds to change and why it responds that way.

Software changes because it can.

Responses to Change

How does software respond to change? Foote and Yoder identify three scenarios.

The way software responds to change depends on its qualities.

- Some software can be produced so cheaply, it is considered disposable. Disposable software is generally discarded and replaced in response to change. Generated code that marshals remote method calls it an example of disposable software. It is typically discarded and regenerated when the remote method signatures change.

- Some software is so costly to replace or modify, it is immutable. Immutable software is generally preserved in response to change, and then discarded and replaced when it is no longer viable. Legacy applications based on dead technologies are examples of immutable software. Immutable software typically contributes requirements to its successors.

- Software that is economical to maintain is considered mutable. Mutable software evolves in response to change. Its evolution is usually evident in both its structure and its behavior, and usually affects both its design and its implementation.

Since nothing needs to be done about the way disposable software responds to change, and nothing can be done about the way immutable software responds to change, the real issue is the way mutable software responds to change. Let's look more closely at how mutable software evolves.

Software Aging

Software ages as it evolves.

Parnas [Par94] likens the evolution of software to human aging.

> *Programs, like people, get old. We can't prevent aging, but we can understand its causes, takes steps to limit its effects, temporarily reverse some of the damage it has caused, and prepare for the day when the software is no longer viable.*

The principal causes of aging are stagnation, fatigue, brittleness, and redundancy.

The Stagnation Problem

Software stagnates when modifications are deferred.

Software stagnates when the modifications required to keep pace with change are deferred, forcing developers to deal with large amounts of change when the software is finally modified. Since the cost of responding to change increases non-linearly with the size of the change, the cost of modifying stagnant software increases non-linearly with time. When the cost of making the deferred modifications becomes prohibitively high, the organization can no longer afford to modify the software, and the software becomes immutable.

The Fatigue Problem

Fatigue is structural erosion caused by making modifications to software that conflict with its original design. A classic illustration of fatigue in civil engineering is adding stories on to a doghouse to build a skyscraper. Since the doghouse was designed with different goals in mind, it cannot support the new stories. Fatigue in software is manifested by the degradation of operational qualities, such as usability, reliability, performance, and supportability. Why would one make suboptimal modifications? We can identify at least three reasons:

Fatigue is structural erosion caused by modification.

- *Malpractice.* Software is sometimes modified in suboptimal ways because the people making the modifications do not understand the original design or lack the competence to work within its bounds.
- *Expediency.* Software is sometimes modified in suboptimal ways intentionally to address other more pressing concerns, such as time-to-market requirements or cost constraints.
- *Brittleness.* Software is sometimes modified in suboptimal ways because the required modifications are poorly accommodated by the original design.

Of course, these reasons can occur in combination. Brittleness and expediency are often combined, for example, when it is deemed too expensive or time consuming to change the original design to accommodate a large modification. Brittleness can also be combined with malpractice, when the original design is changed to accommodate a large modification by people who do not understand the original design, or who lack the competence to change it effectively.

The Brittleness Problem

Brittleness is a measure of how much structural erosion is caused by a given change. It is generally determined by how well the software anticipates such change. Software that does

Brittleness is a measure of how much damage is caused by a given change.

not anticipate the modifications it receives suffers more structural erosion when the modifications are made than software that does anticipate them. Since we cannot know precisely what will change, we cannot entirely eliminate brittleness. We can only make educated guesses and prepare for change accordingly. For example, when building an application with J2EE, we must decide up front which components will be remotely accessible and which will be local. Many aspects of the design and implementation of each component are driven by this decision. If we later find that a component designed to be local must become remotely accessible, we will have to modify it in a way that will affect its clients. The brittleness problem is also called the preplanning problem.

The Redundancy Problem

Redundant versions must be kept synchronized as defects are discovered, or as requirements change.

Requirements imposed on a shared component tend to evolve differently over time for different clients, creating conflicts. Rather than modify the component to address the new requirements, the quickest and easiest solution is usually to copy it and to modify the copy. Once redundant versions exist, they must be kept synchronized as defects are discovered or requirements change. The classic example is the familiar customer database. Most companies have many customer databases, each serving a different purpose, such as order fulfillment or customer relationship management. While these databases usually contain large amounts of redundant information, they usually differ in some ways, as well, creating partially redundant subsets of the information, usually organized differently. When customer information changes, the company must identify the affected databases, and determine how each one must be updated. In some large enterprise shops, more than 90% of the network bandwidth and computing resources, not to mention costly human working hours, are spent keeping partially redundant databases synchronized.

Software As Simulation

We will adopt a different point of view toward problems and solutions.

To understand why change causes these problems, we need to take a closer look at how software is developed, and the role played by requirements. This requires us to adopt a different point of view toward problems and solutions. As developers, we think of requirements as describing the problem to be solved. In this section, however, we will see that the requirements actually represent a negotiated agreement between the customer and the developers regarding the software to be developed to solve a real world problem. In other words, they describe the solution from the customer's point of view.

We will start by thinking of software as a simulation medium. When it runs, software instantiates computational objects that often simulate real world objects. A word processor, for example, simulates real entities like documents, and real processes like editing or searching. From this perspective, software development is developing simulations. Of course, the computational objects that appear in simulations form models of the real world that can and often do differ from their real world counterparts in ways that change how we interact with them. For example, searching electronic documents is faster than searching paper documents, so we search electronic documents more frequently. Simulation is almost always associated with modeling.

Computational objects simulate real world objects.

The relationship between computational objects and real world entities can be defined in terms of *domains* and *mappings* between them. A domain is a subject area or a family of related objects. For example, the Online Commerce domain contains processes for selling products online, such as Order Entry and Order Fulfillment, and entities used by those processes, such as Order, Product, and Customer. From this perspective, the real world defines the problem domain, while the platforms and software architectures that host executables define the solution domain.

A domain is a subject area or a family of objects.

The *problem domain* contains real world objects to be simulated. Unlike the solution domain, it contains processes enacted by humans or by non-computational systems, involving material goods, such as moving books from a shelf to a truck on a forklift to fulfill an Order. These objects may have internal structure that is relevant to the problem. For example, an Order may have properties, such as Order Date, Due Date, and Order Total. We can write assertions regarding problem domain objects. For example, we can require that Order Date must be earlier than the Due Date for all Orders. Problem domain objects can be related to one another. A Customer may be associated with multiple Orders, an Order may be associated with multiple Line Items and a Line Item may be associated with at most one Product. A particular configuration of problem domain objects to be simulated forms the *problem* to be solved.

The problem domain contains real world objects.

Within any given problem domain, there are many problems, some that can be simulated by software, and some that cannot.

The solution domain contains computational objects.

The *solution domain* contains computational objects that reside on an execution platform. Solution domain objects may have internal structure that is relevant to the solution. An Assembly may contain Classes and Resources, for example, and a Class may contain Methods, Variables, Properties, Events, and other Classes. We can also write assertions regarding solution domain objects. To be well formed, for example, a Class might have to declare a name, a default constructor, and a parent Class, while a Method might have to declare an argument list and a return type. Solution domain objects can also be related to one another. For example, one Class might reference another Class or an Interface through a Variable. Solution domain objects generally reside in artifacts called executables. Executables run on platforms that provide the resources required to support their execution. A platform for Online Commerce, for example, might include Microsoft Windows Server, the Microsoft .NET™ Framework, the Common Language Runtime (CLR), Microsoft SQL Server, Microsoft BizTalk Server, and Microsoft Host Integration Server.

There is often more than one way to solve a given problem.

Computational processes and objects often differ from their real world counterparts. One difference is that while they may monitor processes enacted outside the software, such as moving books from a shelf to a truck on a forklift, they do not automate those processes. Instead, they automate information-based processes. When they do, they may add steps, remove steps, change the order of execution, or change the content or structure of an entity. An automated Order Entry process, for example, may include steps that do not appear in its real world counterpart, and an automated Order may include information that does not appear on the equivalent paper form. The distinction between the problem and solution domains is important, as there is often more than one way to solve a given problem. Bidders for contracts often propose different ways to solve the same problem, for example, and the relative merits of the solutions they propose often decide who will win the business.

A solution to a given problem is a configuration of solution domain objects that solves the problem.

Mappings Between Domains

A configuration of solution domain objects that solves a problem forms a *solution* to the problem. For example, a solution

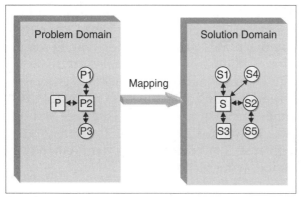

Figure 3.1 A mapping between problem and solution domains

to a problem in the Online Commerce domain might include Classes that represent the Customer and Order entities, and that enact the Create Order, Set Customer For Order, and Add Line Item To Order processes. The relationship between a problem and a solution to that problem can be expressed as a mapping between the problem and solution domains, as illustrated in Figure 3.1. For now, we can think of a mapping as a function that takes a configuration of entities in one domain, and returns a configuration of entities in another domain.

We can now think of software development as the process of finding and rendering well-formed mappings between the problem and solution domains. A mapping is well formed when it maps a problem to a valid solution to that problem. Finding a mapping is a creative activity. The greater the number of possible configurations in a given solution domain, the harder it is to find the ones that solve a given problem. To find a mapping, we make design decisions that select a specific configuration. When a mapping has been found, we capture those decisions by rendering software artifacts. Of course, the mechanical activity of rendering the solution is closely intertwined with the creative activity of finding the solution. We therefore tend to render solutions incrementally, as we find them. This provides feedback that guides our search. In other words, building what we know helps us know what to build. It is useful to distinguish between the two activities, however, since knowing what to build (design) is more challenging than building what we know (implementation).

Finding mappings is hard but rendering them in software, once they have been found, is relatively easy.

We have seen that finding mappings is generally difficult, but we can also see that the level of difficulty varies with the

The gap between the domains is bridged using requirements.

distance between the domains. Mappings are easier to find when the domains are close together (similar), than when they are far apart (dissimilar). This phenomenon is easy to see intuitively. For example, mappings to executables are easier to find from arithmetic expressions than from business processes. Mappings are also easier to find from business processes to C# and the .NET Framework than to assembly language and operating system calls. We call the gap between the domains the *requirements gap*, because it is bridged using requirements, as we shall see in the following sections.

The Role of Requirements

Abstraction makes mappings easier to find.

Abstraction makes mappings between domains easier to find. We said earlier that it removes some information to help us focus on the information that remains. We can use abstraction to remove information about the differences between two domains to make mappings between them easier to find. In other words, we can devise idealized problem and solution domains that contain common features, so that finding mappings between them is easier. This process lets us create an abstract description of the problem and map it to an abstract description of the solution, as shown in Figure 3.2. For example, before writing code for an online ordering system, we would first collect information about how ordering works currently. This is the abstract description of the problem. It would leave out details that

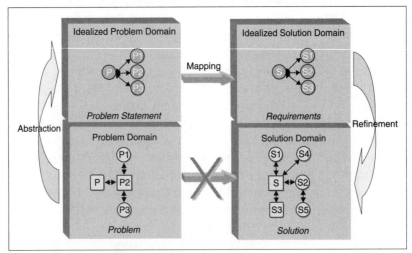

Figure 3.2   Using abstraction to find mappings

were not relevant to automating the process. We would then write an abstract description of the behavior required of the system. It might say, for example, what information an order will contain, how a customer will create and submit orders, and how submitted orders will be filled. This is the abstract description of the solution. We would then use the abstract description of the solution to guide the development of the software.

We can now give familiar names to the abstract descriptions. The abstract problem description is really the *problem statement*, and the abstract solution description is really the *requirements*. If the requirements form a solution to the problem statement, then the executables should form a solution to the real world problem. Of course, it usually doesn't look like this in practice. We have intentionally elaborated some of the details that are usually taken for granted to show how abstraction is used to make mappings easier to find. We can now see how the abstraction gap is created. It comes from using abstraction to describe the solution.

The abstraction gap comes from using abstraction to describe the solution.

Calling the requirements a description of the solution, rather than a description of the problem, may seem odd. Recall, however, that the notions of problem and solution are relative, and may change depending on our point of view. Under fixed conditions, where the requirements do not change for a limited period of time, they do represent the problem to be solved. One of the goals of iterative development is to create limited periods of stability in requirements. Ultimately, however, the problem to be solved is a real world problem that can never be fully described by requirements for more than a limited period of time, since the real world is constantly changing. Consider what would happen if the software satisfied the requirements, but the requirements did not solve the real world problem. Obviously, it is the solution to the real world problem that matters. The requirements are only a temporary proxy for the real world problem. They provide a view of the problem that does not include information irrelevant to the system being developed. They also provide a view of the problem designed to satisfy budgets, schedules, and other external constraints. The requirements are a model of the actual problem.

The requirements are only a temporary proxy for the real world problem.

Choosing a Mapping

In practice, there are many possible mappings between the problem and solution domains. Of those, only a few involve

There are many candidate mappings.

problems that we are interested in solving. We tend to think in terms of solving a specific problem, but in practice, we are usually interested in solving a family of related problems. These problems can differ in various ways, such as which steps are included in a given process, in what order the steps are performed, which entities are affected, which properties are defined on a given entity, and what type of information is stored by a given property. For example, there are many ways to define Order Entry. Some might initiate billing when an Order is placed, others might defer billing until the Order is filled. Some might aggregate unfilled Orders from the same Customer, others might preserve individual Order identity. Some might support different discount schedules for different Customers, others might support general promotions. Of course, there also can be more than one solution for each of these problems, as we have seen. Different solutions can serve the needs of different users, execute on different platforms, or demonstrate different operational qualities. We can now see that there are usually many mappings, each of which is a candidate for development.

We choose mappings that satisfy the stakeholders from among the candidate mappings by approximation.

Of course, among the candidate mappings, some might be preferred over others. Some ways of looking at the problem might make more sense to the end users than others, and some ways of solving the problem might have better operational qualities than others in terms of usability, reliability, performance, supportability, etc. How then do we choose a mapping? In theory, we could render all of the candidate mappings, evaluate each one, and then select the best one. In practice, of course, that would not be practical, so we settle for an approximation. Usually, we make an initial guess and then refine it iteratively until the stakeholders are satisfied. Each iteration selects a mapping (actually just a partial mapping, since we only build part of the solution—the rest is supplied by existing abstractions, as we shall see), renders it, and then evaluates the results. If the stakeholders are satisfied, then we continue toward the completion of that mapping. Otherwise, we modify the selection and repeat the process. When we intertwine the selection and rendering steps, as described earlier, this begins to resemble what we know as software development.

We can reduce the number of iterations by making a good initial guess.

Negotiating Requirements

Since each iteration can be quite expensive, it is generally important to make a good initial guess. The better the guess, the less we have to refine it through iteration. The initial guess is often defined through a process of negotiation, where negotiators seek to reconcile competing concerns such as budget, schedule, and quality to satisfy constraints imposed by the implementation technologies, or by interfaces to existing software. This familiar process is known as defining requirements. It usually produces an initial description of the solution, called the functional requirements, and a set of service level agreements that impose constraints on the solution and the development process, called the non-functional requirements. We can think of requirements as the result of a guess at an acceptable mapping. They describe an idealized solution to an idealized problem.

Unfortunately, the process of negotiation involves at least two parties, each with a different perspective.

There are at least two parties, and therefore at least two perspectives.

- The users have a perspective based on their knowledge of the real world in which the problem exists.

- The developers have a perspective based on their knowledge of the technology domain in which the solution must be expressed.

Each party brings to the negotiating table an abstraction of reality instead of detailed descriptions of the actual problem and solution. They do this for three reasons:

Each party brings an abstraction to the negotiating table.

- To communicate effectively with their negotiating counterparts. For example, the users may not fully understand the technologies used to implement the solution, and the developers may not fully understand the real world problem.

- To prevent unimportant details from derailing the negotiations. Exposing all of the details of either the actual problem or the actual solution (i.e., the implementation) can be counterproductive at some points in the negotiation.

- Because often neither the actual solution nor the actual problem is completely known during the negotiations. Until the software has reached a level of completeness and stability, many details of the implementation may change.

The goal of negotiation is to create a mapping between the abstractions.

The goal of the negotiation is to create a mapping between the abstractions. When the abstraction of the solution (i.e., the requirements) is mapped to the abstraction of the problem (i.e., the implicit problem statement assumed by the users), then the process is considered complete. The users think they know what they are buying, and the developers think they know what they are building. Of course, both parties are wrong to some degree. Since they are dealing with abstractions of the underlying problems and solutions, there is room for misunderstanding. What the users think they are buying is not quite what the developers think they are building. There is also room for each party to make mistakes or invalid assumptions when they create and manipulate abstractions of reality.

- The problem that the users describe may not be the one that actually needs to be solved to meet the real world business need. For example, they make assumptions about what the software should do top meet the business needs, These assumptions may prove to be at least partially incorrect when the software is actually deployed.

- The solution that the developers describe may not be the one that they will actually develop. They make assumptions about what they can build with a given set of resources, how they can build it, and how it will perform. These assumptions may prove to be at least partially incorrect when the software is actually developed.

Iterative development distributes requirements definition over many small negotiations.

Because the assumptions made by both parties may be at least partially incorrect, they should be validated early, and revalidated frequently during development. One way to do this is to prototype the solution during requirements definition to ensure that the requirements meet the real world business need, and to prove that they can be implemented as planned. An even better approach is to use iterative development to define, prioritize, implement, and modify the requirements over many short iterations. New requirements can be added between iterations, and existing requirements can be modified or removed, through a process called scoping. This process distributes requirements definition over many small negotiations, allowing both sides to make adjustments as the software is developed. With iterative development, the negotiators gradually reach consensus, as they learn more about both the problem and the solution.

Requirements as Specifications

We said that the requirements are an approximation of the solution. For example, they might describe the screens to be displayed, the interactions to occur between users and screens, and the transitions to occur among screens. An important distinction between the requirements and the executables is that the requirements specify the results of execution without describing how they are obtained, while the executables provide an implementation that executes on a particular platform. We can therefore think of the requirements as specifications, and the executables as their implementation. This relationship is often obscured in practice, since it is hard to write requirements without being prescriptive. Likewise, the specifications of declarative executables, such as database schemas, resemble their implementations.

The requirements are specifications and the executables are their implementations.

Some familiar platforms, such as spreadsheets and workflow engines, execute the requirements directly. This direct mapping lets us run them, evaluate the results, and then determine whether or not they need improvement in real time. This mapping also provides interesting insights regarding the problem of deriving executables from requirements:

Executable requirements provide interesting insights.

- Differences between specifications and implementations can be reduced, or completely eliminated, for narrow problem domains. The narrower the problem domain, the smaller the differences.

- Specialized languages based on the natural vocabulary of the problem domain make it easier to express solutions to problems.

Sources of Change

We can now see that the net effect of change is to invalidate software, meaning that it causes software to stop providing a valid solution to a valid problem. Since software is developed to solve problems, it is susceptible to changes in the problem and solution domains.

Change invalidates software.

Changes in the Problem Domain

Changes in the problem domain can invalidate the requirements. For example, when a process changes, software that implements the process can become incorrect. These changes

Business evolution and user demand drive problem domain changes.

can be a consequence of changes in the business, as it switches its partners, products and processes in response to competition, economic conditions, consumer sentiment and other market forces. Changes can also be driven by user demand, as they become more reliant on a system, and tend to demand modifications more frequently.

Changes in the Solution Domain

Technology evolution and other factors drive solution domain changes.

Changes in the solution domain can invalidate the executables. For example, when a platform vendor stops supporting the middleware used to implement an application, the application can become difficult or expensive to maintain. Changes can be driven by a number of sources, including changes in neighboring systems or in non-functional requirements. One of the most important sources is the tendency of the industry to introduce new technology, a phenomenon we call technology evolution. A measure of the rate of technology evolution is that three of the four technologies now receiving the most attention (i.e., Web services, Microsoft .NET, Enterprise Java, and Linux) are less than five years old.

Technology evolution can be difficult to predict.

Technology evolution would be easier to manage if it was easier to predict. Until a few years ago, it looked like IIOP and DCOM would be widely used for remote service invocation. Since administrators were reluctant to open firewalls to these protocols, however, HTTP-based protocols are now used almost exclusively for remote service invocation.

Rapid technology evolution creates instability.

The effects of technology evolution are often compounded by the instability of new technologies. XML based technologies are revolutionizing information packaging and exchange, and enabling new application architectures. Like most new technologies, however, they are changing rapidly as they mature. DTDs have been replaced by XSDs. Bulk XML document exchange has been replaced by passing documents as arguments to remote procedure calls using SOAP over HTTP. The World Wide Web Consortium (W3C) and other standards organizations will bring many more changes to these technologies over the next few years.

Current Methods and Practices

How does object orientation deal with change?

We said earlier that change is a fundamental force in software development, and that every software development paradigm has been motivated at least in part by the need to deal with change. How does object orientation deal with change? The answer to this question will help identify some of the chronic problems that it cannot solve, and some of the critical innovations needed to overcome them. While attacking complexity was the primary motivation for most of the features that collectively form the paradigm of object orientation, dealing with change has become the primary focus of innovation on that foundation in recent years. We will focus on three of the problems identified at the start of this chapter: stagnation, fatigue, and brittleness. Preventing redundancy is difficult with current methods and practices, because it requires a longer time horizon than a single project. We will return to this point in Chapter 4.

Preventing Stagnation

The first line of defense in dealing with change is preventing stagnation. Responding to changes in requirements and technologies as they occur helps reduce the amount of change that must be tackled at any one time, and keeps the resulting modifications modest. The most common methods for preventing stagnation are iterative and agile development.

Preventing stagnation is the first line of defense.

Iterative Development

Iterative development is one of the earliest practices in object orientation, and is used almost universally to prevent stagnation. Traditional waterfall processes developed software sequentially, progressing from requirements capture to analysis, design and then implementation. In contrast, iterative development breaks the project into iterations, capturing and implementing a subset of the requirements, and refining work already started within each iteration. Requirements and technologies change only between iterations, providing periods of stability, which helps reduce the amount of change that must be tackled at any one time.

Iterative development is used almost universally to prevent stagnation.

Iterative development can be practiced across as well as within product releases. New development that starts with existing software can be seen as maintenance or enhancement. From this point of view, most software development is incremental and ongoing. We can think of iterations and product releases as points on a time line with different iteration lengths.

Iterative development can be practiced across product releases.

Of course, there are other important differences between completing an iteration and releasing a product. The similarities can be exploited, however, by applying iterative development principles to a series of product releases.

Agile Development

Agility is the capacity to rapidly and cheaply change the software under development in response to changes.

It is widely recognized that agility is a key to successful software development. Agility is the capacity to rapidly and cheaply change the software under development in response to changes in requirements or technology. One reason for the popularity of agile development is that formal processes tend to be overly prescriptive, making the organizations that adopt them less competitive by slowing their responses to changes in the marketplace. Agile development methods include eXtreme Programming (XP), Dynamic System Development Method (DSDM), and Scrum. Since agile development is based on iterative development, it is inherently iterative and incremental, and emphasizes demonstrating the software early and often, which means keeping it building and working. Most methods require a daily build, and testing early in the life cycle. Some require test harnesses to be developed before the application software. Agile development also emphasizes keeping documentation to an absolute minimum, since it is a maintenance burden, but does not directly contribute to producing executables. Most importantly, agile development deals effectively with the requirements gap by involving the customer in the development process, enabling them to validate the requirements as they are being implemented. Agile development methods are optimized for dealing with change, as we said in Chapter 2. Specifically, they are optimized for preventing stagnation.

Some useful insights into agile development are provided by Berrisford [Ber04], who seeks to provide a measurable definition of agility by drawing from the Agile Manifesto, the bill of principles to which agile development methods should adhere. We prefer this list to the actual manifesto, since it is more succinctly stated, adds several important points, and replaces a few questionable assertions with more realistic ones.

- *Time or Cash Box Delivery.* This means being willing to implement only a subset of the requirements, or being willing to relax operational requirements (e.g., usability, reliability, performance, etc.) to keep time to market or costs within predefined limits.

■ *Maintain Continuous and Close User Involvement.* This means having one or more of the business stakeholders embedded in the development team.

■ *Empower a Small Team to Get the Job Done.* This means organizing projects around motivated and competent individuals, giving them the necessary resources and organizational support and trusting them with the outcome. It also means cooperating with other teams by sharing only necessary interface definitions.

■ *Focus on Code and Tests not Specifications.* This means that the primary measure of progress is working software, and that face-to-face communication among the members of the project team should replace documentation. It also means documenting behavior in test cases, rather than documents, and disseminating knowledge about the software by encouraging communication among the team members.

■ *Develop Iteratively According to Priorities.* This means delivering software early and frequently, using iterations that range in length from two weeks to two months. It also means prioritizing the requirements to ensure that the functionality of greatest value to the business stakeholders is delivered first.

■ *Refactor Continuously.* This means reorganizing program and data structures as new requirements are addressed and as existing implementations are refined.

■ *Plan to Continue Development Indefinitely.* This means that the project team should be able to maintain a constant pace, maintaining and enhancing the software continuously as requirements are added, removed or modified, and as technologies change.

■ *Promote Simplicity.* This means paying attention to design and maximizing the amount of work not done by defining and reusing useful abstractions. Note that a balance must be struck between satisfying this assertion simultaneously with the first in the list. Sometimes the justification of "You aren't going to need it again" overpowers the need to simplify using abstractions.

Reducing Brittleness

Reducing brittleness is the second line of defense.

Since brittleness creates fatigue, reducing brittleness is the second line of defense in dealing with change. Recall that software suffers the most structural erosion when it does not anticipate the modifications it receives. This suggests that brittleness can be reduced by anticipating various classes of modifications and designing the software to accommodate them. The most common techniques for reducing brittleness in object-oriented software are encapsulation and adaptive design.

Encapsulation

Encapsulation reduces brittleness.

One of the promises of object orientation was to reduce brittleness by encapsulation. Since encapsulation hides implementations, it lets them change without affecting their clients. In other words, it localizes modifications and prevents them from propagating in an uncontrolled manner through the software. According to Wegner [Weg78],

> *Large systems should be constructed to be evolutionary so that modifications [in response to] changing requirements, improved implementation methods, or the discovery of errors may be easily made. Construction of systems for evolution may require greater overhead during development, but may result in enormous savings during operation and maintenance.*

This is illustrated in Figure 3.3. The persistent objects are protected from changes in the database schema by data access

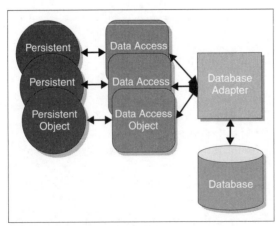

Figure 3.3   Reducing brittleness

objects, which are protected from changes in the database product by the database adapter.

Adaptive Design

One of the objectives of design patterns is to make software less brittle by partitioning responsibility among components according to rate of change and reason for change. This is called adaptive design. To paraphrase the Gang of Four:

Adaptive design reduces brittleness.

> *Patterns help to avoid redesign by ensuring that a system can change in specific ways. Each pattern lets some aspect of the system structure vary independently of other aspects, making the system more robust to a particular kind of change.*

The Strategy pattern, for example, moves each variable portion of an algorithm into a class with a well-defined interface. This design makes it possible to change the behavior of the algorithm by replacing the class. Adaptive design can be applied at many levels of granularity. The Shearing Layers pattern, for example, groups components into layers according to their expected rates of change, as illustrated in Figure 3.4. We cannot know precisely what will change, but we can make educated guesses and prepare for modifications accordingly, as we said earlier. In Chapter 4, we will discover ways to make better educated guesses.

Adaptive design can be applied at many levels of granularity.

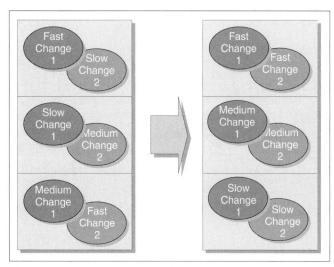

Figure 3.4   Layering software by rate of change

Reducing Fatigue

Reducing fatigue is the third line of defense.

Since fatigue is the inevitable consequence of making modifications, the third line of defense is reducing the amount of fatigue created by a given modification. This can be accomplished by reorganizing the software, changing the design to accommodate the modification. This widely used practice is known as *refactoring*.

Refactoring

Refactoring rejuvenates software.

Refactoring was popularized in the late nineties in the landmark book by that name by Martin Fowler [Fow99]. It improves the operational qualities of a piece of software by changing its structure without changing its externally observable behavior. It starts by changing the design, reallocating responsibility among components, and changing component boundaries. It then brings the implementation into conformance with the new design.

Figure 3.5 shows a design to be refactored. Figure 3.6 shows the result of refactoring.

In Figure 3.6, common aspects of the compensation computation have been moved from the HourlyEmployee and SalariedEmployee classes to the `getCompensation()` method in the Employee class, and the abstract methods `getBase()` and `getBonus()` have been added to provide variability points for the subclasses.

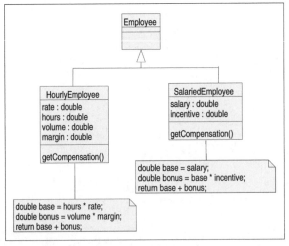

Figure 3.5   A design to be refactored

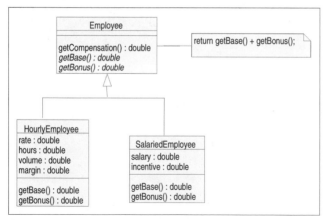

Figure 3.6 The result of refactoring

While it is better to refactor when a modification is made, it is possible to refactor later, to reverse malpractice, for example. Redesign is expensive, and the redesign mandated by refactoring is no exception. However, if refactoring is required, then not refactoring may be more expensive since software degrades more quickly when it is poorly organized. Also, refactoring is more expensive when undertaken later in the life cycle, especially after software is in production.

Refactoring is expensive but less so when done early in the life cycle.

Refactoring can be performed at many levels of abstraction. At the level of software architecture, responsibilities can be moved among components, new components can be introduced, and existing components can be combined or eliminated, to change the operational qualities of a system. At the level of design, methods and variables can be moved between related classes, or along the inheritance hierarchy, to encapsulate design decisions in independent objects. At the level of implementation, lines of code can be rearranged to make better use of language features, or to implement better programming practices.

Software can be refactored at different levels of abstraction.

Patterns describe best practices in solving design and implementation problems. Anti-patterns, on the other hand, describe commonly occurring bad practices in design and implementation. Both patterns and anti-patterns can be used in refactoring. Anti-patterns suggest areas that need refactoring, while patterns suggest structural forms that should result from refactoring. Architectural patterns can be used to refactor systems, design patterns can be used to refactor components, and language idioms can be used to refactor classes and methods written in a specific programming language.

Patterns and anti-patterns can be used in refactoring.

Paradigm Shift

We hire people who build doghouses, give them cranes and ask them to build skyscrapers.
Then we're surprised when they fail.

Eileen Steets Quann

We said in Chapter 1 that if we are indeed at a juncture of discontinuous innovation, then we should be able to identify chronic problems with the current paradigm, as well as critical innovations that solve those problems at the cost of changes in accepted methods and practices. Having studied complexity and change, we are now ready for this analysis.

Chronic Problems

Like all paradigms, object orientation cannot solve certain problems. These are the chronic problems that demonstrate the limits of the paradigm. Some of them have resisted solution since the inception of the paradigm, while others have only recently come to light. In the Preface, we said that these problems fall into four categories: monolithic construction, excessive generality, one-off development, and process immaturity. We will look at problems in each of these categories in this section. As we shall see, many of these problems arise from tensions between methods used to deal with complexity and practices used to deal with change.

This chapter looks at the chronic problems that object orientation cannot solve and at critical innovations that can help solve them.

Monolithic Construction

We have not yet learned to assemble reusable components on a commercially significant scale.

It has long been recognized that one of the keys to productivity is building new components or systems by assembling existing ones. Development by assembly was one of the most important changes promulgated by the industrial revolution, enabling industries previously based on craftsmanship to meet the demands of an increasingly industrialized society. It was also part of the vision espoused by the early pioneers of object orientation, who predicted that new software would some day be assembled from existing objects. Unfortunately, we have not yet learned to assemble reusable components on a commercially significant scale. This is disappointing, since object orientation appears to be equipped to solve the problem. Its basic metaphor is encapsulation, which partitions a problem into opaque pieces, as we have seen. Of course, to be useful, partitioning must be accompanied by assembly. Unless we can assemble the pieces to produce a solution to the problem, we have gained nothing by encapsulation. Development by assembly should therefore be a natural consequence of the object-oriented paradigm.

Software is still produced almost entirely by construction from scratch.

We now know that objects are too fine-grained and context-dependent to be units of development by assembly. When Component Based Development (CBD) appeared, there was broad expectation that it would correct this problem by providing a coarser-grained and less context-dependent component model, fulfilling the vision with only a modest change to the basic paradigm. Unfortunately, despite the promise of CBD, software is still produced almost entirely by construction from scratch. Some observers blame the poor supply of reusable components, or the difficulty of finding the right components to solve a given problem. However, research and observation both suggest that these problems are symptoms of more fundamental problems, such as platform specific protocols, weak packaging, eager encapsulation, and the Not Invented Here syndrome. Let's look at each of these problems in turn.

MONOLITHIC

According to Wikipedia, a monolithic object is created in one piece, without any subcomponents. A monolithic program behaves as a single program, rather than as a collection of intercommunicating programs.

Platform Specific Protocols

Current component assembly technologies depend too heavily on specific platforms, making it difficult to assemble components across platform boundaries, even when the boundaries in question are between different versions and/or configurations of the same products. CORBA and DCOM were the dominant technologies when CBD appeared. They were replaced, respectively, with Java Remote Method Invocation and .NET Remoting. While all of these technologies have succeeded in some ways, none of them has been able to support a component marketplace, or enable secure and efficient distributed interaction at the scales needed to automate business processes that span organizational boundaries. The problem is that they are closely tied to the technologies used to implement the components. This requires interacting components to be based on version compatible instances of the same implementation technologies. Components based on Java RMI, for example, do not interoperate well with components based on .NET Remoting, or even with components based on different versions of RMI, in some cases.

It is difficult to assemble components across platform boundaries.

Weak Packaging

Current component specification and packaging technologies do not capture enough information about the properties of components and about how they interact, making it hard to predict the properties of software developed by assembly. For example, given an arbitrary set of components, it is generally quite difficult to determine what they do, what dependencies they have, what resources they may consume, what performance they may exhibit, or what vulnerabilities they may create in an assembled system. When these unstated dependencies and assumptions conflict, architectural mismatches occur, making assembly difficult or impossible, or degrading the operational qualities of the resulting system. According to Garlan [GAO95], conflicting assumptions can be made about the components, the ways in which they interact, the structure of the system, and the processes used to produce an assembled system.

Weak specification and packaging technologies cause architectural mismatch.

Mismatched assumptions about components can contribute to excessive code size and degrade the operational qualities of the software.

Assumptions about Components

Conflicting assumptions about components can include:

- *Which Supporting Services Are Required.* Components generally include or require the inclusion of infrastructure that supplies services like security, persistence or transactions. Since comparable but different infrastructure may be supplied or required by other components, or by the underlying platform, redundant infrastructure packages may be included in the assembled system.

- *Which Components Are Responsible for Controlling Execution.* Components can make conflicting assumptions about which components will control execution. For example, some components use an event loop to organize interaction among modules, and provide access to services through call backs. If more than one of the components in an assembled system takes this approach, then adapters or mediators must be developed to allow the components to coexist effectively.

- *How Information Structures Should Be Manipulated.* Components can make conflicting assumptions about which components will be responsible for instantiating, copying or destroying other components. They can also make invalid assumptions about information structures maintained by other components, such as assuming that nested nodes in a tree can be added or deleted independently, while the tree control requires them to be added or deleted only by their parents.

These kinds of mismatches can contribute to excessive code size, or to problems with operational qualities, such as usability, reliability, performance, supportability, and especially security.

Assumptions about Relationships

Mismatched assumptions about the relationships between components can require extensive changes to the components or extensive adaptation or mediation.

Conflicting assumptions about the relationships between components can include:

- *How Related Components Will Interact.* For example, some components assume a broadcast pattern, in which components publish messages asynchronously to tell others about events or state changes, while other components assume a synchronous request/response pattern. These mismatches impose awkward requirements on components, such as requiring components that must be small and lightweight for other reasons to manage multiple asynchronous data streams.

- *How Information Will Be Communicated in Interactions.* For example, one component might assume synchronous interaction with discrete typed values as arguments, while another might assume asynchronous interaction with serialized information streamed between components.

These kinds of mismatches can require extensive changes to the components or the construction of extensive adaptation or mediation code to bridge the differences between them.

Assumptions about Architecture

Conflicting assumptions can also be made about the architecture of the assembled system and about the presence or absence of components playing certain roles. For example, one component might assume that component interaction will be mediated by a transaction monitor, while another might assume that peers will interact directly. These kinds of mismatches can cause reliability problems, such as data corruptions and deadlocks in concurrent execution scenarios.

Mismatched architectural assumptions can cause reliability problems.

Assumptions about Process

Conflicting assumptions can also be made about the process used to produce the assembled system. For example, a tool supplied by one component might generate distributed method invocation code from method signatures, while a tool supplied by another component might generate classes from models, requiring developers to write a script that extracts method signatures from classes generated by the second tool if they contain methods that will be invoked remotely. These kinds of mismatches can make builds complex and labor intensive.

Mismatched process assumptions can make builds labor-intensive and complex.

Eager Encapsulation

Current component implementation technologies generally use eager encapsulation mechanisms, such as monolithic class definitions, that make component boundaries difficult to change. This means that components cannot be easily adapted during the assembly process to accommodate the differences between them, or to make them fit into different contexts. For example, dependencies on specific infrastructure, such as CORBA, are usually woven into the implementations of business components, making it impossible to use them with different infrastructure. Eager encapsulation intertwines the intrinsic or functional aspects of a component with the contextual or non-functional aspects, exposing them to changes in the contextual aspects.

Eager encapsulation makes component boundaries difficult to change.

There is a key tradeoff between encapsulation and agility.

There is a key tradeoff between encapsulation and agility. Encapsulation increases agility by reducing complexity. It is faster to extend a framework, for example, than to write equivalent functionality from scratch because many design decisions are made in advance by the framework. However, eager encapsulation limits agility because the intrinsic or functional aspects of a component cannot be easily separated from the contextual or non-functional aspects, making it hard to move them across component boundaries when refactoring is necessary to accommodate new requirements. Eager encapsulation is a minor concern when all of the source code can be modified, but it can be a major concern when the components come from different suppliers, or when some of them are only available at runtime, as in the case of Web services.

Not Invented Here Syndrome

It is more economical in the large to reuse imperfect components that already exist than to develop perfect new ones from scratch.

Finally, one of the most pervasive and insidious causes of monolithic construction is the infamous Not Invented Here (NIH) syndrome. Victims afflicted with this disease generally distrust anything developed outside their immediate organization, invariably choosing to build their own implementation of a required component rather than take a hard dependency on another organization by consuming an implementation that already exists. Sadly, victims also invariably underestimate the cost of developing, maintaining, and enhancing their proprietary implementation, usually by at least an order of magnitude. Of course, since no responsible decision maker would choose such an approach without a compelling reason, some fault must be found with the externally supplied implementation. While such grievances may be quite legitimate, more often than not, they are rather marginal. For example, a third-party XML parser might be seen as unusable because it is does more than is strictly required for the application in question, such as primitive type conversion, which has performance and memory footprint costs. Of course, experience in many other industries demonstrates that it is more economical in the large to reuse imperfect components that already exist than to develop perfect new ones from scratch.

The problem is with the immaturity of relationships between consumers and suppliers, and with the resulting lack of established practices and enabling technologies.

Before we vilify the victims of this disease much further, we should point out that their reluctance to take dependencies on external suppliers may not be completely unwarranted. Given the cost of finding existing components that can satisfy specific requirements, the cost of adapting them to new environments, and the cost of finding defects in them once they have been applied, it may indeed be less costly and less risky to develop new components from scratch than to reuse existing ones in specific situations. In other words, the disease is often the result of having been burned by suppliers who did not deliver on commitments. Such experiences and the skepticism they produce tend to accompany ad hoc reuse, where consumers attempt to reuse individual components opportunistically, in ways that were never anticipated by their designs or implementations. Put another way, the problem is not with the victims, but with the immaturity of relationships between consumers and suppliers in the software industry. There is a lack of established practices and enabling technologies required to make reuse predictable, sustainable, and mutually beneficial for consumers and suppliers.

Of course, there is a bootstrapping problem. No project owner wants to push the envelope of established practice for the long-term benefit of the industry, by trying to make reuse work on his project. The problem is too large for any project or any small number of projects to solve because it requires the creation of a market place for reusable components. Changes are needed on an industrial scale to realign every day thinking and practice about reuse. We will look at critical innovations that can bring about such pervasive changes later in this chapter, and we will show how they can be applied successfully in Chapter 5.

Changes are needed on an industrial scale to realign every day thinking and practice.

Gratuitous Generality

Current software development methods and technologies generally give developers more degrees of freedom than are necessary for most applications. Most business applications, for example, consist of a few basic patterns. They read information from a database, wrap it in business rules, present it to a user, let the user act on it under the governance of those rules, and then write the results back to the database. Of course, this is an over simplification, since real world business applications generally contain a variety of additional challenges, such as interactions with legacy systems, massive amounts of data, massive numbers of concurrent users, or severe quality of service constraints that make the implementation of these basic patterns a lot more challenging than it sounds. We contend, however, having developed many business applications, that while there are always wrinkles that make each project unique and specifics that always vary, such as the names of the

We need general-purpose 3GLs only for a small part of the typical business application.

There is much more benefit to be gained by moving to even higher levels of abstraction.

Most of the work can be made faster and cheaper by using constrained configuration mechanisms.

UML has succeeded as sketching medium, but not as a model-driven development or execution language.

entities and the rule content, the vast majority of the work does not change much from project to project. Do we really need general purpose, Turing complete, third generation languages (3GLs) like C# and Java for more than a small part of the typical business application? Probably not.

Recall from Chapter 2 that raising the level of abstraction reduces the scope of the abstractions and the amount of control over the details of the implementation given to developers. Recall, also, that the result of these losses is a significant increase in the power of the abstractions, enabling them to provide far more of the solution for a problem in the target domain than lower level abstractions. We pointed out there that business application developers would much rather use higher level abstractions, such as those provided by C# and Java, and by their accompanying frameworks, the .NET Framework and J2EE, than assembly language and operating system calls. Just as moving from assembly language to C# yields significant benefits for business application development, such as higher productivity, lower defect levels, and easier maintenance and enhancement, there is much more benefit to be gained by moving to even higher levels of abstraction.

We are not advocating the use of a closed-end language like a 4GL, nor the use of a single language for all aspects of development. We think business application developers will work with 3GLs for the foreseeable future. However, we think that the latitude afforded by 3GLs is needed only for a small part of the typical business application. Most of the work can be made faster, cheaper, and less risky by using constrained configuration mechanisms like property settings, wizards, feature models (discussed in Chapter 10), model-driven development, and pattern application.

If building business applications entirely with 3GLs is counter productive, then why is it the mainstream practice? We think the blame lies with three chronic problems of object orientation: weak modeling languages, weak metadata management, and weak code generation. Let's look at each of these problems more closely.

Weak Modeling Languages

Using models to raise the level of abstraction and to automate development has been a compelling but unrealized vision for 20 years. The single largest impediment to realizing this vision has been the promulgation of imprecise general-purpose modeling languages as both de facto and de jure standards. Since it combined concepts from several object-oriented methods, the Unified Modeling Language™ (UML) became a rallying point for a model-based approach to development. Despite a large number of UML tools, however, UML has not done much to raise the level of abstraction at which developers write source artifacts, or to automate development. Its primary contribution has been to design, since it lacks the focus and semantic rigor required to contribute to implementation, and most of that contribution has taken the form of informal models sketched on white boards. Most of the progress in automating development has been based on programming languages and structured markup languages like XML and HTML. Fowler puts this eloquently, identifying three different goals espoused for UML: informal design, which he calls sketching; model-driven development, which he calls blueprinting; and direct execution where models are interpreted. He claims that UML has succeeded in the first goal by establishing a widely used visual vocabulary, but not in the other two.

One of the reasons for this failure is lack of precision. Development requires precise languages. While much has been done to ensure the precision of general purpose programming languages like C# and Java, much less has been done to ensure the precision of languages offering higher level abstractions. UML and its derivatives have demonstrated over the course of many years that they are incapable of providing such levels of precision. This is not surprising, since they were designed for documentation, not development. Unfortunately, those who stood to profit have long held them to be the only legitimate languages for object-oriented modeling, and have supported their claims with marketing dollars. Despite disappointing results, the industry has therefore been slow to see the problems with UML, and to invest in precise modeling languages designed for development not documentation.

UML lacks the precision required to automate development.

Another reason is poor support for component-based development concepts, such as component specification and assembly. Rather than offer nothing, which might have been preferable, UML provides many gratuitously different, incomplete and incompatible ways to model components, none of which accurately reflects the component architectures in common use today. By offering many ways to solve the same problem, it

UML does not support CBD well.

creates confusion, especially since it does not apply the various mechanisms consistently.

UML is too general for real domains and has weak extensibility mechanisms that make it hard to focus.

A third reason, one that makes it wholly unsuitable for model-driven development, is its generality, combined with weak extensibility mechanisms. UML models anything and nothing at the same time. Tightly bound initially to programming language concepts in vogue at the time of its creation, UML was later given simple extensibility mechanisms similar to text macros, to give it some hope of modeling real domains. Since then, a vast number of features have been added, many of them driven through the crack in the door created by extensibility. Most of this work was undertaken without clear statements of requirements or adequate attention to conceptual partitioning. Due to the weakness of its extensibility mechanisms, efforts to focus UML on real domains have not been successful. The resulting semantic ambiguity and lack of organization have prompted a redesign, but the new version presents an even larger and more complex language that is just as ambiguous and disorganized as its precursor. As we show in Chapter 8 and Appendix B, UML falls short of providing the high fidelity domain-specific modeling capabilities required by the forms of automation described in this book. Its main contribution to automation has been the concept of a modeling language supported by a metamodel. Commercial model-driven development tools will be based on technologies designed for development, not documentation.

Weak Code Generation

CASE failed because code appeared only near the end of the project.

An earlier generation of products, called Computer Aided Software Engineering (CASE) tools, tried to use models to automate development. These products failed for the following reasons:

- Customers were uncomfortable spending most of their time on models, with the promise of code appearing only near the end of the project. This required enormous confidence in the tools, and in the longevity of their vendors.

Poor quality code was generated from platform-independent models.

- They promised to generate code for multiple platforms from platform independent models, allowing customers to preserve investments in the models as the platform . technologies changed underneath them. Of course, a similar promise is offered by byte code languages, such as C# and Java, and by earlier generations of programming languages that provided some measure of insulation from hardware and operating system changes. With a few notable exceptions, however, most attempts at code generation from platform-independent models failed miserably. Unlike byte coded language compilers, CASE tools failed to exploit platform features effectively, producing naïve, inefficient, least common denominator implementations.

- Their round-trip engineering features generally produced poor results. They tried to fill the gap between the models and the platform by generating large amounts of source code. The resulting complexity overwhelmed developers, causing them to abandon the models and write code by hand, at a certain point in the development process. Generic class modeling tools based on UML exhibit similar problems. After a few round trips, the synchronization falls apart, and the models are abandoned, making them ineffective as source artifacts.

Round-trip engineering did not work well.

Weak Metadata Integration

The opportunity to automate more of the software life cycle by integrating metadata from various tools has long been recognized. Information captured by requirements, for example, can be used to drive test case definition and test harness development. Test results can be used to drive defect record creation, and can be correlated with design information to scope defects to specific components. Information about infrastructure dependencies can be used to validate component deployment scenarios and to drive automatic infrastructure provisioning in a target execution environment. Many other forms of automation are also possible, as described in Chapter 7.

Metadata from tools can be used to automate the software life cycle.

CASE tools also promised to standardize life cycle metadata, but failed to deliver on the promise. Standardization attempts, such as the AD/Cycle initiative led by IBM in the late 1980s, were unsuccessful. These efforts made great progress in modeling metadata, but because the models had to satisfy the requirements of tools from multiple vendors, they were complex and could not be changed quickly as technologies and methodologies changed because even minor changes required consensus among the vendors.

CASE tools also failed to standardize life cycle metadata.

Information managed by development tools is still poorly integrated across the life cycle due to tension between file and database resident information and due to attempts to standardize metadata implementation formats and repository architectures.

Information managed by development tools is still poorly integrated across the life cycle. At least two major sources of difficulty can be identified:

- One source of difficulty is the tension between file resident information like source code and database resident information like defect records. File resident information generally requires little if any infrastructure, and can be easily organized, viewed, and edited using simple tools, while database resident information generally requires much more infrastructure and can only be organized, viewed or edited using specialized tools. File resident information also fits more naturally into file-based development processes, such as build and source control. Database resident information, on the other hand, can be queried and updated much more easily in bulk. It also supports much richer relationships between pieces of information.

- Another source of difficulty is the failure to distinguish between metadata integration and metadata unification. Metadata integration requires only that the metadata suppliers and consumers to agree on common interchange formats. Metadata unification, on the other hand, requires them to share standard implementation formats, or even standard repository architectures. Metadata unification is not required, since metadata integration can support rich product interaction, as electronic commerce has amply demonstrated.

These observations lead to a discussion of the infamous repository issue that has burned many development tool vendors, some of them many times, but we will defer that discussion until Chapter 7.

One-Off Development

One-off development treats every software product as unique.

One-off development treats every software product as unique, despite the fact that most software products are more similar to others than they are different from them. Currently, most software product planning focuses on the delivery of a single version of a single product, despite the fact that returns on investment in software development would be far higher if multiple versions or multiple products were taken into account. Failing to leverage commonality across products impedes the harvesting, classification, and packaging of knowledge, such as the documentation of prescriptive guidance, recommended practices and patterns, or the development of reusable components.

The assumption of one-off development is so deeply ingrained in this industry that most of us are not conscious of either the practice or the alternatives. Most widely used development processes, whether formal or informal, are designed to support the development of a single product in isolation from others. This affects both their overall structure and their content. For example, both XP and UP assume that every product will be designed and developed independently from first principles to accommodate its unique requirements, and neither of them provides guidance for supplying or consuming reusable assets, or facilitates communication between consumers and suppliers of reusable assets.

Most development processes are designed to support one-off development.

One-off development permits only an ad hoc and opportunistic approach to reuse, since there is no context for predicting what might be reused, or the situations in which the reuse might occur. It also creates a phenomenon called organizational dementia. An organization afflicted by this disease cannot capture knowledge in reusable forms. It therefore cannot leverage experience or lessons learned in subsequent efforts, and must constantly rediscover what it already knows. Documenting patterns and practices is a step in the right direction because it focuses on capturing and reusing knowledge across multiple versions or multiple products. Later in this chapter, we will consider a critical innovation that goes much further in the same direction.

One-off development permits only ad hoc reuse and fosters organizational dementia.

Process Immaturity

One of the most challenging problems in software development today is managing the development process, especially when multiple groups must collaborate to develop a single product. According to Booch, a development process is a collection of practices designed to promote high quality, efficient resource allocation, and effective cost and time management. While methods vary widely, as we have seen, most organizations use some form of process, and yet few of them can consistently develop software that satisfies requirements on schedule and within budget. This problem suggests that current methods and practices are immature.

Few organizations can develop satisfactory software on schedule and within budget.

Most development processes tend to one of two extremes.

Most development processes in use today tend to one of two extremes: either they use excessive formalism to promote cross-group collaboration at the cost of agility, or they throw formalism to the wind and permit excessive autonomy to promote agility at the cost of cross-group collaboration. As we will show here, these extremes reflect a tension between the need to deal with complexity and the need to deal with change. Later in this chapter, we will suggest an approach that helps organizations deal with complexity, while preserving their ability to respond rapidly to change.

Excessive Formalism

Formal processes are optimized for dealing with complexity.

We said earlier that formal processes are optimized for dealing with complexity. By defining the development process in detail, formalism provides structure that helps the participants organize, understand, and reason about the software, development tasks, the development environment, and development organization. This kind of structure is absolutely essential when multiple groups must collaborate to develop a single product. In such an environment, changing an interface on which other groups depend can break the build, and changing the behavior of a component on which they depend can create usability issues, defects, security holes or performance problems. Changes to shared interfaces and components must therefore be carefully orchestrated. This orchestration prevents all groups from freely changing the software, and therefore limits their agility. It also requires the kind of structure described earlier. Collaborating groups must have a common understanding of shared components, common expectations as to how and when they might change, and common policies regarding tools, directory structure, file formats, and many other parts of the development environment.

Formal processes are often overly prescriptive.

Unfortunately, the industry has a tendency to become overly prescriptive, assuming that developers are naïve and uninformed, and attempting to use formal processes to prevent them from making mistakes by telling them what to build, how to build, and what skills are required to perform certain tasks. Examples of excessive formalism abound, and often involve heavy-handed application of the UP. Another problem with formality is sheer size and weight. Even though most of the material in a process like the UP is relevant to some project at some time, its scope is daunting. Although the material is well organized, using it can require a serious time commitment because of the quantity. It can take much longer than expected to sift through it, find bits relevant to a problem and apply them. There are many cross-references that must be checked to determine whether or not they are required for a given situation. As we shall see, this kind of experience results from naïve application of the UP, and can be avoided through customization.

Excessive Autonomy

Frustration with the glacial pace of development that accompanies excessive formality spawned a global revolt among developers near the turn of the millennium, creating a movement complete with a manifesto, recognized leadership, and annual conferences. Of course, we are describing the agile development movement. Agile methods are the epitome of informality. We said earlier that informal processes are optimized for dealing with change by:

Informal processes are optimized for dealing with change.

- Keeping the team small, which allows it to rely on verbal communication, reducing the need for specifications.

- Working in small iterations, which keeps the software building and running, helping the team interact with business stakeholders to validate requirements.

- Refactoring constantly reduces fatigue, which makes the software more pliable and subsequent changes easier.

Agile methods work exceptionally well for small projects staffed by small teams of expert developers that can work autonomously. They create significant problems, however, when applied on larger scales. Trying to go faster by increasing agility is like trying to make a company more profitable by cutting costs. Both work well up to a point, and improve the health of the organization, but then they have the opposite effect, as necessary infrastructure is jettisoned along with the unnecessary. Berrisford [Ber04] observes that highly agile parallel development increases architectural mismatch, because teams work as independently as possible. Making the teams agree on a common architecture helps ensure that the components they develop can be integrated without extensive changes, adaptation or mediation, but it reduces agility at the same time by involving more people, requiring more documentation, and forcing teams to synchronize their iterations. It also creates inflexible

Agile methods work well for small projects, but not for larger ones.

requirements, since none of the teams sharing a component can change its interfaces without consulting the others. Likewise, refactoring is also harder, since shared interfaces become boundaries that cannot be crossed without consultation.

Adhering to agile development principles when scaling up can create problems.

Of course, refusing to relax some of the principles of agile development when faced with a requirement to scale up can create the opposite problems. Not agreeing on a common architecture ensures that there will be problems with architectural mismatch and unpredictable results when components from multiple teams are assembled, and that extensive changes, adaptation and/or mediation, will be required. It also ensures that the system will exhibit operational quality problems, such as poor usability, high defect levels, security vulnerabilities, and poor performance.

Agile methods can create supportability problems because agile teams do not produce much design documentation.

Agile methods can also create supportability problems because agile teams usually do not produce much design documentation. The lack of documentation makes it hard to determine after the fact what design decisions were made, what alternatives were considered, and what rationale was used to make the decision. Of course, if maintenance and enhancement are ongoing, and the team does not lose any members, then the knowledge required to keep up the software may still be fresh in the minds of the team members. There is significant risk in relying on memory alone, however, since people forget details with the passage of time, and change projects fairly frequently. While the code provides some documentation, there is also significant risk in relying on code alone, since code quality varies widely, and since source code contains many low-level details and accidental complexities that blur its essential behaviors and properties. Thus, a new team called upon to maintain or enhance the software may not be able to understand it quickly enough to maintain it effectively. These conditions can lead to yet another form of NIH syndrome, where the new team decides that it is better to rewrite a component than to try to maintain it. While rewriting may not be entirely unwarranted in some cases, it is usually a somewhat specious conclusion. Moreover, the cost of rewriting a non-trivial component is usually underestimated by at least an order of magnitude.

Geographical distribution can exacerbate these problems.

Geographical distribution can exacerbate these problems, not because people forget or move on, but because they are not available when needed, or because technology limitations and time zone differences restrict high bandwidth communication. We have come to appreciate the value of documentation after leading projects involving teams in Europe and the US West Coast. Given the timezone differences, opportunities for interactive communication were limited and documentation helped make the most of the time we did have together.

Critical Innovations

In this section, we describe critical innovations that solve these chronic problems by taking new ground in the struggle against complexity and change. As we said in the Preface, we have noticed that some of the most significant gains have been produced by a recurring pattern that integrates four practices to automate software development tasks. A framework is developed to bootstrap implementations of products based on a common architectural style. Products are then created by adapting, configuring, and assembling framework components. A language to support this process is defined and supported by tools. The tools then help developers engage customers and respond to changes in requirements rapidly by building software incrementally, keeping it running as changes are made, and capturing design decisions in forms that directly produce executables. We therefore consider critical innovations in four areas suggested by the pattern: systematic reuse, development by assembly, model-driven development, and process frameworks. According to the characterization of paradigm shifts provided in Chapter 1, these innovations should build on the strengths of object orientation while addressing some of the weaknesses that gave rise to the chronic problems described earlier.

We consider critical innovations in four areas: systematic reuse, development by assembly, model-driven development, and process frameworks.

Systematic Reuse

We saw earlier that an ad hoc and opportunistic approach to reuse usually falls short of expectations. The main problem with such an approach is lack of context for reuse. It is challenging, if not impossible, to determine what functionality a component should possess and how it should be implemented to be reusable in arbitrary contexts. It is much easier to build components that are reusable in the context of a specific domain or family of systems. For example, the .NET Framework defines a family of rich client user interfaces on the Microsoft Windows platform. It is much easier to build reusable user

It is hard to make a component reusable in arbitrary contexts.

interface components for the .NET Framework than for arbitrary platforms. While this may seem obvious, too many reuse efforts fail to specify the contexts in which the components are expected to be reused.

Software product families enable systematic reuse.

One of the most important innovations in software development is defining a family of software products, whose members vary, while sharing many common features. According to Parnas [Par76], such a family provides a context in which the problems common to the family members can be solved collectively. Program families enable a more systematic approach to reuse, by letting us identify and differentiate between features that remain more or less constant over multiple products and those that vary.

A software product family may consist of either components or whole products.

A software product family may consist of either components or whole products. For example, one family might contain variants of a portfolio management application, and another might contain variants of a user interaction framework used by portfolio management and customer relationship management applications. Software product families are created by Systems Integrators (SIs), when they migrate an application from customer to customer, or build new applications by customizing existing ones. They are also created by Independent Software Vendors (ISVs) when they develop multiple applications in a domain like Customer Relationship Management (CRM), or multiple versions of one application through maintenance and enhancement. They are also created by IT organizations when they customize applications, develop multiple related applications, or multiple versions of one application through maintenance and enhancement.

Software Product Lines

Software product lines exploit systematic reuse.

A software product line exploits these observations, identifying the common features and recurring forms of variation in a specific domain to produce a family of software products more quickly, more cheaply and with less risk and higher quality than would be feasible by producing them individually. Rather than hope naively for ad hoc reuse opportunities to serendipitously arise under arbitrary circumstances, a software product line systematically captures knowledge of how to produce the family members, makes it available in the form of reusable assets, such as components, processes, and tools, and then applies those assets to produce the family members. Products developed as the members of a family reuse requirements, architectures, frameworks, components, tests and many other assets.

Of course, there is a cost to developing a product line in order to realize these benefits. In other words, product lines exhibit a classical cost-benefit trade-off. While the benefit side of the equation cannot be increased through the production of many copies, as we shall see in Chapter 5, it can be increased through the production of many related but unique variants, as documented by many case studies [CN01]. Developing technologies to enable the construction and operation of software product lines is the first step toward industrialization. In addition, the cost side of the equation can be reduced by making product lines less expensive to build. Reducing the cost of building software product lines is the second step toward industrialization.

A software product line exhibits a classical cost-benefit tradeoff.

Figure 4.1 describes the major tasks performed and the major artifacts produced and consumed in a product line.

Product line developers build *production assets* applied by product developers to produce product line members in much the same way that platform developers build device drivers and operating systems used by application developers to produce applications. The production assets include *implementation assets*, such as languages, patterns and frameworks used to implement the family members, and *process assets*, such as micro processes that provide guidance for using specific implementation assets, and tools that automate parts of the

Product line developers provide assets used by product developers to produce product line members.

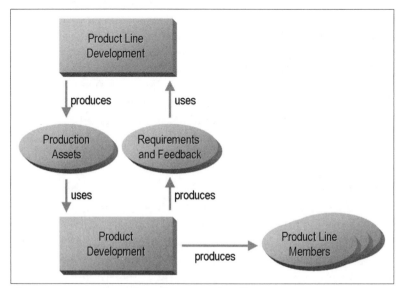

Figure 4.1 Overview of a software product line

process. A key step in developing the production assets is to produce one or more *domain models* that describe the common features of problems in domains addressed by the product line, and recurring forms of variation. These models become detailed descriptions of the problem domains. They collectively define the scope of the product line, and can be used to qualify prospective family members. In Chapter 10, we will look at how requirements for family members are derived from these models, and how variations in requirements map to variations in architecture, implementation, executables, the development process, the project environment, and other aspects of product development.

Differences from One-Off Development

Family-based development differs from one-off development in many ways, including differences in planning horizon, development processes, organizational structure, and development activities.

Planning Horizon

One-off development and family-based development have different planning horizons.

One-off development is organized around an individual product. Every task is geared to that product, including budgeting, scheduling, staffing, process definition, project definition, requirements capture, requirements analysis, technology selection, design, development, test development, test deployment, production deployment, monitoring, maintenance, configuration management, and many other tasks. Of course, there may be accidental continuity from product to product, and even some intentional cross-project planning, but generally there is no systematic reuse. Software product lines take a different approach. Since the production assets must be reused to be cost effective, software product lines impose a planning horizon that spans multiple products. This affects all of these tasks, changing their focus from an individual product to a family of products.

Development Processes

Software product lines use two distinct but related processes.

One-off development starts by capturing requirements and finishes with the delivery of a completed product. Software product lines, on the other hand, use two distinct but related processes, one for developing reusable assets and one for applying them. The two processes are generally quite different.

- Product line developers harvest common features from individual products, and build implementation assets, such as frameworks and class libraries, that implement them. They also define product families, package abstractions for product developers, define the product development process, and build tools and guidance to help the product developers apply the other assets.

- Product developers select, parameterize, and assemble assets supplied by the product line developers, and build, configure, deploy, test, and debug the resulting products. This process requires less knowledge of implementation technologies than one-off development, but more knowledge of the requirements, architecture, components, practices, and tools associated with specific problem domains.

As a consequence of focusing on systematic reuse, software product lines also use cross-project resources, such as repositories for storing and managing assets. We will look at these processes and the resources used to support them in Chapter 10.

Organizational Structure

One-off development generally uses a job shop organization, where developers build one-off products by hand from scratch either on their own or in small teams. While the integration of components requires collaboration, each developer or small team builds whole components, controlling every aspect of their development. Software product lines generally use a supply chain organization, where the two distinct but related processes drive consumer supplier relationships between distinct but related teams. One team develops and maintains production assets. The other team develops and maintains products using the production assets. If the products are production assets used by other teams, then the structure repeats, creating a network of consumers and suppliers. We will look at other ways to organize software product lines in Chapter 10.

One-off development and family-based development use different organizational structures.

Development by Assembly

We have looked at some chronic problems that make it difficult to develop software by assembly. We will now look at five critical innovations that resolve these problems, making it easier to assemble independently developed components across platform boundaries with predictable results. These include platform independent protocols, self-description, deferred encapsulation, assembly by orchestration, and architecture-driven development.

AN EXAMPLE OF DEVELOPMENT BY ASSEMBLY

J2EE provides two of the five critical innovations for development by assembly: self-description and deferred encapsulation. Using metadata files called deployment descriptors, it requires component suppliers to provide information that consumers can use to make better decisions about which components to include in an assembly, and to bridge several differences between components during the assembly process, such as role names and resource locations. It also separates several of the contextual aspects of a component, such as persistence, transactions and security from the intrinsic aspects, allowing infrastructure dependencies to be satisfied uniformly for every component in an assembled system.

Platform Independent Protocols

Web services technologies succeed where earlier component assembly technologies failed.

Web services technologies succeed where earlier component assembly technologies failed by separating the technologies used to specify and assemble components from the technologies used to implement them. Because XML is a technology for managing information, not a technology for constructing components, Web services require the use of wrappers to map web method invocations onto local method invocations based on the underlying component implementation technology. While CORBA attempted to use a similar strategy, its complexity required major investment by platform vendors, which limited its scope. The simplicity of XML-based protocols significantly lowers the barrier to implementation, ensuring their greater ubiquity. By encoding remote method invocation requests as XML, they avoid the interoperability problems of Java Remote Method Invocation and .NET Remoting caused by platform specific remote procedure call encoding and argument marshalling. By obtaining broad industry agreement through standards organizations, Web services technologies have also designed platform interoperability from the beginning.

Self-Description

Self-description reduces architectural mismatch by improving component packaging to define assumptions, dependencies, behavior, resource consumption, performance, certifications and other characteristics of the components explicitly. The metadata it provides can be used to automate component discovery, selection, licensing, acquisition, installation, adaptation, assembly, testing, configuration, deployment, monitoring, and management.

Self-description reduces mismatch.

The most important form of self-description is describing component assumptions, dependencies and behavior, so that developers can reason about interactions between components, and so that tools can validate assemblies. The most widely used forms of specification in object orientation are class and interface declarations. They declare behaviors offered by a class, but only imply significant assumptions and dependencies by naming other classes and interfaces in method signatures. Contracts are a richer form of specification. A contract is an agreement that governs the interactions between components. It is not enough to know how to invoke a component. We must also know which sequences of invocations are valid interactions. A contract therefore describes interaction sequences called protocols, responses to protocol violations and other unexpected conditions. For example, the contract between a seller and a buyer will specify that a *cancel order* message for an item from the seller must be preceded by a *place order* message for that item from the buyer.

Contracts are richer than interfaces.

Of course, contracts are worthless unless enforced. There are three ways to enforce contracts: we can refuse to assemble components with mismatched contracts, or we can use the information supplied by the contracts either to provide adapters that let the components interact directly, or to mediate their interactions. Garlan proposes using cookbooks of standard adaptation techniques, and tools that perform automatic wrapper generation and data transformation. One of the most promising adaptation strategies is to publish incomplete components that can be completed at assembly time with encapsulated aspects that provide the code required for assembly. We will explain these concepts in the next section.

Contracts are worthless unless enforced.

Web services technology uses the Web Service Description Language (WSDL) to define Web services. A WSDL file is an XML file that describes a Web service by specifying how it is

CBD maps well to Web service technology.

invoked and what it returns. It can be advertised in a catalog and used by tools to generate adapters or client side code. A WSDL file is the Web service equivalent of an interface specification, since it says nothing about the implementation of the Web service it describes, and can be generated by tools using component composition techniques. However, since WSDL files do not specify sequencing, they are not contracts, and therefore do not support robust Web service assembly. The second generation of Web services technology now under development will provide these missing ingredients.

Certification is an important aspect of self-description.

Another important aspect of self-description is certification. If components can be certified to have only the stated dependencies, to consume only the stated resources, to exhibit the stated performance characteristics under certain conditions, or to be free of the stated vulnerabilities, then it becomes possible to reason about the functional and operational characteristics of an assembly consisting of those components. This is being studied at the Software Engineering Institute (SEI) at Carnegie Mellon, where it is known as Predictable Assembly from Certifiable Components (PACC).

Deferred Encapsulation

Deferred encapsulation reduces architectural mismatch by weaving adaptations into published components.

We have seen that static encapsulation decreases the probability that a component can be used in an assembly by early binding its functional or intrinsic aspects to non-functional or contextual ones. Deferred encapsulation reduces architectural mismatch by enabling developers to publish partially encapsulated components that can be adapted to new contexts by selecting and weaving appropriate non-functional or contextual aspects with their functional or intrinsic ones. The final form of a component used in a specific assembly can then be determined by the context in which it is placed. This approach improves agility by making component boundaries more flexible, and reduces architectural mismatch by making it easy to adapt mismatched components at assembly time. It also allows functional or intrinsic aspects to be refactored across component boundaries by removing non-functional or contextual assumptions from them. Valid adaptations can be identified in advance, and in some cases can even be performed automatically, given a formal description of the context into which the finished component will be placed.

Deferred encapsulation is an adaptation of Aspect Oriented Programming (AOP). Recall from Chapter 2 that AOP is a method for separating and then recombining, respectively, different aspects of a system. Deferred encapsulation differs from AOP by weaving encapsulated aspects, while AOP, as commonly practiced, weaves unencapsulated lines of source code. Weaving unencapsulated aspects produces the same problems as assembling poorly packaged components, namely architectural mismatch and unpredictable results. Indeed, source code based aspect weaving is even more prone to these problems than component assembly, because components have interfaces that describe their behavior and some packaging that helps to prevent undocumented dependencies. The lack of packaging in AOP makes it hard for developers to reason about the compatibility of the aspects and the functional features into which they are woven. It also obfuscates characteristics of the resulting implementations, and makes it almost impossible for tools to validate aspect weavings.

Deferred encapsulation weaves encapsulated aspects not raw source code.

A second distinction is that AOP weaves aspects during component development, while deferred encapsulation weaves them later, such as during component assembly or deployment. This distinction is important because the contexts into which a component may be placed may not be known until long after the component has been published. In fact, in order to support development by assembly, as described by this book, third parties must be able to predictably assemble and deploy independently developed components. This predictability requires a formal approach to aspect partitioning, encapsulation, specification, and packaging. Enterprise JavaBeans, which provide a limited form of deferred encapsulation, illustrate this requirement. The deployment descriptor defines a contract between a developer who builds the functional kernel of the component, an assembler who weaves aspects into the component at assembly time, and a deployer who weaves aspects into the component at deployment time. As this example suggests, deferred encapsulation can also be progressive, meaning that it can occur in stages, with some aspects woven at each stage and some aspects left unbound to be woven in later stages.

Deferred encapsulation weaves aspects after component development is completed.

A third distinction is that deferred encapsulation is architecture driven, while AOP is not. The aspects separated from the functional kernel must be defined in advance, in the context

Deferred encapsulation is architecture driven.

of an architecture for deferred encapsulation. Here again, J2EE offers an excellent illustration. This distinction is really a consequence of the other two. We will return to the topic of architecture-driven development in the next section.

Architecture-Driven Development

Software architectures can be used to reason about the operational qualities of software.

We have seen that in order to satisfy non-functional requirements, such as performance or security, design decisions must impart specific operational qualities to the software. How can we determine what qualities will be imparted by a given design decision? Software architectures provide high-level descriptions of software, exposing its structure by hiding details. We can use these descriptions to reason about the operational qualities of the software, and to predict the effects of specific design decisions by observing how they change the structure. Once a structure is in place that satisfies the non-functional requirements, subsequent design decisions can then be constrained to either preserve the structure or change it in controlled ways.

Architecture promotes the availability of well-matched components.

While preventing the assembly of mismatched components better than constructing invalid assemblies, it does not necessarily promote the availability of well-matched components. Ensuring this availability is the purpose of architecture. According to Shaw and Garlan [GS93], a software architecture describes the components to be assembled, the interactions that can occur among them, and the acceptable patterns of composition. This process reduces the risk of architectural mismatch by imposing common assumptions and constraining design decisions.

Development by assembly will not be realized on an industrial scale without architecture-driven development.

Of course, developing software architectures is challenging. It takes most architects many years to become proficient with even a limited number of architectural styles or application domains. Development by assembly will not be realized on an industrial scale without significant progress in architectural practice, and much greater reliance on architecture in software development. These are the goals of architecture-driven development, which includes:

- Standards for describing, reviewing, and using architectures that make them more portable across organizations, projects, and technologies.
- Methods for predicting the effects of design decisions.

- Patterns or architectural styles that codify design expertise, helping designers to exploit recurring patterns of component partitioning.

Architectural Styles

According to Garlan [Gar96], an architectural style is a recurring pattern of software organization that provides an abstract framework for a family of systems. An architectural style defines a set of rules that specify the kinds of components that can be used to assemble a system, the kinds of relationships that can be used in their assembly, constraints on the way they are assembled, and assumptions about the meaning of an assembly. For example, a Web service composition style might specify the use of components offering ports defined by Web services, and related by wires connecting ports, with the constraint that two ports may not be connected by a wire unless they are compatible, and with the assumption that communication over a wire uses Web service messages. Other examples of architectural styles include the dataflow, micro-kernel, layered, pipes and filters, and model view controller styles.

An architectural style is a pattern that provides an abstract framework for a family of systems.

An architectural style improves partitioning and promotes design reuse by providing solutions with well-known properties to frequently recurring problems. It also promotes

An architectural style improves partitioning and promotes reuse.

- Implementation reuse by identifying common structural elements shared by systems based on the style,

- Understanding by defining standard architectures (e.g., client server),

- Interoperability by defining standard communication mechanisms (e.g., Web service protocols),

- Visualization by defining standard representations (e.g., boxes and lines for Web service assembly),

- Tool development by defining constraints that must be enforced,

- Analysis by identifying salient characteristics of systems based on the style (e.g., performance in a Web service assembly).

Architectural Description Standards

An architectural description is a document that defines a software architecture. IEEE 1471, Recommended Practice for

IEEE 1471 provides guidelines for architectural description.

Architectural Description, provides some guidelines for architectural description. According to these guidelines, a system has one or more stakeholders. A stakeholder has specific concerns or interests regarding some aspect of the system. To be useful to a community of stakeholders, an architectural description must have a format and organization that the stakeholders understand. An Architectural Description Standard (ADS) is a template for describing the architecture of a family of systems.

A viewpoint provides a pattern for describing a given aspect of a software product.

A *viewpoint* formally defines a perspective from which a given aspect of a software product can be described, and provides a pattern for producing such a description, defining its scope, purpose and audience, and the conventions, languages, and methods used to produce conforming views. The salient elements used to specify a viewpoint include

- An identifier and other introductory information (e.g., author, date, document reference, etc.)
- The concerns addressed by the viewpoint
- The conventions, languages, and methods used to produce views that conform to the viewpoint
- Consistency and completeness tests for conforming views

A view describes a software product from a given viewpoint.

A *view* describes a software product from a given viewpoint. A view is semantically closed, meaning that it describes the entire software product from that perspective. A view consists of one or more artifacts, each developed according to the requirements of the viewpoint. The view is an instance of the viewpoint, and must conform to the viewpoint to be well formed. A view that conforms to a web page layout viewpoint, for example, should describe the web page layout of a specific software product, and should use the notation defined by the viewpoint for describing web page layouts. The salient elements used to specify a view include:

- An identifier and other introductory information (e.g., author, date, document reference, etc.)
- The identifier of the viewpoint to which the view conforms

■ A description of the software product constructed using the conventions, languages and methods defined by that viewpoint

To understand the distinction between a view and its viewpoint, consider a logical database design for a business application. The logical database design forms a view of the application, or more precisely, one of its components. The aspect described by the design and the language used by the design are defined by the logical database design viewpoint. Many business applications could be described using the same viewpoint, yielding many views, each describing the logical database design of some business application. The views would use the same language and describe the same aspect of their subject applications. A view of a software product may consist of views of its components from the same viewpoint.

A view of a software product may consist of views of its components.

According to IEEE 1471, an architectural description must identify the viewpoints it uses and the rationale for using them. An architectural description standard (ADS) for a specific purpose can be defined by enumerating the set of viewpoints to be used. For example, an ADS for consumer to business web applications might require one viewpoint for web page layout and one for business data layout. Each view within an architectural description must conform to one of the viewpoints defined by the ADS on which it is based. Figure 4.2 shows the relationships between these concepts [IEEE 1471].

An architectural description must identify the viewpoints it uses and the rationale for using them.

Assembly by Orchestration

Given adequate contractual mechanisms, Web services can be assembled using an orchestration engine, such as Microsoft BizTalk Server. An orchestration engine uses a model of workflow among services to manage the sequences of messages exchanged between them. Assembly by orchestration makes development by assembly much easier, since Web services have far fewer dependencies on one another than binary components. Unlike classes, Web services do not have to reside within the same executable. Unlike components that use platform specific protocols, they can be assembled across platform boundaries. Two Web services can interact if their contracts are compatible. They can be developed and deployed independently,

Web services can be assembled using an orchestration engine.

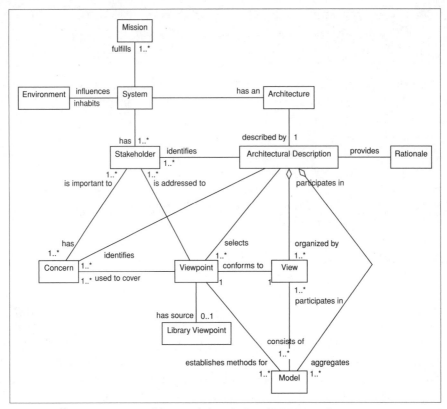

Figure 4.2 An architectural description (IEEE P1471)

and then assembled at runtime using orchestration. If appropriate interception and redirection services are available, they may even reside in different organizations. In other words, assembly by orchestration eliminates design, compile and deployment time dependencies between components.

Assembly by orchestration is a form of mediation.

Assembly by orchestration is a form of mediation, as described by the Mediator pattern published by the Gang Of Four. A mediator orchestrates interactions among components that would not otherwise be able to interact. A mediator has powerful properties. One of these is the ability to filter or translate information being passed between the interacting components. Another is the ability to monitor an interaction, maintaining state across multiple calls, if necessary. This property allows mediators to reason about interactions, and to change them, if necessary. Mediators can perform a variety of useful functions, such as logging, enforcing security policy, and bridging between different technologies or different versions of the same technology. A mediator can also become part of the functional portion of an assembly, enforcing business rules or performing business functions, such as brokering commercial transactions. We will revisit these topics in Chapter 13.

Model-Driven Development

Instead of relying on brute force to plow through enormous amounts of fine-grained detail, we can reduce complexity, increase agility, and improve the longevity of the products we build by raising the level of abstraction for developers. This observation is the key to automating much more of the rote and menial work required by current methods and practices. This is one of the key ideas in Software Factories.

Of course, the level of abstraction has been raised many times since the inception of the current object-oriented paradigm. Platform technology has become increasingly powerful, from class libraries, to component frameworks, distributed component middleware, and asynchronous, loosely coupled Web service infrastructure. What must be done, then, to provide the kind of automation we have described? Recall from Chapter 2 that abstractions can be packaged either as languages or as platform extensions, such as libraries and frameworks. A significant difference between these forms of packaging is that language-based abstractions can be used by tools for automatic refinement, and to generate metadata that can be used to automate other aspects of the software development process, as we have seen. Unfortunately, while these innovations in platform technology advanced the state of the art by giving us new abstractions for solving problems, they did not give us languages based on those abstractions. This conundrum is why we express such coarse-grained concepts as credit authorization using such fine-grained concepts as strings and integers. This imbalance is slowly being corrected by specialized XML-based languages, such as Business Process Execution Language (BPEL), which is a language for specifying the orchestration of business processes. We can accelerate this trend by defining specialized languages for more domains, including business domains, such as Customer Relationship Management and Sales Force Automation, architecture domains, such as service composition and multi-tier thin client applications, and technology oriented domains, such as Web service deployment and message payload design. While most of these languages

The current paradigm has stopped short of giving developers formal languages to express new platform abstractions.

will probably be XML-based, XML is not a hard requirement. Of course, XML may not be the most appropriate language for human consumption, even if it is used as a serialization format to support interoperability. As we shall see in Chapter 8, given a formal definition for a language, it is relatively easy to serialize the metadata it manipulates using a variety of formats.

MDD uses information captured by models to automate development processes.

Unfortunately, defining new languages is not easy, at least not currently. Unless we can find ways to make it faster, cheaper, and easier, it will not be cost effective to provide automatic refinement or other forms of automation for narrow domains. To solve this problem, therefore, we return to visual modeling. Now, however, our interest is not creating design documentation, but rather using models to capture information in forms that can be processed easily. This approach is what we call model-driven development (MDD). Rather than expressing developer intent informally, MDD uses models to capture intent precisely, and to fully or partially automate its implementation using automatic refinement, either by compiling models to produce executables, or by using them to facilitate the manual development of executables, as shown in Figure 4.3. The MDD approach is quite valuable because the intent is currently lost in low-level artifacts, such as source code files, where it is difficult to track, maintain or enhance consistently, due to the number

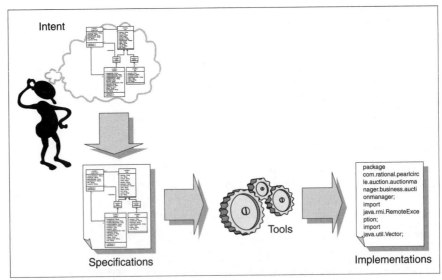

Figure 4.3　Using tools to automate implementation

of independent elements within those artifacts that must be synchronized to add, remove or modify a feature.

Some development activities, such as building, deploying, and debugging, are partially or completely automated today using information captured by source code files and other implementation artifacts. Using information captured by models, MDD can also provide more extensive automation of these activities, and more advanced forms of automation, such as debugging with models and automatically configuring tools. Here are some more examples:

MDD can provide more extensive automation and more advanced forms of automation.

- Routine tasks, such as generating one kind of artifact from another, can often be fully automated. For example, test harnesses can often be generated automatically from user interface models, to confirm that appropriate transitions between Web pages occur in response to simulated user actions.

- Other tasks, such as resolving differences between artifacts, can be partially automated. For example, differences between columns in a table and fields on a form might be flagged as issues for the user to resolve.

- Adapters, such as Web service wrappers, can be generated automatically from models to bridge differences in implementation technologies. Models can also be used to drive transformation, mediation, and other adaptive integration mechanisms.

- Models can be used to define the configurations of artifacts that comprise deployment units, and to automate the deployment process. Models of deployment environments can be used to validate or constrain designs, so that implementations of those designs deploy to them correctly.

- Models can be used to describe configurations of deployed components, capturing information about operational characteristics, such as load balancing, fail over, and resource allocation policies, and to automate management activities, such as data collection and reporting.

- Models can be used to migrate software to new implementation technologies, and to enable faster and more accurate modifications in response to changing requirements and environments.

We can avoid the pitfalls that caused CASE to fail, but realize the benefits it sought to provide, through critical innovations that provide high fidelity modeling languages, code generation of the quality expected from programming language compilers, and ways to define and manage relationships between models and other development artifacts. Let's look at each of these in turn.

Domain Specific Languages

We use models as source code not as documentation.

In this book, we are interested in models that can be processed by tools. We are not interested, for example, in models rendered by hand on white boards, or on note pads. Unfortunately, models have been used to date mainly as documents intended more for human consumption than for compilation and computation. This situation has created the widely held impression that models are not first class development artifacts with the significance as source code. Unfortunately, this impression has been reinforced by standards like UML and fads like CASE, both of which promised more than they were able to deliver. We propose to use models in much the same way as we currently use source code. Models used in this way cannot be written in languages designed for documentation.

Model used for computation must be precise, meaning that they are unambiguous. We will look at what this means formally in Chapter 8, but we can start the discussion here by noting that to be precise a modeling language must be designed for a specific purpose. A modeling language is a visual type system for specifying model-based programs. It raises the level of abstraction, bringing the implementation closer to the vocabulary understood by subject matter experts, domain experts, engineers, and end-users. This has several consequences:

- The purpose for which the modeling language is designed should be explicitly stated, so that an observer familiar with that purpose can evaluate the language and determine whether or not it fulfills its charter.

- The concepts that appear in the modeling language must be understood by people familiar with its purpose. A modeling language for developing and assembling Web services, for example, should contain concepts like Web services, web methods, protocols, and connections between Web services based on protocols. Similarly, a language used to visualize and edit C# source code should contain concepts that appear in C#, such as classes, and members, such as fields, methods, properties, events, and delegates.

- The modeling language should use names for those concepts that are familiar to the people who work with them. For example, a C# developer will find a model that contains fields and methods more natural than a model that contains attributes and operations.

- The notation for the modeling language, whether graphical or textual, should be easy to use for the purpose in question. Things that people who work with the concepts do often should be easy to do. For example, it should be easy to manipulate an inheritance hierarchy in a language used to visualize and edit C# source code.

- The modeling language should have a well-defined set of rules, called a grammar, governing the way the concepts can be combined to form expressions. This grammar makes it possible to use tools to validate the expressions, and to help the user write them.

- The meaning of every well-formed expression should be well defined, so that users can build models that other users understand, so that tools can generate valid implementations from models, and so that the metadata captured by models does what is expected when used for tasks like configuring a server.

A modeling language that meets these criteria is called a Domain Specific Language (DSL), because it models concepts found in a specific domain. A well-defined DSL is a powerful implementation language, providing much greater rigor than a general purpose modeling language like UML. A DSL may have either textual or graphical notation.

Framework Completion

We said earlier that CASE tools tried to fill the gap between abstractions used in the models and the platform by generating large amounts of source code, as illustrated in Figure 4.4(a). One of the keys to more effective code generation is to move the model closer to the platform, as illustrated in Figure 4.4(b). For example, a tool designed for a specific programming language

Move the model closer to the platform.

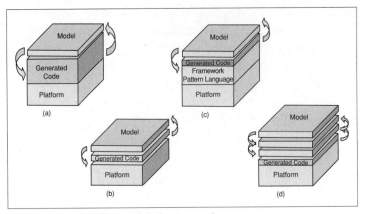

Figure 4.4   Models and application code

can provide high fidelity visualization by using the programming language type system, rather than a type system defined by a general purpose modeling language. The model becomes a view of the source code, allowing the developer to manipulate the program graphically at a higher level of abstraction, rather than textually at a lower level of abstraction. The tool adds value by exposing relationships and dependencies that are hard to see in the source code and suppresses uninteresting details. It also saves time and effort by generating the code for program structures like class and method declarations. It may also support programming idioms like properties with accessor methods, or relationships based on collections. As we shall see in Chapter 6, assisted pattern authoring, application and evaluation, and assisted refactoring can be particularly powerful additions to this kind of development tool.

Move the platform closer to the model.

Of course, moving the model closer to the platform, as just described, reduces its power, by constraining it to use abstractions already defined by the platform, or only slightly higher, such as simple programming idioms. Another approach is to keep the model at a high level of abstraction, and to move the platform closer to the model, as illustrated in Figure 4.4(c). This approach can be implemented using frameworks or transformations. We will look at frameworks here, and at transformations in the next section.

Replace brute-force code generation with framework completion.

We can use a framework to implement the abstractions that appear in the models, and use the models to complete extension points in the framework. Conversely, the models help users complete the framework by representing concepts that appear in the framework, and by exposing its extension points in intuitive ways. Let's consider the example of user interface form design in Microsoft Windows. When Windows was first introduced, only expert programmers could build Windows applications. When Microsoft Visual Basic was introduced, the Form and Control abstractions let a much larger number of developers do the same. Forms and Controls are part of a graphical DSL for Windows based user interface design implemented by the .NET Framework. The Form designer generates snippets of code to complete extension points in the framework. We call this framework completion, to contrast it with brute-force code generation. With framework completion, tools generate snippets of code from DSL-based models to complete framework extension points. Similarly, database design tools use DSLs that represent tables and columns defined by the underlying DBMS, and expose extension points in the DBMS through table names, column names, types and properties, the placement of columns within tables, and connections between columns. Some hand coding is required to complete most implementations, since only part of the solution can be generated. We will revisit the issue of combining handwritten and generated code in Chapter 15.

We said earlier that unless we can find ways to make it faster, cheaper, and easier to develop DSLs, it will not be cost effective to provide automatic refinement or other forms of automation for narrow domains. For one thing, language and framework design requires experience with the target domain. In other words, we need to consider many examples before deciding what to generalize. Also, there must be an ongoing demand for solving problems in the target domain, so that we can amortize the cost of developing the language and the framework over many projects. Finally, we will find that as the language and the framework are used, requirements will change, technologies will change, and forward and backward compatibility issues will appear as time passes. These requirements are tailor made for software product lines. Working with a software product family helps to identify common abstractions that should be represented by the language and implemented by the framework, as well as the recurring forms of variation that should become extension points. It also provides a way to amortize the cost, since the language, framework and supporting tools become production assets used to produce many software products. While this is helpful, we can also look for ways to make language and framework design easier using tools. We will return to this topic in Chapter 8.

Building a language and framework for a narrow domain makes more economic sense in the context of a software product family.

Model Transformation

Bridge large gaps using progressive transformation.

We can combine the preceding approaches by building a low level DSL that is close to the platform, instead of a framework or pattern language, and a high-level DSL that contains powerful abstractions. We can then build models based on the low-level DSL from models based on the high level DSL manually, semi-automatically or automatically. The low-level DSL is easier to implement than the high level one, since it uses abstractions that are closer to the platform. Of course, we can build more than two DSLs to span a wide gap, leading to progressive transformation, where models written using the highest level DSLs are transformed into executables using a series of refinements, as shown in Figure 4.4(d). This is exactly how modern programming language compilers work, transforming specifications written in a relatively high-level language like Java or C# first into an intermediate representation like byte code or IL, and then into a binary format for a target platform using just-in-time (JIT) compilation. Let's look more closely at model transformation.

Pattern-Based Transformation

Patterns can be used for model transformation.

Transformations are inherently parameterized, and bind objects in source models as arguments, creating or modifying objects in target models. A transformation can be seen as mapping a pattern of objects in the source model to a pattern of objects in the target model, as illustrated in Figure 4.5. Using patterns

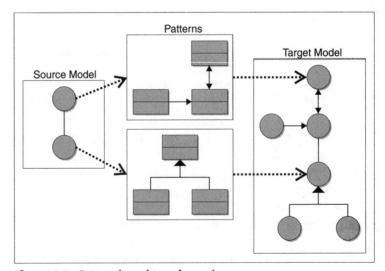

Figure 4.5   Pattern based transformation

to describe mappings has led to new approaches to model representation, transformation, and constraint. Of course, not all patterns can be applied automatically, because in many cases, the mapping between the models cannot be fully defined in advance. In these cases, the patterns must be applied by hand, often with support from a tool. Once they have been applied, however, they can generally be evaluated automatically, as described earlier.

Figure 4.6 shows a Business Entity pattern, which is an abstraction that helps a designer implement persistent objects. This abstraction is quite common in business applications. It can be implemented by writing either large amounts of data access code for a framework like Java Database Connectivity (JDBC), moderate amounts of O/R mapping code, which maps objects in memory to relations in the database) for a framework like TopLink, or small amounts of entity persistence code for a framework like Enterprise JavaBeans.

The pattern describes the implementation of a business entity in terms of classes, their placement in a project, default XML schemas used to externalize its state in Web service messages, an O/R mapping file that describes its persistence in a database table, a SQL DDL file that defines the database table and a SQL DML file that defines a set of stored procedures for creating, reading, updating, and deleting the entity. In the diagram, the pattern is applied to the Customer Type Model in the Customer Management component. Its parameters are bound at the time of application. Type Model is bound to Customer Type Model, and Operations is bound to the operations on Customer

A pattern can be applied to generate implementation artifacts or to update them incrementally as the model changes.

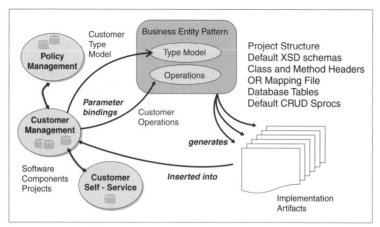

Figure 4.6 Applying a Business Entity Pattern

Management. After its parameters have been bound, the pattern can be evaluated to generate implementation artifacts for all of the entities in Customer Type Model. It can also be reevaluated if Customer Type Model is changed to add fields to an entity, for example, incrementally updating the implementation artifacts.

Patterns can also be applied by hand and evaluated automatically.

Of course, we can also apply patterns directly to the implementations, instead of building models and using patterns to generate the implementations. Generally, this involves applying patterns by hand, but then evaluating them automatically. A pattern language helps make this easier, because it defines patterns that can be combined in different ways to solve different kinds of problems. Core J2EE Design Patterns is an example of a pattern language. Of course, since frameworks are based on patterns, as noted by Johnson, we can also use patterns to direct the assembly of framework components.

A pattern language is a DSL in incubation.

Note that we can now automate framework-based development using either DSLs or pattern languages. The difference is primarily a trade-off between complexity and control. Since a pattern language lets the underlying implementations show through, the developer has more control over them, but must also assume more responsibility. A DSL hides the implementations of abstractions, reducing complexity, but gives the developer less control over them. At this point, it may not come as a surprise that pattern languages and DSLs are closely related. In fact, a pattern language is a DSL in incubation. When the abstractions defined by a pattern language have become so well understood that we are no longer interested in seeing their implementations, we can encapsulate them as a DSL. This approach lets us think in terms of the abstractions, not in terms of their implementations. Where do the patterns go when we create a DSL? They are still used to implement the abstractions through transformation, but they are no longer applied manually by the developer. Instead, they are applied automatically by a tool to implement models written by the developer using the DSL. Of course, this is how programming language compilers work. They automatically apply patterns in a lower level language to implement expressions written by developers in a higher level language. Recall from Chapter 2 that features implemented by programming languages often codify patterns and idioms defined by programmers using lower level languages. We will look at all of these topics in depth in Chapter 6.

Types of Transformations

Transformations can be characterized as horizontal, vertical, or oblique, as described by Czarnecki.

Vertical transformations implement refinements.

- Vertical transformations are mostly refinement transformations that map higher level models to lower level models, such as SQL DDL files, to general purpose programming language source code, or to other low level development artifacts. For example, a transformation from a model that describes a business process to models that describe the collaborating Web services that implement the business process is a vertical transformation.

- Horizontal transformations may be refactoring or delocalizing transformations.

  Horizontal transformations may refactor or delocalize.

  - Refactoring transformations reorganize a specification to improve its design without changing its meaning. Refactoring can be applied to both tree and graph-based languages. We will have more to say about refactoring with models in Chapter 7.

  - Delocalizing transformations are used for optimization, or to compose parts of the same implementation that are specified independently. General purpose programming language compilers use horizontal transformations to optimize generated binary code to improve performance, and aspect weaving uses them to compose independently specified aspects. Like refactoring, aspect weaving can be applied to both tree and graph-based languages. At any level of abstraction, aspects can be specified independently, and then woven into the functional modules automatically when mapping to lower levels of abstraction, by an aspect weaver. Separating aspects from functional modules makes maintenance easier by separating intrinsic and contextual concerns. We will have more to say about using aspects with models in Chapter 7.

- Oblique transformations combine horizontal and vertical transformations. General purpose programming language compilers generally perform oblique transformations, combining a vertical transformation

  Oblique transformations combine the two.

that generates binary code from the source code, and a horizontal transformation that optimizes the generated binary code.

Implementing Transformations

Transformations can be used for continuous synchronization and assisted reconciliation.

Up to this point, we have talked only about generation, where one artifact is created or updated from another in a single pass. Transformations can also be used to support continuous synchronization, where two artifacts are kept synchronized incrementally as either of them changes. Transformations can also drive assisted reconciliation, where the tools identify misalignments among artifacts, but let humans correct them, perhaps by suggesting a menu of possible corrections, or perhaps by waiting for the human to make arbitrary changes. We will have more to say about implementing transformations in Chapters 14 and 15.

Process Frameworks

The key to process maturity is making agility scale up.

The key to process maturity is preserving agility while scaling up to high complexity created by project size, geographical distribution, or the passage of time. As we have seen, some amount of structure increases agility by reducing the amount of work that must be done. This principle can be applied in the context of a software product family to manage complexity without reducing agility using process frameworks. Two related innovations are constraint-based scheduling and active guidance, which we discuss below.

Using a process only makes sense if it provides a net time savings.

Of course, it only makes sense to use a process if doing so provides a net savings of time. This suggests, once again, a family-based approach. A process framework is a structure that organizes the micro processes used to build the artifacts that comprise the product family members. For example, a process framework for a family of simple three tier applications might contain a micro process for building the user interface tier, a micro process for building the business logic tier, and a micro process for building the data access tier. Of course, in practice, process frameworks are much more complex than suggested by this example. Building each part of the architecture usually involves multiple micro processes in even the simplest product family. Building the data access tier, for example, usually involves logical and physical data modeling, tuning and administration. Developing a process framework for a software product line makes sense because the cost can be effectively amortized over the production of many products. This leads to an important insight.

One of the complaints against formal processes is that they are too abstract. The guidance they offer is obvious to a seasoned developer, but not concrete enough for a novice to apply. To be valuable, a formal process must therefore be tailored to the specifics of the current project. Of course, since every organization and every project within the same organization are unique in many ways, it is impossible to publish a process that meets the needs of all projects.

Formal processes are too abstract.

Hopefully, this sounds familiar by now. We know how to solve this kind of problem. Rather than throw out the baby with the bath water, we can specialize and tailor a formal process for a specific product family. This is exactly what happens with the UP, in most cases. Indeed, the UP would not have succeeded in the marketplace if an industry to customize it had not arisen. Some of the vendors customize the UP for specific customers, often mixing in some ingredients from other processes like XP. Others, such as System Integrators and ISVs, tailor processes to support a specific product or consulting practice. Either way, the key to using any process effectively is to make it highly specific to a given project, so that it contains only immediately usable material, organized according to the needs of the project. The change produced by this type of customization is often quite profound, yielding a result that looks very little like the original. A highly focused process will contain detailed information about the project, such as tool configuration, paths to network shares, developer set up instructions, pointers to documentation for APIs that the team will use, names of key contact people for important process steps like CM, defect tracking or builds, team policies regarding check-in, coding style and peer review, and many other details specific to the project, and to any larger project to which it belongs, as well as to the team, and any larger organization to which it belongs. Indeed, the UP is actually a process model designed to be used in this manner. Unfortunately, many of its users simply try to apply the generic defaults, with less than satisfying results.

The key to using any process effectively is making it highly specific to a given project.

As with other forms of systematic reuse, this kind of customization makes sense only when we can use it more than once. When that is the case, however, it can be highly cost effective. Also, reusing highly focused process assets increases

Reusing highly focused process assets increases agility.

agility by eliminating work, just as any reusing other asset does. As Jacobson likes to say, the fastest way to build something is to reuse something that already exists, especially when the reusable asset is designed to be customizable and extensible. This statement is true for any wheel that can be systematically reused, rather than reinvented, including development processes.

Constraint-Based Scheduling

Constraint-based scheduling balances agility and structure.

Constraint-based scheduling is a method for organizing development that balances the need for agility with the need for some amount of structure. Instead of prescribing a process, constraint-based scheduling provides guidance, and imposes constraints on development artifacts. This approach fosters agility by letting a work flow arise dynamically and opportunistically within the constraints, adapting to the innumerable variations in circumstances that will inevitably occur, while at the same time incorporating lessons learned to minimize the amount of time and money wasted on needless rediscovery of existing knowledge.

A process framework defines the space of possible processes.

A process framework essentially decomposes a process into micro processes attached to various types of development artifacts. These micro processes describe the requirements for producing artifacts of the types to which they are attached. This description can enumerate key decision points, analyze the trade-offs associated with each decision point, describe required or optional activities, and enumerate the resources required and the results produced by each activity. Constraints are added to describe the preconditions that must be satisfied before an artifact is produced, the postconditions that must be satisfied after it is produced, and the invariants that must hold when the artifacts have stabilized. For example, we might require scoping and requirements capture to be performed before an iteration begins, and exit criteria to be satisfied before it can end. We might also require that all source code checked into source control build and unit test correctly. We call this structure a process framework because it defines the space of possible processes that could emerge, depending on the needs and circumstances of any given project, instead of prescribing one general purpose process for all projects. Two innovations related to process frameworks are constraint-based scheduling and active guidance.

Once a process framework is defined, micro processes can be stitched together dynamically to support any work flow that the project requires, including top-down, bottom-up, outside in, test then code or code then test, in any combination, as long as the constraints are satisfied. The work flow can also be resource driven, allowing work to be scheduled to maximize overall throughput using methods like PERT and CPM, and to be started when the required resources become available. Many different kinds of resources can drive the scheduling, including artifacts like requirements, test plans or source code, people like developers with specific skills, products like configuration management or defect tracking systems, and facilities, such as the opening of a port or the allocation of storage on a server.

Any work flow can occur that does not violate the constraints.

Note that a process framework need not be large or elaborate, and may contain as much or as little detail as desired. This flexibility provides a way to scale a process up or down, depending on the circumstances. For example, a small and highly agile team might use minimal framework that provides only a few key practice recommendations. A larger organization, on the other hand, might add quite a lot of detail around the build process, check in procedures, testing procedures or rules governing shared components. The UP could be made less prescriptive by recasting it using micro processes and constraints, supported by active guidance tools, which are the topic of the next section.

A process framework need not be large or elaborate.

Active Guidance

Active guidance is a term used to describe an approach to developer assistance that uses software agents to monitor activities performed by the developer in real time to evaluate constraints defined by a process framework, in the context of a development tool, as described by Jacobson [Jac04]. For example, noticing that the developer is attempting to check in changes to source code, a software agent might interfere to prevent the check in because the file has not been successfully compiled or unit tested since the changes were made. A more proactive agent might first disable the check in command when there is nothing ready to check in, then notify the developer when a file has been modified that a build is required, next notify the developer when a build has succeeded that unit tests need to be run, and finally enable the check in command when the unit tests have succeeded. It might also provide a console

Active guidance uses agents to evaluate constraints defined by a process framework in real time in the context of a development tool.

that shows tasks in progress and the conditions preventing them from being completed successfully, or tasks that can be scheduled when tasks in progress are completed successfully. Such an agent might take some of its rules from the project plan, some from a generic process framework developed by encoding a general purpose process like the UP, and some from a domain specific process framework maintained by the project team.

Agents should never interfere by insisting on unimportant but time-consuming tasks.

One of the keys to making active guidance effective is ensuring that the agents never interfere by insisting on unimportant but time-consuming tasks. One way to do this is to differentiate between minor side effects and major consequences in rules. Another is to let developers override a rule, recording the override, so that it can be queried later. A common use for active guidance is developer training, since it can be more effective than passive help. For experienced users, it can naturally recede into the background and serve as a simple real time peer reviewer, catching things that the developer knows are incorrect but has overlooked, in much the same way as a compiler does. An example of a product that provides active guidance is Jaczone WayPointer™ [Jac04].

Software Factories

Software products are in some respects like tangible products of conventional engineering disciplines such as bridges, buildings, and computers. But there are also certain important differences that give software development a unique flavor.

Peter Wegner

In this chapter, we describe the industrialization of software development. We then introduce Software Factories as a way of promoting and supporting industrialization. Next, we look at how Software Factories are implemented and we provide a simple Software Factory example. From there we look at the implications of industrialization. Finally, we briefly consider what must be done to realize this vision, setting the stage for Part 2.

Industrializing Software Development

We suggested in the Preface and in Chapter 1 that the next development paradigm will industrialize software development, moving the industry toward maturity. What does industrialization mean in this industry? We cannot know with certainty until it happens, of course. We can, however, make educated guesses by looking at how this industry has evolved to date. We can also gain some insight by looking at what industrialization has meant in other industries, and by comparing them with this

The next paradigm will industrialize software development.

industry, to reason about how our experience may be similar to or different from theirs.

Ironically, most of the processes in other industries are automated by software systems.

We said earlier that other industries learned how to customize and assemble standard components to produce similar but distinct products, to standardize, integrate and automate production processes, to develop extensible tools and configure them to automate repetitive tasks, to leverage customer and supplier relationships to reduce costs and risks, to automate the production of product variants using product lines, and to distribute production across supply chains composed of highly specialized and interdependent suppliers. In the automotive industry, for example, cars and trucks are end products assembled from standard components supplied by a large number of upstream suppliers, who assembled those components, in turn, from components produced even further upstream. Of course, supply chains are not unique to industries based on physical goods. They are also found in financial services, mortgage lending, music, television and film production, publishing and many other industries based on information and digital property rights. Ironically, most of the production processes in these industries are automated by software systems. In this case, the saying is true that the cobbler's children have no shoes.

Others have made apples-to-oranges comparisons.

Others have drawn and debated such analogies between the software industry and industries based on physical goods. Some of the discussion has involved an apples-to-oranges comparison, however, between the production of physical goods, on one hand, and the development of software, on the other. The key to clearing up the confusion is to understand the economics of reuse.

The Economics of Reuse

Raising the level of abstraction requires an investment in reusable production assets.

Recall from Chapter 2 that reusing solutions to common subproblems in a given domain can reduce the total cost of solving multiple problems in the domain. Reuse can also reduce the total time to market and improve product quality [JGJ97]. To realize a return on the investments we make in developing the solutions, we must reuse them enough to more than recover the cost of their development, either directly through cost reductions, or indirectly, through time to market reductions and quality improvements. In other words, we can think of the solutions from an investment perspective as production assets. We have already seen some production assets, such as languages, tools, patterns, and frameworks. These production assets are called implementation assets, since they are used directly in product implementations. The implementation assets are accompanied by process assets that support their application, such as test cases and harnesses, and design or user documentation. Finally, the process assets are supported by tools and other automation assets. We can now define a production asset as a software artifact explicitly intended to provide a return on investment through reuse.

Recall from Chapter 4 that an ad hoc approach to reuse tends to produce marginal results, and often leads to frustration and then from there to skepticism regarding the idea of reusing code developed by others. To realize the benefits of reuse described earlier, we must adopt a more mature approach that involves identifying the common subproblems in a given domain, and developing integrated collections of production assets that can be reused to solve those problems predictably. The goal of this approach, called systematic reuse, is to increase the returns on investments in production assets through economies of scale and scope.

Reuse must be systematic, rather than ad hoc, to be effective.

Economies of Scale and Scope

Economies of scope are often confused with economies of scale. While both reduce time and cost and improve product quality by producing multiple products collectively, rather than individually, they are otherwise quite different. To clear up this confusion, we will define both terms, and look at how and where both phenomena arise.

Economies of scope and scale are different.

Economies of scale arise when multiple identical instances of a single design are produced collectively, rather than individually, as illustrated in Figure 5.1. They arise in the production of products, such as machine screws, when production assets, such as machine tools, are used to produce multiple identical product instances. A design is generally created, along with initial instances, called prototypes, by a resource intensive process, called development, performed by engineers. Many additional instances, called copies, are generally produced by another process, called production, performed by machines and low-cost labor, to satisfy market demand at low cost. We can think of economies of scale as reducing the cost of solving the same problem in the same way multiple times by reducing the cost of producing each solution.

Economies of scale arise when production assets are reused to mass produce copies of a prototype.

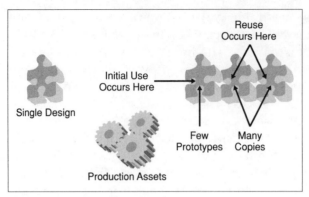

Figure 5.1   Economies of scale

Economies of scope arise when production assets are reused to develop multiple similar but distinct designs and prototypes.

Economies of scope arise when multiple similar but distinct designs and prototypes are produced collectively, rather than individually, as illustrated in Figure 5.2. In automobile manufacturing, for example, multiple similar but distinct product designs are often developed by composing existing designs, such as chassis, body, interior, and drive train designs, and variants or models are often developed by varying features, such as engine and trim level, in an existing design. In other words, the same practices, processes, tools, and materials are used to design and prototype multiple similar but distinct products. Note how this ties directly to the concept of software product lines introduced in Chapter 4. The same is true in commercial construction, where multiple bridges or skyscrapers seldom have the same design. However, an interesting twist in commercial construction is that usually, only one or two instances are produced

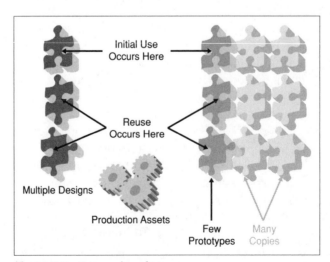

Figure 5.2   Economies of scope

from every successful design, so economies of scale are rarely realized. For this reason, economies of scope are the primary means of systematic reuse in commercial construction. In automobile manufacturing, where many identical instances are usually produced from every successful design, economies of scope are usually complemented by economies of scale, as suggested by the illustration. We can think of economies of scope as reducing the cost of solving multiple similar but distinct problems in a given domain by collectively solving their common subproblems and then assembling, adapting, and configuring the resulting partial solutions to solve the top-level problems.

Systematic Software Reuse

Software is like automobile manufacturing in some markets, and like commercial construction in others. In markets where copies are mass produced, such as consumer desktop programs like word processors, software exhibits economies of scale, like automobile manufacturing. In these markets, as in automobile manufacturing, development and production are distinctly different processes. A design is developed, along with an initial instance, called a master, by a resource intensive process, called development, performed by engineers. The other instances, called copies, are produced by a different process, called duplication, performed by machines and low-cost labor to satisfy market demand at low cost.

Software can exhibit economies of scale in some markets, and can be mass produced using duplication.

Of course, there are important differences between the two industries, such as the cost of producing and consuming copies. In automobile manufacturing, as in other heavy industries, producing copies consumes expensive resources, while in software it consumes inexpensive digital and paper media. In this sense, software is also like the entertainment industry, where the ease and low cost of producing and distributing copies has led to problems with licensing and protecting property rights. Another difference between software and automobile manufacturing is that software is generally more expensive to consume because of customization. In software, customization can range from preference setting to programming, while automobiles generally require only minimal customization. At high enough levels of customization, such as for packaged enterprise applications, copies effectively become similar but distinct products and economies of scale disappear.

Economies of scale are lost at high levels of customization.

In some markets, like the enterprise, where business applications are developed for competitive advantage and copies are

Software exhibits economies of scope.

rarely mass produced, software rarely exhibits economies of scale. In these markets, it can only exhibit economies of scope, like commercial construction. Economies of scope can be realized when market size is limited or extensive customization is required. These economies arise when the same practices, processes, tools, and materials are used to develop multiple similar but distinct designs and their first few instances. Since economies of scale rarely arise in these markets, economies of scope are the primary means of systematic reuse.

Economies of scope arise in development, while economies of scale arise in production.

We can now see where apples have been compared with oranges in the debate about the industrialization of software. The production process in physical industries has been naively compared with the development process in software. In other words, we cannot compare the software industry with industries based on physical goods by looking for the economies of scale that accompany the production of physical goods in the software development process. We can, however, expect the industrialization of software development to exploit economies of scope, especially for markets with limited distribution. Wegner notes that because software is logical not physical, costs are concentrated in development rather than in production (i.e., the cost of producing copies of existing software is negligible), and that since software does not wear out, its reliability depends on logical qualities like correctness and robustness, rather than physical qualities like hardness and malleability.

Industrialization will exploit economies of scope.

Since economies of scale arise in production, while economies of scope arise in development, some observers have erroneously concluded that software is fundamentally different from physical industries. This conclusion is flattering because it makes software seem special, deflecting criticism from other industries and from the financial community, who claim that like other industries, the software industry should be expected to produce net positive returns on investment, instead of the opposite, and should ultimately be judged along with other potential investments solely on the basis of economic merit [Car04]. Surely, the economic realities will eventually prevail. Software is fundamentally like every other industry, i.e. engineers develop designs and prototypes, while copies are produced mechanically to serve mass markets. Hopefully, the software industry will embrace industrialization before the financial community stops buying excuses, and takes its money entirely offshore. Software Factories and supply chains are key steps on the road to industrialization.

Integrating the Critical Innovations

We said in Chapter 1 that Software Factories integrate critical innovations to define a highly automated approach to software development that exploits economies of scope. We then identified the critical innovations in Chapter 4, and showed how they solve chronic problems that object orientation has not been able to overcome. To summarize that discussion, the critical innovations include:

- Building families of similar but distinct software products to enable a more systematic approach to reuse.

- Assembling self-describing service components using new encapsulation, packaging, and orchestration technologies.

- Developing domain specific languages and tools using new language definition, code generation, and tool development technologies that reduce the amount of handwritten code.

- Using constraint-based scheduling and active guidance in the context of a process framework to scale up to larger projects, geographical distribution and extended product life cycles without losing agility.

While each of these technologies is mature enough to be deployed on an industrial scale, their integration produces a whole that is greater than the sum of its parts.

In the Preface and in Chapter 4, we suggested that Software Factories apply these critical innovations to a four-part pattern that has occurred repeatedly throughout the evolution of software development. As we explained there, this pattern involves:

- Developing frameworks to bootstrap implementations of products based on common architectural styles.

- Developing language-based tools to support the development of products by adapting, configuring, and assembling framework-based components.

- Using the tools to engage customers and to respond to changes in requirements rapidly by building software incrementally, keeping it running as changes are made.

- Capturing design decisions in a form that directly produces executables.

Software Factories integrate critical innovations to form a highly automated approach to software development.

Software Factories apply these critical innovations to a familiar four-part pattern for automating development, making it much cheaper to implement.

We then gave examples of the application of this pattern to two domains: user interface construction and database design. We then observed that applying this pattern is extremely expensive, and that because of the cost it only makes economic sense in broad horizontal domains such as user interface construction and data access. Finally, we suggested that new technologies can be used to reduce the cost dramatically, making it economically feasible to realize the resulting productivity gains in narrow vertical domains, such as health care and financial services.

Developing language-based tools is valuable but expensive.

Two parts of this pattern are already cost effective, namely developing frameworks, and using agile methods to engage customers and to respond rapidly to changes in requirements. Recall from Chapter 3, however, that pressure to deliver results quickly from individual projects can make it hard to develop frameworks, which must usually be generalized from multiple projects. The other two parts are not as cost effective. According to Roberts and Johnson, the use of a well-designed framework can reduce the cost of developing an application by an order of magnitude [RJ96]. Using a framework can be difficult, however. A framework represents an archetypical product, such as an application or subsystem, which can be completed or specialized to satisfy variations in requirements. Mapping the requirements of each product variant onto the framework is a non-trivial problem that generally requires the expertise of an architect or senior developer. Roberts and Johnson observe that language-based tools can encapsulate the abstractions defined by a framework, helping users think in terms of the abstractions.

Software Factories use language-based tools to map variations in requirements to framework completions.

Software Factories use language-based tools to map variations in requirements to framework completions. This mapping is a form of guidance provided by architects or senior developers during the development of the Software Factory, and then reused during product development, often by much less experienced developers. Language-based tools also promote agility by capturing requirements in forms that customers better understand, and by propagating changes in requirements to implementations more quickly. Unfortunately, developing such tools to automate the assembly process is currently well beyond the reach of most organizations. If this part of the pattern can be made as cost effective as the others, then we will be close to realizing the vision we described.

What Is a Software Factory?

Answering this question in detail will take the rest of this book. However, we can offer a brief definition to provide an anchor for discussion:

We define the term Software Factory.

> A **software factory** is a **software product line** that configures extensible tools, processes, and content using a software factory template based on a **software factory schema** to automate the development and maintenance of variants of an archetypical product by adapting, assembling, and configuring framework-based components.

The central elements of a Software Factory are a software factory schema and a software factory template based on the software factory schema. The software factory template configures extensible tools, processes, and content to form a production facility for the product family. A schematic of a Software Factory is provided in Figure 5.3. We will use this diagram to look

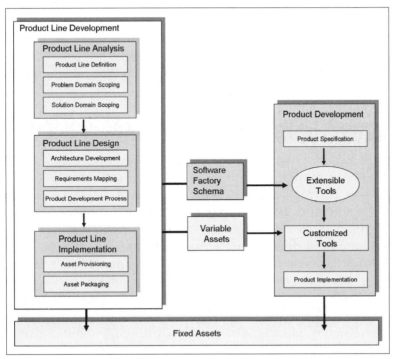

Figure 5.3   A software factory

at each of the parts of a Software Factory in turn. We will then talk about how to build a Software Factory, and how to build a software product using a Software Factory.

HISTORY OF THE TERM

According to Merriam Webster, a factory is a highly organized production facility that produces members of a product line using standardized parts, tools, and production processes. Historically, the term Software Factory has been used to describe large commercial efforts to automate software development along similar lines. Salient features of these efforts include systematic reuse and continuous process improvement. According to Aaen, the term suggests a commitment to long-term integrated efforts to optimize software development methods and practices over the course of multiple projects [ABM97].

What Is a Software Factory Schema?

Use different models to describe different perspectives and different levels of abstraction.

The need for a software factory schema becomes apparent when we recognize that we need a way to categorize and summarize development artifacts, such as XML documents, models, configuration files, build scripts, source code files, SQL files, localization files, deployment manifests, and test case definitions, in an orderly way, and a way to define relationships between them, so that we can maintain consistency among them. A common approach is to use a grid, as shown in Figure 5.4. The columns define concerns, while the rows define levels of abstraction. We have chosen column and row labels that are fairly intuitive to most developers, but others have described grids with more elaborate labeling.[1] Each cell defines a perspective or *viewpoint* from which we can build some aspect of the software. For example, for a 3-tiered application, one cell might define a logical view of the presentation tier, and another might define a conceptual view of the data tier. Once the grid has been constructed, we can populate it with development artifacts for a specific software product.

The software factory schema defines the artifacts and the assets used to build them.

Of course, the grid can be used to build more than one software product. Before it has been populated with specific development artifacts, it defines the development bill of materials required to build the members of a software product family. Taking a cue from software product lines, we can go one step further and add information to each cell identifying the

• Use Cases And Scenarios • Business Goals And Objectives	• Business Entities And Relationships	• Business Processes • Service Factoring	• Service Distribution • Quality Of Service Strategy
• Workflow Models • Role Definitions	• Message Schemas And Document Specifications	• Service Interactions • Service Definitions • Object Models	• Logical Server Types • Service Mappings
• Process Specification	• Database Schemas • Data Access Strategy	• Detailed Design • Technology Dependent Design	• Physical Servers • Software Installed • Network Layout

Figure 5.4   A grid for categorizing development artifacts

production assets used to build the development artifacts required from that perspective, including such as DSLs, patterns, frameworks and tools. If we also identify the micro processes used for each cell, we can also think of this grid as a process framework for producing the family members.

The grid itself is not an innovation. What is novel is applying the grid to a product family, identifying production assets for each cell, and defining mappings between and within the cells that can be used to fully or partially automate model transformations, code generation, pattern application, test harness construction, user interface layout, database schema design, and many other development tasks. As we have seen, we must use first-class development artifacts based on high fidelity languages, such as XML, C#, and SQL, in order to provide this automation. For models, this means using DSLs, not general purpose modeling languages designed for documentation. In some cases, the artifacts described by viewpoints are models, but this is frequently not the case. They can be any source artifacts based on formal languages, such as high-level work flow scripts, general purpose programming language source code files, WSDL files, or SQL data definition language (DDL) files.

Note that the viewpoints define not only the languages used to develop the artifacts they describe, but also requirements on the artifacts, usually expressed as constraints or patterns. For example, a software factory schema might contain two

Applying the grid to a product line and mapping production assets to the cells is novel.

Viewpoints also impose requirements on the artifacts they describe and can use the languages of other viewpoints.

viewpoints that both use the same class modeling DSL. We might require all of the classes modeled from one of these viewpoints to inherit, either directly or indirectly, from classes supplied by a user interface widget framework associated with the viewpoint. Similarly, we might require all of the classes modeled from the other viewpoint to play defined roles in one of several business entity implementation patterns associated with the viewpoint. In a real software factory schema, the same languages are typically used by multiple viewpoints, especially viewpoints close to the platform based on general purpose programming languages.

Software Factory Schemas as Graphs

A software factory schema is actually a directed graph whose nodes are viewpoints and whose edges are computable relationships between viewpoints called mappings.

Of course, even a highly decorated and detailed grid is a gross over simplification of reality. A software factory schema is actually a directed graph whose nodes are viewpoints and whose edges are computable relationships between viewpoints called mappings. This structure allows nodes that would have been non-adjacent in a grid representation to be related. It also relaxes the artificial constraint imposed by a grid representation, which requires the viewpoints to fit into neat classification schemes, creating rows and columns. Finally, and most importantly, it allows the schema to reflect the software architecture. So, for example, a schema for a family of business applications might contain several clusters of viewpoints, one for each subsystem such as customer management, catalog management, order management or order fulfillment. The viewpoints in each cluster might then be further grouped into subsets reflecting the layered architecture of that subsystem, as illustrated in Figure 5.5. We'll use this software factory schema as the basis for our software factory example in Chapter 16. Of course, the grid is a useful simplification because it is easier to visualize. We will therefore use both of these representations at times to suit our purposes, and we will even use the two somewhat interchangeably. Keep in mind, however, that the graph is the most accurate representation, and that the grid is merely a useful abstraction of the graph.

A software factory schema describes the artifacts that must be developed to produce a software product.

We call the graph a *software factory schema* because it describes the artifacts that must be developed to produce a software product, just as an XML schema describes the elements and attributes that must be created to form a document, and as a database schema describes the rows that must be created to populate the database. We can now see how the software

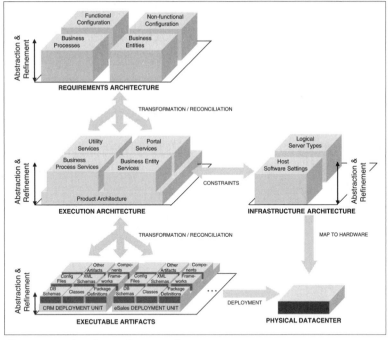

Figure 5.5 A software factory schema

factory schema ties together the critical innovations described in Chapter 4. Like an Architectural Description Standard (ADS), a software factory schema is a template for describing the members of a software product family. Despite this similarity, however, there are several major differences between a software factory schema and an ADS:

- While an ADS deals only with architecture, a software factory schema deals with many other aspects of a software product family, such as requirements, implementation, deployment, testing, instrumentation, debugging, management, maintenance, and enhancement.

- While an ADS organizes design documentation, a software factory schema organizes development artifacts.

- While an ADS implies a software product family, it does not explicitly identify one, or incorporate mechanisms to support family based development, such as a way to express how the members of the family differ from a family archetype. A software factory schema, on the other hand, targets a specific software product family and can be instantiated and customized to describe a specific family member in terms of its differences from the family archetype.

- While an ADS does not necessarily support automation, a software factory schema can be implemented by a software factory template to automate software development tasks, as we shall see shortly.

A software factory schema provides a multi-dimensional separation of concerns.

Of course, the essential property of a software factory schema is that it provides a multi-dimensional separation of concerns based on various aspects of the artifacts being organized, such as their level of abstraction, position within architecture, functionality or operational qualities. According to Coplien [Cop99]:

> *We can analyze the application domain using principles of commonality and variation to divide it into subdomains, each of which may be suitable for design under a specific paradigm.*

We can now see the grid as a two dimensional projection of the graph that plots one or more aspects on the horizontal axis and different levels of abstraction on the vertical axis. Another two-dimensional projection is an aspect plane, which projects related viewpoints from the graph for a specific aspect, providing a consolidated view from that viewpoint. Examples of aspects planes are distribution, security, and transaction planes.

A software factory schema is like a recipe that defines the ingredients, tools, and preparation process for a family of software products.

We can also think of a software factory schema as a recipe for building a family of software products. Clearly, the viewpoints define the ingredients and the tools used to prepare them, but where is the process of preparing them described? Recall from Chapter 4 that a process framework can be constructed by defining the micro process required to develop each member of a set of interrelated artifacts, and by defining constraints regarding the preconditions that must be satisfied before an artifact is produced, the postconditions that must be satisfied after it is produced, and the invariants that must hold when the artifacts have stabilized. This framework defines the space of possible processes that could emerge, depending on the needs and circumstances of a given project. Clearly, there is a resemblance between a process framework and a software factory schema. Indeed, the viewpoints of a software factory schema already define micro processes for producing the artifacts they describe. This relationship means that we can produce a process framework from a software factory schema simply by adding constraints to govern the order of execution. We now have a complete recipe for the members of a product family. It defines the ingredients, the tools used to prepare them, and the process of preparing them.

Relationships Between Viewpoints

Generally, when we describe a product using multiple artifacts, information captured by one artifact may be related to information captured by another. For example, a model describing a database schema might be a refinement of a model describing business entities. Similarly, information captured by one artifact may overlap with information captured by others. For example, a model of the structure of a business entity might refer to the same classes as a model that describes security policy for all of the business entities in an assembly. Clearly, we must define relationships between the artifacts to maintain consistency as changes are made. For example, if the name of a business entity changes in one of the two models in the previous example, then it should also change in the other.

We need to maintain consistency as artifacts change.

We define relationships between artifacts by defining relationships between the viewpoints that describe those artifacts. Relationships between viewpoints are defined in terms of mappings. A mapping encapsulates knowledge about how to implement artifacts described by one viewpoint in terms of artifacts described by another, and makes that knowledge available for reuse. A forward mapping defines how artifacts described by a target viewpoint are derived from artifacts described by a source viewpoint. An inverse mapping defines a similar relationship, but in the opposite direction. In either direction, the derivation may be either partial or complete. With complete derivation, the target artifact is completely defined by the source artifact. With partial derivation, the target artifact is partially defined by the source artifact, and must be completed using information from some other source.

Relationships between artifacts are defined by relationships between viewpoints.

If a mapping is computable, then we can partially or completely generate artifacts described by the target viewpoint from artifacts described by the source viewpoint. To define a computable mapping, we must have formal descriptions of both the source and target viewpoints, meaning that formal languages must be used to express the artifacts they describe. The language of the source viewpoint defines elements that can appear in the artifacts it describes, and the kinds of expressions

Computable mappings can be used to generate artifacts.

that can be formed by combining them. The language of the target viewpoint defines elements that can be used to realize expressions in artifacts described by the source viewpoint, and rules for combining them.

Computations across mappings are called transformations.

Computations across mappings are called transformations. A transformation reads expressions from one or more source artifacts, and writes expressions to one or more target artifacts. Transformations may be fully manual, fully automatic, or somewhere in between, depending on the amount of variability required. If infinite variability is required, then the transformation must be fully manual. If no variability is required, then the transformation can be fully automatic. Partially automatic transformations may involve interactive construction of the results, subject to constraints imposed by the source artifacts. For example, we might need to manually lay out a user interface, constrained by the requirement that every field on a form must map to a property of an object returned by a business operation, and that every property must be displayed by a field. In other cases, we might examine the results of a transformation and change the source artifacts or the transformation parameters to change the results. Some changes may be made directly to the results for optimization or customization. Some of these may be local to the results, while others may be reflected back into the source artifacts. We'll return to study mappings and transformations based upon them in Chapters 14 and 15.

Customizing Relationships

The ability to customize mappings is critical to high fidelity transformation and code generation.

The ability to customize relationships is critical to high fidelity transformation and code generation. For example, there are three well-known ways to represent inheritance when storing objects in a database, as illustrated in Figure 5.6. The top one stores the instances of each class in a separate table. The middle one stores only the additional columns used by Class2 in a separate table. The bottom one stores instances of both classes in a single table, using a discriminator, T_Class12_1D, to identify the class of object stored in each row, and placing NULLs in the columns for the unused attributes in rows containing instances of Class1. Each of these representations exhibits optimal performance for certain access patterns. To tune the performance of object persistence, we must be able to customize mappings between business entity models and database schemas. This diagram is based on the notation defined in Naiburg and

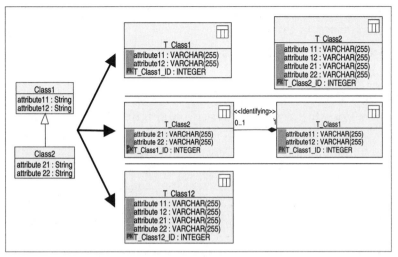

Figure 5.6   Three ways to represent inheritance

Maksimchuk [NM01]. In the figure, PK stands for "primary key" and PFK stands for "parent foreign key".

Setting parameter values is the simplest form of customization, as shown in Figure 5.7, a screen shot from IBM Rational Rose XDE. Parameters are useful because they clearly capture design decisions. Patterns offer more advanced customization with minimal effort. Pattern-based transformations are described in Chapters 7 and 15. More advanced customization can be provided using compiler extensions, such as templates,

Several mechanisms are available for customizing transformations.

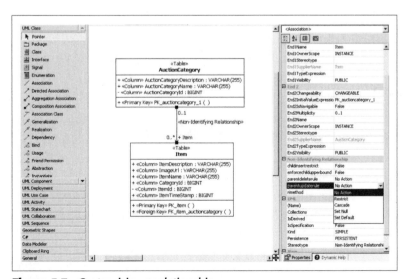

Figure 5.7   Customizing a relationship

scripts, and compiled extensions. We will look at some of these mechanisms in Chapter 7.

Synchronizing Artifacts

Synchronization using mappings to keep artifacts consistent.

Once we have two or more related artifacts, we can use transformations to keep them synchronized during development. Changes to the artifacts or parameter values may invalidate the relationship between them. When that happens, the transformations must be recalculated, or the inconsistencies must be flagged for the user to correct manually. Recalculating the transformations automatically as the user works is called synchronization. Synchronization eliminates the work of keeping artifacts consistent by hand. A business entity model and a database schema might be synchronized, for example, so that when changes are made to one, they are reflected automatically in the other.

Even partial synchronization is an improvement over manual housekeeping.

A model that acts as the source of a synchronized update on one occasion may act as the target on another. Synchronization may occur immediately upon any change to a participating artifact, at specific times, such as when focus changes in a tool, or only when explicitly requested. When artifacts are synchronized, it may not be possible to resolve the discrepancies between them automatically. In this case, we may have to compare the two artifacts and merge the changes. Even partial synchronization is an improvement over manual housekeeping, where elements affected by a change must be identified by visual inspection, compile errors or defects manifested at runtime. Other synchronization aids include restricting user actions to those that produce valid relationships among artifacts, and synchronizing subsets of artifacts, such as method signatures, but not method bodies.

Configuring a Software Factory Schema

We must configure the software factory schema for building any given member of the product family.

An important aspect of using a software factory schema is configuration. A raw software factory schema is a recipe for building a family of software products. However, for any given project, we only care about one software product, the one we have been charged with building. We must therefore configure the software factory schema to create a recipe for building a specific member of the product family. This process is similar to what cooks perform when they modify a recipe before using it, based on special requirements, such as the number of servings required, the ingredients or tools available, or the time available before the meal must be served. This modification is actually quite straight forward, and consists of simple configuration for the most part, as we will show in Chapters 11 and 16. We can now see that in order to support this kind of configuration, a software factory schema must contain both fixed parts and variable parts. The fixed parts remain the same for every member of the product family, while the variable parts change to accommodate unique requirements. A software factory schema for Online Order Entry Systems, for example, might include viewpoints that describe the artifacts and tools used to build personalization subsystems. For some members of the family, however, a personalization subsystem may not be required. Before we set out to build such a system, we would first remove the viewpoints related to the construction of personalization subsystems, configuring our project structure and tools accordingly.

What Is a Software Factory Template?

Now, the software factory process described thus far is quite appealing, but as of yet, it is all on paper. If all we have is the software factory schema, then we can describe the assets used to build the family members, but we do not actually have the assets. To actually build a member of the product family, we must implement the software factory schema, defining the DSLs, patterns, frameworks, and tools it describes, packaging them, and making them available to product developers. Collectively, these assets form a *software factory template*. A software factory template includes code and metadata that can be loaded into extensible tools, like an Interactive Development Environment (IDE) or an enterprise life cycle tool suite, to automate the development and maintenance of family members. We call the code and metadata a software factory template because it configures the tools to produce a specific type of software, just as a document template loaded into a desktop productivity tool like Microsoft Word or Excel configures it to produce of a specific type of document. Like a software factory schema, a software factory template must be configured for building a specific family member. While configuring a schema customizes the description of the software factory, configuring a

We need a software factory template that implements the software factory schema to build a family member.

template customizes the tools and other pieces of the development environment used to build the family member.

Building a Software Factory

Building a Software Factory is a special case of building a software product line.

We are now ready to talk about building a Software Factory. Since a Software Factory is a kind of software product line, building one is a special case of building a software product line. An in-depth discussion of software product line development will have to wait until Chapter 11. We will use terms defined there, and provide brief definitions for some of them. Building a Software Factory involves the following activities:

- Building a software factory schema that describes the software factory. This is a specialization of the two product line activities:

  - *Product Line Analysis* defines what products the Software Factory will develop. The central activity in Product Line Analysis is defining a scope that identifies the software products that will be developed and maintained using the Software Factory. The scope is defined, not by enumerating specific product descriptions, but rather by describing the problem domain that the products address. Product Line Analysis produces, among other things, product line requirements. The product line requirements are organized into viewpoints that become part of the software factory schema.

  - *Product Line Design* defines how the Software Factory will develop products within its scope. The central activity in Product Line Design is defining an architecture for the target software product family. This architecture is similar to the architecture for a single product, except that it is designed to support variation among the family members. Product Line Design produces several other artifacts, including a requirements mapping, which we will discuss shortly, the product development process, and a plan for using tools to automate parts of the product development process. These artifacts also contribute to the software factory schema: the architecture is organized into viewpoints, the requirements mapping is expressed using relationships between viewpoints, and the product development process is expressed as micro processes attached to the viewpoints.

- Building a software factory template that instantiates the software product line. This is a specialization of Product Line Implementation. The software factory template packages the production assets for the Software Factory, including requirements assets like specification languages, implementation assets, like patterns, frameworks and components, process assets, like development tools, testing assets, like test harnesses, unit tests, and integration test suites, and deployment assets, like configurations for logical hosts to which family members will be deployed. The software factory template must ensure that there are no large discontinuities between artifacts described by different viewpoints, that any visible artifact used in the Software Factory can be changed, and that there are no irreversible steps in the product development process.

Once we have developed the first cut of the Software Factory, we then maintain it continuously, collecting feedback as family members are developed, which we can use to refine its definition and implementation. As we said earlier, the most expensive part of developing a Software Factory is building the languages and tools that automate product development. Of course, there are many other significant challenges, such as performing the domain analysis necessary to devise the appropriate software factory schema, and developing the infrastructure needed to support the creation, configuration, and installation of software factory templates. We will address domain analysis in Chapter 11, infrastructure development in Chapters 14 and 15, and technologies that make language and tool development cheaper, faster, and easier in Chapters 8 and 9.

We maintain it as family members are developed.

Building a Software Product

Of course, the goal of building a Software Factory is to rapidly develop members of its product family. As you have probably guessed, building a product using a Software Factory is a special case of building one using a software product line. An in-depth discussion of this topic will again have to wait until Chapter 11, but we will again use terms defined there, and

Building a product using a Software Factory is a special case of building one using a software product line.

provide brief definitions for some of them. Building a product using a Software Factory involves the following activities:

- *Problem Analysis* determines whether or not the product is in scope for the Software Factory. Depending on the fit, we may choose to build some or all of it outside the Software Factory. We may still choose to build a product that fits poorly within the Software Factory, changing the software factory schema and template to accommodate it.

- *Product Specification* defines the product requirements in terms of differences from the product line requirements. A range of product specification mechanisms can be used, depending on the extent of the differences in requirements, including property sheets, wizards, feature models, visual models, and tabular or hierarchically structured prose.

- *Product Design* maps the differences in requirements to differences in the product line architecture and the product development process, producing a customized product architecture, and a customized product development process.

- *Product Implementation* involves familiar activities, such as component and unit test development and build, unit test execution, and component assembly. A range of product implementation mechanisms can be used to develop the implementation, depending on the extent of the differences in design, such as property sheets, wizards, and feature models that configure components, visual models that assemble components and generate other artifacts, including models, code and configuration files, and source code that completes frameworks, or that creates, modifies, extends or adapts components.

- *Product Deployment* involves creating or reusing default deployment constraints, logical host configurations and executable to logical host mappings, by provisioning facilities, validating host configurations, reconfiguring hosts by installing and configuring the required resources, and installing and configuring the executables being deployed.

- *Product Testing* involves creating or reusing test assets, including test cases, test harnesses, test data sets, test scripts and applying instrumentation and measurement tools.

Of course, most, if not all, of these steps must be performed to develop a software product, regardless of whether or not a software factory is used. Using a software factory ensures that the work is done in an orderly fashion, under the control of a process framework. It also reduces the amount of work to be done by reusing existing production assets.

The product assets, including the requirements, develop- *The software* ment process, architecture, components, deployment config- *factory schema* uration, and tests are specified, reused, managed, and orga- *and template can* nized from multiple viewpoints, as defined by the software *be configured or* factory schema. The software factory schema can be configured *reconfigured at* or reconfigured at any point by adding, dropping or modifying *any point.* viewpoints and the relationships between them. The software factory template must also be configured along with the software factory schema. Examples of software factory template configuration include selecting the subsystems and components to be developed, selecting the patterns to be applied and the frameworks to be extended, modifying the project structure and policies, and configuring the execution environment. For example, enabling content personalization for an online commerce application might cause the following things to happen:

- A folder for the personalization subsystem is added to the project being used to build the application.

- The framework and accompanying patterns for the personalization subsystem are imported into the project.

- The viewpoint used to configure personalization is added to the schema, causing the personalization configuration tool to appear on the menu.

- The Front Controller pattern is applied automatically in the transformation between the user interaction model and the web front-end design model, and appears in the designer where we model the web front-end design, instead of the Page Controller pattern, so that the start up page will vector to different pages for different users, instead of showing the same content to all users.

- The project policy on the folder for the presentation layer is modified so that we cannot create a class that derives from PageController.

Development Process

We can work in any way we choose, provided that the process constraints defined in the software factory schema are satisfied.

Product development is organized and constrained by the development process that was defined when the Software Factory was developed, and then customized during the configuration of the software factory schema for the product under development. We can work top-down from requirements to executables, keeping related artifacts synchronized. For example, we can develop a business entity model, use it to produce a logical data model and then use that to produce an optimized database schema. We can also leverage constraints defined by horizontal mappings between viewpoints. For example, information about the deployment environment (e.g., the available protocols and services) can be used to constrain designs of service interactions (e.g., by limiting them to the protocols and services available in the deployment environment), to ensure that the implementations of the service interactions will deploy correctly in the deployment environment. We can also work bottom-up, developing test harnesses and custom components for various parts of the product, and testing as we work. When the software factory schema is completely populated, the process is complete. We can work in any way we choose, according to the needs of the project, the environment and the circumstances that arise, provided that the process constraints defined in the software factory schema are satisfied. Note that bottom-up software development occurs mainly during the implementation of the Software Factory, as languages, patterns, frameworks, and components are developed to supply abstractions for product development. A certain amount of bottom-up work will always occur in product development, however, since each product has unique requirements that may not be addressed by the preexisting abstractions. Once the configured software factory schema has been adequately populated, meaning that we have developed artifacts for a working subset of the viewpoints, we should be able to rapidly modify the implementation by changing those artifacts. This rapid feedback allows us to scale up to significant levels of complexity without losing agility. In addition to rapid modification, another benefit of this approach is the ability to use tools to validate software as it evolves, and to track and manage dependencies among its components.

Variability Mechanisms

We said earlier that a range of mechanisms could be used for product specification and implementation, depending on the extent of the differences between the product under development and the archetypical product defined by a Software Factory. This flexibility is what makes Software Factories so much faster than one-off product development. *With Software Factories, we gradually move from the totally open-ended hand coding that forms the bulk of software development today, to more constrained forms of specification that rely on predefined abstractions.*

Moving from totally open-ended hand coding to more constrained forms of specification is the key to accelerating software development.

Czarnecki and Eisenecker [CHE04] define a spectrum of variability mechanisms that ranges from routine configuration, through staged configuration based on feature models, to creative construction using visual modeling, as illustrated in Figure 5.8. Open ended hand coding, which is not shown in the diagram, lies to the right of creative construction with a graph-like language. Patterns represent an interesting point on this spectrum between visual modeling and open ended hand coding, as described in Chapter 6.

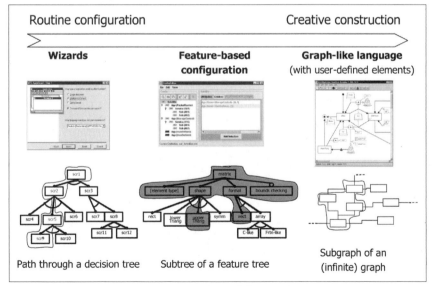

Figure 5.8 A spectrum of constrained variability mechanisms
Used with permission from K. Czarnecki and U. Eisenecker.

A Software Factory Example

We provide a brief example here. See Chapter 16 for a much more detailed example.

We will provide only a brief example here, since a highly detailed example is provided in Chapter 16. Imagine an Independent Software Vendor (ISV) that sells Online Order Entry applications to its customers. The stakeholders at the company work with the product line developers at the company to scope the product family and evaluate the business case. Satisfied that they can achieve their goals, they decide to invest in a Software Factory to reduce cost and time to market, and to increase quality. The product line developers use the results of the analysis to jump-start the development of a software factory schema, shown in Figure 5.9. (This is the bottom-right hand corner of the grid from Figure 5.4, populated for the Software Factory used in this example.) In the diagram, rectangles represent viewpoints, dashed lines represent refinements, and solid lines represent constraints.

Viewpoints describe the artifacts and the assets used to build them.

Recall that each viewpoint describes more than just development artifacts. It also describes:

- DSLs used to build artifacts based on the viewpoint
- Refactorings that can improve artifacts based on the viewpoint
- Aspects that are applicable to artifacts based on the viewpoint

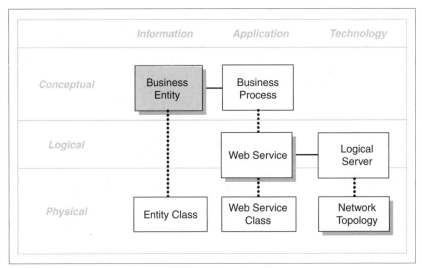

Figure 5.9   A simple software factory schema

- Micro processes used to produce artifacts based on the viewpoint

- Constraints implied by artifacts based on related viewpoints

- Frameworks that support the implementation of artifacts based on the viewpoint

- Mappings that support transformations within artifacts based on the viewpoint

Most of the viewpoints shown here describe models based on a single DSL. The only exceptions are the Entity Class and Web Service Class viewpoints, which both describe C# source code files. The figure illustrates the following:

The ISV defines a simple software factory schema.

- The Business Entity viewpoint defines the business entity abstraction, which describes efficient, message-driven, loosely coupled data services that map onto an object-relational framework. Examples of business entities include Customer and Order.

- The Business Process viewpoint defines the business activity, role and dependency abstractions, and a taxonomy of process patterns that can be used to compose them, forming business process specifications. An example of a business process is Enter Negotiated Order, which might use three process patterns: one for a User Interface Process to build a shopping cart, one for a sequential process to submit the order and perform credit checks, and one for a rule-driven process to calculate the discount.

- These two viewpoints map onto a Web service viewpoint that describes Web service collaborations in a service-oriented application architecture. The Web service viewpoint is used to describe how the business entities and processes are implemented as Web services, how the messages they exchange are defined and what protocols are used to support their interactions, using abstractions that hide the underlying details of the Web service implementations. Patterns of Web service interaction, such as *service façade, service interface* and *gateway*, can be applied to ensure that the architecture of an application uses best practices [MS03]. Security policy can be specified as an aspect and applied to every

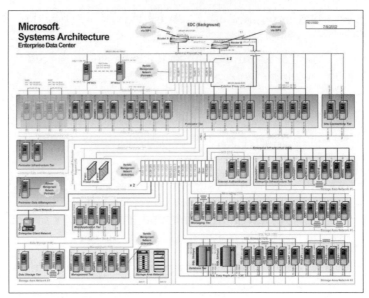

Figure 5.10   A logical data center configuration

operation defined within any group of selected service ports.

■ The Logical Systems Architecture viewpoint describes data center configurations. It lets a network architect create scale invariant data center configurations in terms of logical servers and connections, and their installed software and configuration settings. These will become deployment targets for the Web services. Standard configurations of data centers like the Microsoft Systems Architecture for Enterprise Data Centers shown in Figure 5.10 can be applied to models based on this viewpoint.

■ Information from one model influences the development of others. Examples are the interactions between business entities and processes, and between Web services and logical servers. This last one is particularly interesting because it can be used to design for deployment. Feeding knowledge of the deployment infrastructure into Web service designs constrains those designs to prevent deployment problems. Similarly, working this in reverse, if a Web service is to be deployed on a given logical server type, then we can validate that the server on which it will be deployed is of the correct type, that it has the right software installed, and that it is configured correctly. This approach, called

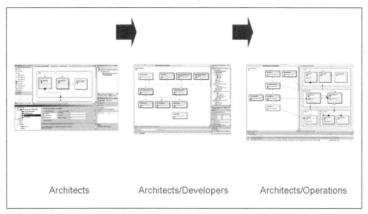

Architects   Architects/Developers   Architects/Operations

Figure 5.11 Design for deployment

Design for Deployment, is illustrated in Figure 5.11, which shows screen shots from Microsoft Visual Studio.

■ Mappings between the viewpoints support synchronization between models at design time. Partial implementations of the Web services are generated from the models in the form of classes that complete a framework, such as ASP.NET, and various configuration and policy files.

With the software factory schema completed, the product line developers build a software factory template based on the software factory schema for the enterprise life cycle suite used by their company for application development. They use ASP.NET and a Web service assembly tool that they developed for an earlier Software Factory to jump-start the effort. They experiment with and test the assets as they develop them, using them to build prototype applications. Experience with the assets leads to two changes in the software factory schema: the addition of patterns to the Web Service Class viewpoint and the addition of an entity framework to the Entity Class viewpoint.

The ISV builds a software factory template based on the schema, builds some prototype applications, and revises the schema.

When the company is ready to pilot the Software Factory, a pilot project team loads the software factory template into installations of the enterprise life cycle suite, configuring it for rapid Online Order Entry application development. Next, the pilot project team works with an early access partner to define the application to be built. They start by agreeing on a time limit, a cost limit and a process for the project. With these defined, they capture the high-level requirements using the product specification tools supplied by the product line development team. About 75% of the application can be rapidly

The ISV works with an early access partner to define a pilot application, and revises the factory.

developed using the Software Factory, most of it by code generation. The rest of it will be developed manually by the pilot project team. The pilot project team revises the software factory schema and the software factory template to accommodate the part of the application to be developed by hand.

The pilot project team customizes the requirements and the product development process and rapidly builds a working prototype.

Next, the team prioritizes high-level requirements, and defines project iterations, including requirements and exit constraints for each iteration, knowing as they do that the plan will change. They start the first iteration by capturing detailed requirements using the product specification tools. They quickly produce a working prototype using the Business Entity and Business Process modeling tools supplied by the product line development team, binding web methods to operations on entities, and accepting the default generated implementations. Reviewing the prototype with the customer, they modify the requirements, and revise the prototype. The customer agrees that the new prototype looks good. This completes the first iteration. One week has passed.

The pilot project team refines the requirements, and then customizes the architecture and the deployment configuration.

The team starts the second iteration by capturing additional requirements using the product specification tools. They now use the Entity Class viewpoint to write custom C# code to add business logic to the entities generated from the models. Then, they use Web Service viewpoint to modify the architecture, applying a façade pattern. After each round of changes, they test the working software to ensure that all is well, and repair defects revealed by testing. Next, they specify a custom security policy required by the customer as an aspect and apply it to all of the web methods on the façade. They update the deployment configuration to incorporate settings required by the custom security policy, and then test the software again to ensure that all is well. After repairing a few more defects in their handwritten business logic, they have a working application ready for customer review. This completes the second iteration. Another two weeks have passed.

The pilot project team builds the part of the application that was outside the scope of the factory.

Finally, the team sets out to build the custom part of the application that was not in scope for the Software Factory. During this time, they make numerous changes to the factory part of the application to accommodate requirements from the custom part, including writing custom message handlers for the Web service façade. After a long defect repair phase in the custom part of the application, the pilot project is finished. It took three months from beginning to end. Note that the factory part of the application covered 75% of the functionality but took about 25% of the time, while the custom part had exactly the opposite profile, since it was entirely coded by hand from scratch. The customer is ecstatic and immediately asks for changes. Since the definition of the application was captured, from its requirements through its deployment configuration, costing and implementing those changes is much easier than it would have been without a software factory.

We hope this simple example provides a feeling for the software factory approach. Obviously many details have been omitted, such as how performance is optimized, and how variabilities in requirements are translated into variabilities in the architecture, the implementation, the deployment configuration, the test plan, and other parts of the software life cycle. We provide a detailed example in Chapter 16 that addresses these issues.

A much more detailed example is provided in Chapter 16.

Implications of Software Factories

Software Factories move software development toward industrialization. As we said in the Preface, one of our goals is to show how new technologies can be used to reduce the cost of providing automation, making it feasible to realize the resulting productivity gains not only in broad horizontal domains, such as user interface construction and data access, but also in narrow vertical domains, such as health care and financial services. In this section, we explore the implications of Software Factories, describing how the industry might look when Software Factories are widely used. In painting the vision, we necessarily gloss over many issues. This does not mean that we have ignored them. We spend much of the book identifying them and suggesting strategies for resolving them. While this is only a vision, it is close enough to reality to start guiding our thinking now.

We look at how the industry will change as software factories become widespread.

Development by Assembly

Application developers will build a small part of each application, typically less than a third. The rest will come from existing components.[2] Application development will consist primarily of component customization, adaptation, extension, and assembly. Instead of writing large amounts of new code, they will obtain most of the functionality they need from ready-built and built-to-order components provided under contract by suppliers, each of whom will do the same.

Only a small part of each application will be developed from scratch.

Software Supply Chains

Supply chains will emerge to feed the demand for components.

Supply chains will emerge to feed the demand for components. According to Lee and Billington [LB94], a supply chain is a network that starts with raw materials, transforms them into intermediate goods, and then into final products delivered to customers through a distribution system. Each participant consumes logical and/or physical products from one or more upstream suppliers, adds value, usually by incorporating them into more complex products, and supplies the results to downstream consumers.

Specification formats, packaging formats, architectures, and patterns will be standardized.

Products developed by a supply chain span organizations, separating consumers from suppliers. This will create pressure to standardize:

- Product specification formats, to streamline negotiations between consumers and suppliers.

- Assets for common domains, especially architectures and patterns, to make independently developed components easier to assemble across platform boundaries with predictable results.

- Packaging formats containing component metadata, to make components easier to discover, select, license, configure, install, adapt, assemble, deploy, monitor, and manage.

Common components will be commoditized and custom suppliers will appear specializing in a wide variety of domains, making software that would be too expensive to build by current methods readily available.

Software factories can be partitioned, to form supply chains. One way to do this is to obtain components from upstream suppliers.

HOW SUPPLY CHAINS FORM

Software Factories can be partitioned, either vertically or horizontally, to shift responsibility to external suppliers, creating supply chains.

- ◆ **A vertical partition lets a Software Factory assemble components provided by upstream suppliers. Imagine, for example, that the entity framework in the preceding example came from an Independent Software Vendor (ISV).**

- ◆ **A horizontal partition separates product line and product developers at the same level of the supply chain. This can take one of two forms:**

- **Product line development is outsourced. Imagine, for example, that instead of working for the ISV in the previous example, the product line developers who developed the Software Factory worked for an outside Systems Integrator (SI). Instead of building Software Factories for in-house developers, they build them for developers in customer organizations.**

- **Product development is outsourced. Imagine, for example, that the product developers in the preceding example work for the SI, using the Software Factory developed by the product line developers working for the ISV. The product developers may be located off shore, in lower cost labor markets.**

Another way to partition a factory is to outsource product or product line development.

Of course, both types of partition can appear anywhere in the factory, and can be combined in arbitrary ways. They can also disappear and reappear, as dictated by business conditions. In mature industries, many levels of suppliers contribute to final products, and there is constant churn, as suppliers enter or leave relationships.

These types of partitions can be combined.

Relationship Management

Customer and partner relationship management will become more important. Service level agreements will govern transactions between consumers and suppliers. Repairs and assistance will be provided under warranty. Consumers will lease components from suppliers, and receive patches and upgrades systematically. Dynamic upgrade mechanisms will become much less intrusive. Tools that manage the configurations of deployed products will become critical parts of the platform. Data from interactions with customers and partners will be collected and analyzed to improve service levels, to optimize production and delivery, and to plan product offerings.

Managing customer and partner relationships will become more important.

Domain Specific Assets

Product developers will rarely use general purpose programming languages, except for small parts of the product. Instead, they will use tools that look like user interface builders to assemble framework-based components using domain-specific languages. These languages and tools will be inexpensive to build, enabling organizations with domain expertise to build

Product line developers will build assets used by product developers.

them cost effectively for vertical domains, such as banking and health care. Product line developers will often use general purpose programming languages to build the production assets used by product developers, in much the same way that operating system developers build device drivers and other system software used by application developers today.

Organizational Changes

Much about development and development organizations will change.

Everyone with a stake in software development will be affected by its industrialization. Developers will take on more specialized roles, as processes are standardized and automated. This evolution will promote role standardization and professional organizations that more closely resemble those found in other industries. Developers and architects will become licensed practitioners, and some standards will become legally enforceable. There is already momentum toward licensing practitioners, and identifying knowledge required for competent practice. Of course, certifying that a developer knows certain facts does not guarantee that they can build software, just as knowing accounting rules does not guarantee that a CPA will exercise good judgment. Peer review boards have started to appear. Board certification will require the presentation and defense of work done in the field before a panel of practitioners. Suppliers will acquire the skills and incentives needed to build Software Factories and to participate in supply chains. They will refactor existing products into families. Consumers will exploit the faster turnaround, higher quality and lower costs made possible by industrialization.

Mass Customization of Software

Software may eventually be mass customized like PCs ordered on the web today.

Some industries, such as the web-based PC business, produce product variants on demand cheaply and quickly for individual customers today. While software product mass customization is a long term vision, the broad adoption of Software Factories will make it possible. Mass customization occurs in other industries today when businesses optimize their internal value chains. According to Porter, a value chain is a sequence of value adding activities within a single organization, connecting its supply side with its demand side. Value chain optimization requires integrating business processes like Customer Relationship Management, demand management, product definition,

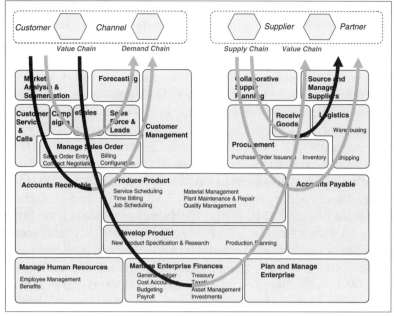

Figure 5.12 Internal value chain optimization

product design, product assembly, and supply chain management, as illustrated in Figure 5.12. Software product mass customization cannot occur until software suppliers optimize their value chains. Imagine ordering a customized financial services application from a web site, the same way customized PCs are ordered today, using a long running ordering process containing many more steps, with the same level of confidence and comparable delivery times.

Realizing the Software Factory Vision

Realizing this vision will require us to think differently about the economics of software development. For example, organizations with problem domain knowledge, such as field organizations, Independent Software Vendors (ISVs), Systems Integrators (SIs) and enterprise IT departments, will capture knowledge in languages, frameworks, patterns and tools. Instead of producing raw knowledge artifacts, such as blueprints and whitepapers, knowledge centers will become tool, process and content suppliers, a business that is economically viable only for a limited class of vendors today. These new assets will

This is a vision for the next decade, but it has already started to appear.

Software Factories put these ideas together.

automate the development of product families in specific domains, allowing users to assemble family members from common components using combinations of standard patterns.

Software Factories are based on the convergence of key ideas in systematic reuse, development by assembly, model-driven development, and process frameworks. Many of these ideas are not new. What is new is their synthesis into an integrated and increasingly automated approach that lets organizations with domain expertise implement the four-part Software Factory pattern, building languages, patterns, frameworks, and tools to automate development in narrow domains. It is said that we overestimate what can be done in 5 years, but underestimate what can be done in 10 years. We think key pieces of the Software Factory vision will be realized, some quickly, and some over the next decade. Commercial tools that can host Software Factories are available now, including Microsoft Visual Studio and IBM WebSphere® Studio. DSL technology is much newer than most of the other technologies, and relies on families of extensible languages, as we shall see in Chapter 9. However, DSL development tools and frameworks are currently under development (for example, the GME project [KSLB03]), and have already started to appear in commercial form.

On to Part II.

The next part of the book, Part II, describes the critical innovations in greater detail.

Notes

1. The grid as described by John Zachman in his Enterprise Architecture Framework contains six columns and five rows. See *www.zifa.com*.
2. While these numbers may look unreasonable, many case studies have shown that even higher levels of reuse can be achieved and sustained using software product lines [CN01, Bos00, WL99].

Critical Innovations

People are so tuned in to the near term that they aren't thinking in terms of decades. Yet, over the long run, we have a chance of fundamentally changing humanity. Many people sense this, but don't want to think about it because the change is too profound.

W. Daniel Hillis

The road map shown in Figure P2.1 describes Part II. As indicated by the road map, Part II consists of several threads, each describing one of the critical innovations introduced in Part I. While the threads can easily be read in parallel, the chapters in each thread should be read sequentially.

Chapters 6 through 9 discuss model-driven development. Chapters 6 and 7 describe models, patterns, and programming with models. Chapters 8 and 9 explore language anatomy and tools for building families of languages.

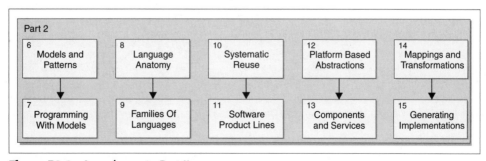

Figure P2.1 A road map to Part II

Chapters 10 and 11 discuss family-based development. Chapter 10 lays the groundwork by describing systematic reuse. Chapter 11 describes software product lines, one of the most important innovations.

Chapters 12 and 13 discuss development by assembly. Chapter 12 looks at platform-based abstractions, including classes, libraries, and frameworks, and Chapter 13 discusses components and services, and introduces the concept of assembly by orchestration.

Chapters 14 and 15 discuss generative programming. Chapter 14 talks about mappings and transformations. Chapter 15 then looks at how code and other implementation artifacts can be generated from models.

Models and Patterns

Interface design and functional factoring constitute the key intellectual content of software and are far more difficult to create or recreate than code.

Peter Deutsch

In this chapter, we consider mechanisms for raising the level of abstraction. We start by looking at how abstractions can bridge the abstraction gap. Next, we look at how patterns can be used to define abstractions, and how they can be woven into informal languages. Finally, we look at how pattern languages can be encapsulated to create formal languages, and at how models can be used as development artifacts.

Intent versus Implementation

We have already looked at the concepts of specification and implementation. We said that specification deals with *what*, while implementation deals with *how*, and that what looks like implementation from above looks like specification from below. We stated that source code is specification from the point of view of a compiler, and that we think of source code as implementation because it is the lowest level specification that we see. We said that in the context of a product family, we can map from abstract specification artifacts like requirements to concrete ones like architectures and components. Using

Most information about the software above the level of source code is captured informally, or lost.

current methods and tools, however, most information above the level of source code is not captured by abstract specification artifacts. Instead, it is either captured informally, or not captured at all.

This is the information that tells us what we are building, and why we are building it a certain way.

This information includes requirements, as well as the design decisions that map from those requirements to executables. We saw that the design decisions from the source code down are made automatically by compilers, while the ones from the requirements to the source code are generally made by developers using progressive refinement and progressive abstraction. We called the earliest and most coarse-grained design decisions architecture, and we showed how the rationale behind design decisions captures tradeoffs between alternative implementation strategies. We also saw that this information tells us what we are building, and why we are building it a certain way, and that losing it makes maintenance and enhancement costly.

Can this information be captured and used by tools?

These observations lead to several questions. Is this information as important as we have suggested? If so, then why do we only capture it informally, if at all? Could we capture more of it, or capture it more formally, so that it can be used by tools? Where do the parts we don't capture at all reside during the development process, and what happens to them when the process is finished? We will answer these questions in this chapter. First, let's look at the value of the information, at where it resides during the development process, and at what happens to it when the process is finished. We will start by considering intent, and its relationship to implementation.

What Is Intent?

When developers write code, they maintain mental images of the software that represent their intent.

According to Simonyi [Sim99], the information that we have been describing is called *intent* because it is what developers intend when they write software. It consists of mental images of requirements that must be satisfied, and of design decisions that must be made to map the requirements to implementation artifacts. For example, developers building an online commerce system keep mental images of the business process to be automated, such as Order Entry, and of the business entities it manipulates, such as Order, Product, and Customer. An implementation is a rendering of intent using specific implementation technologies. Of course, the same intent can often be rendered using alternative implementation technologies, yielding similar but different implementations. Online commerce systems can be implemented using either C# and the .NET Framework, or Java and the Java Development Kit (JDK), for example. The selection of one over the other would make some tasks easier and others harder, and would impose different tradeoffs in usability, reliability, performance, security, and other qualities of service, but the functionality could be implemented using either technology.

Capturing Intent

An implementation may imply the intent that led to its development, but it does not express the intent explicitly. The implementation is a rendering of the intent using terms defined by the implementation technologies, instead of the terms that appear naturally in the intent. The intent cannot be extracted from it easily, even by the author, once it has been rendered, due to feature delocalization. More importantly, the intent cannot be extracted automatically, making it inaccessible to tools. For example, developers writing an online commerce system may know that several classes collectively implement the Order Entry process. The configuration management tool, however, cannot glean that information from the source code, and therefore cannot check the consistency or completeness of the implementation, or perform operations on the files that contain those classes, without being told what to do by the developers, usually in some other language. For example, the developers may have to list the files in a manifest used by the configuration management tool. This situation puts the burden of keeping the manifest synchronized with changes in the business process on the developers. When classes are added to the business process, the files for the classes must be added to the manifest. In the same way, the developers may have to render their intent in many other forms to describe the business process to build scripts, the deployment process, the test environment and the defect-tracking tool. A lot of the work that occupies the developers day in and day out now consists of keeping the files that implement the business process synchronized.

Code cannot capture intent directly.

Jacobson estimates that as much as 80% of the work done by a typical developer is rote work, while as little as 20% is creative work [Jac04]. He points out, however, that the level of rote work may not feel high to the developer because rote tasks and creative tasks tend to be finely interleaved during development. If we could change that ratio, say to 50/50, we

Too much of the work is rote rather than creative.

would clearly increase productivity. We would also increase agility, since developers would have to do less rote work to make a given change. We would probably make development more enjoyable, as well, by reducing the amount of time spent on uninteresting tasks, and increasing the amount spent on creative ones.

Intent is discarded when the implementation is done.

What happens to the intent, once it has been used to guide the development of the implementation? Sometimes, it is captured by documents describing the requirements or the design. As we have seen, however, these documents tend to get out of date as the software changes, because they are not really part of the implementation. In most cases, it is simply discarded when the implementation is done. Of course, some of it may still remain in the minds of the developers, but it generally cannot be completely recovered or reconstructed, especially after the passage of time.

The benefits of RAD could be extended if tools could capture and use more of the intent.

The inability to express intent formally and completely is costly. If developers could express intent directly, then tools could use that information in powerful ways. We see this principle in action in Rapid Application Development (RAD) environments. For example, if a tool knows that we are building a Web service, it can generate a WSDL file from an existing interface, or generate adapter code to expose the interface using an appropriate binding, such as SOAP over HTTP. Or, if a tool knows that we are building a user interface control triggered by a button push, it can generate the code required to subscribe to the button push event, and the skeleton of an event handler that must be completed by hand. The benefits of RAD could be extended significantly, if more intent could be captured. For example,

- Cost and time-to-market could be reduced by automating tedious and mundane programming activities. Currently, developers render most of the implementation by hand. Clearly, this is inefficient, since many implementations at least partially resemble other ones. This recurring code should not be repeatedly reconstructed by hand.

- Quality could be improved by automatically implementing proven practices that embody the experience of expert developers. When code is written by hand, functional defects, performance bottlenecks, security holes, and other problems are created, and must be removed through testing and defect correction.

- Software evolution and migration could be made much easier and more efficient.

In order to capture more intent, developers would have to express it more directly. They would have to name either the concepts that they intend to implement, or some pieces that they could assemble to implement those concepts. For example, to express the intent to develop a Web service, a developer would have to name either the concept of a Web service, or some pieces that they could assemble to implement a Web service, such as a component, a service endpoint, or port that can be attached to the component, and a service interface that describes the service offered by the component through the port. In other words, instead of rendering implementations in languages defined by the implementation technologies, they would have to render specifications in languages defined by the intent.

Intent can be expressed by naming concepts.

We saw how product families enable us to identify commonalities and variabilities among family members, and how product lines exploit these to simplify development. We also saw that the commonalities include common requirements and common architecture, in addition to common implementation components. In other words, the members of a product family share pieces of common intent. This suggests that we should be able to define abstractions that capture those pieces of common intent. Although each abstraction would capture only a small piece of the intent for a given product, it would capture more than the abstractions or primitives from which it was defined. Raising the level of abstraction in this way would let us render intent in terms of these new abstractions, not in terms of the original implementation technologies.

Abstractions can be defined in advance to capture common intent in the context of a product family.

A Closer Look at Patterns

We are now ready to look at why we don't capture intent completely or formally, and at how that might change. We have talked quite a lot about patterns. Patterns are vehicles for encapsulating knowledge. They map concepts that cannot be expressed directly using implementation technologies

Patterns capture intent, and map it to implementation.

onto configurations of concepts defined by implementation technologies. In other words, patterns capture intent, and map it to implementation. This is why they are so effective.

Creating and Using Patterns

The strategy described by a pattern is used when the pattern is applied—a solution based on the strategy is produced by when the pattern is evaluated.

Recall that a pattern provides a strategy for solving a recurring problem in a specific context. The strategy described by a pattern is used when the pattern is applied to some development artifacts. It may make sense to apply a pattern more than once to the same development artifacts. A solution based on the strategy is produced by when the pattern is evaluated, either by hand, or with the help of a tool. Since a pattern is often evaluated when it is applied, this may seem to be a useless distinction. Its value is seen when the development artifacts change, however, since the pattern must be reevaluated but not reapplied. Say we apply a pattern to two classes, A and B, which adds a field to B whose type is A. Now, if we rename A to C, we do not have to add another field to B. Instead, we have to change type of the field we already added from A to C. The solution produced by evaluating the pattern may or may not reside in the same domain as the problem. For example, solutions to problems in the domain of Web service applications may reside in the domain of C# applications. When this occurs, we are using the pattern to define the relationship between a problem domain and a solution domain. For example, we might define the relationship between the domain of Web service applications and the domain of C# applications by defining a pattern of classes used to implement a Web service. Let's look more closely at how patterns are applied and evaluated.

To use a pattern, we must first recognize the opportunity.

In order to use a pattern, we must do four things:

1. We must recognize the opportunity to apply the pattern. This means that we must understand and recognize the context in which the recurring problem solved by the pattern is frequently encountered, and recognize an actual problem encountered during development as being an instance of the recurring problem. For example, in order to use the Observer pattern, shown in Figure 6.1, to make a ToolTip appear after the cursor has hovered over a target for a specified amount of time, we must understand that the Observer pattern is used to solve problems that arise when one object is required to track

changes in the state of another. We must also recognize that the ToolTip problem demonstrates this requirement.

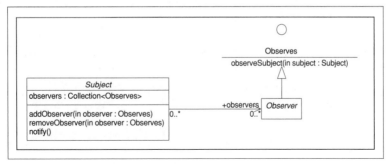

Figure 6.1 The observer pattern

2. We then apply the pattern by mapping each element in the recurring problem to a corresponding element in the actual problem. This restates the recurring problem in the vocabulary used by the actual problem. For example, in order to apply the Observer pattern, we map class `Subject` described by the pattern definition to the `Timer` class, class `Observer` described by the pattern definition to the `ToolTip` class, and the signature of the `observeSubject(in subject: Subject)` method defined on `Observer` to an actual signature by replacing `Subject` with `Timer`, as illustrated in Figure 6.2.

We then apply the pattern by restating the recurring problem in the vocabulary of the actual problem.

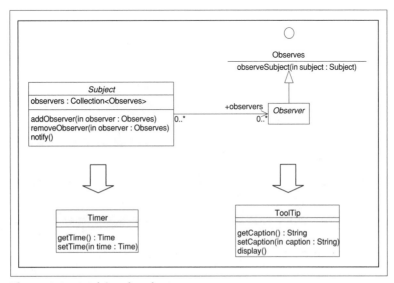

Figure 6.2 Applying the observer pattern

We then evaluate the pattern by restating the solution in the vocabulary of the actual problem.

3. We then evaluate the pattern, selecting a solution strategy, a variation, or an implementation option, if they are offered. We then restate the selected solution strategy, with any variation or implementation option, using the mappings we created in step 2. This restates the solution in the vocabulary used by the actual problem. Finally, we merge the restated solution with any existing implementation elements. For example, to evaluate the Observer pattern, we do the following, as illustrated in Figure 6.3:

   ■ Merge the features of `Subject`, i.e., the `Collection <Observes>` observers field, the `addObserver (observer: Observes)` method, and the `removeObserver(observer: Observes)` method, with the methods and fields already defined on the `Timer` class.

   ■ Merge the features of `Observer`, i.e., the `observeSubject(in subject: Subject)` method and the `Observes` interface, with the methods and interfaces already defined on the `ToolTip` class.

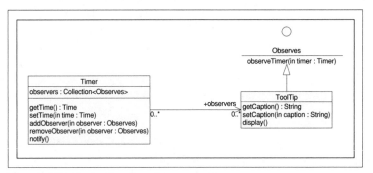

Figure 6.3   Evaluating the observer pattern

Finally, we reevaluate or remove the pattern as appropriate.

4. We then repeat the evaluation of the pattern whenever there is a change in any of the actual problem elements mapped during the application of the pattern. For example, if the `Timer` class is renamed to `Clock`, then we reevaluate the pattern by changing the signature of the method we added to the `ToolTip` class from `observeTimer(Timer subject)` to `observeClock(Clock subject)`, as illustrated in Figure 6.4.

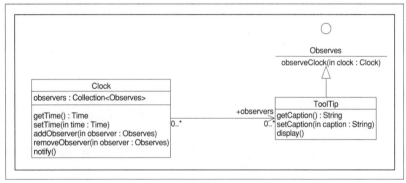

Figure 6.4 Reevaluating the observer pattern

Weaving Patterns into Languages

According to Alexander [AIS+77],

> *No pattern is an isolated entity. Each pattern can exist . . . only to the extent that it is supported by other patterns.*

No pattern is an isolated entity.

Buschmann notes that while many patterns in the literature refer to others, most of these references fail to explain how the patterns can be composed to form solutions to larger problems [Bus00a]. Contexts and problem descriptions are usually stated as generally as possible, so that each pattern can be applied in a wide variety of situations. In addition, solution descriptions and implementation guidelines tend to assume that patterns are applied in isolation, and do not attempt to address issues that arise when multiple patterns are applied in overlapping ways, such as the order in which they can be applied. This situation is problematic, since the features introduced by applying one pattern may be required by the next. A larger context is therefore needed to describe the larger problems that can be solved by combining patterns, and to address issues that arise when patterns are used in combination. This context is provided by a pattern language.

A larger context is needed to describe the larger problems that can be solved by combining patterns.

What Is a Pattern Language?

A pattern language is a set of patterns and relationships among them that can be used to systematically solve coarse-grained problems. Any language defines a set of abstractions, which form its vocabulary, and a set of rules, which form its grammar,

A pattern language is a set of patterns and relationships among them.

for combining those abstractions to create expressions. Both the vocabulary and the grammar of a pattern language can be expressed as patterns. The vocabulary of Core J2EE Design Patterns, for example, includes abstractions like Business Delegate, Data Access Object and Service Locator, and the grammar lets Business Delegate be combined with Service Locator, but not with Data Access Object. Another good example of a pattern language is provided by Trowbridge [MS03]. This language describes related patterns for .NET applications. One of its most interesting features is the use of a graphical notation to describe relationships between patterns like specialization and association. This is a step toward developing a formal language by encapsulating the pattern language. We will return to this idea later in this chapter.

The patterns used by a pattern language must be used within the language.

The patterns in a pattern language are usually designed to be used within the context of the language. They therefore tend to be tightly coupled, and may be difficult or impossible to use in isolation. They are typically related either by containment or by association. When patterns are related by containment, a more coarse-grained pattern uses more fine-grained patterns to express solutions. When two patterns are related by association, the responsibilities they impose on common components are combined, so that the components play roles in both patterns.

The guidelines of all of the patterns in a language form a highly configurable process for applying the language.

A pattern language also provides guidelines to show how the patterns can be composed to form solutions to specific problems. These guidelines may prescribe a process for applying the patterns, or they may merely define constraints that govern their application, such as the order in which they may be applied. We can think of the implementation guidelines supplied by each pattern as a small piece of a larger development process, as suggested by Buschmann. These micro processes often refer to other patterns that complement the one being described. The implementation guidelines of all of the patterns in the language are like process building blocks that collectively form a highly configurable process framework for applying the language. We have seen this kind of process framework before, in Chapter 4. It is much more focused than a general purpose development process and describes specific design strategies. The pattern language described by Schmidt, for example, constrains the order of pattern application by containment, listing coarse-grained patterns as entry points to the language, and then showing how the fine-grained patterns they contain are used to apply them [POSA2].

A pattern language can be extended by adding patterns, either to address new problems, or to provide alternatives to current solutions. When patterns are added, they must be integrated by identifying their relationships with the existing patterns. As the language grows, it becomes more specific to a particular problem domain, and describes more of the architecture of the applications in that domain.

A pattern language can be extended by adding patterns.

According to Schmidt, the trend in the patterns community is toward defining pattern languages, rather than stand-alone patterns. He also predicts the integration of existing stand-alone patterns into pattern languages, and observes that many of the published patterns can be woven into a single pattern language for developing middleware and distributed applications. In addition, as the pattern coverage in a given domain becomes more complete, there will be increasing recognition that the patterns can be formed into a language to solve more coarse-grained problems in the domain.

The trend in the patterns community is toward defining pattern languages.

This trend was predicted by Johnson and others investigating frameworks [Joh97]. Noting that most of the pattern literature takes the form of catalogs of relatively independent patterns, they suggested that groups of related patterns would gradually be integrated to form pattern languages, and that pattern languages would gradually be codified to form frameworks that support the reuse of software architectures.

Pattern languages support architecture reuse.

Characteristics of Pattern Languages

Some writers have suggested that pattern languages should be computationally complete, providing at least one pattern for every aspect of the implementation of the architecture supported by the language. However, it is reasonable to consider the use of multiple pattern languages, each addressing a different part of the architecture, and to compose them to form a complete solution. For example, we might use a different pattern language for each tier of a distributed business application. As we shall see, we can use modeling languages in a similar fashion. This result is quite convenient, because we already have a mechanism for organizing and describing the parts of an architecture, and for identifying the patterns, languages, frameworks, tools, guidance, and other assets used to develop each part. This mechanism is the software factory schema described in Chapter 5.

Pattern languages can be composed.

According to Schmidt, a pattern language should satisfy these requirements.

- Provide a complete set of patterns, including patterns that support the specification of an architecture, patterns that help with refining it, and patterns that help with implementation using specific technologies.

- Describe its patterns uniformly, using a common schema, so that the patterns can be easily searched and compared with one another.

- Expose the relationships between the patterns, including refinement or containment, association and dependencies in the order of pattern application.

- Provide a structure that makes it easy for users to rapidly locate the patterns they need and to explore alternative compositions of patterns.

- Support the construction of implementations by providing guidelines for the application and implementation of the patterns.

- Support its own evolution, explaining how both the constituent patterns and the rules governing their composition may be changed.

Patterns in Product Families

Patterns reflect commonalities among products.

Alexander observes that patterns in solutions are derived from patterns in problems [Ale79]. Patterns in problems reflect commonalities among the problems. We have seen how product families capture commonalities and variabilities among products that can be exploited by product lines. This suggests that patterns and pattern languages actually describe product families, rather than individual products.

A pattern language can form a conceptual framework for developing applications in a domain.

Buschmann notes that a pattern language may be able to describe solutions to most of the problems in a domain, from analysis to implementation [Bus00b]. Such a language forms a conceptual framework for developing software products in a given domain, like a simple software factory schema. Like a framework, a pattern language embodies an architecture. Unlike a framework, however, it does not provide a specific implementation. A framework essentially renders a pattern language using specific implementation technologies, and can be used to develop implementations for requirements expressed using the pattern language, like a simple a software factory template.

In fact, after surveying the pattern literature, Schmidt suggests that many of the most widely applied patterns are derived from or used to document frameworks, that the patterns can be considered abstract descriptions of those frameworks, and that conversely, the frameworks can be viewed as reifications of the patterns. He also recounts the observation that mature frameworks exhibit high pattern density. As we shall see shortly, we can similarly combine modeling languages to form a conceptual framework for developing products in a specific domain.

It is interesting to consider the possibility of defining a framework as a pattern language, and at least partially generating it on demand using application specific technologies and assumptions. For example, we might generate a framework used by distributed applications using either remote procedure calls or web methods, depending on the application requirements. Different combinations of predefined and generated implementation strategies could be used for different frameworks, with predefined implementations being preferred for features that are common to multiple applications, and generated implementations being preferred for features that can vary.

A framework defined as a pattern language can be at least partially generated on demand.

Most of us instinctively try to make new abstractions as general as possible. There is a direct tradeoff, however, between generality and power, as we have seen. The more general an abstraction, the wider its application, but the smaller its contribution. Applying this lesson to patterns, we quickly discover that we have to reduce scope in order to develop genuinely reusable patterns. This makes pattern languages both more specialized and more powerful than general purpose programming languages. They are domain specific languages that solve recurring problems in specific problem domains. A clear trend toward increasing domain specificity can be seen in pattern language publications. While early pattern languages, like those defined by [GHJV95] and [POSA1], were quite general, recent ones are more domain specific. This is evident in [POSA2], in the Pattern Languages of Program Design (PLoPD) series, in pattern conference proceedings, and in pattern languages like the ones we mentioned earlier.

Pattern languages are domain specific languages.

Encapsulating Pattern Languages

As noted by the Gang Of Four, patterns give names to the problems and solutions they describe, adding them to the design vocabulary. A pattern name encapsulates multiple pieces of

Pattern names are abstractions that create a new language.

information, such as the problem to be solved, the solution strategy, and the assumptions made about context. Using a pattern name can communicate all of this information. Pattern names are abstractions that encapsulate implementation knowledge, creating a new and more powerful language. We can take this further by encapsulating pattern specifications, creating formal languages. Before we can show how that is done, however, we need to look more closely at encapsulation.

What Is Encapsulation?

In addition to removing details, encapsulation defines a new vocabulary in terms of the original one.

Encapsulation is an interesting form of abstraction. (See Appendix A for a brief description of different forms of abstraction.) In addition to removing details from a description, it defines a new vocabulary. Let's return to the spider map that we saw in Chapter 2, shown again in Figure 6.5. In addition to removing streets, it defines a new vocabulary containing terms like *bus route, bus stop,* and *transfer point*. Bus routes appear as colored lines on the map, bus stops appear as labeled circles on the colored lines, and transfer points appear as groups of connected bus stops. The new vocabulary can be used in place of

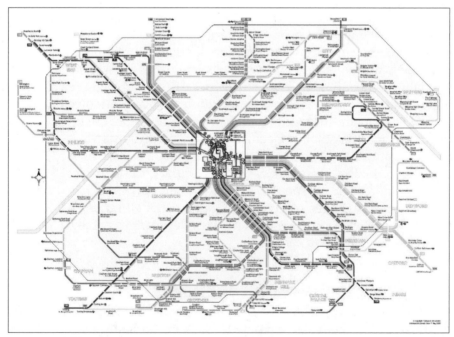

Figure 6.5   London Transport spider map

the original one, allowing the construction of more concise descriptions. Using a spider map, for example, we plan bus trips in terms of bus stops, not in terms of street segments. Some terms in the new vocabulary are defined by configurations of terms in the original vocabulary. Such a configuration is called an *expression*. For example, the term *bus stop* can be defined by the expression *street address*. By defining the new vocabulary using the original one, encapsulation creates a mapping between the two vocabularies that can be used to *translate* expressions written in the new vocabulary into expressions written in the original one. We can translate a sequence of bus stops into a sequence of street addresses, and then into a sequence of street segments, for example, where a sequence is an ordered list.

Some terms in the new vocabulary may be defined in terms of their peers. The term *bus route segment*, for example, can be defined as an ordered pair of bus stops, the term *bus route* can be defined as a sequence of bus route segments, and the term *transfer point* can be defined as a bus stop that appears in two or more bus routes. Using these new definitions, we can rewrite a bus route as a sequence of street segments.

Some terms in the new vocabulary are defined in terms of their peers.

Of course, this discussion presumes that we know how write valid expressions using the terms that comprise each vocabulary. This information is provided by *well-formedness* or *composition rules* that tell us how the terms that comprise a given vocabulary can be combined in meaningful ways. For example, we might define rules requiring that each bus route segment in a sequence except the last one have exactly one successor, and that the starting bus stop in each bus route segment except the first one be the ending bus stop of its predecessor. The set of well-formedness or composition rules that governs the use of a vocabulary is called the *grammar* for that vocabulary. A vocabulary and its grammar form a language.

A vocabulary and its grammar form a language.

We now see that we can define a new language by creating a new vocabulary through encapsulation and by providing a grammar that governs its use. These languages may be informal, like our bus route language, or they may be formal, like C#. C# is defined in terms of an intermediate language called IL. As we would expect, it contains terms defined by encapsulating configurations of IL terms, and can be used in place of IL to construct more concise descriptions of programs. Defining C# using IL creates a mapping between the languages that can be used to translate C# expressions into IL expressions.

Each term in the new language encapsulates an expression in the original one.

Because C# is a formal language, the translation can be performed by a compiler. We will define the properties of a formal language in Chapter 8, and show that only formal languages can be translated automatically.

Encapsulation and translation can be progressive.

Encapsulation can be performed progressively, creating a series of languages, each defined in terms of its predecessor. While C# is defined in terms in IL, for example, IL is defined in terms of processor instruction sets. Translation can follow these definitions. A program written in C#, for example, can be compiled into IL by the C# compiler, and then into processor instructions by a just-in-time (JIT) compiler.

Defining Languages with Encapsulation

Encapsulation separates what from how and captures implementation knowledge that is reused by the process of translation.

As Cleaveland observes, encapsulation separates the concerns of two parties, one concerned with specification, and one concerned with implementation [Cle01]. A *specification* says *what* do without saying how. An *implementation* implements or realizes a specification by doing what the specification describes. It supplies knowledge of *how* to do what is specified. We could plan bus travel from Tower Hill to Elephant and Castle, for example, as a sequence of bus stops. This plan would form a specification for the travel. Using the mappings that we defined earlier, we could implement this plan by translating it into a sequence of street segments. A specification is much simpler than its implementation, and provides a more efficient description of the subject. The sequence of bus stops is much simpler than the sequence of street segments, for example, and provides a more efficient description of the travel. In other words, a specification is more abstract than its implementation. The details it hides are referred to as *implementation details*. A specification is also more general than its implementation because it can support more than one implementation. As long as the bus arrives at the bus stops indicated on its route, for example, the driver might be able to use different sequences of street segments to drive between the stops on different occasions. On the other hand, a specification cannot be executed directly. In order to do what a specification describes, we must implement it by translating it into an implementation expressed using the original language.

For example, in order to realize the bus travel described by a bus travel plan, we must translate the plan into a sequence of street segments. An implementation must either be directly executable by an interpreter, or indirectly executable by further translation into a form that is directly executable by an interpreter. A sequence of street segments, for example, can be executed directly by a driver. We now see that encapsulation captures knowledge about how to implement specifications written in the new language using expressions written in the original one. This knowledge resides in the mapping between the two languages created by encapsulation, and is reused by the process of translation. For example, knowing how to translate bus routes into sequences of street segments means that we know how to implement bus travel plans. In the same way, the C# compiler captures knowledge about how to implement expressions written in C# using expressions written in IL, and a JIT compiler captures knowledge about how to implement expressions written in IL using configurations of processor instructions.

We said earlier that a specification provides a more efficient description than an implementation. This efficiency is a property of the language used to write the specification. A more efficient language conveys the same amount of information about its intended purpose in fewer terms than a less efficient one. For example, the language of bus routes is more efficient than the language of street segments for describing bus travel. Another word for efficiency is power. A language that supports more efficient communication than another one is more powerful than the other one for its intended purpose. Note that because it serves a more specific purpose, a more powerful language is less general than a less powerful one. The language of bus routes, for example, is less general than the language of street segments. The language of street segments can be used for a much larger number of purposes. Since the new language contains terms created by abstraction, or more precisely by encapsulation, we refer to those terms as abstractions. A more powerful language contains more powerful abstractions than a less powerful one for its intended purpose. The language of bus routes, for example, contains more powerful abstractions than the language of street segments for the purpose of bus travel. We can now see that a specification written in a more powerful language is more abstract than one written in a less powerful language. A program written in C#, for example, is more abstract than one written in the processor instruction set.

A more powerful language supports more efficient communication about its intended purpose.

C# is less general and more powerful than the processor instruction set for its intended purpose. The details removed to create this more abstract specification are the details of its implementation in the less powerful language. Those details can be reconstructed using the mapping created by encapsulation when the more powerful language was defined.

Programming languages have become more abstract and more powerful over time.

Over time, the descriptions of software written by developers have steadily become more abstract, as the languages used to write those descriptions have steadily become more powerful. The earliest programs were written in the processor instruction set of the target platform, and were entered directly into memory using hardware devices like switches or keypads. From there, we migrated to assembly language, then to languages like FORTRAN and COBOL, then to structured languages like C and Pascal. Object-oriented languages have changed little since the inception of the current paradigm, however. Byte code-based intermediate languages are a major improvement over directly compiled languages like C++, of course, but for those of us who started with Smalltalk, the relatively recent adoption of languages like Java and C# feels more like rediscovery of effective language design principles than innovation. Of course, the newer languages offer many significant improvements like compilation, namespaces, and packaging. C#, in particular, takes an additional step by supporting common programming idioms, such as properties, events and delegates, which make it more powerful for user interface development.

Formalizing Pattern Languages

We can use encapsulation to create a formal language based on the abstractions defined by a pattern language.

We said earlier that the names of patterns can be seen as abstractions that form a language, and we hinted that a formal language can be defined by encapsulating pattern specifications. Recall that encapsulation creates a new description called a specification to replace an existing description called an implementation. Recall, also, that the specification is expressed using a new language created by the process of encapsulation, and that the new language is defined by a mapping to the language in which the implementation is written. We can use encapsulation to create a formal language based on the abstractions defined by a pattern language. For example, instead of applying the Core J2EE Design Pattern language directly to

Java source code, we might define a language that encodes the abstractions it defines, like Front Controller, View Dispatcher, Business Delegate, Session Facade, and Service Locator. Given such a language, we could specify J2EE-based applications explicitly using these abstractions. The architecture of an application specified this way would be immediately evident in the specifications we produced. In addition, it would be much easier to modify, perhaps by changing the pattern applications to accommodate a design change, or by choosing different implementation strategies for the patterns, to accommodate changes in requirements, or new assumptions about the conditions under which the application will run. The mapping from our new language to Java is provided by the patterns themselves. They describe the implementations that must be created to translate specifications based on our new language into Java.

We now observe that a pattern language is a step toward defining a modeling language. Most formal languages encode patterns or programming idioms that are already used widely by convention in lower-level languages. C#, for example, encodes the programming idioms for user interface development that are already used widely by convention in Java, such as properties, events, and delegates. The pattern definitions are then used by the compiler for the new language to generate implementations from specifications written in the new language. The difference between a pattern language and a modeling language is that a pattern language lets the underlying implementations of the abstractions it defines show through, while a modeling language at least partially encapsulates them. A pattern language is a white-box language, and a modeling language is a black-or gray-box language, depending on how completely it encapsulates the implementations of the abstractions it defines. We can now call the new language that we defined earlier a modeling language.

A pattern language is a step toward defining a modeling language.

An excellent example of a formalized pattern language is the Enterprise Integration Patterns language by Hohpe and Woolf [HW04]. Figure 6.6 shows how patterns are mapped to language elements.

Figure 6.7 shows how language elements can be combined to form expressions, such as the composite message processor in this example. Such an expression can be implemented by applying the patterns associated with the language elements.

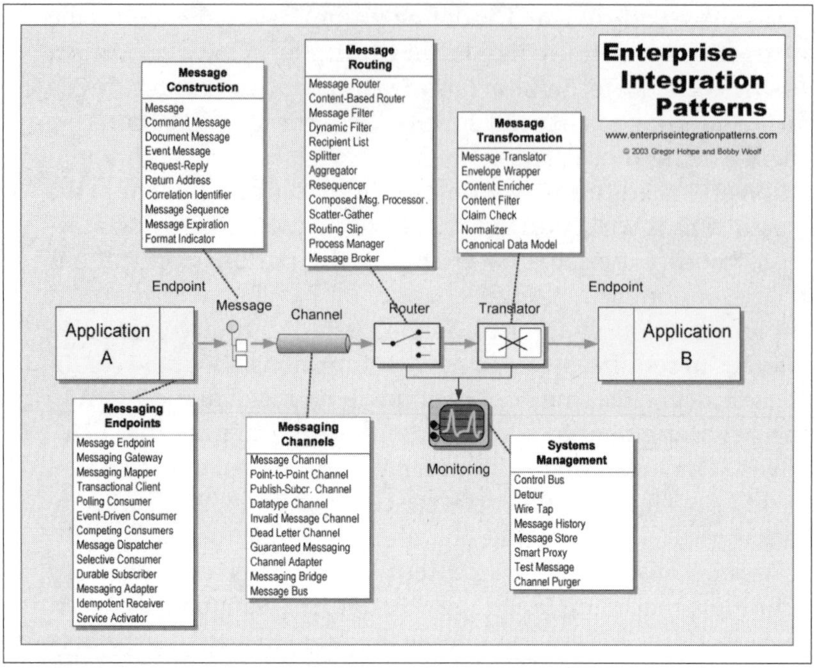

Figure 6.6 Mapping patterns to language elements

Used by permission from Gregor Hohpe, Bobby Woolf, *Enterprise Integration Patterns*, Addison-Wesley, 2003.

What Are Models?

Modeling languages are used to build models. To fully understand modeling languages, we need to understand models. We have talked a lot about models in this book without defining

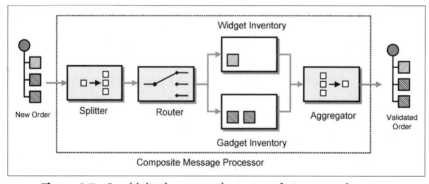

Figure 6.7 Combining language elements to form expressions

Used by permission from Gregor Hohpe, Bobby Woolf, *Enterprise Integration Patterns*, Addison-Wesley, 2003.

them. We will provide a formal definition in Chapter 8. For the purposes of this chapter, we will use an informal definition, as described next.

Models as Abstractions

Recall that a model is an abstract description of software that hides information about some aspects of the software to present a simpler description of others. The model illustrated in Figure 6.8, for example, describes entities in a payroll application. It specifies their attributes and operations, and the relationships between them. Figure 6.8 shows the Business Entity Designer from Microsoft Corporation.

A model is an abstract description of software.

The model in Figure 6.9 describes the user interface of the same application. It specifies the screens defined by the user interface, the information they display, the user actions they support, the input forms they use to collect information, and the navigation paths between them.

This model describes the user interface of the same application.

Neither model states how the constructs it describes are implemented. The entities in Figure 6.8, for example, could be implemented with either the Microsoft Business Framework or Enterprise JavaBeans. Similarly, the model in Figure 6.9 does not state how information displayed on the screens is formatted. The screens and transitions it describes could be implemented using either ASP.NET or Java Server Pages.

The Implementations are not exposed.

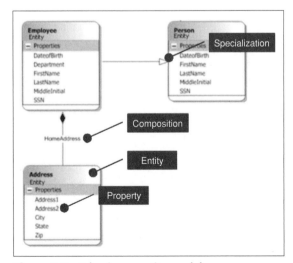

Figure 6.8 A business entity model

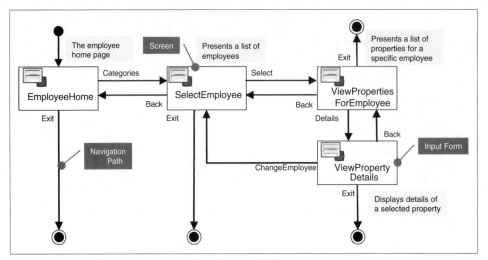

Figure 6.9   A user interface model

Models separate concerns.

Recall that abstraction can be used to separate concerns. Models can be used to separate concerns by isolating information about specific aspects of the software, so that it can be managed independently. The model in Figure 6.9 isolates information about the navigational aspects of the user interface, for example. Developers can build user interaction scenarios using this kind of model without thinking about layout or formatting. Layout and formatting can then be specified independently, perhaps by people with different skills. We will return to the concept of using multiple models to describe different aspects of the same piece of software in Chapter 7.

Model Visualization

Models can be visualized graphically.

Readers who know the UML may associate models with graphical visualization. While graphical visualization can make models easier to understand, models do not have to be visualized graphically. In fact, they can be rendered in a variety of nongraphical notations, as we shall see shortly. We provide a formal definition of notation in Chapter 8, and show how it relates to the other parts of a language. For the purposes of this chapter, we define a notation as a medium in which a language-based artifact is rendered for human consumption. Of course, models can be visualized graphically, as illustrated by the preceding examples.

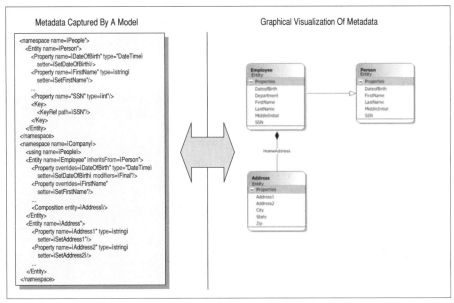

Figure 6.10 Visualizing information graphically

It is important to distinguish between the information captured by a model and the visualization of that information, as illustrated by Figure 6.10. The information captured by the model shown in Figure 6.8 appears on the left of Figure 6.10, rendered as XML, while the graphical visualization of that information shown in Figure 6.8 appears on the right. The point of the diagram, of course, is that the information and its visualization are not the same. The information may be rendered in many different ways, some of which may use graphical notations, and some of which may not. Making this distinction is important for the purpose of this chapter, and generally for the purpose of understanding software factories, because we rely on models to capture information that can be used to automate various aspects of the software development process. This situation is complicated by the popularity of the UML, a language designed for graphical visualization that cannot be used effectively, as defined by its specification, to provide the kinds of automation that we require. We discuss the shortcomings of UML in Appendix B. Readers who are not versed in language design should read Chapter 8, which provides a primer, before attempting to read Appendix B. We will return to the topic of how models capture information shortly.

It is important to distinguish between the metadata captured by a model and a visualization of metadata.

```
Process {
 Activity "Authorize Credit Card" {
 port: ProvidedInterfacePort "Pending Credit Requests"
 port: RequiredInterfacePort "Approved Credit Requests"
 connection: "c1" connects "Pending Credit Requests" to "Requests In"
 connection: "c2" connects "Requests Out" to "Approved Credit Requests"
 messages: "m1"
 messages: "m2"
 Activity "Check Credit" {
 port: ProvidedInterfacePort "Requests In"
 port: RequiredInterfacePort "Requests Out"
 owner: Activity "Authorize Credit Card"
 performedBy: Actor "Credit Clerk"
 usesResource: Resource "Customer Database"
 performedBy: Actor "Credit Approval Officer"
 }
 Actor "Credit Clerk" {
 owner: Activity "Authorize Credit Card"
 performs: Activity "Check Credit"
 }
 Resource "Customer Database" {
 owner: Activity "Authorize Credit Card"
 artifactFor: Activity "Check Credit"
 }
 Actor "Credit Approval Officer" {
 owner: Activity "Authorize Credit Card"
 performs: Activity "Check Credit"
 }
 }
}
```

Figure 6.11   A textual notation

Graphical visualization does not have to use schematic notations.

Of course, when we do visualize models graphically, we are not obliged to use schematic notations like those defined by UML. A schematic notation usually uses geometric shapes like boxes and lines, sometimes enhanced by stylistic images, often annotated with text and icons.

Models can be rendered using textual and widget notations.

We said earlier that models can be rendered using a variety of notations. These include textual notations, like the one in Figure 6.11, and widget based notations, like the one in Figure 6.12, from IBM WebSphere Studio, which uses user interface widgets, such as wizards, dialogues, forms and editors. Figure 6.11 is an excerpt of a model rendered using a schematic notation in Chapter 7, shown in Figure 7.28.

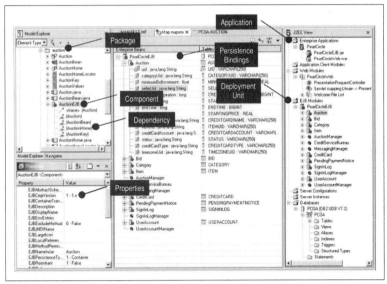

Figure 6.12   Visualizing models non-graphically

Models as Metadata

We said earlier that we must distinguish between the information captured by a model and the visualization of that information because software factories rely on models to capture information that can be used to automate various aspects of the software development process. This information, called metadata, can describe various aspects of software products and the software development process, such as the names of the classes and packages in a project, the properties of a user interface control, the programmatic interface published by a Web service, the build order dependencies among multiple projects, or the resource requirements that must be satisfied when a component is deployed. It can be used by editors, compilers, debuggers and other tools, to provide various forms of automation, as we shall see in Chapter 7. We now define a formal model as an artifact that captures metadata in a form that can be interpreted by humans and processed by tools. Of course, this definition is not sufficient, since some artifacts that satisfy it, such as databases, are generally not considered models. We will refine this definition in the next few sections. Note, however, that it excludes descriptions of software that cannot be processed by tools, such as diagrams drawn on whiteboards. By this definition, such a diagram is not a formal model, because

A formal model is an artifact that captures metadata in a form that can be interpreted by humans and processed by tools.

it does not capture metadata in a form that can be processed by tools. On the other hand, a WSDL file is a formal model by this definition, since we do not require the use of UML notation or graphical visualization. In this book, we are interested only in formal models. We will therefore drop the modifier and refer to them simply as models, unless the context requires us to do otherwise.

Models as Development Artifacts

Formal models can be used to automate software development.

Advanced or extensive use of metadata to automate development is the hallmark of rapid application development (RAD). Not surprisingly, RAD tools are based on formal models. They usually do not maintain persistent models, however. Instead, they often build models on the fly by extracting information from other development artifacts, such as source code files, use them to support automation, and then discard them when the session ends. In some cases, however, they do maintain persistent models like configuration files, build manifests and project files, which capture information that cannot be extracted from other development artifacts.

Model Partitioning

We must be able to express models as files in order to make them accessible to development tools.

Now, since most development tools operate mainly on files, we might surmise that we must be able to express models as files in order to make them accessible to development tools. While this might seem to be an important point, the UML specification does not address it directly, leaving the relationship between UML-based models and files open to interpretation. Tool vendors have therefore found it difficult to integrate UML-based models into the development process, and to exchange UML-based models as development artifacts. The main problem is one of scope. How much information does a model contain? If it contains too much information to fit conveniently into one file, then how should the information be partitioned across multiple files? Once the information is partitioned, how can it be reconstituted later?

The scope of a UML model is a whole system, so models tend to span files.

According to the UML specification, a model captures a view of a system. It is an abstraction of the system, with a specific purpose that determines what is to be included in the model and what is irrelevant. The model completely describes those aspects of the system that are relevant to its purpose, at the appropriate level of detail. How much of a system does a UML model describe? According to IEEE 1471, a view is a representation of a whole system from the perspective of a related set of concerns. By these definitions, then, a model describes a whole system, not a part of a system. Of course, since the definition given by the UML specification is rather vague, we are merely surmising that this is what it means, using another established standard to define the terms it uses. An indication that this is the correct interpretation is that the UML does not say how the description of a system should be partitioned. Of course, it does provide the concept of a package, and several kinds of dependency relationships that can be used to create references between packages, but it does not define a notion of package type, a way to define the scope of information captured by a package of a given type, or a way to assert that a package of a given type is a complete description of a subject. In addition, it does not say how packages relate to files or directories.

- Should we assume that every package maps to a single file?
- Where does the mapping from packages to files reside?
- Does the name of a package match the name of the file to which it maps?
- What happens when a package contains other packages?
- Does the parent package map to a file and a directory?
- Does the name of the file to which the parent package maps within the directory conflict with the names of child packages?
- What happens when a file or directory is moved, deleted or renamed in the file system but not in the modeling tool?

Like so many of the mechanisms in UML, packages are close to what we need, but do not quite satisfy our requirements. One way to solve these problems might be to define some rules. For example, we could require that every package maps either to a file by the same name, or to a directory by the same name containing a file with the same name of a different type, and that direct manipulation of the file system is prevented by making the files and directories comprising a model read-only. This would let us partition a model across multiple files. Of course, if we define our own rules, without support from

Like many UML mechanisms, packages are not quite what we need.

the standard, then our partitioning scheme may not work with other tools. Perhaps we could get around that problem by serializing the entire model into a single file? This would probably be a rather inconvenient way to work with other tools, such as a configuration management tool, since it would force a developer to check out the entire model to make any changes. Instead of defining a top-level construct like a model and partitioning it into multiple files, most development tools work with one file at a time. When they work with information that spans multiple files, they generally work with a package that aggregates those files, such as a Java Archive (JAR) or an assembly in .NET. In other words, most development tools use a bottom-up approach, not a top-down approach to partitioning information. The partitioning model implied by the UML definitions of model and package is therefore difficult to use in the context of a typical development process. Readers who have used products from well-known modeling tool companies that partition models across multiple files using rules like the ones we have just described will know this from experience.

We require a model to be a well-formed unit of processing or compilation.

We subscribe to the assertion that a model describes a system from a specific perspective, but we do not require that a model describe a whole system from that perspective. Instead, we require a model to be a unit of processing or compilation as defined by the language in which it is expressed, and to contain only semantically complete and well-formed closures. A *closure* is the set of objects that can be reached from a root by traversing designated links, and that satisfy designated constraints. The closure of a UML class, for example, includes its attributes and operations, but not the associations in which it participates. To be *semantically complete*, a closure must have a specific meaning. Such a model can reside in a file, and may describe only part of a system from a given perspective.

Model References

Elements in one model must be able to refer to elements in others.

Given the ability to partition metadata across multiple models, in a manner similar to the way source code can be partitioned among multiple files, we must either require that every model be entirely self contained, or allow elements in one model to refer directly to elements in others. Since entirely self-contained models would be unwieldy and create source code control problems, we need a way to establish, maintain, and resolve references between models. Since files are the standard units of

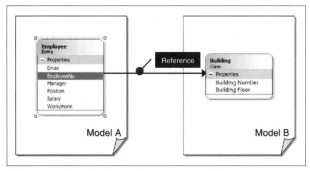

Figure 6.13   References between models

information management in software development, we must be able to resolve model references to model elements stored in model files, as illustrated in Figure 6.13. Figure 6.13 is from the Business Entity Designer by Microsoft Corporation.

A good precedent for solving this problem has been established by programming languages like C# and Java. Source code can easily be partitioned among many files by the developer to simplify source code control and other artifact management tasks. This does not present a problem, since types defined in one file can easily reference types defined in other files, usually on the basis of a qualified name. For example, in .NET, a class defined in one file can extend a class defined in another file by referring to the target class using its name. Class names are qualified by the namespaces in which they reside. Namespaces are declared in files where classes are defined, and imported into the files where they are referenced with using statements. For example, in the code snippet shown in Figure 6.14, we import several namespaces at the top of the file with using statements. We then declare the namespace `Employee` and define the class `Employee` within its scope. Note that class `Employee` derives from another class named `EmployeeBase`, which is defined by the Microsoft Business Framework in the namespace `Microsoft.BusinessFramework.Entity`. Note, also, that we were able to refer to class `Employee Base` using only its unqualified name because we imported the namespace in which it is defined. With this approach, a type must be uniquely defined within some context, except for its version and its locale, by its fully qualified name. We will return to the question of context shortly.

A similar approach can be taken with models serialized as XML. Namespaces can be declared in model files, model

A good precedent for solving this problem has been established by programming languages.

A similar approach can be taken with models serialized as XML.

```
using System;
using System.Data.SqlTypes;
using Microsoft;
using Microsoft.BusinessFramework;
using Microsoft.BusinessFramework.Entity;


namespace Employee
{
  [Serializable]
  public partial class Employee : EmployeeBase
  {
    protected override int getEmployeeNo()
    {
      // Get logic for EmployeeNo goes here
      return base.getEmployeeNo();
    }
    protected override void setEmployeeNo(int value)
    {
      // Before set logic for EmployeeNo goes here
      base.setEmployeeNo(value);
      // After set logic for EmployeeNo goes here
    }
  }
}
```

Figure 6.14   Name-based references in source code

element names can be scoped by the namespaces in which they are defined, model elements can refer to other model elements by name, and namespaces can be imported into model files with using statements. With this approach, a model element must be uniquely defined within some context, except for its version and its locale, by its fully qualified name. This imposes two requirements on model elements:

- Every model element must have a name.
- Every model element must be defined in the scope of a namespace.
- Every model element must have a unique fully qualified name within the context in which model references are resolved.

We will return to the question of context shortly.

We can now declare namespaces in model files. For example, a namespace statement might have the form:

```
<namespace name="Employee"/>
```

The name of a model element can then be declared in the scope of a namespace. For example, a model file might declare a model element like this:

```
<Entity name="Employee"/>
```

Here, the name of the model element is `Employee`. If this declaration appeared within the scope of the namespace used in the previous illustration, then its name would be `Employee.Employee`. A model element can now be referenced using its fully qualified name. For example, we might add a reference to an existing entity from which the entity declared in the previous example inherits like this:

```
<Entity name="Employee" inheritsFrom="com.somevendor.People
.Person"/>
```

The fully qualified name of an element can be implied when the reference appears within the scope of a using statement. A using statement in a model file might have the form:

```
<using name="com.somevendor.People"/>
```

We can now rewrite the model element declaration from the previous example within the scope of this using statement like this:

```
<Entity name="Employee" inheritsFrom="Person">
```

One of the most important aspects of model references is that the context in which they are resolved must be external to the model, permitting references to be resolved in different ways under different circumstances. For example, we may need to resolve references between models in the context of the folder hierarchy for a development environment. In .NET, such a hierarchy is called a solution, and consists of possibly many projects, each of which has a root folder within the solution, and possibly some subfolders. Two kinds of references are used to resolve model references within a tool working with a solution. Project references are used to resolve them to elements that reside in model files in other projects within the solution. Assembly references are used to resolve them to elements that reside in assemblies. Of course, while this is quite a convenient way to define the reference resolution context at development time, it does not work well at runtime. At runtime, we will have to resolve model references in the context of an installed image, not in the context of a development environment. The installed image will consist of assemblies placed at known locations in the

The context in which references are resolved must be external to the model.

file system and registered with the .NET runtime. This is analogous to the JARs and class path used by the Java runtime. Regardless of the specifics of a given context, the key to robust reference resolution is keeping the context external to the model, so that it can vary. Of course, this is the way type references are resolved in modern programming languages. In Java, for example, a type reference based on package and type name is resolved at runtime by the class loader. Trying to define the reference resolution context within the model using a package structure is a serious flaw in UML. This forces tools that use UML to map the package structure in the model to the actual context in which model references must be resolved. This generally produces poor results because the tools do not have control over those contexts, and therefore cannot maintain the mappings reliably.

Model Versions

Now that we know how to partition models effectively, store them in files reliably, and create, resolve, and maintain references among them, we must know how to manage model versions effectively. There are several issues to be considered.

How do we determine whether or not a model was created by an earlier or later version of the software that interacts with it?

One issue is software compatibility. How do we determine whether or not a model was created by an earlier or later version of the software that interacts with it? There are three parts to the answer to this question.

1. We must define what we mean by version. A version identifier usually consists of several version numbers, such as major and minor version numbers, that can be used to determine how a version of a file relates to a version of the software. Assemblies in .NET use a four-part version number, consisting of major and minor version numbers, followed by a build number and an update number.

2. Since compatibility may be affected by other factors, especially the culture for which a file was localized, we must include such factors when defining compatibility. Assemblies in .NET use a two-part culture descriptor that identifies both a language and a locale (e.g., en-US for English in the United States and en-UK for English in the United Kingdom). Different localizations of the same

model will have the same version number, but different cultures.

3. We need to define what compatibility means. Is a file compatible with the software if it has exactly the same version number, or does it only have to have the same major version number and a minor version number no greater than the minor version number of the software? Is the en-US culture compatible with the en-UK culture? A compatibility policy is required to address these issues.

Another issue is scoping model reference resolution by version. How do we ensure that a model reference will resolve to the right version of a model? There are two ways to do this. One is to place the version identifier in the reference. This has the advantage of recording the information in the model, but it has the disadvantage of being harder to maintain by hand. Since version dependencies are often determined by builds, a better approach is to place the version identifier on a container that holds the model. This keeps the reference simple, but allows it to be scoped to a container that carries the appropriate version identifier at resolution time. Examples of version identifying containers include .NET assemblies and digitally signed model files.

How do we ensure that a model reference will resolve to the right version of a model?

A third issue is model integrity, as hinted at in the preceding paragraph. How do we ensure that a model has not been modified so that its version identifier is no longer accurate? This can be done by placing the model files in a digitally signed container during the build process. A digital signature provides a way to assert that the contents of the container have not been modified since the container was signed. Assemblies in .NET can be digitally signed for this purpose. A digital signature typically contains the following parts:

How do we ensure that a model has not been modified so that its version identifier is no longer accurate?

- A header, which identifies the methods used to create a digest from the file, the digest, and the algorithm used to generate the signature value from the digest.
- The signature value, which is a private key encryption of the digest.
- A public key, which is used to decrypt the signature value and verify that it matches the digest.

Note that XML files can be digitally signed using schema elements and algorithms standardized by the W3C. This makes it possible to compile a model file into a signed XML document. Placing a version identifier in the document at the time of compilation makes it possible to use the document as a stand-alone artifact that does not have to reside in any other container in order to be referenced reliably.

Modeling or Programming?

Some widely used terms related to programming and modeling are not well defined.

Clearly, mechanisms like those described previously pave the way for treating models as first class development artifacts, along side source code files and other XML files. This now begs a difficult question. What is the difference between programming and modeling? Lack of clarity around the terms *programming* and *modeling* has fostered some widely held misconceptions. We have been using the terms rather loosely up to this point, relying on the reader's intuition to supply their meaning. The problem with trying to define them more precisely is that they are used widely and inconsistently throughout the industry. In addition, there are no well-established definitions to which we can turn. On the other hand, we cannot leave them entirely undefined. Since they are widely used to discuss many of the topics addressed in this book, and since some of the discussion here is quite a departure from widely held notions regarding those topics, we need to provide some definitions. We therefore provide our preferred interpretations. We will refine these definitions in Chapter 8, where we can be more precise.

Notation is not a reliable basis for distinguishing between modeling and programming languages.

Notation is sometimes used to informally distinguish programming languages from modeling languages. However, this is not a reliable practice.

■ Because most programming languages have historically used textual notations, it is often assumed, incorrectly, that a programming language must be textual. Examples of graphical programming languages abound. An interesting one is the graphical programming language that accompanies Lego Mindstorms, a product used to build robots. Like many graphical programming languages, it defines graphical elements for performing arithmetic and other kinds of operations, and for creating program control structures like loops, conditional branches and procedures. The converse also does not hold. A textual language is not necessarily a programming language. XML is a well-known textual language, for example, but few people would consider it a programming language.

- Similarly, because most modeling languages have historically used graphical notations, it is often assumed, incorrectly, that a modeling language must be graphical. Also, the legacy created by graphical modeling languages designed for documentation and the failure of highly visible attempts to use them to generate software has created the widely held misconceptions that graphical modeling languages are not an effective medium for programming, that all programming languages must therefore be textual, and that all graphical languages must therefore be modeling languages. As we have seen, models can use a wide variety of notations, including schematic, stylistic, textual, and widget-based notations. They can also be used as an effective software development medium, as we will see later.

Style of specification, which may range from imperative to declarative, is also used to informally distinguish programming languages from modeling languages. Here, again, there are no well-established definitions. One way to distinguish between them is to note that statements in a declarative language are assertions or constraints that must be satisfied, while the statements of an imperative language are instructions to be executed. Another is to note that the order in which the statements are evaluated does not affect the meaning of a specification written in a declarative language, but it does affect the meaning of one written in an imperative language. To make matters worse, most languages contain both declarative and imperative features, and there is an increasing trend toward the use of declarative features in primarily imperative languages, such as C# attributes. The best we can do in most cases is to say that a language is *mainly* imperative or declarative. With this caveat, we adopt the definition provided by Coenen [Coe00]: An *imperative* specification describes instructions to be executed without describing the desired results of execution; a *declarative* one describes the desired results of execution without describing how they are obtained. Now that we have defined these terms, let's look at how they relate to the notions of programming and

Style of specification is not a reliable basis for distinguishing between modeling and programming languages.

modeling. As we shall see, we cannot use the style of specification to distinguish programming languages from modeling languages.

- Because most programming languages have historically been primarily imperative, it is often assumed, incorrectly, that a programming language must be primarily imperative. Logic and functional programming languages, however, are primarily declarative, and some primarily declarative languages, such as Prolog, have imperative features for controlling the order of evaluation.

- Similarly, because modeling languages have historically been primarily declarative, it is often assumed, incorrectly, that a modeling language must be primarily declarative. However, some modeling languages, such as the state machine language defined by the UML, are primarily imperative.

Both models and programs are specifications of software.

Clearly, both models and programs are specifications of software. Programs specify execution, meaning that they can be readily transformed into executable instructions. Note, however, that they can also specify declarative aspects of the software, such as its structure. Models usually specify aspects of the software other than execution, such as structure, packaging or deployment. Since we do not prevent them from specifying execution, however, we can think of a program as a kind of model. Rather than swim against the tide by giving these terms precise definitions, we use them imprecisely with these observations in mind. At the same time, we note that they do not effectively describe many of the languages commonly used to specify software. SQL, which is textual and declarative, is neither a programming language nor a modeling language. We therefore prefer to use terms introduced by Czarnecki, which reflect our focus on specificity [CE00]. The term *general purpose language* (GPL) refers to a language that encodes generic abstractions, and the term *domain specific language* (DSL) refers to a language that encodes abstractions used in a narrow domain. These terms are independent of both style of specification and notation.

The term source code refers to expressions written in the textual notation of a programming language.

We can now recap our definition of a model as an artifact that captures metadata in a form that can be interpreted by humans, and which forms a unit of processing or compilation, as defined by its language of expression, containing semantically complete and well-formed closures. Note that a model is not analogous to a *program* because that term implies completeness. A program includes everything required for execution, other than an execution environment. We therefore use the term *source code* or *program fragment* to describe compilation units, such as class files, written in the textual notation of a programming language, as we have defined that term, which do not contain complete programs. Since modeling subsumes programming, we could say with reasonable confidence that a program is a kind of model, and that source code is a textual rendering of that kind of model. While this might be defensible, it muddies the water, since the term *source code* is widely contrasted with the term *model*, as when we say that source code is generated from a model. We prefer to reserve the term *source code* for expressions written in the textual notation of a programming language. While these artifacts are specifications from the point of view of a compiler, developers often think of them as being *the* implementation. For this reason, the term *source code* also suggests a specification that is compiled into a form that is not intended for human consumption. A model, on the other hand, may be compiled into a form like source code that is intended for human consumption. Of course, a model can also be compiled directly into executables.

CHAPTER 7

Programming with Models

Our human civilization rests on the power of abstraction insofar as the volume of specific cases handled by an abstraction is typically much greater than the overhead of the abstraction mechanism itself.

Charles Simonyi

In this chapter, we discuss model-driven development, a technique for using metadata captured by models to automate software development tasks. We start by looking at how metadata can be used to support automation. Next, we look at tasks that can be fully or partially automated using metadata, including pattern application, refactoring, build, deployment, testing, and debugging. We then talk about viewpoints and how they can be used to identify the various aspects of a software product to be modeled and the relationships between them. From there, we look at various ways to model software, and we discuss the requirements for modeling for automation. Finally, we introduce the concept of domain specific languages and consider their business and technical ramifications.

Model-Driven Development

Now that we have defined the term model, we are ready to look at how models can be used to automate development. Recall that using models to automate development is called

MDD is programming with models.

model-driven development (MDD). We can think of MDD as programming with models. In this section, we will see how models can be used to generate software, to automate design, refactoring, deployment, builds and testing, and to debug software.

- Routine tasks, such as generating one kind of artifact from another, can usually be fully automated. For example, test harnesses can usually be generated automatically from user interface models to confirm that appropriate page transitions occur in response to simulated user actions.

- Other tasks can be partially automated, such as resolving differences between artifacts. For example, differences between columns in a table and fields on a form might be flagged for the user, then automatically corrected once the user decides how to resolve them.

- Models can be used to integrate incompatible implementation technologies. Adapters, such as Web service wrappers, can be generated automatically from the models to bridge the differences in implementation technologies. They can also be used for reflection, protocol configuration, and other adaptive integration mechanisms.

- Models can be used to migrate software to different implementation technologies, and to enable faster and more accurate responses to changes in requirements.

MDD uses DSLs to capture intent and provide automation.

The essential features of MDD are:

- Using domain specific languages to write specifications of software that capture developer intent in computational forms.

- Isolating and encapsulating variability points, so that many behavior variations can be achieved by configuration and assembly, instead of by coding.

- Using model-driven development environments to facilitate the instantiation, parameterization, and assembly of components, and to automatically generate partial or complete implementations from specifications.

- Using supporting tools, such as compilers and debuggers, and other forms of automation to exploit the expressions of intent captured by specifications.

Generating Software

Perhaps the most important form of automation is generating implementations from specifications of intent. A *specification* says *what* do without saying how, while an *implementation* implements or realizes a specification by doing what the specification says. It supplies knowledge of *how* to do what is specified. A Web service specified by a WSDL file is implemented by a configuration of classes and methods that instantiate and enact behaviors described by the WSDL file. The process of deciding how to implement a specification of intent using a given set of implementation technologies is called *design*.

Capturing Intent, Revisited

Most development artifacts, like source code and XML files, capture implementations of intent written in the vocabulary of the implementation technologies. This information can be interpreted by tools to provide basic automation, such as editing, compilation, and debugging. Since the intent is expressed informally, using documents or whiteboard drawings, and only indirectly encoded in implementations, it can be extracted and interpreted by tools only to a limited degree. The implementations are produced by hand from these informal descriptions. Both the intent and the knowledge of how the implementations were produced from it are usually lost, as illustrated in Figure 7.1.

Implementations are currently produced by hand from informal descriptions of intent.

Models can be used to explicitly capture intent in forms that tools can interpret to provide more advanced forms of automation. This requires the use of languages that can be used by

Models can be used to explicitly capture intent in forms that tools can interpret to provide more advanced forms of automation.

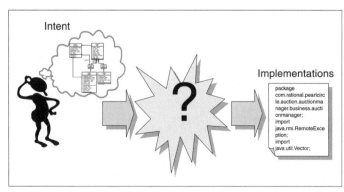

Figure 7.1   Implementing intent by hand

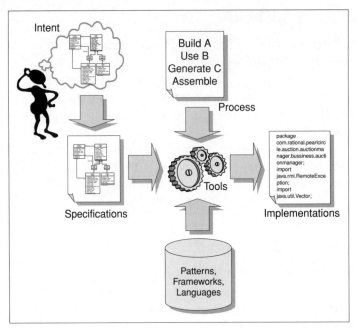

Figure 7.2   Implementing intent automatically

developers to express intent. These languages must use terms that represent concepts used in the expression of intent, and grammars that define how those terms may be combined to form valid expressions of intent. Intent can then be expressed directly by developers using these languages and then captured explicitly using models. Implementations can then be produced from the models using tools. Both the intent and knowledge of how the implementations were produced from it are preserved, and can be reused systematically, as shown in Figure 7.2. This process does not automate design. It automates the selection, composition, customization, and application of predefined design fragments, under the direction of a developer, according to predefined rules, to implement planned variations in specifications. In other words, it performs automatic configuration.

An Example of Capturing Intent

Let's look at an example of capturing intent. Consider the whiteboard drawing shown in Figure 7.3. It is an informal expression of intent that describes a distributed system for an outdoor outfitter. The information expressed by this drawing cannot be used by tools.

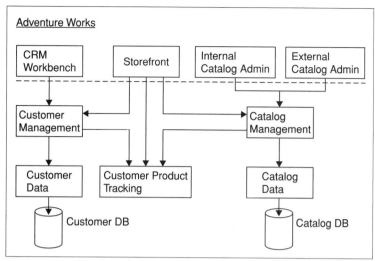

Figure 7.3 An informal expression of intent

Now, consider the diagram shown in Figure 7.4, a screen shot from Microsoft Visual Studio. It is a formal expression of intent that describes the same system as Figure 7.3. Clearly, the information expressed by this diagram can be used by tools.

Many parts of the implementation of the system, such as project structure, classes, and configuration files that implement

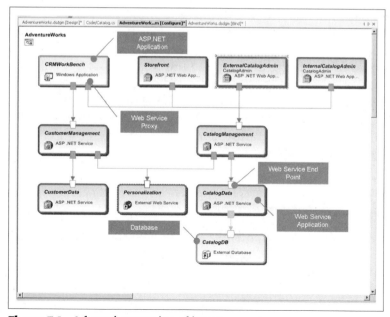

Figure 7.4 A formal expression of intent

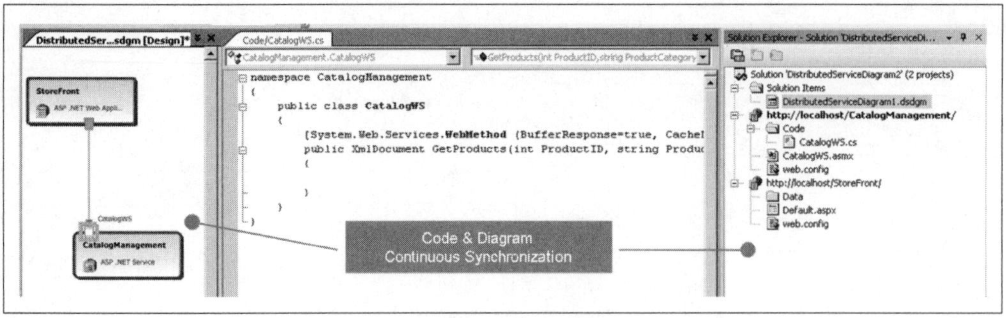

Figure 7.5   Generating implementation from intent

the Web services, have been generated from the model by the tool, as shown in Figure 7.5, also from Microsoft Visual Studio. The developers can now continue working with this solution, adding handwritten code to provide the behaviors exposed by the Web services, or using other models, such as the one shown in Figure 7.7 to generate additional code.

Class Modeling, Revisited

Code visualization must be a high fidelity representation of the source code.

Recall from Chapter 2 that code visualization based on general purpose modeling languages can actually be less appealing than working directly with the source code, since it does not use the programming language terminology, and does not capture all of the features expressible in source code. To be genuinely useful, it must be a high fidelity representation of the source code, giving the user the impression that the diagram is just another view of the source code. Figure 7.6 shows a diagram based on a high fidelity modeling language designed for C# in Microsoft Visual Studio. The diagram is showing source code from the System.Xml namespace supplied by the .NET Framework.

Code Generation, Revisited

A high fidelity code model can be used to automate code generation from higher-level models.

Once we have a high fidelity domain specific language available for a programming language, we can use it to automate code generation from higher-level models. Figure 7.7 shows how a business entity is implemented by a pattern of four C# classes using the modeling language shown in Figure 7.6. The

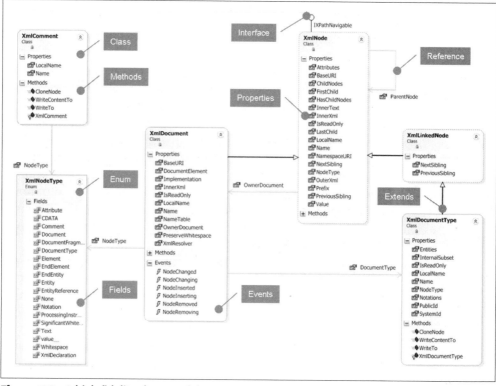

Figure 7.6 A high fidelity class model

business entity modeling tool can let the user toggle the representation of the business entity back and forth between the more abstract view on the left and the more concrete view on the right. This makes it easy to write code that interacts with code generated from abstractions like business entities.

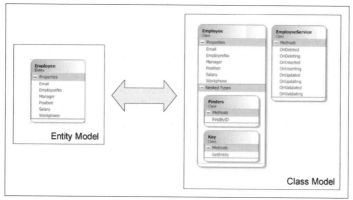

Figure 7.7 Generating classes from entities

Automating Patterns

Patterns can be automated using models.

We are now ready to look at how models can be used to automate patterns. Tools can help pattern authors create, package, and publish patterns, and can help pattern users find, manage, apply, and evaluate them. Patterns can also be applied automatically by tools to implement transformations. Some commentators question the value of automating patterns. Their main concerns are that patterns must be well understood to be used correctly, and that patterns should not prescribe specific implementations, so that they can be used in many contexts. These concerns are compounded when two or more patterns are applied to the same design, since responsibilities imposed by multiple patterns may have to be merged into a single component. We will address these issues in turn.

Pattern automation is a labor-saving feature like automatic completion in language sensitive editors.

While we agree that patterns must be understood to be applied correctly, we do not think automation necessarily prevents a user from understanding patterns, especially if it is based on user gestures.

- If the decision to apply a pattern remains in the hands of the user, then automation is merely a labor saving feature similar to automatic completion in language sensitive editors. The decision to apply a pattern and the selection of a specific solution variant or implementation strategy is still based on value judgments driven by considering the forces that give rise to the problem being solved and the best way to resolve them for a specific instance of the problem. Once the pattern has been applied, the user is free to decide whether to accept the results or to back them out and try another approach to solving the problem.

- If the decision to apply a pattern is delegated to a tool, then most tools will do a poor job in the absence of significant constraints. Automatic pattern application is probably intractable in the context of one-off development. However, a product family provides a context in which recurring problems can be effectively mapped to appropriate solution strategies. Using an architecture for the members of a product family provided by a product line, we can place each pattern application in a specific context within the architecture, allowing rules written in advance by human authors to determine when and how a given pattern is applied automatically. This is how modern language compilers work.

While patterns should be usable in a variety of contexts, partially generating some of their implementation makes sense, especially if done in a flexible way that lets the developer tune the generated implementation. This is more tractable in the context of a product family, where the set of required implementation variations can be partly constrained.

It is possible to provide a tool that evaluates a pattern once, when it is applied by the user, given a set of arguments. This has several drawbacks.

It is possible to provide a tool that evaluates a pattern once when it is applied by the user.

- It may be difficult to understand the design goals of the resulting implementation, since the patterns applied to produce the implementation may be difficult to identify later.

- It is not possible to automatically reevaluate a pattern application when the values of its arguments change. The user is therefore responsible for ensuring that invariants defined by patterns already applied to the development artifacts are maintained as the artifacts change.

- If multiple patterns are applied to the same development artifacts, the results of one application may become the starting point for another, obfuscating the results of applying each pattern, and making it difficult to discover the order in which patterns were applied, to back them out correctly.

A better approach is to keep track of the patterns applied, the arguments bound by each pattern application, and the results of evaluating each pattern application. A tool that provides this kind of automation usually provides at least two pattern-oriented views:

A better tool keeps track of patterns applied, arguments bound, and the results of evaluation.

- A view of the development artifacts, showing how the pattern has been applied. This is essential to keeping the developer in control of the process. There should be no mystery when a pattern is applied.

- A view that enumerates pattern applications, which can be used to navigate to the arguments and to the results of evaluation. This helps the user determine which patterns have been applied, in what order, using what arguments.

A good tool can help with pattern creation, packaging, and presentation.

Such a tool can help the pattern author by:

- Automating the creation of model fragments used to build patterns through gestures like selection or drag and drop
- Providing a user interface, such as a wizard, which helps the author identify the elements to be parameterized, and describe the properties of each parameter
- Packaging pattern specifications and making them available to pattern users (e.g., in libraries or through a search feature)

A good tool can help with pattern application, evaluation, and enforcement.

It can also help the pattern user by:

- Supporting the application of patterns by
  - Displaying libraries of available patterns, or providing a pattern search feature
  - Providing a user interface, such as a wizard, which helps the user bind arguments to pattern parameters
- Evaluating patterns applied by the user, both upon their initial application, and again when the values of arguments bound to their parameters change
- Checking that the results of pattern evaluation continue to satisfy invariants defined by the patterns
- Preventing unintended modification of pattern applications when the development artifacts are edited

Automation changes pattern application and evaluation in two ways.

When patterns are applied or evaluated by hand, all four of the steps described in Chapter 6 are applied to source code files. Automation usually changes this in the two following ways:

1. Only the first of the four steps (i.e., recognizing the opportunity to apply the pattern) is performed manually. The rest of the steps are performed partially or completely automatically.

    - The second step can be partially manual, when the user applies the pattern explicitly. It can also be completely automatic. Note that when a pattern is applied automatically by a tool, the opportunity was recognized by the tool developer. In this case, the user may not be aware that a pattern is being applied, since the pattern application and evaluation may be performed internally within the tool.

■ The third and fourth steps are usually performed completely automatically by the pattern engine. They can also be partially automated by letting the user trigger evaluation explicitly.

2. Patterns are applied directly only to models. Because models can be mapped to other types of artifacts, however, patterns can be applied indirectly to other types of artifacts, such as source code files or project structures, through models. A parameterized template, such as a code template, can often be attached to a pattern to customize the artifacts generated from the model to which the pattern is applied.

Patterns are applied directly only to models.

Pattern Engines

Pattern automation is generally performed by a pattern engine. Most pattern engines help the user with authoring, management, and application, and automatically evaluate pattern applications. Some allow multiple patterns to be applied to the same artifact, merging the results. A pattern engine may also leave the pattern applications attached to a model, to document design decisions, to allow automatic reevaluation when the model changes, and to prevent constraint violations when the model is edited. Pattern automation can be used to support prescriptive design practices, to provide active guidance once patterns have been applied, to support refactoring, to transform or generate artifacts, and to configure and populate project environments to jumpstart development.

A pattern engine performs the kinds of automations described above.

A pattern engine can be designed independently of any specific editor, so that a consistent approach can be used across editors, and so that adding pattern capability to new editors is relatively easy. To support patterns, an editor must host the pattern engine by defining a modeling language over which patterns will be supported. It must also provide facilities for computing, duplicating, and merging object graphs. Since these same facilities are required by other editor functions, such as drag/drop and copy/paste, the cost of supporting patterns can be a relatively modest increment over the cost of building the editor. The editor user interface must also be aware of the

A pattern engine can be designed independently of any specific editor.

pattern engine, and must be capable of displaying patterns, parameters, and applications. Again, however, these are quite modest requirements for patterns that are essentially parameterized fragments of models already supported by the host editor.

Pattern Specifications

A pattern engine uses executable pattern specifications.

A pattern engine uses executable pattern specifications. In addition to the content that appears in a document-based specification, an executable specification contains a pattern body, as described next. It may also contain scripts or custom code supplied by the pattern author to support solution variants, custom implementation strategies, or custom scenarios for applying and/or evaluating the pattern. An executable pattern specification may also contain pattern parameters and external artifacts, as described next.

Pattern Bodies

The body of a pattern defines how its outputs depend on its inputs.

The body of a pattern defines how its outputs depend on its inputs. Pattern bodies are usually based on parameterized model fragments called prototypes. A prototype is a degenerate pattern (i.e., a pattern that has no parameters) expressed in terms of the modeling language defined by the host editor. We can think of a prototype as a piece of model boilerplate. Adding parameters to the prototype makes it a pattern that can be applied in a variety of contexts by binding arguments to the parameters. The most general form of pattern body is rule-based.

A prototype is defined by a closure.

A prototype is defined by a *closure*, which is a well-formed model fragment (i.e., a graph of model elements) with a designated root. A closure is defined by enumerating model elements reachable from the root by traversing designated relationships, such as the relationships that identify the Fields, Methods, and Properties of a Class, and which satisfy designated constraints, such as being publicly visible. Various kinds of closures can be defined by varying the relationships used for traversal. The closures that form prototypes are based primarily on containment.

Pattern Parameters

A pattern is usually parameterized.

A pattern is usually parameterized. A parameter is usually based on an element in the prototype, such as a class or method, or on an element property, such as the type of a field. A parameter may be read and/or written during evaluation. When a pattern is applied, arguments are bound to these elements. When the application is evaluated, the values of arguments read are merged with values of the corresponding elements in the prototype, and then the values of arguments to be written are merged with the values of the arguments to which they are bound. Parameters often have properties that can be set by the pattern author, such as name, type, direction, multiplicity, and default value.

External Artifacts

A model is usually only a partial description of the software. Additional information is then provided by artifacts outside the model, such as source code or configuration files. Depending on the tool, the relationship between the model and these external artifacts may take one of three forms:

Artifacts outside the model may be affected by pattern application.

- *The model is master.* All external artifacts can be generated completely from the model. If the external artifacts are source code files, then all of the source code is generated completely from the model. The external artifacts can either be stored, or generated on demand. In the event of a conflict between the model and the external artifacts, the external artifacts are discarded and regenerated from the model.

- *One or more external artifacts are master.* The model can be generated completely from the external artifact. The model stores only semantically insignificant information, such as information describing the visualization of the software. In the event of a conflict between the external artifacts and the model, the model is discarded and regenerated from the external artifacts.

- *The model and external artifacts are joint masters.* The model cannot be generated completely from the external artifacts, and some or all of the external artifacts cannot be generated from the model. Usually, multiple masters arise when handwritten source code must be composed with generated source code. This composition can be challenging, but can also be quite effective. It can be done at design time, using a model aware source code editor, at compile time, using partial classes or class templates, or at runtime, using delegation or inheritance.

We will look at these mechanisms in detail in Chapter 15. Conflict resolution can be more complex with multiple masters, since changes from multiple artifacts may have to be interleaved, with help from the user to resolve ambiguities.

When an external artifact is a sole or joint master, a pattern that defines a model fragment does not contain enough information to completely describe the software. A pattern that defines only a class diagram fragment, for example, does not contain enough information to generate the bodies of methods on classes in the diagram. In these situations, a pattern must be accompanied by one or more external artifact fragments, such as source code templates, that provide the remainder of information required to completely describe the software.

Pattern Application

A pattern is applied by binding arguments to its parameters.

A pattern is applied by binding arguments to its parameters. Arguments can be bound manually by the user, or automatically by a tool. When a pattern is applied to a model, a record of the application is usually stored in a model, at least temporarily, to support evaluation. It can remain in the model to support reevaluation until removed manually, or it can be removed automatically:

- Manual removal makes it easy to practice a style of development where applying a pattern is a way of setting policy. The pattern application governs the target model to ensure its well formedness based on the pattern definition through reevaluation and by constraining edits. Pattern applications left in a model document design decisions and help ensure that they are implemented correctly.

- Automatic removal immediately following evaluation makes it easy to practice a style of development where applying a pattern is a way of performing an operation on a model. Pattern application, evaluation, and automatic removal form an atomic operation.

A tool may reapply a pattern every time two models must be synchronized.

When a tool uses a pattern to implement a mapping between two models, it usually reapplies the pattern every time the models must be synchronized. For example, a tool that generates C# classes to implement business entities might use a pattern that describes the implementation of a single business entity in terms of a collaboration of C# classes, as illustrated in Figure 7.7. It might then apply this pattern automatically to each of the selected business entities whenever the user asks it to generate code. The user of this tool might not even know that a pattern is being used to generate the implementations.

Pattern Evaluation

To produce a result, a pattern, or more accurately, a pattern application, must be evaluated. Evaluating a pattern may change elements of the development artifacts bound to the parameters. Patterns are usually evaluated immediately after they have been applied, giving the false impression that the results are produced by pattern application.

A pattern must be evaluated to produce a result.

Patterns can also be reevaluated when the values of their arguments change. For example, assume that we apply the Observer pattern by binding the `Timer` class to the `Subject` parameter and the `ToolTip` class to the `Observer` parameter, as shown in Chapter 6. Now, when the `Name` of the `Timer` class changes to `Clock`, the signature of the `observeTimer (Timer subject)` method becomes `observeClock(Clock subject)`. This is the result of reevaluating the pattern, not reapplying it. Reapplying the pattern would mean repeating the process of binding the `Timer` class, now named `Clock`, to the `Subject` parameter and binding the `ToolTip` class, which did not change, to the `Observer` parameter. There is no need to reapply the pattern, since we still want it to apply to the same two classes, even though the name of one of them has changed.

Patterns can also be reevaluated when the values of their arguments change.

Separating pattern evaluation from pattern application lets us apply a pattern once, and then evaluate it repeatedly as its arguments change. Pattern evaluation can be triggered by a variety of events, such as user gestures or synchronization. If a pattern is *idempotent*, then evaluating it repeatedly with the same arguments yields identical results. Only idempotent patterns should be reevaluated when their argument values change.

A pattern engine must be able to locate the definition of an applied pattern to evaluate it. If evaluation is performed immediately after pattern application, then this requirement can be satisfied trivially because the pattern definition is available when the pattern is applied. If evaluation is requested

We must be able to locate the definition of an applied pattern to evaluate it

later, however, such as when a pattern application attached to a model is reevaluated, then the pattern definition may no longer be available. The pattern engine must therefore be able to locate the pattern definition, using a reference held by the target model. If the pattern is a model, then this is simply a model reference, as described in Chapter 6.

Pattern Application Example

Here is another example.[1] Figure 7.8 shows a pattern to be applied in IBM Rational Rose XDE. This is one of the Core J2EE Design Patterns called BusinessDelegate. It insulates presentation tier components from a business service to minimize the effects of implementation changes, ensure efficient use of network resources consumed by calling the business service, and hide the complexity of the distributed interface exposed by the business service. It does this by providing a client-side proxy for the business service, called BusinessDelegate. The client-side proxy exposes methods that access the business service indirectly. It also uses ServiceLocator, another Core J2EE Design Pattern, to create an instance of the business service.

The pattern takes three parameters, as shown in Figure 7.8, the BusinessHome, the BusinessService, and an optional Client.

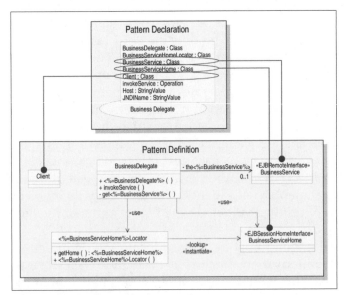

Figure 7.8   A pattern to be applied

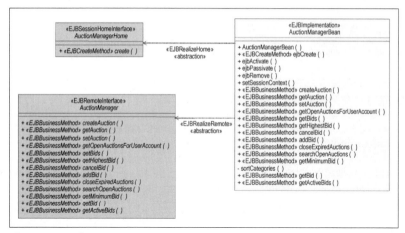

Figure 7.9 The pattern arguments

The lines emanating from the pattern declaration show how parameters in the pattern declaration map to objects in the pattern definition. Figure 7.9 shows the model to which the pattern will be applied, also in IBM Rational Rose XDE. AuctionManager is a business service based on an EJB session bean. We will bind its home and remote interfaces, shown in blue, to the BusinessHome and BusinessService parameters, respectively. No value will be supplied for the optional Client parameter.

Figure 7.10 shows the result of pattern evaluation, also in IBM Rational Rose XDE. The shaded classes and their relationships

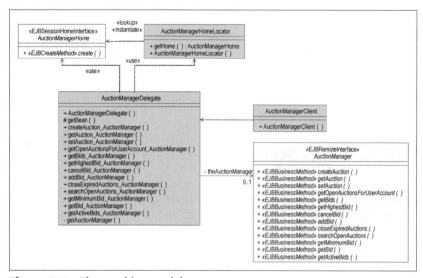

Figure 7.10 The resulting model

```
java.util.Hashtable env = new java.util.Hashtable();
env.put("java.naming.Context.PROVIDER_URL", "iiop://<%=Host%>");
env.put("java.naming.Context.INITIAL_CONTEXT_FACTORY",
"com.ibm.ejs.ns.jndi.CNInitialContextFactory");
javax.naming.InitialContext jndiContext = new
javax.naming.InitialContext(env);
Object ref = jndiContext.lookup("<%=JNDIName%>");
<%=BusinessServiceHome%> home = (<%=BusinessServiceHome%>)
javax.rmi.PortableRemoteObject.narrow(ref,
<%=BusinessServiceHome%>.class);
return (<%=BusinessServiceHome%>)
javax.rmi.PortableRemoteObject.narrow(ref,
<%=BusinessServiceHome%>.class);
```

Figure 7.11 A code template

to the other classes were created by the pattern. The pattern created a new Client, since we did not supply a value for the argument.

The code template from IBM Rational Rose XDE shown in Figure 7.11 is used by the getHome method of the Home Locator class. It is evaluated when the ServiceLocator pattern is evaluated, with its parameters bound in the context of the BusinessDelegate pattern:

Figure 7.12 shows the code generated by IBM Rational Rose XDE from the code template shown in Figure 7.11 during the evaluation of the BusinessDelegate pattern in this example.

```
public AuctionManagerHome getHome() throws LocatorException {
  try {
    Hashtable env = new Hashtable();
    env.put("java.naming.Context.PROVIDER_URL", "iiop:///");
    env.put("java.naming.Context.INITIAL_CONTEXT_FACTORY",
"com.ibm.ejs.ns.jndi.CNInitialContextFactory");
    InitialContext jndiContext = new InitialContext(env);
    Object ref = jndiContext.lookup("AuctionManager");
    AuctionManagerHome home = (AuctionManagerHome)
    PortableRemoteObject.narrow(ref, AuctionManagerHome.class);
    return (AuctionManagerHome)
javax.rmi.PortableRemoteObject.narrow(ref, AuctionManagerHome.class);
  } catch (Exception e) {
    throw new LocatorException(e.toString());
  }
}
```

Figure 7.12 The generated code

Automating Refactoring

Recall from Chapter 2 that refactoring involves changing the structure of the software without changing its externally visible behavior, and that it usually involves migrating members from one class to another, collapsing or expanding an inheritance hierarchy, and similar types of transformations. Refactoring can be automated using high fidelity domain specific models tuned to the underlying programming language. Here, again, as with pattern automation, the goal is to assist the developer by offering labor saving features. For example, dragging a method from one class to another or right-clicking an inheritance line to collapse a subclass into its parent in Figure 7.6 is much faster and less error-prone that doing this in source code, especially if the classes involved are in different files or different namespaces. The tool can automatically fix up class declarations, method declarations, references to classes and other pieces of code as the user makes changes on the diagram. Refactoring can also be done with higher-level models. For example, we might choose to collapse Employee back into Person in Figure 7.27.

Automating Builds

Models can capture build information, including the artifacts that participate in builds, and dependencies among them. Figure 7.13 shows solution configurations in Microsoft Visual Studio. Using these screens, the tool captures information about the projects included in each configuration, the dependencies between them, and the desired build order.

Models can capture build information, including the artifacts that participate in builds, and dependencies among them.

Automating Deployment

Models can capture information about deployment, including the configurations of the executables being deployed, capacities and configurations of hardware or software resources required by the executables or available in the deployment environment, policies required by the executables or available in the deployment environment, and bindings between service access points in the actual resources and logical resources referenced by the executables. J2EE-based executables, for example, use XML documents called deployment descriptors to describe logical resource references. Figure 7.14 shows a pair of models describing logical resource references and their bindings for an

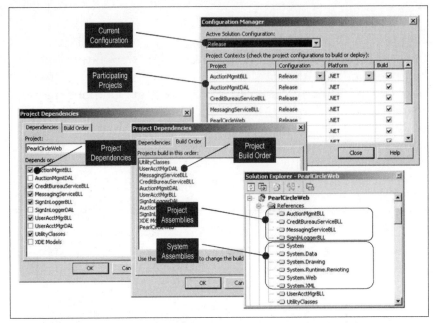

Figure 7.13 Solution configurations in Microsoft Visual Studio .NET

Enterprise JavaBean in IBM WebSphere Studio. This information can be used to automate deployment tasks, such as determining which resources can be used to host specific executables, installing the executables on the resources, configuring the executables to use the resources, and configuring the resources as required by the executables.

In some environments, such as those based on .NET Distributed Systems Initiative, model-based information can be

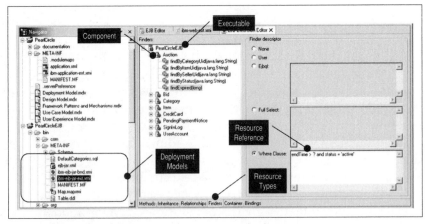

Figure 7.14 Models used to automate deployment

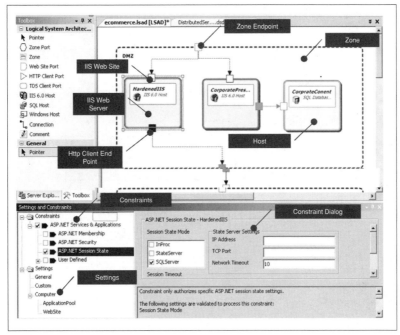

Figure 7.15 A logical model of a deployment environment

used to provision or configure resources on demand. Figure 7.15 shows a model of a logical deployment environment used by the Microsoft Dynamic Systems Initiative in Microsoft Visual Studio. Using this model, logical host type configurations can be defined by describing the runtime settings required on hosts of those types, and by defining additional constraints on their configuration.

Models of deployment environments can also be used to constrain design, so that executables based on the design satisfy predefined non-functional requirements when deployed. Figure 7.16 shows components being mapped to logical host types to define deployment requirements in Microsoft Visual Studio. Models can also describe deployed components, capturing information about configurations and operational characteristics like load balancing, fail over, and resource allocation, and to automate operational tasks like execution monitoring and management.

Automated testing using model-based information is more efficient and less labor-intensive than manual methods.

Automating Testing

Testing is a hard part of the software life cycle to automate well, and has traditionally involved tedious manual activity

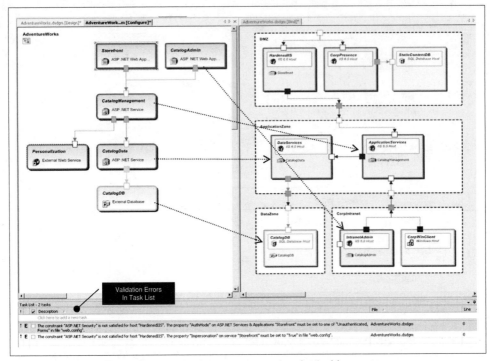

Figure 7.16 Mapping components to logical host types

that lacks the appeal of writing code. Automated testing using model-based information is more efficient and less labor-intensive than manual methods. Instead of developing test cases, test scripts, and test data sets by hand, for example, we can generate and apply them based on declarative information captured by models describing desired outcomes of execution. We can also configure and control tests, and monitor their execution using models.

Debugging with Models

Model debuggers provide a model-based view of a running system, letting the user control the system using modeling language expressions. While code-based views may also be used at times, model-based views help the user think in terms of the intent that motivated the development of the executables. Figure 7.17 shows a debugging session in Microsoft Visual Studio using the model from Figure 7.4. The highlighted path shows that the debugger stopped on a message from CRMWorkBench to CatalogManagement.

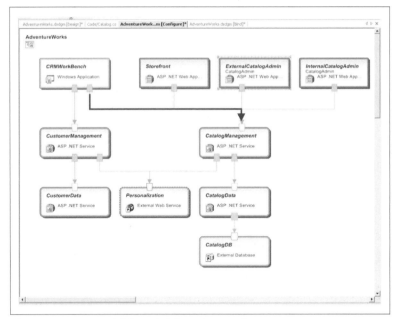

Figure 7.17   A model-based debugging session

Using Multiple Views

To be used effectively for automation, a model must capture a limited amount of information, focusing on a specific aspect of the software. This means that we must usually develop multiple models to completely describe a piece of software, each model focusing on a different aspect. These descriptions are called views. For a business application, for example, we might use views describing how the application presents data to the user, how it interacts with the user, how the user interactions invoke the business logic, how the business logic is structured, how the business logic uses business data, and how the business data is stored in a database. Different views usually interest different audiences. For example, a DBA may be interested in a view of the database schema, while a developer may be interested in a view of the user interface.

A model must focus on a specific aspect of the software.

Architectural Description

A significant amount of thought has been given to the question of what views to use to model software, and how to organize

Architectural description principles can be applied to MDD.

them into coherent descriptions of the software. The most formal work done to date in this regard is in the domain of architectural description. This work is not directly applicable because architectural description uses abridged specifications that describe only those aspects of the software deemed to be architecturally significant, while MDD uses more complete specifications. Despite this difference, principles from the field of architectural description can be applied to model-driven development.

A viewpoint can specify the language(s) used by conforming views.

Specifically, a viewpoint can specify the modeling language(s) used by conforming views because different modeling languages may be needed to capture different kinds of information. For example, state transition diagrams can be used to describe object behavior as responses to events, but they cannot be used to describe classes and relationships. Class diagrams, on the other hand, can be used to describe classes and relationships, but cannot be used to describe object behavior as responses to events. The language used for a viewpoint can be an existing modeling language. However, if no existing modeling language captures the information associated with a viewpoint, then a domain specific language can be created to support the viewpoint.

Domain Specificity

A DSL specifies software from a specific viewpoint.

We can now refine the definitions we gave earlier. A domain specific language (DSL) is a language that enables the specification of software from a specific viewpoint. It defines abstractions that encode the vocabulary of the domain that is the focus of the viewpoint. A general-purpose language (GPL) is not viewpoint based. Instead, a GPL supports only generic, undifferentiated specification.

Multiple DSLs are needed to describe a business application.

As we saw earlier, we generally develop a DSL to capture information about some aspect of the members of a family of software products. Multiple DSLs are needed to describe the typical business application. Modern business applications can be quite complex, both structurally and behaviorally. They frequently cover multiple functional domains, and contain many different implementation mechanisms. For example, the online auction exemplar used in this chapter is a relatively simple business application by industry standards, but it contains five major functional areas, and is broken into six distinct architectural layers. Obviously, we should not expect a single language to adequately capture its complexity.

Domain Specific Tools

To use DSLs, we need tools that understand them, including:

To use DSLs, we need tools that understand them.

- Editors for creating and maintaining specifications. For simple languages, existing textual editors may be adequate. For complex languages, syntax-directed textual or graphical editors may be required for editing and validation.

- Language processors, such as preprocessors, compilers or an interactive generation environment, for producing implementations from models.

- Debugging tools to debug implementations using the language.

- Tools that automate other development tasks using metadata captured by models based on the language, including test generation and execution, instrumentation and measurement, configuration management and deployment.

DSLs for popular domains like Enterprise Application Integration or Web Services Definition will be defined primarily by standards bodies like the W3C, or by vendors like Microsoft or IBM. These standardized DSLs will be supported by products and services from multiple vendors. However, they will also be slow to evolve, since new versions of the languages and tools must be released to distribute new abstractions, or to improve the definitions or implementations of existing abstractions.

Standardized DSLs will be supported by multiple vendors.

Custom DSLs provide an alternative to standardized DSLs and third-party tools. Of course, there are risks, as well as benefits, to developing proprietary languages, such as migrating developer skills, and maintaining the language and tools. These risks may be outweighed, however, by benefits like higher fidelity code generation and more comprehensive automation for a specific software product family. To realize these benefits, we need efficient technologies for developing custom DSLs like those described in Chapter 9.

Custom DSLs can offer advantages if tooling can be automated.

As Czarnecki observes, DSLs can be implemented as stand-alone languages or as extensions to existing languages [CE00].

DSLs can be implemented by extending existing languages or as stand-alone languages.

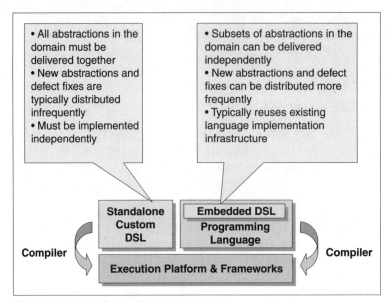

Figure 7.18   Implementing custom DSLs

Most IDEs are developed from scratch. They are therefore expensive to develop, and must target broad domains, such as .NET or J2EE, to be cost effective. This limits the levels of specificity and automation that vendors can afford to provide. In software factories, custom DSLs and tools can be developed for much narrower domains by exploiting extensibility features provided by general-purpose tools and technologies. Instead of new languages developed from scratch, for example, we can extend existing languages like XML. Instead of building new compilers, editors, and debuggers from scratch, we can build plug-ins for existing IDEs. This makes it easier to build special-purpose IDEs that target narrow software product families, providing high levels of specificity and automation at relatively low cost. The differences between these approaches are illustrated in Figure 7.18.

Levels of Specificity

Specificity is the key to achieving commercially significant levels of reuse.

Historically, the software industry has stayed at relatively low levels of specificity, compared with more mature industries, where specialized products and services are ubiquitous. The economics of software development reflect this tendency, rewarding generic products that can be used in many applications, but which contribute little to their development. The fact that applications are built primarily by hand shows that reusable components are not available for the vast majority of the features they require. Achieving the levels of reuse required to create significant economies of scope requires much higher levels of specificity, and a migration from highly generic products, such as tools and libraries for general purpose programming languages like Java and C#, to highly specialized products, such as tools and frameworks for vertical domains like Banking and Insurance. In order for this migration to occur, companies with domain knowledge must become producers of reusable components that support the application development in those domains. Barriers to component development must be lowered, so that domain knowledge holders can develop components in house. A component outsourcing industry may also help to implement custom components from specifications supplied by the domain knowledge holders. Both solutions can be seen in other industries. For example, in the consumer electronics industry, there are companies that build their own branded components, and there are companies that build components branded by others on a contract basis. Of course, this requires new composition mechanisms, like the ones we discussed in Chapter 4, since software component assembly requires much higher levels of adaptation than the assembly of hardware components. It also requires the standardization of specification formats and packaging technologies, since current solutions are too informal to support third-party component assembly, and much more agile customer and supplier relationship management, since software development involves much higher levels of iteration.

Why has the software industry stayed at such low levels of specificity? The answer is partly a matter of technology and partly a matter of economics. On the technology front, there are two reasons for producing generic components:

The software industry has stayed at relatively low levels of specificity for both technical and economic reasons.

- Before we can build specialized components, we need a mature foundation of generic ones that protects them from platform technology churn. Early attempts to build specialized components produced several high-profile failures, as platform technology churn rendered the components obsolete before they could produce a significant return on investment.

- The more specialized a component, the more assumptions it makes about the context in which it is used. A credit authorization service, for example, must make assumptions about application architecture, communication protocols, security threats, and business models that do not have to be made by a user interface widget. A specialized component must therefore be more adaptable, or more loosely coupled to its context, than a generic one, to be reusable. Unfortunately, loosely coupled architectures, implementation technologies, and packaging mechanisms are much harder to build than tightly coupled ones, and require more processing resources.

Markets for high-value components are hard to bootstrap.

On the economic front, the answer is also simple. The more specific a component, the more value it provides, but the smaller its market. In an immature industry, where there are few suppliers from which to choose, most consumers will build high-value components, instead of buying them, to avoid the risk of big ticket purchases, no matter how much more expensive it is to build them. Obviously, this creates a self-fulfilling prophecy, since few suppliers will build high-value components for a reluctant market.

Modeling Aspects

Recall from Chapter 2 that AOP uses aspectual decomposition and composition to separate and then recombine, respectively, different aspects of a system. Let's look at this process more closely.

Aspectual Decomposition

Certain aspects of a system are hard to develop using only functional mechanisms.

Conventional software development emphasizes the partitioning of a system into functional components and the subsequent assembly of those components to form its implementation. Conventional programming languages provide mechanisms, such as classes, to support these processes, which are called functional decomposition and composition, respectively. AOP recognizes that certain aspects of a system, such as distribution, security, concurrency, transactions, and persistence, are hard to develop using only functional mechanisms. Some aspects cross the boundaries of functional modules, e.g., transaction contexts or threads of execution. These aspects generally represent non-functional requirements, and are implemented by configuring system services. Others arise from separable concerns like security that add content to more than one functional module, or from variations, such as distribution, that rearrange the content of multiple functional modules.

Aspects tend to be scattered throughout the software, interspersed with functional code. Because they are not well localized, they are often difficult to understand and maintain. This problem is known as code tangling. Code tangling can also result from optimizations that rearrange the code to improve some operational quality, such as performance. Unfortunately, aspects cannot be created or destroyed by rearranging the code. Localizing their implementations delocalizes the implementations of other aspects or functional components. For example, when we rearrange code to clean up security concerns, the implementation of distribution may become more complex. This is illustrated in Figure 7.19, where Aspect B is localized on the left, and Aspect A is localized on the right.

Because aspects tend to be scattered throughout the software, they are difficult to understand and maintain.

Conventional software development methods do not provide ways to specify aspects apart from functional components, or to weave their implementations into functional components. Using these methods, we write the tangled code by hand. AOP addresses this problem by separating aspects from functional components, and by automatically composing their implementations to produce the tangled code, as illustrated in Figure 7.20.

Aspect-oriented programming separates aspects from functional components, and automatically composes their implementations to produce the tangled code.

The process of separating aspects is called aspectual decomposition.

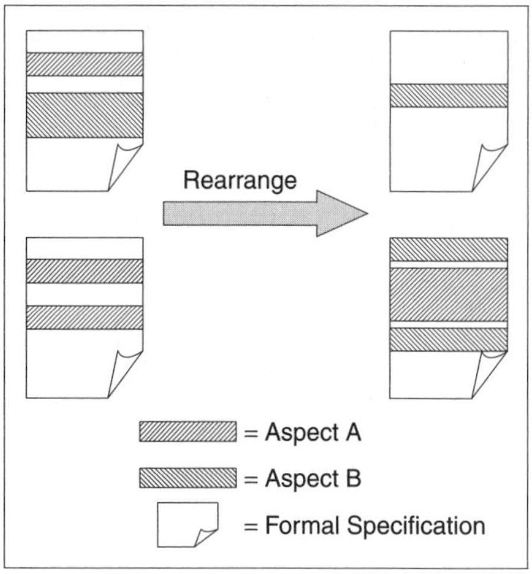

Figure 7.19 Localizing aspects by rearranging code

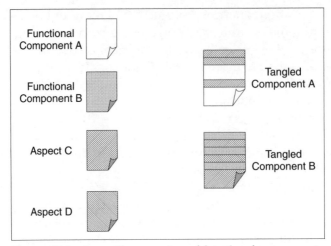

Figure 7.20 Separating aspects and functional components

The process of separating aspects is called aspectual decomposition. Aspectual decomposition involves the following activities:

- Separating and localizing aspects, so that they become easier to analyze and implement.

- Specifying aspects using languages that provide appropriate notations and semantics. As with functional abstractions, we can reduce complexity by defining aspectual abstractions.

Aspectual Composition

The process of combining aspects with functional components is called aspectual composition.

Once aspects have been specified independently, their implementations can then be combined with the implementations of functional components. This process, described in Appendix A, is called *aspectual composition*. Aspectual composition involves the following activities:

- Defining how aspects are implemented. An aspect extends or modifies the semantics of the functional components with which it is composed. Aspects are therefore typically implemented in one of the following ways:

  - By modifying the implementations of functional components. For example, by changing the signatures of the methods in a Java interface to throw remote exceptions if the interface will be accessed remotely.

- By adding program fragments to the implementations of functional components. For example, by calling out to check for appropriate authorization at the beginning of a method.

- Automatically weaving the implementations of aspects and functional components. This involves processing separated specifications for one or more aspects and functional components to produce one or more tangled components.

Weaving can be performed using interpretation or generation. Object-oriented programming mechanisms including design patterns like Adapter, Bridge, Mediator, and Strategy, and idioms like Dynamic Inheritance and Delegation, can be used to perform interpretive weaving. These mechanisms can cause problems, however, such as object identity leakage when multiple objects implement what looks like one object, inability to support compositions that were not anticipated, and inability to identify compositions once they have been implemented. Generative mechanisms avoid these problems, and provide additional advantages, such as looser coupling between the aspects and the functional components, greater variation of binding times and modes, and less intrusion functional components. Czarnecki [CE00] describes these topics in much more depth. Two characteristics of aspects that influence their use are coupling and binding times and modes.

Weaving can be performed using either interpretation or generation.

One of the goals of AOP is adapting functional components to different contexts by weaving them with different aspects. Some adaptations, such as security policy, can be performed using variability points in the components, such as method preambles. Others, such as instrumentation for performance or coverage, can be implemented by generative methods, such as byte code insertion. As we saw in Chapter 4, variable encapsulation uses the principles of AOP to make component adaptation more robust.

Aspect weaving can be used to adapt functional components.

Coupling

Coupling is a measure of how much the specification of an aspect depends on the specifications of functional components. When they are tightly coupled, small changes in functional

Coupling is a measure of how much the specification of an aspect depends on the specifications of functional components.

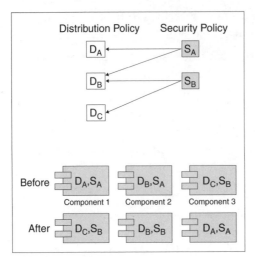

Figure 7.21   Coupling between distribution and security

components, such as renaming a class, invalidate aspect specifications. When they are loosely coupled, large changes in functional components, like merging classes, are required to invalidate aspect specifications. Dependencies are created at join points, where aspect specifications refer to functional component specifications. Three types of join points can be identified:

- *References to Specific Program Elements.* For example, security code may refer to a specific variable or invoke a specific method.

- *References to Specific Program Contexts.* For example, security code may access security credentials passed in the transaction context.

- *References to Specific Program Elements Residing in Multiple Components.* For example, security code may navigate an object graph by traversing relationships.

Coupling can also exist between aspects.

Aspects can be bound to functional components at various times and in various ways.

Coupling can also exist between aspects. For example, a security policy that applies to distributed components can depend on the distribution policy, so that the security policy cannot be bound until the distribution policy is bound, and must be rebound when the distribution policy changes, as illustrated in Figure 7.21.

Binding Times and Modes

Aspects can be bound to functional components at various times and in various ways. For example, a security policy can be bound statically at development time by adding code that

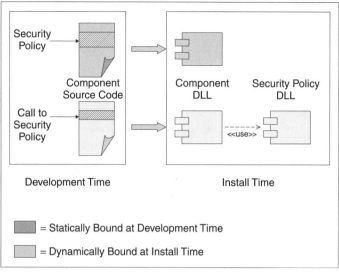

Figure 7.22   Aspect binding times and modes

implements the policy to the functional components. The same policy can be bound dynamically at installation time by adding code to the functional components that looks up and calls a policy object specified when the functional components are installed. These alternatives are illustrated in Figure 7.22.

Aspect Frameworks

AOP assumes that different types of systems may have different aspects. For this reason, it does not define a fixed set of general-purpose aspects, and focuses instead on mechanisms for specifying and weaving aspects. A fixed set of aspects, called an aspect framework, can be defined for a given product family, along with the necessary specification languages and composition mechanisms. Product line practices can then be used to develop and apply aspect frameworks. For example, we might define an aspect framework that defines aspects like distribution, security, transactions and persistence, and mechanisms for weaving them with business components.

A fixed set of aspects can be defined for a product family.

How to Model Software

Now that we know how and why models capture information about software, we are ready to ask what information should be captured. The answer to this question varies by product family. We can identify several types of information that can be captured, however, and several characteristics of the models that capture it, including level of abstraction and style of specification.

Types of Information

Three areas should be modeled to support integration and interoperability: the integration context, the contracts governing the interactions, and the implementation of the components.

The first step in deciding what to model is defining the scope of the information that must be captured. In the context of a Software Factory, this scope is defined by the software factory schema for a specific product family. For the purposes of this chapter, we will focus on ways of defining scope that are common to all product families. We start by observing that some information is shared across multiple product families when their members interact. We therefore consider integration and interoperability requirements when defining the scope of the information that must be captured. These requirements can surface in many areas of the software. For example, data models must be shared to support data integration, component contracts must be shared to support application integration, and business process and entity models must be shared to support business integration. Generally, there are three areas of interest that should be modeled independently to support integration and interoperability: the integration context, the contracts governing the interactions of the components, and the implementation of the components. For example, Figure 7.23

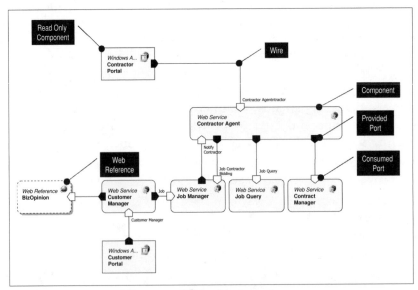

Figure 7.23   Modeling assemblies of web services

identifies each of these areas of interest for an assembly of Web services. The integration context is described by the entire assembly. The contracts governing the interactions of the Web services are described by the ports and the wires that connect them. The implementations of the Web services are described by the components. The view shown in the figure captures only the integration context. Additional views are required to capture descriptions of the contracts and component implementations.

Next, we can identify several kinds of information that can be captured in each area of interest. In software factories, we typically model behavior, structure, artifacts, and qualities of service. These aspects are highly interdependent. Qualities of service are realized by behavior, behavior is realized by structure, and structure is realized by artifacts.

Several types of information are relevant in each area of interest.

Behavior

To model behavior, we create views that describe what the software does, how it interacts with users or with other systems, and how its structural units collaborate to perform these functions. Examples of behavioral views include sequence and collaboration diagrams, which describe component interactions, and views that describe processes, such as activity graphs and flow graphs like the view shown in Figure 7.24 from the designer for the Microsoft BizTalk server. Colored Petri-Nets are widely used for modeling business processes. A process modeling language for information commerce appears in [AW01].

Structure

To model structure, we create views that describe how the software is organized into units like classes or components, how the units are composed, and what information they manipulate. Structural modeling is particularly useful for showing a component is implemented in terms of other components. For example, we might create a view that describes the set of classes that implement a business entity, as shown in Figure 7.7. Structural views are by far the most common in current practice.

Artifacts

To model artifacts, we create views that describe the development, deployment, and execution artifacts used by the software.

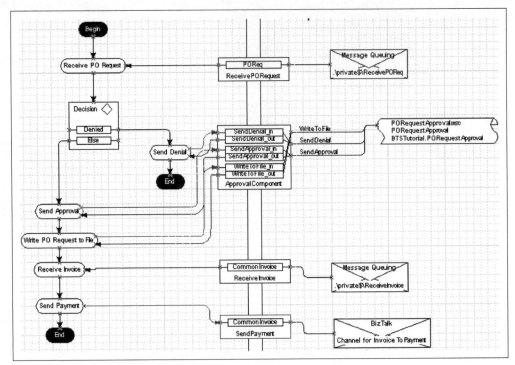

Figure 7.24   A behavioral view

For example, we might create views that describe the class files, resource files, and archive files that comprise the executables for an application, as shown in Figure 7.25, a screen shot from IBM WebSphere Studio, or views that describe the physical design of a database.

Level of Abstraction

Views can be developed at different levels of abstraction. A more abstract view captures less detailed information than a less abstract one.

Views can be defined at different levels of abstraction. A more abstract view captures less detail than a less abstract one. The view in Figure 7.26, for example, describes three business entities without saying how they will be implemented. A less abstract view captures more detailed information than a more abstract one. The view that appeared previously in Figure 7.7, for example, describes the implementation of the Employee entity in Figure 7.26. The view in Figure 7.7 refines the one in Figure 7.26, meaning that it describes the same subject in greater detail. In Figure 7.7, Employee has been realized as a set of four classes. Another view could be created describing the realization of Address.

Figure 7.25   An artifact view

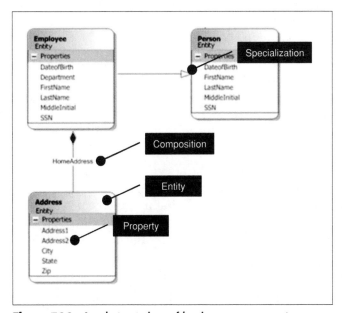

Figure 7.26   An abstract view of business components

The more abstract the view, the less we must specify to describe the software.

A more abstract view is more concise. The more abstract the view, the less we must specify to describe the software. With just a few symbols, for example, the view in Figure 7.26 describes concepts that take several diagrams to express at the level of abstraction of the view in Figure 7.7. Similarly, the view in Figure 7.7 hides large amounts of detail compared to the source code files, XML files, and other artifacts used to implement the business entities. These terms are relative, of course. The view in Figure 7.7 is less abstract than the view in Figure 7.26, but more abstract than C# source code. A developer who uses the view in Figure 7.7 must know more about C# than one who uses the view in Figure 7.26, but not as much as one who hand codes the business entities.

Conceptual, Logical, Physical

Three commonly used but informal characterizations of the level of abstraction are conceptual, logical, and physical.

Despite the relative terminology, we can characterize levels of abstraction by the kind of information they capture relative to specific implementation technologies. Three commonly used characterizations are conceptual, logical, and physical. As with the definitions we offered in Chapter 6, these definitions are not formal, and represent only our preferences. They could be replaced by different definitions that reflect the preferences of different commentators. Note, also, that they are not absolute. We can easily have views at more or less than three levels of abstraction. We have chosen to use these terms only because they offer useful characterizations.

- A *physical* view captures information about constructs that exist outside the realm of execution of the software being modeled, such as files and directories. Physical constructs are defined by the implementation technologies, and can be used to implement logical constructs.[2]

- A *logical* view is a more abstract view that captures information about constructs that exist within the realm of execution of the software being modeled, such as the classes it defines and the objects it instantiates. Logical constructs are explicitly defined by the developer using the implementation technologies, and can be used to implement conceptual constructs.

- A *conceptual* view is a more abstract view that captures information about constructs that are implied by the execution of the software being modeled, such as the business processes it supports. Conceptual constructs are defined by the intent of the developer and cannot be explicitly defined using the implementation technologies. They must be encoded indirectly using configurations of logical constructs. Of course, we can define them explicitly by developing new languages that raise the level of abstraction, as we have seen. Raising the level of abstraction turns some conceptual constructs into logical ones.

For example, a conceptual view of a business process might describe flows of control or information, a logical view might describe messages and message processing classes, and a physical view might describe the files that comprise its executables.

Conceptual models can be used to support integration and interoperability. In many cases, different implementations of shared concepts must be integrated. For example, the same conceptual data model may be realized differently in different databases. Different table names, column names, and types may be used for essentially the same information. Conceptual models can be used to hide implementation differences that would prevent them from interoperating. We can then use the models to describe integrations, and to generate adapters that bridge implementation differences. This approach is described by D'Souza [Dso02].

Conceptual models can be used to support integration and interoperability.

We can apply these characterizations to the types of views defined earlier. An artifact view is always physical. Structural, behavioral, and quality of service views are logical if the constructs they model can be explicitly defined using the implementation technologies. Otherwise, they are conceptual. For Enterprise JavaBeans, for example, transaction isolation levels can be defined explicitly, so a view that describes them is logical. For plain Java classes, however, they cannot be defined explicitly, so a view that describes them is conceptual.

Platform Independence

Another important characterization is platform independence. A view that does not imply specific platform technologies is platform independent. A platform-independent view can be used more effectively than a platform-specific view to migrate software to a different platform. A platform-specific view depends on technologies supplied by the platform. If the software is migrated to a different platform, the view must be

Any view that captures enough content to generate usable software will contain some platform dependencies.

modified to reflect the changes. The view in Figure 7.7, for example, is specific to the Microsoft Business Framework, while the view in Figure 7.26 could be implemented using either MBF or J2EE, but it assumes some kind of distributed component architecture. Of course, the view in Figure 7.26 does not provide nearly as much information as the view in Figure 7.7. Platform-independent views generally elide significant amounts of information to minimize platform dependencies. This limits their use to special tasks, such as migration. Of course, all views make some platform assumptions, so all of these terms are relative. Views can vary in degree of platform specificity, assuming general classes of technology, such as distributed component architectures, platform standards, such as .NET or J2EE, specific products, such as SQL Server, or specific product versions, such as SQL Server 2003. The view in Figure 7.23, for example, depends on a general class of technology, i.e., Web services, not on specific products or product versions. In practice, any view that captures enough content to generate usable software will contain some platform dependencies.

Computation Independence

Computation-independent views describe information and processes in a real world problem domain without specifying how they are automated.

Another important characterization is computation independence. Views that describe information and processes in a real world problem domain without specifying how they are automated are computation independent. A computation-independent view is always conceptual. Figure 7.27 from [OMG ptc/04-01-10] for example, shows a computation-independent view of part of an order management process. In this diagram, an activity called Authorize Credit Card contains an activity called Check Credit. Ports called Pending Credit Requests and Approved Credit Requests on Authorize Credit Card support connections to other activities. Within Authorize Credit Card, connection c1 connects Pending Credit Requests to a port on Check Credit called Requests In using a message schema m1. Similarly, connection c2 connects a port on Check Credit called Requests Out to Approved Credit Requests using a message schema m2. When Pending Credit Requests and Approved Credit Requests, are connected, Authorize Credit Card routes messages arriving from merchants on Pending Credit Requests to Check Credit for processing, and messages processed by Check Credit to Approved Credit Requests. The primary actors in this process, Credit Clerk and Credit

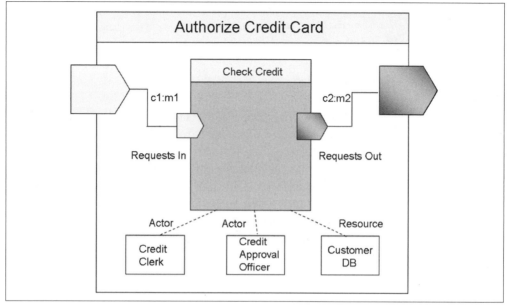

Figure 7.27   A computation-independent view

Approval Officer, are humans. The model does not say how they perform the activities and whether or not the flows of information among them are automated.

Style of Specification

We have already discussed style of specification at length. Using the definitions in Chapter 6, we now observe that a view can be imperative, meaning that it describes instructions to be executed but not the desired results of execution, or declarative, meaning that it describes the desired results of execution but not how they should be obtained. Behavioral views are primarily imperative, while the other types of views are primarily declarative. Of course, as we said earlier, the two styles of specification are often mixed.

Behavioral views are imperative, the others are primarily declarative.

Declarative Specification

Declarative specification is not as well understood as imperative specification, since most development is performed using imperative languages. SQL offers a familiar example of declarative specification. Using SQL, we tell a DBMS what data to fetch, and it decides how to satisfy the request. We do not provide explicit instructions, telling it how to fetch the

When we specify software declaratively, we do not provide explicit instructions to define its implementation.

```
Document ("myDocument.xml") myPackage {
  class [self.priority = #HIGH and self.cost = 25]
}
```

Figure 7.28 A declarative query

data. Similarly, when we specify software declaratively, we do not provide explicit instructions to define its implementation. Instead, we specify what it should do, and how it should be organized. In some cases, it is possible to automatically generate an implementation for a declarative specification, as we have seen. In other cases, we may need to provide one manually, or with assistance from tools that use the declarative specification to provide assistance, such as generating partial class and method definitions that must be completed by hand. Because they elide information about order of execution, declarative views are often more abstract than imperative ones. For example, Figure 7.28 shows a declarative query that locates elements in an XML document whose priority is "HIGH" and whose cost is 25. Implementing this query imperatively with Visual Basic takes about 150 lines of code.

Complementary Styles

Declarative and imperative styles of specification are complementary

Declarative and imperative styles of specification are complementary and can be used to provide complementary views of the same software. For example, when configuring a database, imperative scripts, like triggers and stored procedures, are often written to complement declarative data definition and manipulation language expressions. Of course, the most common use of complementary specification styles is the generation of imperative specifications from declarative ones. Modern Interactive Development Environments (IDEs), for example, usually generate imperative implementations from declarative specifications for user interfaces. Figure 7.29 shows a declarative user interface specification in Borland JBuilder.

Figure 7.30 shows the imperative implementation generated from the declarative specification also in Borland JBuilder.

Adding Code to Models

Declarative models are frequently augmented with imperative code.

Declarative models are frequently augmented with imperative code. Experience has shown that up to 70% of the structure and

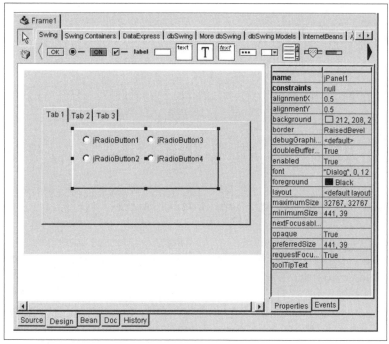

Figure 7.29   A declarative specification

```
public class Frame1 extends JFrame {
    //Main UI panel
    JPanel contentPane;

    //Tabbed pane and layouts for pane 1 and pane 2
    //Pane 3 uses a null layout
    JTabbedPane jTabbedPane1 = new JTabbedPane();
    JPanel jPanel1 = new JPanel();
    JPanel jPanel2 = new JPanel();
    JPanel jPanel3 = new JPanel();
    FlowLayout flowLayout1_panel1 = new FlowLayout();
    FlowLayout flowLayout1_panel2 = new FlowLayout();

    //Radio buttons on pane 1; buttons are in a
    //mutually exclusive button group
    JRadioButton jRadioButton1 = new JRadioButton();
    JRadioButton jRadioButton2 = new JRadioButton();
    JRadioButton jRadioButton3 = new JRadioButton();
    JRadioButton jRadioButton4 = new JRadioButton();
    ButtonGroup buttonGroup1 = new ButtonGroup();

    //Labels on pane 2
    JLabel jLabel1 = new JLabel();
    JLabel jLabel2 = new JLabel();
```

Frame1.java   1:1   Insert

Source Design Bean Doc History

Figure 7.30   An imperative implementation

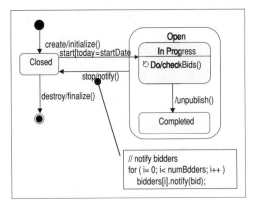

Figure 7.31   Code added to a state transition diagram

behavior of most business applications can be specified declaratively. Imperative code is required to specify the remainder. Most of this code is used to define custom business rules or logic that cannot be expressed declaratively. It usually refers to model elements by name, and calls services supplied by frameworks that accompany the modeling languages, such as setting the value of a property, creating an instance of a type, or adding an instance to a relationship. Figure 7.31 shows some code added to a model to customize the behavior of a state transition. In this example, the code in the box is executed when the transition named "stop" occurs between states "Completed" and "Closed". The code sends a notification to each bidder.

Domain-Specific Languages

Organizations with domain knowledge must supply DSLs for their domains.

Programming with models requires a wide array of modeling languages capturing a wide variety of metadata. Since the languages we will use for this purpose are specific to fairly narrow domains, we are not likely to be able to buy them off the shelf from platform vendors, who have traditionally been the suppliers of languages and tools for software development. Organizations with domain knowledge will have to become proficient in building them. This has both business and technical ramifications.

New business models are required to support the development of languages and tools for narrow domains.

Business Ramifications

On the business front, new business models are required to support the development of languages and tools for narrow domains. Consider how platform vendors do business today. As we have seen, there is an inverse relationship between the level of abstraction of a language and the scope of the domain it can serve. There is also a direct relationship between the level of abstraction and power. It is therefore no surprise that platform vendors typically build low-level, general-purpose languages and tools that help to solve relatively small amounts of the problems facing business application developers. They do this because current business models reward high volumes and low price points. Ironically, the platforms on which the software runs are much more expensive. Over time, the disproportionate valuation of platforms relative to tools has devalued tools to the point where they are effectively commodities. This makes it difficult for vendors to sell more advanced tools profitably. This is a fundamental driver in the disparity between progress in platform technology and progress in development technology. We think the time has come when the pendulum will start to swing the other way. The industry is beginning to recognize that its most severe bottleneck is not the platform technology, but the cost and risk of software development, and that investing in more powerful tools would provide the greatest return on investment at this point in its evolution. To realize the benefits of MDD, third-party organizations with domain knowledge, such as Independent Software Vendors (ISVs), Systems Integrators (SIs) and enterprises, must become profitable suppliers of domain specific languages and tools.

Technical Ramifications

This now leads to the question of how hard it is to build DSLs. Observers close to the industry know that building languages and the tools that support them, such as editors, compilers, and debuggers, is a difficult proposition requiring much more skill than building applications. Will we make the software development bottleneck even worse by placing an even more onerous technical challenge on the third-party organizations we described earlier? No. We propose to address this question in two ways:

We must tackle the cost of building DSLs.

- By recognizing the value of working within product families using product line principles, organizations can leverage the skills of their most talented developers much more effectively, making them product line

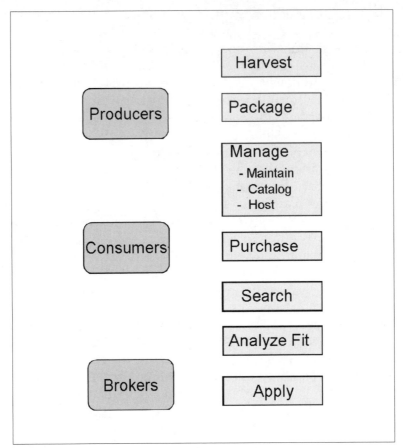

Figure 7.32 Working with product line assets

developers, who build the languages and tools used by product developers. This already happens to some extent in most organizations, but much more could be done to empower product line developers. For example, they could have much better technology for identifying, harvesting, refining, documenting, testing, packaging, and supporting assets for explicit reuse, as illustrated in Figure 7.32. Similarly, product developers could have much better technology for finding, analyzing, purchasing, installing, and applying those assets within the development environments they already use.

■ New technologies are now available that can make the development of languages and tools much easier, moving the task from the realm of rocket science to the realm of development that most third-party organizations can reasonably undertake.

Next Steps

Assuming that the business and technical challenges can be met, and that third-party organizations with domain knowledge can be empowered to develop domain specific languages and tools, what happens to the platform vendors, and the existing business models? We think that like all paradigm shifts, this one will move forward under its own momentum, leaving some elements of the status quo behind. Also, as in all paradigm shifts, we think there is tremendous opportunity for those who made the existing paradigm successful in its day to be among the first to profit from new business models and new technologies. Indeed, some platform vendors will recognize and exploit the opportunity by providing better support for product line practices in their existing tools, while others will fail to make the transition because the current paradigm is too deeply ingrained in their thinking. Also, at the end of the day, software runs on platforms. This means that platform vendors will provide concrete languages and tools targeted by transformations from higher-level abstractions.

Of course, model-driven development, as described here, is not the whole story. Development by assembly also plays a significant role. We will look at innovations in assembly in Chapters 12 and 13, and at methods for generating implementations in Chapters 14 and 15. Before we look at the other pieces of the picture, however, we will look at new technologies that make the development of languages and tools much easier in Chapters 8 and 9.

Notes

1. This example is based on Pearl Circle Online Auction (PCOA), an application described in [EHK02], and uses an implementation of the Core J2EE Design Patterns from IBM.
2. Of course, these constructs are as ephemeral as any other constructs made of bits. We use the term physical to convey that they are perhaps more permanent than constructs described using either of the other terms defined here. We do not intend to imply that they are literally physical.

CHAPTER 8

Language Anatomy

By Steve Cook and Stuart Kent

The good thing about bubbles and arrows, as opposed to programs, is that they never crash.

Bertrand Meyer

In Chapter 7, we saw that models play a different role in software factories than they have traditionally played in software development. Instead of modeling to provide documentation for human consumption, we use models as development artifacts that are processed by tools to generate implementations, or to automate other aspects of the software development process. We also saw that the modeling languages used in software factories must be defined as rigorously as programming languages. In this chapter, we look at how languages are defined, at the relationship between modeling and programming languages, and at ways to define and implement domain specific languages. We also show how textual and graphical languages can be integrated.

This chapter investigates languages that can be processed by machine.

   The first step in studying language anatomy is to differentiate between natural and formal languages. *Natural languages*, such as English, art, sculpture and music, are evolving organic phenomena. Given the current state of the art, they are too complex to be processed effectively by machine for the purposes of software development. *Formal languages*, however, are specifically designed for machine processing.[1] These are the languages we focus on in this chapter.

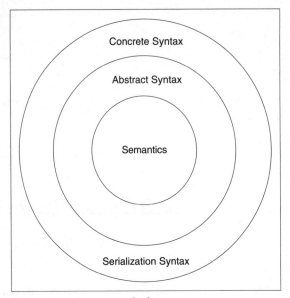

Figure 8.1   Anatomy of a language

The anatomy of a formal language includes a semantics, an abstract syntax, and one or more concrete or serialization syntaxes.

Figure 8.1 shows the high-level anatomy of a formal language. In this diagram, the concentric circles represent an architectural topology. They show which parts of a language are directly related to each other. As the diagram shows, the Abstract Syntax is directly related to the Semantics, and the Concrete Syntaxes are directly related to the Abstract Syntax. Semantics is related to the Concrete and Serialization Syntaxes only indirectly, however, through the mediation of the Abstract Syntax. The Abstract Syntax characterizes the essential concepts and structure of expressions in a language. Abstract syntax is the most necessary part of the definition from a machine processing perspective. Concrete and Serialization syntaxes say how these abstract concepts are realized in a concrete notation such as text or graphics. There can be many of these. Semantics gives meaning to the abstract concepts. There is usually one of these.[2] Let's look briefly at each of these elements, starting with the abstract syntax.

The abstract syntax defines elements and composition rules.

- The *abstract syntax* of a language characterizes, in an abstract form, the kinds of elements that make up the language, and the rules for how those elements may be combined. The kinds of elements that make up English, for example, include nouns, verbs, and adjectives, and the rules for combining them are given by English grammar.

- The *semantics* of a language define its meaning. The term is used widely when defining formal languages. The semantics of formal languages are easier to pin down than the semantics of natural languages, such as English, where about the best one can do is write a dictionary. A dictionary describes the meaning of each word by explaining it using other words of the language, or, indeed using words of another language, in the case of bilingual dictionaries. There are then rules for composing the meanings of words to construct the meanings of expressions formed by composing the words. These rules are largely unwritten and depend heavily on context (i.e., their meaning varies significantly according to the context in which they are used). Indeed, despite some claims to the contrary [Mon74], it is virtually impossible to capture these rules accurately or precisely because of this dependence on context. The problem of meaning is even more difficult for other natural languages, such as music, where the meanings of individual elements, such as notes, cannot be defined explicitly. In contrast, for formal languages, it is possible to be entirely explicit about how meanings of expressions are composed from the individual language elements, and it is essential to do so in order to define how to process the language consistently. We can now define a *formal language* more precisely as a machine processable language that has well defined semantics. We shall identify and explore two ways to define semantics for formal languages in this chapter. Note that this definition creates a category of machine processable languages that do not have well defined semantics. Such languages can be processed in ways that rely on human interpretation, such as rendering diagrams, but unless they are extended or modified to give them a well-defined semantics, they cannot be processed effectively to produce software products, since the meanings of expressions in such languages cannot be determined precisely. We will refer to them as *semi-formal languages*. The Unified Modeling Language (UML) is a well-known example of a semi-formal language; see Appendix B.

  The semantics define the meaning of the language.

- A *concrete syntax* defines how the language elements appear in a concrete, human-usable form. There are

  A concrete syntax is a human usable form.

many different forms of concrete syntax. The two most common forms for English are the written (textual) and spoken forms. Concrete syntaxes for primarily imperative languages are often textual, while concrete syntaxes for primarily declarative languages often combine graphics, text, and conventions by which users may interact with the graphics and the text under the auspices of tools. However, these distinctions are not absolute and exceptions abound. Another term for concrete syntax is *notation*.

- A *serialization syntax* is like a concrete syntax, except that it does not have to be human-usable. A serialization syntax is used to persist and interchange language expressions in serialized form.

A serialization syntax does not have to be humanusable.

The remainder of this chapter describes each of these elements in depth. First, we introduce an example language, which we use to illustrate the concepts. Armed with this language, we show how abstract syntax is described, and we discuss abstract syntax graphs (ASGs), abstract syntax trees (ASTs) and the relationship between them. Next, we show how concrete syntax, serialization syntax, and semantics are described. Finally, we discuss the relationship between programming and modeling languages, and we precisely define some key terms throughout the book.

Example Language

We use a simple example language called OSL to explain the concepts introduced above.

There is nothing to say that a domain specific language should be purely textual or purely graphical. Our expectation is that most domain specific languages will be a mixture of both. So to illustrate how to define the parts of a language, we'll use an example language that combines both graphical and textual elements. The sole purpose of this language is to give detail to our illustration: since we believe it should be easy to define new languages, we permit ourselves to define a small one just for this. As well as showing how to combine textual and graphical elements, our example language will allow approaches to defining textual and graphical languages to be contrasted and compared.

In the example language, *classes* can have *attributes* and *methods*, which may assign values to attributes. Classes can also be

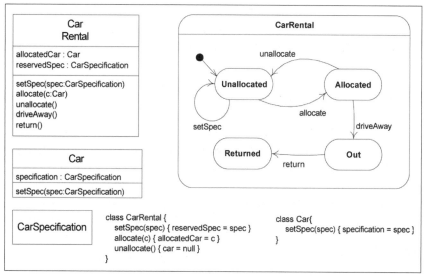

Figure 8.2   Example OSL model

associated with *state machines* that place some constraints on the order in which methods can be invoked. *Our Simple Language (OSL)* is introduced informally by way of Figure 8.2.

This represents a (grossly simplified) fragment of a model for a car rental administration system. The focus is on the `Car-Rental` class. A car rental object represents a record of the rental of a car, from initial inception to the final return of the car. A car rental object has attributes recording which specification of car has been reserved, and which specific car has been allocated to fulfill the rental. There are methods to set the car specification, allocate a car, unallocate the car, record the fact that the car has been driven away and then returned. There is a fragment of text in the model which defines which attributes are set and how for each of the methods. For example, `allo-cate(c:Car)` sets the attribute `allocatedCar` to `c`.

The figure represents part of a car rental administration system.

UML-like notation is used to depict classes, although in OSL only attributes are permitted—there are no associations.

A class may have a state machine. The state machine associated with the `CarRental` class is depicted on the right of the diagram, also using UML-like notation. A state in a state machine is shown by a box with rounded corners. A state machine has a root state, which has the same name as the class with which the machine is associated. A state can contain other states; in this case the root state contains four other states, which are connected by transitions, represented as arrows. `Unallocated`

OSL uses UML-like notation.

The state machine constrains the order in which methods can be invoked.

is annotated as the initial state, by targeting it with an arrow from a black circle. A transition has a source state and a target state; it must be labeled by one of the methods of the class.

The meaning of this state machine can be summarized as follows. When a CarRental object is created it is put into the Unallocated state. Thereafter the state machine constrains the order in which methods may be invoked on the object, by following transitions from state to state: only methods labeling transitions sourced on a state can be performed from that state, and when they have finished executing, the object moves into the target state. Only the setSpec and allocate methods may be performed from the Unallocated state. The setSpec method takes the object back into the Unallocated state; the allocate method takes the object into the Allocated state. From Allocated it is possible to unallocate or driveAway. The latter changes the state to Out; then it is only possible to return, at which point the state changes to Returned and no more methods can be performed.

There are many different state machine notations and semantics.

There are notations for state machines that are richer than this one, and some that are less rich. There is also a range of different semantics that can be given to any notation. There are two kinds of semantics for state machines. One is where the state machine should be seen as constraining the order in which transitions can be taken; the machine itself does not cause execution of methods, rather it constrains the choices that can be made at each step. The semantics for state machines in OSL is of this kind. The other kind is where the machine is used to drive execution; during execution there is an algorithm that refers to the state machine to choose which method to invoke next, by selecting from the set of possible transitions from the current state. The algorithm is simplest if the machine is deterministic, so that there is only one transition that can be taken at any time from any state. The definition of such semantics can get tricky as the notation gets richer, in particular, when guarded transitions and orthogonal states are admitted.

Because OSL mixes textual and graphical syntax does not mean it is not a programming language.

Before leaving this section, observe that OSL uses a mixture of graphical and textual notation. The graphical notation has text embedded, and there is a separate text fragment defining the body of the methods. Because of its graphical notation, many people would classify it as a modeling language, rather than a programming language. This is misleading. One could come up with a purely textual syntax for this language, where information currently conveyed through diagrams is conveyed through text, instead. Such a definition is provided later, in the section on concrete syntax. Similarly, one could come up with a partially graphical notation for a language like C# or Java (probably some fragment of class diagram notation). Furthermore, one could imagine interpreting OSL, just as one would a programming language. What would the interpreter do? It would start by asking the user what kind of object to create. `CarRental` might be the answer. Then, it would display the choice of methods available to be called on that object, say through a pop-up menu in a GUI. At this point, the available methods on `CarRental` would be `setSpec` and `allocate`. At any time, new objects could be created. So, the user might ask it to create a `CarSpecification` object, and then pass this object as argument to the `setSpec` method, and so on. Because this interpretation process involves non-determinism, it is sometimes referred to as the "animation of a specification" rather than the "execution of a program". Provide a richer language, including standard datatypes like `Boolean`, `String` and `Integer`, and a richer statement language for method bodies, and one would have a programming language, interpretable by machine, quite suitable for defining simple business processes that act on object-oriented databases.

Abstract Syntax

Abstract syntax characterizes, in an abstract form, the kinds of elements that make up the language and the rules for how those elements may be combined. There are atomic elements and composite elements; the rules indicate how composite elements are formed by combining other elements, which can either be composite or atomic.

Abstract syntax characterizes kinds of language element, and rules for composing them.

   There are different ways in which the different kinds of elements and rules can be defined. We'll look at two here, context-free grammars and metamodels, since they have been the main approaches to defining the abstract syntax of textual and graphical languages, respectively. A more traditional view would restrict the use of the term "abstract syntax" to that which can be expressed by a context-free grammar, and would regard the additional capabilities provided by metamodels as falling into the area of semantics. Because we are interested in languages that mix text and graphics, however, we prefer a broader definition of abstract syntax, which includes the additional capabilities provided by metamodels.

Context-Free Grammars and BNF

Context-free grammars are traditionally used to define the syntax of programming languages.

Context-free grammars (CFGs) are traditionally used to define the syntax (both concrete and abstract) of programming languages. Although they are tuned for processing text, this does not mean that they cannot be used in the definition of graphical languages, such as OSL.

There are different flavors of context-free grammar with subtly different characteristics that affect how the language can be processed by a machine. We won't go into that here; see [Wat91]. A context-free grammar definition consists of a set of productions, where the left-hand side is called a non-terminal (symbol) and the right-hand side details an internal structure for a given non-terminal in terms of other non-terminals and terminals. A non-terminal is a composite language element and a terminal is an atomic one. One non-terminal is singled out to be the start symbol, which represents the top-level elements of the language, which for a programming language would be programs.

BNF is a common notation for CFGs.

A context-free grammar for the abstract syntax of OSL is given below. It is expressed using a form of Backus-Naur form (BNF) notation, a common notation for CFGs, as shown in Figure 8.3.

BNF NOTATION

BNF notation is very simple. A production is of the form X ::= Y, where X is a non-terminal and Y is some expression involving terminals and non-terminals. Thinking in terms of trees, this rule means that an X node has as children whatever types of elements that Y allows. Y can be formed as follows:

- ◆ Y1 Y2 ... YN means that X has a sequence of Y1, ..., YN as children
- ◆ Y1 | Y2 | ... | YN means that X has one of Y1, ..., YN as children
- ◆ brackets can be used when combining these together, as in X ::= (Y1 | Y2) Y3 which is different from X ::= Y1 | (Y2 Y3)

◆ *** and + can be used to indicate a sequence of zero (respectively one) or more elements of the same type, and ? to indicate that the element is optional. So X ::= (Y1 Y2)* (Y3)+ Y4? means that X has as children a (possibly empty) sequence of pairs of Y1 Y2 elements, followed by a non-empty sequence of Y3 elements, followed, optionally, by a Y4 element.**

In this example, the start symbol is `Model`. A model has a sequence of model elements as children, where model elements, in this case, can only be classes. A class has a name, followed by a sequence of features, followed, optionally, by a state machine. A feature may either be an attribute or a method. And so on. Because the BNF is for constructing trees, it is not possible to share nodes between different parents—if you did, you would end up with a graph. However, there are places where a graph would be more natural. For example, a transition

The BNF for OSL starts at Model and builds a tree, although in some places a graph would be more natural.

```
1.    Model ::= (ModelElement)*
2.    ModelElement ::= Class
3.    Class ::= ClassName (Features)* (StateMachine)?
4.    ClassName ::= Identifier
5.    Feature ::= Attribute | Method
6.    Attribute ::= AttributeName TypeRef
7.    AttributeName ::= Identifier
8.    TypeRef ::= Identifier
9.    Method ::= MethodName (Argument)* Statement
10.   MethodName ::= Identifier
11.   Argument ::= ArgumentName TypeRef
12.   ArgumentName ::= Identifier
13.   Statement ::= (Statement)* | AssignmentStatement
14.   AssignmentStatement ::= LHS RHS
15.   LHS ::= AttributeRef
16.   AttributeRef ::= Identifier
17.   RHS ::= AttributeRef | ArgumentRef
18.   ArgumentRef ::= Identifier
19.   StateMachine ::= State
20.   State ::= StateName (StartState)? (State)* (Transition)*
21.   StateName ::= Identifier
22.   StartState ::= StateRef
23.   Transition ::= MethodRef StateRef
24.   MethodRef ::= Identifier
25.   StateRef ::= Identifier
```

Figure 8.3 BNF abstract syntax

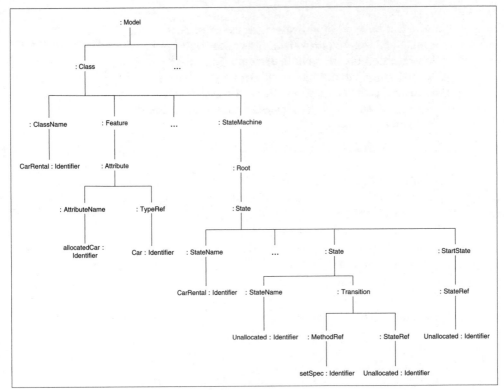

Figure 8.4 AST for car rental model

(defined on line 23) needs to refer to a target state (the state that the transition is a child of is assumed to be the source state), which will already be a child of some other state. As a transition cannot have this state as its child (the state already has a parent), it is necessary instead for it to have a reference to the state. In this grammar the references are plain identifiers.

Figure 8.4 shows the abstract syntax of a fragment of the car rental model as a tree conforming to this grammar. Because it is a tree, we call it an Abstract Syntax Tree, or AST for short.

Identifier is used in place of terminal symbols.

This grammar actually has no terminal symbols. Instead, there is a single non-terminal symbol (Identifier) that is not on the left-hand side of any rule. This is common practice when defining an abstract syntax, as one does not generally want to be specific about the concrete form that identifiers can take. The definition of Identifier as allowed sequences of particular symbols would be provided as part of the lexical grammar (see the section on concrete syntax).

Metamodels

Metamodeling is another approach to the definition of the abstract syntax of languages, which has grown in popularity since it was used to define the abstract syntax of UML [OMG formal/03-03-01]. Metamodeling has come to mean the construction of an object-oriented model of the abstract syntax of a language. For UML, this is expressed in a subset of UML. A metamodel characterizes language elements as classes, and relationships between them using attributes and associations. There are various flavors of metamodeling, which tend to differ mostly in the nature of associations that are permitted (unary versus binary versus n'ary, with qualifiers or not, and so on). A metamodel of the abstract syntax of our state machine language appears in Figure 8.5.

Metamodels are used to define the abstract syntax of modeling languages. Metamodels are usually object-oriented.

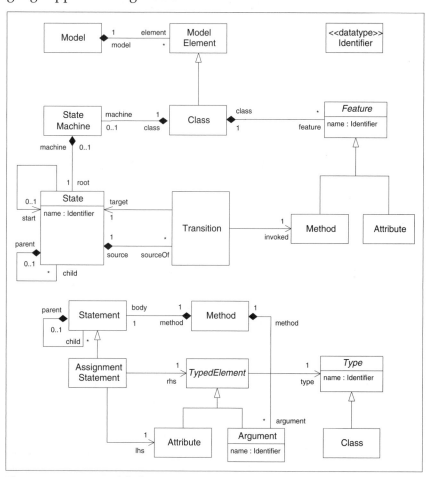

Figure 8.5   Metamodel abstract syntax

METAMODEL NOTATION

The metamodel notation used here is UML-like. It reuses UML notation, but has semantics precisely defined specifically for metamodeling.

This sidebar provides a detailed and systematic, though informal, definition of the semantics of the notation, which should be sufficient to understand the example. However, we would have to use the techniques described in the *Semantics* section later to provide a definition precise enough to support machine processing of this language. Some familiarity with OO concepts is assumed.

The language comprises classes, represented by the box-symbol used by UML. Classes can have attributes, whose types are datatypes, and associations, which refer from one class to another.

Classes have instances, which are objects with identity. Objects can have exactly the same state (represented by values of their attributes) yet different identities.

Classes may inherit from (zero, one or more) other classes. This means that objects of the subclass are also objects of the superclass, and, therefore, must have values for the attributes and associations defined by the superclass.

Classes may be abstract (the name is shown in italics) or concrete. An instance of an abstract class must also be an instance of one of its concrete subclasses.

Attributes are declared inside a compartment of a class rectangle, using the form x : Y, where x is the name of the attribute and Y is its type. An attribute of an object has a value of the type for which it is declared.

Associations are represented by lines between classes. Associations combine the concept of a mathematical relation with the idea of navigability. They may be unidirectional, indicated by an arrowhead, or bidirectional, indicated by an absence of arrowheads. Association ends may be marked with a multiplicity, which is restricted to be one of 0..1, 1, and *. 0..1 means that the corresponding association refers to a single object of the target class, or null. 1 means that it can never be null. * means that it refers to a sequence of objects of the target class. We choose sequences, as they can easily be converted into sets, if necessary, whereas the converse is not so easy.

A bidirectional association represents a pair of unidirectional associations, where one is the inverse of the other—if a is the inverse of b, then for any value x in a, x.b.a contains x, where x.b

(continued)

METAMODEL NOTATION *(continued)*

is the set of values obtained by navigating b from x, and x.b.a is the set of values obtained by navigating a from all values in x.b and concatenating the results.

One end of an association may be shown as composite (indicated by a black diamond). If class A has a composite association to class B (black diamond appears at the A end) labeled b, then the values of x.b for any x of class A are said to be owned by x. This has deletion semantics—if x is deleted then all x.b's will be deleted also. In contrast, if b was non-composite then the values in x.b would not get deleted when x was deleted; they are only being referred to by x, and will be owned by some other element. We often refer to composite associations as ownership associations.

Datatypes are primitive, in the sense that when a metamodel is processed, e.g., to generate code for a modeling tool, a datatype will map to a predefined type implemented in the supporting framework. It is assumed that it is at least possible to ask whether or not two values of a datatype are equal.

It is an underlying assumption of the metamodeling language used here, that all elements except a single root element must be owned by some other element; thus there must be at least one composite association targeted on every concrete class except one. The idea that a single root element simplifies how to think about a model was identified in Syntropy [CD94], in which it was called the "initial object".

The metamodel corresponds systematically to the BNF definition.

With careful observation, we can see that the metamodel mimics the BNF definition. For example, the first BNF rule `Model ::= (ModelElement)*` is mimicked by the ownership association between `Model` and `ModelElement` in the metamodel. `Model` is the only class that is not the target of an ownership association.

In general, non-terminals in the BNF are represented as classes in the metamodel (though see below). Ownership associations correspond to production rules: they are sourced on the class representing the non-terminal on the left-hand side of a production, and targeted on an element in the right-hand side of the production rule. Thus a `Model` owns `ModelElements` (corresponding to production 1), and a `Class` owns `Features` and an optional `StateMachine` (corresponding to production 3). `Identifier` has been modeled as a datatype. Hence the attribute `name:Identifier` is declared inside `Class`.

Some non-terminals in the BNF definition were used in order to make the definition more readable, for example `ClassName`. These have been omitted in the metamodel definition, where other techniques are available to improve readability, such as giving names to attributes.

Multiplicities are given to associations corresponding to the *, + and ? annotations in the BNF as follows:

- **BNF** * annotation, meaning zero or more, maps to the * annotation in the model which also means zero or more.

- **BNF** + annotation, meaning one or more, maps to 1..* in the model.

- **BNF** ? annotation, meaning optional, maps to 0..1 in the model.

- No annotation on the BNF maps to 1 in the model.

For example, classes have a sequence of features (* multiplicity, * annotation used in production 3), but only optionally a state machine (0..1 multiplicity, ? annotation used in production 3), and a state machine must have a root state (1 multiplicity, no annotation in production 19).

All ownership associations are bidirectional. This allows a child to navigate back up to its parent, which can be useful when writing well-formedness constraints (see later). The multiplicity on the reverse end is 1, if there is only one possible kind of owner (for example, features can only be owned by classes), otherwise it is 0..1 (states can be owned by a state machine or other states).

The non-composite associations are derived from those BNF rules where it has been necessary to have a reference to some other node in the tree. One advantage of a metamodel is that objects can directly reference other objects; an instance of a metamodel is not an object tree, but an object graph. For example, in production 23 a transition has a reference to a method and a reference to a state. These become associations in the metamodel, labeled `invoked` and `target`, respectively. Reference associations are all unidirectional, to accurately reflect the BNF grammar.

Where a BNF rule specifies alternatives, there are different ways of representing them in a metamodel.

Where a rule is of the form X ::= Y1 | ... | YN, Y1 ... YN have been made subclasses of X. This captures the idea that X can be any one of these. For example, `Attribute` and `Method` inherit from `Feature`, by production 5. This raises an interesting question as to what to do with rules of the form X ::= Y, where Y has no further structure. There are two cases worthy of note in the BNF: productions 2 and 19. Production 2 states that a model element has a class, and this we have shown on the metamodel by `Class` inheriting from `ModelElement`. That is, class is a kind of model element. This decision comes from the expectation that there may be other model elements to be introduced in a future version of the grammar, when production 2 would then take on the form X = Y1 | ... | YN. In contrast production 19 says that a `StateMachine` has a `State`. There is no expectation that a `StateMachine` will in future be a State or something else. Furthermore, if `State` inherited from `StateMachine` then it must be owned by a class, which conflicts with the possibility that it might be owned by a `State`. We conclude that this relationship should be represented some other way. One option, which is our design choice, is to represent it as an ownership association in the metamodel. Another option might be for `StateMachine` to inherit from `State`, but then it would be possible to have state machines as child states of other states, which is not what is intended here.

Abstract Syntax Graphs

Figure 8.6 shows a fragment of the car rental model as an instance of the metamodel, notated using UML-like object diagram notation. An object is depicted by a box, and the metamodel class[3] of the object is shown in the form :X. Some objects have more than one class, by inheritance. For example, an Attribute is also a Feature. Values for metamodel attributes are shown in an attribute compartment. Reference and ownership links between objects are depicted using the lines one would expect. Comparing this with the equivalent AST representation, notice that the ownership links, by themselves, form a tree; add the reference links and you have a graph. This is, therefore, an *abstract syntax graph* (*ASG*). Furthermore, the ability to put attribute values in a compartment of an object helps to make the diagram concise.

A metamodel represents an abstract syntax graph (ASG).

Finally, the reader should beware that not all metamodels are built as systematically as this, and certainly not to correspond so neatly with BNF—although it might be a good idea if they were. Doing so here enables us to compare and contrast the two styles of definition.

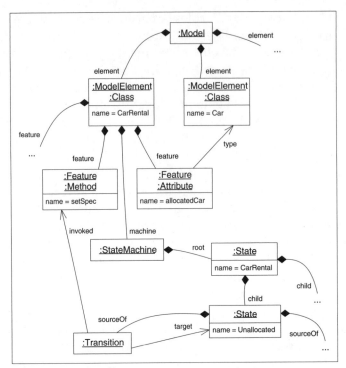

Figure 8.6   Car rental model as metamodel instance

UNIFIED MODELING LANGUAGE

The Unified Modeling Language (UML) is a well-known notation that is useful for documenting object-oriented systems. In this chapter, we are using the UML notation in a couple of different ways: OSL is like a subset of UML, and we also use a UML-like language for metamodeling. The UML standard itself is a large and complex set of documents, which specifies abstract, concrete, and serialization syntaxes, and informal semantics. Unfortunately, these specifications are insufficiently precise to make UML usable on its own as a language for defining machine-processable artifacts. Appendix B discusses UML and its related technologies in some depth, and concludes that UML as defined is not very suitable as a basis for the definition of domain specific languages.

Once a text has been parsed into an AST, identifiers must be bound.

Well-Formedness Rules

In textual language processing, a text consisting of a long sequence of characters must first be analyzed and translated into an abstract syntax tree. This process is known as parsing. Once the text has been parsed, some contextual analysis must be performed. The first phase of this analysis is called *identification* or *binding* [Wat93]. This associates each application of an identifier with its declaration. For example, it would associate the `StateRef` child of the `Transition` node at the bottom of the AST in Figure 8.4 with the `State` node whose `StateName` resolves to `Unallocated`. How we store this information is not relevant here. Suffice it to say that we would use some kind of look up table. See [Wat93] for more detail.

In the process of identification, scope rules are enforced. These ensure that, for example, a transition is between two states in scope, which, in this case, means the states must belong to the same state machine; also that the identifier for a transition must identify a method for the class with which the state machine is associated.

Scope rules are enforced.

OBJECT CONSTRAINT LANGUAGE

UML has its own language for expressing constraints, called the Object Constraint Language, or OCL for short. We use an OCL-like language in this chapter to express well-formedness rules and other constraints.

A class may have a set of constraints associated with it. A constraint is an equation that must hold before and after every change to the class. The two sides of the equation are expressions that refer to the attributes and associations of the class, and other objects that can be navigated to via these attributes and associations. OCL expressions can also use arithmetical and logical operators such as +, -, and, or.

Taking the car rental system as an example, there might be a constraint on the `CarRental` class that the allocated car must have the same specification as the requested car. In OCL this would be written as follows:

```
CarRental
  allocatedCar.specification = reservedSpec
```

An OCL expression must hold true for all objects of the class within which it is written. The expression is actually written in the context of an arbitrary object, which is denoted in OCL by the keyword `self`. So the previous expression could have been written as follows:

```
CarRental
  self.allocatedCar.specification = self.reservedSpec
```

(continued)

OCL expressions often denote collections of objects, rather than single objects. The language includes a library of operations that manipulate collections; for example, the `select` operation takes a collection and extracts from it the subcollection for which the select expression holds. Taking the same example, if `cars` represents a set of Cars and `carSpec` represents a CarSpecification, the expression

```
cars->select(specification = carSpec)
```

results in the subcollection of `cars` whose specification is `carSpec`. Note that collection operations are applied using an arrow, rather than a dot.

OCL expressions can also be used to define the results of *query* methods on classes, i.e., methods that do not change the state of the object. An example appears in the well-formedness rules in the main text.

OCL can be used to express scope rules.

Using OCL we can express one of the scope rules suggested above:

```
Transition
    target.root().machine = source.root().machine
```

which says that there is a constraint on the `Transition` class requiring the machine of the root of the target state to be the same as the machine of the root of the source state for all transitions. `root()` is a method on the `State` class, defined recursively as follows:

```
State::root() : State {
    if parent = null then self else parent.root()
}
```

That is, if the state has no parent then the root is itself, otherwise, it is the root of the parent state.

OCL can also be used to do type checking.

The second phase of contextual analysis is type checking. This has to check, for example, that the type of thing assigned to an attribute in a method body is the same as the type of that attribute. This can be captured in a well-formedness rule as:

```
AssignmentStatement
    lhs.type = rhs.type
```

Comparison of CFGs and Metamodels

So far, the differences between the metamodeling approach and the CFG approach to defining abstract syntax can be summarized as follows.

There are several differences between metamodels and CFGs.

- In a metamodel, the ability to give names to attributes can make it easier to record the intentions of the language designer. For example, in the BNF production 22 there is no indication that `StateRef` actually refers to the target of the transition. This is sometimes got around in BNF by allowing labels to be used within productions, so production 22 might have been written

  ```
  Transition ::=  invoked MethodRef  target StateRef
  ```

  where **invoked** and **target** are just convenient labels to aid readability.

- Related to the first point, is the tendency in a CFG to introduce additional levels of indirection to improve readability. For example, the rules for State has `StartState` on the right-hand side that is then resolved to `StateRef`. This enhances readability—it is redundant otherwise.

- Partly due to the previous point, there are a number of rules of the form X ::= Y, where Y has no further structure. We have discussed various ways in which rules such as these can be represented in the metamodel, where intuition about the language designer's probable intentions is used to inform the decision on which representation to choose. In these cases the metamodel is able to record a language designer's intentions more clearly than a CFG.

- A metamodel specifies a family of object graphs, whereas a CFG specifies a family of trees. So in a metamodel, direct referencing of objects by objects other than the owner can easily be achieved using plain attributes. In contrast, CFGs require Ref non-terminals to be introduced. It is only the names of these non-terminals that give a clue to the language designer's intentions. Furthermore, an abstract syntax tree needs to undergo further processing to resolve these references (known as *identification* or *binding*) before any semantic processing can take place.

- The fact that classes define a self-contained namespace, means that it is not necessary to distinguish between, e.g., ClassName, AttributeName, and so on in a metamodel. The fact that an attribute `name` is declared inside `Class` and `Attribute`, respectively, is sufficient qualification.

- The metamodel can be viewed as a diagram, which, arguably, makes it easier to understand the definition. On the other hand, there is no reason why a metamodel could not be expressed textually; or, for that matter, why a CFG could not be expressed graphically.

- A metamodel definition with well-formedness rules is more complete than a CFG definition, where implicit rules are built into the code that does contextual analysis—identification and type checking.

A metamodel is richer in what it can express.

In summary, there are many similarities between a CFG and a metamodel. However, a metamodel is richer in what it can express and is able to make finer-grained distinctions in the definition of a language. A CFG is optimized for machine processing of text, as generation of ASTs from text strings can be easily automated, by looking for separators such as commas and brackets. But before ASTs can be used as input to any form of semantic processing they have to undergo a further phase of contextual analysis, which through the process of identification, effectively turns an AST into an ASG. In this way, ASTs are a natural stepping stone to ASGs for formal textual languages. However, graphical languages are generally graph-structured not tree-structured. This, perhaps, is one reason why metamodeling has emerged as the preferred way of defining the abstract syntax of languages, such as UML, which use graph-based syntaxes extensively.

To process mixed languages effectively, we must integrate the approaches.

In conclusion, to process mixed graphical and textual languages effectively, we must integrate the CFG approach with the metamodeling approach. The richer and more complete definition of abstract syntax is a metamodel, whose instances are abstract syntax graphs (ASGs) not trees (ASTs). Well-formedness rules explicitly capture rules that are usually implicit in the implementations of tools that process ASTs. CFGs should be seen as useful stepping stones for processing textual parts of language, where the end result of that processing should be an ASG in preparation for semantic processing.

Concrete Syntax

The purpose of a concrete syntax is to render language elements and combinations thereof in a form that can be interpreted and produced by users of the language. For mechanical users of the language we use a particular kind of concrete syntax that we call serialization syntax, which is dealt with in the next section. Here we are particularly concerned with the form of the concrete syntax that is used by human users. We consider both text and graphics.

A textual representation of an expression is simply a string of characters, which may contain delimiters, line breaks, comments, and so on. In order to convert that string into an abstract syntax tree (AST), we must go through a process called parsing, which has two main steps:

To convert a textual representation into an AST it must be parsed.

- Lexical analysis, which converts the string into a sequence of separate tokens such as names and numbers. This is the process where recognition of delimiters, escape sequences, comments, and white space is important. A lexical grammar can be used to define how tokens are identified and separated.

- Syntactic analysis, which converts the sequence of tokens into an abstract syntax tree (AST). This is the process where such concepts as bracketing and operator precedence are important.

The reverse process, to output a string from an AST is straightforward: a simple tree-walking algorithm traverses the tree in the appropriate order, emitting appropriate textual tokens for each node that it encounters, and keeping track of the output position in order to emit appropriate formatting information.

Outputting text from an AST is simple.

We will not go into further detail on handling textual concrete syntaxes, since that is a widely understood subject. Our main focus here is the definition of graphical concrete syntaxes. As graphical languages like UML have emerged in the industry, it is notable that little work has been done on the rigorous definition of graphical concrete syntax, or on the mapping of the concrete syntax to the abstract, and that little or no support has been given to the developers of tools that process graphics, as well as text. In contrast, techniques have been developed over many years for processing textual languages, focusing on automated parsing and analysis. There are also tools that process

Our focus is the definition of graphical concrete syntaxes, an overlooked subject in the industry.

tree-based grammars to partially generate programs that automate tasks like parsing textual concrete syntax and rendering equivalent abstract syntax. We want to treat both models and programs as first-class development artifacts, subjecting them to machine processing. We also wish to use languages for modeling and programming that have interactive graphical content. These goals imply that the techniques used for the definition of interactive graphical languages and for the development of interactive graphical tools must be on a par with those for textual languages. Furthermore, as graphical syntax almost always embeds textual syntax, and sometimes gets mixed with it for coverage of the whole language, metamodeling techniques must be integrated with techniques for processing CFGs. We will see later that this is an achievable goal, and we will outline what needs to be done to achieve it.

We introduce a technique for representing the concrete syntax of a graphical language.

We introduce here a technique for defining a concrete syntax for an interactive graphical language. We return to our example language, and look first at the part of it that depicts state machines. Our objective is to create a representation that shows efficiently how a state machine is represented on a two-dimensional surface by interactive shapes. Such a representation can be used by tool developers to manually construct appropriate interfaces to interact with the concrete syntax, or even to wholly or partially generate such tools.

Here are some observations that characterize this syntax.

Figure 8.7 shows the state machine from our earlier example, depicted graphically. Our representation for graphical concrete syntax must describe what symbols are used to represent the

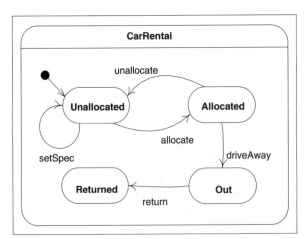

Figure 8.7 A state machine in graphical concrete syntax

information, and how these symbols are laid out. Here is a set of observations that characterize this syntax:

- A state is depicted by a rectangle with rounded corners. We call this a *roundangle*.

- The name of a state without children appears in the centre of its roundangle.

- The name of a state with children appears in a compartment at the top of its roundangle, separated by a straight line.

- A state machine has no separate notation; it is depicted by the symbol for its root state.

- Child states are topologically nested (i.e., placed anywhere, as opposed to being listed or laid out on a grid) inside their parents, in the compartment below the straight line, and may not overlap.

- Transitions are represented by arrows from the source state to the target state.

- The names of the methods corresponding to transitions appear adjacent to the transition arrows.

- The start state is designated by a small black blob connected to it via an arrow.

SUBTLETIES OF NOTATION AND INTERACTION

The conscientious reader will notice that many additional questions might be asked about this characterization, such as these:

- ◆ How are symbols selected, moved, copied, and deleted?

- ◆ Are transitions allowed to cross each other, or to cross state symbols?

- ◆ Are the sizes of symbols calculated from their contents, or separately determined?

- ◆ What typefaces are permitted for text embedded within the diagram?

- ◆ Are there any restrictions on the lengths of lines?

- ◆ How is the positioning of the names of transitions determined?

(continued)

Such questions would have to be addressed in a complete treatment, but our purpose here is only to show some basic principles, so we omit the details. In practice, effective treatment of such subtleties can make all the difference between a good and a poor implementation. Other elements of user interface behavior, such as zooming, collapsing, hiding, and mode-handling are also crucial aspects of the overall user experience. Providing a really effective user interface to a graphical language remains something of an art form, and it is a pity that most currently available tools that support graphical modeling languages are not very good at it, compared with interactive design tools for other disciplines.

We annotate the metamodel.

We represent these observations in the form of annotations that label the metamodel. Figure 8.8 shows the part of the OSL metamodel that defines state machines, decorated by

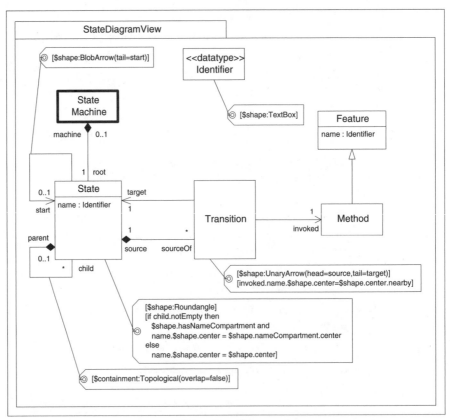

Figure 8.8   Annotated metamodel for state diagram view

annotations that define how the represent elements are depicted in a view called StateDiagramView, i.e., so that they look like Figure 8.7.

The annotations in Figure 8.8 comprise a set of constraints that can potentially be transformed into executable code that implements a graphical editor.

Firstly, notice that this metamodel has been enclosed in a context called StateDiagramView. In general, concepts in a language may be depicted in many views, and in one or more different ways in each view. The annotations in this figure show how these concepts are depicted in this particular view.

The annotated metamodel defines one kind of diagram.

Within this view, the class StateMachine has been shown with a thick black line around it. What this tells us is that in order to create one of these diagrams, the abstract syntax must be traversed as a tree, starting from a particular StateMachine, and following the ownership (black diamond) links.

Each annotation consists of a set of constraints, each contained in square brackets, and written using an extended version of our OCL-like language. Many of the constraints contain the term $shape. This word denotes an object that represents the graphical shape that corresponds, on this diagram, to the annotated element.[4] When an element has a $shape there is a constraint on its type; for example, the [$shape: Roundangle] constraint on State tells us that the shape object for a State has the type Roundangle. Similarly, the [$shape: UnaryArrow(head=source, tail=target)] constraint for Transition tells us that the shape for a Transition has the type UnaryArrow, and furthermore this arrow is constrained so that its head is tied to the source State, and its tail to the target State.

The term $shape refers to the graphical shape that depicts the annotated element.

Constraints that annotate a composite association specify how the containment corresponding to that ownership is manifested graphically. In the case of the ownership by States of other, nested States, the constraint $containment: Topological(overlap=false) tells us that the symbols for child states are topologically nested within the area that depicts the parent State. As with $shape, the term $containment defines the visualization of the associated element only for the current diagram.

The term $containment indicates how ownership is shown.

The remaining constraints define relative positioning of the shapes. For example, the constraint [invoked.name.$shape .center=$shape.center.nearby] on Transition tells us that the TextBox, that is, the shape corresponding to the name

Other constraints define positioning.

Figure 8.9 Concrete syntax for an OSL class

of the invoked method has its center at a place that is near the center of the shape corresponding to the Transition. A full interactive implementation of `nearby` is clearly a complex matter, but need not be exposed at the level of these constraints.

Constraints use navigation expressions.

Within constraints such as the one in the previous paragraph are navigation expressions that refer both to the metamodel attributes (such as `invoked.name`), as well as to attributes which are assumed to be defined in the definitions of the types of object used in the graphical syntax (such as `$shape.center`). The definitions of these graphical types are not included here; they would appear in a separate library of shapes designed for the assembly of concrete graphical syntaxes.

A concrete syntax for classes also handles embedded text.

We use a similar approach to show how the graphical syntax for OSL classes, such as the one shown in Figure 8.9, is specified. There is an additional matter to be handled here, which is that the lines of text embedded in the diagram that represent the attributes and methods have a textual concrete syntax that can be conveniently specified using BNF. We see in Figure 8.10 that this is dealt with by constraining `$shape` to have the type `BNFTextBox`, which takes two parameters, the first being the identity of the model element that is to be rendered in a textual syntax, and the second being a string that represents the right-hand side of the BNF production rule required to render the model element.

The format of embedded text is defined by a grammar string.

The parameter MethodGrammar is a string of the following form:

```
MethodGrammer = "name '('argument.name ':' argument
.type.name ')'"
```

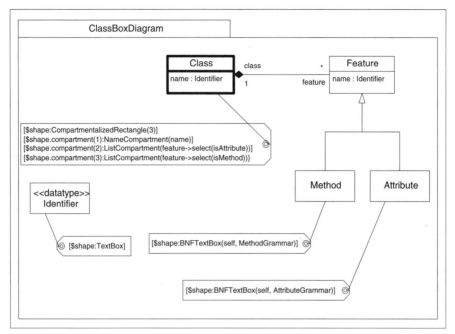

Figure 8.10 Annotated metamodel for class notation

where the navigation expressions such as argument.type .name follow the associations defined in the metamodel shown in Figure 8.5, starting at the method object itself. Thus for the method setSpec of the class CarRental, this rule produces the text "setSpec(spec:CarSpecification)", which is placed in a suitably sized box and inserted into the diagram.

The annotations on the metamodel show what kinds of shapes can be associated with the elements in the abstract syntax graph, and how these shapes are constrained. What they do not, and in general cannot, show is the actual layout of these shapes within these constraints in any particular case. Usually, layout is determined by the user by interacting with the shapes using the mechanisms of the design tool's graphical drawing surface, in order to create an aesthetically pleasing result that communicates the intent of the model effectively. This means that for a particular model, layout information has to be stored in addition to elements of the abstract syntax. Layout can include positioning information for shapes as well as color, density, line width, typeface, and similar information. What layout information is actually stored is determined by the graphical library that defines the kinds of shapes and their interactive behavior. Layout information is normally kept in

Layout information must be stored for particular models.

```
<Class name = 'CarRental'>
    <Attribute name = 'allocatedCar' type = 'Car' />
    <Attribute name = 'reservedSpec' type = 'CarSpecification' />
    <Method name = 'setSpec'>
            <Argument name = 'spec' type = 'CarSpecification' />
    </Method>
    <Method name = 'allocate'>
            <Argument name = 'c' type = 'Car' />
    </Method>
    <Method name = 'unallocate' />
    <Method name = 'driveAway' />
    <Method name = 'return' />
</Class>
```

Figure 8.11   XML for ASG fragment of car rental model

the same physical store as the elements in the abstract syntax graph, so that the information can be persisted and serialized in the same way.

Serialization Syntax

The primary purpose of serialization syntax is to render expressions of the language in a form that allows them to be persisted or interchanged between tools.

The primary purpose of serialization syntax is to render expressions of the language and associated layout information in a form that allows them to be persisted or interchanged between tools. One option is to use one of the existing concrete syntaxes. So, for example, the standard way to persisting or interchange expressions in C# or Java is using their textual notations. Another, increasingly popular, alternative is to use XML. Using XML the CarRental class in our sample OSL model could be serialized as shown in Figure 8.11.

XML NOTATION

XML is, essentially, a notation for describing tree structures. Nodes in the tree are represented by paired opening and closing tags, which take the form <a ...> and </a>, respectively. Nodes in the tree are typed by the label of the tag which is a in <a>; the opening and closing tags must use the same label. Child nodes are shown by nesting tag pairs within the tag pair for the parent node. In the example, the section <class ...> ...</class> represents a class node. Its children are attribute and method nodes.

(continued)

XML NOTATION *(continued)*

A node may also be attributed, which is shown by placing the attributes with their values within the opening tag. In the example, class nodes have name attributes, and the value of the name attribute for the class that is serialized is 'CarRental'.

Finally, if a node only has attributes, but no children, then the closing tag can be omitted, and instead a forward slash can be inserted at the end of the opening tag, as in <a ... />. This has been done for attribute and argument nodes, and some method nodes, in the example.

That is, a class has a name and is composed of attributes and methods. Attributes and methods each have names, and methods may also have arguments. Arguments each have a name, and attributes and arguments have a type. As OSL is quite simple, it is sufficient to refer to the type using the name of the class. One could produce a corresponding XML Schema Definition (XSD), which would define the tags allowed in XML documents for OSL, the attributes associated with those tags and which tags could be nested within which others. Translations between XML documents in this form and OSL ASGs would be relatively straightforward to define and implement.

One could produce a corresponding XML Schema Definition.

In this example, we have essentially designed XML syntax specifically for OSL. A different approach would be to design a general scheme for mapping ASGs to XML that will work with any metamodel. Consider how this might work. Every class in a metamodel maps to a tag in the XML, where the name of the tag is the name of the class. So, for the fragment of OSL covered by the XML previously, there would be tags for Class, Attribute, Method and Argument. We exclude abstract classes in this mapping. Containment relationships can be shown by nesting elements, though to deal with cases where there may be two containment relationships between the same two classes (for example, if OSL was extended to have public and private features), a tag must also be introduced for the role name of the relationship; e.g., feature in the model. Datatype attributes in the metamodel would be treated as tag attributes in the XML, so Class has a name attribute, for example. Reference associations between classes, for example, the type of an Attribute, could be dealt with by including an attribute in the tag for the source of the reference, whose value is the value

Another approach would be to design a general serialization scheme that will work with any metamodel.

```
<Class name = 'Car' id = '1'>
...
</Class>
<Class name = 'CarSpecification' id = '2'>
...
</Class>
<Class name = 'CarRental' id = '3'>
     <feature>
             <Attribute name = 'allocatedCar' type = '1' id = '3.1'/>
             <Attribute name = 'reservedSpec' type = '2' id = '3.2'/>
             <Method name = 'setSpec' id = '3.3'>
                    <Argument name = 'spec' type = '2' id = '3.3.1' />
             </Method>
             <Method name = 'allocate' id = '3.4'>
                    <Argument name = 'c' type = '2' id = '3.4.1' />
             </Method>
             <Method name = 'unallocate' id = '3.5'/>
             <Method name = 'driveAway' id = '3.6'/>
             <Method name = 'return' id = '3.7'/>
     </feature>
</Class>
```

Figure 8.12   XML generated using generic scheme

of a distinguishing attribute of the thing being referenced, for example, the value of the name attribute for Class. However, this presumes that every class in the metamodel has appropriate distinguishing attributes, such as a name attribute. As this can not be guaranteed, a more general approach is to implicitly assume that every class in the metamodel has an id attribute, and that the value of this attribute will be unique among objects. If we apply these rules, the XML for the CarRental class would appear as Figure 8.12.

The general scheme is more verbose.

This is more verbose than the simple version, but only a little. Surely the slight inefficiencies could be overlooked, given the potential benefit of the generic approach; once the general scheme has been defined, we get serialization for free every time a new language is defined.

There is a more serious drawback—the format is brittle.

Unfortunately, there is another drawback to this approach which has more serious consequences. The mapping between metamodel and XML is fixed by the general scheme; it is defined once and applies to all metamodels. This means that whenever the metamodel changes the XML format is likely to change, making the XML format brittle. For example, an earlier metamodel for OSL may not have had a Feature class, and instead had containment associations directly from `Class` to `Attribute` and `Method`, labeled `attribute` and `method`, respectively. Making this change to the metamodel would cause the XML in Figure 8.12 to change.

So, using a generic scheme, the XML format is sensitive to any change being made in the metamodel or the generic mapping rules, and as new versions of the metamodel or rules are developed, there is no guarantee that XML documents conforming to the format dictated by older versions will match the format of XML corresponding to the new versions. This means that any tools based on the old versions will not be able to exchange models with tools based on the new versions, and that updating a tool to the new version will require migration tools to be built to protect the investment of those using the old version. It is imperative, therefore, that changes to serialization syntax are made infrequently.

The generated XML format is sensitive to any change being made in the metamodel.

But metamodels may be refactored for all sorts of good reasons, for example, to accommodate new language extensions, or to organize languages into a family, or just to improve the efficiency of tools (in the final section we shall discuss the generation of modeling tools from metamodel definitions).

Metamodels may change for good reasons.

In other words, metamodels and serialization syntax should be allowed to change at different rates, and not be lock-stepped by a general XML mapping scheme. Instead, the XML syntax should be designed on a language-by-language basis, so that the language designer has the flexibility to change the mapping to accommodate different rates of change on either side. This does not preclude the use of tools that capture good practice to help the designer build an XML syntax as quickly and effectively as possible.

Metamodels and serialization syntax should not be lockstepped.

Semantics

Semantics is a technical term for "meaning", which is often used in the definition of formal languages. There are two styles of semantics that we'll consider here: *translational* and *trace-based*. These were chosen because they have particular practical relevance to the automated processing of domain specific languages. It is possible to define semantics using either style more or less formally. Various approaches to the form in which semantics are defined are also discussed.

There are two styles of semantics: translational and trace-based.

Translational Semantics

We can translate one language into another that has semantics.

The essence of a translational approach to semantics is to translate expressions in a language under study into another language that already has semantics. For example, the semantics of a programming language like C# can be defined by translation to the intermediate language IL, whose semantics can then be defined by translation to the instruction set of a particular CPU platform.

Translations may be defined informally, or formally, perhaps by a compiler.

Each of these translation steps may be defined informally, by describing the translation rules using a natural language, possibly illustrated by examples. They may also be defined formally using another formal language. In this case, to gain the most practical benefit, the second language might be a directly executable language, such as a machine instruction language, or, it might be a language that can be translated into a directly executable language. C#, for example, is first translated into IL, as described earlier. From there, the IL can be directly executed by the common language runtime (CLR), or it can be translated again into the instruction language of the host machine by the just-in-time (JIT) compiler.

USING MATHEMATICS TO DEFINE LANGUAGES

Mathematics is a formal language that can be used to define the semantics of other languages. When the term *formal semantics* is used in the literature, it usually means semantics expressed using the language of mathematics. For example, there are now mathematical semantics for IL [GS01]. The advantage of using mathematics is that one can use it to prove interesting properties of the language in question, such as the property of type safety, which requires that well-typed programs do not lead to untrapped execution errors. It is worthwhile constructing such semantics for languages, such as IL, which are then used as the basis of semantics for many other languages.

A mathematical semantics can also be useful as a reference against which to compare other semantics. There are many different translations from IL to the instructions sets of specific platforms. How does one guarantee that these are equivalent, in the sense that a piece of IL code compiled to different platforms has the same behavior to an external observer when executed? One approach is to make some observations for various test examples; another is to use the mathematical semantics as a reference point when defining these translations. In practice, one uses a combination of both.

SELF-DEFINITION AND THE BOOTSTRAP

If a language is defined using another language, the question that always arises is: What is used to define that other language? Is there ever a point at which we can stop? This applies not only to the definition of semantics, but also to the definition of syntax. There is a neat way out of this conundrum, which is to define the other language in itself, or possibly a kernel of itself. This may seem like a circular definition—Okay, it is a circular definition—but this is not a problem provided at least one of two conditions is satisfied:

◆ The language (or the kernel used) is small enough for its semantics to be understood by a large enough community that can agree. A reason for using mathematics to define other languages is that there is a large community with a rich heritage who are able to agree on a context independent meaning for the language of mathematics. The way that meaning surfaces is through axiomatic rules, the basis of proof, which, given a starting set of expressions in the language, will tell you what other expressions can be deduced. For example, a rule of algebra is that if $x - y > z$ then $x > y + z$; another is that $0 + y = y$. Using these rules one can deduce that if $x - y > 0$, then $x > y$.

◆ The language used to describe the semantics can be directly connected to observations of the real world. What is meant by this will become clearer when trace-based semantics is discussed later. However, it might be worth observing that the rules of algebra can be tested by filling in actual numbers for x, y, and z, and numbers can be directly related to reality by counting things.

Defining a language in itself has a very practical benefit: the bootstrap. This has been used in the development of programming languages for many years. One starts by defining the syntax of a kernel of a programming language, say in BNF, then one constructs a compiler or interpreter using some other language, which may just be machine instructions for a particular platform. When that is working sufficiently (not necessarily perfectly) one rewrites the compiler using the same programming language kernel, which is now executable. Thereafter, one uses the current version of the programming language to write the compiler (and, possibly, other language processing tools) for the next version. At each stage, one is bootstrapping the language from one version to the next.

In .NET, all programming languages are translated into IL.

In .NET, all source programming languages, including C#, Visual Basic and many others, are translated into IL. This lets programmers mix programming languages when writing applications, choosing them according to their suitability for the task at hand. For example, APL is a great language for engineering and financial calculations, but it is not much good for writing GUIs. In .NET, we might use VB for the GUI, but use APL for the under-the-bonnet stuff. Given this architecture, a lot of effort can be put into defining IL, and into understanding its semantics, knowing that that effort will be paid back many times over, once for every programming language that is mapped into IL.

Translation is usually the best way to give semantics to a programming language.

Translation is usually the most effective way to give semantics to a language. More generally, depending on the domains in which they operate, the semantics of domain specific languages are often, but not always, given most effectively by translation, sometimes into other domain specific languages, and sometimes into general-purpose languages. If the abstract syntaxes of both languages are defined as metamodels (sometimes they are not, such as when the target of the translation is a tree-based language), then it may also be possible to define the translation as a metamodel. A pattern for doing this is given in [AK02].

Trace-Based Semantics

A trace-based approach to semantics defines the meaning of a language in terms of its execution traces.

A trace-based approach to semantics defines the meaning of a language in terms of execution traces.[5] In order to understand how a program works, we execute it and watch what happens. Observations can be made in at least two ways.

- We can observe the output of the program. This may work provided the programmer has been thoughtful enough to make sure the program outputs enough information to support meaningful observations.

- We can use a debugging tool. This is generally more effective, especially when the intricate workings of the program must be understood. A debugging tool exposes the execution traces generated by the program in a form that lets us determine exactly what is going on. Given a debugging tool, and an understanding of the execution traces exposed by that debugging tool, then the meanings of language expressions used in a set of example programs can be understood by executing the programs and observing the execution traces exposed by the debugging tool.

In either case, success can be measured by the ability to write programs that generate the expected traces when executed.

In a trace-based semantics, an execution trace language is constructed and then mapped to expressions in the language whose semantics is being defined. The debugging tool in the preceding scenario uses an execution trace language to expose execution traces. An execution trace language may be either graphical or textual, and is usually highly interactive.

We can define the mapping between execution traces and language expressions *constructively*, using composition to show how an execution trace is generated by a program based on that language. For each atomic statement in a program (i.e., each statement that is not composed of other statements), we define its meaning by describing how it produces a new state (e.g., a configuration of objects with new attribute values) from a given state (e.g., a configuration of objects with given attribute values). Next, we define composite statements (i.e., statements that are composed of other statements), and show how each one produces a new state from a given state, using the meanings of its component statements. Finally, we use these definitions to construct an execution trace from a program, given a particular starting state.

Take `Statement` defined in OSL, as an example. A statement is a sequence of statements or an assignment statement. An assignment statement is an atomic statement: it is not composed of any other language elements, though it does reference a left-hand side and a right-hand side. The meaning of an assignment statement can be expressed in terms of its effect on a given starting state, where an attribute of the object denoted by the variable `self` is set to a particular value, to produce a new state, where the attribute is set to hold the value denoted by the expression on the right-hand side of the statement (which will either be another attribute or an argument of the method in which the assignment statement appears). The meaning of a composite statement is given by successively executing the sequence of statements from the starting state, where the starting state of the next statement is the state reached by executing the current one.

A language of execution traces is constructed and related to expressions in the language whose semantics is being defined.

The meaning of a statement can be expressed constructively in terms of its effect on a given state.

Alternatively, define the rules that say whether or not a given trace is valid.

Defining the mapping between traces and language expressions *constructively* is appropriate for imperative languages, since we can use expressions based on them to generate execution traces, given a particular starting state. However, it is not appropriate for declarative languages, since we can use expressions based on them only to constrain the range of execution traces that can be generated, given a particular starting state. We can also describe the mapping *descriptively* by defining rules that say whether or not a given trace is a valid trace of a particular declarative expression. Since the descriptive approach also works for imperative languages, it is more general than the constructive approach. Note, however, that unless the language permits the expression of concurrent executions there will only be one valid trace per starting state for a particular imperative expression.

The language for defining traces has a similar anatomy to the one it gives traces for.

It is possible to produce a descriptive definition of the semantics for a given language using the concepts already introduced for defining syntax by defining a language of execution traces. For example, the abstract syntax of a fragment of the trace language for OSL, is captured by Figure 8.13. Beginning at the top right, this exposes a model trace, which consists of a set of object traces. An object trace has a sequence of object values, and optionally, a state machine trace. A state machine trace has a sequence of state machine values, each of which has a single state value. The connection between object values and state machine values is exposed by a reference from `ObjectValue` to `StateMachineValue`. An `ObjectValue` also has a set of attribute values—there will be one for each attribute in the object's class. A `StateValue` can be the source of at most one transition occurrence (there will be no transition from the final state reached). This transition occurrence refers to a method invocation which has the effect of transforming an object value (`pre`) to another value (`post`), in the context of the method arguments. As methods can only set attributes in OSL, the difference between these object values, if any, will be in the attribute values they hold. Not all invocations must be associated with a transition occurrence (there may be methods not mentioned in the state diagram), and this is allowed by the definition.

An example trace.

Figure 8.14 shows a trace of the car rental model, using an invented concrete syntax for the trace language. The diagram provides a view on a model trace, which in this case contains three object traces each depicted by a line. An object trace is

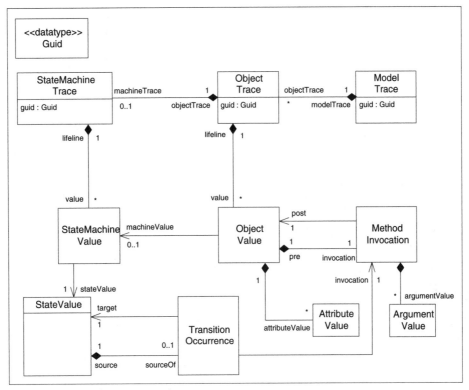

Figure 8.13 AS for OSL trace language

a sequence of object values, each of which is depicted by the UML notation for objects (a box). The guids (globally unique identifiers) of the object traces are shown as the part of the name preceding the colon of the first object value of the object trace. The class of the object trace (see Figure 8.15) is shown after the colon. Subsequent object values do not need to carry this information. If an object value is associated with a statemachine value, this is shown by including a state symbol inside the object value. Attribute values are shown in the form x = v, where x is the attribute name and v the value. In this case attribute values are either null, or references to other objects (01 and 02). Method invocations are indicated by a left to right arrow, labeled by the method and with argument values shown between brackets. The pre value of the method invocation is the object value just preceding it, and the post value is the one just following it. A transition occurrence is implicit in the method invocation, with the source (resp. target) state value being the value of the pre (resp. post) object value.

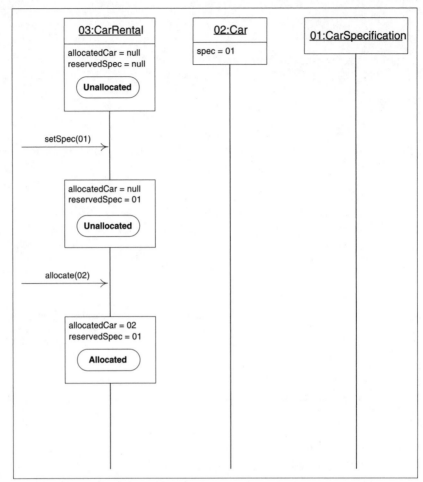

Figure 8.14 A trace of the car rental model

Additional well-formedness rules are needed, both for the trace language itself, and for its relationship to OSL.

There are several well-formedness rules that need to be associated with this definition. For example, a sequence of consecutive object values in the object trace can be associated with the same state machine value, as the state value may not have changed because a method was invoked without causing a transition to occur (some methods may not be mentioned on a state diagram). These rules could be encoded in OCL, although we will refrain from doing this here.

The relationship between the trace language and OSL is captured, in part, by Figure 8.15. In fact, this is part of the definition of the abstract syntax of the trace language, which is dependent on the abstract syntax of OSL.

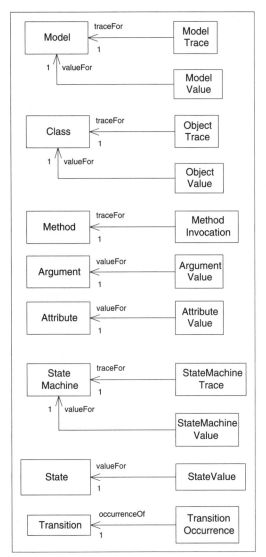

Figure 8.15 Relationship between OSL and OSL trace language

The more subtle aspects of the relationship are captured as well-formedness rules, for example, the root of the state corresponding to the state value of a machine value must be the root of the machine corresponding to that machine value; there must be exactly one attribute value in an object value, for each attribute in the class corresponding to the attribute value; the method associated with a method invocation referenced by a transition occurrence must be the method referenced by the corresponding transition. Other examples of using metamodels to define trace-based semantics can be found in [KGR99, CEK+00, AK02, 2U03].

The semantics of the trace language itself are defined by observation.

Finally, we return to the question of how to define the semantics of the trace language itself. We would argue that defining an explicit semantics is not necessary. At some point an external connection to reality has to be made and this cannot be explicitly written down. Traces are relatively easy to connect to reality: given an object, one can point to a concrete thing and say "this represents that"; it is much harder to find the concrete thing that corresponds to a class—one can only point to examples of things that may or may not be in that class. For further discussion of issues such as these see [Mon74].

Programming versus Modeling

The colloquial definitions arose historically, through differences in the concerns of platform and development tool vendors, and were cemented by popular development methodologies.

We discussed the distinction between programming and modeling in Chapter 7. As we suggested there, the colloquial definitions of these terms arose historically. Because platform vendors are generally more concerned with machine execution than with developer productivity, they tend to create imperative languages. Since development tools are an afterthought for many of them, they tend to create tree-based languages with textual notations, which are easier to process than graph-based languages, as we have seen. On the other hand, because development tool vendors are generally more concerned with developer productivity than with machine execution, they tend to create graph-based languages, which provide more expressive power than tree-based languages, as we have also seen. Since they are generally not interested in defining new platforms, they tend to create declarative languages. These historical accidents were firmly cemented into the collective thinking of the industry by the broad adoption of OOA& D in the early 1990s. Declarative graphical languages offered by development tool vendors were used to document software products, and textual imperative languages offered by platform vendors were used to implement them. This also established the widely held misconception that textual languages are more effective than graphical ones for developing software.

Recent trends suggest that the distinction between programming and modeling languages may soon become entirely irrelevant. While it is common to serialize declarative metadata using serialization syntaxes, such as XML, imperative logic has been serialized using textual notations designed for human consumption, and associated with programming languages. This is starting to change, however, as serialization syntaxes are increasingly intertwined with traditional programming language notations, as illustrated by the historical progression described below.

The definitions of software products will soon contain large amounts of declarative metadata, in addition to imperative logic, serialized using formats intended more for tools than for human consumption.

- Comment syntaxes, such as javadoc and xdoc, were added to programming languages to generate documentation.

- Markup language syntaxes, such as JSP and ASP.NET, were added to programming languages to describe web page layout.

- XML documents carrying declarative metadata, such as J2EE deployment descriptors, were added to packages containing compiled source code.

- XML fragments and language attributes, such as C# attributes, were added to programming languages to capture declarative metadata.

If this trend continues, it will not be long before software specifications contain large amounts of declarative metadata, in addition to imperative logic, using serialized formats intended more for tools than for human consumption.

Notes

1. Some authors would reserve the term "formal language" to mean a language specifically intended for treatment as a mathematical object. Our use of the term "formal" is wider, and includes all languages intended for processing by machines.
2. Some languages, such as Harel's Statecharts, have been given more than one semantics. We can see this as one language with many semantics, or many languages that share the same abstract and concrete syntax.

3. There is scope for confusion in the fact that OSL has Classes and Attributes, and its metamodel also has classes and attributes. We have attempted to alleviate this by capitalizing the names of metamodel classes such as Class and Attribute.

4. It is occasionally meaningful for an element to be represented by more than one shape on a diagram; additional shapes would have different names.

5. The term *trace-based semantics* is used in the formal semantics community in a specific way that involves a lot more mathematical rigor than we are applying here, including formal definitions for equivalence classes of traces. Our use of the term is looser, but in the same spirit.

Families of Languages

By Steve Cook and Stuart Kent

*The only rock I know that stays steady, the only institution
I know that works, is the family.*

Lee Iacocca

In the previous chapter we discussed in detail the parts of a formal language, and we showed how domain specific languages are defined in terms of these parts. In this chapter, we build on these ideas to show language components can be defined, and how families of languages can be defined using those components. We then describe the tools required to rapidly design and implement language family members.

Language Families

Chapter 5 showed how systematic reuse in software development can be achieved by defining families of related software products, and by developing assets that can be used to produce the family members from specifications of their variable features. The previous chapter described the elements used to construct a single domain specific language. We now observe that domain specific languages can be considered software products, and that economies of scope can be achieved in families of domain specific languages using the techniques described

DSLs are software products, and economies of scope can be achieved in families of DSLs using product line principles.

in Chapter 5. In addition, since software factories rely heavily on domain specific languages to support automation, as described in Chapter 7, the economical development of domain-specific languages is a key to the broad adoption of software factories.

Our metamodeling language is a DSL for defining DSLs.

All of the examples in the previous chapter were described using a UML-like metamodeling language, and a textual constraint language for describing well-formedness rules and annotations. We can think of the combination of these languages as a *domain specific language for defining domain specific languages*. It should be apparent with a little thought that this language can also be used to describe itself. With this observation, we see the possibility of bootstrapping a complete technology for the economical development of software factories. We will return to this topic in more depth in the second section of this chapter, where we discuss tools for defining and implementing domain specific languages.

We have effectively defined a family of DSLs.

In order to define a family of domain specific languages, we must identify the common and variable problem features among the family members. In order to develop a product line to produce the family members, we must develop common solution features with well-defined variation points. In fact, this is what we have been doing all along. In the previous chapter we effectively defined a family of domain specific languages, whose members have both graphical and textual components, and whose anatomies include concrete syntax, serialization syntax, abstract syntax, and semantics. We also identified variations in syntax and semantics, and we showed how they map to variations in language implementation using definitions based on metamodels, constraints that define their well-formedness, and annotations that map them to reusable concrete visual elements.

The language anatomy that we have described forms the product family architecture.

Armed with an understanding of this anatomy, we can observe that multiple domain specific languages of significant complexity have recognizably similar parts. In other words, the language anatomy that we have described defines the architecture of the family members. Recall from Chapter 4 that the architecture for the product family is the central asset of a software product line. A quick inventory shows that in addition to the architecture, we have the metamodeling and constraint languages and the processes for developing family members. With these assets already in hand, we can realize economies of scope in the production of domain specific languages by developing, components, patterns, and tools, and by reusing all of these assets systematically to assemble new languages from specifications.

Let's focus first on language components. One of the keys will be to define them at the right level of granularity. A single class is too small to be a meaningful language component. Languages can be successfully assembled from components that are larger than classes, however, and that may even be complete languages.

DSLs can be assembled from language components.

Observe that Our Simple Language (OSL) can be thought of as consisting of three smaller languages: a language for including model elements in models, a state modeling language, and a class modeling language. In fact the class modeling language can be decomposed further into even smaller languages. We will leave that as an exercise for the reader. It is easy to envisage other uses for the three sublanguages in other contexts:

OSL consists of three smaller languages.

- Almost every language will require the ability to include model elements in models.

- The class modeling language is a simple version of the metamodeling language that we have used throughout this chapter, although the metamodeling language has no associated concept of state machines.

- The state modeling language, on the other hand, might be used with many kinds of things other than classes, such as user interfaces, Web services, protocols, or hardware components.

Furthermore, each of these sublanguages can be defined completely in terms of concrete syntax, abstract syntax, and semantics. A very common mistake made by modeling language designers is to concentrate only on the abstract syntax. Typically, the reasoning goes a bit like this. Since a metamodel is more-or-less equivalent to an object-oriented program, and since the primary reuse mechanism in object-oriented programming is inheritance, it is appropriate to use inheritance as the primary mechanism for constructing new languages from existing ones. In practice, this approach is rarely successful. It makes the erroneous assumption that a single class is the appropriate unit of language composition. Instead, as we will show, a much

Each sub language is a complete language, and can be parameterized to form a pattern or template.

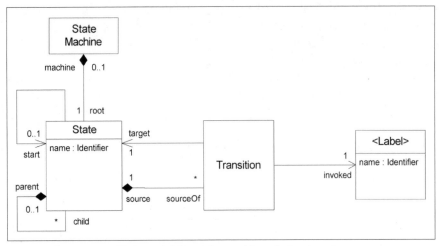

Figure 9.1   Metamodel for state machine abstract syntax

more effective technique is to construct whole components, including concrete syntax, abstract syntax, and semantics, to parameterize these components to form patterns or templates, and to use model mapping techniques to assemble them into composite languages.

We look in detail at the state machine sublanguage.

In the interests of space, we will look at just one of the sublanguages, the state machine language, and show how it can be separately defined and composed with other language components. Once we understand the technology for putting these parts together, the assembly of larger languages from smaller ones becomes quite natural.

Figure 9.1 shows the abstract syntax for the state modeling language on its own. This differs slightly from the metamodel for the complete OSL in which it was combined with the class modeling language, because transitions now refer simply to labels, instead of to methods. In the componentized version we can think of the Label class as a *parameter* of the state modeling language definition, which can be combined with something

We can combine the state modeling sub language with the class modeling sublanguage using a glue model.

else when the state modeling language is combined with another language component. We indicate this on the diagram by surrounding the name of the class with angle brackets. By doing this, we effectively turn the state modeling language definition into a pattern or template definition.

Figure 9.2 shows the metamodel for the semantic domain, and Figure 9.3 shows the semantic mapping.

We can also define a graphical notation for this language, as shown in Figure 9.4. This is the same as the graphical notation

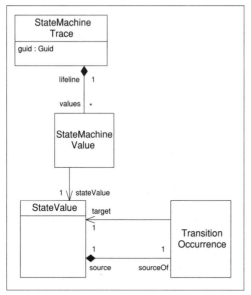

Figure 9.2 Metamodel for state machine semantics

definition in the previous chapter, except that transitions refer to labels instead of methods.

We now have a complete definition of the state modeling sublanguage, including concrete syntax, abstract syntax, and trace semantics. We now show how to combine it with a similar definition of the class modeling sub language. There are two stages to this process.

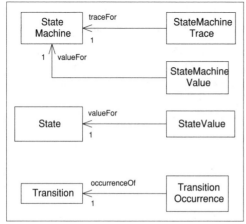

Figure 9.3 State machine semantic mapping

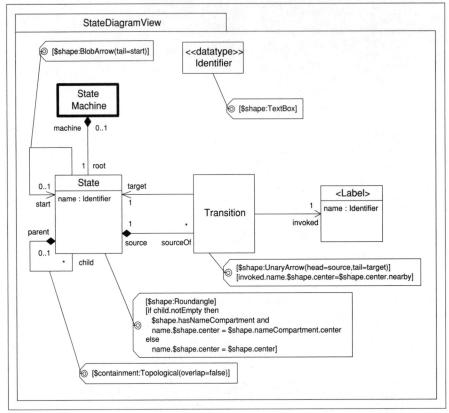

Figure 9.4 Concrete syntax for state modeling sublanguage

- First, we build a "glue" model, which defines how the class metamodel and the state metamodel are connected. A fragment of this model showing the part related to the abstract syntax is shown in Figure 9.5; other parts of the glue model concern the semantics and semantic mapping.

- Then, we merge the definitions of the two languages with the glue model, in order to create the composite language, substituting `Method` for `Label`, as indicated in Figure 9.6. The rules for merging are straightforward, and are basically these: when two metamodels

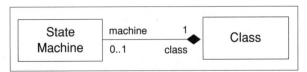

Figure 9.5 Fragment of glue model

contain classes of the same name, those classes are merged, and when two classes contain attributes of the same name and type, those attributes are merged.

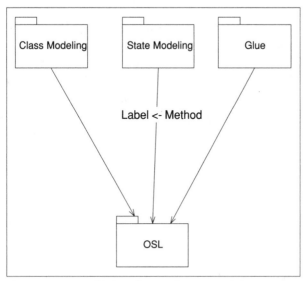

Figure 9.6   Combining class and state modeling

The preceding ideas are based on recent attempts at defining language families, in particular [CEK+00, 2U03, CEK03], which use the package template idea proposed by [DW98]. Attempts to provide a more formal treatment for this idea, such as [CEK02], have led us to conclude that model merging, including parameter substitution, is a special case of the model mapping problem, which is discussed in more detail in Chapter 7. As that chapter points out, there are many possible ways of implementing transformations between sets of models. The key observation is that both composite languages and language components can be defined as models, and as such can be subjected to model mapping techniques, just like models for any other domain.

Model merging is a special case of model mapping.

With the caveat that additional work would be required to define the product line scope more carefully, to describe the process in more detail, and to package the assets for consumption, we now have all of the elements needed to support a product line for this family of domain specific languages, except tools. These are the subjects of the next section.

Tool Factories

A tool factory is a software factory used to build tools for the members of a family of DSLs from specifications of the family members

Now that we have described how all of the parts of a DSL can be defined in a machine-processable way and put together to construct complete languages, we are ready to talk about tools that can process these definitions and turn them into tools for working with DSLs. A *tool factory* is a software factory used to build tools that manipulate and process the members of a family of DSLs from specifications of the family members. A software factory for building software factories may include tool factories for one or more families of DSLs, plus factories for the other assets that make up a software factory template, such as patterns, architectures, frameworks, and processes. We describe the architecture of a tool factory next, before discussing the state of the art in automating tool development.

Tool Factory Architecture

The Language Designer is a tool for designing family members.

Figure 9.7 gives a bird's eye view of the architecture of a tool factory for a family F of domain specific languages. In the diagram, ovals represent tools, rectangles with folded corners represent artifacts, solid arrows represent derivation, and dashed arrows represent generation. The Language Designer is a tool

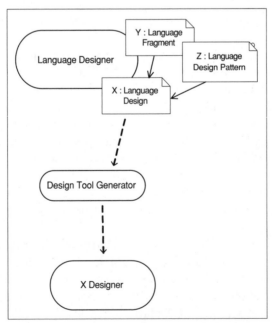

Figure 9.7 Overview architecture of a tool factory

for designing family members. The diagram shows a design for some language, X, created in the Language Designer. The design of X includes all of the pieces described in the previous chapter, including concrete syntax, abstract syntax, serialization syntax, and semantics.

The design of X is created in the Language Designer from language fragment, Y, and language design pattern, Z, defined for the language family, F. Language designs created in the Language Designer are fed into a Design Tool Generator, which generates part of a design tool for X. We use the term *designer* to mean a design tool, and the term *X-designer* to mean a design tool for the language named X.

The design tool for X is partially generated.

Figure 9.8 gives one perspective on the architecture of an X-designer, in terms of functional components. At the heart of the

At the heart of a designer is an in-memory-store (IMS).

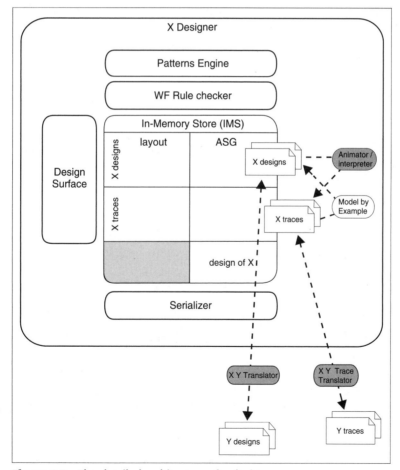

Figure 9.8 The detailed architecture of a designer

architecture is an *In-Memory Store* (IMS), which stores both the ASG and layout information for designs and traces expressed in the language X. The format of the information is dictated by the definition of X and its trace language, as discussed in the previous chapter. The IMS also stores a definition of X, which can be read by code that needs to interpret the language.

Several components work off the IMS.

The rest of the components work off the IMS. The *Design Surface* lets the user manipulate expressions and traces of X through their respective graphical and textual concrete syntaxes. It interacts with ASGs and layout information stored in the IMS, and manages graphical layout, as well as the display and parsing of text embedded in diagrams. The *Serializer* serializes ASGs and layout information from the IMS using the serialization syntaxes.

The Rule Checker checks the well-formedness rules.

The *Rule Checker* checks well-formedness rules over information stored in the IMS. Static code could be generated from rules language expressions, but a more powerful alternative is to enable the Rule Checker to interpret the rules language expressions dynamically. This lets the language designer experiment with rules before fixing them in the language definition. It also lets the language user build queries that retrieve information from models, and filters that control the display of models. Interpretation also makes the pattern engine, and external tools, such as the translators shown on the diagram, more powerful and easier to build.

The Pattern Engine supports the definition, application and evaluation of patterns.

We said in Chapter 6 that patterns can be defined, applied, and evaluated using tools. The *Pattern Engine* is a language-independent component that implements the model mapping techniques described in Chapter 15. It uses the IMS, the design surface and language specific extensions, to provide those automations. A critical component of the Pattern Engine is a Merge Engine, which merges the results of pattern evaluations with each other, and with the existing elements in the target models. The Pattern Engine can also store pattern applications in the IMS, so that they can be edited and reevaluated when the values of their arguments change, as described in Chapter 6.

Trace-based semantics are used by the 'Animator/ Interpreter' and 'Model by Example' components.

We also said in Chapter 6 that models can be animated or interpreted, and used to trace execution. The *Animator/Interpreter* and *Model by Example* components implement these automations using the trace-based semantics for X:

- The *Animator/Interpreter* implements the mapping from models to traces to provide either an interpreter, for an imperative language, or an animator, for a declarative language. An animator asks the user to decide any non-deterministic choices that it cannot resolve, while an interpreter always makes a choice.

- *Model by Example* implements the mapping in the opposite direction. It can automatically construct a partial model from example traces developed by the user (e.g., to illustrate particular problem scenarios) or recorded by an execution-tracing tool.

The *XY Translator* and *XY Trace Translator* are examples of tools that interact with designers. If Y is a general-purpose programming language, then the XY Translator might generate Y based code from X based models. However, if X is a business processes modeling language, and Y is a software architecture modeling language, the XY Translator might reconcile X and Y based models manipulated independently and concurrently by different users, as described in Chapter 4. In either case, the XY Translator would interact with the designers, but would not be embedded in them.

Translators generate code or models from models, or reconcile models that are edited concurrently.

The *XY Trace Translator* might be used, for example, to monitor execution traces generated by an X based system, and to display them through X based models. If X is a declarative language, then the XY Trace Translator might also be used for testing, by checking the traces against the X based models, to see if they satisfy them. If X is a business process modeling language, then the XY Trace Translator might also be used to generate a dashboard, where traces of the running business processes could be tracked.

A trace translator can be used for testing and dashboarding.

Figure 9.9 gives another perspective of the makeup of the X-designer. While our long-term vision is to generate complete

In the near term, part of an X-designer will be handcrafted.

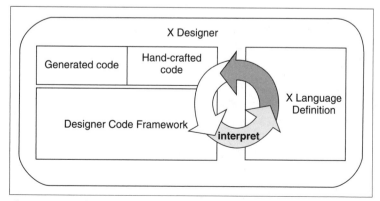

Figure 9.9 Where the code comes from

designers from language definitions, this will certainly not happen soon, so we expect some handcoding to take place. In keeping with the philosophy of software factories, code generation works best when the generated code completes an existing framework. Of course, there is a tradeoff between placing functionality in the generated code, and placing it in the framework. In practice, a combination of the two approaches usually works best.

The Language Designer is just another X-designer.

The Language Designer is just another X-designer, where X is the language for designing languages (LDL). Hence, it should have the same architecture as other designers, as illustrated in Figure 9.10. In particular, it is worth noting that in this case the pattern engine can be used to support the definition of language families. Figure 9.10 provides the last twist in the tale, observing that it should be possible to generate the LDL-designer from a definition of the language for designing languages (LDL). This allows the tool factory to bootstrap itself from one version to the next. In addition, provided the LDL is rich enough, it should be possible to define a mapping from

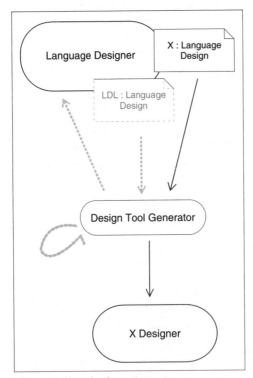

Figure 9.10 The bootstrap

language designs into the programming languages and frameworks used to implement designers, allowing the design tool generator to be bootstrapped, as well.

The State of the Art

Tools already exist that implement some of this architecture. We consider them in increasing order of how much they support.

Tools already exist that implement some of this architecture, but most of them implement a set of languages.

- First, there are conventional development environments, which only deal with textual programming languages. These can be very sophisticated in their support for program development, but they generally do not support graphical languages, nor the definition of new languages.

- Then, there are tools that support a fixed set of graphical languages, typically used for documentation within a specific development process. These tools generally do not support the definition of new languages.

- Then, there are tools that support a fixed set of graphical languages, together with code generation, intended for tighter integration into a specific development process. Sometimes such tools also provide "reverse engineering" facilities that translate code into diagrams.

  These tools generally do not support the definition of new languages, although some of the most sophisticated do allow the definition of minor extensions to their existing languages, often using facilities for defining and applying patterns. These tools often expose APIs that can be used to control them programmatically. These APIs typically covers the manipulation of models and diagrams. Some tools even provide their own scripting languages, which manipulate these APIs, letting users define patterns, serialization syntaxes, well-formedness rules, and even animations.

None of the tools listed so far provide any significant capabilities for designing new languages. Tools that do provide such capabilities are often called "meta-tools", because they interpret a metamodel to implement a language. Over the last few years, several meta-tools have been made commercially

Tools that interpret language definitions are called "meta-tools."

available. They support the definition and interpretation of ASGs and graphical notations, and usually provide ASG-driven scripting languages.

There are some pitfalls to be avoided with meta-tools.

Experience with commercial meta-tools reveals some pitfalls to be avoided:

- Because meta-tools usually interpret language definitions, instead of compiling them, performance, error-handling, and scalability to large models can be problems. Interpretation is attractive because it offers the advantage of flexibility, but this should not be bought at the cost of performance, error-handling, and scalability.

- Because meta-tools often interpret well-formedness rules immediately, they prevent the user from creating ill-formed models. Since ill-formed models are valid steps on the way to well-formed models, a tool that does not permit the creation of ill-formed models typically suffers usability problems.

Instead of interpreting language definitions, a better approach is to provide a library of language definition components in an IDE, and to let the user assemble languages from them using ordinary programming techniques.

Open-source meta-tools have appeared based on the OMG MOF.

Some open-source meta-tools have appeared based on the OMG Meta Object Facility (MOF). They generally take an abstract syntax expressed in MOF, and generate an in-memory store and serializer for that abstract syntax. The serializer implements the generic metamodel to XML mapping defined by the OMG XML Metadata Interchange (XMI®). These tools use a mixture of code generation and metamodel interpretation, and generate simple, form-based UIs to support interaction with the in-memory store. Examples include the Eclipse Modeling Framework and the NetBeans Metadata Repository, both of which are open source. Some commercial tools, such as IBM WebSphere Studio, are partially generated from these implementations.

KMF allows well-formedness rules to be interpreted.

The Kent Modeling Framework is a research vehicle that is similar to these MOF-based tools. In addition it accepts metamodels annotated with well-formedness rules expressed in OCL, and generates well-formedness rule checking code. Furthermore, it is able to interpret OCL expressions from within the generated tool. One of many applications of this feature is the ability to experiment with well-formedness rules over test populations as the metamodel is being designed.

Another research vehicle that explores similar ideas is the Generic Modeling Environment [LMB+] developed at the Institute for Software Integrated Systems at Vanderbilt University. GME is a configurable tool kit for creating domain-specific modeling environments. Its architecture is similar to the one described earlier, including support for constraints using OCL, and metamodel construction using a UML-like metamodeling language. GME is also defined in itself and bootstrapped, using the techniques we described earlier. GME claims to reduce the time needed to develop a modeling environment for the integrated simulation of embedded systems from several person-years down to one person-month.

GME is another research environment that demonstrates substantial productivity gains.

These tools have their strengths and weaknesses. EMF [EMF] and MDR [MDR] are focused on generating code that integrates with specific tools (Eclipse and Netbeans). However, they lack support for well-formedness rules and concrete syntax. KMF [KMF] provides this support, but the framework used by the generated code is primitive compared with the frameworks that sit beneath Eclipse and Netbeans. The main elements in our architecture that have been absent from most other meta-tools to date are dynamic pattern reevaluation, support for trace-based semantics, good model reconciliation, and self-definition. Without these elements, it is difficult to reuse language components, to build model-by-example or dashboard features, or to build the complete set of domain specific languages required by the schema for a software factory. In all of these cases, the usability of the designers could be improved significantly, and certainly is not on par with Interactive Development Environments (IDEs) from major vendors, such as Microsoft Visual Studio. For the user who wants to build a software factory today, however, existing tools can be integrated with an IDE to provide a significant portion of the tool factory.

These tools have their strengths and weaknesses.

Moving these tools into the mainstream is primarily an economic and cultural problem, not a technical one. A full-fledged tool factory is not a mass-market item; its customers will be organizations setting up software factories. In order to provide the economies that customers would expect to derive from this exercise, the tools would have to exhibit a level of engineering comparable to the IDEs available from major vendors.

Moving such tools into the mainstream is primarily an economic and cultural problem.

Furthermore, the tools produced by a tool factory must offer their users similar standards of usability to overcome their natural reluctance to use tools that do not demonstrably improve their productivity. We think we have shown that a significant amount of the theory necessary to build such tool factories is well known, however, and that tool factories are starting to appear in the marketplace today.

CHAPTER 10

Systematic Reuse

The software industry has a long history of recreating incompatible solutions to problems that are already solved

Pattern Oriented Software Architecture, Volume 2

In this chapter, we will look at family-based development, a critical innovation in development process that lays the foundation for software factories. We start with software product families, looking at why they are important, and how they arise. Next, we will see how systematic reuse relies on exploiting commonalities among the members of software product families. From there, we will examine software product lines. Finally, we will explore how software product lines can be connected to form software supply chains.

Software Product Families

Recall from Chapter 5 that economies of scope arise when multiple similar but distinct designs and prototypes are produced collectively, rather than individually, and that systematic software reuse exploits economies of scope. In this section, we will see that economies of scope arise naturally in families. Parnas [Par76] defines a family as a set of problems whose common subproblems can be solved collectively. We can generalize this definition to product families, specifically to software product

Economies of scope arise naturally in families.

families, where a product may be an end product, such as an application, or a component of an end product, such as a Web service.

Software as a Product

All software is produced to be consumed by a customer, if only by its producer.

Of course, you may not be accustomed to thinking of software as a product. If you've been developing software on a contract basis, or developing components of an end product for internal customers, you may draw a distinction between the product sold to a consumer in a shrink-wrapped box and the software you write. By talking about software products, we do not mean to limit our scope to shrink-wrapped software developers. On the contrary, software product families arise in many service-oriented scenarios, as we shall see later in this chapter. Our goal in talking about software products is to emphasize that all software is produced to be consumed by a customer, if only by its producer, and that in most cases, there are real costs associated with producing and consuming software, even if there is no explicit exchange of money. Only by thinking about software as a product can we make development economically sustainable, and create the commercial infrastructures, such as supply chains, that support mature industries.

How Families Are Formed

The members of a family form the leaves of a decision tree.

Working within a family reduces the number of features and relationships among them that must be considered simultaneously to decompose a problem or to compose a solution. To see this, think of the members of the family as the leaves of a tree, where each node is a design decision taken during development. We saw such a tree in Chapter 2, leading to alternative solutions to a given problem. We can now expand the tree to include solutions to multiple problems, as illustrated in Figure 10.1, where S1 through S3 are solutions to P1, S4 through S6 are solutions to P2, and S7 through SC are solutions to P3.

Product families are formed by feature prioritization.

Stepping back further, we can think of this decision tree as a subset of a much larger one that includes the solutions to all possible problems. Let's collapse each subtree that describes the solutions to each problem into a single node, and think of it as a product, as illustrated in Figure 10.2. We can now see that the members of a product family are differentiated from all other products by features common to all of the family

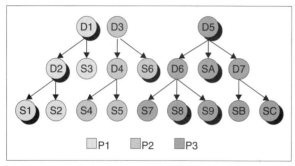

Figure 10.1   Solutions to multiple problems

members.[1] For example, all members of the Online Commerce Systems family let customers place orders for products through a user interface. Their common features include managing customers, showing a product catalog, and accepting orders. Common features, called commonalities, are represented by nodes that appear in all of the paths that lead to family members. C1 and C2 in Figure 10.2 represent common features. P1 through P6 are members of a product family defined by C1 and C2. The members of a product family are differentiated from each other by features unique to some members or common to only a subset of members. Variable features, called variabilities, are represented by nodes that appear in only some of the paths that lead to family members. V1 through V3 in Figure 10.2 represent variable features. Of course, changing the order in which design decisions are taken yields different paths, and therefore different product families. Placing a feature closer to the root of the tree makes it common to more products. In other words, product families are formed by feature prioritization.

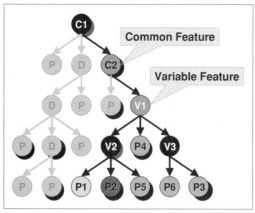

Figure 10.2   Common and variable features

Working Within a Family

We can standardize how family members are specified by constraining how problems can vary.

Now that have defined product families, let's look at how they change the way we produce software products. Working within a family simplifies problem decomposition because the common problem features can be assumed. Any family member can be specified entirely in terms of variable problem features. For example, when we specify an Online Commerce System, we do not have to say that it manages customers, exposes a product catalog or accepts orders. However, we might have to say how it adds customers, how its product catalog is organized, and how it validates orders. If we plan to develop multiple Online Commerce Systems, we might even develop forms to collect this information. By constraining how problems can vary within a family, we can standardize the way family members are specified.

We can standardize how family members are implemented by constraining how solutions can vary.

Working within a family simplifies solution composition, as well. Recall from Chapter 2 that raising the level of abstraction involves developing solutions to common subproblems in a given domain, which can be composed to completely or partially solve multiple problems in the domain. We can now think of a product family as forming such a domain, where the members of the family are the problems in the domain, and their common features are the common subproblems. This means that we can reduce the total cost of developing multiple family members by developing solutions to their common features. For example, we might develop an Online Commerce framework that provides classes for managing customers, exposing a product catalog, and accepting orders. To support the required variations among family members, we might parameterize the classes, provide hooks for policy objects and method overrides, and provide tools that let developers assemble the classes or configure them by setting property values. Since the common solution features are implemented in advance, they can be assumed. This means that any family member can be implemented entirely in terms of variable ones. These are the parts of its implementation that are not shared by all of the family members. For example, we might develop a specific Online Commerce System by assembling, configuring, and extending the framework described previously. By constraining how solutions can vary within a family, we can standardize the way family members are implemented.

To build a family member, we only have to supply solutions to variable problem features.

Now, since every family member can be specified in terms of variable problem features, and implemented in terms of

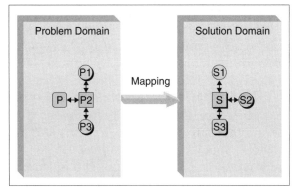

Figure 10.3   Mapping all common features in advance

variable solution features, we can ignore the common features, and focus only on the variable ones. This reduces the scope of the problem to be solved. Instead of solving the entire problem, we only have to solve the portions that are variable. It also reduces the scope of the solution to be supplied. Instead of supplying the entire solution, we only have to supply the portions that are variable. In other words, to build a family member, we only have to supply solutions to variable problem features.

Solving Problems in Advance

Recall from Chapter 3 that developing software involves finding and rendering mappings between domains. When we develop the common solution features for a product family, we find and render part of the mapping for all family members in advance. Specifically, we find and render the part of the mapping that relates the common problem features to the common solution features, as illustrated in Figure 10.3.

We may also be able to find some variable parts of the mapping in advance, as illustrated in Figure 10.4.

By developing common solution features, we find part of the mapping for every family member in advance.

By constraining how both problems and solutions can vary, we improve our ability to anticipate and accommodate change using adaptive design.

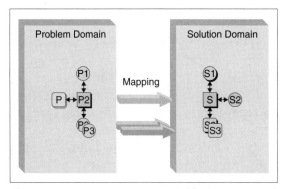

Figure 10.4   Mapping some variable features in advance

- In some cases, we may know enough about the possible problem variations to supply the corresponding solution variations in advance. For example, if we know exactly how certain portions of an algorithm can vary, then we can use the Strategy pattern to extract them using a common interface, we can provide a class to implement each variation, and we can let each family member instantiate the class that satisfies its requirements. We might even provide a tool that contains a pick list showing the options, and let the developer choose one. This is the case, for example, with the transaction policy for an Enterprise JavaBean. It must be one of the policies supported by the architecture.

- In other cases, we may only know enough to constrain the solution variations. For example, if we know that certain portions of an algorithm can vary, but not exactly how, then we can use the Strategy pattern again. This time, however, we cannot provide a class to implement each variation, so we must let each family member provide a strategy class that satisfies its requirements. Of course, in this case, we can still constrain the variations by defining the interface to which strategy classes must conform. This is the case, for example, with Enterprise JavaBean activation and passivation. A container requires a bean to save or restore its state on demand, and requires the bean to provide methods that it can call for this purpose.

By constraining how both problems and solutions can vary within a family, we improve our ability to anticipate and accommodate change using adaptive design.

The Role of Architecture

Defining a software architecture is the most important aspect of developing a software product line.

Obviously, working within a family changes the way we make design decisions. It binds some design decisions in advance, constrains some design decisions, and leaves some design decisions open. This should sound familiar. These are the terms we used to define an architecture. It should come as no surprise, then, that developing an architecture is a central aspect of working within a family, as noted by Clements and Northrop [CN01]. Note, however, that the architecture we are talking about here describes an entire family, not just an individual product. In the same way that the architecture for an individual product reduces the complexity of problems that must be solved to produce the product, the architecture for a product family reduces the complexity of problems that must be solved to produce the family members.

Fine, you say, to bind design decisions in advance for a problem sitting in front of us. But, how can we do that for an entire family of problems, some of which we may not even know about? We have already seen how rapidly requirements and technologies can change, and how hard it can be to anticipate and accommodate the changes. Weiss and Lai [WL99] answer this question with three interesting hypotheses.

How can we bind design decisions in advance for an entire family of problems?

- The *redevelopment hypothesis* holds that most software development is redevelopment that consists of building variations on existing products, and that the variations have more in common with each other than not.

- The *oracle hypothesis* holds that we can predict at least some of the changes that may be made to a product over its lifetime, and that some of these changes are based on well-known patterns of variation.

- The *organizational hypothesis* holds that it is possible to organize both software and software development resources, such as processes and people, to take advantage of predicted changes.

Although these hypotheses may not be widely understood, or even recognized, they are responsible for many software development practices, including adaptive design, the development of patterns and architectures that enable adaptive design, and the embodiment of those patterns and architectures in frameworks, such as the JDK and the .NET Framework. There is no point in adaptive design unless we are reasonably confident that some kinds of changes will occur more often others, based on predictable patterns; that we can take advantage of those patterns to avoid some amount of rework by separating those aspects of products that change at different rates or for different reasons; and that we can organize both the software and the way we develop it to take advantage of this knowledge.

These hypotheses are responsible for adaptive design and its manifestations.

Since the principles of adaptive design can be applied to multiple products, as well as to individual products, as we saw in Chapter 2, we can now extend these hypotheses to say that we can identify families of products whose members have more in

Working within a family applies the principles of adaptive design to multiple products.

common with each other than not; that we can predict at least some of the variations that may occur in a product family; that some of these variations are based on well-known patterns; and that we can define an architecture and a development process for a product family that reduces the total cost and time to market of developing the family members, and improves overall product quality. In other words, working within a family applies the principles of adaptive design to multiple products. As we shall see, this is the basis for software product lines.

Commonality and Variability

Every feature is a point of standardization or customization.

How should we define the commonalities and variabilities for a product family? Defining a commonality increases the level of standardization in a family, since it makes a feature mandatory for all of the family members. Conversely, defining a variability increases the level of customization in a family, since it makes a feature optional for some of the family members. Since every feature must be either mandatory or optional, every feature is a point of standardization or customization. This leads to a simple guideline for defining commonalities and variabilities: make things that must be standardized common, and everything else variable. Of course, without perfect foresight, the initial definitions are bound to be incorrect, and changing requirements may force the revision of definitions that were previously correct. In practice, however, this guideline works reasonably well.

Defining commonalities and variabilities is the basis of abstraction.

Clearly, when we define commonalities and variabilities, we emphasize some concerns (i.e., the variabilities), while ignoring others (i.e., the commonalities). This should sound familiar. These are the terms we used to define abstraction. It should come as no surprise, then, that separating commonalities and variabilities is the basis of abstraction, as noted by Coplien [Cop99]. When we create an abstraction, concerns we ignore become commonalities, and concerns we emphasize become variabilities. Abstraction mechanisms are tools that help us package abstractions by codifying patterns for separating commonality and variability. Design patterns, for example, codify patterns for separating commonality and variability in classes, as noted by Shaw [Sha84].

A product family provides a context for raising the level of abstraction.

We can now see that a product family provides a context for raising the level of abstraction. By separating the commonalities and variabilities of its members, it helps identify the

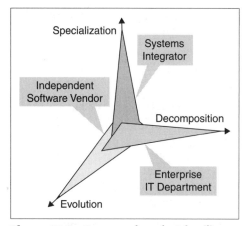

Figure 10.5   Sources of product families

abstractions that need to be developed to solve their common subproblems. In addition, a product family provides a scoping mechanism for grouping and naming abstractions. This scoping mechanism is glaringly absent from the pattern literature, where the context in which a problem is frequently encountered often receives only passing mention, and most of the attention is given to describing the problem. This suggests that patterns can be made more effective by identifying the specific software product families to which they can be applied. Since patterns can be composed to form architectures, as we have seen, this suggests developing canonical architectures for families of software products with a common structure as pattern languages.

Where Families Are Found

At this point, you may be wondering why, if product families are so important, you haven't seen many. If you are accustomed to thinking of software products as individuals, as we were before we started thinking about software factories, you may have seen many product families without recognizing them. Product families naturally arise in many scenarios, including evolution, specialization, and decomposition, as shown in Figure 10.5.

Product families are formed by many common scenarios.

- Evolution forms a family from multiple versions of the same product over time. This scenario is common among Independent Software Vendors (ISVs), who issue multiple releases.

- Specialization forms a family from multiple instances of the same product with different features or different configurations of the same features. This scenario is common among Systems Integrators (SIs), who address the needs of multiple customers.

- Decomposition forms a family from multiple products that solve related problems. This scenario is common among enterprise IT departments, who produce different applications to automate different aspects of the same business.

Features can be defined in many ways.

To make this more concrete, let's look at some areas where features can define a product family, including requirements, architecture, and implementation.

- *Requirements.* We have already seen a family of Online Commerce Systems defined by their common and variable requirements. All of the family members let customers place orders to purchase products interactively. Their common requirements include managing customers, showing a product catalog, and accepting orders. Their variable requirements may include how customers are added, how the product catalog is organized, what kinds of products are offered, and how orders are validated.

- *Architecture.* We can also define a family of products based on architecture. For example, all members of the family of Business Component Systems are organized as federations of interacting business components, as defined by Herzum and Sims [HS00]. Their common features include a graph-based overall structure, where each member of the graph is a potentially distributed component or subsystem consisting of multiple layers, possibly distributed across multiple physical tiers, and where the interaction among the components is loosely coupled and based on XML message exchange. Their variable features may include the way the layers interact, which layers are physically distributed, and how each component accesses data or interacts with users.

- *Implementation.* We can also define a family of products based on implementation technology. For example, all members of the family of .NET Based Systems are implemented using .NET languages and the .NET

Framework. The common features include the mandatory components of .NET, such as the common language runtime. Their variable features include a wide variety of optional .NET components, such as ASP.NET for web-based user interfaces, or ADO.NET for database access.

Of course, as we can see from these examples, different kinds of features may not always be orthogonal. For example, Online Commerce Systems may or may not be Business Component Systems, and these, in turn may or may not be .NET Based Systems. The more we can align the features of a product family across the various levels of abstraction, the more value we can derive from working within the product family. For example, we can derive more value from working within a family of Online Commerce Systems that are Business Component Systems based on .NET than we can from working within a family of Online Commerce Systems that have different architectures and implementation technologies. Also, while we can define a product family at any level of abstraction, the higher the level of abstraction, the greater the value we can derive from working within the product family. Conversely, the higher the level of abstraction, the narrower the family. This is an instance of the tradeoff that we saw in Chapter 2 between the power and scope of an abstraction. There is one important exception to this rule. Below the level of abstraction of the development artifacts, we have some room to manoeuvre. For example, as long as the developer always works with a language such as C# or Java, we can vary those aspects of the implementation technology hidden by the language, such as the type of hardware on which the software will be deployed.

The more we can align the features of a product family across the various levels of abstraction, the more value we can derive from working within the product family.

Software Product Lines

We are now ready to look at software product lines. From a marketing perspective, a product line is a set of products with a common, managed set of features for some target market segments. A software product line adds the concept that the products are software products built from a common set of production assets. The production assets capture knowledge about how to produce the family members, and make it available for reuse to produce the family members. Of course, product lines

A software product line is a production capacity for a family of software products.

are not a new idea. They have been understood since the inception of the industrial revolution, and form the basis of modern industry. The new idea is using product lines to produce software products. While new to many people, this idea has been around for some time, and has been used enough to demonstrate viability, as documented by many observers.

Creating Economies of Scope

A software product line creates economies of scope.

A software product line exploits the benefits of working within a product family to create economies of scope in the development process. We saw earlier that we can develop any family member by supplying only the variable solution features that must be added to common solution features defined in advance to implement the variable problem features. We also saw that by constraining the way problem features can vary, we can standardize the way family members are specified, and that by constraining the way solution features can vary, we can standardize the way they are implemented. A software product line exploits these observations as follows.

- It identifies the common problem features for the product family in advance, and provides a standard way to specify variations.
- It identifies and implements the common solution features for the product family in advance, and provides standard ways to implement variations.
- It defines a mapping between the variable problem and solution features for the product family in advance, so that developing a family member is at least partially deterministic.

The degree of determinism depends on how much is known about the range of variation for each variable feature.

The degree of determinism depends on how much is known about the range of variation for each variable problem feature. The range of variation defines how a feature may vary.

- When the range of variation is completely known, the software product line can implement each one in advance. For example, it might define specific configurations of library classes that implement specific state management policies, and provide a tool for selecting the policy, as illustrated in Figure 10.6. In this

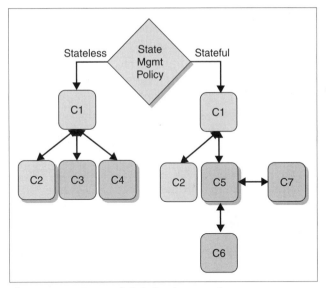

Figure 10.6 Deterministic implementation

case, implementing the feature is a matter of configuration.

- When the range of variation is only partially known, the software product line can constrain the implementation strategy by providing an architecture and implementation components. It might provide a framework, for example, that can be used to build the user interface. In this case, implementing the feature may be a matter of assembly, extension and configuration.

- When the range of variation is unknown, the software product line may only be able to constrain the implementation, by providing extension points in the architecture and implementation components. For example, it might provide an interface to which custom security policy implementations must conform.

This leads to the question of how much determinism makes sense. For some product families, such as embedded telecommunications and automotive systems, near total determinism is often appropriate. The FAST method developed at Bell Labs supports the development of highly deterministic software product lines that use program generators to implement most of each family member automatically. This is useful when the range of variation for the variables feature can be specified

Software product lines yield significant benefits even for highly unpredictable product families.

precisely. For most product families, however, this is not possible for the majority of the variable features, since variations may be dictated by market changes, technology evolution, or other unpredictable forces. For some product families, it may not be possible even to identify the variable features in advance, much less to specify ranges of variation. These product families require a much less deterministic approach. Software product lines yield significant benefits even for highly unpredictable product families, however, since even modest levels of systematic reuse can substantially reduce cost, reduce time to market, and improve product quality.

Required Adaptations

Product lines require significant adaptations.

We can see from this discussion that product lines significantly change the way we develop software. Since they create economies of scope, they also change the business of developing software. These process and business changes ultimately require changes in the organizational structure. We will defer discussion of business adaptations to Chapter 9, and turn to the process and organizational adaptations.

Process Adaptations

A product line uses two distinct but interacting development processes.

We said earlier that product lines significantly change the development process. Recall from Chapter 2 that a development process is a set of best practices designed to promote product quality, efficient resource allocation, and effective budget and schedule management. Most modern software development uses some development process, ranging from the ad hoc to the prescriptive. These processes generally start by capturing the requirements for an individual product, and end with its delivery. By contrast, a product line uses two distinct but interacting development processes, one that produces production assets, called product line development, and a second that applies the production assets to produce products, called product development.[2]

As illustrated in Figure 10.7, there are two interactions between these processes, the delivery of production assets from product line to product development, and the delivery of feedback in the opposite direction. Product line development defines the kinds of products developed, and provides the

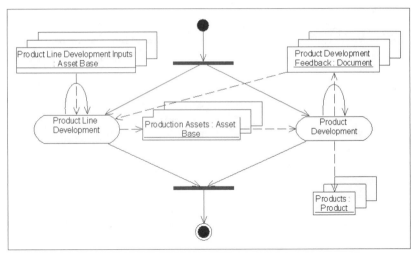

Figure 10.7 Product line development processes

implementation, process and automation assets used to develop them. Product development provides feedback, such as
updated product requirements, defect reports or enhancement
requests for production assets, and product development process metrics. This feedback is used in product line development to continuously improve the production assets. In practice, these two processes may be separated to varying degrees.
At one end of the spectrum, they may reside in different organizations, and their interaction may be commercial. At the
other end, it may not even be possible to tell them apart, since
they may be completely interleaved, and practiced in parallel
by the same people. Of course, the software life cycle doesn't
end with development. It also includes deployment, maintenance and enhancement. We will look at how product lines
affect these phases of the software life cycle in Chapter 11.

At first glance, the two processes might appear to be merely
different instances of the same process. Closer examination reveals significant differences between them [CKPW95]. They
produce different products to satisfy different requirements
through different activities, and they change for different reasons at different rates. These differences are summarized in
Table 10.1, and described in greater detail in Chapter 16. They
are intrinsic to the way products are developed in a product
line, and do not depend on how distinctly the practice of the
two processes may be separated.

*They produce
different products
against different
requirements
through different
activities.*

Table 10.1 Different development processes

PRODUCT LINE DEVELOPMENT	PRODUCT DEVELOPMENT
Produces production assets for product development	Produces a product for consumers outside the product line using production assets supplied by product line development
Must satisfy the fixed and variable requirements of multiple products	Must satisfy the variable requirements of a single product
Uses the same process for every product family	Uses a different process defined by product line development for every product family

We suggest definitions for these processes, that can be changed, replaced, extended or discarded altogether.

In practice, these processes may be more or less formally defined. At one end of the spectrum, a highly deterministic product line may define them so formally, they can be fully automated. At the other end, a highly opportunistic product line may define them so informally that their definitions are passed on entirely by word of mouth. Many software development shops fall more toward the latter end of the spectrum today, and may implement product lines without recognizing them. While we are not fond of ceremony, case studies show that some formality can yield significant benefits. We therefore set a relatively low bar, compared with methods like FAST, but one that is more formal than current practice in most organizations. While this bar admits significant variation in the way these processes are defined, we suggest some definitions, to provide scaffolding on which we can hang the discussion of salient product lines features. We define each process in terms of its constituent activities and the artifacts they produce and consume. However, our definitions are not prescriptive. They can be changed, replaced, extended, or discarded altogether.

Figure 10.8 summarizes the activities that comprise product line development, and Figure 10.9 summarizes the artifacts they produce and consume.

Figure 10.10 summarizes the activities that comprise product development, and Figure 10.11 summarizes the artifacts they produce and consume.

```
□ 📁 Product Line Analysis
    ⊞ 📁 Product Line Definition
    ⊞ 📁 Problem Domain Scoping
    ⊞ 📁 Solution Domain Scoping
       📁 Business Case Analysis
□ 📁 Product Line Design
       📁 Product Line Architecture Development
       📁 Product Line Architecture Mapping
       📁 Product Development Process Definition
       📁 Product Development Process Automation
□ 📁 Product Line Implementation
    ⊞ 📁 Implementation Asset Provisioning
    ⊞ 📁 Process Asset Provisioning
    📁 Production Asset Packaging
    📁 Production Asset Release
```

Figure 10.8   Product line development activities

```
    📁 Product Line Development Inputs
□ 📁 Production Assets
    □ 📁 Product Line Specification
        □ 📁 Product Line Definition
            📁 Content Description
            📁 Context Description
            📁 Stakeholder Description
            📁 Domain Glossary
            📁 Product Examples
        📁 Problem Domain Model
        📁 Product Line Requirements
        📁 Business Case Model
        📁 Product Line Scope
    📁 Product Line Architecture
    📁 Requirements Mapping
    📁 Product Development Process
    📁 Process Automation Plan
    □ 📁 Product Line Implementation
        □ 📁 Implementation Assets
            📁 Components
        □ 📁 Process Assets
            📁 Development Tools
            📁 Development Resources
            📁 Process Documentation
```

Figure 10.9   Product line development artifacts

```
⊞ 📁 Problem Analysis
⊞ 📁 Product Specification
□ 📁 Product Implementation
    □ 📁 Executable Implementation
        ⊞ 📁 Architecture Derivation
        ⊞ 📁 Product Assembly
           📁 Product Build
           📁 Unit Test Development
           📁 Unit Test Execution
    ⊞ 📁 Test Case Implementation
    ⊞ 📁 Product Deployment
    ⊞ 📁 Product Testing
⊞ 📁 Collateral Development
    📁 Product Evaluation
    📁 Product Packaging
    📁 Product Release
```

Figure 10.10   Product development activities

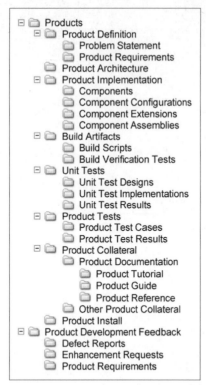

Figure 10.11   Product development artifacts

Organizational Adaptations

A product line uses two distinct but interacting teams.

We will look at the organizational adaptations required to use product lines more closely in Chapter 17. For now, we only need to make one important point. Since the two processes involve different skills and rewards, as summarized in Table 10.2, product lines tend to create two teams. Product lines clearly promote greater specialization of roles than one-off product development. While there is some role specialization in software today, between the manager and developer roles, for example, there is no consistent specialization of the developer role. Role specialization tends to increase as an industry matures, driven by increasing standardization of practices. Product lines can be supported by a variety of organizational structures, ranging from one team wearing all the hats to multiple teams wearing single hats. For now, we assume a distinct product line development team supporting some number of distinct product development teams.

Table 10.2 Different skills and rewards

PRODUCT LINE DEVELOPMENT	PRODUCT DEVELOPMENT
Requires synthesis skills for generalizing components from multiple products and parameterizing them for variations	Requires analysis skills for decomposing products in terms of existing components
Rewards technical innovations that improve product development	Rewards delivery of products that satisfy customer requirements

Software Supply Chains

Looking around the industry today, we see only a few cases of systematic family based product development, most notably the packaged enterprise applications, such as Enterprise Resource Planning (ERP), Supply Chain Management (SCM) and Customer Relationship Management (CRM). Why don't we see more product lines? One reason may be lack of knowledge. Product line practices are not well understood in the software industry. Another reason may be inertia. Established practices are often difficult to replace, especially when the changes involve not only technical, but business and organizational adaptation. We will look at some of these issues in Chapter 17. Perhaps the most significant reason, however, is the cost of providing the tools and infrastructure required to support a product line. As we have seen, one of the goals of software factories is to make it inexpensive to implement software product lines, and one of the keys to realizing this goal is avoiding the mistake of trying to build everything required to support a software product line from scratch. In other words, one of the keys to reducing costs is consuming some assets from external suppliers, instead of building them all in-house.

One of the keys to reducing costs is consuming some assets from external suppliers, instead of building them all in-house.

As an industry matures economically, a pattern of interaction emerges between consumers and suppliers, called a supply chain. In a supply chain, product lines are connected, so that the outputs from one or more upstream product lines become the inputs to one or more downstream product lines. Of course, the upstream product lines can supply either implementation assets, such as components, or process assets, such as tools and process documentation, to the downstream ones.

Product lines connect to form supply chains.

There are important differences between these two types of assets in a supply chain. Since products produced by downstream product lines incorporate implementation assets supplied by upstream ones, the downstream product lines have narrower scope and produce larger products than the upstream ones. For example, a supplier of Online Commerce Systems that consumes a user interface framework has a narrower focus and produces larger products than the supplier of the user interface framework. This may not hold for process assets. The user interface framework supplier, for example, may consume configuration management and defect tracking tools that are both larger and narrower in scope than the user interface frameworks its supplies.

An important prerequisite for a supply chain is aligning the architectures and processes of the participating product lines.

An important prerequisite for a supply chain is aligning the architectures and processes of the participating product lines. As we have seen, one of the main impediments to component composition is architecture mismatch. If components are not designed with compatible assumptions about how they will interact with each other and with the platforms on which they execute, then they cannot be assembled without extensive modification, adaptation or mediation. The less compatible these assumptions, the greater the level of architecture mismatch, and the greater the amount of adaptation required to assemble the components. At some level of architecture mismatch, it may not be possible to assemble the components successfully. Similar alignment issues apply to the development process for product lines that seek to consume or supply process assets. For example, a product line that uses testing tools from one supplier may not be able to consume defect-tracking tools from another supplier, if they cannot be integrated with the testing tools. In many cases, integration requires the tools to make compatible assumptions about the development process.

Constraints propagate downstream through a supply chain.

One way to ensure the required alignment is to enable constraints to propagate downstream, by including them explicitly in the asset packages. Simple examples of such constraint propagation already exist between development and deployment tools, where a development tool places constraints on the configuration of the target platform in the deployable package. The deployment tool then picks up these constraints and either configures the target platform as necessary to satisfy the constraints, or validates that the target platform is correctly configured and disallows deployment if the constraints are violated. Constraint propagation has some interesting effects on the downstream product lines. They may inherit common requirements from the supplier and bind some of its variable requirements. For example, the Online Commerce System supplier may inherit common user interface requirements from the user interface framework supplier, such as the requirement that all Online Commerce System user interfaces be Web-based. Similarly, the architectures of downstream product lines may inherit or aggregate some parts of the architectures of their suppliers. For example, the Online Commerce System supplier inherits the user interface portion of its architecture from the user interface framework supplier. Finally, the downstream product lines may adapt or aggregate components from their suppliers. For example, the Online Commerce System supplier may extend the user interface framework with a custom control for browsing product catalogs.

Some of the most advanced examples of software supply chains can be found in embedded software development within the automotive and telecommunications industries.[3] The architectural alignment issues described earlier have been major challenges for these pioneers. Daimler Chrysler, for example, works as a system integrator, prescribing the overall architecture for the systems they place in their automotive products, while relying on commissioned suppliers, such as Bosch and Siemens, for most of the software components. Managing the relationship between the system integrator and the component suppliers is extremely challenging. The challenges include specifying commissioned components effectively without seeing the source code used to implement them, while keeping the number of iterations and revisions low to manage costs, deciding what knowledge to keep in-house and what to outsource, and protecting the intellectual property of each party, some of whom may be competing with each other in different settings.

Fine, you say, these kinds of relationships already exist. While this is certainly true, the level of interdependency in the software industry is much lower than in more mature industries. This is good news, however, since it means that we have an opportunity to significantly reduce costs, reduce time to market, and improve the quality of software products by increasing the level of interdependency, and by taking advantage of lessons learned in other industries about how to make supply chains more efficient. Exploring this opportunity further is unfortunately beyond the scope of this book. We hope to see books on the market soon that address this subject.

Notes

1. We use the terms *design decision* and *feature* interchangeably, since design decisions select features, as we saw in Chapter 2.
2. Some commentators call the former domain engineering and the latter application engineering.
3. Thanks to Krzysztof Czarnecki for sharing with us his experiences with software supply chains at Mercedes.

Software Product Lines

The value of an abstraction increases with its specificity to some problem domain.
Michael Jackson

In this chapter, we will look at how software product lines can be used to develop the members of a software product family.

Product Line Development

The goal of product line development is to supply production assets for a product family. We can think of product line development as product line analysis, design, and implementation, as illustrated in Figure 11.1. These activities are iterative and parallel, not sequential, and can be undertaken in any order, as soon as the artifacts and other required resources are available, as indicated by the diagram. Product line analysis produces a product line specification. Product line design produces a product line architecture and a product development process. Product line implementation implements the product line architecture and the product development process.

According to Clements and Northrop [CN01], external inputs to product line development include existing production assets and product and production constraints.

- While many of the production assets used by a product line may be developed by the product line, existing

The goal of product line development is to supply production assets for a product family.

External inputs to product line development include existing production assets and product and production constraints.

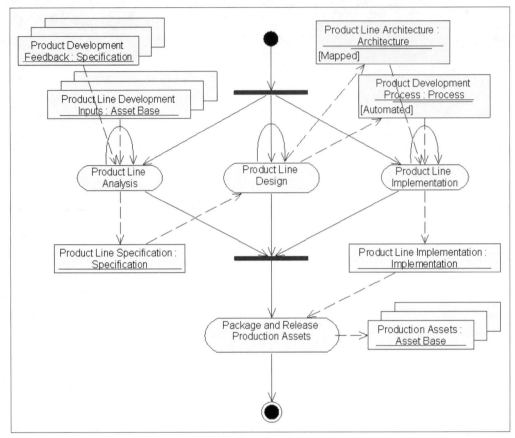

Figure 11.1 Product line development

production assets, such as architectural styles, patterns, languages, architectures, frameworks, libraries, assemblies, programs, processes, and tools can be used to bootstrap the product line.

- Product constraints are requirements imposed on the products developed by the product line, such as standards, external interfaces, or localization, packaging, licensing, installation, operational and administrative requirements.

- Production constraints are requirements imposed on the product development process by the product line, such as technology, vendor or platform preferences, acceptance and reporting criteria, budget and schedule constraints, or development policies and guidelines.

Feedback from product development provides an internal input to product line development, as described earlier. The output of product line development is the collection of production assets used by product development.

Product Line Analysis

The purpose of product line analysis is to decide *what* products the product line will develop. Product line analysis includes product line definition, problem and solution domain scoping, business case analysis, and scope evaluation. It produces a product line definition, problem statements to be solved, a problem domain model, requirements for products to be developed, a product line requirements specification, a business case model, and a product line scope specification, as illustrated in Figure 11.2. These artifacts comprise the product line

The purpose of product line analysis is to decide what *products the product line will develop.*

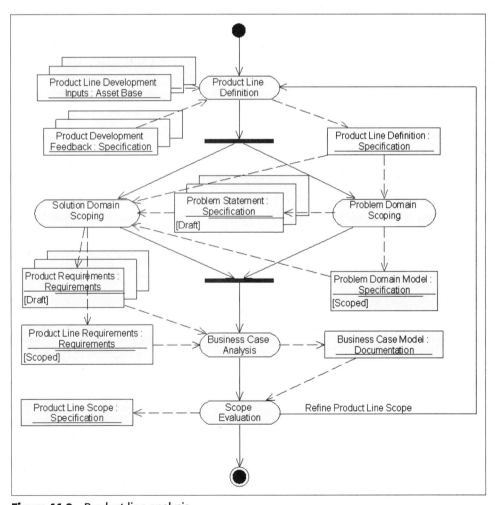

Figure 11.2   Product line analysis

specification. Product line analysis should run concurrently with other product line and product development activities to maintain and enhance these artifacts. For example, the product line specification may change in response to requests received before, during or after product line design and implementation or product development.

Product Line Definition

Product line definition describes the problems that the product line is expected to solve and the products it is expected to produce to solve those problems.

Product line definition describes the problems that the product line is expected to solve and the products it is expected to produce to solve those problems. It can also describe the context in which these problems are encountered, and in which the products it produces are expected to be used. For example, if the product line will produce a component of another product, we can describe that product and the problem it solves. Product line definition can also describe the stakeholders, such as investors, managers, developers, customers, and users, and their concerns or expectations. It can also produce a glossary that describes the vocabulary of the problem domain, and examples of known problems and existing products in the domain, as illustrated in Figure 11.3.

Problem domain scoping identifies and selects the problems that will be solved by the product line.

Problem Domain Scoping

Problem domain scoping identifies and selects the problems that will be solved by the product line. It can produce a problem

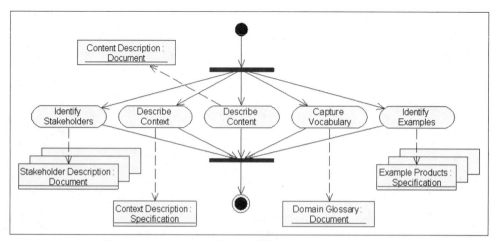

Figure 11.3   Product line definition

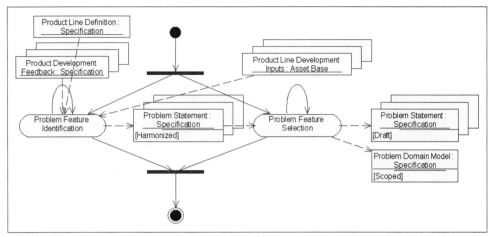

Figure 11.4   Problem domain scoping

domain model and draft statements of the problems that will be solved by the product line. Recall that a product line cannot fully solve variable features whose ranges of variation are unknown. This means that the product line may solve only a subset of a given problem. We must therefore identify not only the problems that will be solved, but also the features of those problems that will be solved by the product line, as illustrated in Figure 11.4. For example, a product line for Online Commerce Systems may address the feature of offering new products from the primary supplier, but not the feature of offering new and used products from alternative suppliers. While a product line may be able to build most of a product that requires an unsupported feature, the parts of the product related to this feature will have to be custom developed. Bosch provides an excellent analysis of problem domain scoping at the feature level.

Problem Feature Identification

To identify the problem features that will be solved by the product line, we must first identify some problems that may be partially or completely solved by the product line. We will call them candidate problems. We should be able to identify a number of candidate problems based on the product line definition. We can then identify candidate problem features by writing problem statements for the candidate problems. Because the same feature may be described differently by different problem statements, we must then harmonize the feature definitions, so

To identify the problem features that will be solved by the product line, we must first identify some problems that may be partially or completely solved by the product line.

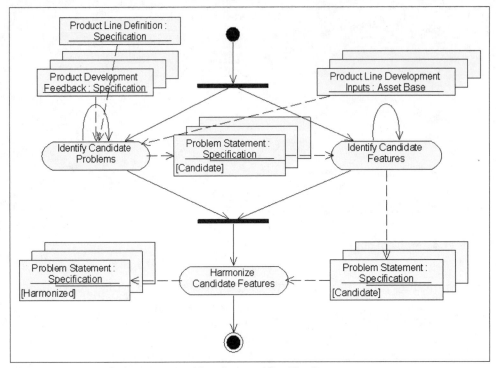

Figure 11.5   Problem feature identification

that we can compare them across problem boundaries, as illustrated in Figure 11.5.

Problem Feature Selection

When the candidate feature descriptions have been harmonized, we can select the ones that will be solved by the product line.

When the candidate feature descriptions have been harmonized, we can select the ones that will be solved by the product line, as illustrated in Figure 11.6. Typically, the selection is based on the number of candidate problems in which a candidate feature appears, on whether or not it is variable, and if so, on how much is known about its range of variation. A candidate feature that appears in a large number of candidate problems should probably be solved by the product line if it is common to all of the candidate problems, or if its range of variation is either partially or completely known.

Problem Feature Modeling

A domain model describes the problems in a domain.

A model of the problem domain can be used to support the selection of candidate problems and features, and the writing of

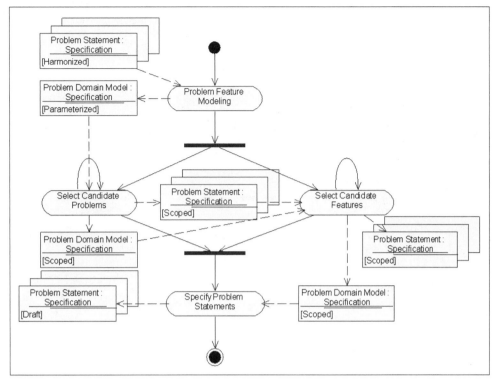

Figure 11.6   Problem feature selection

problem statements. A problem domain model is an idealized description of a problem domain that hides information that is not relevant to defining the scope of the product line. For example, a model of the Online Commerce domain used to scope a product line for Online Commerce Systems might hide all information not related to Order Entry.

Unfortunately, the term "domain model" is heavily overloaded in the industry. It can describe common and variable features of a problem domain, according to Neighbors, features of a specific problem, according to Kruchten [Kru00], units of information managed by products in a domain, according to Fowler, or generative facilities for a product family, according to Czarnecki and Eisenecker [CE00]. We use a problem domain model to separate the common and variable features of the problems that will be solved by the product line. Our use of the term is therefore closest to the definition given by Neighbors. To model a problem domain, we classify each candidate feature as either common or variable, and we parameterize each

We use a domain model to identify and separate the common and variable features of the problems that will be solved by the product line.

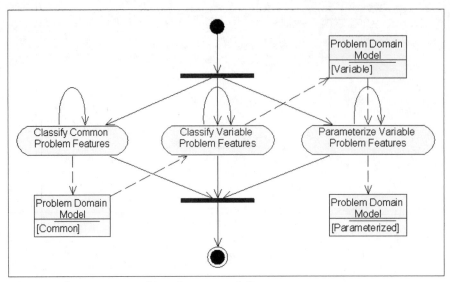

Figure 11.7   Problem feature modeling

variable feature to describe its range of variation, binding time, binding owner, and default binding, as described by Weiss and Lai. This process is necessarily iterative because classifying a feature may reveal tradeoffs that force earlier classification decisions to be revisited. The common features and ranges of variation collectively define the problem domain scope. These activities are illustrated in Figure 11.7.

There are several ways to express this information.   Problem feature modeling is expected to produce a specification that describes these classifications and parameterizations. There are several ways to express this information. Business Entity and Process models, like the ones shown next, can be used to describe the structural and behavioral aspects, respectively, of a problem domain. While popular, these types of models are of limited value, since they cannot separate commonalities from variabilities, or define parameters of variation. Jacobson [JGJ97] addresses this issue by adding a variation point construct to the modeling language. Natural language can also be used to describe domains, but such descriptions can be difficult to automate. Use cases are a well-known form of natural language description, and can express some forms of variation using extension and inclusion, as noted by Cockburn [Coc00]. A use case describes the aspects of an abstract process seen by one of its participants. Activity Graphs can also be used to specify use cases, as exemplified by Cheesman and Daniels [CD01].

BUSINESS PROCESS AND ENTITY MODELS

Business Entity and Process models can be used to describe some of the structural and behavioral aspects, of a problem domain.

Figure 11.8 shows part of a business entity model for the Online Commerce domain. It describes business entities involved in Order Entry.

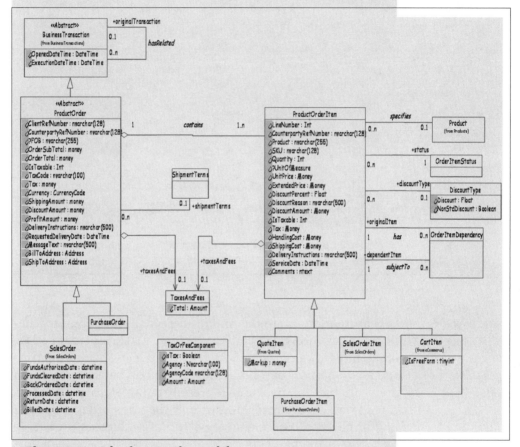

Figure 11.8   A business entity model

Figure 11.9 shows part of a business process model for the Online Commerce domain. It describes business processes involved in Order Entry.

While popular, these types of models are of limited value, since they cannot separate commonalities from variabilities, or represent parameters of variation.

(continued)

BUSINESS PROCESS AND ENTITY MODELS *(continued)*

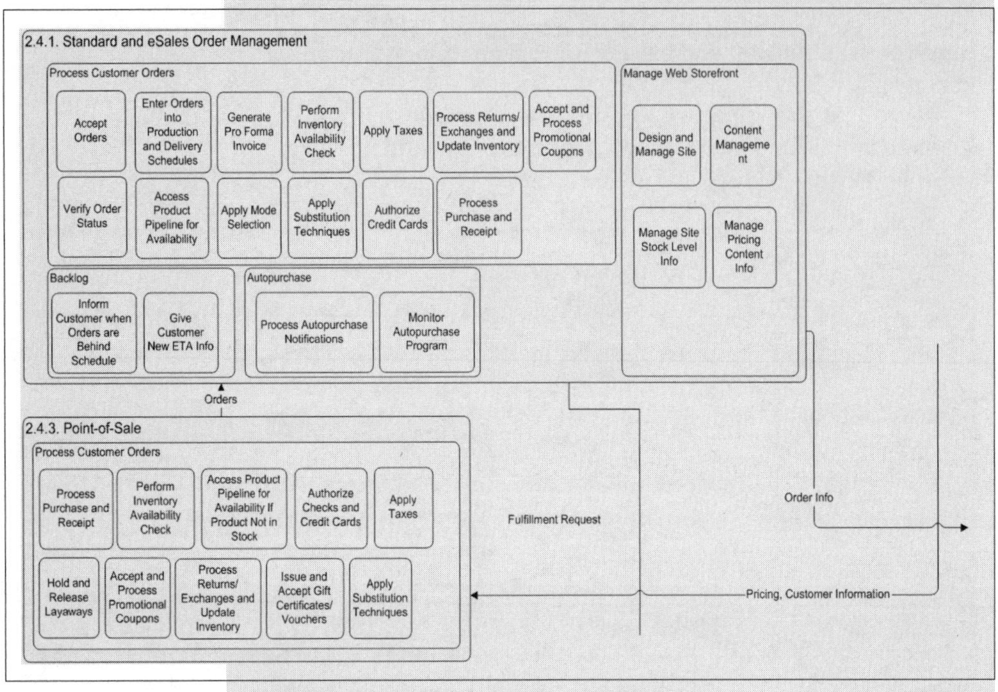

Figure 11.9 A business process model

Feature models are the preferred domain modeling mechanism for product lines.

Feature models are the preferred domain modeling mechanism for product lines. Unlike mechanisms designed for modeling individual problems, feature models are designed to model domains. They explicitly distinguish between common and variable features, and represent parameters of variation directly as constraints. In addition, they are independent of any implementation technology, and are therefore preferable to mechanisms like genericity and inheritance. The elements of a feature model are features, not objects. A feature may be atomic or composite. An atomic feature is a unit of functionality that cannot be subdivided. A composite feature, by contrast, is a unit of functionality composed of subsidiary features. The subsidiary features that contribute to a composite may be mandatory, optional or alternative, and may be related to one another through various types of constraints, such as exclusion, where one feature cannot coexist with another, and inclusion, where one feature requires the existence of another. Predicates and cardinalities can also be used to describe more complex

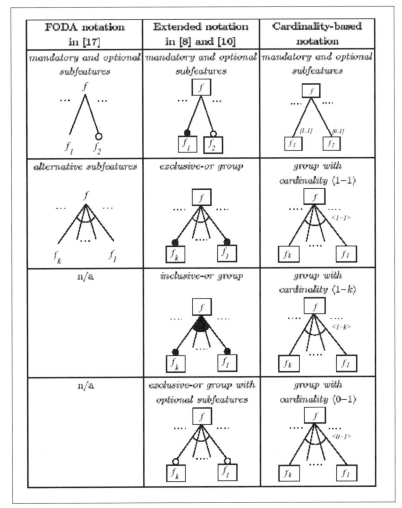

Figure 11.10 Feature modeling notation

Used with permission from K. Czarnecki, S. Helsen, U. Eisenecker. Staged Configuration Using Feature Models. Proceedings Of Software Product Line Conference 2004.

relationships. Feature models can also be mapped easily to XML schemas, which makes them convenient for describing configuration. We will return to this topic shortly. Czarnecki [CHE04] describes feature model notations, as illustrated in Figure 11.10, and provides a formal semantics for cardinality-based feature models by translation to context-free grammars.

The feature model in Figure 11.11 uses the cardinality-based notation shown in the right-most column of Figure 11.10. It indicates that a security profile has a password policy and zero or more permission sets. The password policy may indicate

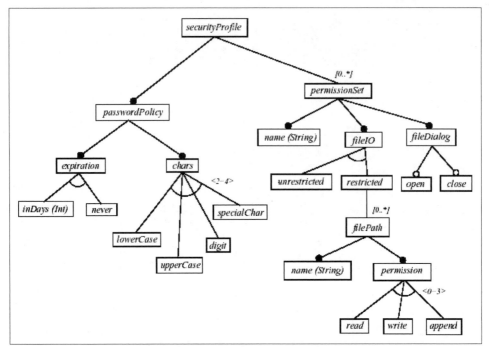

Figure 11.11   A feature model of security policy
Used with permission from K. Czarnecki, S. Helsen, U. Eisenecker. Staged
Configuration Using Feature Models. Proceedings Of Software Product Line
Conference 2004.

that a password never expires, or that it expires on some number of days. It also requires that at least two different types
of characters be used in passwords. The permission set defines
execution permissions. For example, File IO can either be unrestricted or restricted to a set of file paths, and for each file path,
any combination of read, write, and append may be selected.

*A problem
statement binds
variable features.*

A problem statement provides bindings for variable features in a problem domain model. When a problem domain
is described by a feature model, problem statements can be expressed as specializations of the problem domain model that
describe the features of specific problems. We will look at feature model specialization in the next section. These problem
statements can be rendered as XML documents based on the
XML schema derived from the feature model.

Solution Domain Scoping

*Solution domain
scoping produces
the product line
requirements.*

Solution domain scoping mirrors problem domain scoping,
except that instead of the problem domain model and draft
problem statements, it produces product line requirements and

draft product requirements. The product line requirements define common and variable requirements for all of the products that the product line is expected to produce. They define how the members of the product family will solve the problems in the problem domain. Recall from Chapter 2 that the requirements for an individual product are defined by negotiation, and provide a contract between negotiators. The same is true for the product line requirements.

Up to this point, we have been concerned with building products that solve real world problems. Now, however, to focus on producing executables for each family member from requirements in the context of the product line, we will adopt the perspective regarding problems and solutions used in Chapter 2. Recall that within a single iteration of an individual product, we can let the requirements represent the problem to be solved, so that we can use progressive refinement and abstraction to develop executables that implement them. In the same way, within a single iteration of the product line, we can let the product line requirements represent the problem domain, so that we can use progressive refinement and abstraction to develop the executables for family members from their variable requirements. The wrinkle this time is that the common requirements can be assumed. We can therefore specify any product within the product line scope entirely in terms of its variable requirements. The common design features and implementation components can also be assumed, as we have seen, so we can implement any product within the scope of the product line by supplying only the variable design features and implementation components that must be added to the common ones to implement its variable requirements.

We can implement any product within the scope of the product line by supplying only the variable design features and implementation components required to implement its variable requirements.

In addition to describing requirements, solution domain scoping can define the parameters of variation for each variable requirement, indicating when, how, and by whom it must be specified during product development. These parameters can be defined in terms of the following properties:

The product line requirements indicate when, how, and by whom each requirement is specified.

- *Binding time* defines when a requirement is specified. Common requirements are specified during product line development. Variable requirements are specified during product development, or later.

- *Binding mode* defines how a requirement is specified, and when, if ever, an existing requirement can be changed. The information used to specify the requirement, such as a resource location or policy value, is called the requirement binding. The binding mode may also include an XML schema that describes valid requirement bindings. The schema may define the multiplicity, type, default, and constraints for the value of the requirement binding, as well as nested schemas for complex values, such as localization files.

- *Binding role* defines who specifies a requirement, such as product line owners, product line developers, product owners, product developers, third parties or end users.

Specification aids can be developed to standardize requirements specification.

We saw earlier that requirements separate the concerns of the negotiators and define a contract between them. They do the same thing for product and product line developers. Product line developers are concerned with identifying and implementing the common requirements, while product developers are concerned with specifying and implementing the variable features. The product line requirements separate these concerns by defining how products are specified. A product is specified by providing bindings for the variable requirements, and descriptions for any requirements that fall outside the product line scope. Product specification aids can be developed to simplify the process. Some methods, such as FAST [WL99], use specification languages and tools to capture and analyze product specifications.

A PRODUCT LINE FOR FAMILY OF MEALS

Product specifications can be produced by specializing product line requirements expressed as feature models.

We can think of the product line requirements as a menu used to order products. To press this analogy further, the products are like meals served by a restaurant. Product line stakeholders are like customers who order meals from the menu. A product specification is like a specific meal order. The product developers are like cooks who prepare the meals described by the orders, and who may modify meal definitions, or prepare meals outside the menu. The product line developers are like chefs who decide what will appear on the menu, and what ingredients, processes, and kitchen equipment will be used to prepare them. To turn this analogy around, a restaurant is like a product line for a family of meals.

We said earlier that feature models can be used for configuration, meaning that they can be used, not only to describe variability, but also to support the process of selecting specific variations. Feature models can therefore be used to describe the valid configurations for members of a software product family. In other words, product line requirements can be expressed using feature models. A product specification can then be expressed as bindings for variable features in the model, in the same way that a problem statement can be expressed as bindings for variable features in a problem domain model. Since feature models and their bindings map easily to XML schemas and XML, this provides a good foundation for product line implementation, as we shall see shortly. According to Czarnecki, the process of binding variable features is called specialization, and produces a feature model that contains less variability than its predecessor. Three kinds of transformations can be performed to specialize a feature model:

- Refining feature cardinalities, reducing the range of variability in the number of instances of the feature. For example, the cardinality 1..*, meaning one or more, could be reduced to 1, meaning exactly 1.

- Removing a subfeature from a group, reducing the range of variability in the choices available. For example, one engine type could be removed from a set of two alternative engine types in the configuration of a car.

- Assigning a value of the appropriate type to a feature, reducing the range of variability in the set of possible values that could be assigned.

As Czarnecki points out, feature models are especially useful in the context of a software supply chain, since they can be used to support staged configuration, where features are selected in stages, and each stage refines the configuration specified by its predecessor. A security feature model is created by partially specializing the one shown in Figure 11.12. This feature model requires all passwords to expire in 30 days, requires passwords to use three or four different kinds of characters, and restricts File IO and file dialog permissions for the Internet.

Feature models can be used to support staged configuration.

Business Case Analysis

Business case analysis determines the return on investment for the product line over its life cycle. It is generally based on estimates of the number of products in the domain, the cost of developing, maintaining, and enhancing each product in the context of the product line, the cost of developing, maintaining,

Business case analysis determines the return on investment for the product line.

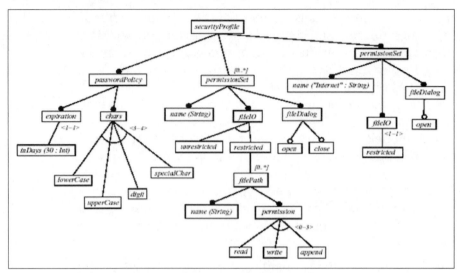

Figure 11.12   A security feature model specialization

Used with permission from K. Czarnecki, S. Helsen, U. Eisenecker. Staged Configuration Using Feature Models. Proceedings Of Software Product Line Conference 2004.

and enhancing a product as an individual, and the cost of developing, maintaining, and enhancing the product line. This information can be captured by a financial model, which can be used to determine the product line scope. Business case analysis is generally performed after product line definition, problem domain scoping, and solution domain scoping, so that these estimates can be based on the results. Weiss and Lai provide an excellent discussion of business case analysis.

Scope Evaluation

The product line scope identifies the products that will be produced by the product line.

All of the artifacts produced up to this point by product line analysis activities can be used to define the product line scope. The product line scope identifies the products that will be produced by the product line. It includes all products that solve problems in the associated problem domain, and that can be developed in a way that satisfies the product and production constraints. Defining the product line scope is inherently an iterative activity. Scope evaluation is the last step in the process.

Product line scoping occurs throughout product line development.

In scope evaluation, we consider the business case and decide what adjustments, if any, should be made to the product line scope to improve the business case.

While product line scoping, as an activity, is often associated with product line analysis, in practice, it occurs continuously during product line development, as product development provides feedback, and decisions that affect the product line scope are taken.

- Decisions taken during problem domain scoping determine what problems can be solved by product family members.

- Decisions taken during problem domain modeling regarding the identification and separation of the common and variable problem features determine how problems will be specified.

- Decisions taken during solution domain scoping determine how product family members will solve problems in the problem domain.

- Decisions taken during product line design and implementation determine product constraints, such as the architecture, and implementation components that will be used to produce family members.

- Decisions taken during the development and automation of product development process determine production constraints, such as the development activities that will be used to produce family members and the tools that will be used to automate those activities.

Product Line Design

The purpose of product line design is to decide *how* the product line will develop products. Product line design includes product line architecture development and mapping, and the definition and automation of the product development process, as illustrated in Figure 11.13. It produces a product line architecture and a mapping from the product line requirements to the architecture, and a specification and an automation plan for the product development process. Product line design should run concurrently with other product line and product development activities to maintain and enhance these artifacts. For example, the requirements mapping may be revised during product line implementation, or when the implementation components are revised in response to product development feedback. Similarly, the automation plan may change in response to tool changes during process asset provisioning, or in response to defect reports or enhancement requests received before, during or after product development.

The purpose of product line design is to decide how the product line will develop products.

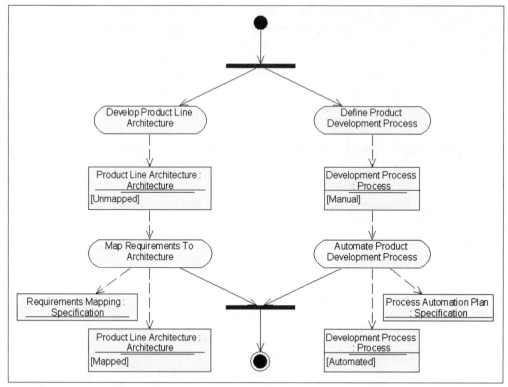

Figure 11.13   Product line design

Product Line Architecture Development

Product line architecture describes the common high-level design features of the products.

This activity produces a product line architecture that describes the common high-level design features of the products that will be produced by the product line. This includes the basic partitioning of products into components, the allocation of responsibility among components, the contracts offered by the components, the relationships and interactions among components, and the technologies used to implement the components. We saw earlier that developing an architecture is a central aspect of working within a family. It should therefore come as no surprise that the product line architecture is the most important asset produced by product line development.

It distinguishes between the common and variable design features.

A product line architecture is like an architecture for an individual product, since most individual product architectures are abstract enough to admit a variety of implementations. However, while an individual product architecture assumes a single outcome, a product line architecture must address variation among the family members. In other words, it must distinguish between their common and variable design features. The product line architecture also defines the process used to customize the product line architecture, and an architectural description standard (ADS) for the product line. The ADS describes the structure of the architecture for each family member. In addition, it provides styles, patterns, and mechanisms to be used by those product architectures, and it defines constraints, policies, and guidelines that govern the way they are developed.

The common design features are described in the usual way, by identifying the architecturally significant requirements and the design decisions taken to satisfy them, as described in the SARA report [SARA]. In other words, the common design features for a product family are described in exactly the same way as the architecturally significant design features for an individual product. The architecturally significant requirements for a product line are a subset of the common product line requirements.

The common design features are described in the usual way.

The variable design features cannot be described in the same way because we may not know how to implement a given variable requirement in advance. The variable design features may therefore be expressed as variability points, which are points where the architecture can vary to accommodate the implementation of variable requirements. Recall from Chapter 2 that the mapping between problem and solution features is generally complex. One variability point may therefore support many variable requirements. Conversely, one variable requirement may be supported by many variability points. Recall that the degree of determinism in a product line depends on how much is known about the ranges of variation for the variable features. We are now ready to see how this principle is supported by the product line architecture. The possible variations at a given variability point depend on how much is known about the ranges of variation of the requirements supported by the variability point.

Variability points let the architecture vary to accommodate the implementation of variable requirements.

- When the ranges of variation are fully known, the possible architecture variations can be completely defined. In this case, specific requirements variations, such as specific transaction policies, can be mapped directly to specific architecture variations, such as specific configurations of library classes.

- When the ranges of variation are partially known, the possible architecture variations can be partially defined.

In this case, general requirements variations, such as specific user interfaces, can be mapped to general architecture variations, such as those supported by a user interface framework.

- When the ranges of variation are unknown, the possible architecture variations cannot be defined beyond specifying the constraints that must be satisfied by the implementation of the family member.

Product Line Requirements Mapping

We can exploit our knowledge of variable requirements and variability points to produce a mapping between them.

We can exploit our knowledge of variable requirements and variability points to produce a mapping between them. This mapping can be used during product development to accelerate the process of deciding how each variable requirement will be implemented. It identifies the major design decisions that correspond to each variable requirement, and indicates when, how, and by whom those design decision are taken. By definition, design decisions against common requirements are taken during product line development (e.g., during the development of the product line architecture, during the development and automation of the product development process, during the mapping of the product line requirements to variability points, or during the provisioning of the implementation components). Design decisions against variable requirements can be taken during product line development, if enough is known about their ranges of variation. Otherwise, they can be taken at product development time (e.g., during the derivation of the product architecture or product production plan, during the construction of the product implementation, at product deployment or initialization time, or during execution).

Product Development Process Definition

Process definition describes the common and variable features of the product development process.

According to Jackson, the value of a method increases with its level of specificity to some problem domain (epigraph). It therefore seems reasonable for a product line to define a process for developing product family members. Process definition describes the common and variable features of the product development process. It produces a process that identifies the production assets and explains when, how, and by whom they are used to develop the product family members. It may describe the activities performed, the artifacts they produce or consume, and guidelines, conventions, and policies for using the production assets. It also defines how product specifications become orders for product development, how components are provisioned and used to fill those orders, and how change requests and special requirements are handled.

Product Development Process Automation

The product development process may be fully manual, partially automated or fully automated. If it is at least partially automated, then we need to decide which tools will be used, and how to automate specific tasks. These decisions can be captured in an automation plan that describes the flow of control and artifacts among the tools. Like other product line artifacts, it has both fixed and variable elements. Developing tools is an expensive task. Models and patterns can be used to dramatically reduce the cost of automating product lines.

An automation plan describes the flow of control and artifacts among tools.

Product Line Implementation

The purpose of product line implementation is to provision the implementation assets required by the product line architecture and the process assets required by the process automation plan. Product line implementation includes implementation and process asset provisioning and packaging, as illustrated in Figure 11.14. It produces the implementation and process assets, and modifies the product line architecture and the product development process. Product line implementation should run concurrently with other product line and product development activities to maintain and enhance these artifacts. For example, implementation components may be revised in response to changes in the product line scope, or in response to enhancement requests or defect reports received before, during or after product development.

The purpose of product line implementation is to provision the implementation assets required by the product line architecture and process assets required by the process automation plan.

Implementation Asset Provisioning

Implementation asset provisioning provides the components required to build family members by buying them from suppliers, developing them in-house, mining them from existing products, or commissioning them to be developed externally, as illustrated in Figure 11.15. Each component may be accompanied by contracts, design and user documentation, testing artifacts, tools, and a description of a micro process used to customize and apply the component during product development.

Implementation asset provisioning provides the implementation components.

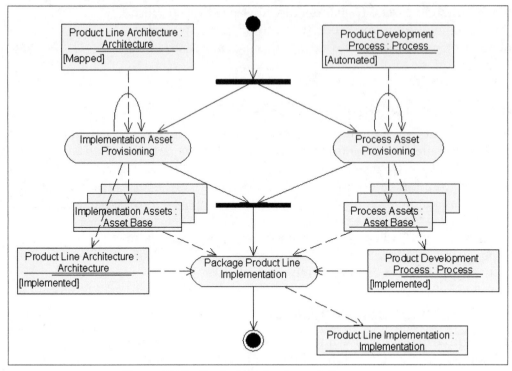

Figure 11.14   Product line implementation

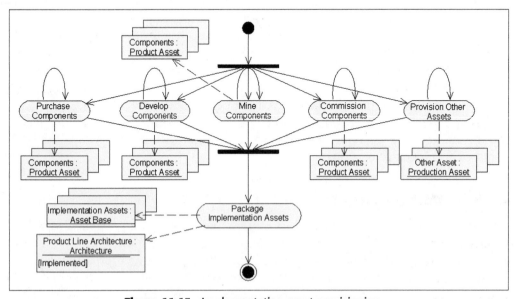

Figure 11.15   Implementation asset provisioning

These assets may also be packaged, stored, versioned, maintained, and enhanced by this activity.

Variability points in the product line architecture are implemented by assembling and configuring the components. Fine-grained variability points can be implemented using association, aggregation, invocation, inheritance, delegation, parameterization and inclusion. Medium-grained variability points can be implemented using adaptation, decoration, mediation, interception, visitation and observation. Coarse-grained variability points can be implemented using assembly. Many of these mechanisms are supported by design or architectural patterns.

Variability points are implemented using variability mechanisms.

Process Asset Provisioning

Process asset provisioning implements the product development process by providing tools, documentation, and other resources, as illustrated in Figure 11.16. Tools can be developed from scratch or by extending existing tool frameworks.

The production plan is automated by developing tools.

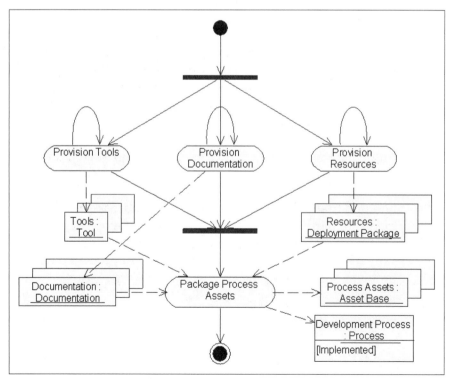

Figure 11.16 Process asset provisioning

Product Development

The goal of product development is to produce a member of a product family.

The goal of product development is to produce a member of a product family. Inputs to product development include the production assets and the requirements for the product family member to be developed. Its output is the product family member. The product development process is usually defined by product line development, as we have seen. In this section, we therefore present an abstract product development process. In practice, the product development process will be much more specific, and much less prescriptive. We can think of product development as consisting of problem analysis, product specification, product and collateral implementation, product evaluation, and product packaging and release, as illustrated in Figure 11.17.

Problem Analysis

The purpose of problem analysis is to decide what *problem to solve.*

The purpose of problem analysis is to decide *what* problem to solve. It includes validating the problem features against the features in the problem domain to ensure that the problem falls within the scope of the product line, identifying the features of the problem that are addressed by the product line, describing the features of the problem not addressed by the product line, and pruning the problem statement by resolving overlaps, extras, and conflicts between the problem and the problem domain, as illustrated in Figure 11.18. Since the product line requirements represent the problem domain within a single iteration of the product line, as we have seen, problem analysis is a short activity that serves only to determine which parts of the problem to be solved are in scope for the product line, and to support the negotiation of product specific requirements for parts of the problem that are out of scope. It produces a problem statement describing the problem to be solved, possibly by updating a draft problem statement produced during problem domain scoping.

Product Specification

The purpose of product specification is to decide what *product to develop to solve the specified problem.*

The purpose of product specification is to decide *what* product to develop to solve the specified problem. Product specification includes validating the product requirements against the product line requirements to determine which parts of the

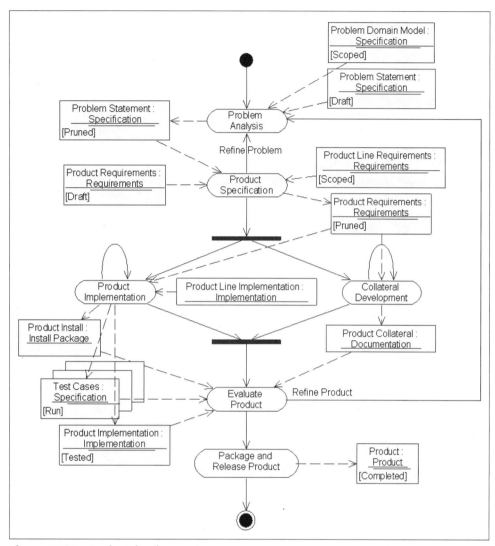

Figure 11.17 Product development

product are in scope to be developed using the product line and how, providing bindings for the parameters of variation, defining requirements for parts of the problem not addressed by the product line, and pruning the results by resolving overlaps, extras, and conflicts with the product line requirements, as illustrated in Figure 11.19. It produces product requirements that specify the product to be developed, possibly by updating draft product requirements produced during solution domain scoping. Product specification may include a business case analysis to determine whether or not the product should be developed within the product line, including estimates of the

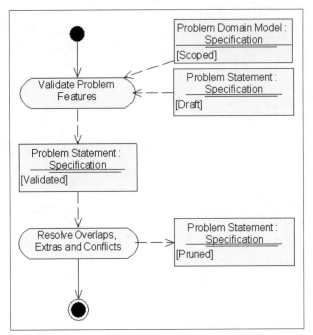

Figure 11.18   Problem analysis

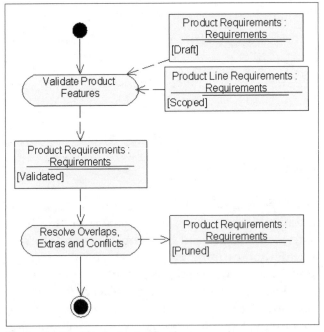

Figure 11.19   Product specification

cost of developing, maintaining, and enhancing it within the product line and as an individual product, and the cost of modifying the product line to develop the product. The product line may develop all, part or none of the product.

Collateral Development

The purpose of collateral development is to produce the product collateral, such as user documentation, packaging, marketing collateral, and any other artifacts that are part of the product, but that are not executable. The production assets may include assets that support collateral development, such as a collateral development process, collateral development tools, and collateral resources, such as style sheets, standard artwork, and document templates.

Product Implementation

The purpose of product implementation is to produce the specified product. It includes product design, executable and test case development, and testing, as illustrated in Figure 11.20. It produces a production plan, a product architecture, a product implementation, a product install, test cases, and test results.

The purpose of product implementation is to produce the specified product.

Product Design

The purpose of product design is to decide *how* to develop the product. Product design includes process customization and architecture derivation, as illustrated in Figure 11.21. It produces a product architecture and a production plan.

The purpose of product design is to decide how *to develop the product.*

Process Customization

Process customization produces a production plan that describes how the product will be developed. The production plan is derived from the product development process, and takes into account the variable requirements, requirements outside the product line scope, and any other product specific concerns.

Architecture Derivation

Architecture derivation produces a product architecture that describes the product implementation. This architecture is derived from the product line architecture, as illustrated in

The product architecture is derived from the product line architecture.

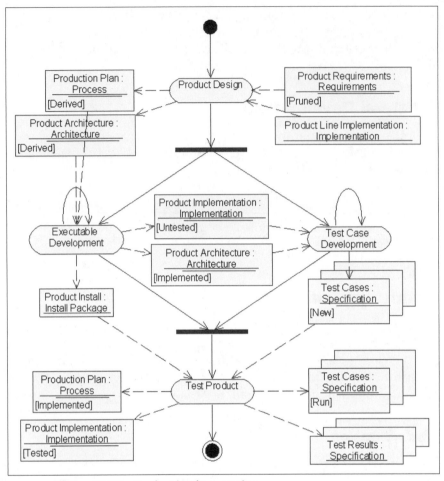

Figure 11.20 Product implementation

Figure 11.22. This includes validating the product line architecture, which confirms that the product implementation can conform to the product line architecture; selecting variants and options, deciding what implementation components to use, and how to configure, assemble, adapt or extend them to satisfy the product requirements, and identifying any required components that are not supplied by the product line; extending the product architecture to address any unique requirements; optimizing the architecture; and evaluating the architecture to confirm that it will satisfy both the functional and operational requirements. See Bosch [Bos00] for a detailed and comprehensive treatment of architecture derivation in a product line context.

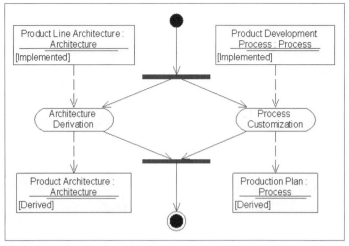

Figure 11.21   Product design

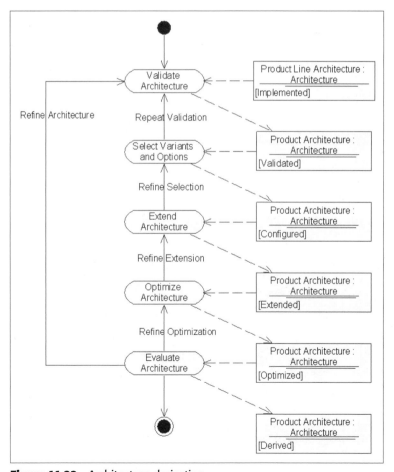

Figure 11.22   Architecture derivation

Test Case Development

The purpose of test case development is to design and implement test cases for the specified product. This is similar to test case development for an individual product, except that the product line may provide production assets to support test case development for family members, including test harnesses, generators, and execution environments, a product testing process and tools.

The purpose of executable development is to produce executables for the product from the product requirements.

Executable Development

The purpose of executable development is to develop executables that satisfy the product requirements. This activity includes product assembly and build, and unit test development, build and execution, as shown in Figure 11.23. It produces the product implementation, a product install image, unit tests,

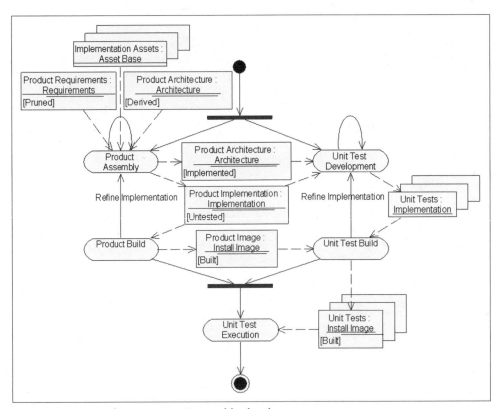

Figure 11.23   Executable development

and unit test results, and it may modify the product architecture. Note that the vast majority of the time spent during one-off product development involves these activities. When products are developed in the context of a product line, much less time is spent on these activities than with one-off product development.

Unit Test Development

Unit test development produces unit tests for the product implementation. This is similar to unit test development for an individual product, except that the product line may provide production assets to support unit test development for family members, including test harnesses, generators, and execution environments, a unit test process and tools.

Product Assembly

The purpose of product assembly is to implement the product according to the product architecture and the production plan by integrating the implementation components supplied by the product line. The components may be used without modification, or configured or adapted as necessary. Components that are required but not supplied by the product line may be provisioned by purchasing them from suppliers, developing them in-house, mining them from existing products, or commissioning them externally, as illustrated in Figure 11.24. Generally, provisioned components are product specific, since they address variable requirements by definition. In some cases, however, they may be added to the product line and made available to be reused in the development of other family members. In this case, the product line requirements must be updated to describe the variable requirements addressed by the new components, the product line architecture must be updated to include them, and the requirements mapping must be updated to relate these additions. Because product assembly is so central to product development, and because software factories automate product assembly using models and patterns, we devote an entire chapter to this subject (Chapter 13).

Product and Unit Test Build

Product and unit test build produce executables from the implementations of the product and the unit tests. This is similar

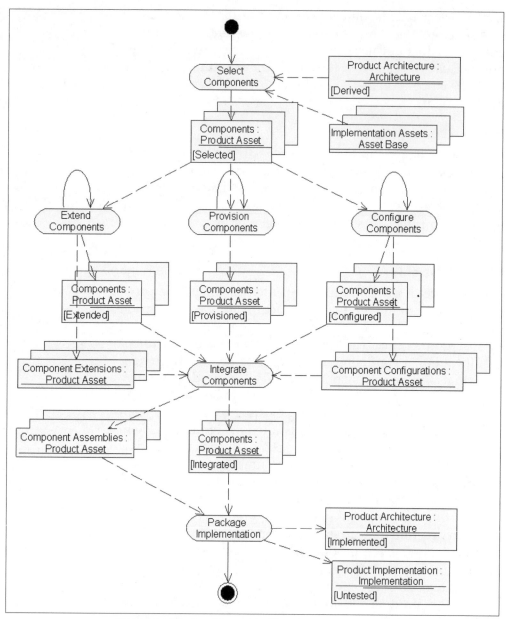

Figure 11.24 Product assembly

to the build process for an individual product, except that the product line may provide production assets to support the build process for family members, including build scripts, build verification tests, and build environments, a build process and tools.

Product Line Evolution

Product line evolution is a special case of product evolution. Recall from Chapter 3 that the primary sources of change for business applications are business and technology evolution. These factors also drive the evolution of product lines for business applications. In general, product lines change as their family members change. These changes are introduced as family member requirements and target platforms change. Recall, also, how software can respond to change. Disposable software is discarded and replaced. Unmaintainable software is preserved until it is no longer viable, then discarded and replaced. Mutable software evolves. All three of these types of software with their associated responses to change may be present in a product line, or in the family members it produces, maintains and enhances. Again, recall the effects of change, and the phenomenon of software aging. Product lines, like individual products, grow old. Like individual products, they experience fatigue and stagnation, and they must anticipate and accommodate modification to avoid brittleness. As we saw earlier, adaptive design is one of the most important strategies for mitigating the effects of change. We have also seen how product lines apply the principles of adaptive design across multiple products. This lets them accommodate change on a larger scale than individual product development. An interesting quality of product lines is that the interaction between the two processes tends to balance short and long term concerns, letting both evolve efficiently. Product line development provides stability by changing slowly in response to long-term concerns, and product development provides adaptability by allowing rapid change in response to short-term concerns.

Product line evolution is a special case of product evolution.

Product Line Deployment

A topic related to product line evolution is product line deployment. We have not yet considered how product lines are deployed. There are two major aspects to product line deployment, start up and operation. Start up is the transition from individual product development to family-based product development. Operation is the ongoing development of the product family. We will look at both in Chapter 16.

Platform-Based Abstractions

That Moore's Law drives complexity is axiomatic. That the growth of complexity represents novel challenges to designers and architects is not news. But why this is the case is less obvious; the answer offers some tantalizing indications of the course architecture will take in the next few years.

Chris Hamlin

In this chapter, we look at how platform-based abstractions can be used in a software product line to support development by assembly. We start by describing three types of platform-based abstractions, classes, components, and services. Next, we compare these, looking at how each is defined, and at how well each supports systematic reuse and development by assembly. Finally, we describe classes, libraries, and frameworks in depth.

Challenges created by platform complexity and technology evolution have similar effects on both hardware and software design, and are being solved in similar ways in both industries.

Platform-Based Abstractions

In the chapter epigraph, Chris Hamlin of LSI Logic Corporation [Ham02], is thinking of the issues of complexity in semiconductor technology. The designers and architects he has in mind are those concerned with the rapidly increasing complexity of new hardware design at the deep submicron geometry level and advanced material science. According to Hamlin,

The future of semiconductor design lies in adopting a platform approach to taming the costs and risks of complexity. Such an approach, involving higher levels of abstraction, offers customers access to complex high-performance functions while insulating them from the increasing difficulty of reliably implementing such blocks in advanced processes. In addition, the customers' value-adding design activities are no longer held hostage to growing topological complexity.

Challenges created by platform complexity and technology evolution have similar effects on both hardware and software design, and are being solved in similar ways in both industries. A growing set of ideas known in the electronic engineering community as *platform-based design* are gaining hold in the area of submicron electronic design (see [San02] for an introduction), based on layers of successive platform-based abstractions. The history of rising levels of abstraction in that community in response to design and platform complexity, as shown in Figure 12.1, looks very familiar.

Recall the definition of platform-based abstractions.

In Chapter 2, we showed how the level of abstraction can be raised to make software development easier, and how a meet-in-the-middle approach works best—progressive refinements

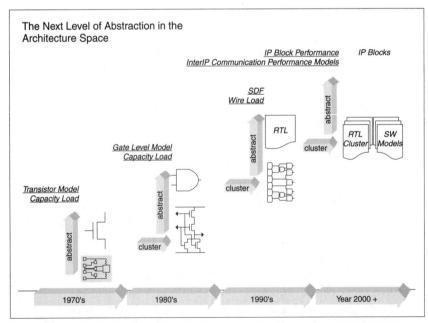

Figure 12.1   Platform-based abstractions in electronic engineering (from [San02])

of requirements meet progressive abstractions of potential implementations. Each new set of abstractions defines a new layer, or platform, and uses design choices communicated by its user through variation mechanisms like parameters to select an implementation at the layer below.

The increasing complexity and functionality of platform technology demands ongoing development of new platform-based abstractions to support software design and construction. Unfortunately, not all platform-based abstractions are suitable for systematic reuse in software product lines. In this chapter, we show what makes an abstraction suitable for systematic reuse, and we describe several kinds of platform-based abstractions. Since our focus is on the transition from the existing paradigm of object orientation to a new paradigm of industrialized software development, as we explained in Chapter 5, we assume that the basic constructs from which we can construct new platform-based abstractions are the existing constructs of object orientation, such as classes and class libraries, class frameworks, and components.

We show what makes an abstraction suitable for systematic reuse, and we describe several kinds of platform-based abstractions.

Platform-Based Abstractions in Product Lines

In Chapter 11, we showed how product lines promote systematic reuse. Making systematic reuse achievable in the software industry is the key contribution of product line practices. Reuse has been a long-term goal in software development, but it has not been realized on a large scale. Some kinds of software products have been successfully reused, such as operating systems, middleware, and class libraries. Systematic reuse of higher-level abstractions has proved more difficult, however. As Bosch points out [Bos00], software is generally reused successfully across multiple versions of a single product, but ad hoc reuse based on the field of dreams model (*build-it-and-they-will-come*) has generally been unsuccessful. Feature modeling, domain specific languages and patterns provide a foundation for systematic reuse, as we have shown in Chapter 8. Let's look at several kinds of software constructs that may be candidates for expressing systematically reusable platform-based abstractions.

Feature modelling, domain specific languages and patterns provide a foundation for systematic reuse.

Programming Language Classes

A *class* is the basic unit of program modularization and encapsulation in an object-oriented programming language. A class

Classes and class libraries are the mainstay of reuse today.

is therefore a language-based abstraction. A class provides a common description for its instances, each of which is an object that encapsulates state and behavior. The behavior is supplied by code that is uniquely privileged to change the state. While it is possible to provide a systematically reusable platform-based abstraction consisting of only a single class, it is more common to provide a group of related classes that must be used together. A predefined class or group of related classes made available to clients at runtime through a platform-based abstraction. One or more of these abstractions may be packaged together in the form of a *class library*. Class libraries are by far the most common packaging mechanism for platform-based abstractions in use today. Many prebuilt, pretested abstractions are available, saving huge amounts of development time. Examples include math libraries, string libraries, event and exception handling libraries, database access libraries, and user interface widget libraries.

Software Components

Components have contractually specified interfaces and are independently deployable.

Generally, a class is not an independent unit of deployment. It does not exist outside the programming environment in which it is defined, except in source code form. To enter into the world of independently deployable platform-based abstractions, we need a *software component*. A software component has almost as many definitions as authors who describe them. In this book, we will start with the definition quoted by many, offered by Szyperski [Szy99] at the 1996 European Conference on Object-Oriented Programming.

> *A software component is a unit of composition with contractually specified interfaces and context dependencies only. A software component can be deployed independently and is subject to composition by third parties.*

This definition introduces several key concepts. It links the term *interface* with the phrase *contractually specified*, and mentions *context dependencies*. We will analyze this definition in a later section, because we need to understand exactly what the minimum functionality should be for an interface, and assess how much of a contract most interface mechanisms really support. In particular, we're interested in how an interface is used at runtime to manage interaction with the component. In addition, we'll need to understand what Szyperski meant by context dependencies, since a key property of a platform-based abstraction is the dependency it has on its underlying execution platform. We will also see how component-based development methods help developers specify, implement, and compose systems from collections of components.

Service Components

We define a *service component* as a component that offers its capabilities to its consumers as services. A service is offered by a service provider. An authorized client can use a service without knowing how it is implemented or where it is deployed. This means that a service is both opaque and location-independent. A service component uses richer interface mechanisms that offer higher qualities of service to its consumers and a richer specification to its implementers. Service components can be organized to form applications using an architectural style called a Service Oriented Architecture (SOA). We will explore several SOAs and their facilities for extension and composition in later sections.

A service component is a component that offers its capabilities to its consumers as services.

While service-oriented applications do not require Web service technology, interest in loosely coupled, message-driven architectures seems to be driven by existing and emerging standards-based Web service interoperability protocols. Using Web service technology allows organizations to build highly composable applications, whose components are distributed across multiple heterogeneous platforms, and which incorporate services outside the organization, possibly in partner companies, government departments or standards organizations. Web service technology reduces dependencies between service components by using canonical wire formats. We will look at the implications of Web service technology for the construction of systematically reusable platform-based abstractions in a later section.

Web service technology reduces dependencies between service components by using canonical wire formats.

Properties of Platform-Based Abstractions

A number of common threads appear throughout these introductory remarks on platform-based abstractions. In this section, we revisit these threads as seven properties of

We identify seven key properties of platform-based abstractions.

platform-based abstractions: definition, discovery, composability, adaptability, deployment, distribution, and organization. We then characterize several well-known platform-based abstraction mechanisms in terms of these properties.

Definition

Specification must be separated from implementation.

The definition property deals with the distinction between specification and implementation. A specification describes *what* an abstraction does (i.e., how it will behave when used). Given knowledge only of a specification, a client can use an abstraction without knowing *how* it is implemented. The implementation of the abstraction uses code, data or other artifacts, in order to provide behavior that conforms to the specification.

Specifications can be weak, strong, formal or informal.

Specifications may be informal, perhaps expressed as natural language text, or formal, expressed using a specification or modeling language with precise syntax. Specifications may be weak, meaning that they say little about using the interface, even though they may describe precisely how its methods should be called or how messages passed to those methods should be formed. A strong specification would stipulate this additional information, identifying sequences of calls that produce valid behaviors or sequences that produce error conditions.

Formal specifications support reasoning and implementation substitution.

Clearly, formal specifications are preferable to informal ones, since they can serve as metadata that an abstraction exposes to tools, platforms, and customers. Exposing the specification as metadata, particularly at runtime, is an important step toward providing a high value, systematically reusable abstraction, since it allows a consumer to reason about the abstraction and its properties. Also, when an abstraction provides a formal specification, clients write to its specification, not to its implementation. Any other implementation of the same specification is a candidate for substitution for the original.

Discovery

Abstractions that expose metadata are easier to discover.

The discovery property deals with how easy it is to find either a known instance of a known platform-based abstraction, or an unknown instance of an unknown platform-based abstraction that is well suited to a specific purpose. Abstractions that expose metadata are easier to discover through metadata access techniques like reflection, as in Java and .NET languages, and like publication to queryable catalogs, as in UDDI for Web services. The richer the metadata exposed by an abstraction, the easier it is to find the abstraction. Strong formal specifications provide much richer metadata than class names or method signatures. Without metadata, discovery techniques are limited to scanning for names, keywords, comments or annotations.

Composability

No abstraction works alone, so understanding how multiple abstractions work together is important. What restrictions, if any, govern the composition of the abstractions (e.g., does the composition mechanism rely on a specific language or runtime)? What assumptions does each abstraction make about others (e.g., does a component start its own transaction, or does rely on receiving a context from the caller)? Can new abstractions be created by composing existing ones?

Composability deals with how abstractions work together.

Adaptability

The adaptability property deals with how easy it is to reuse the abstraction in a different context. We met white-box and black-box mechanisms in Chapter 2. White-box mechanisms offer the most flexibility since the implementation of the abstraction, if supplied at all, is exposed, and can often be extended. Blackbox mechanisms are opaque. Bosch points out [Bos00] that the popular notion of software components as "Lego bricks" that can be snapped together without adaptation is largely myth. To be systematically reusable, an abstraction must anticipate and accommodate adaptation, either through some internal variability mechanisms, or through external adapters. Note that accommodating adaptation through external adapters may sound easy. Can't any component be adapted to any context by wrapping it in adapter code? Unfortunately not, as Bosch points out. There may be differences in control between a component and its context (i.e., some components expect to initiate interaction, some expect to be called), differences in calling style (e.g., some components pass arguments by reference, some pass by value), or dependencies that cannot be resolved (e.g., a component may require access to a legacy system that is not available outside its home data center).

Adaptability deals with how easy it is to reuse the abstraction in a different context.

Deployment

Deployment deals with resolving dependencies on the execution platform.

The deployment property deals with resolving dependencies on the execution platform to install and execute an abstraction. How is the abstraction installed in an execution environment (e.g., what registry keys must be set)? What services does the abstraction require from the execution environment (e.g., Java Remote Method Invocation)? How are the required services bound to the abstraction (e.g., through a configuration file or user interface)? What other software must be deployed with the abstraction (e.g., the server side for the client side stubs)?

Distribution

Distribution concerns the capability for remote server deployment.

Deployment and Distribution are separate properties but tightly related. Distribution concerns whether it is possible to design an application from platform-based abstractions such as classes and components in a way that permits their deployment on remote, but networked servers. Distribution affects design, since the ability to exploit distributed execution environments is hard to add to a design built without them.

Deployment can also affect design, since in most cases, knowledge of the target infrastructure upon which classes or components will be deployed can and should, influence aspects of design. For example, if a component is designed to accept certificated security, but its target server software does not support that option, then a deployment problem is being wrongly designed in.

Organization

Frameworks apply an organizing architecture

Although individual platform-based abstractions are often useful, usually it is a related collection of abstractions that offers the most value to a consumer developer. An organizing architecture for the abstractions makes clear the structural relationships between abstractions, and their behavioral dependencies.

We will see that a useful organizing architecture for reuse with a software product line is a software framework. Software frameworks apply architecture to a collection of classes and components in a way that encourages reuse and custom extension by defining extension points in the framework that support the variable features of the product family.

Classes, Libraries, and Frameworks

Programming language classes offer an excellent way to structure an otherwise monolithic program, imposing encapsulation boundaries and providing developer abstractions that can simplify development, debugging, and maintenance. However a class scores poorly as a useful platform-based abstraction mechanism when assessed in terms of the properties described earlier.

Specification and Implementation are usually not distinguished in classes.

Typically, a programming language class such as those found natively in C++, Java or C#, provides little support for the separation of its specification from its implementation in terms of the method code and data elements. Each class is an encapsulated unit, enforced by the syntax and semantics of classes in the language.

Interfaces are supported by most modern OO programming languages, but usually as a supplement to the principal class declaration. Interfaces provide a way to extend the definition of a class by grouping related methods and their parameters into a language construct. Classes which implement the interface provide their own implementation code for the methods in the interface. Interfaces thus provide a kind of partial separate specification for a user of the class, albeit a weak one (methods only). As well as providing a partial separate specification, an interface provides a degree of substitution for a consumer of the class.

Discovery is usually weak, as the only way to find classes is keyword searches (when provided) or inspection through browsers.

Discovery is difficult unless class metadata is available.

Class-based systems like the Microsoft CLR-based languages and Java, permit reflection of metadata about classes. Metadata available from reflection includes inherited classes, methods and parameters, and a list of methods called from within method bodies. This allows the metadata to be extracted into a database that may be used to search for classes, to provide for hyperlinking between methods and even some where-used analysis across the members of the library. Reflection can overcome some of the limitations of classes that have no natural runtime specification. But reflection is often an inefficient process, and places too great a burden on the developer of the consuming class.

White-box extensions are the most common.

White-box customization is the most common form of extension, since the rarity of specification languages makes black-box working very difficult. Users of the class library can make their own extensions by defining new classes which inherit from those supplied in the library, enabling the library to become customized for a particular application, or set of users. Care is required however, that critical classes are not changed inadvertently with unpredictable consequences to other users. Because extensions are permitted, class design by inexperienced programmers may become encapsulated in name only, with defined methods that depend too tightly on one underlying implementation, and may reveal more of the inner workings of the inherited class than its original designer intended.

Composability is limited due to deployment dependencies.

In addition to composability gained from inheritance of classes in the library, client code wishing to use a class provided as part of a library must directly call the individual methods, and is thus bound strongly to that implementation. Individual instances of the class, the objects in the system, lie within the programming environment, often making it difficult for client code which calls the methods to operate in an altogether different environment. Standards for most of the commonly used OOPLs exist either as *de facto* or *de jure*, enabling most libraries written in Smalltalk, C++, and Java to be used in a standard way. Class libraries which are part of proprietary 4GLs are usually callable only through that environment. Therefore, in many cases, all or much of the library ends up (statically or dynamically) linked to the client execution unit, and is not separately deployable.

Distributed object technology allows for remoting.

Technology for distributed objects became a reality in the 1990s with the advent of CORBA object request brokers and Microsoft's remote object technology known as DCOM. Distributed object technology allowed for platform-based abstractions to be distributed across remote servers.

But lack of variability mechanisms makes them poor for product line feature mapping.

Overall, potential for reuse with class libraries is quite high. Many useful functions exist as class libraries, often in key areas such as GUI building, mathematics, engineering, and other domains. But their lack of any dependable interface at run-time means that classes are a poor choice for platform-based abstraction in a product line supported by a software factory. Class libraries add little or no meaningful architecture to an application using them. But the big weakness as a platform-based abstraction for product line feature mapping is their lack of variability mechanisms, because control predominantly lies in the calling code.

Class Frameworks

Class frameworks impose a well-defined organizing architecture for a collection of classes designed for custom extension and reuse. In fact, with a class library, the application developer defines the application architecture. With a framework, the framework defines the application architecture Here is a definition of a class framework from Johnson and Foote [JF88]

Class frameworks impose architecture on applications that use them.

> *A framework is a set of classes that embodies an abstract design for solutions to a family of related problems.*

According to Roberts and Johnson, frameworks embody the theory of a problem domain, and are always the result of domain analysis [RJ97]. They assert that developing a framework makes sense only when many applications are going to be developed within a specific problem domain, so that the cost of developing the framework can be recovered from the savings that result from applying it.

A framework may address all or only part of an application's architecture. For example, a user interface framework addresses only the user interface portions of the application, while an object-relational mapping framework addresses only the portions related to the persistence of business entities.

Gamma predicted that frameworks would become increasingly important due to the levels of reuse they provide, that large applications would consist of layers of cooperating frameworks, and that most of the code in applications would either be supplied by frameworks or be framework completion code. All of these predictions have been realized in examples like J2EE and the .NET Framework [GHJV95].

Framework Structures

A framework is defined as a number of concrete and abstract classes and a definition of the way instances of these classes interrelate. The concrete classes typically implement the interrelationships between the classes. The abstract classes constitute the extension points at which the framework can be used or adapted. An extension point is a part of the framework

Structure of frameworks provides clear extension points.

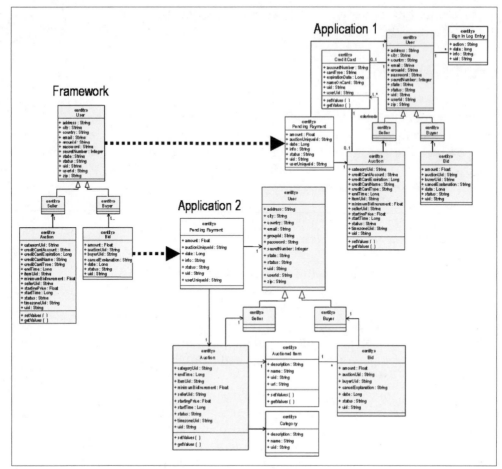

Figure 12.2 Completing a framework

for which the implementation is not given. Typically, only the specification of the interface is provided by the framework and the developer chooses how these extension points should be adapted to implement specific variability features of the product line (see Figure 12.2).

Parameterization is often used to accommodate architectural variation and to permit customization of the implementations. Other extension mechanisms, such as class and interface inheritance, method overrides and delegation, may also be used. These mechanisms constitute the *variation points* of the framework.

Control inversion of frameworks influences composability.

Frameworks often impose architectural structure on an application using them because of a characteristic known as *inversion of control*. This refers to an architectural feature of

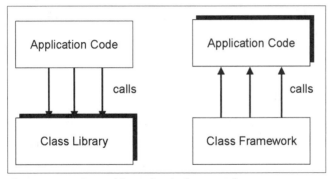

Figure 12.3 Control inversion in frameworks

frameworks in which the framework plays the role of a main program in coordinating and sequencing application activity. The consumer of a framework provides methods that override specific framework behaviors to tailor it for a specific application. The core of the framework is dynamically shared among all applications derived from it (see Figure 12.3). This allows a framework to serve as the nucleus of a family of related applications as evolving requirements cause its members to diverge [Foo88].

Frameworks and Patterns

Patterns play an important role in developing frameworks. Design patterns help developers choose design alternatives that make software more reusable and avoid design alternatives that make it less reusable.

We use patterns while building frameworks.

Frameworks typically emerge during the refactoring that occurs when software is consolidated. Foote describes the life cycle of software as consisting of a series of prototyping, expansionary, and consolidating phases [Foo92]. Consolidation involves refactoring the software to improve its organization without changing its behavior.

During refactoring, the reusable parts of the design and implementation are separated from the application specific parts, the decomposition of the software is revisited, the assignment of responsibilities is refined, and the interfaces are improved [GHJV95].

Changes to framework code may have wide effects, so we must build them accordingly.

Another general principle articulated by Roberts and Johnson, known as the Pluggable Objects pattern, involves encapsulating the areas of the framework code that change most often.

The ability to anticipate and accommodate change is even more important in application frameworks than it is within individual applications. This is due to the need to reconcile two opposing forces:

- Frameworks must support the union of the requirements of the applications that reuse them. Because they are exposed to change in any of the applications, they have greater exposure to change than any of the applications have individually.

- Changes to frameworks have wider repercussions than changes to individual applications, and therefore are potentially more destabilizing. In keeping with the readily observable phenomenon that wide acceptance and deployment creates resistance to change, stability is more important in frameworks than in the applications that use them [FY99].

It is therefore more important to use agile methods in application framework development than in application development. For example,

- Frameworks should be constantly refactored as they change to support new requirements. This keeps them easy to maintain by preserving their architectural integrity.

- Frameworks should be constantly tested as they change to support new requirements. This ensures that they do not compromise the reliability of the applications that incorporate them.

- Frameworks should use mechanisms that encapsulate change, such as those described by the pattern literature [POSA1]. This reduces the cost of supporting new requirements by minimizing the effects of change.

Framework Adaptability

White-box extension methods involve inheritance and programming.

White-box extension methods for frameworks use patterns like Template Method and Factory Method [GHJV95] to encapsulate reusable behavior, and primarily involve extension by subclassing. In other words, the principal composition mechanism is inheritance.

Inheritance is a static composition mechanism, and creates strong coupling between a superclass and the subclasses derived from it. On the other hand, it permits the subclass to modify the behavior supplied by the superclass, enabling adaptations that were not envisioned by the developer of the superclass.

Completing a white-box framework requires knowledge of the framework implementation, since applications must inherit from framework classes and override their methods. Since this can lead to problematic inconsistencies, this can be avoided through language mechanisms that block overriding, such as using the keyword `final`. But the key idea is that extending a white-box framework involves programming and a detailed understanding of the class structure of the framework.

Black-box extension methods for frameworks use patterns like Decorator and Visitor to encapsulate reusable behavior, and primarily involve extension by assembly. In other words, the principal composition mechanism is association.

Black-box extension methods involve association and assembly.

Association is a dynamic composition mechanism that allows relationships between objects to change during execution. While it is more flexible than inheritance, the compositions it creates are not as easy to discover by examining the source code [RJ97].

Completing a black-box framework requires knowledge of only the framework specification, since applications provide parameters and compose framework classes by association. Completing a black-box framework involves parameterization and assembly.

Inheritance is used in a black-box framework to help application developers locate and apply reusable classes by organizing into hierarchies.

Johnson and Foote observe that frameworks typically evolve from white-box frameworks to black-box, as the most stable and widely used abstractions and their implementations are encapsulated and parameterized [JF88]. The refactoring that occurs during consolidation tends to produce many new abstractions, often by decomposing existing abstractions and recomposing them using association rather than generalization. As a framework evolves, portions of the framework emerge as distinct components.

Frameworks can be developed by extracting reusable abstractions from multiple applications.

Building Frameworks

The patterns literature contains a number of pattern languages that provide insight into the challenges associated with developing frameworks. A good example is the Pattern Language For Evolving Frameworks, by Roberts and Johnson [RJ97].

Application frameworks are developed by extracting reusable abstractions from multiple applications. The more applications considered when designing the framework, the more general the result. Roberts and Johnson suggest that three archetypes are optimal, applying the well-known Rule Of Three [Tra88]. They identify the central challenge in designing a framework: domain experts don't know how to encode the abstractions that characterize the domain, but developers don't know the domain well enough to derive the abstractions.

Many important abstractions are discovered only after a framework has been reused, especially those that are artifacts of framework design, rather than elements of the domain vocabulary (see Figure 12.4).

Teams may work in succession or in parallel.

Roberts and Johnson identify two primary ways to develop a framework:

- Have the same team build multiple applications in succession, reusing the designs and the code. This approach leads more rapidly to the identification and extraction of reusable abstractions than the others, but tends to produce less general results.

- Have multiple teams build multiple applications in parallel, independently. This approach improves generality by introducing a greater diversity of perspectives, but takes longer to produce results. They recommend using an independent reuse team that mines the reusable abstractions from the archetypes.

In either case, the applications can be prototyped, rather than taken to completion, in order to accelerate the development of the framework, but this produces less mature frameworks that suffer more modification during application development than frameworks based on completed archetypes.

Of course, frameworks are often developed after the fact, mining the reusable abstractions from existing applications that are discovered to be archetypical of the domain.

During the initial stages of framework development, reusable abstractions may be identified and extracted using a technique known as programming by difference, described by Johnson and Foote [JF88]. In essence, this amounts to identifying candidate abstractions by noting the portions of the archetypes,

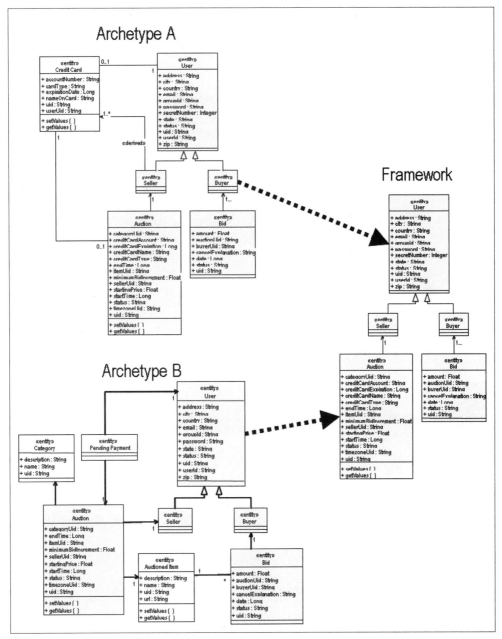

Figure 12.4 Building a framework from archetypes

either at the method, class or component level, that exhibit the least amount of variability.

The preceding methods for building frameworks are best suited to the construction of generic, widely applicable frameworks, which will be potentially used across multiple product

Modeling class frameworks with tools.

lines. Frameworks may also be built that are suited to more specific uses within a domain defined by a product line. Both domain specific and domain independent class frameworks will become part of the product line assets.

As we showed in Chapter 11, product lines set the context for commonality and variability across products. When models are used to define product line artifacts as shown in Chapter 6, then these models may be used to help build domain specific frameworks. The metamodel of the domain, itself derived from the feature analysis of the domain, models the key reusable abstractions in the domain. These abstractions are used to define a domain specific language and corresponding tools with which to describe the variabilities and to enable transformation into framework completion code. The metamodel of domain abstractions is also used to define the framework classes, which may then be refined into a more detailed implementation

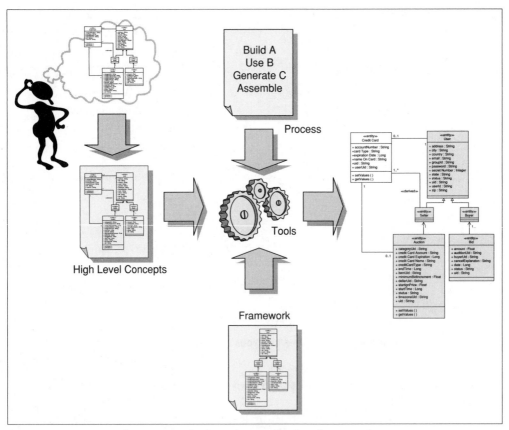

Figure 12.5 Systematic use of a class framework

model of the framework. Such a detailed model may be hand-crafted or automatically generated as a class framework.

Requirements of a toolset to be found in a product line software factory would include:

- Support for domain modeling, especially feature analysis and type modeling to build domain metamodel incorporating commonalities and variabilities.

- Support for refactoring, pattern extraction, and pattern instantiation.

- Generation of classes that constitute the framework from domain metamodel.

- Generation of completion code from domain specific languages and tools (see Figure 12.5)

We will study methods by which domain specific languages and abstract metamodels can be implemented in software factories using generative techniques in Chapter 15.

Summary

In this chapter we've discussed a number of possible ways to extend an execution platform by providing higher-level abstractions. We've looked at classes, class libraries, class frameworks, components, and service components, assessing each for the main attributes that help to map product line feature models and DSLs to the execution environment.

We saw that the critical criteria included the capability to adapt—important to implement product line variabilities. Equally important is the capability to expose as much information as possible in a schematized form—this enables runtime use of component metadata, discovery, and the processing of metadata at design time through tools. With well-formed computer processable metadata, tools may implement patterns of components with variation points, generate code to fill variation points in frameworks and components, and ensure product developers work within carefully designed application architectures designed to maximize reuse and flexibility across the product family.

CHAPTER 13

Components and Services

The correction of programming errors depends almost entirely on the skill and speed of a mathematician, and there is no doubt that it is a very difficult and laborious operation to get a long programme right.

B. V. Bowden

In this chapter, we look at components and services in depth. We start by defining components more precisely, discussing interfaces and dependencies, and describing component-based development methods. Next, we consider the migration now taking place from components to services. We look at how services change the partitioning of responsibility, focusing on message sequencing, protocol design, and service level agreements. From there, we consider how contracts can be used in software product lines, and we look at service-oriented architectures. Finally, we discuss Web services technology and assembly by orchestration.

Software Components

Definition

As we'll show, a software component is a platform-based abstraction mechanism that is a far more useful basis for the implementation of product line features. Szyperski's [Szy99] definition, repeated from Chapter 12 is:

A component metamodel illustrates the key ideas of component specification and implementation.

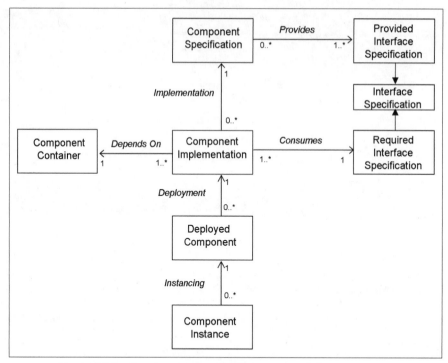

Figure 13.1   Component specification metamodel

A software component is a unit of composition with contractually specified interfaces and context dependencies only. A software component can be deployed independently and is subject to composition by third parties.

To help explain the ideas behind this definition we'll use a simplified metamodel of component definition, as shown in Figure 13.1, which is an extension and variation of that provided by Cheesman and Daniels [CD01].

The key idea behind a software component is the separation of a component specification from a component implementation. A component specification describes what the component does, and how it behaves when its capabilities are used by others. Given knowledge solely of the specification, any potential user, or client, of those capabilities can focus on its part of the overall solution without concern as to how those capabilities are actually implemented. The capabilities will be implemented by some developer who provides an implementation for the component by supplying code and data structures that meet the specification. In general, more than one implementation for a component specification may exist, each one differing in some aspect, such as platform, performance or cost. Changes to implementations, or indeed substitution of one implementation for another, must not disrupt clients who have been implemented to depend only on the component specification.

The capabilities of a component specification are described by a collection of one or more interface specifications, each of which describes a related group of capabilities. Interface specifications are, of course, potentially reusable across many component specifications, as in the case of an interface description for Address Management that may be shared by the specification for a Customer Information component and for a Personal Information Manager component.

Interface specifications are reusable ...

As a programming language abstraction, an interface is essentially a collection of related methods for which a class that implements the interface must provide an implementation. As such, it is a concept available at design time but not at runtime. For a software component, the interface specifications provided by a component specification must be available at deployment time and potentially at runtime. Interface specifications provide important metadata about the component that can be used to help discovery and validation that correct communication between components is occurring.

.. and must be available at runtime as metadata.

The interface specifications are important elements driving the mapping to feature models in the product line domains. The component specification describes the abstractions that are surfaced by the component. If component specifications already exist in a reusable component they can be matched to feature models for fit. Discrepancies lead to a decision to adapt the component or build another. If no existing component specification can be discovered in the product line assets, one can be built using a process of refinement that derives interface specifications from feature models.

Interface specifications map to product line feature model.

To ensure these processes work effectively, and to ensure well-formed interface specification metadata can be relied upon at runtime, a well-defined interface specification language is critical.

And are defined by interface specification languages.

Interface Specifications

Techniques for describing interface specifications have been evolving for as long as programming languages have been

Brief history of interface languages.

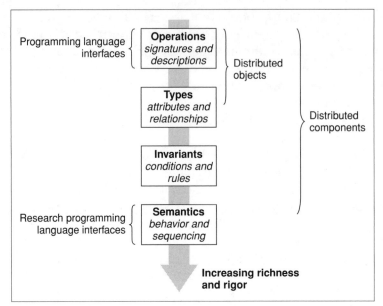

Figure 13.2 Elements of an interface specification

around. In Figure 13.2 we show the main elements of an interface specification language and indicate how various component approaches have added richness and rigor to interface specifications.

Programming language interfaces only define methods.

We mentioned earlier that general programming languages such as C++, Java, and C# have language facilities for defining interfaces. These allow for a description of a group of related methods specified by name, along with return types and parameter names and types. Languages such as Modula and Ada elevated the importance of meta descriptions of programming classes that allowed consuming code to rely only on an available module descriptions, and not depend on implementations of them that might be built in parallel, or for some time in the project, not at all. This made distribute development teams, common in large government or military contracts, much easier to manage. Again, these module meta descriptions were restricted to entry point or method names and parameter types.

But distributed object systems require a common type system.

A Specification Type Model

As distributed object systems became available, such as COM and DCOM from Microsoft, or the OMG CORBA 2.0 implementations, interface specifications became more important since it was imperative that a component developer have a detailed guarantee of the capabilities of a remote component that may be operating in another execution environment. These distributed object systems provided Interface Description Language (IDL), which defined not only the entry point descriptions, but added a definition of the type system that could be assumed common across all implementation of the standard. This is unnecessary in programming language interface descriptions since the type system is already predefined by the language specification, but essential when there may be multiple implementations of the common distributed object specification.

Despite having the same acronym, both CORBA 2.0 implementations and Microsoft DCOM had different IDL specifications, but several software products successfully formed bridges between the two, permitting a degree of interoperability. Today, as we'll see later, the same IDL function is provided by the standard definition of WSDL for interoperation between different Web service implementations. WSDL has the type system inherent in XSD type specifications.

While operations and types are adequate for small granularity distributed objects, they are inadequate as the basis for larger granularity distributed components. Although the types and operations elements provide an indication of how a component may be used, they are missing vital information that concerns, for example, how complex user-defined types are related, what changes to the internal state of the component are caused by the operations, and the correct sequence in which operations should be called.

A specification model can describe relationships between types.

More detailed interface specification languages therefore must add the additional elements illustrated in Figure 13.2. In the Catalysis component-based development method devised by D'Souza and Wills [DW99], interface specifications are described using models based on a well-formed underlying interface specification metamodel. An example of an interface specification model is shown in Figure 13.3.

The figure shows an interface specification model for an Order Manager component interface. The specification type model now shows more detailed information about the type system a component that implements this interface must conform to. The figure does not show primitive types that should also be defined, and imported into each interface specification. The type model acts as a vocabulary for the operations, and can form the basis for specifying the additional elements of the

And provide a vocabulary for defining invariants and behavior.

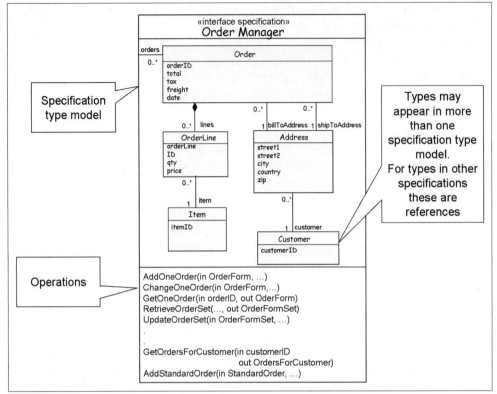

Figure 13.3   Interface specification model

interface specification—any invariants that must hold and the semantics of the behavior of its operations. These semantics must be unambiguous, yet sufficiently rigorous to ensure precise and predictable outcomes during the interaction, and to form the basis of an implementation project for a developer of the component.

It's worth emphasizing that the specification model is not necessarily at all related to any data structures that may actually be used by a developer in an implementation—it represents the "what" of the component. The developer's task is to manifest the behavior described in each interface specification—he produces the "how" of the component. No actual data structures used in implementations surface through the interface.

The specification model does however provide a vocabulary for types which are derivable from the model to be used as parameters to operations. Three such structures are shown in Figure 13.4.

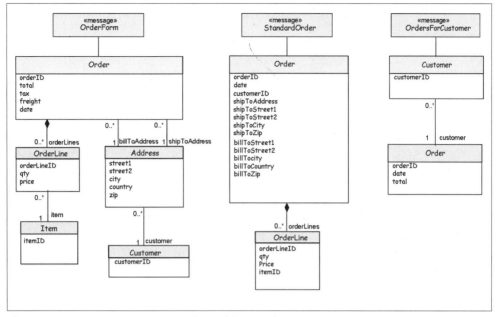

Figure 13.4 Parameter structures derived from order manager specification model

Types may be reused across multiple interface specifications. In this case a good design rule mentioned by Cheesman and Daniels [CD01] is to ensure that in all but one of the specification models the types simply carry the locator attribute (an identifier or other universal locator such as a URI). At implementation time, design patterns such as Observer may be used to ensure the components are synchronized.

Types are reusable across more than one specification model.

Specification of Invariants

Any rules that hold for the particular interactions we specify in the interface for a component must be clearly stated. Rules that hold for all scenarios in the behavior of a component are known as *invariants*. These benefit from both a formal, precise description, and an informal, helpful explanation. Invariant descriptions complete the type definition, and should be added to the specification model. As with operation specifications, they are expressed solely in terms of the common vocabulary provided by the specification model. For example, suppose we wish to limit the component Order Manager to small organizations, we could insist that it is banned from handling any orders that would contain over time more than 20 lines, and

Invariants model the constraints of the interface, and rules which hold for all operations.

that no order could exceed a value of $5000. Invariants would hold:

> **Invariant 1:**   For every order looked after by Order Manager, the number of OrderLines for the order may not exceed 20
>
> `For Every` order:Order Manager • count(order.lines) < 21
>
> **Invariant 2:**   For every order looked after by Order Manager, the total value of the order must not exceed $5,000
>
> `For Every` order:Order Manager • order.total < 5001

While both of these invariants could be specified formally in some language supported by the underlying specification metamodel,[1] some, such as invariant #1 could be depicted graphically using cardinality constraint symbols (0..20). Of course, a complete specification of the invariant would also include the notification sent to the client if the invariant is broken.

Specification of Behavior

Techniques for specification of behavior exist but are not widely used.

Fully specifying the behavior of a component by declaratively describing the effects of operations given in the interface specifications remains largely a research goal. Formal, declarative languages for describing interface behavior do exist. These are based on two seminal papers by Hoare as explained by Gary Leavens [Lea99]:

> *Hoare's paper "An Axiomatic Basis for Computer Programming" [Hoa69], used two predicates over program states to specify a computation. The first predicate specifies the requirements on the state before the computation; it is called the computation's precondition. The second predicate specifies the desired final state; it is called the computation's postcondition.*

> *Hoare's paper "Proof of correctness of data representations" [Hoa72], described the verification of abstract data type (ADT) implementations. In this paper Hoare introduced the use of an abstraction function that maps the implementation data structure (e.g., an array) to a mathematical value space (e.g., a set). The elements of this value space are thus called abstract values [LG86]. The idea is that one specifies the ADT using the abstract values, which allows clients of the ADT's operations to reason about calls without worrying about the details of the implementation.*

Examples of interface specification languages include VDM [Jon80] and Z [PST96], though these are not widely used in commercial application development. These languages are based on mathematical logic, which provides unambiguous specifications that may be analyzed using mathematical methods. Using mathematical languages also means that there exists opportunity to prove that an implementation of the interface conforms to its specification.

Early efforts at the Laboratory of Computer Science at MIT focused on algebraic methods of specification, first of abstract data type specifications, but later to program modules (see [GH93] and [Lar99]). These projects matured into the Larch project, which has produced interface specification languages for a variety of programming languages including Smalltalk, C++, and Java.

Larch is a well-known project to build formal specifications of several common languages.

Defining Larch specifications, which share some common ideas with those of Eiffel [Mey97] for observing the *Design by Contract* paradigm, consist of writing various assertions as annotations to the program source text. These essentially define invariants and preconditions and postconditions to methods of classes to form a complete specification of the class. See [Lea99] for a worked example of Larch for C++, which is beyond the scope of this book to run through.

In Catalysis, D'Souza and Wills [DW99] pick up this theme of declarative behavior specifications and use the component interface specification model as the vocabulary from which to write preconditions and postconditions for each operation in the interface. Catalysis is extended and simplified by Cheesman and Daniels [CD01], who choose to use OCL [WK99] to describe the behavior conditions. Again, it is only the vocabulary defined in the interface specification model plus any types provided as parameters that may be mentioned in these conditions. For example, with the interface model that appeared in Figure 13.3, we might write the following OCL:

Catalysis uses a logic language to define behavior of component interface specifications.

```
Operation: GetOneOrder( in ord : orderId, out of: OrderForm)
PreCondition:
  --- orderID is a valid order
  Order -> exists( o | o.orderID = ord )
PostCondition:
  --- the orderForm returned is the one whose orderID
  --- matches that provided on input
  Let theOrder = Order->select( o | o.orderID = ord) in
  result.orderID = theOrder.orderID and
  result.total = theOrder.total and
```

```
--- and so on for all members of the OrderForm type
--- structure shown in Figure 13.4
--- Note that the OCL keyword result refers to the
--- OrderForm structure
```

Interface Specification Adaptability

Adaptability of specifications and implementations is possible for white-box components.

As we mentioned before, the reuse of component assets as unchangeable Lego bricks has been pointed out by Bosch [Bos00] to be mostly a myth. Even in the well-framed context of the product line, there may be a breakdown of some of the assumptions that led to the creation of a planned reusable component that requires the product developer to adapt the component to the new circumstance. If the component specification is changed, careful checking of all usages of that component will be required to avoid invalidating existing application code.

For white-box components whose specification and implementation code is available, the developer may add functionality to the interface specification, or may override and delete functionality. The developer may then modify and add to the implementation code to meet the requirements of the new interface specification.

Black-box components extend the interface but not the implementation.

For black-box components, the component may only be adapted at the interface specification—the internal implementation code must be used as is. Two techniques are available for the product developer to adapt black-box components in this way.

- *Planned expansion* may be accomplished by designing generic operations whose actual parameters provide specific types that conform to the interface specification type model. For example, in the interface specification model in Figure 13.3, we may imagine an operation called OrderQuery whose parameters include the orderID of an order managed by Order Manager, but which includes a list of specification types for which actual data must be returned. Generally speaking, query operations such as these may be added to a specification with straight-forward preconditions, but care must be taken that new operations do not have behavior inconsistent with existing operation specifications.

- *Wrapping* the component specification with a new one is another common component adaptation mechanism.

Wrappers encapsulate an existing specification, and provide new implementation code that is implemented using new code, or calls to operations of the wrapped interface using the existing implementation. Wrappers must assume the responsibility for all previous operations offered by the wrapped specification, and have the added benefit that they themselves may be reusable across more than one original specification. Wrappers are also composable in that they themselves may be subject to further wrapping.

Discovery of Components

The interface specification model has one further utility within the product line assets, or even a wider context than a product line. We have already noted that the model provides a vocabulary for specification of a component's behavior and constraints, and that this vocabulary offers a richer description of the component than is given by simply listing the operations and their parameters.

Query of model metadata can assist catalog search and discovery.

This richer description may be exploited when data representations of the type graph and its operations and constraints are stored in a catalog of specifications as metadata that can be searched using rich queries. Existing catalog mechanisms for discovery, such as UDDI, do not offer this degree of capability (although UDDI may be extended to accomplish this). Product line asset catalogs should be capable of this level of discovery, and software factories should make use of them to ensure assets are discoverable and reused.

Component Dependencies

We said earlier in the chapter that classes and class libraries make a poor choice for product line platform-based abstraction, mostly due to their weak variability mechanisms, lack of architectural structure, and lack of metadata describing interfaces at runtime or design time. Class frameworks address the first two of these issues convincingly and therefore are more suitable as platform-based abstraction mechanisms.

To be good platform-based abstractions components must compose and interact.

Distributed software components have restricted variability mechanisms but rich interface description that can be exploited at both runtime and design time. Their ability to impose architectural constraints on the product line family members depends on their ability to compose and to form interactions with other components and frameworks.

Provided and Required Interfaces

Required interfaces complete the abstraction of a component.

The component interface specifications we have described thus far are more correctly described as *Provided Interfaces* since they describe operations that the component implementing the interface *provides* to others. Since applications are typically built from components that interact, and we require a description of any one component that can be independent of others, it is necessary to also specify what operations a component *requires* from others. These interface specifications are called *Required Interfaces*.

Required interface specifications group related operations that will be provided by other components and a supporting type model vocabulary as the basis for describing the required behavior and invariants.

Matching required and provided interfaces can be defined in metadata ...

Components may be composed by specifying how a required interface should be matched to a provided interface. This allows for a specification of how components interact to be defined independently of the technology that actually enables the interaction. This is very important when establishing a component architecture for a product line, since we wish to ensure interaction between components is describable with metadata which itself can become an asset for the product line that can be analyzed, cataloged and used to generate actual code and data structures required by the components at runtime when they have been deployed in their distributed servers.

...which drive the definition of special ports attached to the component implementation ...

Once all the required and provided interfaces are known, the component can be prepared for its implementation. Each provided interface specification will be made available as metadata describing a *port* that will provide access to the interface implementations. A port is a network addressable endpoint that is associated with a particular implementation of the component specification. Depending on the framework used for component interaction, each provided port will need some implementation within the software component that is responsible for receiving calls or messages to the operation, marshalling parameters, converting types, checking validity and security aspects, etc.

Each required interface specification will be made available as metadata describing a required port that manages interaction

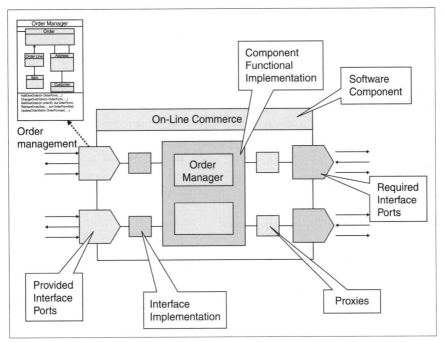

Figure 13.5 Elements of component specification and implementation

with components providing operations to it. Again, depending on the framework used for component interaction, each required port will need a proxy capable of marshalling parameters, handling validity and security aspects, and handling the outgoing addressability of the target provided interface port. These concepts are illustrated in Figure 13.5.

Of course, at runtime, distributed components interact through a component interaction environment which is responsible for providing services to the components to support interaction, as shown in Figure 13.6. These services would include remote procedure calls, messaging, location resolution, name resolution, security, and routing, all of which help to abstract from the component functional implementation code the details of how the interaction takes place. Historically, component interaction environments included implementations of the OMG CORBA 2.0 specification and the Microsoft DCOM environment. These environments themselves take the form of collections of components and frameworks which implement the various services. The completion of these frameworks, whether by tooling or manual coding can be driven from the specification of matching required and provided interfaces.

…and are used to generate extension code for interaction environments.

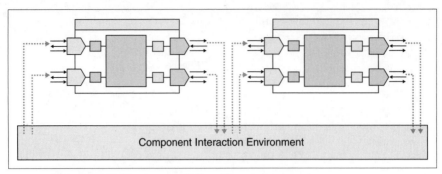

Figure 13.6 Component interaction environment

Container Dependencies

Containers provide other services than remote invocation.

In addition to the impact of the component interaction environment on the component implementation, there will also be dependencies on other services. It's common to refer to a collection of runtime services that a component may depend on as a *container*. In reality, the container is a set of frameworks and components that together provide services such as session state management, object persistence, and object state serialization. An example is J2EE, which provides exactly these services and more through frameworks which are completed by Java developers using manual completion or IDE-based tools and generators. Microsoft provides the same kind of services through namespaces within the overall .NET Framework for developers.

Deployment manifests are schematized artifacts describing dependencies.

Component deployment requires that all dependencies—container and interaction environments—are explicitly defined in a deployment manifest. Ideally, deployment manifests are artifacts with well-formed metadata that allows for search, analysis and reflection by deployment and management tools. Since deployment manifests may be predicted by product line architects, they may be reusable and extendable and therefore become part of the product line assets.

Component-Based Development

CBD can address the key issues in defining a software architecture for a product line.

Component-based development (CBD) is a set of techniques, tools, and processes for designing and building applications from the kind of large granularity, distributed components we've been looking at. The central challenges CBD addresses are the following:

1. How should interface specifications be determined from an analysis of the domain? How should domains be analyzed such that interface specifications are products of the process?

2. When interfaces specifications are designed, how should they be allocated to component specifications? How should the interaction between components be determined?

3. How can interaction between software components be used to impose architectural standards on a family of applications?

Now it is not the intention of this book to give a detailed account of how various approaches to CBD can address these issues. Rather it is our intention to briefly summarize works of a few other authors who do, to various degrees, address these questions. In this chapter, we will demonstrate that CBD is a maturing discipline, and that techniques and tools have been, or can be, defined to economically create a platform of predefined component abstractions within the context of a product line. Recall we are not endorsing the approach to reusable components we call *build-it-and-they'll-come* that has largely been unsuccessful. We are endorsing the premise that within the well-defined context provided by product line feature analysis of commonalities and variabilities, it is possible to design software architecture and an implementation strategy based on a set of interacting software components. As we'll show, we believe the next step for CBD is to embrace Development by Assembly in which self-describing components interact through independent protocols, and components are assembled using declarative orchestration mechanism, and configured by software factories using deferred encapsulation devices such as DSL-based aspects.

A Survey of Key CBD Techniques

D'Souza and Wills defined one of the first rigorous and comprehensive CBD methods known as Catalysis [DW98]. Catalysis was built on an earlier work on formalizing object-oriented design in the Syntropy method by Cook and Daniels [CD94], and the Fusion method by Coleman [Col93], and on Wills' PhD thesis on formal specification languages like VDM and Z.

Catalysis is based on types, collaborations and refinement.

Our use of terminology in this chapter has been strongly influenced by Catalysis and its derivatives. Catalysis describes three main levels of abstraction:

- Domain analysis, by which the authors mean any problem analysis not necessarily bounded by the interests of a product family as we have used the term.
- Component specification, which includes the notions of interface specification.
- Component implementation, in which specifications are refined into implementations.

Catalysis also uses three main concepts:

- A Type which is equivalent to an interface specification in the preceding text, and which is used to specify the external behavior of an object, such as an Order Manager. A type has a specification type model, a set of invariants, and a set of operations with preconditions and postconditions much as described previously, and says nothing about its potential implementation.
- A Collaboration, which is the communal behavior, or *joint action* in Catalysis, of a group of objects focused on solving a particular part of the problem. For example, the group of objects involved in the orders-to-cash joint action might include Order Manager and Inventory Manager, and others. The objects in the collaboration are really *roles*, since they are more accurately roles played by objects within the context of the collaboration.
- Refinement, used in Catalysis as we have used the term in this book to mean the process of meaningfully relating descriptions of types and collaborations at different levels of abstraction. For example, the orders-to-cash joint action may be refined to produce a more detailed collaboration that includes joint actions such as check stock collaboration between Order Manager and Inventory Manager, and enter sale between Order Manager and Account Manager. After successive refinements, we may reach the stage where it is possible to localize a joint action to a *local action* that becomes part of the behavior of one type—an operation

it must support. Thus, the check stock joint action
may be refined into actions like check stock on hand,
find substitute product, find reorder delay,
all of which may become local actions, or operations, of
Inventory Manager.

In the process of performing domain analysis, component
specification, and component implementation, various models involving different perspectives of types and collaborations
are used. For example, in domain analysis, collaborations may
summarize substantial business processes, with roles representing organization units. Refinement is used to decompose
these into smaller subprocesses so that the roles represent significant business entities. Subprocesses are joint actions, which
may be further refined as described earlier until detailed descriptions of types are discovered.

*Many specific
modeling
languages are
used during the
Catalysis process.*

When detailed component specification takes place, use cases
are used to help decompose joint actions into local actions, and
filmstrip scenarios are used to discover the effects of local actions, and their preconditions and postconditions. These latter
concepts may also be discovered or verified by the use of state
charts. Interaction diagrams are also used to analyze joint actions.

Once the types are refined to a level where further decomposition would involve restricting implementation options, the
type specifications may be gathered into components for implementation to begin. Catalysis assumed that implementation
would then be tool-supported with as much code generated
from the type models as possible.

Traceability back to early stages of specification must be managed by tools since all refinements can be expressed in metadata describing the exact transformation that had occurred between more abstract types and collaborations, and more detailed ones. We'll return to this key issue as we study generative
implementation for software factories in Chapters 14 and 15.

Perhaps one of the most novel and important aspects of
Catalysis is its use of the notion of frameworks. D'Souza and
Wills generalize frameworks to describe any recurring patterns of the three main concepts—types, collaborations, and
refinements. Variation points in the frameworks are matched to
model elements during the process of framework instantiation.
Figure 13.7 shows an example of a collaboration framework

*Frameworks in
Catalysis are
patterns of types,
collaborations,
and refinements.*

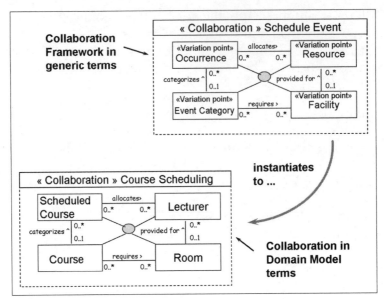

Figure 13.7   Framework instantiation by term substitution

expressed with generic variation points, which is matched to specific terms in a target model to produce a collaboration instance.

In practice, domain and specification models can be built up from successive applications of frameworks, and frameworks can be composed to form new frameworks. Collaboration Frameworks may have more complex substitutions than we've shown here, such as abstract actions that represent some partial specification of an actual concrete action in some domain. For more details on Frameworks in Catalysis, see [LSOW].

Catalysis built-in precision and traceability to support tooling.

Catalysis demonstrated that it was possible to describe a path from requirements analysis of a well-defined domain, through to specifications of components, with metadata tracing through the levels of abstraction, and well-defined artifacts at each step. Component interactions and component interfaces could be modeled precisely using structured metadata at all levels so full analysis and traceability was possible. This precision and the mappings between metadata artifacts were built-in to support tooling. Pluggable frameworks provided mechanisms for variability and composability. Catalysis was the basis for several tool product lines (for example, CA-Advantage, Select Software) that included generation techniques to provide component implementations from the component specifications. Most criticism leveled at the approach was due to its apparent complexity and reliance on formal specification methods.

Building on Catalysis

Cheesman and Daniels described a method heavily inspired by Catalysis they called UML Components [CD01]. The end goal was the same for UML Components: how to get from a rich model of requirements for a domain to a set of implementable but abstract component specifications. But UML Components was a vastly simpler approach than Catalysis—Cheesman and Daniels maintained most of the strengths of Catalysis, but were able to condense a description of it to more easily comprehended text. UML Components offered two important innovations over Catalysis:

UML Components simplified Catalysis without losing the key ideas.

- UML Components articulated a development process as a simple yet systematic sequence of steps, including a detailed description of artifact workflow, where Catalysis had left the actual development process to be deduced from a set of process patterns.

- Cheesman and Daniels showed how ordinary, standard UML notation could be used to describe component and interface specifications, and how other UML diagrams, such as use case and interaction diagrams, could be informally used to help derive specifications. For example, they showed how interface specification type models could be built using extended UML class diagrams by using a simple profile of UML stereotypes. They showed how standard OCL could be used for invariants, and for preconditions and postconditions.

We have only had the space to touch on a few of the published techniques for CBD. For further information, the reader is directed to other examples such as the method Korba [Atki02], which is a full-fledged CBD approach, and the work of Select Software in developing a CBD method called Perspective and a commercially available toolset [App03]. Bosch [Bos00] offers a different approach to the definition of CBD, but wraps in the product line story. Weiss and Lai [WL99] define a detailed development process called FAST based on product line engineering and CBD. We always find much to admire in articles published by the CBDiForum consulting group [CBDi].

Further reading on CBD.

Defining Product Line Component Architectures

The product line defines components and frameworks that will support commonalities and variabilities.

So far in this chapter, we've studied the two main types of software artifact that are available to the product line architect as he considers how to implement the commonalities and variabilities of the product family—software frameworks and software components. These artifacts are preferable since they support planned adaptability mechanisms, and they may be described using metadata that can be derived from domain models and processed by software factory tools. Software frameworks may incorporate design patterns, and impose an architecture on the use of a group of software classes. Patterns of interacting software components may also be defined.

A software architecture for the product line constrains how the components and frameworks may interact.

But in addition to specifying and providing adaptable, reusable components as part of the product line, the product line architect needs to be able to specify the overarching architecture of the members of the product family. The architecture sets the guidelines for the product developer by specifying what kinds of interactions are permissible between components and frameworks for products in the family. In other words, the product line describes not just what components and frameworks should be used, but the constraints on the way in which they can be used. This is an important consideration since component interaction environments, such as CORBA, provide a way to allow general-purpose components and application specific components (see Figure 13.8) to be composed in rich and potentially baffling ways, as well as providing common components such as brokerage, security, and name resolution. A software architecture therefore overlays a discipline on how the component interaction environment must actually be used.

The product developer uses tools that must support the architecture.

Recall from Chapters 10 and 11 that the product line architect also defines domain specific languages and tools to help the product developer build members of the family. The product developer uses these to build the completion code for frameworks, the adaptability mechanism for software components, and using other patterns and components provided to him, sets about building the applications. The tools that the developer uses should be constrained to work within the architecture defined for the product family as part of the product line assets. How then should product architectures be defined such that they can be processed and used by tools in this way?

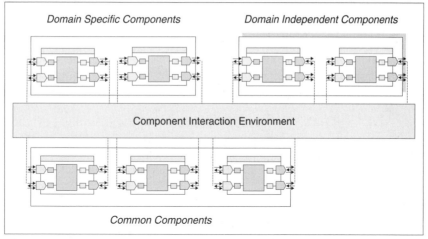

Figure 13.8   Component categories in a component interaction environment

Using Architecture Patterns

Software architectures are defined using architectural patterns. Architectural patterns impose an architectural style over the use of components and frameworks. An architecture pattern

Software architectures are defined using architectural patterns.

"...expresses a fundamental structural organization schema for software systems. It provides a set of pre-defined subsystems, specifies their responsibilities, and includes rules and guidelines for organizing the relationships between them." [POSA]

A commonly adopted style for building modern web-based applications uses the Layers pattern as defined in the [POSA]. An architecture based on this pattern offers many benefits to architects, such as easier maintenance due to lower coupling between components, and well-ordered dependencies between layers. A derivation of the Layers pattern is shown in Figure 13.9 involving three layers where each layer is dependent only on the layer beneath it, and components assigned to each role must be of a specific component type—that is, components that perform a predetermined role in the overall architecture.

Other patterns could be specified along with this pattern, such as the *Observer* pattern to manage dependencies between the Business Layer and the Presentation layer, and *Front Controller* and *Model-View-Controller* applied to the Presentation Layer. For details of these patterns, see [POSA], [GHJV] and [Fow02].

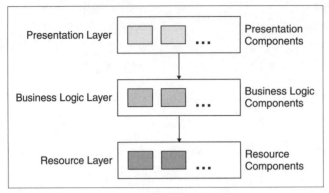

Figure 13.9 Three-layer application pattern

An example of architecture from The Business Component Factory book.

Different architectural styles may impose yet further constraints on the Layered architecture pattern. Herzum and Sims, for example, in addition to providing an excellent account of component-based development from domain models to implementation, define the concept of a *business component* as illustrated in Figure 13.10 [HS00]. Applications are composed from interacting business components using notions of component

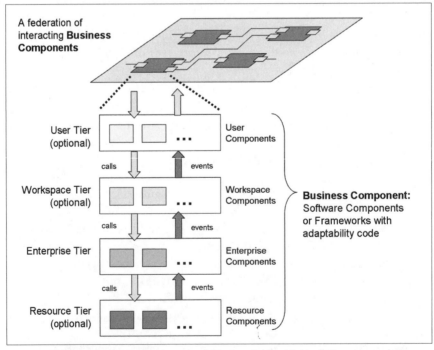

Figure 13.10 Component architecture in the style of Herzum and Sims [HS00]

interfaces as we've described earlier. Each business component encapsulates the implementation of a business concept or business process, and is itself a composition of software components, each of which plays a specific role in a specific layer of implementation. Thus, as Herzum and Sims say, a business component is a unifying concept across the distribution tiers.[2] Herzum and Sims describe in detail how business components and their constituent parts are defined and interrelated to construct effective business applications. The User Tier handles the representation of the business component on a user interface device. It handles forms and controls that edit and display data relevant to the business component. The Workspace Tier handles all logic necessary to support a user that requires access to enterprise resources. The Enterprise Tier processes the core business rules, validation, and interaction between enterprise components and frameworks. The Resource Tier manages physical access to shared resources.

The architecture in Figure 13.10 is a popular one for many business applications today. A Web service façade is used to provide the mechanism for describing interactions between the business components. The façade passes control to the lower levels of components and framework code, J2EE, for example, using high-bandwidth, tightly coupled remote procedure calls. At deployment time, the tiers map well to server clusters that provide front-end services running a web server, middleware servers running an application server, and back-end server clusters running DBMS software.

Jacobson, Griss and Jonsson [JGJ97], who also give an excellent account of another variant of component-based development, offer a different approach to layered architecture. Their architectural style, which emphasizes planned reuse via carefully designed component variation points as we've discussed earlier, is based on the concept of *component systems*. A component system is a pattern describing the composition of closely related components and frameworks, along with configuration components describing completion code for their variation points, and one or more façade components whose task is to expose features of the components and frameworks in that component system. Applications are built by describing the interaction between *application systems* and component systems. Application systems, which are derived from application system families, are compositions of components that manifest the use cases to consumers of the application.

And another from the Software Reuse book.

Defining Architectural Patterns

Architectures define component types.

Within architectural styles there is usually a taxonomy of component types. For example, some components manage business rules concerning a business concept. These are called Entity Business Components by Herzum and Sims. Other components implement business processes. These are called Use Case components in Jacobson, Griss and Jonsson, and called Process Business Components by Herzum and Sims. Process components implement various kinds of processes. Each kind of process must have common features that define what it is to be a process—they must be able to be suspended and resumed with state maintained, they manage state separately for each consumer of the process component, they implement the idea of state changes and actions that can move the process from one state to another. But a process component that manages, for example, the dialog with a single user—a User Interaction Process—may be used in a different layer from one that orchestrates the interaction between a number of business logic components.

We'd like a way to define architectural patterns ...

Each of the particular component architectures we've mentioned, and many variants of them, has advantages and disadvantages. The point is that the product architecture, whatever it should be to support the requirements of a particular product line, needs to be defined in a way that can be used to manage subsequent development of the products in that family. From our understanding of how architects wish to express product architectures for their product lines, we can see that the metadata required to express architectural patterns needs:

- A concept to describe the types of component, for example, the properties of user interface process components, entity components, and orchestration process components.

- A concept for organizing types of components into groups, for example, we may define a layer in the architectural descriptions above as a group.

- A concept of constraint on what types of component may belong in each group. For example, we may demand that only User Components and User Interface Process Components may be placed in the User Layer.

- A concept of dependency between groups that constrains how components in one group may interact with those in another. For example, we may constrain components in the Presentation Layer to only interact with components in the Business Logic Layer.

- A concept to describe the nature of the interaction between components in different groups. For example, we may stipulate that .NET Remoting should be used as the protocol for communication between Presentation Layer and the Business Logic Layer, or that Java events and callbacks must be used from the Business Layer to the Presentation Layer.

- A concept that allows related design patterns to be associated with component groups. For example, that the Observer or Façade pattern should be considered for the Business Logic Layer.

Of course, we are now treating the subject of defining architectural styles as a domain in its own right. We've been discussing examples of architectural patterns, and teasing out some commonalities and differences. The concepts in the preceding list could be used to construct a metamodel of architectural patterns and a specific language and tool for defining them. Such a tool could be used by product line architects to specify their product family architectures, and the artifact thus produced—a meta description of the architecture and its constraints—could be made available to the development tools used by the product developer to build members of the product family. With this metadata installed, the development environment can ensure that design and implementation decisions made by the developer conform to the intended product line architecture. We'll return to this idea in Chapter 16 as we illustrate the construction of a Software Factory, and provide some concrete examples of patterns used to formulate a product line architecture.

...using a metamodel and tool specific to the task and then to install architectural constraints in the product developers' tools.

Note that an architectural pattern is not the same as a component pattern. The latter is a prototypical set of related components that may be instantiated using domain parameters to make instances of components during the development of a particular product. A component pattern may cause instances of components to be created in one or more than one layers, for example. On the other hand, an architectural pattern is a prototypical set of related elements of the metamodel that represents the concepts in the previous paragraph. An architecture pattern causes instances of tool constraints, and project structures, folders, packages, and policies to be created.

From Components to Services

Components are good platform mechanisms for implanting abstractions ...

So far we have looked at the key platform-based abstractions that are well-suited to provide a basis for implementing product line commonalities and variabilities. Components and frameworks suitably constrained by a well-specified product line software architecture become the core of the product line assets. But there are still some weaknesses.

As we've looked into platform-based abstractions, one of the criteria we've used to judge an abstraction mechanism was the degree to which it could be schematized—represented by a metamodel which could become the basis of computer processable artifact for use in a modeling tool, a code generator or as a constraint on either. Schematized artifacts also support variability more readily than those expressed only in code.

...but still miss opportunity to describe information in metadata.

But in two clear cases, we have still left crucial information in code which could potentially be further schematized. These are: the full description of a component interface specification; and a description of the interaction between components—a literal schema of the component collaborations. First, we'll look at how we can complete the specification of a component interface, and then investigate how interactions between components can be described in terms of a business protocol—a schematized description of the requests and responses of participating components.

Service Components

We need to add more rigor to interface specifications.

In Figure 13.2, we saw the elements of an interface specification. In Figure 13.11 we repeat the figure but with some extended elements. To reach a stage where the interaction between components may be reliably and fully specific, we must have a more formal model of how a provided interface behaves with respect to any of the required interfaces of its potential consumers. Such a formal relationship is called a contract. In addition to the elements of an interface specification described earlier, an interface specification that is part of a contract must have its behavior specified and its obligations described in a Service-Level Agreement (SLA).

Service components' interfaces become contracts.

We will assert that a *service component* is a software component:

- Which is large granularity, typically providing for a single business process or concept

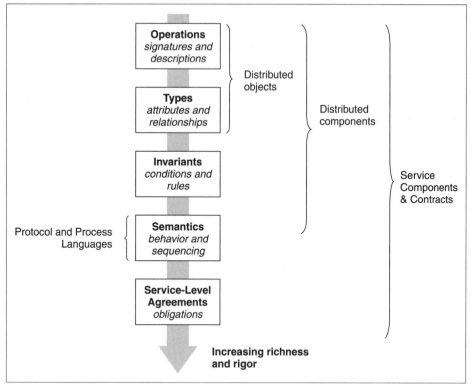

Figure 13.11   Elements of a service component interface specification

- Which may be interacted with asynchronously
- Whose interface specification behavior is fully defined in terms of sequences of emitted and received messages
- Whose obligations are described in an SLA

Service components offer services to one another that are governed by contracts, may engage in meaningful dialogs with others and understand conversation state, and meet their contractual obligations. Service component interface specifications must contain all these elements.

Business Protocols and Contracts

When service components interact in support of some business process, they interchange messages according to a *business protocol*. We append the word *business* to *protocol*, to differentiate between these protocol definitions and much lower network-level protocols, such as *http*. A *contract*[3] is the specification of the requirements on provided interfaces and required interfaces

A business protocol defines how services interact.

They may be defined independently by organizations.

An example of a business protocol implementation.

Contracts describe the behavior of parties in the protocol when implemented.

which are implementing a business protocol. Hence, we say that a contract governs the interaction between one or more service components and implements a business protocol.

Business protocols can be defined independently of contracts which implement them. For example, the organization RosettaNet has defined well over a hundred protocol definitions which can be composed into various actual protocols that support business-to-business service interaction. Called Partner Interface Processes (PIP) by RosettaNet, they have helped organizations begin service-based business-to-business operations, since the PIPs have been defined in conjunction with a large number of contributing member companies. Figure 13.12 illustrates a segment of a business protocol implementation for online order entry, using terminology borrowed from Rosetta Net PIPs PIP3A1, PIP3A2, PIP3A3, PIP3A4 [ROSETTA].

A business protocol must define what happens when two or more parties conduct an interaction. What it does not stipulate is how the parties perform actions on receiving a message, or what they do in order to produce an emitted message. In other words, the business protocol is a subset of the business process.

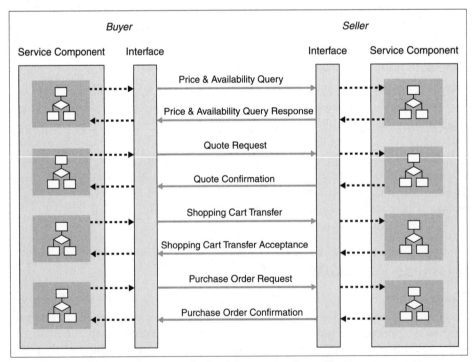

Figure 13.12   Part of a business protocol specification

RosettaNet publish business process descriptions showing the activities of the process, to provide a context for the protocol description. Although the overall business process from which the business protocol is derived may indicate what each party is *supposed* to be doing when a message is received, the contract specification does not reveal how messages are *actually* processed when received or processed before being emitted. Instead, we need to ensure that as much information relevant to proper functioning of the protocol is contained in metadata that describes the contract.

Message Sequencing

A business protocol must define the schemas that describe data contained in messages and any constraints the data is subject to. This corresponds to the kind of interface specification model we described earlier in the chapter. When dealing with message-based service description, the messages emitted and received take the place of operations and events described for software components. Protocols are state machines—they describe valid sequences of messages that can change the state of the process, or conversation, in which the parties are participating. This state machine must be decomposed into a state machine for each party to enable the contract specification for each participating member to be defined.

Protocols are state machines for the interaction.

We looked earlier at the use of preconditions and postconditions as a way to define behavior of a specification. Another approach is to describe the valid sequences of messages using a regular expression derived from the state machine of each participant. As Figure 13.12 shows, these sequencing expressions will be inversions of one another—an emitted message from one is the received message for the other. For example, a sequencing expression from the Sellers perspective would add information to a contract as follows:

A sequencing expression adds behavior information to the contract.

- The Buyer/Seller protocol is a dialog between a contract specification of the role of Buyer, and the role of Seller; the Buyer initiates the dialog.

- The Seller receives a `Price & Availability Query` message.

- The dialog is suspended until the Seller emits a `Price & Availability Query Response` message back to the Seller.

- The combination of Price & Availability Query followed by Price and Availability Query Response may occur any number of times. Notice that this fact about the protocol is hard to show in protocol interaction diagrams like Figure 13.12.

- This combination is ended when a Quote Request message is received by the Seller.

- The dialog is suspended until the Seller emits a Quote Confirmation message.

- The combination of Quote Request followed by Price and Quote Confirmation may occur any number of times.

- This combination is ended when a Shopping Cart Transfer message is received by the Seller.

- And so on.

Such sequencing expressions can be readily schematized and produced as additional elements on an interface expression.

Designing Protocols

Protocol design is a very challenging problem—some issues.

But protocol design is a very challenging problem. Even apparently simple protocols turn into complex ones as some of the following protocol issues are considered:

- *Request Response Pairs*: Should every message have an acknowledge message back to the sender? Doing so increases the protocol complexity, but not doing so requires the protocol to know when the most recent interchange has been received. For example, the Seller only knows that the last Price and Availability Query Response was received by the Buyer when it receives the first Quote Request message.

- *Deadlocks*: In which the protocol is in suspension with each party waiting for input from another party.

- *Livelocks*: In which the protocol is busy going nowhere. Interaction between the parties is looping with no hope of ending or making progress toward the next state.

- *Error States and Exceptions*: Have all possible errors and exceptions been considered? What happens if the Buyer emits a Quote Request before receiving the Price and

`Availability Query Response` from the Seller? Is that allowed? Or not?

- Even when acknowledgements are part of the protocol, how does the last message sender in the protocol know that its message was received?

- When services are collaborating across unreliable networks (such as the Internet), underlying message transport software will often send messages multiple times as intermittent network problems cause receive errors or timeouts. What happens if these resends actually do arrive? Unless reliable messaging frameworks offer a service level that guarantees messages arrive *once* and *in order* then messages must be designed to be received multiple times. Messages designed in this way are called *idempotent*. Designing idempotency into message protocols can eliminate great complexity in the processing of contracts at either end.

Protocol design and validation is a complex topic, which has been the subject of a great deal of research and engineering. Much of the work in this area has been inspired by the early work of Hoare in describing Communicating Sequential Processes (CSP) [Hoa85]. Each state machine that is described as part of the contract implementing the protocol is a *sequential process*. Hoare described a calculus for synchronizing the effects of these processes. Milner defined the π-calculus to achieve the same end, but added the capability to deal with mobile sequential processes—those between which communication could be broken and resumed—obviously a good thing for business protocols across mobile or static end points using the modern Internet. Although not for the mathematically fainthearted, Milner's work [Mil99] was the basis for the process language XLANG that is part of the Microsoft BizTalk Server product line. For a highly readable yet detailed account of protocol design issues, and examples of algorithms and languages which can specify processes and validate the protocols in which they are involved, see the work of Gerald Holzmann [Hol91].

Further reading on protocol design.

Representing SLAs

We have said that the contract specification—that part of a protocol which is to be supported by a service component that

Service Level Agreements specify obligations.

implements its role in the protocol—requires an element which describes the obligations for the contracts. For example, how long should the Buyer wait for a response from the Seller after it has sent a `Price & Availability Query` message? Is two minutes acceptable? Or, two hours? To depend on a service, these levels of service must be made explicit in a SLA that is supplied by the implementer of the contract. These obligations are to be met by the implementer, or the contract can be deemed at fault.

Typical elements in a SLA would include:

- Time to acknowledge receipt of message.

- Time to respond to action requested.

- Is authorization required, and if so, what kind? For example, are certificates required, and if so who is to be the issuing authority?

- Is non-repudiation required? This is a common requirement for business-to-business applications. These applications must ensure that a party cannot subsequently repudiate (reject) a transaction that has been accepted as final. For example, in addition to authenticating the Buyer, the Seller will also "time stamp" the transaction, so it cannot be claimed subsequently that the transaction was not authorized or not valid. Often the non-repudiation requirement is met by a trusted third-party service provider. This, however, increases the complexity of the collaboration protocols.

Contracts as Product Line Assets

Contracts are schemas and may also be patterns.

The information elements that make up a contract specification can all be described in a schema which can become a product line asset. These may then be used by product developers as they put together the service components that constitute a product. Since they are schematized, they may have an underlying metamodel which can be manipulated using software factory tools. Contract schemas may be parameterized to account for product line variabilities—forming contract patterns. For example, the Buyer/Seller contract specification may define Buyer and Seller as variation points which can be instantiated on to multiple pairs of service components to build different product family members. Contract patterns are a good example of a deferred encapsulation technique that allows variation of standard product line assets to take place at component assembly time.

Metamodels of the concepts underlying service component definition and service interactions and contracts may be used by graphical tools that can help the design and implementation of product family members.

Tools help with interaction design.

Service-Oriented Architectures

A Service-Oriented Architecture (SOA) breaks applications into large granularity service components, whose interactions may be bi-directional and asynchronous and are governed by properly specified message-based contracts as we have described. There is much interest in SOAs since one of their principal benefits is the loose coupling inherent in the contract-based approach. Loosely coupled application components are easier to change, are easier to join together using specialized service components that implement different process patterns. This makes SOA an excellent approach to support flexibility in shifting requirements for business processes. Since the service components tend to be defined to match business concepts and business processes, the mapping between business models and technology-independent design models is much tighter.

SOA describes applications as loosely coupled service components and contracts.

We showed earlier that a software component architecture imposes a structure and constraints on how components work together. An SOA imposes a structure and constraints on a set of collaborating service components. Recall that in Figure 13.10, we showed an example of component architecture. In that architecture, only the highest-level components could be potentially drawn as service components with contracts governing their interactions. In an SOA, some of the interactions between components in the vertical implementation stack could also be governed by contracts, and therefore potentially become service components. This allows, for example, a service component that implements a business process or workflow to be reused across more than one highest level service—defined in way that it can orchestrate lower level services, each of which can be used by more than one process or workflow.

It allows for contracts and services to be defined at lower levels of implementation.

An example of an SOA ...

Figure 13.13 illustrates an SOA that pushes service components lower into the stack to achieve higher degrees of reuse and greater degrees of flexibility. It achieves this by allowing for asynchronous, loosely coupled layers of process components

... that involves reusable workflow, user process, and business rules services.

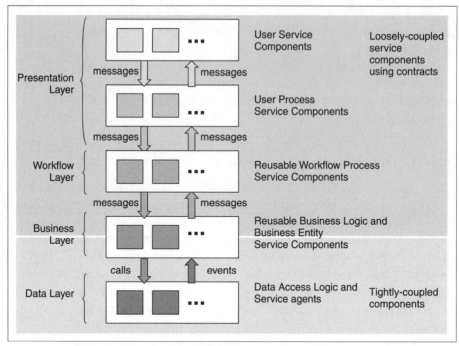

Figure 13.13   Service-oriented component architecture

which support user interaction and workflow orchestration of lower level services. Note that tight coupling is still shown for the lowest level services, since typically data access layers and service agents (components whose job is to manage interaction with other services) are not reusable between Business Layers.

Patterns of SOA are possible too.

Of course, the architecture in Figure 13.13 is only a prototype arrangement of layers, constraints, and component types. Just as we said earlier, such a prototype may be defined as a pattern of elements of an architecture definition metamodel to produce a schema of architectural constraints to be installed in a product developer's toolset.

Web Services Technology

Web services implement SOA with open and widely accepted standards.

Web service technology may be seen as the latest in a series of technologies for implementing SOAs (see Figure 13.14). Although still in its infancy, Web services have caught the attention of software package vendors, software platform companies, and most importantly, developers and architects in business IT departments. Web services are based on widely

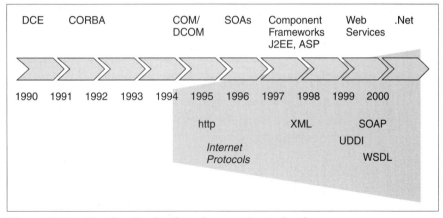

Figure 13.14 Timeline for distributed computing technology

accepted open standards such as XML and SOAP, which themselves are based on Internet standard protocols such as *http*. As such, Web service technology has industry-wide buy-in, and promises at long last a platform for interoperable distributed applications which acknowledges that most organizations operate on heterogeneous computing platforms.

Web services can be used as to impose a component architecture on applications, although the reality of some of the technological shortcomings of Web services currently means that the technology is rarely used for the components requiring tight coupling. Early successes in using Web services have been applications that connect existing information systems to Web service technology. This enables new modes of use, for example, allowing thin-client user interfaces to older applications, but also new categories of users—the so-called "edge applications" applications that connect an organization to customers, employees or other companies [HB01].

Early use focuses on edge applications, EAI and thin client wrappers.

Another class of applications for which Web services have been appropriate is application integration, often called EAI— enterprise application integration. EAI, which arises from the need to support cross-functional business processes that involve interlinking of existing functionally oriented applications. Existing applications often expose functionality in limited ways, and it's not untypical for an enterprise to have core business applications running on a variety of database, middleware, and operating system platforms. Used as facades to existing functionality, Web services provide the required interoperability.

What's Different This Time?

How do Web services differ from other distributed platforms?

We will emphasize four areas in which Web services look to offer attractive advantages over previous SOA technology:

- *Ubiquitous Connectivity*: With Web services, application data and functionality can be accessed anywhere it resides. No platform bridges are required. Mocking the early claim for Java, people have said Web services means "write-once, use anywhere".

- *Internet Standards*: As we have said, Web services are built on widely accepted open standards which are being evolved by open committees. Web services run just as well across both Internet and corporate intranets.

- *True Black-Box Components*: To use a Web service, no consideration need be given to implementation technology, platform specifics, and container dependencies.

- *No Explicit Programming Model*: With the interface described as metadata in the WSDL format, a Web service offers no restrictions on programming language concepts at the endpoints. The SOAP format defines how methods are invoked. CORBA primarily prescribed a programmatic interaction at the object level that required developers to know the structure of classes at the remote end.

But also has triggered efforts in standardizing common process and data semantics.

The other significant differentiator for Web services is that it is not only about the technology and standards that enable basic and advanced component interaction. Via a succession of proposed standards, efforts have been directed at security, reliable messaging, and transactions. These form the basis for Web service interoperability There are two other domains that complete the holistic view of distributed computing. These are Web service Data Semantics and Web service Process Semantics (Figure 13.15).

Web Service Data Semantics

Web service data semantics concern the meaning of data exchanged.

Web service data semantics concerns the meaning of data as it is exchanged between Web services. While XML schemas such can govern the format of message data interchanged, they cannot dictate that say, a customer name element means the

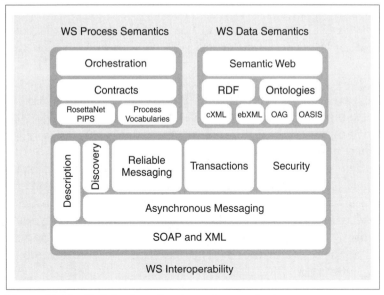

Figure 13.15   Holistic view of web service standards

same to both Seller and Buyer. The Buyer may issue the `name` element of type `string` with `first name` and `last name` separated by a space. The Seller may expect a single string with last name followed by first name separated by a comma. Who decides the correct meaning of a customer name field? As another example, who should decide the meaning of the term `credit rating` or `discount`? Web services that interchange data often have to run transformations between formats.

But another approach is to build a standard dictionary of terms so that message schemas can always draw from definitions that are universally agreed to. Actually, "universally agreed to" is a stretch. More likely is that vocabularies, or ontologies as they are sometimes known, which are specific to a domain can be defined by industry groups, such as cXML and trading consortia. For instance, a large company such as Ford may define exactly the purchase order form schema they expect their thousands of supply chain partners to use. Otherwise, groups such as OASIS and RosettaNet offer libraries of standard schemas that can be used in defining business protocols.

While these proprietary ontologies are a step in the right direction, many feel that there should be a consistent way to describe the meaning of data across the Internet. This is the Semantic Web idea. It would rely on a language that is richer

Shared ontologies and schemas help form supply chains between product lines.

The semantic web comprises composable definitions of vocabularies.

than today's XML Schema for describing syntax and some amount of semantics, such as RDF [W3C RDF], which is published and still evolving at the W3C. Think of XML Schema as a way to describe valid message formats, where RDF is a way to describe data models. RDF is based on a graph model of related resources, especially tuned to the needs of the web. For example, resources are URLs, and there is no central authority owning all definitions. So an `order` resource may be defined by one authority missing the concept of `discount`. The resource `discount` may be defined by another authority and combined with order to form a vocabulary of orders that includes discount. Vocabularies such as the Dublin Core [DublinCore] have been defined in RDF, but an effort to specify a generic language for describing ontologies in RDF is underway at the W3C in the OWL project for the Web Ontology Language [W3C OWL04].

Vocabularies are product line assets and can constrain variation points in contracts.

For product line engineering, it is enough for us to know that the semantics of data is increasingly being schematized beyond the syntax of messages. Ontologies and domain-specific vocabularies to be used by product engineers are assets in the product line. Variation points in contract definitions can be constrained to prespecified vocabularies, enforcing the product line architecture more firmly.

WS Process Semantics

The Web service messaging services are being filled out.

Building on the core interoperability standards for messaging over the internet, Web service standards have addressed more advanced functions such as security, transaction, and reliable messaging. With these in place the industry is set to interchange secure messages, asynchronously with guaranteed delivery, in order, and once only. Web service process semantics refers to the specification of higher-level meaning to Web service interactions that utilize these base services.

We need a language for specifying contracts.

We saw earlier how business protocols lead to the definition of contracts for Web service component interfaces. We also discussed the efforts undertaken by organizations such as RosettaNet that have defined protocols that can be adapted and reused by trading partners. These are the equivalent to data vocabularies on the process side—they are vocabularies for contract specifications. What must be supplied are the languages for expressing contracts that can become widely accepted by the Web service community. The W3C is working on a standard for expressing these known as Message Exchange Patterns (MEP) [W3C MEP], but so far these have not risen to the challenge of all elements of a contract specification as described earlier.

However, contracts as we've discussed them so far have been between two parties. There are many circumstances where we want to implement collaborations which have more than two parties. When we want to describe multiparty contracts, additional concepts must be defined. For example, suppose we have three Web services that are a Buyer, a Seller, and a Credit Checker. The Buyer may send a purchase order to the Seller, but the Seller must send the Buyer's details to the Credit Checker for order validation. With each service communicating asynchronously in a reliable fashion, it is necessary to include in the definition the *correlation* or *coordination* information that allows the contract between Buyer and Seller, and the contract between Seller and Credit Checker to understand that it is the same purchase order in each case.

But contracts get more complex when they involve more than two parties.

Defining these more complex relationships between contracts and addressing issues such as message correlation and scope of transactions has raised interest in languages that define the *orchestration* of Web services, sometimes referred to as *choreography* of Web services. A language now widely accepted by the software industry for doing this is Business Process Execution Language for Web services or BPEL for Web services [BPEL]. A detailed look into BPEL is not possible here, but briefly, BPEL allows a developer to specify how a group of Web services work together to provide an implementation of a business process. It breaks down some of the opacity of the Web service, by specifying some part of how a Web service must provide an implementation that ensures that correlated messages and interleaving of transactions across service boundaries needs to take place.

Then you need languages to describe orchestration …

So in addition to being a language for expressing executable business processes, BPEL may also be used to specify business protocols by using a restricted subset of the language. Internal details like the use of lower level components and databases, complex data manipulation, business logic for determining how messages are processed, and so on are omitted from such a view. It is possible to represent RosettaNet PIPs in BPEL, and we expect to find libraries of business protocols that can be combined and adapted by developers and architects becoming available in the near future.

...which are great for use as product line assets.

As with Web service data semantics, the ability to define Web service process semantics in a schematized form makes Web services a desirable platform for implementing abstractions in a product line. Patterns of protocols and executable processes are easily represented and may be cataloged and used in product development. Combined with standard data vocabularies, patterns of federated Web services with clear variation points are a powerful asset for systematic reuse and processing by software factories.

Summary

In Chapter 12, we discussed a number of possible ways to extend an execution platform by providing higher-level abstractions. We saw that the critical criteria included the capability to adapt—important to implement product line variabilities. Equally important is the capability to expose as much information as possible in a schematized form—this enables runtime use of component metadata, discovery, and the processing of metadata at design time through tools. With well-formed computer processable metadata, tools may implement patterns of components with variation points, generate code to fill variation points in frameworks and components, and ensure product developers work within carefully designed application architectures designed to maximize reuse and flexibility across the product family.

In this chapter, we have focused in on software components, and particularly a form of component we called service component that uses a strong notion of a contract with which to govern its dealings with others. Contract bearing components can be the foundation of well-formed product line architectures, which can be defined using patterns and implemented on various technologies. One of the most important technologies is Web services. Although still in its infancy, Web service technology promises to grow into the heterogeneous component assembly platform most enterprises have been dreaming about for a decade or more. With rapid progression in component-based development methods, and the industry's focus on orchestration of services to maximize flexibility and maintainability of distributed systems, the stage is set for an architecturally-driven approach to model-driven development of product families.

Notes

1. UML, for example, provides OCL for this purpose.
2. Herzum and Sims actually use the term *tier* here where we have used *layer*.
3. The term *contract* was probably first used in this context by a seminal paper on behavioral specification by Helm, Holland and Gangopadhyay [HHG90].

CHAPTER 14

Mappings and Transformations

Once you know the pattern, a lot of design decisions follow automatically.
The Gang Of Four

Relationships between viewpoints play a key role in software factories, as we have seen. In this chapter, we look at how we can express those relationships as mappings between DSLs, at how transformations based on those mappings can be used to optimize DSL-based specifications, and at how to synchronize and reconcile models based on DSLs with general-purpose programming language source code files. Since general-purpose programming language compilers use transformations based on mappings, we apply lessons learned in compiler development of to the transformation of DSL-based models. We discuss the taxonomy of transformations and solutions to common model transformation problems, including the composition problem and the traceability problem.

Transformations

Let's start by establishing a vocabulary for relationships between viewpoints. In this section, we discuss the taxonomy of transformations. Many of the concepts we will cover are discussed in depth in the seminal book on Generative Programming by Czarnecki and Eisenecker [CE00].

Types of Transformation

Transformation changes representation but preserves semantics.

A compiler for a General-Purpose Programming Language (GPL) applies a succession of transformations to a program expressed in the concrete syntax of the GPL. First, it builds an abstract syntax tree (AST) that describes the program, and then it produces an executable description of the program in a language appropriate for the target platform. At each point in the succession of transformations, care is taken to ensure that the original intent and semantics of the program are preserved. All transformations used for language translation must provide this guarantee.

A transformation creates an instance of a mapping.

We saw in Chapter 2 that a transformation is a process that creates or modifies one or more output specifications, from one or more input specifications. Since each input specification is expressed in the language of an input domain, and each output specification is expressed in the language of an output domain, we can think of a transformation as creating an instance of a relationship between the input and output domains. This relationship is called a mapping.

Transformations may be vertical, horizontal or oblique.

Several types of transformation can be identified based on the way their input and output domains are related:

- A *vertical transformation* writes the input specifications to the output specifications at a different level of abstraction. A transformation that lowers the level of abstraction is a *refinement*. A transformation that raises the level of abstraction is an *abstraction*. The input and output domains of a vertical transformation are always different.

- A *horizontal transformation*, on the other hand, changes the structure of the input specifications, or weaves multiple specifications into a single output specification, without changing the level of abstraction. It may also preserve the languages in which the input specifications are expressed, meaning that its input and output domains may be the same.

- A compiler often runs horizontal transformations against an abstract syntax tree before running the vertical transformations that render its executable representation. From the outside, the compiler appears to perform a single transformation that combines horizontal and vertical actions. This is called an *oblique transformation* [CE00].

Note that in the preceding description, we said that a compiler primarily runs transformations against the abstract syntax representation of an input program. It is usually more effective to apply transformations to an abstract syntax representation than to a concrete syntax representation, so that variations in the concrete syntax do not affect the transformation engine. In addition, the abstract syntax representation supports more powerful transformations. Although both allow the program to be broken into well-defined tokens, the abstract syntax representation generalizes those tokens, identifying them as instances of types defined by a language grammar. This lets them participate in expressions with complex structures and semantics.

Transformations are applied to abstract syntax representations.

Recall from Chapter 8 that the abstract syntax for a DSL may be described by a metamodel, that its instances are called abstract syntax graphs (ASGs), and that unlike ASTs, which are based on tree-structured context-free grammars, ASGs are directed graphs based on graph-structured grammars defined by metamodels. The key point is that there is no difference between the role of a DSL and the role of a GPL in the development process. Each defines an abstract syntax used to specify a piece of software, and both participate in a progressive transformation process that produces an executable implementation, as described in Chapter 2, and as shown in Figure 14.1.

Although DSLs and GPLs have different concrete and abstract syntax representations, they serve the same purpose in the development process.

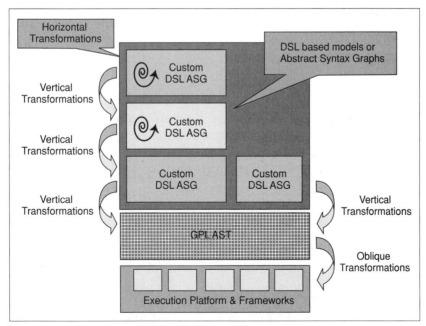

Figure 14.1 Transformations between ASGs and ASTs

In no sense is a DSL an inferior player. As we pointed out in Chapter 8, DSLs are development languages, not documentation languages, and DSL-based models are development artifacts, not documentation artifacts. Although DSLs and GPLs have different forms of abstract syntax, and may have different kinds of notations, they ultimately serve the same function, which is to specify software in a form that can be processed by tools to produce executable implementations.

Vertical Transformations

There are several kinds of refinements.

Vertical transformations are also called refinements. Several kinds of refinements can be identified, as described in Appendix A. Briefly these are:

- *Specialization*, in which configurations of less specialized objects in the input specifications are transformed into configurations of more specialized objects in the output specifications.

- *Elaboration*, in which less detailed configurations of objects in the input specification are transformed into more detailed configurations of objects in the output specifications.

- *Realization*, in which configurations of objects in the input specifications are transformed into objects in the output specifications that represent their implementations. Note that these implementations may not yet be executable.

- *Derivation*, in which new configurations of objects in the input specifications are derived from existing configurations of objects in the input specifications.

- *Decomposition*, in which individual objects in the input specifications are transformed into configurations of objects in the output specifications.

To illustrate these concepts, we'll look at some refinements performed by GPL compilers, some model refinements, where the input specifications are DSL based models, but the output specifications are GPL source code files, XML files, and other low level artifacts, and some model-to-model refinements, where both the input and output specifications are DSL based models.

A simple example is introduced.

Consider the simple business application specification shown in Figure 14.2. It contains views conforming to three

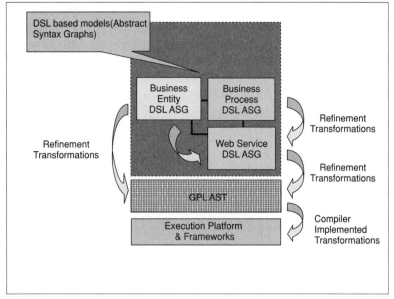

Figure 14.2   A simple application specification

viewpoints: Business Entity, Business Process, and Web Service. Each view contains one or more models based on a DSL defined by its viewpoint.

- The Business Entity DSL defines Business Entity and Business Entity Component abstractions, which can be used to specify message-driven, loosely coupled data services that map to implementations based on an Object-Relational Mapping framework.

- The Business Process DSL defines Business Process, Business Activity, Role and Dependency abstractions, and a taxonomy of composition mechanisms that can be used to specify sequences of Business Activities.

- These two DSLs map to the Web Service DSL, which can be used to specify service-oriented application architectures by describing how responsibility is partitioned among Web service components, what messages they exchange, and what contract protocols they use, while hiding their implementations.

DSLs used in the example are defined.

The mappings between the viewpoints describe how abstractions defined by the Business Entity and Business Process DSLs are realized by abstractions defined by the Web Service DSL.

Higher-level abstractions have complex mappings to GPLs.

Some abstractions, such as Class, Method, and Field, are supplied by the GPLs into which we generate the implementations of models. Other abstractions, such as Business Entity, Bi-Directional Relationship, Form and Control, are higher-level abstractions supplied by the modeling languages. Because they are primitives in the modeling languages, but not in the GPLs, they must be implemented by combining GPL language primitives, using patterns, frameworks and tools.

- Some higher-level abstractions can be implemented as programming language types. An event, for example, can be implemented as a class that supports a designated interface.

- Most higher-level abstractions cannot be implemented as programming language types because they are too large. Their implementations span multiple programming language types, and may involve other kinds of artifacts, such as XML files or SQL files, in addition to source code. The implementation of a Business Entity for example, might consist of several classes, metadata stored in an XML file, and a set of SQL DDL files that defines database tables, views, and stored procedures.

Business Entity to GPL

The mapping from the Business Entity DSL to a GPL.

The following mappings relate abstractions defined by the Business Entity DSL to abstractions defined by a GPL.

- Each Business Entity maps to four classes representing the Business Entity, its primary key, a factory for creating, reading, updating and deleting Business Entity instances, and an agent that can be used to remotely connect to the Business Entity.

- Each relationship among Business Entities maps to a member variable of one Business Entity whose type is a collection of instances of the Business Entity at the other end of the relationship.

- Each property of a Business Entity maps to a member variable in the class that represents the Business Entity.

- Some properties of a Business Entity maps to parameters of methods for creating, reading, updating, and deleting instances of the Business Entity on the class that represents the Business Entity factory.

Business Process to Web Service

The following mappings relate abstractions defined by the Business Process DSL to abstractions defined by the Web Service DSL.

The mapping from the Business Process DSL to the Web Service DSL.

- Each activity in a Business Process Component maps to a Web service component with appropriate ports.

- Each artifact flow between business activities maps to a message that supports the collaboration between the Web service components that implement the activities.

- Each group of activities designated as a scheduled sequential process maps to a scheduled process Web service component with appropriate ports. Each activity in the group maps to a Web service component with appropriate ports, as before, but with connections to the Web service components that represent the activities immediately preceding and following it in the scheduled sequential process. This mapping can be implemented using decomposition and elaboration.

- Each business interaction maps to a contract and an inverse contract.

Business Entity to Web Service

The following mappings relate abstractions defined by the Business Entity DSL to abstractions defined by the Web Service DSL.

The mapping from the Business Entity DSL to the Web Service DSL.

- Each business entity component maps to a component embedded in a Web service component, either as indicated by the designer, or using an algorithm that chooses the Web service component to minimize the number of cross Web service message exchanges required to access the business entities from activities in other Web service components.

Web Service to GPL

The following mappings relate abstractions defined by the Web Service DSL to abstractions defined by a GPL, such as C#.

The mapping from the Web Service DSL to a GPL.

- Each Web service component object maps to the appropriate C# implementation concepts. For example, using ASP.NET Web service technology, each Web service maps to a Web service project, a Web service configuration file, a C# based `.asmx` file for each port, a method on the `.asmx` class attributed as `[web method]` for each port operation, and a WSDL file.

- Each message maps to a class that derives from the C# Message class, with appropriate members for each message element.

- Each scheduled Web service component maps to a Microsoft BizTalk Web service with a schedule that references all of the Web services that implement activities coordinated by the schedule.

GPL to Executables

Vertical transformations performed by GPL compilers.

GPL compilers generate binary code for a target platform, or byte code for jitting or for interpretation by a virtual machine.[1] As we said earlier, they generally perform both vertical and horizontal transformations. Vertical transformations performed by GPL compilers typically include (see [CE00] for a complete list):

- Implementing abstract data types as machine data types.

- Implementing conditional logic expressions in terms of machine instructions.

Implementing arithmetic expressions based on the operators they contain and the types of their operands.

- Implementing method calls by building virtual function tables and stack frame linkages

Horizontal Transformations

Horizontal transformations perform refactoring, optimization, or delocalization.

Horizontal transformations generally *refactor, optimize,* or *delocalize* a source specification. Refactoring, which is widely applied to GPL-based source code files, is equally applicable to DSL-based models. Fowler has published a widely read catalog of refactoring transformations for object-oriented GPLs like C# and Java [Fow99]. Common examples include moving a block of code into a new method, or replacing error handling code with an `Exception`. Generally, optimization and delocalization are performed by black-box transformations, since they obfuscate the realization of higher-level abstractions in the output specifications, while refactoring is performed by white-box transformations, since they are intended to improve the structure of specifications consumed by developers.

Optimization transformations improve characteristics of a specification, such as its performance or resource usage. Examples of performance transformations include unreachable code removal, loop optimizations, common sub-expression elimination, and *inlining*, where a procedure call is replaced by an expansion of the procedure implementation using the arguments passed in the call. *Interleaving* is a storage access optimization. For arithmetic operations on the corresponding elements of two arrays, such as might be common in programs using arrays to represent matrices, a compiler can arrange the storage allocation such that the corresponding elements are in the same memory block. Similar techniques are used to optimize table storage by optimizing query processors in SQL database systems. See [CE00] for more about optimizing transformations. These types of optimizations can also be applied to the implementations of DSL-based models. The schema for a graph of business entities, for example, can be optimized by grouping columns that are frequently accessed together by operations on the entities.

Optimization transformations improve characteristics like performance or resource usage.

Delocalization and Aspect-Oriented Programming

Delocalization is a particularly important kind of horizontal transformation because it is used to implement aspects. Recall from Chapter 7 that aspects are characteristics of an application that cut across its modular structure, and they typically derive from non-functional requirements, such as security, instrumentation, and error handling, while modular structure typically derives from functional requirements (Figure 14.3).

Delocalization can be used to implement aspects.

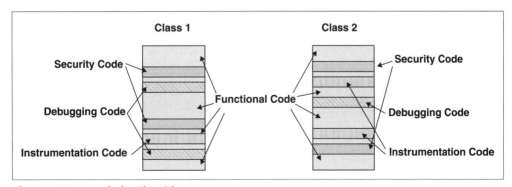

Figure 14.3 Tangled code without aspects

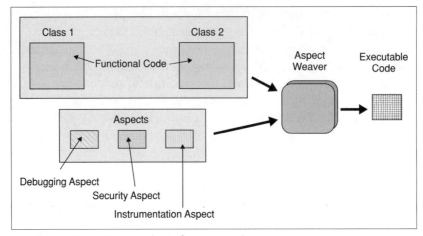

Figure 14.4   Aspect-oriented programming

As noted earlier, aspects are typically spread throughout other modules, making the implementations of both the aspectual and functional requirements hard to trace and hard to evolve.

As described in Chapter 7, we can localize an aspect by defining it in one place, and letting a delocalizing transformation weave its implementation into the functional modules prior to compilation. This lets the developer treat the aspect as a unit, and it removes the aspect from the functional code, making that simpler, as well (Figure 14.4).

Most experience with aspects has focused on adding aspect support to GPLs.

Experience with implementing aspects to date has focused on adding aspects to GPL based source code, but as we've pointed out, the concepts apply equally well to DSL based models. In Aspect-Oriented Programming (AOP), aspects are defined in either the host language, or in an aspect language, markers are placed in the source program to define the points where aspects may be inserted, and an aspect-weaving step is added to the compilation process. AspectJ, a project at Xerox PARC [Kis02, KLM97] was is a prototypical implementation of AOP. Built as an extension to Java, it illustrates many AOP concepts and introduces AOP terminology.

- *Join Point:* A position in the functional code where an aspect may be inserted. AspectJ defines 11 of these, including method calls, exception execution, and field assignment. All of them are recognized by the AspectJ compiler.

- *Pointcut:* A collection of join points with optional qualifiers. For example, a pointcut for a method call join point might specify the return value type and parameter types that must be present for the aspect to be inserted.

- *Advice:* Code to be inserted before and/or after the code identified by a point cut.
- *Introduction:* The addition of new behavior or members into a type by aspect weaving.

An AOP Example Using AspectJ

As an example, imagine that we have a package that defines data type abstractions like binary trees, stacks, and queues using linked lists constructed from nodes of type SLNode containing a data field of type Object, and a next pointer to the next node in the list [Jen98]. We want to build an aspect that will trace the use of features in this package to help with debugging. The aspect is partially defined in the listing in Figure 14.5.

A node debugging example.

```
Public aspect NodeDebugging
{
    pointcut nodepc1(SLNode n) : target(n) &&
        call(public * SLNode.*(Object));

    before(SLNode n) : nodePc1(n)
    {
        // code that prints tracing information for
        // calls to SLNode methods which take object
        // as an argument
    }

    after(SLNode n) : target(n) &&
        call(public Object SLNode.getNext());
    {
        // code to print tracing information for
        // calls to the SLNode.getNext method
    }

    private boolean SLNode.printingDisabled = false ;

    private void SLNode.printObject (object O)
    {
        // code for new method inserted in SLNode
    }
}
```

Figure 14.5 Listing for the NodeDebugging aspect

This listing illustrates AOP concepts using AspectJ. The aspect NodeDebugging defines the following:

- The pointcut nodePc1, defined as any calls to public methods of the class SLNode which take an Object reference as an argument.

- Before advice that inserts code to be executed before the public method is called. In this case, it is code that will print tracing information.

- After advice that inserts code to be executed after the getNext method of SLNode is executed. Its job is to print additional tracing information when this method specifically is called. Note that this after advice does not specify a pointcut as did the before advice. It relies on the method call join point defined by AspectJ.

- Two introductions that add members to SLNode for use by this aspect: a Boolean variable called printing Disabled and a method called printObject.

Other AOP approaches.

AspectJ describes its aspects using extensions to the Java language. These are fed into an aspect weaver immediately prior to compilation. The resulting code is not intended to be maintained, and is an intermediate artifact in the AspectJ compilation process. AOP can be implemented in other ways. Any implementation must provide two things :

- A way to define aspects and pointcuts.
- A way to perform aspect weaving.

In addition to language extensions, aspects can be described with aspect-specific languages or class libraries based on the host programming language. Czarnecki and Eisenecker describe an earlier version of AspectJ that supported two different kinds of aspects, and a language for defining aspects of each type. One of the languages, called Cool, was used to define synchronization aspects for Java programs. The other, called Ridl, was used to define remote method invocation and parameter serialization. In AspectJ, weaving is implemented as a compile time transformation of the source files. It could also be implemented against the abstract syntax trees.

```
Public class SLNode
{
    private Object m_data ;
    private SLNode m_next ;

    public SLNode()
    {
        data = null ;
    }

    [NodeDebugging("In SLNode constructor"]
    public SLNode(Object data)
    {
        m_data = data ;
    }

    [NodeDugging("In SLNode getNextMethod"]
    public Object getNext()
    {
        return m_next ;
    }

    // Other SLNode methods here

}
```

Figure 14.6 Aspects in .NET using metaattributes

An AOP Example Using .NET

Another implementation of AOP uses meta programming constructs called attributes to create custom extensions to Microsoft .NET programming languages [SFS02]. Aspects are implemented as .NET language attributes. Point cuts are defined by placing the attributes in the source code, as illustrated in Figure 14.6. Join points occur wherever the .NET languages allow attributes to appear. As you can see, .NET language attributes can take parameters—in this case, a String to be written.

An example using meta programming features in .NET.

The implementation of the aspect is a class that derives from System.Reflection.Attribute. Notice from the listing in Figure 14.7 that attribute definitions may be attributed—in this case, by a usage attribute that allows the aspect user to attach the aspect to class members, and that prevents them from attaching more than one instance of it to the same class member.

.NET provides mechanisms for language extension.

All that remains for the aspect implementer is to create the context in which code inserted by the aspect will execute. This

```
Using System ;
Using System.Reflection ;

[AttributeUsage( AtributeTargets.ClassMembers,
                 AllowMultiples = false ) ]
Public class NodeDebugging : Attribute
{
    public NodeDebugging (String s)
    {
        Console.WriteLine ( s ) ;
    }
}
```

Figure 14.7   Implementation of NodeDebugging attribute

requires intercepting calls to instrumented methods, and modifying the call context. The .NET runtime has hooks that make it easy to manipulate call contexts and to add interceptors before and/or after calls.

Aspect weaving can happen at runtime too.

Aspect weaving is not restricted to compile time transformations—aspects can be woven at runtime using mechanisms based on reflection, which enable weaver code to inspect metadata provided by the runtime system describing compiled units.

Examples of Aspects in DSLs

Aspects can be implemented using DSLs.

We have seen how aspects can be implemented using general-purpose programming languages. Now, let's look at an example based on a DSL. The Web Service DSL from Figure 14.2 supports the specification of two kinds of policy:

- Security policies can be defined and then applied to multiple ports associated with multiple Web service components. For example, we might require all operations offered by selected ports to use certificate-based security and a specific license server.

- Deployment settings required of server software that hosts Web service components can be defined and then applied to multiple Web service components. For example, we might indicate that several Web service components require specific settings for Authentication Mode and Session State on the server software that hosts them.

If these policies are defined as aspects of the Web Service DSL, then we can specify them independently of the Web service models, in a policy editor window, for example, and then attach them to the ports or web service components using simple drag and drop gestures. The DSL compiler can then weave their implementations with the implementations of the target model elements, and can reweave them when they change.

In cases where a language does not support aspects, and cannot be extended to do so, aspects can be introduced at a higher level of abstraction, and then woven when generating down to the original language. For example, if the Web Service DSL did not support the specification of policy aspects, and could not be extended to do so, we might add those capabilities to the Business Entity and Process DSLs, use them to specify security and deployment policies in Business Entity and Process models, and then weave the implementations of those policies with implementations of Business Entity and Process abstractions when generating down to the Web Service DSL. Although this localizes the aspects at the higher level of abstraction, it scatters them throughout the specifications expressed in the original language. It may also be awkward for the user, since the aspects may not be relevant to the concerns expressed at the higher level of abstraction. A user working with Business Process models, for example, may not know how the Business Processes are implemented, and therefore may not know how to apply deployment policies to them.

Aspects can be applied at higher levels of abstraction, or using aspect languages at the same level of abstraction.

A second approach is to create new languages for the aspects we need to specify, and to identify the join points where aspects based on those languages can attach to modular specifications based on the original language. We can then specify aspects using the new languages, and weave them with modular specifications based on the original language before compiling. For example, we might create new Security and Deployment Policy DSLs, use them to specify policies, and then weave the policies into Web service specifications before we generate C# code. Although this approach does not require the original language to know about the aspect languages, it does require the aspect languages to know about the original language. This is the approach used by AspectJ.

Sometimes, the results of a refinement transformation are resources like schemas, configuration files, project definitions, and folders. Resources may also benefit from delocalizing transformations, since the same information is often repeated in

They can also be applied to resources and other types of artifacts.

multiple items, and since any one item is often a tangle of multiple concerns. For example, a Visual Studio .NET project file can capture policies. We might want to create a policy restricting the kinds of items that can be added to a project. We might want to say, for example, that a project representing the data access tier of an application may not contain UI widgets. This kind of policy is an aspect with respect to the project system, and can be expressed using the Visual Studio Template Definition Language, which is a project system aspect language.

Remember that there are problems with AOP.

In Chapter 4, we listed some of the problems with AOP. As commonly practiced, AOP weaves unencapsulated source code, creating architectural mismatch problems similar to those created by poor component packaging. This lack of encapsulation in AOP makes it hard for developers to reason about the compatibility of aspects with the functional code into which they are woven and hard for tools to validate aspect weavings. We described deferred encapsulation as an adaptation of AOP that weaves encapsulated aspects with component implementations later in the development process, such as at assembly or deployment time. Since DSL-based abstractions can be implemented by artifacts other than source code files, DSLs provide a stronger basis for deferred encapsulation. For example, the Web service security policy aspect described earlier might be implemented as configuration file statements interpreted at runtime.

Transformation Problems

Special problems occur at boundary between models and source code.

We have seen how vertical transformations, especially refinement transformations, and horizontal transformations, especially aspectual transformations, can be applied to abstract syntax representations of both general-purpose programming languages (ASTs) and DSL-based models (ASGs). In the process of moving from higher, more problem specific, levels of abstraction to lower, more implementation specific levels of abstraction, there are more similarities than differences between these two forms of specification, as we have noted. DSL models are first class development artifacts, not mere documentation that creates overhead, like the models produced by many CASE products in the past. In this section, we look at problems that beset transformation systems. Most of these problems affect transformations between models, as well as transformations from models to source code. However, there are some thorny issues that we cannot sweep under the carpet at the boundary between models and source code. Weak transformations across this boundary were a major factor in the failure of CASE products.

Model-to-Model Transformations

Robust model-to-model transformation is a prerequisite to the effective use of DSLs in software factories, where mappings between viewpoints in software schemas must be computable. Since most relationships between abstractions are reversible, we prefer to use the term *model synchronization*. The primary goal of model synchronization is to provide a robust and efficient way to reconcile differences between models and to bring them into full or partial conformance with one another. Model synchronization mechanisms must address scenarios that arise in the context of a software factory, where the contents of one model are often related to the contents of many others. As a general goal, we are interested in supporting model synchronization, not only synchronously, as models are being edited, but also asynchronously, after edits have been made. This will let us reason about conflicts between sets of changes made concurrently by different team members, for example, an important problem that remains to be solved effectively by products in the market.

Robust model synchronization is required in software factories.

We are interested in making model synchronization easy to specify and implement, and especially in replacing the error-prone and inefficient event-based approaches often found in model-driven development tools available today. Event handlers usually fire on changes to specific types of model elements, either when the changes occur, or after transactions in which the changes occur, and they usually attempt to respond to the changes immediately. This approach is satisfactory for certain tasks, such as collecting data about fine-grained changes made to a model by a complex operation, but it is quite unsatisfactory for synchronizing models, especially when there are many complex synchronization requirements, as is often the case.

Model mappings should be easy to specify and easy to implement.

The following problems tend to occur with event-based synchronization:

- It is often hard for an event handler to determine conclusively what operation caused the event to occur.

There are many problems with event-based approaches to model synchronization.

This ambiguity makes it difficult to write different strategies for propagating changes caused by different operations.

- Because events usually listen to operations on individual element types, it is often difficult to write sets of rules that act in concert to efficiently propagate coarse-grained changes. Strategies for propagating coarse-grained changes are often distributed among the handlers for many fine-grained events, and are therefore difficult to maintain.

- The order in which events will occur is often difficult to predict. This makes it hard for a developer writing an event handler to determine how far a top-level operation might or might not have progressed when the handler receives control. It also makes strategies for propagating coarse-grained changes hard to design and implement.

- Event handlers often respond immediately to the changes that cause them to fire. Since this can cause additional event handlers to fire, the execution of multiple event handlers is often interleaved. When combined with uncertainty about order of execution, this interleaving can make it quite difficult to isolate the execution of any one handler for the purposes of debugging, and tends to introduce subtle defects created by unanticipated interactions between handlers that are hard to reproduce.

- Because event handlers interact entirely through side effects, it is generally necessary to observe or predict all possible interactions among the members of any given set of event handlers in order to determine the aggregate behavior of a system. This task is hard enough when all of the handlers are implemented by the same developer, and it is harder still when they are implemented by different developers, especially when the developers are on different teams, but it is almost impossible when the set of handlers cannot be known in advance. This wreaks havoc with plug-in based extensibility models for model-driven development tools, where the set of plug-ins that will be loaded, and therefore the set of possible interactions is determined at runtime based on configuration, and therefore cannot be known in advance.

Lazy loading further exacerbates these problems. A simpler and more declarative way to describe and maintain mappings between models is highly desirable. In fact, mappings can be modeled. This makes it possible to generate model synchronization code from the mapping models, or to build an interpreter that executes them directly. In these solutions, synchronization is performed by translating journals of operations performed against a source model into update scripts that can be executed against the target, models to bring them into conformance with the source model. The update scripts can be played against the target models immediately, while the source model is being edited, or later, when changes from multiple editing sessions are reconciled.

We need a more declarative way to specify mappings and an engine that knows what operations to perform.

Model-to-Code Transformations

Consider a more detailed drill in to the DSLs shown earlier in Figure 14.2, and again in Figure 14.8. In many cases, a model-to-code transformation cannot directly create or manipulate ASTs for generated code, and must therefore generate code using its concrete syntax. Backward traceability from the code to the model may have to be implemented by convention, if the

Editing generated source code can destroy traceability.

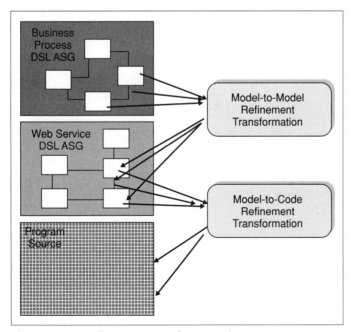

Figure 14.8   Refinement as code generation

transformation is required be reversible, such as using a pre-defined programming model, where method signatures are recognized by the reverse engineering tool, or where metadata is embedded in comments. Both of these conventions are used by popular user interface builders. Once generation has been performed, backward traceability may be destroyed if users are allowed to edit the generated code.

This problem usually does not arise at boundaries between models, since model editors, whether graphical or textual, tend to be designed to work with multiple levels of abstraction, and usually manage traceability between DSLs automatically. If a user wants to change a Web service that was generated to implement a business process, for example, their editor might constrain their edits to be consistent with the business process model, or it might reflect their edits into the business process model. In either case, consistency between the two models would be preserved.

Unconstrained editing of generated models is just as dangerous as unconstrained editing of source code. It does not cause as much trouble only because the same tool is usually used to maintain both models. Moving forward into a world where we treat models like source code, making them live in files and compiling them, it is much less likely that the same tool will be used at every level of abstraction.

Since higher level abstractions are so frequently implemented using GPLs, we will highlight special problems and solutions for this scenario.

Preventing Uncontrolled Edits

Ideally, users should not edit generated artifacts.

Ideally, users should not edit generated artifacts. There are some legitimate reasons for editing them, however, as we shall see. There are also some illegitimate reasons, such as:

- Improving performance.
- Making them prettier, more readable, or less obtrusive.
- Making them conform to coding standards.
- Fixing bugs.

Obviously, if generated code performs poorly, is not readable, does not conform to coding standards, or contains defects, then there is a problem with the generator.

When abstractions are implemented by transformation, there is often a legitimate need to extend the generated implementations with custom logic. For example, when a user defines a business entity in a DSL based model, the modeling tool will typically generate most of the implementation as classes that derive from framework classes, written in an underlying GPL. The user may then need to add custom code written in the underlying GPL to the generated implementation. In this situation, we need a way to compose the custom code with the generated implementation. In the next section, we'll look at two mechanisms that allows the user to directly edit generated artifacts: *markers* and *hidden regions*. Next, we'll look at several mechanisms that separate the user code from the generated code, and then compose them to produce a complete implementation.

The need to add logic creates a composition problem.

Protecting Generated Code

For mechanisms that allow the user to directly edit generated artifacts, the primary goal is to protect the generated code. A simple form of protection is to place *markers* around the generated code. Often the markers are pairs of comments that delimit the region containing the generated code. They usually warn the user not to edit anything within the delimited region. Markers are merely advisory. Any changes made between them by the user will be lost if the code is regenerated.

Markers place boundaries around generated code.

Markers can be also used with models. Model markers take the form of annotations on the ASG that can be interpreted by the editor when displaying the concrete syntax. A graphical rendering of a marked model might, for example, display the marked parts using a different color scheme.

Instead of human readable markers, some generators use language directives to delimit generated regions. The marked regions can be hidden by a language sensitive editor, which helps to protect them. A good example is the Windows Form Designer in Microsoft Visual Studio .NET. It defines a DSL whose abstractions support Windows user interface construction, such as Form, Control, and Button. It generates code into hidden regions. It also generates skeletons in visible regions for event handlers that must be completed by the user. No roundtripping is performed, so changes made by the user may be lost when the form is edited. Like human readable markers,

Hidden regions keep generated code out of sight, but do not prevent editing.

hidden regions can also be used in graphical or textual model editors.

Solving the Composition Problem

There are several mechanisms for composing user code with generated code. A primary distinction can be drawn between these mechanisms based on binding time.

Design Time Techniques

At design time, we can use protected regions or special code windows.

Design time binding merges user code with generated code in shared artifacts before compilation. This strategy requires the use of mechanisms that prevent the user from modifying the generated code. Some editors lock delimited regions to prevent editing. The user edits only the unrestricted regions. In some tools, such as early versions of Visual Basic, the user adds code to an abstraction in a special window.

Compile Time Techniques—Partial Specifications

At compile time we can use partial specifications.

Compile time binding merges user code with generated code during the compilation process. Methods vary in terms of when the merge is performed. One approach is to merge source code before the compiler is called (e.g., the C macro preprocessor). A better approach is to merge *partial specifications* in compiled form during compilation.

Partial classes allow transformations to build chunks of a class that can be hidden.

Partial specifications are GPL source code fragments or fragments of DSL-based models that can be merged in a modular fashion. Each of the fragments is incomplete on its own, but when all of the fragments are combined, the result forms a complete implementation. Generated code is placed in fully protected read-only fragments that cannot be edited by the user. Users are allowed to edit writable fragments.

The *partial classes* supported by the Microsoft Visual Basic and C# language compilers in Visual Studio 2005 are examples of partial specifications. In this version of Visual Studio, the Windows Form Designer generates partial classes to implement controls, and puts them into read-only files, which are hidden by default, but can be made visible for perusal. The user then adds custom logic to partial classes stored in writable files. At compilation time, the compiler combines the partial classes to form a complete implementation.

```
namespace CustomerManager
{
    public class Service1 : System.Web.WebService
    {
        public Service1() {...}

        [WebMethod]
        public string AcceptJob(string CustomerName, string JobDetails)
        {
            // This method is generated as a requirement for the WSDL
            // generation by the ASP.Net system
            SafeService1 safe = new SafeService1() ;
            Safe.HelperLogic(CustomerName, JobDetails) ;
            return safe.AcceptJob(CustomerName. JobDetails) ;
        }
        //other web methods here
    }
    public partial class SafeService1
    {
        public SafeService()  {...}

        public string AcceptJob(string CustomerName, string JobDetails)
        {
            // Here is the developer-added business logic for
            // Accepting a job

        }
    }
}
// ...and in a separate file ...
namespace CustomerManager
{
    public partial class SafeService1
    {
        public string HelperLogic(string CustomerName, string JobDetails)
        {
            // Here lives the helper code for handling
            // SOAP Headers to extract conversation ID
            // and restoring conversation state
        }
    }
}
```

Figure 14.9 Partial class implementation of helper logic

With this approach, the members of a class are distributed among multiple partial class declarations residing in separate files. The compiler merges these declarations into a single class during compilation. A partial class declaration in C# is created by using the `partial` keyword, as illustrated in Figure 14.9. In this example, the class named SafeService1 is created by combining the two parts.

Runtime Techniques–Delegated Classes

Runtime binding merges user code with generated code at run-time using call backs to registered objects. A variety of runtime

At runtime, we can use delegated classes.

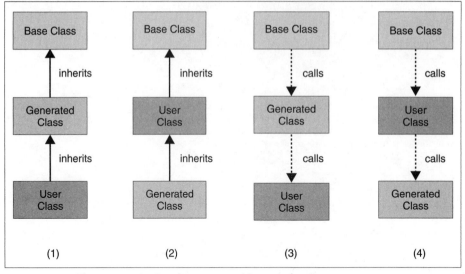

Figure 14.10 Runtime composition mechanisms

binding mechanisms based on delegation are described by design patterns, many of which were documented by the Gang of Four [GHJV95]. These include Observer, Adapter, Strategy, Abstract Factory, Mediator, Decorator, Proxy, Command, and Chain of Responsibility. Two advantages of runtime binding are the use of interfaces to formalize the contract between the user code and the generated code, and the ability to change the implementation at runtime using substitution. A minor disadvantage is the runtime overhead of the additional method invocation. Several mechanisms based on runtime binding are popular in component programming models. These are illustrated in Figure 14.10. All four of them are used in the Enterprise JavaBeans architecture.

- *User Subclass:* The user subclasses a generated class. Abstract methods in the generated class define explicit override points. The user supplied subclass overrides the abstract methods, and brackets calls to the generated base class with preamble and postamble code.

- *Generated Subclass:* The user supplies an abstract class that is later subclassed by a generated class. Abstract methods in the user class define explicit override points. The generated subclass overrides the abstract methods, and brackets calls to the user supplied base class with preamble and postamble code.

- *User Delegate:* The user supplies a delegate class that is called by the generated class. The generated class calls the user supplied class at designated points, such as before and after setting a property value. In many cases, the generated class is a proxy for the user supplied class.

- *Generated Delegate:* The user supplies a facade class that calls a generated delegate class at designated points. For example, a user supplied class might call a generated delegate class to set and get property values.

One of the primary complaints against runtime composition is the need to provide two class names. This problem can be solved in several ways:

- *By Naming Convention:* For example, in the Enterprise JavaBeans architecture, if the name of the bean is MyBean, then the generated bean class is called MyBean, the generated home class is called MyBeanHome, and the handwritten delegate is called MyBeanImpl by convention.

- *By Name Mangling:* For example, in the Enterprise JavaBeans architecture, the name of the generated bean implementation subclass is generated by a tool using a tool specific name mangling scheme.

- *By Name Space:* Instead of using either of the two preceding methods, generated classes can be given the same name as user classes, but in a different name space. For example, a user supplied partial class that implements a Customer entity might be named mycompany.CRM.Customer, while a generated partial class for the same entity might be named mycompany.CRM.impl.Customer.

Solving the Traceability Problem

So, we can prevent the editing of generated code and models, while letting the user extend them, but to really make transformations trustworthy, we must fundamentally solve the traceability problem. Recall that traceability is the ability to relate generated code or model elements to the model elements from which they were derived. A common approach to solving this problem is to leave comments in generated code or tags on generated model elements that identify the model elements from

Traceability must be preserved when generating code or models from models.

which they were derived. These identifiers, which are often GUIDs, can obfuscate the generated artifacts. Worse, they can be separated from the code they adorn by edits that move the code around.

Code Models are the answer.

This is clearly unacceptable for software factories, where models participate in the development process on an equal footing with source code derived from them, and with resources and other development artifacts. A better approach is to define *code models* for the underlying GPLs.

A code model is a set of APIs offered by a tool for programmatically reading and writing code. With a code model, transformations can treat GPL source code as just another type of model in the software factory schema. As long as the code model can issue change events when the user changes the code, the transformation system can ensure that the relevant model elements are kept up-to-date. Transformation systems that use code models can provide traceability between generated code elements and model elements by storing the names of the generated code elements in the model elements (e.g., namespace.classname.membername). Code generation using a code model effectively replaces the model-to-code refinement transformation at the bottom of the stack with a model-to-model refinement transformation, as illustrated in Figure 14.11. Examples of code models are provided in Visual Studio .NET for Visual Basic and C#. These models provide read-write programmatic access to classes and their members, and to other parts of the source code file, such as using statements, with change events.

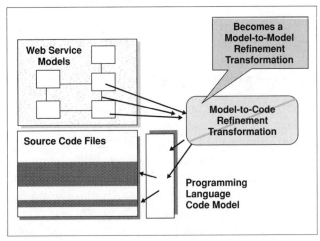

Figure 14.11 Code generation using a code model

If code is generated only through the code model, then the traceability problem can be solved, and the historically poor quality of round-tripping features in modeling tools can be replaced by continuous, high-fidelity code and model synchronization. Code models, partial classes, and delegation collectively provide a basis for the kinds of robust transformations required by software factories. In the next chapter, we'll look at how transformations are implemented.

The goal is to view generation as model synchronization.

Summary

In this chapter, we set out to explain how DSL based models could be mapped to executables. We have stressed that these models should be seen no differently from the general-purpose programming language source code that forms the mainstay of current software development methods and practices. Although they may require graphical editors, DSL based models can be as rich and powerful as GPL source code, and should never be seen as mere documentation. Both DSLs and GPLs are implemented by progressive transformation systems commonly known as compilers or code generators.

A significant difference between DSLs and GPLs is that most GPLs are based on context-free grammars that map to hierarchical data structures called ASTs, while most DSLs are based on metamodels that map to graph based data structures called ASGs. For most purposes, however, this difference can be safely ignored. Transformations can be implemented either between DSL based models, or between DSL based models and GPL source code. Historically, transformation systems have struggled with the boundary between models and GPL source code, since ASTs were rarely exposed, forcing the use of concrete syntax for code generation. Code models, partial specifications, and delegation can be used to solve this problem, allowing transformation systems to become important parts of software factories.

Notes

1. Jitting is just-in-time (JIT) compilation of intermediate code generated by the compiler into native code for the target platform at run time.

CHAPTER 15

Generating Implementations

The laws of physics are in place but the universe is very young. We're very early in a revolution that's going to have very long legs.

John Doerr

Now that we understand the fundamentals of transformation, we are ready to look at ways to represent and implement transformations. We start by showing how rules can be used to describe mappings, and we describe several ways to implement them. Next, we talk about implementing horizontal transformations, including aspectual and refactoring transformations. From there, we show how patterns can be defined using mapping rules. Finally, we discuss transformation systems, and describe various ways to implement generators.

Describing Transformations

We have discussed transformations that act on either ASGs— the data structures used to implement DSL based models, or on ASTs—the data structures produced by compilers from source code. These data structures are instances of metamodels, as described in Chapter 8. To discuss transformations in more general terms, we will need to talk about metamodels, not about models. Recall that models are instances of metamodels, meaning that they contain instances of classes defined in

We need some precise definitions to help us describe transformation in more general terms.

metamodels. We will also need more precise definitions of transformation concepts.

We use the term *model transformation* to describe the process of transforming a source *model* to produce a target *model*. A model transformation is performed across a relationship between the metamodels that describe the source and target models. Such a relationship is called a *model mapping*. A model mapping maps types and relationships in one or more source metamodels onto types and relationships in one or more target metamodels, as illustrated in Figure 15.1. In a horizontal mapping, the source and target metamodels are the same.

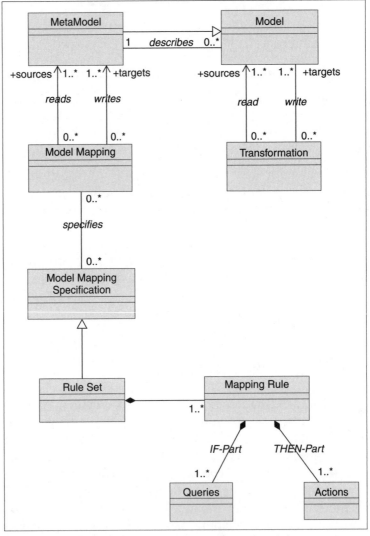

Figure 15.1   Metamodel for mapping and transformation

A model mapping is specified by a *model mapping specification*. Model mapping specifications can be expressed using a number of different mechanisms. We will use *mapping rules*. Other widely used model mapping specification mechanisms include tables, functions and natural language prose. A mapping rule is defined by specifying:

- Configurations of objects in the source models to which the rule applies.

- Configurations of objects in the target models that will be created, updated or deleted by the rule.

Viewing the mapping rule as a function, the first of these two configurations defines the input parameters, while the second defines the output parameters. A third type of parameter, called a mapping parameter, changes the mapping between the input and output parameters. Formally, there is no difference between the input parameters and the mapping parameters. Both determine the output parameters. In practice, however, it is often convenient to distinguish between the two, by allowing input parameters to come only from source models, and allowing mapping parameters to come only from the environment in which the rule is applied. The mapping parameters serve as tuning knobs, letting the user change the results produced by applying the rule to a given set of source models.

A mapping rule matches objects in the source model and creates, updates, or deletes objects in the target model.

Mapping Rules Have IF-THEN Parts

A mapping rule can be expressed in a general way as an IF/THEN rule, in which the IF parts consists of a parameterized query against the source models, and the THEN parts consists of parameterized action clauses to be performed against the target models, as illustrated in Figure 15.2. To execute a mapping

A mapping rule specification consists of a declarative IF part and an imperative THEN part.

```
IF
    {parameterized query of objects in source1} and
    {parameterized query of objects in source2} and
    ...
THEN
    {action to be taken in target1}
    {action to be taken in target2}
    ...
```

Figure 15.2   The structure of a rule

rule, we first execute the IF part, evaluating each clause in the query, binding each parameter to matching objects in the source models. If the query succeeds, then the bindings are passed to the THEN parts, where they are substituted for the corresponding parameters in the action clauses, causing the specified actions to be performed.

For example, here is one of the mapping rules described in Chapter 14. It deals with one aspect of the mapping between Business Process and Web Service models:

Each artifact flow between business activities maps to a message that supports the collaboration between the Web service components that implement those activities

Informally, we might express this rule using the pseudo-code shown in Figure 15.3.

```
IF
    // First query the BP_DSL model for bindings
    {BP_DSL: ?ba1 is a business activity} and
    {BP_DSL: ?ba2 is a business activity} and
    {BP_DSL: ?ba1 is not the same as ?ba2} and
    {BP_DSL: ?af1 is the artifact flow between ?ba1 and ?ba2}
    ...
THEN
    {WS_DSL: create a new message object ?m1}
    {WS_DSL: set the name property of the message to
            the name of the artifact flow ?af1}
    // Build the web service model as an elaboration
    // of the business activities
    {WS_DSL: create a new web service ?ws1}
    {WS_DSL: set name property of ?ws1 to the name of ?ba1}
    {WS_DSL: create a new web service ?ws2}
    {WS_DSL: set name property of ?ws2 to the name of ?ba2}
    {WS_DSL: associate ?m1 to ?ws1}
    {WS_DSL: associate ?m1 to ?ws2}
    // Now set up traceability relationships
    {WS_DSL: set implements property of ?ws1 to ?ba1}
    {WS_DSL: set implements property of ?ws2 to ?ba2}
    {BP_DSL: set implemented by property of ?ba1 to ?ws1}
    {BP_DSL: set implemented by property of ?ba2 to ?ws2}
    ...
```

Figure 15.3 A rule that generates message objects

Note that in this example, terms defined by the metamodels are in bold, parameters are indicated by ?x, and each action/ query clause is tagged with the model name to which it applies. So, reading the query clauses in the IF part,

Declaratively specified rules can often be implemented procedurally.

```
{BP_DSL: ?ba1 is a business activity}
```

will bind the parameter ?ba1 to all instances of **business activity** in the source model. The actual implementation of this clause would depend on the data structure used for the ASG, but given, for example, a collection of business activity objects, a crude implementation might translate this clause into an outer `foreach` statement. The second query clause is similar to the first:

```
{BP_DSL: ?ba2 is a business activity}
```

Again, a crude implementation might iterate over the same collection using an inner `foreach` statement. The third query clause excludes all pairs of business activities, whose members are identical. We will see more realistic implementation techniques later in this chapter, but for now, we will continue to use this declarative pseudo-code based specification format to help illustrate transformation concepts.

Using Traceability Information in Rules

It is often a requirement for traceability that at least one action clause in the THEN part record information that can be used to determine whether or not the rule has already been run. This information can be recorded in the source model, in the target model, in both models, or in a third model that contains nothing else.

Traceability information is used by refinement rules...

By including a query clause that tests the traceability information, a rule can detect that a source model element has already been transformed, and take alternative actions. For example, it might stipulate that existing objects in the target model are to be modified, instead of being recreated. In the preceding example, another rule in the model-mapping might contain the IF part shown in Figure 15.4.

In this case, instead of creating new Web services, the THEN part would modify existing Web services that already implement the corresponding business activities.

...and by reverse-refinement rules.

Another use of traceability information is to support *reverse-refinement rules*. A reverse-refinement rule propagates an effect

```
IF
    // First query the BP_DSL model for bindings and check for already
    // implemented business activities
    {BP_DSL: ?ba1 is a business activity} and
    {WS_DSL: ?ws1 is a web service that implements ?ba1) and
    {BP_DSL: ?ba2 is a business activity} and
    {WS_DSL: ?ws2 is a web service that implements ?ba2) and
    {BP_DSL: ?ba1 is not the same as ?ba2} and
    {BP_DSL: ?af1 is the artifact flow between ?ba1 and ?ba2}
    ...
THEN
    ...
```

Figure 15.4 Changing behavior based on previous transformations

from a lower level of abstraction to a higher one, i.e., from the target to the source. Reverse-refinement rules are used to synchronize models, or code and models, when the target is edited. Change events from the target trigger the firing of the rules, the query in the IF part of the reverse-refinement rules match objects in the target, and appropriate synchronizing actions are performed against the source.

For example, we might let a user of the Web Service DSL change the schema of a message, propagating the changes back into the Business Process model. A reverse-refinement rule in this model mapping might look like the one shown in Figure 15.5.

Traceability information can also be recorded using a DSL designed for that purpose.

Another alternative is to record traceability information using a DSL designed for that purpose. This allows us to separate it from the primary content of the source and target models, and to remove or update it without having to modify them. A

```
IF
    // First query the WS_DSL model for bindings and check
    // to see what a changed message implements in the BP_DSL model
    {WS_DSL: WHEN message ?m1 is changed} and
    {WS_DSL: web service ?ws1 emits ?m1} and
    {WS_DSL: web service ?ws2 receives ?m1} and
    {WS_DSL: ?ws1 implements activity ?ba1) and
    {WS_DSL: ?ws2 implements activity ?ba2) and
    {WS_DSL: ?m1 implements artifact ?af1}
    ...
THEN
    // Perform actions on activities ?ba1, ?ba2 and artifact ?af1
    //
    {BP_DSL:  . . . }
    ...
```

Figure 15.5 A rule that checks for traceability links

```
IF
    // First query the Mapping model for bindings and check
    // to see what a changed message implements in the BP_DSL model
    {WS_DSL: WHEN message ?m1 is changed} and
    {WS_DSL: web service ?ws1 emits ?m1} and
    {WS_DSL: web service ?ws2 receives ?m1} and
    {MAPPING: ?ws1 implements activity ?ba1) and
    {MAPPING: ?ws2 implements activity ?ba2) and
    {MAPPING: ?m1 implements artifact ?af1}
...
THEN
    // Perform actions on activities ?ba1, ?ba2 and artifact ?af1
    //
    {BP_DSL:  . . . }
    ...
```

Figure 15.6   A rule that checks for traceability links in a mapping model

generic mapping DSL can be defined that can record traceability between arbitrary sets of source and target models, as long as their metamodels are all expressed in the same language (i.e., as long as they all have the same meta-metamodel). A rule that uses a generic mapping DSL might look like the one shown in Figure 15.6.

Implementing Mapping Rules

Mapping rules can be implemented as specifications similar to the ones shown these examples, using rule based languages like Prolog, or using programming languages like XQuery that provide pattern-matching facilities. They can also be implemented imperatively, using procedural programming languages. We will look at each of these, in turn. Note, however, that regardless of the mechanism used to implement mapping rules, the source and target metamodels always supply the vocabulary used to specify them.

Mapping rules may be implemented using a variety of mechanisms.

Using a Procedural Programming Language

Using a procedural programming language, each rule is typically implemented individually, as a method on a Visitor class [GHJV95]. This is the most laborious approach, since matching and binding must be hand coded, but it is generally also the most efficient, and allows unrestricted expression of both the IF part and THEN part of each rule. For example, if the rule specifications shown earlier as examples were implemented as

Procedural implementations often use the Visitor pattern.

specified, then the resulting transformation system would be extremely inefficient. It would visit each object in the ASG for the Web Service model many times, once for each IF part clause that mentions the object type. A hand coded implementation, on the other hand, would visit each object fewer times, by making a limited number of passes over the ASG, and calling rules implemented as visitation methods when the object is visited.

GPL compilers use similar techniques.

In effect, procedural implementations refactor the mapping rules, grouping the IF part clauses by the object type queried. This is a well-known implementation strategy for general purpose programming language compilers, which often traverse ASTs using visitors to perform static analysis, to optimize the ASTs, and to generate results. When a GPL compiler-compiler is used to build the compiler, the visitation methods, called action routines, are often attached to the abstract syntax using an attributed grammar. While most model compilers are currently written by hand, we have seen one example of a model compiler-compiler that offers similar facilities, allowing action routines to be attached to the metamodel [KC04].

Continuous synchronization uses the Observer pattern.

In some scenarios, continuous synchronization is used for model transformation, rather than compilation. These scenarios typically use the Observer pattern, rather than the Visitor pattern. Each rule is implemented as a class that observes changes to designated objects, or to objects of a designated type. Rules fire continuously as the user edits the source and target models. The whole ASG is rarely traversed in its entirety. Instead, a small part of the ASG is visited on each change notification.

Using an Embedded Query Language

An embedded query language makes query optimization easier...

Using a procedural programming language that has embedded query and pattern matching capabilities, such as Perl or XQuery, some of the query optimization can be delegated to the language runtime. Mapping rules do not have to be refactored to provide an efficient implementation because the runtime schedules rule execution. It also eliminates the need to write matching and binding code.

...But may require model data format adaptation.

A downside is that the language runtime may not be able to access the model data in the format used by the ASG. In this case, an adapter must be written to transform it from the format used by the ASG to the format required by the query language. For example, if the embedded query language is

XPath or XQuery, then the adapter must to make the ASG look like an XML document. Or, if the query language is embedded SQL, then the adapter must to make the ASG look like a SQL database. Of course, the availability of an embedded query language like XQuery or SQL might dictate the design of the ASG.

Using a Rule-Based System

A rule-based system, such as CLIPS or Prolog, can directly execute rules written in a declarative language. In fact, the pseudo-code rule specification language used in this chapter bears a passing resemblance to CLIPS [CLIPS]. Rule-based systems have many in-built mechanisms for efficiently describing, executing, and managing complex rule sets, and can perform the kind of execution optimization discussed earlier. Again, the downside is that these systems typically require their data to be represented in special formats, or to be stored in special purpose storage facilities. Interfacing them efficiently to ASGs for DSL-based models can be a challenging task.

A rule-based system would implement our rules almost as they are!

Implementing THEN parts with Code Templates

When the target model is source code, a common practice is to use code templates or scripts to implement the THEN parts. To illustrate the use of code templates, we'll go back to our stack of DSLs and the examples we've been looking at, and show how the implementer of the Web Service DSL can write a rule to produce some ASP.NET Web service code.

THEN parts for code often use code templates or scripts.

The rule must take each Web service in the source model, follow its relationships in the ASG to each port through which it offers operations, and then gather information about the parameters for each of those operations. The IF part for this rule might look the one shown in Figure 15.7.

A code template example.

The IF part binds objects from the Web Service model to variables. The variables are then used to parameterize the code template supplied by the THEN part. To keep this example simple, we have not shown the details of parameter list handling, which would require breaking into the parameters to access parameter name and type. Also, templates in real products like Microsoft Visual Studio .NET and IBM Rational XDE usually provide facilities for formatting the generated code. Using markup language, such as parameterized spacing and

```
IF
    // First query the WS_DSL model for bindings and check
    // to gather information for the generated code
    {WS_DSL: ?ws1 is a web service} and
    {WS_DSL: ?ws1 offers port ?p1} and
    {WS_DSL: ?p1 request message ?m1) and
    {WS_DSL: ?m1 has parameter list ?pa1) and
    {WS_DSL: ?m1 has return parameter ?rt} and
    ...
THEN
    // Using these bound parameters, match and execute the
    // following code template
    {C#_TEMPLATE:
    using System ;
    using System.Web ;
    using System.Web.Services  ;

    namespace ?ws1
    {
        public class ?p1 : System.Web.WebService
        {
          public ?p1()
          {
          //CODEGEN: This call is required by the ASP.NET Web
          // Services Designer
          InitializeComponent();
          }
          //Hidden Region Below
          Component Designer generated code

          [WebMethod]
          public ?rt.type ?m1(?pa1)
          {

          }
          . . .
        }
    }
    } // End of template
```

Figure 15.7 Using templates in THEN parts

indentation directives, these templates can apply user-defined styles to create standard formatting in the generated code.

Also, while not shown in any of our examples so far, a THEN part might be able to execute more than one template. For example, in addition to generating code, a rule might build project folders and create configuration files.

When a code model is used, the template format looks more like the THEN parts shown in the model-to-model rule

```
IF
    // First query the WS_DSL model for bindings and check
    // to gather information for the generated code
    {WS_DSL: ?ws1 is a web service} and
    {WS_DSL: ?ws1 offers port ?p1} and
    {WS_DSL: ?p1 request message ?m1) and
    {WS_DSL: ?m1 has parameter list ?pa1) and
    {WS_DSL: ?m1 has return parameter ?rt} and
    . . .
THEN
    // Using these bound parameters, match and execute the
    // following code model actions
    {C#_CODE: . . . }  // For using directives and namespace
    {C#_CODE: createClass(?ws1.?p1, "System.Web.WebService") }
    {C#_CODE: createMethod(?ws1.?p1.?m1, ?rt, ?pa1) }
    {C#_CODE: createAttribute(?ws1.?p1.?m1, "WebMethod") }
    . . .
```

Figure 15.8   Using code model calls in THEN parts

examples. Some code models may take formatting information, but this is not shown in Figure 15.8. The API shown here is an example used for illustration purposes only. It is not the actual API for the C# code model in Microsoft Visual Studio .NET.

Specifying Horizontal Transformations

Having looked at vertical transformations, let's now switch to horizontal ones. Recall that horizontal transformations are those in which the source and target models are the same. They are used either to implement delocalizing transformations, like aspect weaving, or to optimize a model before and/or after running a vertical transformation.

Horizontal transformations are either optimizing or aspectual.

Describing Aspect Weaving

Suppose we have a graphical concrete syntax for our Web Service DSL that looks like the one in Figure 15.9.

The figure shows Web service components as boxes of different types. It also shows ports on their edges through which they either provide services or consume services provided by other Web service components. Lines between ports represent sets of messages interchanged between them. This language provides a nice surface on which to design a service-oriented architecture that implements activities within a business process.

An aspect weaving example…

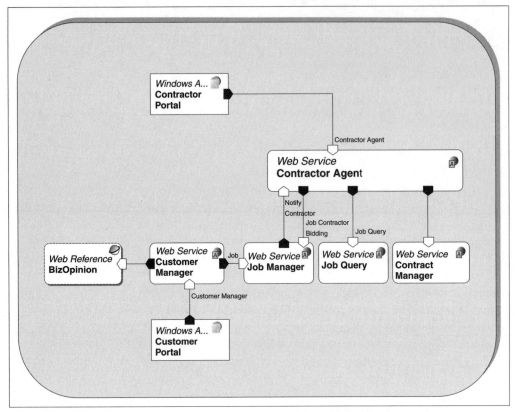

Figure 15.9   Graphical syntax for the web service DSL

...using security policy.

We would like to let the user of this language apply security policies to operations offered by the Web service components. Such a policy might state that certificates are required from a specific issuing authority. Since the same security policy could be applicable to multiple operations across multiple ports, we'd like to treat it as an aspect that is defined once, and then woven into the model in multiple places. Given some graphical capability to define the security policy, and a graphical way to select all Web service components and ports to which the security policy should be applied, the appropriate rule would look something like Figure 15.10.

Note that this rule operates only on models based on the Web Service DSL. A refinement rule could turn this information into code supported by an Aspect-Oriented Programming language like AspectJ, or by language extension attributes in a .NET programming language.

```
IF
    // First query the WS_DSL model for bindings
    // and reference the security policy aspect and
    // the graphically selected web services
    {WS_DSL: ?ws1 is a web service} and
    {WS_DSL: ?ws1 is selected} and
    {WS_DSL: ?ws1 offers port ?p1}
    {WS_DSL: ?p1 request message ?m1) and
    {WS_DSL: ?sp1 is a security policy} and
    . . .
THEN
    // Using these bound parameters, match and execute the
    // following action to weave the aspect into the model
    {WS_DSL:  associate ?sp1 to ?m1}
    . . .
```

Figure 15.10   A rule to weave a security policy to multiple ports

Describing Refactoring Rules

For another horizontal transformation scenario, we show an example of a refactoring rule. A refactoring transformation is typically used to improve the structure of a model to make it easier to read and maintain, to change its operational qualities, or prior to running vertical transformations. *An example of an optimizing rule.*

We will also take this example from the Web Service DSL. Imagine that the tool supporting the graphical syntax shown in Figure 15.9 lets us refine designs by using a predefined set of rules that can be run on demand—perhaps driven by an easy-to-use wizard. For example, it might offer the capability to clone a Web service, and then route all messages to ports on the original service to ports on the clone. Also, it might set tighter security on the clone than on the original.

This transformation is useful, since we often have to perform these actions when we want to create a façade—a service to be offered to customers or partners outside the datacenter firewalls from a less secure "demilitarized" zone (DMZ)—which passes some or all of its operations through to services residing in a more secure zone inside the datacenter firewalls, as shown in Figure 15.11. The façade exposed to the public uses a tighter security policy to prevent access to sensitive information or privileged operations offered by the original Web service. The original Web service, on the other hand, uses a looser security policy, so that the sensitive information and operations can be accessed from within the company.

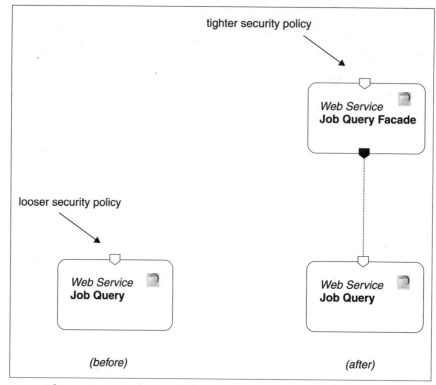

Figure 15.11   Before and after states of refactoring

Using our pseudo-code rule specification language, the wizard might execute the refactoring rule shown in Figure 15.12.

In fact, this example is a good candidate for an oblique transformation, where this refactoring rule is followed by a refinement rule that generates the project folders, configuration entries, and code skeletons required to implement the façade.

Patterns as Sets of Mapping Rules

Rules implement patterns. So far, in our discussion of transformations, mappings, and individual rules, we have used the term "pattern" quite loosely and generally, and without relating it to the more detailed discussion of patterns in Chapters 6 and 7. We can think of a mapping rule as a pattern. Recall from Chapter 2 that a pattern provides a strategy for solving a recurring problem in a specific context. Another way to say the same thing is to say that a pattern defines a mapping between a problem and a solution.

```
IF
    // First query the WS_DSL model for bindings
    // surrounding the graphically selected web services
    // to which we want to add a "façade" service
    {WS_DSL: ?ws1 is a web service} and
    {WS_DSL: ?ws1 is selected} and
    {WS_DSL: ?ws1 offers port ?p1}
    {WS_DSL: ?p1 request message ?m1) and
    . . .
THEN
    // Using these bound parameters, match and execute the
    // following actions to create the façade services into the model
    {WS_DSL:  create a new web service ?wsf}
    {WS_DSL:  create a new port ?p2}
    {WS_DSL:  associate ?p2 to ?wsf as offers}
    {WS_DSL:  create a new request message ?m2}
    {WS_DSL:  set contents of ?m2 equal to ?m1}
    {WS_DSL:  associate ?m2 to ?p2 as receives}
    {WS_DSL:  create a new security policy ?sp2}
    {WS_DSL:  set the value of ?sp2 to "windows Authentication"}
    {WS_DSL:  associate ?sp2 to ?p2 as secures}
    {WS_DSL:  create a new web service reference port ?wsrp1}
    {WS_DSL:  associate ?wsrp1 to ?wsf as consumes}
    {WS_DSL:  associate ?m2 to ?wsrp1 as emits}
    . . .
```

Figure 15.12   A rule to implement the facade pattern

Of course, most of the patterns in use today give informal descriptions of the problems they solve and the solutions they provide. A mapping rule formally defines both the problem and the solution in terms of the source and target metamodels. The problem is defined as the configurations of objects that satisfy the query clauses in the IF part, and the solution (expressed as either an optimization or a refinement) is defined by the configurations of objects produced by the THEN part.

Most of the patterns in use today also give informal descriptions of the contexts in which the problems they solve are encountered. A few also give informal descriptions of the contexts in which the solutions they provide can be applied, but more often than not, the solution context is assumed by the pattern writer, and merely implied by the pattern definition. Usually, it is assumed to be a popular object oriented programming language supported by runtime libraries (e.g., C# and the .NET Framework). Since the pattern reader generally makes the same assumption, failing to describe the solution context is usually not much of a problem. The pattern reader effectively translates the solution provided by the pattern into the assumed solution context.

Most patterns describe the problem context only informally, if at all.

A model-mapping provides a context for mapping rules.

Unlike the descriptions of the problem and the solution, a mapping rule does not directly formalize the description of the problem and solution contexts. Instead, it only implies them by defining a mapping from models that conform to one meta-model onto models that conform to another. Where does the rest of the context description come from? We have been talking all along about mapping rules occurring in the context of a model-mapping, and at the beginning of this chapter, we defined a model-mapping as a relationship between the meta-models describing the sources and the targets of a transformation. The model-mapping therefore provides the context for a mapping rule. It defines the context in which the problem solved by the mapping rule is encountered, and the context in which the solution provided by the mapping rule can be applied. This conclusion is important, since it lets us predict situations in which we can expect to encounter specific recurring problems.

A software factory schema can be formalized by describing artifacts using models and relationships among them using model-mappings.

The preceding statement should sound familiar. Recall from Chapter 4 that working within a product family lets us identify problems common to the family members. In other words, it lets us predict situations in which we can expect to encounter specific recurring problems. As we showed in Chapter 4, it also lets us solve those problems in advance. From these observations, we might conclude that the context provided by working within a product family could consist of model-mappings. Recall from Chapter 5 that a software factory schema describes and organizes the development artifacts used to build product family members, and describes the relationships among them. If the development artifacts are models, or can be described using models (e.g., models of source code), then the relationships among them can be described using model-mappings. The more we formalize the descriptions of the development artifacts and the relationships among them, the more formal the software factory schema becomes, and the more we can automate the development of the product family members using transformations.

Patterns are the seeds of new abstractions.

We can now think of rule sets as formal specifications of patterns. Conversely, we can think of patterns as informal descriptions of transformations. Since patterns are used to capture best practices, we should also be able to capture best practices using rule sets. The patterns community generally frowns on automatic pattern application, however, asserting that patterns encode abstract knowledge that can be applied more effectively by humans than by tools. Most of the attempts to date to automate pattern application in modeling tools support this conviction. Compilers tell a different story, however. Decades of experience with compilers demonstrate that automatic pattern is not only possible, but also highly desirable. This experience suggests that the keys to success are to use formal languages for sources and targets, and to formally define transformations using mapping rules. As we saw in Chapter 6, patterns represent a step in the formation of new language abstractions. Recall that a pattern associates a name with an abstraction, and that if the pattern is applied frequently, then its name becomes part of the design vocabulary. Consider the preceding refactoring rule for a façade service. If this rule is applied frequently, then façade service will become part of the design vocabulary. As we saw in Chapter 6, a group of patterns designed to be used together forms a pattern language, and can be encapsulated to create a DSL. We can therefore think of a pattern language as an emerging DSL containing more abstract concepts than the underlying language in which the patterns are expressed.

Some patterns, like the façade service, describe horizontal transformations. Others describe vertical transformations. Consider any of the refinement rules described in this chapter. Each of them would presumably represent a best practice for mapping some configuration of objects at a higher level of abstraction onto some configuration of objects at a lower level. Patterns are often used as the starting point for defining rules, since they encode best practices, such as how best to implement business activities as Web services, how best to implement Web services in C#, or how best to generate an efficient relational schema from a business entity model.

Patterns are often used as the starting point for defining rules.

Unfortunately, not all useful patterns can be codified as rules. This is because in some cases the problem to which the pattern applies cannot be expressed as queries against a model. This usually occurs when some of the information required to apply the pattern is not captured by any model, and resides only in the head of the pattern reader. Consider, for example, the *layers* pattern [POSA1], which describes the conditions under which it is appropriate to factor an application into communicating layers, such as presentation, business logic, and data access layers. A complex interweaving of these conditions, given performance, scalability and other operational requirements, determines how the layers will map to underlying physical servers and their operating systems and web servers. Although we might be lucky enough to have information about all of

But many patterns rely on human knowledge and cannot be encoded in models.

these factors in a database for a given system, and although we might be able to solve example problems using a rules engine, we would still be a long way from automatically solving arbitrary layering problems with acceptable levels of quality under real world conditions. A more attainable goal would be to solve highly constrained layering problems for a well-defined family of systems. Software systems and deployment environments are already being described using formal models, such as the System Definition Model (SDM) defined by the Dynamic Systems Initiative, an industry effort led by Microsoft [DSI], so we may see tools that can at least evaluate layering strategies for certain families of .NET-based systems in the near future. That said, we should expect many patterns to continue to reside only in documentation for the foreseeable future.

And need to be able to create new patterns from models.

Many useful patterns will come presupplied by DSL implementers. Others will be discovered by users. In either case, there will be a need to extract configurations of objects from models, and to store them as parameterized patterns for later reuse. A graphical DSL editor that satisfied this requirement might provide a way to create IF parts from existing models, and to create THEN parts as parameterized configurations of objects to be created in target models. A graphical editor for the Web Service DSL, for example, might let the user define the IF part for the refactoring rule by selecting the configuration depicted on the left hand side of Figure 15.11, and running a wizard to parameterize elements in the selection, such as the name of the Web service. It might then let the user define the THEN part by selecting the configuration depicted on the left hand side, and running a wizard to bind the parameters to elements in the selection, such as the name of the façade service. With this pattern defined, the user could then select a Web service, and ask the tool to apply it to a Web service. After bringing up a wizard help the user bind the parameters to existing model elements, it would then apply the refactoring described by the rule, generating the façade service and rerouting connectors, as described earlier.

Transformation Systems

We are now ready to look at transformation systems. A transformation system is a tool that fully or partially automates transformations by automatically or interactively applying mapping rules.

Black-Box and White-Box Transformations

In the discussion so far, we've seen several ways to apply mapping rules.

Transformations can be performed manually, automatically or interactively.

- Manually, using hand coding to produce and optimize implementations from formal or informal input specifications.

- Automatically, or in "batch" mode, using transformation systems like compilers that produce and optimize implementations from formal input specifications.

- Interactively, using transformation systems that produce and optimize implementations iteratively and incrementally from formal input specifications. In such an environment, transformations can be applied either on demand, or continuously, by synchronizing the input and output domains, as the user modifies the input specifications, or the mapping parameters.

As these alternatives suggest, a generator is not the only means of performing transformations. Just as we distinguished between white- and black-box abstractions in Chapter 2, we can now differentiate between white- and black-box transformations. A white-box transformation is manual and completely transparent. It is performed by hand by a human. Applying a pattern by hand editing code is an example of a white-box transformation. A black-box transformation, on the other hand, is fully automatic and opaque. Compiling source code is an example of a black-box transformation. In a white-box transformation, the user produces, examines and edits the results of the transformation. In a black-box transformation, the user does not expect to do these things, although it may be possible for the user to examine or even to edit the results of the transformation. Most of the transformations used in every day development are grey-box transformations that fall between these extremes. A grey-box transformation is partially automatic and semi-transparent, and the systems that implement them are usually interactive. Using a visual builder to construct a user interface, writing only the event handlers by hand, is an example of a grey box transformation. Generally, optimizations and delocalizations are performed by black-box transformations, since they tend to obfuscate implementations of higher level abstractions in the output specifications. Refactorings are generally performed by white-box transformations, since they

Generators are not the only way to perform transformations.

are intended to improve the structure of specifications used by humans.

Most transformation systems let the user set mapping parameters.

Most transformation systems let the user set mapping parameters like compiler switches. Some let the user select the rules to be applied. These choices represent design decisions requiring judgment on the part of the user. Consider, for example, the refactoring rule shown in Figure 15.11. This rule might be rewritten, as shown in Figure 15.13, to indicate that user input is required. Of course, in practice, we probably would not query the user interactively during rule execution. Instead, we would use mechanisms that collect this information at more convenient times, such as exposing options that can be set by the user when the tool is idle, or running a wizard before performing a transformation. Default values for these design decisions should be provided by the designer of the model-mapping.

Mappings may vary on a type or instance basis.

Interactive transformation systems make it easy to change mapping parameter values, either by collecting them into user profiles, where they apply to all objects of a given type, or by placing them in source models, as properties of specific objects.

```
IF
    // First query the User for a binding to a web service
    // to which we want to add a "façade" service
    {ASK-USER}: "Select a web service" ?ws1}
    //Verify selected object is a web service
    {WS_DSL: ?ws1 is a web service} and
    {WS_DSL: ?ws1 offers port ?p1}
    {WS_DSL: ?p1 request message ?m1} and
    {ASK-USER: "Define a security policy", ?sp2
            Choices "Windows Authentication",
                    "Passport", "Certification"
            Default "Windows Authentication"}
    //Verify the security policy entered
    {WS_DSL: ?sp2 is a security policy} and
    . . .
THEN
    // Using these bound parameters, match and execute the
    // following actions to create the façade services into the model
    {WS_DSL:   create a new web service ?wsf}
    {WS_DSL:   create a new port ?p2}
    {WS_DSL:   associate ?p2 to ?wsf as offers}
    {WS_DSL:   create a new request message ?m2}
    {WS_DSL:   set contents of ?m2 equal to ?m1}
    {WS_DSL:   associate ?m2 to ?p2 as receives}
    {WS_DSL:   associate ?sp2 to ?p2 as secures}
    {WS_DSL:   create a new web service reference port ?wsrp1}
    {WS_DSL:   associate ?wsrp1 to ?wsf as consumes}
    {WS_DSL:   associate ?m2 to ?wsrp1 as emits}
```

Figure 15.13   Rule showing ask-user elements

With either approach, changing the mapping parameter values changes the way the source model objects are implemented, creating a rapid and highly iterative approach to development, where the user iteratively tweaks the mapping parameter values, and then automatically or semi-automatically regenerates the output specifications. Interactive transformation is often associated with Rapid Application Development (RAD), a project planning methodology focused on minimizing time to market, as described in Chapter 17. An important aspect of interactive transformation is that the mappings can be tuned not only on a type basis (i.e., between DSLs), but also on an instance basis (i.e., between individual models). Different models based on the same DSL, and even different objects within those models, can have different mappings to the underlying implementation language.

Grey-Box Transformation Systems

Here are some examples of the kinds of assistance that a grey-box transformation system can provide:

1. Constraining manually developed output specifications, so that the user cannot produce an implementation of an input specification that is inconsistent with the mapping. This is useful when the mapping between the input and output specifications is not fully defined, i.e., when we do not know enough about the relationship to produce the output specification in its entirety from the input specification, but we do know enough to constrain it. An example of this kind of assistance is generating and reverse engineering the structural portions of the code, while leaving method bodies untouched, and requiring that the structural portions be consistently defined in both the input and output specifications.

   Constraining manually developed output specifications.

2. Suggesting alternative implementations, so that the user must choose one of several possible results, either for the whole input specification, or on an object-by-object basis within the input specification. This is useful when the mapping between the input and output specifications is complete, except for the selection of alternatives, i.e., when we know enough about the relationship to produce multiple alternative output specifications from the input specification, but we have consciously chosen

   Suggesting alternative implementations.

to leave the selection of the alternative to the developer as a means of tuning the results. The selection of alternatives is one end of a spectrum, whose other end is fine-grained tuning of the mappings, as described next.

Auto completion as the developer types.

3. Auto completion as the developer types, so that names of objects defined at the higher level of abstraction are intelligently suggested in context, based on knowledge of their meaning. For example, when a developer is completing method bodies in code whose structural portions have been generated from a model, we can assist them by offering the definitions of classes, properties, events, and methods captured in or referenced by the model using an intelligent editor prompt, such as the IntelliSense® technology in Microsoft Visual Studio. For example, we might suggest method names from the model when the developer is typing a method name within a method body (i.e., to invoke the method), or we might suggest class names from the model when the developer is typing a class name within a method body (i.e., to specify the type of a field, or to qualify a method or property name).

Synchronization of the input and output specifications.

4. Synchronization of the input and output specifications, so that as the developer modifies the output specification manually, changes that violate the mapping are flagged, and automatic corrections are offered. For example, if the developer edits the code to change the signature of a method that was defined in the model, we can flag the inconsistency and offer to correct the code, correct the model, or change the mapping. This is especially important when the names defined in the input specification are used in many different places in one or more output specifications, or when they are mangled in some way.

A classic example of synchronization arises in generating or maintaining source code for Enterprise JavaBeans. Each EJB is defined by anywhere from four to eight specifications, which must be consistent with each other, in order to compile. At a minimum, a remote home interface, a remote bean interface, a bean implementation class, and several entries in a deployment descriptor shared by multiple EJBs must be defined. There may also be a local home interface, a local bean interface, a home implementation class, and a primary key implementation class. The name of the EJB appears in different forms in the specifications. For example, it appears verbatim in the remote bean interface, but is typically mangled to produce the names of the other artifacts using a set of naming patterns.

For example, an EJB named Order would typically include a remote bean interface named Order, a remote home interface named OrderHome, a bean implementation class named OrderImpl, a home implementation class named OrderHomeImpl, a local bean interface named LocalOrder, a local home interface named LocalOrderHome, and a primary key class named OrderKey. As the developer edits the source code or a model of the EJB, these specifications must be kept synchronized. It is especially valuable to flag changes made by the developer that affect multiple specifications. For example, if the developer changes the name of the local bean interface from LocalOrder to LocalOrderForm, we might prompt to change the names of the other parts of the EJB, both in the model and in the other source code files, accordingly. This behavior is provided by Borland's JBuilder, for example.

5. Validation of the output specifications, so that when the developer has finished modifying the output specifications, they can be checked against the knowledge of the higher level abstractions and their mappings to the output specifications to ensure that the output specifications are correct. This may be done either to check edits to the output specifications made outside the development environment, or to compensate for a lack of synchronization. IBM WebSphere Studio, for example, does not provide full synchronization for EJBs, but it does perform a validation pass before attempting to compile the source code files to ensure that they are consistent and well formed.

Validation of the output specifications.

Applying Black-Box Transformations

Generators are development tools that automatically select, schedule, and apply black-box transformations to produce implementations from input specifications. In most cases, they

Generators are development tools that apply sequences of transformations.

also decode input specifications and encode implementations. Input specification decoding is generally called parsing, and is not required when the input specification is an AST or ASG. Implementation encoding is called rendering, and is not required when the output is an AST or ASG. There are many benefits to passing around specifications that do not have to be parsed or rendered. This is what makes XML so powerful. XML is effectively a direct serialization of an ASG. Generators also manage rule sequencing, and make choices when more than one rule could apply, in some cases guided by attributes attached to individual rules. We can identify several ways to implement generators.

Using Meta Programming Facilities

Using meta programming facilities.

Some general-purpose languages have built-in meta programming facilities, such as C++ templates and UML standard extension mechanisms. Language extensions that use these facilities may be able to extend the host language compiler to process new syntactical forms and to perform specialized code generation, error checking and reporting, or optimization for abstractions defined by the extensions.

This approach has several benefits.

- The resulting generators can be distributed as libraries for existing development tools.
- The meta programming facilities are usually optimized for the host language, allowing the generator to take advantage of host language compiler optimizations.
- The meta programming facilities usually operate on the host language source code, not on its abstract syntax representation, which makes them easy to use.

It also has some drawbacks.

- Many host languages do not support notation extensions.
- Developing a generator may be hard if the host language does not provide good meta program debugging facilities.
- Language extensions may conflict with each other, interfere with host language notation, or change the host language implementation in unexpected ways.

Building from Scratch

Generators can be also built from scratch as stand-alone programs either by hand, or with language development tools, such as lexical analyzers and parser generators. This can be expensive, since the abstract syntax representation and the analysis, optimization, and generation components must be custom developed. The resulting generator may also be expensive to adapt to new abstractions, or to interface with other development tools.

Building generators from scratch can be expensive.

Using as Preprocessors

Preprocessors expand macros embedded in a host language, and are deployed in front of the host language compiler. Preprocessors have several drawbacks.

Pre-processors expand macros in the source language.

- Errors in source specifications are reported by the host language compiler in terms of the preprocessor output, not in terms of the preprocessor input.
- Host language debuggers typically do not support debugging in preprocessor languages.
- If the preprocessor does not completely understand the host language, then macros may not be able to access or manipulate portions of the input specification expressed in the host language.

Parametric Modeling

An innovative approach called parametric modeling lets the user build a generator by assembling mapping rules, instead of building source models. Instead of applying rules to models, a parametric generator treats the rules and their parameter bindings as the model. Rules create new target model objects from parameter values, modify target model objects already created by rules, and change parameter values. The generator works like a spreadsheet, automatically propagating changes to parameter value throughout the rule base. With a good library of predefined rules, patterns, and software components, parametric modeling can produce extremely high levels of automation. The primary example is Bowstreet Factory from Bowstreet Software [Bow03].

With parametric modeling, the user builds a generator, not source models.

Using a Generator Framework

Using a generator framework with a software factory.

A generator framework provides an extensible implementation platform used by extension library providers to build generators. This platform may include facilities for developing concrete and abstract syntaxes, for parsing the concrete syntaxes, for editing the abstract syntax, for encoding the abstract syntax, for error diagnosis and reporting, for program analysis, for performing optimizations, for scheduling and invoking transformations, and for rendering generated implementations. Extension libraries provide a convenient way to package and distribute generators. The primary advantage of using a generator framework is lower development cost. The primary disadvantage is that it may lock the extension library provider into a proprietary programming model.

Summary

In Chapter 14, we studied various ways of categorizing mappings between models, and between models and code, and we highlighted issues that must be addressed to support model-driven development in software factories. In this chapter, we looked at how transformations implement these mappings. We introduced a pseudo-code format for expressing mapping rules, and described implementation options based on several different currently available technologies. Finally, we described several types of transformation systems, we looked at several different ways to implement generators.

Software Factories in Depth

Companies are moving as fast as they can, and the marketplace is the judge of who gets these things right.

Bill Gates

The road map shown in Figure P3.1 describes Part III. Part III reviews the concepts introduced in Part I, drawing on material presented in Part II to bring the book to its conclusion. Chapter 16 presents an example of a Software Factory, and Chapter 17 answers Frequently Asked Questions. Appendix A explains forms of abstraction and refinement, and Appendix B describes the Unified Modeling Language.

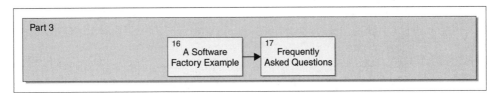

Figure P3.1   A road map to Part III

A Software Factory Example

Because we don't talk about problems, we don't analyze or classify them, and we slip into the childish belief that there can be universal development methods, suitable for solving all development problems.

Michael Jackson

By now, we hope you have a good sense for the software factory methodology and for the critical innovations that make it possible. In this chapter, we illustrate both the methodology and the critical innovations by showing an example of a software factory for a realistic family of applications, and of the process used to build one member of that family within that software factory. Our goal is to show that the methodology can be implemented now, that it can be widely used to complement and eventually replace existing practices, and that it can help move the software industry toward maturity.

A Review of the Approach

In this chapter, we provide practical suggestions for building a software factory using the technologies described in Chapters 6 through 15. We offer a concrete example, showing representative artifacts, explaining how and when each artifact is created or used during either factory or product development. We also point out where the big wins occur along the way, compared with crafting products individually by hand. We also identify areas where new technology needs to be developed, areas where the required technology exists, but has not yet been hardened commercially, and areas where it can be obtained in the form of commercial products.

Building an Online eCommerce Application Family

Back to our fictional software vendor, GSS.

To do this, we return to our fictional software vendor, Greenfield & Short Software, Inc. (GSS), which we first met in Chapter 1, when it was commissioned by our fictional customer, Construction Tools, Inc. (CTI), to build a set of process-oriented connected applications to support electronic commerce and Customer Relationship Management (CRM).

GSS started life as a software company, building custom one-off applications from scratch for manufacturing businesses located on the East Coast. But, after building similar applications on many engagements, including the one for CTI, they decided to change their business model. Instead of a software contracting firm with modest margins, constantly under threat from competitors, they would become a software product company, selling the kinds of applications they were building for customers as software products, with far higher margins. So, after raising some capital, GSS has set about building software products to sell.

They decide to build a software factory.

Knowing their customers, they know that the kind of contracting they used to do—gathering requirements, building the software, installing and interfacing to other business systems—will still be needed, since every customer will have many unique requirements. However, they also know that in order to sell software as a product, they must build reusable applications that meet the needs of many customers. They will succeed if and only if they can efficiently produce custom applications from a set of reusable components, rather than starting from scratch for every customer. They therefore decide to build a software factory.

They plan to exploit a software supply chain using assets from other vendors.

GSS also knows that they cannot expect to build all of the production assets that they will need to build the applications. They will therefore have to acquire some of them from other companies. They will also have to integrate their applications with systems already installed in customer data centers. Using a software factory will pay off handsomely for them, since they know other software component suppliers who are using the same approach, making it easier to obtain components that will fit into their product line architecture. In other words, GSS will exploit a software supply chain enabled by the software factories methodology.

GSS also recognizes that two of their most important assets are their knowledge of the business processes supporting eCommerce and CRM, and their knowledge of how to help their customers implement them. This domain knowledge and the ability to rapidly apply it in the analysis of existing processes and application portfolios are the key competitive advantages that GSS wants to exploit.

Their domain knowledge is their primary competitive advantage.

With these ideas in mind, GSS decides that their software factory should produce process-driven, data-intensive, service-based eCommerce and CRM applications based primarily on the Microsoft .NET platform, with interfaces to other applications and services running on other platforms. They therefore develop the software factory schema summarized in Figure 16.1.

GSS defines their software factory schema

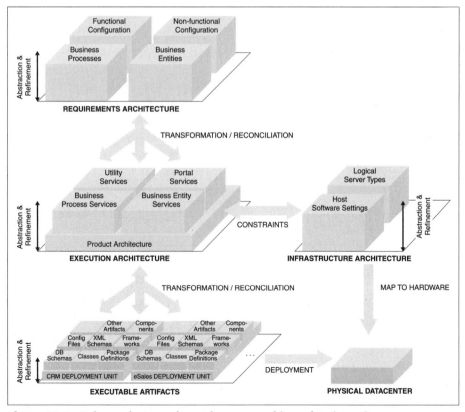

Figure 16.1 Software factory schema for process-driven, data-intensive, service-based eCommerce applications

This chapter will show examples of patterns, DSLs, frameworks, and tools.

During the course of this chapter, we will look at various details from this software factory schema. We will look at the patterns, DSLs, frameworks, tools, and other production assets developed or acquired by GSS to support the viewpoints it defines. We will discuss the variability inherent at every point in the schema, and discuss some of the mechanisms used by GSS to configure the schema to meet the requirements of specific customers. We will see examples of simple mechanisms, such as wizards and the simple inclusion and exclusion of components based on feature requirements. We will also see examples of more complex mechanisms like pattern expansion, where schema-defined patterns are selected by configuration decisions, and merged with existing component interface type models, to produce customized type models that are used to generate specific code within a white-box component implementation. Finally, we will show how these configuration decisions map to customizations of the product architecture. Figure 16.2 presents a simplified view of the sequence of

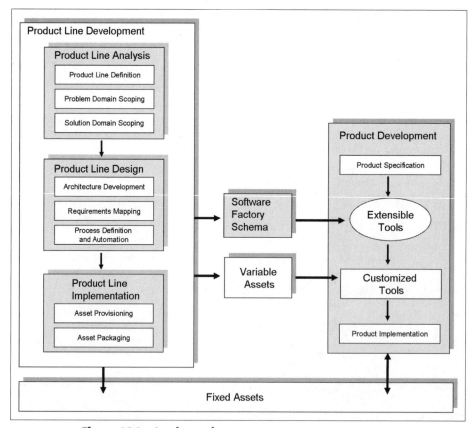

Figure 16.2   A software factory

activities that will drive the rest of the chapter. This process is described in much more detail in Chapter 11. Recall that building and maintaining a software factory is a continuous process consisting of many iterative and parallel activities, most of which can be undertaken in any order, as soon as the necessary resources are available. Recall, also, that software factories are usually the result of both bottom up and top down development, and that they evolve over time. Since we have limited space here, we will present the example linearly, understanding that the process is iterative and incremental in practice, not sequential.

Product Line Analysis

Product Line Analysis is the first group of tasks to be performed in the construction of the software factory. The purpose of this activity is to decide *what* products the software factory will produce. The main deliverables are listed in Figure 16.3. The focus of product line analysis is describing the commonalities and variabilities that characterize the product family. As we describe the deliverables, note the different kinds of variabilities that each of them is capable of describing.

Product Line Definition

In their road show for raising capital, GSS will demonstrate broad knowledge of the online-commerce domain, and will

GSS defines their product family.

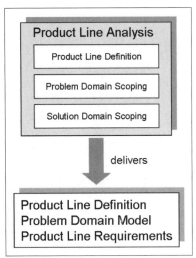

Figure 16.3 Summary of product line analysis tasks and delverables

explain how a modular architecture that supports the variability inherent in the domain will help them build multiple similar but unique applications that meet the specific needs of a wide range of customers. To make this presentation convincing, the GSS marketing team must describe the problems that their customers want to solve, and the products that they should offer to solve them. They must also describe the contexts in which these problems are encountered, and in which customers should be able to use their products to solve them.

Problem Domain Description

GSS describes the problem domain.

GSS describes the problems that their customers want to solve. Their customers want:

- Comprehensive online commerce and customer relationship management;
- Interactions with other businesses, especially their suppliers, their credit authorization partners, and government agencies;
- Interfaces to other software packages, particularly software for employee management and accounting;
- A way to offer self-service and personalization to their customers and suppliers;
- A way to offer selected employees and customers access to alerts and status information using mobile devices.
- Extensive customization features, such as customizing the workflow for processing leads as they arrive, and adding additional data items to online forms.

Business Processes

Business Processes used by their customers.

These problems occur in the context of business processes used by their customers, illustrated in Figure 16.4. These business processes were introduced in Chapter 1. Since the business processes manage customers, we will refer to GSS customers as *installations* from this point forward to avoid confusion with the *customers* managed by the business processes.

Web site Management Process.

The web site management process creates a business web presence and the basic web-based storefront for an installation. It describes how the installation will setup e-mail accounts,

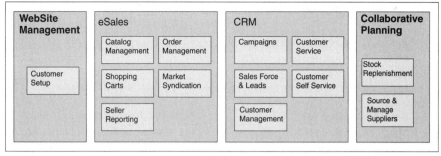

Figure 16.4 Business processes supported

how they will design and manage the layout and content of their web site, how they will register the site with search engines, and how they will subscribe to banner exchange networks.

The Customer Relationship Management process will provide a complete suite of tools to automate and improve customer acquisition, conversion, service, retention, and feedback gathering. It describes the following subprocesses:

Customer Relationship Management Process.

- *Campaigns:* The process that businesses use to create, execute, and track direct marketing campaigns, initially focusing on e-mail direct marketing.

- *Sales Force and Leads:* The process that proscribes how sales people and sales managers track and manage their leads, prospects and current customers, including automated prospecting, sales processes, task management, customer acquisition, team selling, goal setting, and commission tracking.

- *Customer Management:* This process describes how customer information is recorded and used. It defines what happens when a new customer is acquired and what happens when customers ask to be unregistered.

- *Customer Service:* This process describes how customers are enabled to help themselves (e.g., knowledge base access, natural language search, solution rating), how incidents are tracked and escalated, how service representative effectiveness is tracked, how chat, e-mail and phone contacts are routed and queued, and how Service Level Agreements (SLA) are managed.

- *Customer Self-Service:* This process describes the management of a "logged in" customer on the web site, including how the customer checks order and support incident status, how opportunity/sales are handled, and how requests for custom quotes and product configurations are handled.

The eSales Process.

The eSales process describes five primary subprocesses:

- *Catalog Management:* This process consists of a set of catalog management activities that enable a business to enter products and services into their catalog, manage merchandising and configuration rules, and create custom catalogs and pricing.

- *Order Management:* This process describes how an installation manages orders received from any marketplace or partner. It is also the process by which a business defines policies (e.g., discounts) and service providers (e.g., credit card processors) that participate in order processing.

- *Shopping Cart Processing:* This process describes how orders from customers are handled and how customers can get their order history.

- *Market Syndication:* This process defines how an installation submits catalog data to marketplaces, such as eBay.

- *Seller Reporting:* This process gives Sales Management a snapshot of the sales activity across all their partners and marketplaces.

Collaborative Supply Planning Process.

The Collaborative Supply Planning process describes two primary subprocesses:

- *Stock Replenishment:* Stock from inventory is replenished by placing restocking orders to suppliers, and by giving them certain demand information to enable automatic re-stocking and goods receipt.

- *Source and Manage Suppliers:* Suppliers are vetted and selected for close collaboration.

Problem Domain Scoping

GSS must select a subset of problems to solve.

Since GSS cannot solve all of the problems in the domain, they must identify and select a subset of the problems to solve. The subset will be chosen by analyzing the business processes, and will be honed based on knowledge of specific installations. They will produce a problem domain feature model and business process models to document their selections. These artifacts will evolve continuously, as we shall see shortly.

Problem Feature Modeling

The problem domain feature model describes the common and variable features of problems in the target domain. The top-level feature model for the problem domain is shown in Figure 16.5. Feature models are described in detail in Chapter 11. We use the Extended Notation shown in Figure 11.10 in these examples: a filled circle denotes a mandatory feature, an open circle denotes an optional feature, a filled arc denotes inclusive subfeatures (i.e., any of them may be selected), and an open arc denotes exclusive subfeatures (i.e., at most one of them may be selected).

Using feature models to describe the problem domain.

Notice how mandatory and optional features are described by the feature model. For example, although web site management is required by all installations, only some of them require e-mail setup and domain name registration, since many

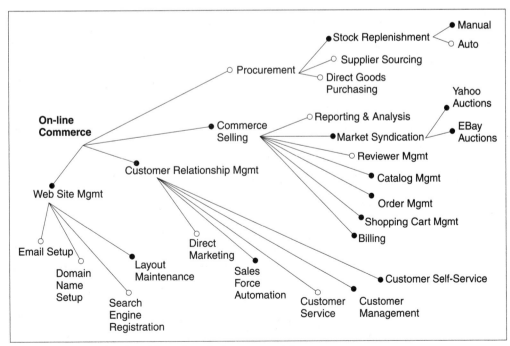

Figure 16.5 Top-level problem domain feature model

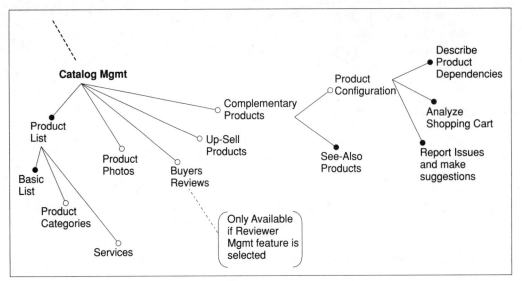

Figure 16.6 Feature model for catalog management

will already have these capabilities. Figure 16.6 shows a further feature analysis of the Catalog Management feature. A feature model can also describe types, cardinalities and other constraints, such as dependencies between features. We show constraints as annotations. For example, in Figure 16.5, we do not allow an installation to have Buyer Reviews for their online catalog entries unless they also have the Reviewer Management feature.

Figure 16.7 shows additional analysis of the Customer Relationship Management features. Of course, these figures show only a subset of the features in this problem domain for the purposes of this chapter. A fully elaborated set of feature models for this problem domain would be quite large, and would contain many more constraints.

Business Process Models

Business process models can be detailed and used for simulation.

GSS draws up Business Process Models that describe the business capabilities of target installations and the high-level dependencies between them. The models describe business events that influence those capabilities, and the information that flows between them. Not much detail is captured at this stage. Only the main successful outcome paths are illustrated. Error handling or exception paths are not yet shown. Although some companies invest heavily in business process modeling,

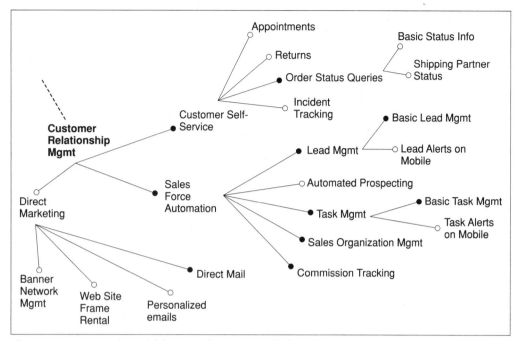

Figure 16.7 Feature model for part of customer relationship management

and use it to perform analysis and simulation to measure current approaches against possible improvements, GSS does not need this level of business process modeling. Their models will be used to check that the feature models correctly describe the problem domain, and to provide context for more detailed models that will be created later.

Solution Domain Scoping

Now that GSS has selected the problems to be solved, they must decide how their products will solve them. This will be done jointly by the Marketing and Product Line Development teams through negotiation, as described in Chapter 2. They will create a solution domain feature model to document the results. This feature model will evolve continuously, as we shall see shortly.

Solution Feature Modeling

The solution domain feature model describes the common and variable features of the product family. It differs from the

Feature models for the solution domain are the result of negotiation.

product domain feature model in several ways:

- The problem domain feature model describes problems without saying how they are solved, while the solution domain feature model describes product features without saying what problems they solve.

- The problem domain feature model may describe physical entities like people, and processes enacted manually, while the solution domain feature model describes only computational processes and entities.

- The problem domain feature model describes problems that may be solved by multiple systems while the solution domain feature model describes only the portion of the solution provided by this system.

- The entities or processes described by the solution domain feature model may contain different properties or steps than those described by the problem domain feature model, since the solution domain feature model describes encodings of the problem domain entities and processes.

During the negotiation, some features requested by the Marketing team are cut and others are modified because the implementation is too costly or too risky. Features required by the implementation that did not surface in problem domain scoping are added. Examples include features for the configuration and administration of data stores.

Features are often removed, added, and modified during negotiation.

Figure 16.8 shows the solution domain feature model during the negotiation. The teams have decided that although *Automated Prospecting* is a powerful feature, the technology required to implement it is too immature, so it has been cut. *Personalized e-mails* for *Direct Marketing* are too expensive given the level of value they provide. The feature *Mail List Setup* was not captured during problem domain scoping, but is required to support the Direct Mail feature.

The product line requirements are produced from the solution domain feature model.

An important artifact, called the product line requirements, is produced from the solution domain feature model. This is a schematized representation that will be used during product development to indicate which optional features are to be included in a particular family member. As the requirements of a prospective installation become known, optional features are selected from the product line requirements. Each optional feature is mapped to variability points in production assets like

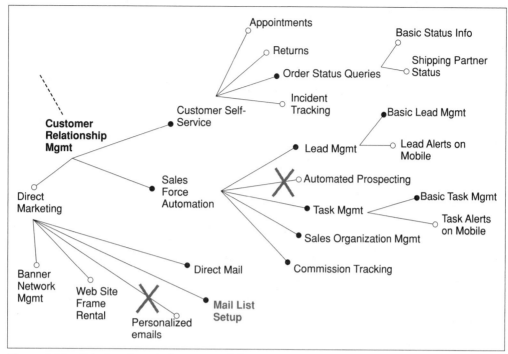

Figure 16.8   Solution domain feature model

the product line architecture and the product development process. These mappings will be explained in the next section as we look at the product line design.

Business Process and Entity Models

There are many different ways to define, document, analyze, and present business processes. It is beyond the scope of this book to explore this topic in depth. In the course of their consulting work, GSS has built a large knowledge base of business process models. They have used Microsoft Visio to produce drawings using their own variation of the notation suggested in [EP00], as illustrated in Figure 16.9. These are preferred by the team, since they facilitate the analysis of process flow and the identification of key business entities, and because they highlight documents that are used to move information between process steps.

Business Processes can be modelled in many ways.

As part of the definition of the software factory, GSS plans to migrate the business process knowledge base to a DSL that they will develop—one that reflects the way they model

But traceability to implementation is a challenge.

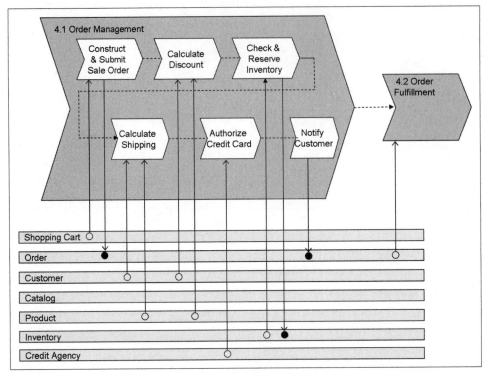

Figure 16.9   Business process model

business processes and from which they can generate models of their implementations. It is worth noting that few commercially available business process modeling tools are capable of generating implementations or models of implementations.

Non-Functional Requirements

Non-functional requirements are also described.

GSS also analyses the non-functional requirements for the product family using feature models. Figure 16.10 shows a partially completed feature model for non-functional requirements. In the interests of keeping these figures readable, much detail is omitted from this figure, since dependencies exist between many of the braches and leaf nodes of the feature model. For example, user response, latency, throughput and efficiency represent trade-offs that will need to be considered carefully for each installation.

Business Case Analysis is closely intertwined with problem and solution domain scoping.

Business Case Analysis

As these activities unfold, and GSS learns more about the costs of solving specific problems, they decide that some of the

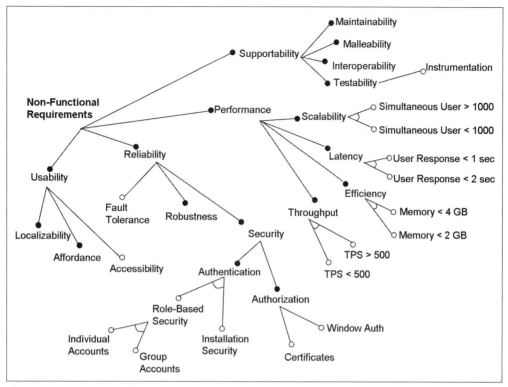

Figure 16.10 Feature diagram for non-functional requirements

problems they were planning to solve are too difficult, and that some of the problems they were not planning to solve can be solved more easily than they thought, creating business opportunities. They also discover that some of the problems they were planning to solve are of less interest to potential installations than they thought, and that some of the problems they were not planning to solve are more important. This kind of evaluation is called business case analysis. It usually runs continuously, fed by the results of problem and solution domain scoping. Of course, the results of business case analysis can cause problem or solution domain scoping to be revisited. In practice, since each of these activities influences the other two, all three must run in parallel. Of course, as products are developed using the software factory, product development feedback will lead to changes in the product line architecture, the product line implementation, the product development process, and other production assets. These changes will in turn lead to changes in development costs, and from there to changes in solution domain scoping. This is analogous to the feedback that occurs during the iterative development of a one-off product, and that leads to changes in the product requirements.

Product Line Design

Product Line Design focuses on the product architectures and the product development process.

Once the purpose and requirements for the product family are known, the GSS product line development team can start designing the software factory. The purpose of product line design is to decide *how* the software factory will produce the products. These tasks and deliverables are summarized in Figure 16.11.

Product Line Architecture Development

The product architecture is designed using patterns.

The GSS product line development team develops the product line architecture by analyzing the product line requirements and by applying architectural and design patterns. Figure 16.12 summarizes the patterns used by the team. Note that this figure does not show all patterns that could be used, nor does it accurately reflect all possible relationships between the patterns. For more information about Architecture and Design patterns, see [Fow03, HW03, MSDN04, GHJV95], where the patterns listed in the figure are defined.

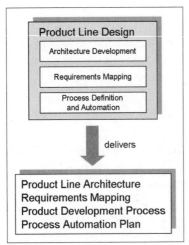

Figure 16.11 Product line design—summarized tasks and deliverables

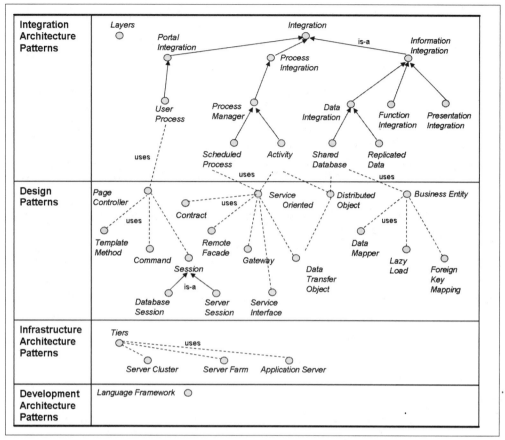

Figure 16.12 Architecture and design patterns

By studying the contexts and forces associated with these patterns, the product line development team composes the product line architecture through successive pattern application. The figure shows examples of pattern composition, where "lower level" patterns such as *Session*, *Command*, and *Page Controller* [GHJV95] are *applied* to form the *User Process* pattern, defined in a following section. It also shows examples of *is-a* relationships between patterns that represent specialization of context or form. The *Session* pattern, for example, is usually implemented using either *Database Session* or *Server Session* [Fow03]. The figure also categorizes the patterns following [MSDN04], separating Integration Architecture patterns concerned with the composition of coarse grained components from design patterns concerned with fine grained component interactions.

Patterns are composed and specialized.

Using Application Architecture Patterns

This product line architecture uses layers of typed services.

To maximize the flexibility of the product family, the product line architecture will use a set of loosely coupled, layered software services. Integration among the layers and between services in the same layer will be based on service integration patterns. Figure 16.13 illustrates the choices made by the GSS product line development team. The architecture uses the *layers* [POSA1] pattern to separate concerns. Service components residing in each layer are typed according to their function. Portal Services implement user scenarios and interactions. Business Process Service components implement business processes defined in the solution domain feature model using variations of the *process manager* [Fow03] pattern. Business Entity Service components implement major business entities defined in the solution domain feature model, and isolate the logic they contain from the physical data structures used by the data services. Business Entity Service components are implemented using the *Business Entity* pattern, discussed later, which in turn uses patterns that implement object-relational mapping, such as *Data Mapper, Foreign Key Mapping,* and *Lazy Load* [Fow03].

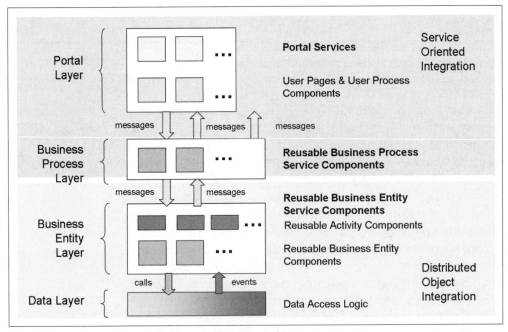

Figure 16.13 Product line architecture summary

Interactions between Portal Service and Business Process Service components are based on the *Service-Oriented* pattern, using message-driven, contract-bearing service interfaces, as described in Chapter 12. These interactions are implemented using Web service technology. Interactions between Business Process Service and Business Entity Service components are based on the *Distributed Object* pattern. Interactions between Activity and Business Entity components are also based on the *Distributed Object* pattern, but must use stateful, tightly coupled connections to meet performance requirements.

Various interaction and design patterns are used to meet product line requirements.

Alternative pattern strategies can be used to adapt the product line architecture to meet varying requirements. Consider the non-functional requirements described in Figure 16.10. Tradeoffs between performance and supportability call for different architectural and design patterns to be used in different installations. For example, an installation that wants to emphasize interoperability over performance might use Web service technology to support interactions between the Business Process and Business Entity Layers.

Some forms of variability can be addressed by varying the patterns.

Using Development Architecture Patterns

While developing the product line architecture, the GSS product line development team watches for opportunities to build special purpose tools that will increase the productivity of the product developers, and ensure that best practices are used when building the product family members. Since the product line architecture requires several different kinds of service component, each based on a different framework, the product line development team will construct DSLs that help product developers use the abstractions surfaced by these frameworks. They will use of the *Language Framework* pattern defined by Roberts and Johnson, and shown in the Development Architecture patterns part of Figure 16.12. This pattern is illustrated in Figure 16.14. We will see examples of the application of this pattern in this section as we look at the DSLs, frameworks, and tools developed by the GSS product line development team.

Using the DSL and Framework pattern to build special purpose tools and languages.

Stakeholder Portal Services

The Stakeholder Portal Services will be implemented using HTML pages based on ASP.NET. From their experience with

Stakeholder portals are Web applications.

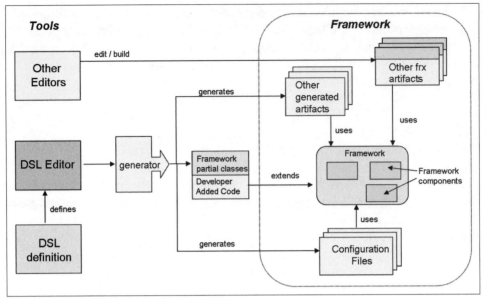

Figure 16.14   Language framework pattern

past projects, the team knows that a common pattern of user interaction, known as *User Process*, can be exploited to implement user interaction scenarios. The product line architecture will incorporate this pattern using a User Process framework, and a User Process DSL.

They are based on the User Process pattern.

The *User Process* pattern is characterized by:

- *Resuming Web Sessions:* This enables users to close browser sessions, and then later return to them with the ability to resume where they left off.

- *Transferring Web Sessions:* This enables one user to suspend a session, and another user to pick it up. It also enables the same user to suspend a session on one device, and then resume it on a different one.

- *Development of Wizard-Based Applications:* This helps developers build wizard that use a consistent style and that store session state until the process ends.

- *Development of Create, Read, Update, Delete (CRUD) Applications:* This helps developers build user interface processes for standard CRUD applications.

- *Development of Discrete Tasks:* This helps developers build encapsulated tasks (for example, Register User and

Checkout) that can be linked to form a User Process. Information can be passed between tasks as required (for example, user details can be passed from Register User to Checkout).

Relationships between User Process and Business Process Service components are shown in Figure 16.15. Here, a User Process steps through a sequence of Web Forms created by server-side ASP.NET pages. The User Process can be suspended by the User at any time, and then resumed later, since the User Process framework automatically stores the session state for each user. Note that BP1 and BP2 are Business Process Services that support the preparation steps in the User Process, while BP3 executes the results of preparation. Note also that BP2 is defined by an Activity schedule, while BP3 is a BPEL schedule. These concepts will be described in the next section.

The User Process pattern makes it easy to build complex user interactions. In this product family, it is used to implement use cases like Submit Orders and Register Customer. Each stakeholder portal is a package of User Processes customized for a specific type of stakeholder.

User Process makes it easy to build user interactions.

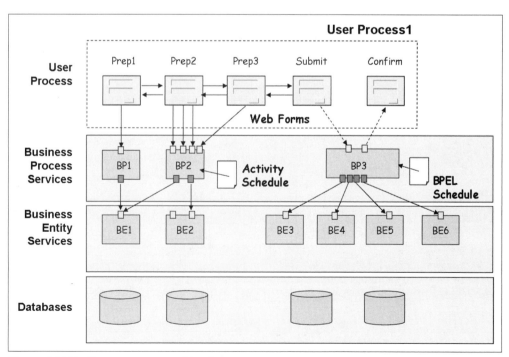

Figure 16.15 User processes and business processes

A DSL and a Framework for User Processes

The User Process pattern is implemented in a framework.

The User Process pattern is implemented in a framework built by GSS as an extension of the framework supplied by Microsoft known as the User Interface Process (UIP) Application Block for .NET, which is published by Microsoft on MSDN.[1] GSS has extended the code supplied by Microsoft and will define a DSL to wrap the framework. The high-level structure of the UIP Application Block is shown in Figure 16.16 [MSDN UIP]. Note how the relationship between tools, DSL and framework is described by the *Language Framework* pattern shown in Figure 16.14.

Developers will build User Processes by designing Web Form pages and writing framework extensions to indicate how control flow through the process should take place, what branching and exit conditions should be executed, and what business process components should be called.

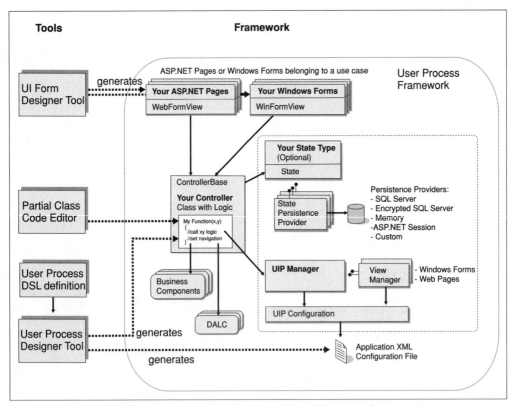

Figure 16.16 User process tools and framework

The goal is to make it easy to build complex, wizard-like sequences of forms while ensuring the use of best practices. GSS has built a metamodel defining User Process concepts, and has used tool-building tools to create a simple visual editor that can be used to build user processes. The tool generates ASP.NET and framework extension code and keeps them synchronized, as described in Chapter 15. The User Process Framework manages links between pages, manages session state for related pages, and calls business process services via agents, which create the necessary message structures.

A metamodel is defined and tool-building tools are used.

Conallen [Cona03] describes generative techniques for web client applications based on a static structure metamodel. GSS developers have built a framework based on a statechart metamodel, however. Their metamodel is very simple, and their graphical syntax is very straightforward. One of their User Process definitions is shown in Figure 16.17. For more information the use of statecharts describing user interaction, see Horrock [Horr99].

The framework is based on a statechart metamodel.

Business Process Services

The Business Process Services implement the business processes defined by the solution domain feature model.

Business Processes are implemented in Business Process Services.

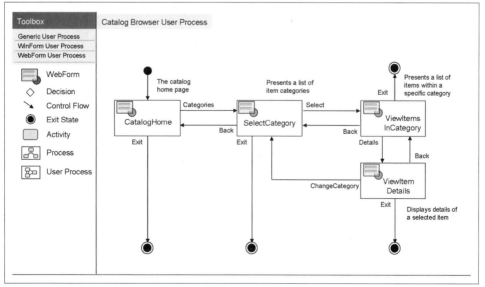

Figure 16.17 Graphical tool for describing a user process.

- They support user interactions using XML messages from the portals. The messages are extensible to allow for data items not defined by the message schemas.

- They implement process rules, and orchestrate loosely coupled message-driven business entity services to accomplish domain specific tasks, and they store information for the portals.

- They manage interactions with existing applications by calling adapters, or wrappers, which are service components that provide access to those applications. For example, after order processing, they feed information to a third party Accounting package supplied by the installation.

- They manage interactions with external companies, such as business-to-business collaborations, with suppliers and government agencies.

GSS decides to use BPEL schedules for flexibility.

GSS has decided to implement business process services using the *Process Manager* [Fow03] pattern, with process details defined in a schematized form, so that they can be changed to satisfy unique installation requirements. They do this by encoding business processes as BPEL schedules hosted within Web services. This allows them to run portal functionality across both intranets and the Internet for business-to-business collaborations.

Examples of Business Process Services.

The following business process services will be implemented:

- Web Site Management
- Direct Marketing Management
- Sales Force Automation
- Customer Self-service
- Market Syndication
- Catalog Management
- Order Management
- Billing
- Shopping Cart Process
- Supplier Sourcing
- Supplier Collaborative Planning

We will show later how patterns and fragments of BPEL schedules are applied to a basic schedule that implements the common features of the product family, to produce a final schedule that also implements selected variable features. An additional benefit from this approach is that installations will be able to further customize these processes, by editing the schedules, and recompiling the affected services.

BPEL allows installations to customize processes.

A DSL and Framework for Activities

Some parts of these business processes are too simple for the overhead of a BPEL engine—they are just simple sequences of synchronous transactions. Rollback after failure is scoped across these sequences, so complex compensation mechanisms are not required. For these kinds of subprocesses, based on the *Activity* pattern, GSS has built a framework that can be used to implement any Activity. They have also developed a DSL to wrap the Activity framework, called Activity Execution Language (AEL). AEL lets GSS describe Activities declaratively, making them easier to change and making it easy to develop patterns and language fragments that can be combined to address variable requirements. The definition of an Activity is called an Activity Schedule.

Another DSL is developed to boost further productivity.

The AEL is based on the *Pipeline* pattern. It defines a simple stateful process as a sequence of steps, each of which may be a call to a service, or to a business entity. An Activity has only a single entry point and all calls block, (i.e., wait for a response before continuing). An Activity wraps each of its steps to a separate transaction, standardizes error conditions arising from failures, and backs out completed steps when failures occur. GSS defines the AEL metamodel, and creates a graphical concrete syntax that lets them creates patterns and Activity model fragments, and will help product developers build specific Activities. Their graphical AEL editor is shown in Figure 16.18.

This DSL will be used to describe Activities.

Business Entity Services

A Business Entity Service manages information for a closely related set of business entities. Each business entity corresponds to an object in the problem domain that must be represented in

Business Entity Services perform information management.

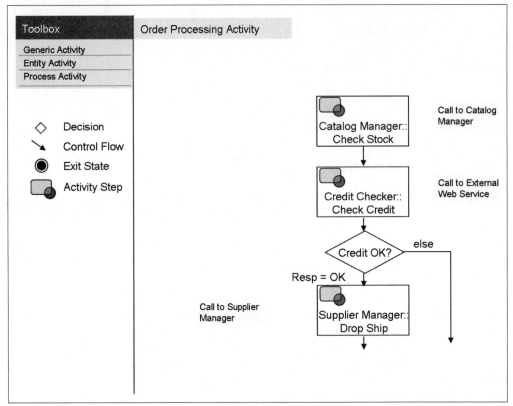

Figure 16.18   A graphical activity editor

the system. Projections of business entity graphs form specification models for ports offered by Business Entity Services, as described in Chapter 12. GSS plans to cut development costs for the data access layer using an object relational (O/R) mapping framework. O/R mapping frameworks are readily available from many vendors, and typically provide a way to define business entities, along with code generators and entity-to-table mapping tools. Some provide visual languages with graphical editors for defining business entities.

GSS will produce interface specification models, and underlying business entity models to support the common features of the product family. They will also define patterns and fragments of business entity models that can be applied to the base models to address variable requirements. The O/R mapping framework will insulate the business logic from the underlying database schemas. Schemas can be varied to address unique installation requirements without affecting the business entities.

GSS will use an O/R framework that automatically generates create, read, update, and delete (CRUD) actions for each business entity, and provides a navigational query language for following relationships between them. The behavior offered by ports on the business entity services is usually a sequence of calls to CRUD actions, wrapped in a transaction. GSS must specify these behaviours declaratively, so that patterns and fragments can be combined to address variable requirements. AEL will be used again for this purpose.

Activities implement service behavior by performing CRUD actions on Business Entities.

A Business Entity Service component is a collection of Business Entities plus a set of Activities that perform sequences of CRUD actions against them, as shown in Figure 16.19.

The following Business Entity Services will be implemented:

A candidate list of business entity services.

- *Order Manager:* Manages all information concerned with orders, including transaction workflow, tax calculations, shipping, payment and fulfillment. The transaction sequences can be customized to address the unique requirements of individual installations.

- *Catalog Manager:* Manages an installation's catalog of products and services. Products from external entities can be included to augment the businesses internal catalog. The service supports custom catalogs and

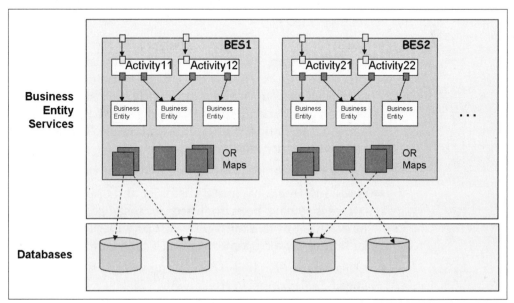

Figure 16.19 Business entity services and business entities

pricing, merchandising cross-sell/up-sell options, soft and hard goods, and services. The Catalog Manager service also manages product dependencies and supports configuration planning. Catalogs may be offered via external auctions and marketplaces. All product data is managed through the catalog service.

- *Supplier Manager:* Manages all information concerned with suppliers. It contains the settings and rules specific to integrating and collaborating with a supplier and definitions of each of the document types exchanged between the installation and its suppliers. This service will include supplier terms and contracts, materials usage and links to supplier component catalogs, demand trends and forecasting, and details of collaborating supply chain data with suppliers.

- *Inventory Manager:* Handles all information concerning stock of goods kept by the installation at various locations.

- *Web Site Manager:* Handles the content and layout of the various pages that constitute the installation's public web sites.

- *Party Manager:* Handles information relating to currently registered customers, suppliers and external merchants with which the installation maintains any kind of relationship.

- *Customer Service Manager:* Manages four core entities and the affiliated objects (notes, appointments, tasks, processes, e-mails, phone calls, meeting notes, quotes, specifications, etc.) needed to provide a consistent view of a customer and all the interactions they have had with a given installation, both offline and online. These four core entities include:

- *Contacts:* Customers who are known to the installation.

- *Leads:* Information about a customer and opportunities before they have been qualified (for instance, leads could be acquired from a third-party list provider or could be submitted by a customer visiting a merchant's web site).

- *Opportunities:* An object containing information about a specific sales opportunity.

- *Incidents:* Information about a customer service request, the resulting resolution, etc.

- *Appointment Manager:* Allows customers to book time periods for services offered by the installation. These appointments are typically used by installations for scheduling visits by service engineers to fix problems and perform repairs. The service manages the inventory of service resources.

- *Sale Force Manager:* Manages the data associated with creating, managing and tracking sales territories, sales goals, sales performance, commission plans, commission modeling, and expense tracking and reporting.

- *Payment Manager:* Manages an installation's information relating to billing their customers.

- *Advertising Manager:* Manages advertisements on the banner exchange network, and supports activities relating to advertisement placing on affiliate web sites.

A DSL and Framework for Web Service Connectivity

We stated earlier that to maximize flexibility and to ensure interoperability between components, Web service technology will be used to implement the *service-oriented interaction* pattern. GSS product developers would like to use a DSL to model the connectivity between their Web services. Such a tool would allow them to focus on service interactions by hiding the Web service implementation technology. It would have to support current Web service implementation technology, such as WSDL, and, more rigorous contract specifications in the future as described in Chapter 13. It should also generate and synchronize Web service development artifacts.

GSS would like a DSL for Web service connectivity design.

Since the product family is primarily targeted to Microsoft Web service technologies, GSS can exploit the Web Service DSL and design tool in Microsoft Visual Studio 2005 for designing connectivity between Web services. This tool lets developers focus on the service interactions, contracts as expressible in WSDL, and policies for ports offered by the services. It also takes care of generating and synchronizing development artifacts, such as .asmx files, project structures, class skeletons and attributes, and configuration files. A partially completed model of the emerging structure of the eCommerce Web services developed using this tool is shown in Figure 16.20.

They use a tool supplied by Microsoft Visual Studio 2005.

The boxes in the diagram represent Web service components. The smaller boxes on their perimeters represent ports through which web service behaviours are offered. Each port

It is another instance of the Framework and DSL pattern.

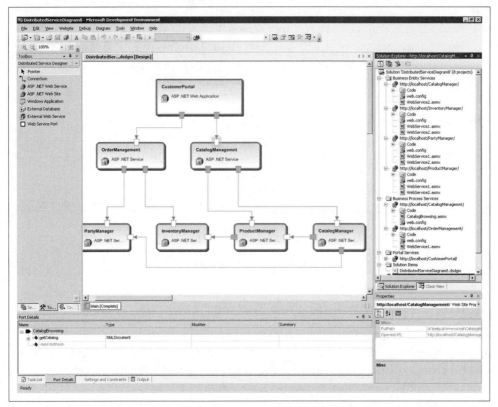

Figure 16.20   Web service connectivity model designer (partial)
Used with permission from Microsoft Corporation.

generates multiple development artifacts required by the
ASP.NET Framework to implement a Web service proxy or
interface class. The lines on the diagram represent messages
exchanged between the ports. Note that this tool, with other
tools supplied by Visual Studio and the underlying ASP.NET
Framework demonstrate the *Language Framework* pattern illustrated in Figure 16.14. Since this tool is extensible, GSS plans to
extend it to capture links to their business process models for
reconciliation and traceability.

Utility Services

*Utility Services
support other
services.*

Utility services support either the business process services or
the business entity services. They include:

- *Authentication:* A service that maintains a database of
  roles and IDs to support role-based security for portal
  users, and that can optionally connect to existing data

sources, such as Active Directory on the Microsoft Windows platform.

- *Rule Engine:* A service that stores, manages, and executes declaratively specified rules used in business processes and business entity activities.

- *Communications:* Services such as instant messaging, e-mail and fax, used to communicate with customers and suppliers.

Product Line Architecture Summary

Figure 16.21 summarizes the product line architecture. While not detailed enough to show variability points in the product line assets, it shows that the product family members will consist of portal services that manage stakeholder interactions, and it identifies the major categories of software services supporting the portal services.

Architecture diagrams…

To convey a high-level description of requirements and how they plan to meet them, GSS describes the services they expect to build or acquire from suppliers to instill confidence in their potential investors. They use the product line architecture diagram, describing the common features and the features that

…convey high level information about product structure.

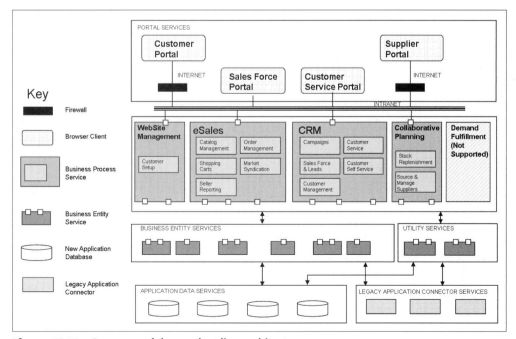

Figure 16.21   Summary of the product line architecture

will vary according to the unique requirements of individual installations. For example, they walk through product catalog construction, presentation, and maintenance, noting the differences between simple catalogs and catalogs that support product photos and customer reviews.

GSS will provide contracts for some of the other services to its suppliers.

As we said earlier, GSS does not plan to build all of the service components by themselves. Instead, they plan to exploit a supply chain of partner companies, who will build some of the service components to the specifications they have defined. For example, GSS has minimal knowledge of stock replenishment processes, but one of their partner companies has deep expertise in this area, and agrees to work with GSS by building the Business Process Services for *Stock Replenishment* and for *Source and Manage Suppliers* using the interface specification models designed by GSS. GSS will provide contracts for the other Business Entity Services that the outsourced services will have to invoke, along with acceptance tests. This increases the probability that the outsourced services will fit into the product line architecture, when delivered.

Legacy connectors expose legacy systems as services.

The last feature of the architecture is legacy connector services. These services implement the *Remote Façade* wrappers, exposing legacy systems as services that can be used by the other services. Behind the facades, they handle communication, data mapping and transformation, and other idiosyncrasies of interacting with the legacy systems.

Technology Mapping

Mapping the Product Line Architecture to implementation technologies.

The last step in defining the product line architecture is to specify how the elements of the architecture map to available technologies. In practice, of course, these tasks are not sequential. The structure of the architecture will be influenced significantly by the hardware and software platforms on which the product family members will run. For example, the decision to use BPEL schedules to implement Business Process Services was predicated on the availability of the Microsoft BizTalk Server. The decision to implement Portal Services using the User Process framework was based on the availability of the User Interface Process Application Block from the Microsoft Patterns and Practices group. The mapping to technology is described in the following section.

The Product Line Architecture is recorded in a schematized form.

The Product Line Development team defines the constraints that complete the description of the product line architecture.

Constraints will define the overall structure, relationships between large components, and technology requirements that must be considered during implementation. These constraints are expressed using an architectural policy mechanism, like the enterprise templates mechanism in Visual Studio. During Production Asset deployment the policies developed using this mechanism will be loaded into the IDE to govern the way projects are structured and the ways items are added to projects,[2] and the message connections and protocols used to implement communication between layers. In addition a default directory structure containing default development artifacts generated from templates may be specified in the product line architecture, giving the user a partially completed product as a starting point. This pre-defined content will be instantiated progressively during product development, as decisions are made regarding the variable features of the family member under construction.

Portal Layer

- Use ASP.NET.
- Use the User Process framework.
- Issue SOAP calls to business process layer using the *Service-Agent* pattern.
- Designed with the Web service design tool.

Business Process Layer

- All messages emitted and received from the Portal layer and other business process layer services are SOAP-based.
- All interface specifications are contracts with SLAs.
- Messages going outside the firewall must be signed and certificated.
- Using AEL and its underlying framework, the Activity pattern is used to create a façade behind every incoming message. This pattern calls an authentication service, and can be extended to perform message transformations before and after the passing control to a business process service.
- All are Web services designed using the Web service design tool.

- Any Business process service that communicates directly with a service outside the firewall is wrapped with a Façade service implementing the *Remote Facade* pattern that replicates its external ports but with tighter security.

- Aspects are defined for non-functional requirements, such as security policies and Instrumentation.

- The portal layer and the Business Process layer and the communication between them are designed using a Web services design tool.

- Business process logic is defined using code, BPEL schedules (use Microsoft BizTalk Server), rules and Activities.

Business Entity Layer

- Interface Specifications are contracts.

- Activities implement each operation in each contract.

- Interface specifications (contracts) are implemented as Microsoft Enterprise services (COM+) using generated code to drive contract sequencing.

- Interface specification models are subsets of the Business Entity graphs. Message schemas are subsets of the interface specification models.

- Use the OR framework for persistence and data access layer generation

- SQL is generated dynamically for each CRUD operation.

- High bandwidth SQL Server connections.

Data Layer

- SQL databases.

- Hand tuned stored procedures provide high performance access to data (reflect back in maps).

Design For Deployment

Many problems surface at deployment time.

Like many other software companies, GSS has little control over the equipment and software installed in customer data centers. They need some knowledge of the kinds of servers, host software, and network protocol settings available in customer data centers in order to proceed with the design and implementation of their product line architecture. They will implement features like security, for example, which require certification servers to be present in the data center to ensure speedy and efficient deployment of applications. In fact, this is a general problem for any Enterprise that is designing complex distributed applications. All too often, problems surface at deployment time, where they are very costly to resolve. The same problems, if caught at design time, would be much cheaper to resolve. These problems could be as simple as incorrect settings on an instance of Microsoft Internet Information Server (IIS), or as profound as mismatched communication protocol settings on switch boxes and firewall devices.

To reduce the number of problems that surface during deployment, GSS realizes that a model of the data center, describing the servers it contains, their settings and the constraints they impose on the applications they host would be of great benefit at design time. By checking the emerging application design against this model, errors could be caught early and fixed cheaply. GSS can even build a model to specify the ideal data center architecture for their installations, and either use it to help installations configure their data centers or to evaluate installation data centers before deployment to explore potential issues. GSS hopes that these capabilities will let them outbid their competitors, who will be forced to charge hefty contingency fees for deployment problems.

A model of the data center could be used at design time to prevent many of these problems.

Fortunately for GSS, they will be able to use the Logical Data Center Designer in Microsoft Visual Studio 2005. This is a graphical tool that helps a data center architect or network expert describe the server types, settings, and network segment protocols found in a data center. This is a scale invariant view, not a physical view, where each box will ultimately map to many physical servers in the data center buildings. This tool is shown in Figure 16.22. Boxes represent servers with known configurations., lines represent traffic using known protocols across known gateways. Dashed boxes represent virtual network segments. Using this tool in combination with the tool illustrated in Figure 16.20. GSS can verify that data center constraints are not violated during design. The Logical Data Center Designer generates schematic information that will be used by future deployment and management tools under the Microsoft Dynamic Systems Initiative [DSI].

GSS plans to use a DSL that describes data center constraints.

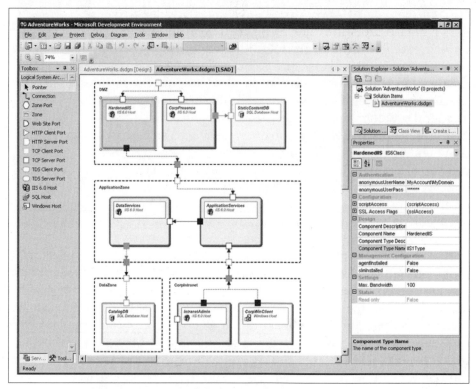

Figure 16.22 Logical data center designer

Product Line Requirements Mapping

Product Line Requirements Mapping.

Product Line Requirements Mapping is a key activity for the product line architect. Its goal is to map variabilities in the product line requirements onto variability mechanisms in the production assets, especially the product line architecture, the implementation components, and the product development process. The mapping shows how each variable feature when selected by an installation, will be implemented in terms of the variability mechanisms in the production assets. Note, however, the mapping may be incomplete as explained in Chapter 4, since the implementations of some variable features will be completely open ended, and cannot be even partially defined in advance.

Dependencies between features must be analyzed.

Dependencies between the variable features must be enforced. For example, appointments are only applicable to Catalogs of service products, offering site visits only to service engineers. In addition, forced feature dependencies may arise. For example, if a feature F1 interacts with F2 then selecting both F1 and F2 should trigger an interaction between the features.

A concrete example will illustrate. Suppose credit checking is a variable feature for Online Commerce. The order processing activity must therefore support being able to skip credit checking. If Credit Checking is selected, then the activity must be able to call Customer Service to query for credit refusals for a registered customer.

The key artifact delivered from this stage of product line development is a feature/asset mapping chart. This shows for every feature what asset or assets support that feature.

Optional and Variable features map to different types of asset.

- Mandatory features typically map to component interface specifications and to interactions between component specifications and to framework specifications.

- Optional features map to alternative asset selections, such as pattern and model fragments that must be applied, or, for large feature areas, to variation points on specific assets, such as component interface specifications, contracts, and frameworks.

- Non-functional requirements like security will map to aspects that can be woven into models and code.

A skeletal feature/asset map is shown in Figure 16.23. A number of items may reside in each of the cells of this map,

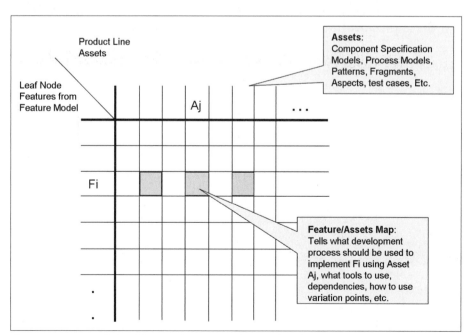

Figure 16.23 A skeletal feature/asset map for product line

The cells contain instructions to the application developer, explaining how to implement a given feature with the assets to which it is mapped. The instructions nominate tools to be used, and development steps to be followed, and explain how variation points in patterns or models should be completed based on the product requirements.

For any given map, the tools to be used and the processes to be followed are gathered into two deliverables: the *Product Development Process Definition*, and the *Product Development Process Automation Plan*, respectively.

Product Line Implementation

Asset Provisioning

Product line assets are built or acquired and packaged ready for use.

Asset Provisioning is the task in which many of the key reusable assets, both fixed and variable are actually acquired from other suppliers or built by GSS product line developers. This includes implementation assets such as contracts and frameworks required by the product line architecture, and process assets such as DSL editors, compilers, and other custom tools, required by the process automation plan. The main tasks and deliverables are summarized in Figure 16.24. We will illustrate the remaining task of Product Line Implementation by showing three product line asset construction scenarios that call attention to

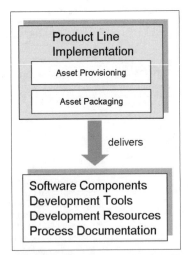

Figure 16.24 Summarized tasks and deliverables from product line implementation

most of the issues that arise when completing the specification and implementation of the software factory.

Defining and Building a Business Entity Service

First, we'll look at the task of building the specification model for one of the Business Entity Services. Before building this detailed model, a number of analysis tasks would have been performed by the product line development team. These include the analysis of the feature models to produce collaboration models for key use cases, and refinement of the business entity models (based on the glossary) to produce specification models. Much of this activity is similar to what is required by CBD, as described in Chapter 13. However, although this approach is good at providing implementations for common features, it is inadequate for describing the variable one. The analysis of variabilities adds additional detail to the models, and provides the basis for building patterns and model fragments that can be selected and applied to the implementations of the common features to address variable requirements.

We'll look at the specification of one of the Business Entity Services.

Figure 16.25 shows the specification model designed for the common features of the Catalog Manager. It offers operations

Catalog Manager, Product Manager, and Party Manager.

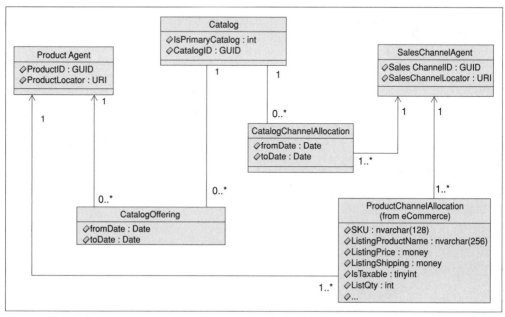

Figure 16.25   Catalog manager interface specification for (common) features

like `Retrieve Products` for a specified Catalog, and is capable of recording the allocation of both catalogs and individual products with external market places. Note that this service has two required ports that allow it to collaborate with Product Manager and Party Manager to obtain product and sales channel information, respectively. These interactions, along with the details of contracts between services, security policies, and protocols are designed using a Web services connectivity designer.

Catalog Manager interface specification for common features.

The Catalog Manager specification model designer has applied the *Service-Agent* interaction pattern as required by the product line architecture, to manage information sourced from other business entity services. The product developer will be instructed by the product development process to replicate any required product or sales channel attributes to Catalog manager agent types, and to implement, publish and subscribe client side logic using the *Observer* pattern.

Analysis of variable features produces other assets.

To support the variable features dealing with Catalog Management, additional production assets must be implemented. Again, these are based on use case analysis and business process modelling performed while identifying the variabilities in the solution domain. The product line architect may produce requirements mappings like the one shown in Figure 16.26.

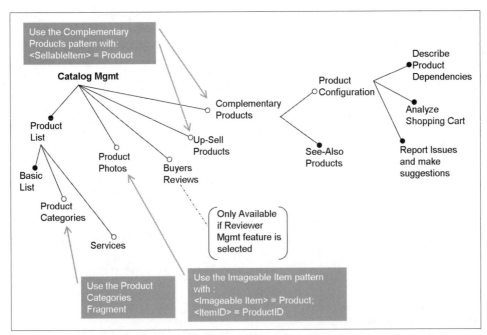

Figure 16.26 Part of the product line feature mapping information

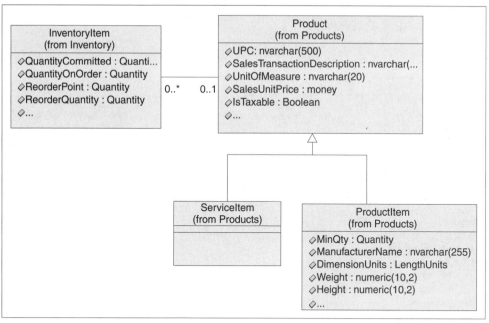

Figure 16.27 Part of the specification model for product manager

For the Product Categories variable feature, the product developer will be prompted to apply the model fragment shown in Figure 16.28. It will be merged into the model shown in Figure 16.27, and will add types that describe a category hierarchy and that define how categories map to Sales Channels. It will also add operations, such as `AllocateProductCategory-ToSalesChannel` to the contract supported by Catalog Manager. Any Activities developed to implement these operations will also be added to the project for Catalog Manager.

The product developer will apply patterns and fragments to customize the specification model.

The requirements mapping also tells the product developer how to add product images to Catalogs, and how to add upsell and see-also product listings. These features, when selected, will require the developer to use the patterns shown in Figure 16.29 and Figure 16.30 with appropriate substitutions at the variation points, as indicated in the mapping instructions summarized previously in Figure 16.26. The patterns were designed using the modeling tool used to define the specification models, but in pattern definition mode, allowing the architect to specify the variation points. Note also that each pattern is a parameterized collaboration and therefore contains template behavior specifications. For example, the *Imageable Item* pattern will be accompanied by templates for the `scrollLeft` and `scrollRight` operations.

Configuration drives selection of the appropriate patterns to fix variabilities.

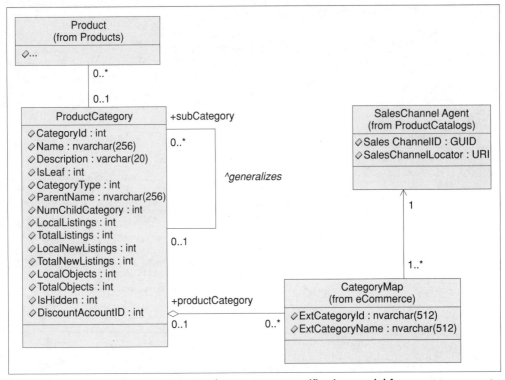

Figure 16.28 Product manager specification model fragment to support categories

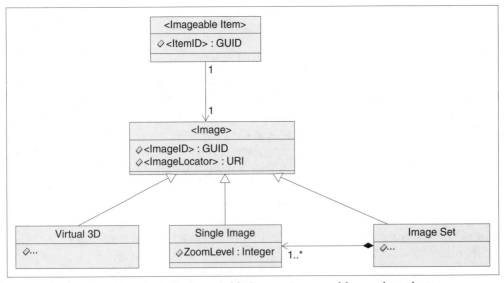

Figure 16.29 Imageable item pattern used for product photos

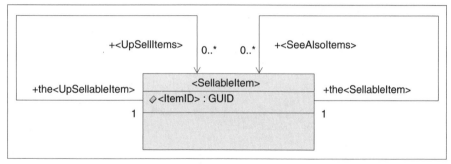

Figure 16.30   Complementary product pattern

Defining and Building an Activity

We saw earlier how an Activity can be used to declaratively specify simple parts of business process services. In that example, we showed an Activity graph that defined how order processing will be performed. Since Activities are defined by models, they can be manipulated by tools and used to generate framework completion code. They also support the kinds of model fragment and pattern extensions used for business entity services. Figure 16.31 shows a model of the order processing Activity that implements the common features of the product family.

Order Processing is an Activity in the product line.

Credit card authentication is a variable feature, and has been mapped to an Activity model fragment, as shown in Figure 16.32. Note that the fragment is parameterized. Actual Activities must therefore be supplied to complete the fragment. Two of the variation points are defined as wildcard matches,

An Activity model fragment for credit checking is provided.

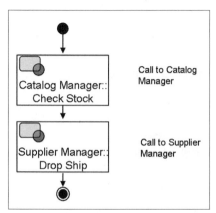

Figure 16.31   Order processing activity for common features

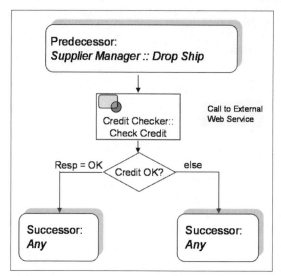

Figure 16.32   Parameterized model fragment for order processing activity

indicating that any task may be supplied as a successor, but only a task of type `Supplier Manager :: Drop Ship` may be supplied as a predecessor. In practice, tasks will be mapped to operations of other services and to business entity actions, which may also have parameterized argument lists.

New steps are added if Customer Service support is also selected.

The feature models (see Figure 16.7) for the product family indicate that Customer Service—the reporting and management of customer complaints, warrantees claims, purchases, and returns—is an optional feature. But if the installation has requested Customer Service, then the order processing Activity should include a task that sends a *purchase-incident* message to the Customer Service Manager. This may require the product developer to use a model fragment indicated by the requirements mapping illustrated in Figure 16.33.

Defining and Building a Business Process Service

BPEL is used to describe more complex processes.

We described earlier how more sophisticated business processes will be beyond the capability of the simple task sequencing given by Activities. This is especially true when service calls are asynchronous, bi-directional and when entering or leaving the context of the installation's datacenter for business-to-business transactions. In these circumstances the product line development team decides that the business processes will be specified as BPEL processes. These allow for the more complex

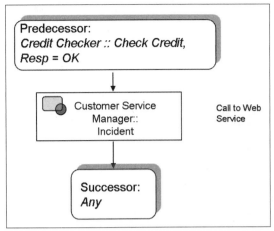

Figure 16.33 Model fragment for customer service dependency in order processing

long-running transactions typical given the characteristics just mentioned, to be declaratively described as a well-formed document with a standard schema, and a precise metamodel. BPEL tools are readily available, including from Microsoft, which may execute BPEL processes using its BizTalk Server product line.

Figure 16.34 shows how a Web services design tool might allow for BPEL schedules to be designed graphically, and shows *Stock Replenishment is*

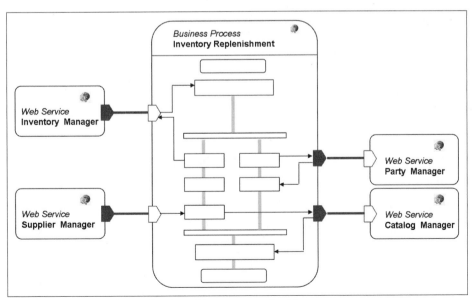

Figure 16.34 Partial specification of inventory replenishment process

*such a service,
involving
orchestration of
internal and
external services.*

the required and provided ports applicable to the schedule, and the contracts the schedule enforces with other Web services, which are said to be orchestrated by the schedule. The context here is the process of Inventory Replenishment. The figure does not attempt to show the actual process logic involved in automatic stock replenishment and demand forecasting. We summarize the structure of BPEL using the state diagram notation common in commercial BPEL design tools. Here we show the services orchestrated and the ports and contracts in use. Each line between ports stands for a set of message schemas for documents interchanged, a sequencing expression that defines the behavior of the contract, and a schematized description of the service level agreement (SLA) enforced by the contract, just as described in Chapter 13.

*Show BPEL
fragment for
process.*

This detail is particularly appropriate when the non-repudiation service feature is requested. This will involve the use of an external non-repudiation service provider who records in a legally binding way, all the transactions that occur between installation and a selected Supplier, to prove success or failure in the event of a dispute. Since this feature is described as optional in the feature model (Figure 16.35), the product line development team describe the contract between a non-repudiation service provider and the installation's replenishment process as a pattern of BPEL and Web service contract elements.

*Use of a non-
repudiation
external service
is an optional
feature.*

*This feature is
optional for those
selecting stock
replenishment.*

Figure 16.36 illustrates the high-level features of the Non-Repudiation contract, expressed using variation points from

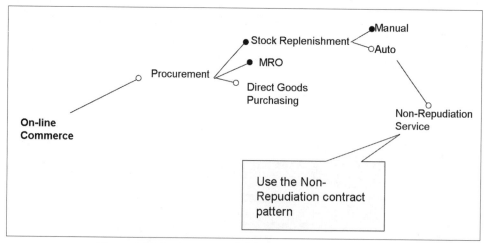

Figure 16.35   Feature model for procurement

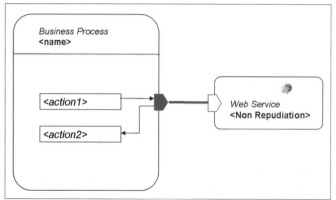

BPEL and Web services design model fragments provide a useful pattern.

Figure 16.36 BPEL model fragment and contract pattern for non-repudiation

the Web services designer metamodel elements, and the BPEL designer metamodel elements. When instantiated with the actual service provider, and any other variation points filled, such as variations in message schemas, the BPEL for the Inventory Replenishment process will be transformed to contain the correct statements required to operate the contract with that service. It is certainly possible with existing technology to imagine a protocol checking validation step which would ensure that the BPEL and its collaborating services is correctly formed, and that all pattern actions have been placed into the BPEL schema in valid positions.

Pattern instantiation creates elements in the BPEL and the Web services design models.

Asset Packaging

Asset Packaging is the activity by which the patterns, frameworks, tools, processes and other production assets are packaged as a software factory template. When the template is loaded into the target development environment, it becomes a software factory that automates the development of eCommerce product family.

Product Development

Product Development is the task performed by product developers. As illustrated in Figure 16.37, the software factory schema along with the variable and fixed assets, such as patterns, frameworks, tools and processes, constituting the

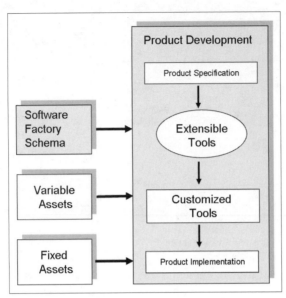

Figure 16.37 Summarized tasks for product engineering

software factory template, are loaded into an extensible development environment.

Product Specification

Product specification is the selection of optional features.

During product specification, GSS sales and support engineers help the installation to express their requirements in terms of the product line requirements, and then map them to the other production assets. This is shown in Figure 16.38. In practice, the product line requirements may be used to drive a configuration tool that helps the product developers select the variable features through a user interface. As a result of creating the product specification, the assets that support common and selected variable features may be loaded into the product developers' shared workspace in the software factory.

In practice, a configuration tool may help, and automatically select product line assets for the developers' workspace in the software factory.

Using a Component Specification Model

We'll look at the definitions of Catalog Manager and Product Manager.

Given the feature selection shown in Figure 16.38, we can look at the final interface specification model for the Catalog and Product Manager Business Entity Services we looked at earlier. The specification model for Catalog Manager itself does not change, but its provided port operations list and sequencing expression, and service level agreements will be amended to provide the new functionality. Operations such

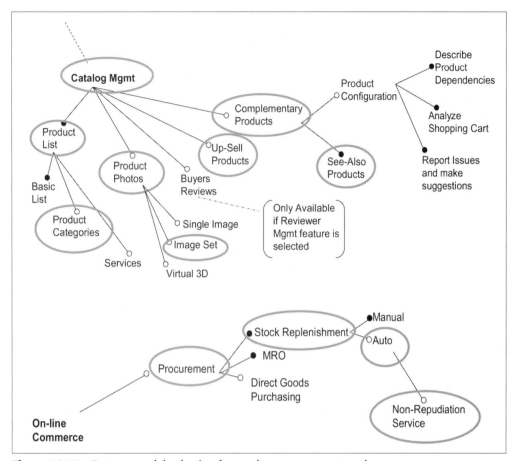

Figure 16.38   Feature model selection for catalog management and procurement

as `getUpSellProducts`, `specifySeeAlsoProducts` and `getImageSet` will now be available.

The specification model and interface behavior for Product Manager will reflect the results of the instantiation of the various patterns and model fragments implied by the selected variable features. This is shown in part in Figure 16.39. These models will be used by the software factory generators to produce much of the code needed to drive the OR framework, and class structures for the developer to finish the remaining business logic by hand.

Which reflect the instantiation of implied patterns and fragments.

Using a Process Model

Given the feature selection shown in Figure 16.38, we can look at the final interface specification model for the Inventory

We'll look at the Inventory Replenishment Service,

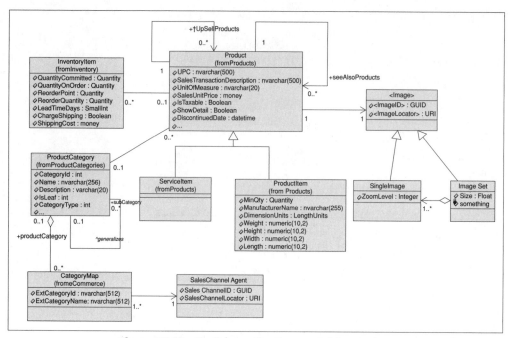

Figure 16.39   Partial specification model for product manager after feature selection

Replenishment Business Process Service we looked at earlier shown in Figure 16.40. Notice that after the non-repudiation service contract pattern has been instantiated, with Acme Trading, providing the non-repudiation services, the BPEL schedule now incorporates the correct actions to accommodate the new collaboration in the long-running replenishment process.

Which now reflects the non-repudiation pattern instantiation.

Now the developer can generate the correct code from the BPEL schedule schema which will drive the Microsoft BizTalk Server engine to orchestrate the Web services according to the predefined product line architecture.

Conclusion

We'll look at the Inventory Replenishment Service.

In this chapter, we have walked through a detailed example of a software factory, focusing on the product line architecture, and we have illustrated the development of a product using the software factory. In this walk through, we have omitted a number of important steps, such as product development process definition and automation, process asset provisioning, process customization, product architecture derivation, product

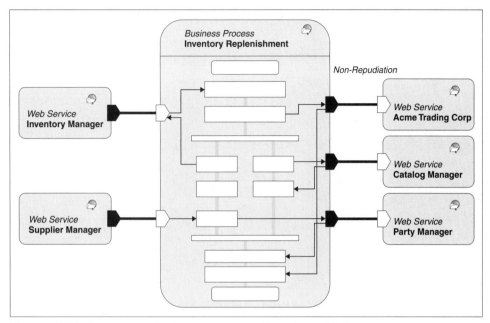

Figure 16.40 Inventory replenishment after configuration with the non-repudiation pattern

implementation, unit test and test case development, product packaging and product release. Chapter 11 provides describes these activities, and provides more information about the activities illustrated by the example. Software factories can be implemented now, as this example demonstrates. Several are being constructed as we go to press, and we expect to see reports of many more in the near future.

Notes

1. The User Interface Process Application Block for .NET, available from the Microsoft Patterns and Practices Group on http://msdn.microsoft.com.

2. Visual Studio .NET has part of this functionality today in Enterprise Templates.

CHAPTER 17

Frequently Asked Questions

A small anarchic community of wireheads and hackers made the mistake of giving fire to the masses. Nobody is going to give it back. It is paradise lost.

John Markoff

At this point, you probably have quite a few questions about Software Factories. This chapter answers the following frequently asked questions:

- How Do Software Factories Differ From ...?
- How Agile Are Software Factories?
- How Will Software Factories Be Adopted?
- How Mature Are Software Factories?
- How Should Software Factories Be Implemented?
- What's Different This Time?

How Do Software Factories Differ From ...?

Borrowing a page from Scott Ambler [Amb02], we can sharpen the definition of Software Factories by comparing them with other things, including Model-Driven Architecture (MDA), Rapid Application Development (RAD), and the Unified Process (UP).

How Do Software Factories Differ from RAD?

Software Factories are domain specific RAD.

A Software Factory is essentially a domain specific Rapid Application Development (RAD) environment. Like general-purpose RAD, it automates development tasks, often using graphical visualizations. How, then, does it differ from general-purpose RAD? The primary difference is that while general-purpose RAD uses only logical information about the software captured by general-purpose development artifacts, a Software Factory also uses conceptual information captured by domain specific models. (See Chapter 4 for the definitions of these terms.) This difference has several significant consequences.

Using Conceptual Information

A Software Factory uses conceptual information captured by domain specific models to provide more extensive and more advanced forms of automation than general-purpose RAD. Let's look at the differences between a general-purpose IDE and the Software Factory from Chapter 16.

Software Factories can automate design.

Unlike general-purpose IDEs, Software Factories can partially automate design. For example, to add a wire to an assembly of Web services, a developer using an IDE writes code, while a developer using the Software Factory drags a connection between the Web services on a design surface, configures the message path properties using a property editor, and lets the tool generate some or all of the code. Some general-purpose modeling tools capture design information. However, these tools are typically unable to leverage that information to automate design because they do not know what it means.

Software Factories can detect design level specification errors.

Unlike general-purpose IDEs, Software Factories understand the rules that govern the selection, configuration, and assembly of design level objects, and can detect design level specification errors. For example, the Software Factory in Chapter 16 knows how to validate Web service assemblies, and can detect an invalid configuration of components, wires, and ports in an assembly of Web services. The Java compiler and XML parser in a general-purpose IDE, on the other hand, can only detect errors in the Java language statements or DTDs that implement various parts of the Web services, since they know nothing about what those artifacts mean.

Software Factories can perform domain specific optimizations.

Unlike general-purpose IDEs, Software Factories can perform domain specific optimizations automatically. This is more effective than performing them by hand in the source code, which leads to errors, reduces productivity, and further obscures the rendering of intent in the implementation. The Java compiler and XML editor in a general-purpose IDE, for example, cannot optimize message routing and transformation in an assembly of Web services. The Java compiler can optimize the byte code it generates, and the XML editor cannot perform any optimizations. The required optimizations must therefore be performed manually by the developer in the Java source code and the XML. The Software Factory in Chapter 16, on the other hand, can automatically perform end-to-end optimizations of Web service assemblies.

Unlike general-purpose IDEs, Software Factories can use design level objects to provide execution visualization, inspection, and debugging. For example, while a Java debugger in a general-purpose IDE steps through Java language statements, the Software Factory in Chapter 16 shows messages flowing through an assembly of Web services. While the general-purpose IDE displays the message contents as raw XML using the XML editor, the Software Factory displays security, routing, and referral information carried in the SOAP message headers. A Software Factory for Business to Business Integration (B2BI) might go even further and display information about the business transaction carried by the message payloads.

Software Factories can use design level objects for many development activities.

Unlike general-purpose IDEs, Software Factories can report errors in terms of design level objects. These error reports are more effective than error reports based on general-purpose implementation technologies, because they do not have to be mentally mapped by the developer to the design. For example, a developer using the Software Factory in Chapter 16 might receive an error report indicating that a message contains a formatting error, while a developer using a general-purpose IDE might see a Null Pointer Exception, and have to discover that it was caused by a message formatting error.

Software Factories can report errors in terms of design level objects.

Unlike general-purpose IDEs, Software Factories can use design information to manage development artifacts. When creating a deployment baseline for a Web service application, for example, a developer using a traditional configuration management and version control (CMVC) system must define the baseline manifest by hand, and may make mistakes, such as omitting files, including the wrong files, or including files that are not required. The CMVC system cannot tell whether or not the configuration of files described by the manifest forms a

Software Factories can use design information to manage development artifacts.

valid Web service application. It can only ensure that the versions of the files listed in the manifest have been included in the baseline. The Software Factory in Chapter 16, on the other hand, generates the manifest from validated models. This ensures that it forms a valid a Web service application.

TRUSTING TOOLS WITH DESIGN DECISIONS

The idea of trusting a tool make design decisions can make developers quite uncomfortable. They feel that they are giving up something important that only humans can do well. One way to get over this worry is to compile something. Compilers decide what instructions to use, how to allocate registers and other processor resources, and how to organize the code they generate for optimal performance. When the authors started programming, we wrote primarily in assembly language, and made most of these decisions ourselves. Despite this concession of responsibility to compilers, however, developers are now more important than ever to society. Perhaps trusting tools to make even more of the rote design decisions is not such a bad proposition.

Automating Design

Patterns are still not widely used by tools.

As we have seen, one of the most important advances in software design has been the use of patterns for capturing and reusing knowledge. Despite their potential application to automation, however, patterns have yet to make a major impact on development tools 20 years after the Gang Of Four. Why have pattern-based tools failed to materialize on a significant scale?

Patterns are intentionally abstract.

As several writers have observed, one of the strengths of a pattern is that it deliberately expresses a solution in abstract, rather than concrete terms. This lets consumers apply it to a wide variety of problem domains, system architectures, implementation technologies, and development processes. At the same time, however, this approach yields a pattern definition that is not formal enough to be applied automatically.

Some decisions must be bound in advance.

As we have seen, a pattern is a template containing unbound design decisions. In order to automate pattern application, development tools must bind some of these design decisions in advance based on assumptions about the problem domain, the system architecture, the implementation technologies, and the development process. Earlier efforts to formalize pattern definitions have been unsuccessful because the bindings they provided worked for some applications, but not for many others. Similarly, the pattern palettes have also been essentially arbitrary, and have typically been chosen to reflect the contents of a popular book, rather than the requirements of a specific product family.

In other words, general-purpose IDEs have been unable to automate pattern application effectively because they are focused on individual systems, and have no basis for choosing bindings. Software Factories, on the other hand, are focused on product families, and can therefore make specific assumptions about the problem domain, the architecture, the implementation technologies, and the development process. This lets them provide appropriate pattern palettes and bindings tuned for individual product families.

Patterns can be automated most effectively in the context of a product family.

Systematic Reuse

As noted previously, general-purpose RAD deals with individual systems, while Software Factories deal with product families. General-purpose IDEs therefore assume the development of new systems from scratch, and generally do not provide processes or mechanisms for harvesting and reusing assets. By contrast, Software Factories provide processes and mechanisms explicitly designed to support the development and application of reusable assets, such as asset repositories, pattern authoring tools, component packaging tools, and language design tools. A Software Factory is therefore better suited than general-purpose RAD to supporting systematic reuse.

A Software Factory is better suited to systematic reuse.

How Do Software Factories Differ from MDA®?

Some of the themes that appear in this book have received a lot of attention from the Object Management Group™ (OMG) in its Model Driven Architecture® (MDA) initiative [ormsc/2001-07-01]. Since MDA claims to enable automation, we should consider whether or not it provides a credible basis for realizing that claim.

The resemblance is only superficial.

Consider the following excerpt from the MDA FAQ [MDA FAQ]:

The MDA is a new way of writing specifications and developing applications, based on a platform-independent model (PIM).

MDA requires the use of UML as a pseudo programming language.

A complete MDA specification consists of a definitive platform-independent base UML model, plus one or more platform-specific models (PSM) and interface definition sets, each describing how the base model is implemented on a different middleware platform. A complete MDA application consists of a definitive PIM, plus one or more PSMs and complete implementations, one on each platform that the application developer decides to support.

This is effectively claiming that UML is a universal programming language. Given the problems with UML described in the next section, this claim seems overreaching. It is also claiming to provide cross platform portability, much like the "write once, run anywhere" claim of Java. However, even Java, which is a programming language, does not achieve portability except at the most basic level. Extensions like Swing achieve portability at the cost of performance, usability, and platform integration, and are routinely replaced with platform specific extensions like SWT. It therefore seems unlikely that this claim can be supported without yet another rewrite of UML, this one much more thorough than the last one, taking care to provide the semantic fidelity required for compilation. Since the recent rewrite took almost three years, we do not expect the necessary revisions to be ready soon. Of course, none of this addresses the real opportunity of model-driven development, which is not to replace programming languages, but to make it cheap and easy to build highly focused modeling languages that can be used to complement programming languages by supporting automation.

MDA says nothing about architecture or software development.

MDA also claims to provide an architecture and a methodology, but it does not concretely address the following questions:

- How software is developed using models.
- What models to build to describe an application.
- How to define relationships between models.
- How to define graphs of interrelated models that help to solve specific problems.
- How models interface with source code.
- How models relate to patterns or frameworks.
- How models relate to architectural styles or architecture description standards.

- How models and modeling tools can be reused systematically.

- How models fit into the development process.

- How models are used throughout the software life cycle.

- How the cost of using models can be reduced by making it cheaper and easier to define them.

It focuses mainly on one aspect of the problem—platform independence, while saying little about many other complex aspects of developing software.

While MDA does recognize the need for domain specific languages, it does not identify the need to focus on families of software products, or the need to use viewpoints to identify the aspects of those families that must be modeled to develop their family members. This is because it focuses only on one-off development. The Software Factory approach, by contrast, concretely defines a family-based development artifact called a software factory schema. A software factory schema defines viewpoints from which the family members are modeled. It also defines the DSLs, patterns, frameworks, tools, micro processes, and other assets used to capture metadata from each viewpoint, and the mappings between models required to support transformation and other forms of automation. A software factory schema also defines the common requirements and architecture for the product family, and maps specific variations in requirements among family members to specific variations in the architecture, the implementation, the development environment, the deployment environment, and many other structures affected by those variations. Finally, a specific Software Factory is a concrete configuration of the tools and artifacts designed to automate the development of a specific software product family, and can be used to actually build the family members.

MDA focuses on one-off development.

Why Don't Software Factories Use UML?

First of all, we want to make it quite clear that we think UML has added a lot of value to application development during the last decade. It has established a set of widely used concepts and diagrammatic conventions in the domain of object-oriented design, and has brought together multiple notational conventions, to the point that diagrams describing classes connected

UML has established a set of widely used concepts and diagrammatic conventions for object oriented design.

by relationships are instantly recognizable by almost all developers. We see no reason to gratuitously diverge from these conventions. Where UML has not established standard concepts or notations, however, we see no reason to use UML, when languages tuned to the target domains can be developed by others, especially those who have domain expertise. The UML deployment diagram type, for example, has not been widely used, and does not describe modern application deployment technology effectively, since it does not provide a way to specify the policies and protocols that govern interactions and dependencies among hardware and software components.

The UML standard has many serious problems.

UML has succeeded, to a large extent, in spite of the UML standard, which is large, complex, hard to understand, inconsistent and redundant in many places, and poorly organized. It provides weak extensibility mechanisms, namely stereotypes and tags, that are little more than text labels, and do not carry semantic significance in modeling tools based on UML, except in special cases where the tool vendor has hard coded meanings for specific collections of stereotypes and tags called profiles. This is unfortunate, since UML, as a general-purpose modeling language, cannot possibly address the requirements of all possible domains in a way that provides real meaning. All domains contain things that can be typed and related, but if that is all the models can say about them, then it is unlikely that robust and performant implementations can be generated from the models for one platform, let alone many platforms with different programming languages, type systems, and runtime frameworks. The problem is that UML does not clearly define the requirements it is intended to address. It does not say clearly what it can and cannot do, or how it should and should not be used. Obviously, it cannot do everything. No language can. It serves telecommunication domains better than business application domains by providing message sequence charts and other elements from telecommunications industry practices, but even then, these features do not appear to have been designed for solving specific classes of problems. These issues are discussed in greater detail in Appendix B.

The severity of these issues should not be underestimated.

The most significant problem with UML, however, is its scope. The most successful standards in the software industry promote interoperability among vendors by defining common interchange formats. UML and its relatives, by contrast, attempt to define a common architecture, expressed as a standard metamodel. They effectively require tool developers to let a standards committee define the most fundamental parts of their implementations. Some might argue that UML tools can be implemented with internal architectures that do not follow the standard. This is true. Our experience has shown that deviation from the standard is actually a necessity, since the standard does not appear to have been designed to support tools. This means that in practice, there are no UML compliant tools, only tools that claim to be compliant. Since compliance is only loosely defined by the specification, UML is essentially a brand that vendors embrace to reap marketing benefits. As long as they use enough of the notation to make their claims plausible, they can take the liberties necessary to field commercial products. Even with these caveats, claiming UML compliance is not an easy decision for tool vendors, especially when they consider that new revisions of the standard usually take quite a long time to come to market. The lack of a road map for UML and other parts of MDA creates additional risk.

A lighter-weight standard for defining DSLs would be more appropriate.

A lighter-weight standard would be more appropriate for the kind of sketching that UML supports so effectively. It is probably no accident that the best selling book on UML is Martin Fowler's *UML Distilled*, now in its third edition [FS97b]. Unlike some other books on UML, this one focuses on teasing out the most useful abstractions, and showing the reader how to apply them in a lightweight fashion. The models used in Software Factories are simple but formal abstractions, highly focused on specific aspects of the requirements, architecture and implementation of well-defined product families. They are based on domain specific languages (DSLs), whose semantics are precise and unambiguous. We define DSLs using small but accurate metamodels, and we define mappings between them, and to other artifacts using computable mapping languages. Martin Fowler uses the term "little languages" to describe this approach.

Why Don't Software Factories Use MOF/XMI?

There are several competing versions of MOF.

MOF is a metalanguage used to build models that define the conceptual structures of other languages. It has mappings to Java and to CORBA. The Java mapping is standardized, though not through the OMG. It is defined by the Java Metadata Integration (JMI) standard published by the Java Community Process (JCP). In practice, there are actually three versions of MOF, the original MOF standard, and two competing versions known as EMOF and CMOF, respectively. The mapping to Java gives MOF most of its value, since defining a metamodel in Java makes it possible to generate an API and code behind it to handle metadata conforming to that metamodel. However, since the two camps that provide implementations are finding it hard to reach agreement, this puts the value of MOF in question. The goal of metalanguage technology is to create language definitions that can be compiled or interpreted to produce partial or complete editors and other tools for those languages. MOF covers only a small part of the tool design space, however, and far more innovation and experience are required in the area of language and tool definition before technologies for the other parts can be effectively standardized.

An XMI based interchange format cannot be changed without changing the metamodel of the target language.

Another OMG standard, XML Metadata Interchange (XMI) is based on MOF. XMI defines production rules for generating XML schemas from MOF metamodels, and for serializing models conforming to a particular MOF metamodel as an XML document. While serializing model based metadata as XML is certainly desirable, and forms the foundation of model processing in Software Factories, as described in Chapters 7 and 8, XMI is strongly coupled to the metamodel of the target language. This means that the interchange format cannot be changed without changing the metamodel, and vice versa. This is a problem, since serialization formats are designed for interchange, while metamodels are part of the internal architecture of the development tool. A vendor who adheres to XMI therefore cannot change its tool architecture without obtaining the consensus of a large number of vendors. Also, the XMI production rules have gone through a number of iterations. Choosing to support XMI therefore means deciding which set of rules to support (XMI 1 or XMI 2, or one of the intermediate versions), and which version of the metamodel for the target modeling language to use. Since the modeling language most commonly used with XMI is UML, there are at least four versions in current use, 1.3, 1.4, 1.5, and 2.0, and undoubtedly more to come. The XMI standard also leaves some room for interpretation in the implementation of the production rules, so that two tools claiming to support the same set of rules and the same UML metamodel versions still may not be able to successfully interchange models. Finally, XMI-based model serializations are difficult to read, since the formats are generated, not developed by hand. Since one of the goals of XML-based metadata interchange is to ensure that the information is human readable, it is probably not advisable to concede readability for the sake of conformance to XMI.

How Do Software Factories Differ from the UP?

Like Software Factories, the Unified Software Development Process (UP) defines an approach to software development that makes extensive use of models. Despite this superficial similarity, however, Software Factories differ radically from the UP. One of the most significant differences is that the UP provides a prescriptive process, while Software Factories provide a non-prescriptive process framework.

A Software Factory and the UP differ significantly.

Software Factories Are not Prescriptive

The development activities suggested in Chapter 11 are highly parallelized, and form constraints based on the availability of artifacts, not on the completion of prescribed sequences of steps. As we pointed out in Chapter 4, this kind of process framework can be used for constraint-based scheduling, which promotes agility. Also, while we do differentiate between product and product line developers, we define those roles quite loosely, and do not suggest any further role refinement within those categories. Instead, we define an overall approach to software development, and a collection of practices and techniques based on that approach. Individual organizations can pick and choose from among them and adapt them to their preferred working styles and to their specific environments and circumstances. Of course, while the UP is generally known as a fixed process, it is actually a process model, accompanied by a fixed process based on that model. It could in theory be used to define domain specific product development processes. It would have to be rewritten in terms of constraints and microprocesses, and focused on a specific domain, however, to be usable in Software Factories.

Software Factories are not prescriptive.

Software Factories are more formal in terms of language definition, but less in terms of process.

We think of Software Factories as a method, not a process. A method is an orderly way of doing things, or a body of systematic techniques in an engineering discipline, according to Merriam Webster. Of course, this does not imply that Software

Factories are informal. On the contrary, in order to support automation, Software Factories must use formal definitions of domains, languages, requirements, patterns, transformations, architectures, frameworks, and components. In fact, while Software Factories are less formal than the UP in terms of prescribing a process, they are much more formal in their treatment of models and modeling languages.

We now discuss other differences.

Now that we have discussed the differences between Software Factories and the UP in terms of process, the remainder of our comparison can focus on differences in approach to software development. The two primary differences are that Software Factories focus on product families, while the UP focuses on individual systems, and that Software Factories use models quite differently from the way the UP uses them.

Software Factories Focus on Product Families

Software Factories focus on exploiting commonality and variability in software product families. By contrast, the UP focuses on one-off development. This difference has many implications.

Software Factories use two interacting processes.

Software Factories use two interacting processes, one for developing the production assets for a product family, and one for developing family members using those assets. This separates the concerns of infrastructure and application developers, while providing communication mechanisms that help them cooperate effectively. In addition, Software Factories explicitly anticipate and accommodate the selection, instantiation, and configuration of production assets during application development.

The UP defines a stand alone process.

The UP, by contrast, defines a stand-alone process. It does not recognize the distinction between infrastructure and application development, or explicitly support the development, management and consumption of production assets. This difference affects every phase of the software life cycle, as illustrated by the following examples:

Software Factories use domain models and per product models.

■ Where Software Factories use a shared domain model to describe the problem domain for a family of systems, and per product models to describe specific family members, the UP uses a per product model to describe both a subset of the problem domain and the problem to be solved in that domain by an individual product.

There is no provision for sharing these models between products, or combining them to form a complete model of the problem domain.

- Where Software Factories use multiple domain specific languages to specify various aspects of a family member and uses automatic transformations when possible to synchronize models and to generate implementations from them, the UP uses one general-purpose modeling language to specify all aspects of the software, and assumes a manual translation from the models to implementation.

  Software Factories use DSLs, not UML.

- Where Software Factories assume that the architecture of a family member is based on a common architecture developed for the family, the UP assumes that the architecture of each product is developed independently.

  Software Factories use an existing architecture.

Note that one of the two Software Factory processes in Software Factories is variable. While the product line development process is largely the same across Software Factories, the product development process is uniquely defined for each Software Factory by the product line developers, often using different languages, different tools, different architectures, and different implementation technologies. A Software Factory can therefore be seen as a domain specific process supported by customized tools, and by domain specific content.

One of the Software Factories processes is variable.

Software Factories Use Models as Source Artifacts

Software Factories use models quite differently from the way the UP uses them. In the UP, models are used primarily as documentation, while in Software Factories they are used as source artifacts. This difference leads to different ways of defining, organizing, and using models.

Unlike Software Factories, the UP uses views as model projections, and does not define domain specific viewpoints. Instead, it prescribes five general-purpose views for all systems (i.e., Use Case, Logical, Deployment, Implementation, and Process), each from what we would call a different viewpoint. There is exactly one view from each viewpoint. The UP also prescribes a fixed set of eight general-purpose models for all systems (i.e., Business, Use Case, Analysis, Design, Data, Implementation, Deployment, and Test), each using a

UP prescribes fixed sets of general-purpose views and models.

general-purpose modeling language. The views are used only to describe the architecturally significant elements of the models. In other words, they are used only to provide a form of summary description of the system. The views were added to the process after the general-purpose models, and are not well integrated into the overall process.

Software Factories let developers define the software factory schema.

Software Factories define domain specific viewpoints, and take a different approach to views. Instead of prescribing a fixed set of general-purpose views for all systems, Software Factories let product line developers define any number of domain specific viewpoints, and allow any number of views to be created from a given viewpoint, as we have seen. Also, instead of defining a fixed set of general-purpose models for all systems, Software Factories let product line developers define the software factory schema for a product family.

Model relationships defined by the UP are not computable.

Like Software Factories, the UP defines relationships between models. Unlike Software Factories, however, these relationships are defined only for the specific models prescribed by the UP. For example, the UP defines relationships between the Use Case Model and the Business, Analysis and Design Models. Also, the relationships defined by the UP are not computable. In other words, they are not mappings, and cannot be used to support automatic transformation. That said, a detailed description of a manual transformation process is provided for some of the relationships. For example, Workers in the Business Model map to either Actors or Use Cases in the Use Case Model, and Entities in the Business Model map to Classes in the Analysis Model. In addition, the nature of the relationships varies depending on the pair of models being related. So, for example, the UP requires the design model to be kept consistent with the implementation model, but does not require the Use Case or Analysis Models to be kept consistent with the Business Model. It also allows the Analysis Model to evolve into the Design Model, and to be discarded once the Design Model is complete. Similarly, the manual transformation process between the Analysis and Design Models is not defined in as much detail as the processes for the Business Model described earlier.

Software Factories define computable mappings and use them for automation.

Software Factories define computable mappings between viewpoints, and use them to support manual, partially automatic or fully automatic transformations of views that conform to those viewpoints, as we have seen. These transformations are used to keep model contents synchronized as they are edited, to reconcile them after they have been edited, or to incrementally rewrite specifications from higher to lower levels of abstraction. Lower-level models can be regenerated from higher-level models at any time. The higher-level models are maintained throughout the entire software life cycle to support development and maintenance, instead of being evolved into lower level models, or discarded.

How Do Software Factories Differ from Agile Modeling?

Agile Modeling [Amb02] is a relatively new approach to modeling based on the values and principles of agile development. There are two obvious differences between Agile Modeling and Software Factories:

There are both obvious differences and obvious similarities.

- Software Factories focus on product families, while Agile Modeling focuses on one-off development.

- Software Factories use models as source artifacts, while Agile Modeling uses them only as a form of documentation.

As we shall see, however, Software Factories and Agile Modeling have much more in common than might be apparent at first glance.

The most important similarity is that both use modeling primarily as a means of developing software, and only secondarily as a form of documentation. Although Agile Modeling does not attempt to use models programmatically, as Software Factories do, it eschews the creation and maintenance of models for the sake of formality. Every model developed in an Agile Modeling project is directly related to rapid construction of working software. Software Factories simply take this emphasis one step further by using tools to capture the intent expressed in agile models and to make it available to developers as generated source code, tool configuration, project structure, and other forms of development automation.

Software Factories take the primary focus of agile modeling one step further.

Ambler explores the life cycle of an agile model, pointing out that like most forms of documentation in agile development, agile models are temporary. They start out as informal sketches created for the purpose of exploring ideas, and are then discarded. Models designed to communicate with an audience may live longer, but most of these are also eventually discarded.

Models in Software Factories stay current because they are used to build executables.

Some temporary models are refined, iteratively, during the course of the project. Of these, some are kept as permanent design documents. Models used in Software Factories can pick up at any point along this life cycle where using a tool makes modeling faster. All of the models from which models, source code or other artifacts are generated are usually permanent, since they are source artifacts. This is not a requirement, however, and the members of a Software Factory team may decide to keep only a subset of the models used to develop the software. Of course, they do so at their own risk, by discarding not mere documentation, but artifacts used in the development of the software. Unlike design documents that become stale as the software evolves, models in Software Factories stay current because they are used to build executables. They therefore provide significant value in as the software evolves, making maintenance and enhancement much easier.

Ambler also takes a similar view of UML. He sees it contributing mostly to sketching, by establishing a widely recognized visual vocabulary for certain types of diagrams. He also finds it insufficient for developing business software, noting that there are many common modeling requirements that it does not address. He also finds it overly complex, noting that the specification is huge, and that 20% of the notation works for 80% of the sketching requirements. Regarding the UML specification, he says [Amb02]:

> On the one hand, it has too little in it, and, on the other hand, it has too much in it.

He then notes that part of the vision behind the creation of modeling languages was to automate development using models, and he identifies several benefits of working at higher levels of abstraction, such as avoiding premature design, making it easy to change the software as the requirements evolve, and making it possible to postpone implementation decisions to the last minute. However, he concludes that UML is not up to the task, and not likely to be any time soon. Finally, he concludes that an easy to use model-driven development tool that generates software appropriate for the target environment, and provides a better return on investment than hand coding, would be agile. We couldn't agree more.

Perhaps the best way to see the similarities between Software Factories and Agile Modeling is to look at the Agile Modeling

Table 17.1   Agile modeling principles

AGILE MODELING PRINCIPLE	SOFTWARE FACTORY REALIZATION
Produce high-quality software that meets the needs of project stakeholders	Every model developed in a Software Factory is used in some way to produce working software.
Make sure the software is robust enough to be maintained and enhanced	Software Factories provide much better traceability and reconstruction than current methods and practices.
Create and keep artifacts as few artifacts as possible	Models developed in a Software Factory are source artifacts not documentation.
Expect change and be prepared to deal with it	Automation provided by Software Factories enables rapid responses to change.
Change the software in small increments	Software Factories can keep models synchronized continuously through incremental transformation.
Build models only when their purpose is clearly defined	Every model developed in a Software Factory is used in some way to produce working software.
Use multiple models each describing a different aspect of the software	Software Factories use multiple models based on viewpoints defined by a Software Factory Schema.
Make permanent artifacts good enough to be reused	Models developed in a Software Factory are good enough to compile.
Obtain feedback and respond quickly before problems become serious	Software Factories can keep models synchronized continuously providing immediate feedback.

principles and practices, and to see how they relate to Software Factories, as described in Tables 17-1 and 17-2. In each table, we summarize an Agile Modeling principle or practice, and then show how it is realized in Software Factories. Not all of the principles and practices of Agile Modeling apply to Software Factories, however. The ones that do not apply are primarily related to the documentation focus of Agile Modeling.

Table 17.2   Agile modeling practices

AGILE MODELING PRACTICE	SOFTWARE FACTORY REALIZATION
Create several models in parallel	Multiple models are created and maintained in parallel in a Software Factory.
Model a bit, code a bit, test a bit, deliver a bit	Software Factories can keep models, source code and other artifacts synchronized continuously.
Use the simplest tool available for the job	DSL-based tools are simpler and more focused than general-purpose modeling tools.
Validate models by implementing them and then testing the implementations	Test cases and harnesses can be generated from models in a Software Factory.

How Agile Are Software Factories?

This is the question that gets asked the most. Since Software Factories do not look a lot like what we currently call agile development, we might be tempted, on first glance, to think that they are not agile. After all, agile methods and practices, they are aligned with agile development principles and practices. Let's look at this alignment more closely.

Agile Development Principles

Software Factories exploit the stability in common requirements to help developers focus on variable ones and respond quickly to changes.

Perhaps the most important principle in agile development is embracing change. Agile methods are based on the assumption that requirements change constantly, and that implementing requirements can cause them to change. At first glance, it might seem that developing reusable assets for software product families would be an impediment to agility. However, in practice, a significant subset of the requirements for a software product family usually remains stable. For example, while there is variation in the way orders are processed, and the data they contain, Order Entry processes always deal with Orders, Customers, and Products in fairly well-known ways. By exploiting stability in the common requirements for a software product family, Software Factories actually increase agility, helping developers to focus on the variable requirements and respond quickly to changes. Few agilists would wish to return to the days of constructing user interfaces by hand, without the aid of a WYSIWYG user interface builder. Even though hand coding is ultimately required to complete a user interface, laying out widgets by specifying coordinates in code is not a productive use of time. There is also no benefit in terms of agility in writing data access code by hand instead of using an RDBMS.

Perhaps the best way to communicate this point is to compare Software Factories with similar methods and practices in use today. The two best analogies are patterns and frameworks. Presumably, most agilists would consider patterns and frameworks to be highly agile, because they save significant amounts of time. The answer given by a pattern author or framework developer might be different, however. Developing these reusable assets involves domain analysis, design, implementation, testing, and documentation. While some of this can be harvested from the examples on which the patterns and frameworks are based, there is still a significant upfront investment that must be made, in order to produce assets that can be readily reused by others. Trying to document a pattern or construct a framework in the middle of a time-critical project is probably not a wise of project stakeholder resources, and may not produce the best results.

Developing Software Factories is like authoring patterns and developing frameworks.

This leads to an important insight. While the product developer seeks to avoid making large upfront investments on a project, the reusable asset developer does not have much of a say in the matter, since their project is a large upfront investment by definition. Reusable asset developers make these investments in order to accelerate development for product developers. This is exactly the rationale for building Software Factories. By investing upfront in the analysis, design, and implementation of reusable assets for a specific family of software products, product line developers accelerate the development of the family members. The only major differences between building Software Factories and authoring patterns or developing frameworks are that we can say a bit more about the target product family with Software Factories, and that the patterns we author and the frameworks we build are accompanied by process assets like custom languages and tools that help product developers apply them even more rapidly. Indeed, Software Factories are the key to making product developers more agile, especially as project size, geographical distribution, and

Product line developers make large up front investments to accelerate product development projects.

project life times grow, as we saw in Chapter 4. By doing some of the work in advance, Software Factories reduce the amount of work that must be done during product development. As Ivar Jacobson likes to say, with a twinkle in his eye, the best way to deliver more software in less time is to develop less software.

Agile Development Practices

Differences in practice between Software Factories and current methods and practices suggest the need to describe what agile development practices look like for Software Factories. Experience has shown that most changes in software products are variations on common themes, not redefinitions of the software product families to which they belong. We can therefore leverage current agile development methods to deal with these kinds of changes. Of course, some changes in software products do affect the definitions of software product families, and the reusable assets developed to support them. Let's consider how both kinds of changes are handled by Software Factories.

Changes Affecting Individual Products

XP suggests that runtime variability points are opportunities to change an individual system without damaging platform-based assets, such as frameworks. Clearly, this practice can be applied in Software Factories. For example, extensibility points in a framework supplied by a Software Factory provide opportunity to modify product family members in a variety of ways without damaging the framework. Software Factories also offer opportunity to apply the same principle using development time variability points. Generation or configuration parameters, for example, can be used to modify product family members in a variety of ways without damaging tool-based assets. Design time variability points anticipate a different class of future changes than runtime variability points. By addressing design time variability as well as runtime variability, Software Factories take this agile development practice one step further.

XP also advocates continual refactoring. Clearly, this practice can also be applied in Software Factories. For example, product family members can be continually refactored throughout their life cycle using visual assembly tools based on DSLs. In this regard, Software Factories make the practice easier to perform,

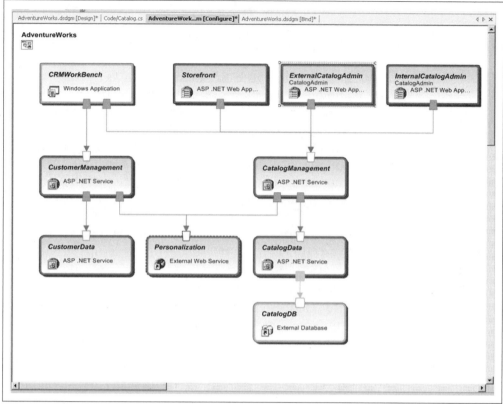

Figure 17.1   A tool for assembling web services

since tool-based refactoring is much faster and more accurate than manual refactoring, as we have seen. We can also apply this principle tuning to design decisions to change the structure of any generated implementations. Tuning design decisions is less expensive than manually refactoring the implementations, since tools carry the burden of modifying the code. For example, instead of manually refactoring all of the Web services handling preamble and postamble methods using chain of responsibility, so that, multiple third parties can participate, we might change a configuration setting in a tool like the one in Microsoft Visual Studio shown in Figure 17.1. The tool would then perform the refactoring automatically, changing the structure of the code while preserving the handwritten method bodies. While a modest amount of manual follow up would be needed to produce the final result, the overall process would be many times faster and much less error-prone using the tool than doing all of the work by hand.

Changes Affecting Software Product Families

Changes affecting software product families can occur in the problem or the solution domain:

- Changes in the problem domain, such as changes in common requirements or in parameters of variation for the software product family, may require changes anywhere in the software factory schema or the production assets, from the requirements framework, through the mappings, to the architecture, the components, the development environment (the default project structure and content, including patterns, frameworks and tools), the development process, the packaging plan, the deployment plan and process, and the execution environment.

- Changes in the solution domain, such as changes in the implementation technologies, or in the development or deployment environments, may only require changes in bottom-end of the software factory schema, and in production assets from the architecture down.

Because a Software Factory provides much better traceability through the software factory schema than current methods and practices, the effects of changes in either domain can be assessed more rapidly and reliably than in products developed in isolation.

How Will Software Factories Be Adopted?

A beachhead for Software Factories has already been established.

The beachhead principle articulated by Geoffrey Moore [Moo02] holds that the most effective way to introduce a new technology is one market segment at a time. This makes the process of transition more manageable, and allows a more focused application of the technology to each market segment. Conveniently, a beachhead for Software Factories has already been established in the area of business application development by the adoption of graphical user interface and database development tools that implement the four-part Software Factory pattern.

Business applications are an important frontier for the software industry.

Business applications are the new frontier, the edge of the charted territory, where innovation is occurring. This is because they exhibit a greater measure of similarity in requirements than other market segments, such as productivity applications,

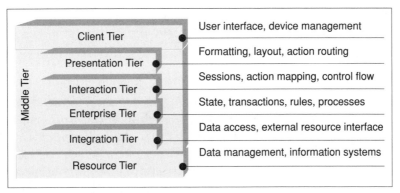

Figure 17.2   Business application tiers

and with the consolidation of platforms, a greater measure of regularity in architecture and implementation technology. They are therefore more susceptible to Software Factories, which exploit commonality among the members of a product family.

The new territory to be claimed by Software Factories lies in what have traditionally been considered the middle tiers of business applications. Figure 17.2 shows the names and functions of tiers in a typical multitier architecture. The interaction, business and integration tiers will be the next areas to benefit from automation.

Software Factories will tackle the middle tiers.

Historically, most of the progress in business application development has been in the client and resource tiers. It is in these parts of the application that the four-part Software Factory pattern has taken hold. The primacy of the front and back ends is now giving way, however, to an increasing emphasis on the rest of the application. Service-oriented architectures, which are the next step forward in business application architecture, as we have seen, are focused entirely on the rest of the application. This turns the picture inside out. Instead of squeezing the middle tiers between the user interface and the database, service-oriented architectures emphasize assemblies of interconnected components. User interfaces and databases appear on the periphery, as views into those assemblies, or as repositories that components use to manage their state, respectively.

The primacy of the front and back ends is giving way.

This shift in focus is motivated by interest in data, application, and business process integration. Also, less has been done to automate development in the middle tiers, so there is a need to bring developer productivity in these areas in line with the front and back ends. Perhaps the reason we started with user interfaces and databases was the presence of fixed boundaries,

Less has been done to automate development in the middle tiers.

namely the display and storage devices, that reduce the complexity of design in these areas by providing structure.

Types of Business Applications

The term business application is commonly used for systems that automate business operations, such as order processing and fulfillment, purchasing, and supply chain management. They are traditionally classified as either packaged or custom.

Packaged applications satisfy generic requirements.

Packaged business applications are supplied by an Independent Software Vendor (ISV), and satisfy generic requirements. Packaged business applications represent the first step toward the four-part Software Factory pattern in the middle tiers, since they provide reusable platform-based abstractions, and can be specialized using custom languages. Examples of packaged business application domains include decision support systems (DSS), data warehousing and online analytical processing (OLAP), Enterprise Resource Planning (ERP), Customer Relationship Management (CRM), and Sales Force Automation (SFA).

Custom business applications are developed specifically for the user, and satisfy custom requirements. Like packaged applications, they are a double-edged sword. While packaged applications dramatically reduce risk, cost, and time to market, they typically impose a standard set of requirements on the customer, and more often than not, the customer changes its business practices to accommodate the software nearly as much as it changes the software to satisfy its unique requirements. With custom applications, of course, the situation is exactly reversed. They can be made to satisfy highly specialized requirements, but at much higher risk, cost, and time to market.

Software Factories provide a middle ground, allowing customers to build variants on an archetypical application to satisfy a wide range of highly specialized requirements, but with much lower risk, cost, and time to market than developing new software from scratch. We expect to see many packaged application vendors recast their products as Software Factories.

Business applications have many interactions.

Business Application Characteristics

On the front end, business applications interact with users or with other applications over internal or external networks.

On the back end, they interact with Enterprise Information Systems (EIS), such as legacy systems, Transaction Processing Monitors (TPM), and Database Management Systems (DBMS). *They manage large amounts of structured information.*

They manage relatively large amounts of structured information compared with productivity applications, using internal representations of business entities. A typical application may manage tens, hundreds, or thousands of business entity types, with thousands, tens of thousands, or millions of instances.

They typically perform relatively small amounts of computation compared with productivity applications. The primary purpose of this computation is to support interactions with users or with other applications, or to process business rules. *They typically perform small amounts of computation.*

Business applications are often deployed into complex environments that can span multiple sites and companies, as illustrated in Figure 17.3 [MSAIDC]. *They are generally complex and volatile.*

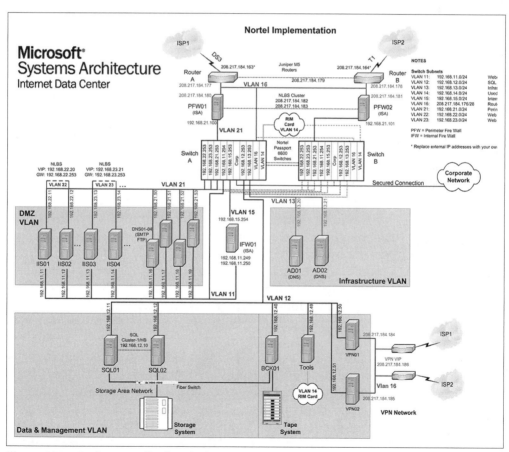

Figure 17.3   Business application deployment environments

When deployed, business applications must satisfy challenging operational requirements to ensure the security, reliability, performance, and availability of business or mission-critical data and processes. These requirements may include protecting information exposed to the Internet, scaling up to millions of users, or remaining online 24 hours a day 7 days a week.

Business application development projects typically involve competing stakeholder concerns. They also typically involve multiple tools, methods, and technologies, and share information, artifacts, and facilities with other projects at different stages of completion. Finally, they must typically respond rapidly to frequently changing requirements driven by changing business conditions.

Despite their complexity and volatility, business applications are rather formulaic, compared with productivity applications. This makes them ideal candidates for the Software Factories approach, which exploits variations on common themes.

How Mature Are Software Factories?

It may take some time for the industry to become comfortable with Software Factories.

RAD environments offering visual languages for instantiating, parameterizing, and assembling component libraries have been widely used for at least 10 years, and tools for developing databases have been part of established practice even longer. In this sense, the industry is already familiar with the concept of working at higher levels of abstraction and letting tools generate implementations. Applying these concepts to other parts of the application architecture is not yet part of established practice, however, and it may take some time for the industry to become comfortable with the idea.

Moore's law makes the speed advantages of hand written code irrelevant over time.

Some readers may remember the transition from assembly language to C for productivity application development on the IBM PC. For some time after C appeared on the scene, developers wrote in C but debugged in assembler. Why? For one thing, debuggers didn't offer C language source code debugging for several years. Also, bugs were frequently found in the assembly code generated by the compilers. In addition, many performance-critical pieces of software were hand coded in assembler because the code generated by the compilers did not make efficient use of machine cycles. Of course, compilers gradually produced faster and more reliable code, and Moore's law gradually made the speed advantages of handwritten assembly language irrelevant for all but the most performance sensitive parts of the operating system.

The transition described earlier was driven by businesses seeking competitive advantage by lowering cost and time to market, and raising product quality, using automation. We should expect to see a similar pattern in the displacement of the current generation of manual software development methods by automated methods using higher-level languages over a period of several years. This displacement will be driven by the economic concerns of software consumers and suppliers.

The transition will be driven by economic concerns.

The least mature aspects of Software Factories are language technology, tool extensibility, pattern composition, deferred encapsulation, and the development of standard DSLs, patterns, frameworks, and tools for popular domains.

Language Technology

UML has proven inadequate as a basis for model compilation, as described in Appendix B. Much higher fidelity languages are required. Modeling technologies that support the necessary levels of semantic formality are just starting to appear, as described in Chapter 8.

Higher fidelity mechanisms are required.

Tool Extensibility

Despite their increasing incorporation of modeling technologies, IDEs are not yet mature in terms of providing automation using those technologies. Most provide simple code visualization or low-level code generation using general-purpose modeling languages. Similarly, despite their increasing integration with IDEs, modeling tools are not yet mature in terms of automating development. Most are still focused on generating code from general-purpose models, such as UML class models. They do not yet address the rest of the software life cycle, or provide robust facilities for rapidly developing domain specific languages and tools. As described in Chapter 9, some IDEs are starting to include metamodeling facilities that can be used to develop formal domain specific languages. These same IDEs also provide robust extensibility mechanisms that can be used to develop editors, compilers, debuggers, and other tools required to make those DSLs available to product developers.

IDEs and modeling tools are not yet mature.

Pattern Composition

Pattern composition is still in its infancy.

Despite the recent appearance of some promising examples, (e.g., [ACM00]), pattern composition is still in its infancy. The patterns community is still thinking primarily about stand-alone patterns. More emphasis is needed on composing patterns to form system and subsystem architectures, more work is needed on relating pattern languages to architectural styles, and more progress is needed in defining rules for pattern composition.

Buschmann has written some useful guidelines.

An example of the latter is Frank Buschmann's paper on pattern application [Bus00a]. It provides general guidelines governing the application of multiple patterns in the context of progressive refinement guided by an architectural vision, explaining how to sequence the application of multiple patterns, how to manage the conflicting priorities of pattern integration and implementation, and how to combine patterns with existing structures whose participants provide similar or related responsibilities.

Hohpe, Woolf and Brown have created a visual pattern language.

Another promising development is the domain specific language for composing Enterprise Application Integration (EAI) patterns developed by Gregor Hohpe and Bobby Woolf, discussed in Chapter 7 [HW03]. This language provides a graphical notation, composition rules, and transformational semantics for assembling independent processes that communicate through asynchronous messaging by composing patterns. It has been applied to the development of traditional EAI systems and Web service assemblies. As the language is quite new, no attempts have yet been made to use it for automation, but they are sure to follow quickly. As more patterns are developed for important business and architectural domains, there will be many more opportunities to define domain specific languages and tools to automate their composition.

Deferred Encapsulation

While the concepts behind deferred encapsulation are quite simple, and have been proven in the lab and in special purpose products, such as container generators for Enterprise JavaBeans, commercially available development tools do not yet support essential aspects of the technology, such as encapsulating aspects, assembling partially encapsulated components, or validating assembled encapsulations. The closest examples are the compilers for CLR languages, such as C# and Visual Basic, available from Microsoft and its partners. Many of these compilers support the use of partial classes, which allow the definition of a class to be broken across multiple files, and then recombined during compilation. Partial classes are used to great advantage in Visual Studio, such as in the tools for the Microsoft Business Framework, for example. These tools support the development of higher-level abstractions using handwritten source and source code generated from simple DSL-based models using partial classes.

Standard Assets for Popular Domains

In order to provide a foundation for Software Factories, standard production assets must be developed for key business and architectural domains. Efforts are under way in a variety of organizations to replace EDI standards with XML-based DSLs defining entity, message, and process models for commerce [AW01]. Examples include ebXML [EBXML], RosettaNet [ROSETTA], and the Internet Open Trading Protocol [IOTP]. We also expect vendors like Microsoft and IBM to publish standard assets for technology domains based on their platforms and for architecture domains based on canonical architectures for those platforms.

Standard specification languages are needed for key domains.

How Should Software Factories Be Implemented?

Software Factories are part of a new paradigm for provisioning software, which combines technologies for automating development with changes in business and management practices. It is a disruptive technology that replaces general-purpose languages with domain specific languages for large parts of the development process, shifts the focus from individual products to product families, significantly increases the level of automation, and relies more on declarative specification and less on imperative specification than current methods and practices. This suggests that their implementation can have significant consequences.

Software Factories are a disruptive technology.

*Software
Factories imply
significant
change.*

According to Jacobson, organizations implementing methods like Software Factories will not realize the benefits of systematic reuse unless they produce related products as members of a product family, make significant investments in production assets, and make significant changes in business models, personnel, process, organization, architecture, tools, and technology [JGJ97]. Some of these issues are reviewed briefly next.

New Development Artifacts

*Developers must
program with
models.*

Software Factories use models to automate application development. Models become primary development artifacts, replacing general-purpose programming language source code. In other words, developers must program with models. This means that they must be conversant in domain specific languages. They must write specifications using those languages, compile them using domain specific compilers, and then discover, locate, and resolve defects in them.

*This has many
implications.*

Because Software Factories use domain specific languages, the abstractions manipulated by developers are close approximations of concepts that occur naturally in the problem domains. Users therefore understand specifications more readily than programs written in general-purpose programming languages. Product developers are no longer the only interpreters of the requirements. Product line developers play a more immediate role, since they develop the domain specific languages and tools used by product developers.

New Development Scope

Because Software Factories focus on families of products, they require a new planning horizon, new development processes, and new organizational structures. These topics were discussed in Chapters 4 and 10.

New Development Activities

Software Factories change application development significantly, as we have seen in Chapters 4 and 10. They also change infrastructure development, but more by giving it focus and formalizing its interactions with application development than by changing or replacing current methods and practices. There are two exceptions:

- In the context of a Software Factory, infrastructure development involves a much higher degree of tool construction than current methods and practices, which focus more on implementation assets like patterns and frameworks than on process assets that support them like guidance and tools.

- In the context of a Software Factory, infrastructure development becomes more distinct, as product line development organizations build more formal relationships with their customers, and go much farther than they currently do in areas like product packaging and support.

See Bosch for an excellent and more detailed discussion of these issues [Bos00].

Implementing Software Factories

Because of these differences, Software Factories should be adopted progressively to give people time to adjust to the changes. In other words, it may be necessary to maintain current operations while transitioning to new practices. This can be done by incrementally increasing either scope or abstraction. These methods are not mutually exclusive, and can be used in combination.

Software Factories should be adopted progressively.

Increasing Scope

An adopting organization can gradually increase the scope of Software Factory usage to include a progressively larger portion of its product development activity. It can start by using Software Factories for a pilot project, for example, or for a subset of the components in each project, while developing other projects, components or final products using traditional methods. Then, over time, it can use Software Factories for additional projects, for more of the components in each project and for final product assembly.

The scope of Software Factory usage can be gradually increased.

Increasing Abstraction

An adopting organization can gradually increase the level of abstraction used with Software Factories. For example, it can

The level of abstraction can be gradually increased.

start by introducing basic Software Factory practices, producing most of the implementation by hand, and then move to more advanced practices over time, relying more heavily on automation, as people become comfortable with each level of practice.

Incremental Adoption

A series of steps is often followed.

According to Jacobson, the typical organization progresses through a series of steps toward systematic reuse.

- The first step in the process is a transition from no reuse to informal code reuse based on copying and adaptation.

- The second is a transition to black-box code reuse, driven by the difficulty of maintaining multiple similar but slightly different copies. This requires identifying, harvesting, refining, documenting, testing, packaging, and supporting components for explicit reuse.

- Next, pressure to support the competing demands of different users forces a transition to a managed reuse process supported by a separate reuse organization.

- From there, higher levels of reuse and greater coverage of the life cycle require a transition to architecture-driven reuse, where reusable components are designed to work together in the context of a shared architecture.

- The final step is a transition to domain specific reuse, where the organization embraces the need to identify domains of interest, and to describe them in sufficient detail to support the development of domain specific production assets.

Software Factories accelerate this progression by providing well-defined methods and practices that help organizations implement systematic reuse.

What's Different This Time?

How many times have we heard this claim?

This book proposes a way to raise the level of abstraction for developers using models, and claims that it will produce faster and more reliable applications in less time and at lower cost than traditional software development methods. How many times have we heard this claim? The number of failed attempts to realize the vision is at least as numerous as the number of times it has been espoused.

Computer Aided Software Engineering (CASE) sought to increase productivity using models, but failed to deliver on its promise, or to replace a significant amount of hand coding with 3GLs. 4GLs also attempted to increase productivity by directly encoding problem domain concepts. Unlike CASE, however, they were commercially successful. The three most popular development tools in terms of number of seats sold, Visual Basic, Power Builder, and DBase (including its variants), are 4GLs. Of course 4GLs have significant limitations, compared to hand coding with 3GLs. Most notable are the requirement to work entirely within the 4GL environment, the use of a single language for all aspects of the problem and an extremely rigid approach to architecture that limits them to dealing with monolithic or simple client/server or web applications.

CASE and 4GLs tried to cover this ground.

Are we grinding the same old axe? Admittedly, our axe resembles earlier ones. But, isn't that how we make progress? We learn from failures, even costly, high-profile ones. We correct their worst mistakes, retain their best contributions, leverage new developments in the industry, and craft an approach that has some things in common with earlier ones, but that also differs from them in significant ways. Are the differences between Software Factories and CASE significant enough to produce a different outcome? What's different this time?

Progress is made by learning from failures.

- Software Factories use formal and complete models that conform to well-defined viewpoints, organized into well-defined schemas. The notations and semantics of the models and the relationships between them are specified completely and unambiguously enough to support synchronization, progressive transformation, and other forms of automation.

Software Factories use formal models with well-defined relationships.

- Software Factories keep high-level models synchronized with low-level models and other development artifacts throughout the development process using much more powerful transformation technologies than earlier efforts. Without this synchronization, maintaining this information would not be cost effective.

Software Factories use tools to synchronize artifacts.

- Software Factories take a more open-ended approach, allowing product line developers to design the software factory schema, and therefore to use any combination of

Software Factories use an open-ended approach.

assets that makes sense. There is no need to use one technique, such as modeling or component assembly, for every aspect of product development.

Software Factories are family based.

■ Software Factories focus on specific software product families, providing a basis for making reusable assets cost effective, while earlier efforts focused on one-off development, making them hard to sustain economically.

Software Factories use DSLs.

■ Software Factories use domain specific languages (DSLs) that explicitly represent problem domain concepts, and domain specific tools that encapsulate knowledge about their implementation. This knowledge can be applied by using these domain specific production assets.

Software Factories use models across the life cycle.

■ Software Factories use models across the whole life cycle (e.g., for testing and debugging), reducing the need to work directly with lower level implementation artifacts. This helps developers think in terms of the concepts encoded in the modeling languages.

Software Factories use file based models.

■ Software Factories define the organization of models and the packaging of information within models to help development tools process models in the file-based world of application development.

Software Factories live in domain organizations.

■ Software Factories are developed and used primarily by organizations with domain expertise. This means that they live close to the requirements that they implement, and can therefore be much more nimble than earlier efforts.

Software Factories are open and extensible.

■ Software Factories are based on ordinary programming languages, patterns, frameworks and other familiar technologies, and do not hide lower level implementation artifacts. This means that they do not lock consumers into fixed architectures or programming models that become obsolete when technologies change.

Abstraction and Refinement

Nothing is really unprecedented. Faced with a new situation, people liken it to familiar ones and shape their response on the basis of the perceived similarities.

M.S. Mahoney

This appendix presents a brief tutorial on abstraction and refinement.

Abstraction is a transformation that maps configurations of objects in one or more input domains to a configuration of objects in an output domain, as shown in Figure A.1. It can be made reflexive using identical input and output domains. Abstraction can remove information from the input configurations, and can change their modular structure. Several forms of abstraction can be identified.[1]

Abstraction is a transformation or mapping.

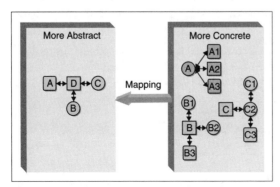

Figure A.1   Abstraction is a transformation

Refinement is the inverse of abstraction.

Refinement is the inverse of abstraction. It maps configurations of objects in an input domain to configurations of objects in one or more output domains. It can be made reflexive using identical input and output domains. Refinement can add information to the input configuration. Like abstraction, it can also change its modular structure. A refinement that expands an object into its constituent parts preserves the modular structure of the object. Although new information has been revealed about the internal structure of the object, the boundaries of the object have not changed, and it may even be identifiable as the original object in the output domain. A refinement that reorganizes a configuration of objects by moving features between classes, or by combining classes to produce a more optimal configuration, does not preserve the structure of the input configuration. Refinements that do not preserve the structure of the input configuration include optimizations and refactorings. Several forms of refinement can be identified, as described next. Each is the inverse of one of the forms of abstraction described in the same section.

Generalization

Generalization maps a more specific configuration to a more general one.

Generalization maps a configuration of more specific objects in an input domain to a configuration of more general objects in an output domain. For example, we can generalize from Manager to Employee, as shown in Figure A.2. Generalization treats more specific objects like more general ones. For example, Managers can be treated as Employees. Generalization always preserves the modular structure of the input configuration.

Specialization is the inverse of generalization.

Specialization is the inverse of generalization. It maps a configuration of more general objects in an input domain to a

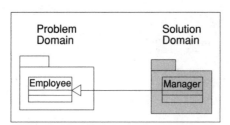

Figure A.2   Generalization

configuration of more specific objects in an output domain. For example, we might specialize from Employee to Manager. Specialization always preserves the modular structure of the input configuration. Specialization treats instances of the more general objects as instances of the more specific ones for the purposes of a specific process. For example, we might treat Employees as Managers in order to let them become consumers of reporting relationships.

Projection

Projection maps a more detailed configuration of objects in an input domain to a less detailed configuration of objects in an output domain. For example, we might create a projection of a configuration of objects by combining objects and by removing properties, operations, and relationships, or by fetching a subset of the columns in a table, as illustrated in Figure A.3.[2] Projection can also change the modular structure of the input configuration by combining or separating objects, or changing the partitioning of properties, operations, and relationships.

Projection maps a more detailed configuration to a less detailed one.

Elaboration is the inverse of projection. It maps a less detailed configuration of objects in an input domain to a more detailed configuration of objects in an output domain. For example, we might create an elaboration of a configuration of objects by adding information about properties, operations, and relationships. Elaboration can also change the modular structure of the input configuration by changing the partitioning of properties, operations, and relationships among the objects.

Elaboration is the inverse of projection.

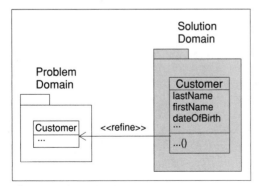

Figure A.3   Projection

Encapsulation

Encapsulation is a form of projection.

Encapsulation is a form of projection that preserves the input configuration in the output domain, and adds a configuration of objects called a specification. In the output domain, the input configuration becomes the implementation. External objects cannot interact with the implementation except through the specification. Encapsulation lets the implementation vary without affecting the specification [GHJV]. In object-oriented languages, specifications are expressed as interfaces. An interface defines a contract between a class and its collaborators. The contract establishes the terms of the collaboration while hiding the implementation of the class from its collaborators. This lets the consumers of the interface collaborate with the suppliers without knowing the implementations of the suppliers or all of the interfaces that the suppliers implement. Abstract classes are like interfaces in terms of encapsulation, but they differ in terms of scope and implementation. An abstract class defines a common interface that can only be used by its subclasses. It may also implement some of the methods in the common interface, making them available to its subclasses. Encapsulation is often used to wrap concrete classes with interfaces. For example, we might encapsulate a configuration of classes implementing an Order Entry process as an EJB session bean. The home and remote interfaces of the EJB session bean form the specification used to access the configuration of concrete classes, as illustrated in Figure A.4.

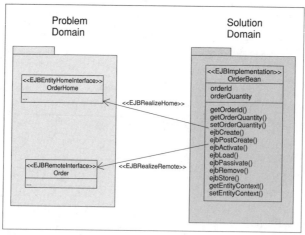

Figure A.4   Encapsulation

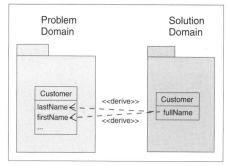

Figure A.5   Derivation

Realization is the inverse of encapsulation. It preserves the input configuration in the output domain, and adds a configuration of objects to the output domain called an implementation. In the output domain, the input configuration is called a specification. External objects cannot interact with the implementation except through the specification. Realization is used frequently to specify configurations of concrete classes that provide implementations of interfaces. For example, the home and remote interfaces of an EJB session bean that represents an Order Entry process might be realized by adding an implementation class, some helper classes and EJB entity beans that represent Orders, Products, and Customers.

Realization is the inverse of encapsulation.

Derivation is a form of realization that implements a configuration of objects in the input domain using other objects in the input domain, as shown in Figure A.5. For example, the property fullName derives from the properties firstName and lastName. Derivation preserves the modular structure of the input configuration.

Derivation is a form of realization.

Composition

Composition maps configurations of objects in one or more inputs domain to a configuration of objects in an output domain. The output configuration must use all of the input configurations. In other words, the input configurations must be collectively sufficient to define the output configuration, and no subset of them may be sufficient [CE00]. Composition can be used to create larger configurations from smaller ones. For example, we might compose classes to form components, and then compose the components to form an Order Entry system, as illustrated in Figure A.6.

Composition combines configurations to form a new one.

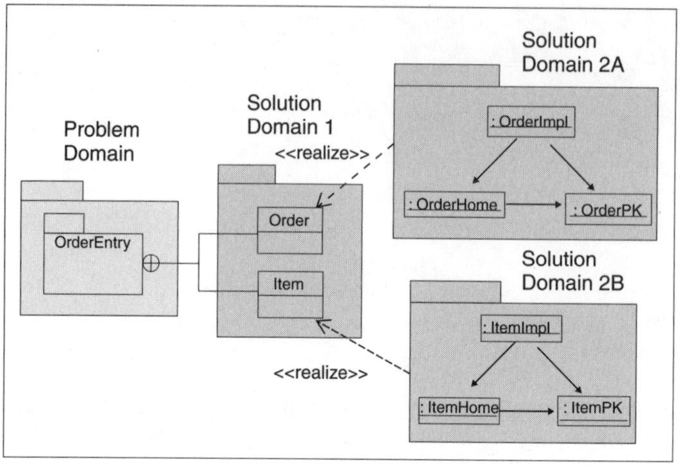

Figure A.6   Functional composition

Compositions may be encapsulated. For example, we might provide interfaces for components from the preceding example to hide the compositions of classes that form their implementations. Composition also provides a way to separate the parts of the software that are expected to vary at different rates or for different reasons. Many object-oriented patterns use composition in this way to specify designs that can adapt to certain kinds of changes. For example, we might use the Strategy pattern to place the variable aspects of an algorithm in a separate object that we can invoke at some point in the algorithm. We can then vary the behavior of the algorithm by replacing the Strategy object [GHJV]. Two types of composition can be defined—functional and aspectual.[3] They are complementary, and are often used together [CE00].

Decomposition is the inverse of composition.

Decomposition is the inverse of composition. It maps a configuration of objects in an input domain to configurations of objects in one or more output domains. Decomposition can be used to create smaller configurations from larger ones. For example, we might decompose an Order Entry system into components, and then decompose the components into classes. Decomposition is often used with realization. For example, the implementation classes we added above might realize interfaces defined by the components. Decomposition provides a way to break out part of an object as a new object, so that it can vary independently, both at development time, meaning that it can be further refined independently, and at runtime, meaning that it can be replaced with another object through association.

In other words, decomposition branches both the refinement process and the architecture. The use of decomposition usually implies a subsequent use of composition to combine the resulting objects. For example, once we have implemented the classes that we specified by decomposing the components in the preceding example, we compose them to implement the components. There are two types of decomposition—functional and aspectual.

Functional Composition

Functional composition maps configurations of objects in a single-input domain to a configuration of objects in an output domain. The examples in the previous section illustrate functional composition. Functional composition preserves the modular structure of the input configurations. It can be used to implement the functional requirements by progressively combining smaller implementations to form larger ones.

Abstraction is transformation

Functional decomposition is the inverse of functional composition. It maps a configuration of objects in an input domain to configurations of objects in a single output domain. The examples in the previous section illustrate functional decomposition. Functional decomposition preserves the modular structure of the input configuration. It can be used to break down the functional requirements by progressively partitioning larger requirements to form smaller ones.

Functional decomposition is the inverse of functional composition.

Aspectual Decomposition

Aspectual composition maps configurations of objects in two or more input domains to a configuration of objects in an output domain. It always changes the modular structure of one of the input configurations and scatters the members of one of the input domains across the members of the others. It can be used to provide implementations for aspects that cut across the modular structure of the software, such as security, persistence, and concurrency. These may be mandated by the non-functional requirements, or they may be artifacts of the design. Each of the input configurations represents some aspect of the output configuration. For example, we might map a database schema and descriptions of EJB entity beans to persistence bindings, collecting the columns of the database schema and the fields of the EJB entity beans into the persistence bindings.

Abstraction is transformation.

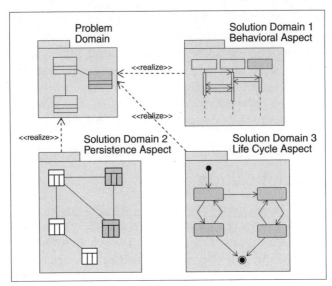

Figure A.7   Aspectual decomposition

Aspectual decomposition is the inverse of aspectual composition.

Aspectual decomposition is the inverse of aspectual composition, as shown in Figure A.7. It maps a configuration of objects in an input domain to configurations of objects in two or more output domains. A property of aspectual decomposition is that the objects in at least one of the output configurations always refer to objects in one or more of the others. Aspectual decomposition can be used to analyze requirements called aspects that cut across the modular structure of the software, such as security, persistence and concurrency. These may be mandated by the non-functional requirements, or they may be artifacts of the design. Each of the output configurations represents some aspect of the input configuration. For example, we might map the deployable descriptions of several EJB entity beans to a database schema, descriptions of the EJB entity beans. In this example, the persistence bindings refer to fields in the EJB entity beans and to columns in the database schema. Aspectual decomposition always changes the modular structure of the input configuration. The preceding example distributes the persistence bindings into the columns of the database schema and the fields of the EJB entity beans.

Subjective decomposition is a form of aspectual decomposition that separates the concerns of different audiences.

Subjective decomposition is a form of aspectual decomposition that separates the concerns of different audiences by creating multiple descriptions of the same subject, each one hiding and exposing different information, as shown in Figure A.8.

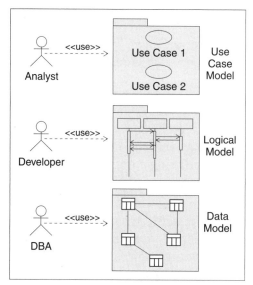

Figure A.8 Abstraction separates concerns

Composition Mechanisms

Most object-oriented programming and modeling languages support several well-known composition mechanisms. These mechanisms create abstractions by composing existing ones, and can be used for both functional and aspectual composition. Composition mechanisms can be classified as static or dynamic, according to when they are bound...

Composition mechanisms let developers build new abstractions from existing ones.

- Static composition mechanisms are bound at development time, when implementations are generated.

- Dynamic composition mechanisms are bound at execution time, when executables are processed.

...Or, as structural or behavioral, according to what they combine.

- Structural composition mechanisms combine smaller structures, such as classes, to form larger structures, such as components.

- Behavioral composition mechanisms combine less complex behaviors, such as analyzing, parsing and generation, to form more complex behaviors, such as compilation.

Association

Association is a static or dynamic structural composition mechanism.

Association is structural composition mechanism, and can be static or dynamic. It defines a simple linkage between two or more objects. An object reference is an example of association. Association can be either static or dynamic.

- Static association is bound at compile time. Inner classes are examples of static association. An inner class can be embedded in an outer class during compilation, so that the linkage between them cannot be changed at runtime.

- Dynamic association is bound at runtime, as objects acquire references to other objects. This makes the relationships harder to see in the implementation, but it makes the implementation more configurable [GHJV]. It also means that the runtime structure of the implementation is not captured effectively by the compile time structure [POSA1].

Association may let the related objects know about each other.

Association may let the related objects know about each other. For example, consider two objects in a database. We might let them know about each other, we might let one to know about the other without being known, or we might let neither know about the other and use a join to maintain the linkage between them. Association does not imply any lifetime coupling between the objects. In other words, neither object owns the other. Associations are generally made and broken frequently, and generally are not long lived [GHJV].

An association has two or more ends.

An association has two or more ends. Each end defines how objects attached to it participate in the association. The following properties are defined for binary associations by the UML [OMG ad/01-02-14].

- Multiplicity—Indicates how many objects at this end may be associated with an object at the other end. For example, a multiplicity of exactly one at this end and a multiplicity of zero or more at the other end describes a one-to-many association.

- Navigability—Indicates whether or not an object at this end can be reached by traversal from an object at the other end. For example, if the association end is navigable, then objects at the other end can know about objects at this end, and may invoke their methods.

- Ordering—Indicates how objects at this end are ordered relative to an object at the other end. An ordering is often implemented using a sorted collection. For example, if the ordering is ascending by last name, then the object at the other end may perform a binary search by last name to locate a specific object on this end.

- Qualification—Indicates how objects at this end are partitioned relative to an object at the other end. A qualification is often implemented using a guarded collection. For example, the qualification for a collection of paid invoices may be that the `boolean` attribute `paid` must be `true`.

- Changeability—Indicates how the participation of the objects at this end may change. For example, an association between two classes may be bound at compile time, while an association between their instances may allow variation at runtime.

Association can be used to move variable elements into new classes [GHJV]. New functionality is obtained by creating configurations that use the new objects. Since the variable elements are no longer part of the original objects, we can no longer modify their behavior directly. They are therefore often parameterized, so that their behavior can be modified by supplying appropriate parameter values, as described next. Association requires the participating objects to be encapsulated [GHJV]. In other words, it does not give consumers visibility into their implementations.

Association can be used to move variable elements into new classes.

Aggregation

Aggregation is a form of association that defines a part/whole relationship like the relationship between a directory and the files it contains. Aggregation is generally less common and longer-lived than association [GHJV]. The most common form of aggregation—composite aggregation—requires that a part be included in at most one whole, and that destroying the whole destroys its parts.[4] Note that the lifetimes of the whole and its parts are not necessarily identical, since parts may be added to the whole after its creation, in some cases. For example, files can be added to an existing directory, but when the directory

Aggregation is a form of association that defines a part/whole relationship.

is destroyed, its contents are also destroyed. Composite aggregation is also called containment.

Procedure Invocation

Procedure invocation is a static or dynamic structural or behavioural form of composition.

Procedure invocation is a behavioral composition mechanism, and can be either static or dynamic. One procedure requests execution of another. Arguments may be passed and return values may be received. It is the most commonly used composition mechanism [GAO94].

Static procedure invocation is bound at compile time.

Static procedure invocation names the procedure to be invoked, and the invocation is bound at compile time. Dynamic procedure invocation invokes a procedure through an indirection mechanism, such as a C++ function pointer, or dynamic method dispatch in Smalltalk, and binds the invocation at runtime.

Inheritance

Inheritance is a static or dynamic structural or behavioural form of composition.

Inheritance can be used for both structural and behavioral composition, and can be either static or dynamic. Inheritance allows a class to reuse the interfaces or implementations of other classes. It combines composition, which is a form of abstraction, with specialization, which is a form of refinement, by composing objects with the objects they specialize.

Static inheritance is easier to see in than association, but makes the code less configurable.

Static inheritance is the most common form. Extending an existing class by name in the declaration of a new Java class is an example of static inheritance. Static inheritance makes relationships easier to observe in the implementation than association, but also makes the implementation less configurable [GHJV]. Dynamic inheritance can be implemented using dynamic parameterization and parameterized inheritance. Changing the class of a Smalltalk object using the become operator is an example of dynamic inheritance.

Inheritance can be used to refactor classes.

Inheritance can be used to move variable elements into one or more classes or interfaces [GHJV]. New functionality can then be obtained by specializing or extending the new classes or interfaces. Since the variable elements are no longer part of the original classes or interfaces, their behavior can no longer be changed by the original class.

Inheritance may violate encapsulation.

Inheritance may give inheriting classes visibility into the implementations of the new classes, effectively violating their encapsulation [GHJV]. It is possible to use inheritance without exposing implementations by keeping the members of the new classes private, or by using only interface inheritance, but that tends to be the exception rather than the rule.

Paramerization

Parameterization can be used for both structural and behavioral composition, and can be either static or dynamic. It replaces part of an implementation with a value supplied by a variable parameter. Dynamic parameterization is the most common form, and is supported by most programming languages by argument passing in procedure invocation. It can also be implemented using association, as illustrated by design patterns, such as Decorator, Flyweight, Command, and Strategy [GHJV]. Dynamic parameterization carries a runtime performance penalty, and may make debugging more difficult, but it allows for runtime variation.

Parameterization is a static or dynamic mechanism for structural or behavioral composition.

Parameterized Inheritance

Inheritance and parameterization can be combined to form parameterized inheritance. With parameterized inheritance, an inherited class or interface is represented by a parameter. C++ template classes demonstrate parameterized inheritance. The order in which inherited class or interface parameters are bound can determine the correctness and the semantics of the implementation [CE].

Inheritance and parameterization can be combined as parameterized inheritance.

Delegation

Delegation is a form of association that simulates inheritance but does not violate encapsulation [GHJV]. It uses an association between two—a consumer and a supplier. The supplier acts like the part of the consumer that would have been supplied by inheritance. In other words, it provides state and behavior that would have been provided by inheritance. The consumer calls the supplier as it would call its superclass. Because the consumer does not actually inherit from the supplier, however, the identity of the consumer must be passed explicitly to the supplier as a parameter value on every call. This lets the supplier call the consumer back to obtain state, or to complete an algorithm, for example, using the Template Method pattern [GHJV].

Delegation simulates inheritance without violating encapsulation.

Notes

1. See [CE00] for more information. See [GHJV] for a discussion of design trade-offs among abstraction mechanisms in programming languages.
2. UML notation is used to show that the problem domain is a refinement of the solution domain. Because abstraction is the inverse of refinement, the solution domain is an abstraction of the problem domain.
3. [CE00] refers to functional composition as modular composition, to emphasize the preservation of module boundaries. The term *functional composition* is more widely used.
4. The UML defines another form of aggregation, shared aggregation, which is not as widely used [OMG ad/01-02-14].

The Unified Modeling Language

By Steve Cook and Stuart Kent

It is important to note that the current description is not a completely formal specification of the language because to do so would have added significant complexity without clear benefit.

UML 2 Specification

This appendix discusses the Unified Modeling Language (UML) and its related technologies, and considers whether or not they provide appropriate artifacts for automating aspects of the software development process as proposed in this book. We will find that although UML contains popular and highly successful standard notations for documenting aspects of software development, it falls well short of being a suitable foundation for formal domain specific languages.

Background and History

The history of the UML[1] started in the early 1990s with the publication of several books about object-oriented graphical modeling languages. Its creation came about when James Rumbaugh, one of the authors of the Object Modeling Technique [RBP+91] joined Rational Software, and started working with Grady Booch, author of another best-selling book on object-oriented modeling [Boo94]. By 1995, Rational had

The UML pooled the ideas of the "Three Amigos".

acquired Objectory, and with it Ivar Jacobson, the main author of a third well-known book on object-oriented development [JCJ+92]. At Rational, these three authors became known as the "Three Amigos". They pooled their ideas and created the first draft of what was then called the Unified Method, which subsequently became the Unified Modeling Language and the associated Unified Process. It is important to note that the "U" in UML means "Unified", and that this refers to the fact that the language was a unification of the ideas of these three authors. The UML is not, and was never intended to be, a Universal Modeling Language.

These three were not the only authors of object-oriented modeling languages in the early 1990s. Other leading figures included Peter Coad [CY90], James Martin and James Odell [MO92], Sally Shlaer and Stephen Mellor [SM88, SM91], and Trygve Reenskaug [Ree96]. A good overview of these and other approaches is given by Ian Graham [Gra93].

The UML was adopted as an OMG standard in 1997.

As books about object-oriented modeling were published, efforts were made by the Object Management Group to initiate standardization. Early efforts met with no success, but when Rational published the Unified Method, it was widely recognized that the time was ripe for standardization. Version 1.1 of UML was adopted as a standard by the OMG in November of 1997. Since then, UML has undergone several minor revisions, from version 1.2 through version 1.5, and one major revision, version 2.0, which has been accepted for adoption, and is being completed as we go to print.

UML is the most successful modeling language.

UML is the most widely adopted object-oriented modeling language by a large margin. It is described by more than one hundred books, supported by multiple commercial tools, used by many other standards as a specification language, taught by many universities, and adopted by many organizations to support the software development process. As a commonly accepted means of expressing and communicating the basic concepts of object-oriented design, UML has been successful.

The UML Specification

UML defines notations, abstract syntax, and informal semantics.

The UML specification defines a set of graphical notations, an abstract syntax, and an informal semantics. (See Chapter 8 for a discussion of formal semantics.) It defines constructs for describing software, for organizing models, and for creating extensions. The user manipulates UML-based models primarily through diagrams, and UML provides several kinds of diagram. Examples of UML diagrams include the Class Diagram and the Activity Diagram. See [OMG ad/03-04-01] for a complete list of UML diagrams.

The UML includes a logical language, the Object Constraint Language (OCL), which is used to express logical conditions on models, such as preconditions, postconditions, and invariants. OCL was introduced into UML as part of the standardization process, and has its roots in the modeling approach called Syntropy [CD94]. OCL is widely used to express well-formedness constraints in the definition of UML itself. Warmer and Kleppe [WK99] is a good introduction to OCL.

UML includes a constraint language called OCL.

The Action Semantics Extensions, a relatively recent addition to UML, defines execution semantics semi-formally for some of the behavioral abstractions [OMG ad/01-08-04]. These extensions were designed to support the construction of executable models.

UML defines execution semantics for some concepts.

Given the quantity and quality of books on the market about UML, there is no need for a tutorial here. The OMG UML home page, at http://www.uml.org, provides introductory information, recommended reading, and references to other resources. Fowler and Scott [FS97b] provide a popular introduction to the language.

There is no need for a tutorial here.

For our purpose, it is worth exploring in depth how UML is defined, and how it fits into a set of related modeling technologies also standardized by the OMG. We do this in order to understand the anatomy of UML in the terms described in Chapter 8, so that we can assess the suitability of UML as a basis for automating aspects of software development. It is important to make this assessment, because UML is often claimed to be a suitable starting point. We propose to show that it is not, for two main reasons:

We show that UML is not as a suitable starting point for automating software development.

- It does not have well-defined semantics, and
- Its definition is not structured in a way that makes it a good basis for defining new languages.

The abstract syntax graph for UML is itself a UML model; more specifically, it is a set of UML package and class diagrams. See [OMG formal/03-03-01] for examples of UML used to define itself. The UML abstract syntax for UML is usually called the UML *metamodel*.

The abstract syntax of UML is defined in UML.

Figure B.1 Use of composition

The definition of UML is bootstrapped.

Now, it may require some mental acrobatics to understand how UML can be defined in UML. If we want to find out what UML means, we go to its definition, and there we find more UML—we have a "chicken and egg" problem. This problem is familiar to programming language developers: a new programming language is often bootstrapped from being initially implemented using a compiler written in something else, to being implemented using a compiler written in a previous version of itself.

UML has semantic uncertainty at its core.

Unlike the bootstrapping of a compiler, however, which is based on execution, the bootstrapping of UML originally rested on a purely informal understanding of the meaning of UML, as defined in the associated books and papers. This is fine for a language primarily intended for documentation, but it is inadequate for a language intended to form executable software artifacts. This basic semantic uncertainty has been at the core of UML since its creation, and remains to this date. A case in point is the meaning of the *black diamond* symbol, which is stated in the UML specification to mean "composition". A typical example of the use of this symbol is shown in Figure B.1. This simple diagram would often be interpreted as saying "a Car has Wheels", with the implication that the Wheels belong to the Car.

The exact meaning of the UML black diamond is ill-defined.

However, defining an exact meaning for this symbol (and the related *white diamond*) has caused immense difficulty in the UML community. The topic of composite objects is complex, and has been the subject of numerous technical papers—see [Civ93] and [KR94]. The black diamond symbol has variously been called composition, ownership, containment, by-value, whole-part, and strong aggregation. We can ask many questions about this symbol, such as:

- Does it imply deletion propagation?
- Does it imply copy propagation?
- Does it imply propagation of any other operations? If so, which?

- Can a part change its whole? If so, when?

- Can a whole change its parts? If so, when?

- Is it permissible for a given part to belong to the same whole more than once?

Some of these questions are answered in the standard definition of UML, in English sentences, but some of them are not. Bear in mind that the answers to these questions are logically independent: any combination of "yes" and "no" answers would be possible. However, whatever the standard says, there are implementations of UML in the marketplace that offer semantics that conflict with each other, and with the standard. For example, although the standard says that deleting the whole causes deletion of the parts, we must question what that would mean in terms of the model in Figure B.1. We can plausibly assume that the figure concerns real cars and wheels, rather than software objects, in which case, it is sensible to ask what it might mean to delete a car, and why doing this to a car would affect its wheels. If delete means destroy, do we always require the wheels to be destroyed in order to conclude that a car has been destroyed? This seems unlikely.

If the model is about real cars and wheels, the concept of delete propagation makes no sense.

On the other hand, if the figure describes classes related by memory references defined in some programming language, then deletion propagation would seem to make sense. If the programming language has automatic garbage collection, however, some more explanation seems necessary. Then again, the figure might represent tables in a relational database, in which case, we could presume that a "cascades delete" integrity rule applies between a Car and its Wheels. But in this case, we need to know when this rule is to be applied. Is it immediate, or should it be deferred until a transaction commits? Since UML contains no concept of a transaction, this question cannot be answered. Since none of these interpretations are expressly established or prohibited by the UML specification, we are left quite uncertain of the meaning of this symbol.

If the model is about software artifacts, many different meanings are possible.

The black diamond symbol is part of the most commonly used area of UML. As a consequence, it is impossible to specify exactly the meaning of any UML model without additional information. When UML is used as an informal means of communicating object-oriented concepts on whiteboards, or in documents, this is not usually a significant drawback. Any information needed to disambiguate the diagrams can be

It is impossible to specify the exact meaning of any UML model without additional information.

communicated using some other means, typically verbally. However, for a language to be usable to drive an automated development process, it is essential for the meaning of the language to be precise. In the case of UML, the language does not provide this precise meaning. It must be added externally, in a manner specific to the context at hand.

UML is essentially just standard abstract and concrete syntax.

The basic difficulty here is that UML is essentially a standardized abstract and concrete syntax. Although it claims to have a standard semantics, in practice it does not. It actually has a wide range of possible semantic interpretations, only some of which are formalized, and many of which are inconsistent with each other. As a language for documentation, and for communicating object-oriented designs, this ambiguity is at worst a minor drawback, and can often be a positive advantage. As a language for driving automated processes, it is a major handicap. Since the language does not intrinsically define an exact meaning, a specific semantic interpretation must be applied from outside. This would perhaps be satisfactory if the language were flexible enough to encourage the assignment of semantics. Unfortunately, however, the way UML has been specified, it is both semantically imprecise and sufficiently restrictive to make the assignment of semantics impractical in many cases. We will see this shortly in our discussion of UML *profiles*.

The OMG Modeling Architecture

The OMG has several modeling standards.

Beside the UML, several other modeling technologies are adopted as standards by the OMG. The Meta Object Facility (MOF) is used for defining metamodels. The XML Metadata Interchange (XMI) is used for defining interchange formats for models and metamodels.

The Four-layer Modeling Architecture underpins the OMG modeling standards.

Underpinning this set of standards is a concept called the Four-layer Modeling Architecture. This is illustrated by Figure B.2, which shows the models defined at each of the four levels and the dependency relationships among them [OMG formal/00-04-03]. Starting from the bottom, this shows some data about two vendors at the *information* level; some data describing the structure of Vendor data at the *model* level; some data describing the structure of model data at the *metamodel* level; and a "hard-wired model" at the *meta-metamodel* level.

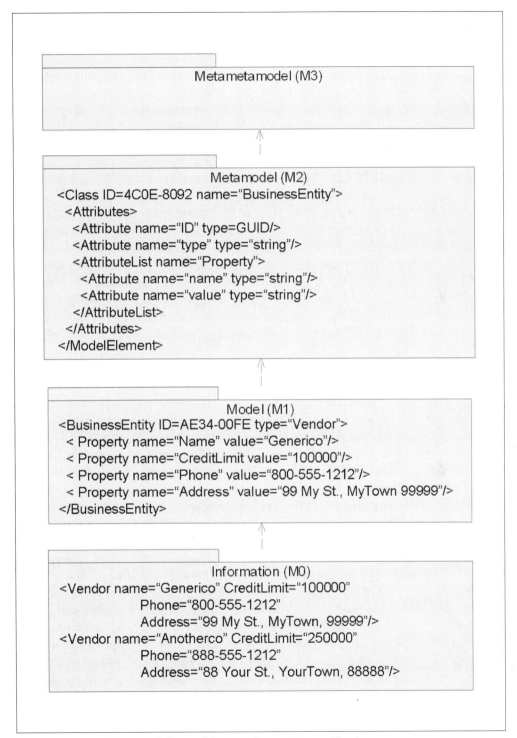

Figure B.2 Four layer modeling architecture from MOF specification

Conventionally, the information level is called M0, the model level M1, the metamodel level M2, and the meta-metamodel level M3.

Level N + 1 defines an abstract syntax for level N.

The relationship between any level and the level below it in this hierarchy is that level N + 1 defines an abstract syntax for level N. For example, a Vendor element at level 0 is expressed using the abstract syntax defined by the BusinessEntity element at level 1, and similarly the abstract syntax for BusinessEntity elements at level 1 is described by MetaClass elements at level 2, which are themselves structured according to the abstract syntax defined by the hard-wiring of MOF itself.

The hard-wiring implements the MOF standard.

The hard-wiring at level M3 implements the MOF standard. Thus, given a MOF implementation, it is possible to define a metamodel (at M2). Equipped with this definition, MOF provides standard ways to populate and manipulate M1 models using CORBA interfaces, and to exchange models and metamodels using XMI. A more complete description of the OMG four-layer architecture can be found in David Frankel's book on *Model-Driven Architecture* [Fra03]. A more complete description of the XMI specification is given in [GDB02].

MOF metamodels are created using concepts similar to UML.

The MOF uses concepts similar to the UML. A metamodel is defined by creating a set of classes,[2] together with attributes, associations, and inheritance relationships. Each class defines a concept that can be used in models. So, for example, in an entity-relationship modeling language defined in MOF, there would likely be classes called Element and Relationship. Unlike UML, though, MOF defines precise meanings for its elements. The MOF specification sets out in detail how classes, associations, and attributes are instantiated, including the meaning of the black diamond symbol. This defines precisely the relationship between metamodels at M2, and models at M1. Additionally, the abstract syntax for MOF is in fact defined in terms of itself, which specifies the relationship between M3 and M2.

MOF does not specify the relationship between M1 and M0.

MOF does not say anything about the semantics of models, or the relationship between models and the information that those models represent. In many cases, models do not specify an abstract syntax for the subject matter they describe. For example, a model of a C# or Java program does not define an abstract syntax. Instead, the model corresponds to the program in ways defined by a mapping from the modeling language to the programming language. Neither does a model of a business process define an abstract syntax. Instead, the model elements correspond to business elements in ways defined by the specification of the modeling language. The four-layer architecture can therefore be confusing because the relationship between M1 and M0 is in general quite different from the relationships between the other levels.

According to the Four-layer Modeling Architecture, the UML is defined in terms of MOF. But we said earlier that the UML is defined in terms of UML. So, what is going on? In fact, the first version of the UML was defined in terms of a subset of itself. The first version of MOF was being defined at the same time, and contained similar but not identical concepts. The committee writing UML then published an additional formulation of UML that mapped the UML-based definition into a MOF-based definition. Doing this helped to firm up the definition of the UML abstract syntax (but not its semantics), because MOF is an implementable specification in which the meanings of constructs like the black diamond discussed earlier are given operational definitions by mapping into executable code. Defining the UML in MOF also established a standard way of serializing UML models using XMI.

According to the Four-layer Modeling Architecture, UML is defined in terms of MOF.

In fact, though certainly the best known, the UML is just one of the OMG standard metamodels. The other significant metamodel adopted by the OMG is the Common Warehouse Metadata (CWM™) model, intended to provide a standard way to describe metadata associated with data warehouses. The CWM metamodel shares some common notions with the UML metamodel. In effect, CWM was created by copying and pasting a subset of the UML metamodel, and extending the result. The designers of CWM originally tried to use the UML metamodel verbatim, but found that the classes in the UML metamodel came with too much baggage for their purposes. For example, in the UML metamodel, there is a class called *Classifier*, which is inherited by the definition of UML Class, and by other metaclasses. CWM required such a metaclass to represent database concepts like Table and Dimension. Unfortunately, UML Classifier includes inheritance, which is not valid for Table or Dimension. For this reason, the CWM architects decided not to extend the UML metamodel directly, and created their own similar but different metamodel. CWM itself provides no standard notation, although its conceptual similarities with the UML allow some aspects of the UML notation to be borrowed.

The other significant metamodel adopted by the OMG is the Common Warehouse Metadata (CWM) model.

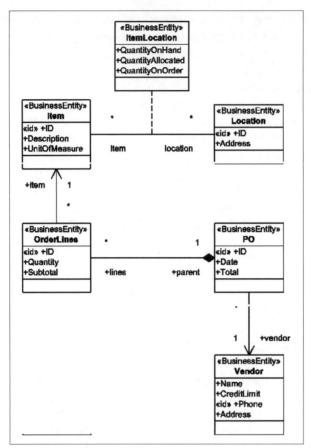

Figure B.3 A back end brokerage system

UML has a set of standard profiles.

Associated with the UML itself is a set of standard *profiles*. A UML profile is a way of configuring the UML definition, so as to specialize its application to a particular domain. This is done by labeling the elements of the model with special labels, called *stereotypes*. An example of a profile is the UML Profile for Enterprise Application Integration (EAI) Systems [OMG formal 04-02-26], which describes UML extensions for modeling things that appear in EAI systems, such as Filters and Operators and Transformers.

Figure B.3 shows how a profile can be used to redefine the UML Class symbol.

The model shown in Figure B.3 demonstrates how the UML Class symbol can be used to represent several different concepts, through the application of a profile. For example, the class symbol with the name Vendor contains the stereotype <<BusinessEntity>>, which declares that the symbol marked Vendor represents a BusinessEntity, instead of a normal

Class. A profile defines a set of stereotypes, and states which UML metaclasses they may decorate, and what extra constraints and properties apply to those metaclasses when decorated in this manner.

There are therefore two alternative ways of defining new abstract syntax using the OMG standards:

Profiles and metamodels are alternatives.

- Defining stand-alone metamodels in MOF

- Defining UML profiles

Indeed, there are standards adopted by the OMG, such as the Software Process Engineering Metamodel [OMG ptc/02-05-04], which provide definitions using both methods, and include a mapping between them. Choosing between these approaches can lead to uncomfortable decisions. It might be attractive to use a UML profile, because this means that existing UML tools will support the new language, in the limited sense of allowing the labels to be placed on the symbols of a UML diagram, as in the example in Figure B.3. Of course, without some means of providing behavior for those symbols, or mappings from those symbols to an implementation language, they will be nothing more than labeled symbols. On the other hand, defining a stand-alone metamodel provides a much more efficient representation of the concepts being defined, and makes it possible to exclude more of the UML definition unrelated to the problem at hand, though usually not all, as illustrated by the problem with the definition of CWM, previously described. In addition, if implementations of the metaclasses can be hosted in a tool, then the metaclasses can have unique behaviors and unique mappings to implementation languages. Also, note that the XMI format for a stand-alone metamodel and for a UML profile that emulates the metamodel are completely different.

It would obviously be desirable to create a UML profile for Java, where UML constructs are mapped onto Java constructs. At first sight this would seem to be a straightforward proposition, since UML and Java are both object-oriented languages. But consider, for example, UML `Interface`. It is defined as follows in the UML 1.5 specification (paraphrased).

It would obviously be desirable to create a UML profile for Java, where UML constructs are mapped onto Java constructs.

An interface describes the externally visible operations of a class, component, or other classifier, without specification of internal structure. Each interface may specify a subset of the behavior of an actual classifier. Interfaces do not have implementations. They lack attributes, states, and associations. They only have operations. Interfaces may have generalization relationships. An interface is formally equivalent to an abstract class with no attributes and no methods and only abstract operations.

UML Interface cannot model Java or C# interfaces.

From this definition, UML `Interface` seems to describe interfaces offered by classes, such as C# or Java interfaces. Unfortunately, however, it cannot be used to model Java interfaces, because they can contain static variables that should be modeled as `Attribute`. So, to define a UML profile for Java, it is necessary either to violate the well-formedness constraints of the UML specification, or to ignore the existing UML concept when defining the corresponding Java concept and use something else, instead, defeating the purpose of the mapping. C# interfaces are even more interesting, because they can contain properties, events, delegates and other features that cannot be completely described even by UML `Class`.[3]

The structure of UML inhibits reuse of its parts.

The basic difficulty is what we referred to earlier. UML is in fact no more than an abstract syntax and notation. It claims to have a reusable semantics, but in practice does not. However, in claiming to have semantics, it has been designed in such a way as to drastically restrict the ways in which it can be successfully applied. We have seen some examples here. CWM could not reuse the abstract syntax of UML because it carried too much baggage. Language profiles cannot reuse the abstract syntax of UML because it is over specified.

What changes are required to make UML more useful?

The UML would be much more usable as a basis for defining domain specific languages if it were explicitly designed as a reusable abstract syntax, with fewer basic concepts, fewer restrictions on how these concepts may be related to each other, and better-developed mechanisms for language extension.

It is possible to construct a domain specific language using MOF, but the available facilities are meager.

Of course, we could ignore UML and define domain specific languages using MOF, following the example of CWM. However, all that MOF provides is a way to define abstract syntax, using basic class inheritance to reuse parts of language definitions. There are no facilities for defining concrete syntax, no facilities for specifying semantics, and no mechanisms for model composition. MOF does not support the kind of language assembly we described in Chapter 8. Furthermore, the serialization mechanism (XMI) suffers from the brittleness of representation problems discussed in Chapter 8, which means that there are increasing numbers of XMI formats out in the marketplace; in the case of UML, one XMI format for every possible combination of the XMI version and the UML meta-model version.

Model-Driven Architecture

In 2001, the OMG introduced a new brand called MDA®: Model Driven Architecture®, as an umbrella for the set of modeling technologies positioned around UML and MOF. The essence of MDA lies in making a distinction between two types of UML based models, Platform-Independent Models (PIMs) and Platform-Specific Models (PSMs). In theory, to build an application using MDA, one would first build a PIM, using an appropriate UML profile, to define the application in a platform-independent manner. One would then find and apply a standard mapping for the target platform, to transform the PIM into a PSM, also based on a profile. Finally, one would generate code for the target platform from the PSM.

In 2001, the OMG introduced MDA.

According to the executive overview on www.omg.org/mda, MDA claims to assure the following benefits:

MDA makes big claims.

- Portability, increasing application reuse and reducing the cost and complexity of application development and management, now and into the future.

- Cross-platform interoperability, using rigorous methods to guarantee that standards based on multiple implementation technologies all implement identical business functions.

- Platform independence, greatly reducing the time, cost and complexity associated with retargeting applications to different platforms—including those yet to be introduced.

- Domain specificity, through domain specific models that enable rapid implementation of new, industry-specific applications over diverse platforms.

- Productivity, by allowing developers, designers, and system administrators to use the languages and concepts they prefer, while allowing seamless communication and integration among them.

MDA is essentially proposing UML as a new universal programming language.

These are big claims. The trouble with them is that the technology is insufficient to bring them about. The idea that UML lies at the heart of MDA is essentially equivalent to proposing UML as a new universal programming language that can be compiled onto every platform. This is very reminiscent of the "write-once, run-anywhere" principle used to promote the Java programming language. There are two main reasons why this will not work for UML.

The semantic distance from UML to any existing platform is too big for effective mapping.

- For any platform, there must be a mapping from the concepts in the language to the concepts supported by the platform. In the case of simple data types, such as integers or strings, it is often possible to do this reasonably efficiently because of similarities between platforms. In the case of more complex types, however, such as the elements of a graphical user interface, starting with platform-independent model and mapping to a platform-specific can create performance penalties, usability issues and other problems that make the results unacceptable to users.

The UML is not a programming language.

- More seriously, the UML is not a programming language. Since it does not have well-defined semantics, as we have seen, anything that purports to be a UML "program" has no guarantee of meaning the same thing on every platform. Any vendor implementing the MDA will need to augment and modify the definition of UML substantially, in order to make it executable. See [MB02], for example, where the authors develop an executable variant of UML, and explicitly spurn various aspects of the standard that don't serve their purpose. This means that any two implementations of MDA based on UML will be significantly different. It is hard to see how this solves problems of portability and interoperability in any way. Furthermore, although UML is not specified precisely enough to be usable as a programming language, neither is it specified flexibly enough to provide suitable building blocks for defining domain specific languages.

We have shown that attempting to use UML as a universal application development language is unworkable, as currently specified. We hope that we have set out a compelling alternative to MDA in the rest of this book.

UML 2

No discussion of UML would be complete without some consideration of version 2, which at the time of writing is undergoing its finalization phase. The need for a new version of UML was identified through a Request for Information issued by the OMG in 1999. A large number of responses were received from both vendors and users of UML. They identified numerous improvements desired by the UML community. These responses were distilled into four Requests for Proposal, covering UML Infrastructure, UML Superstructure, OCL, and UML Diagram Interchange.

UML 2 is being finalized as we go to press.

The last of these is the easiest to explain. Before UML 2 there was no standard way to interchange UML diagrams; only instances of the abstract syntax could be represented using XMI. The existence of the diagram interchange standard makes it possible also to serialize the layout of UML diagrams, which is clearly a very useful capability. The OCL development is a modest improvement on the original OCL, extending its capabilities and also defining an abstract syntax graph for the language itself.

UML 2 Diagram Interchange serializes diagram layout.

The UML Infrastructure RFP is primarily about aligning the core of the UML, i.e., those parts that are used to describe the UML, with the MOF. Here the UML 2 development hit some fundamental problems, which it unfortunately failed to solve. We have already observed that the semantics of UML are imprecise, and indeed must be so in order to make the language flexible enough to be widely useful. We gave the simple examples of the black diamond and UML `Interface`. Another example is the definition of visibility. In UML 2, this is given semantics similar to the Java language, although these semantics are inappropriate for other languages, such as C#, C++ or Eiffel. These are just a few examples of where flexibility is missing. There are many others. The fundamental problem is that MOF requires the meanings of these notions to be precisely and operationally defined, while UML requires these meanings to be highly flexible. By proposing to use the same definition for both of these applications, the UML 2 effort has gone in

The UML 2 Infrastructure aligns the core of UML with MOF, which creates some problems.

diametrically the wrong direction if its goal was to make UML a suitable basis for defining domain specific languages. If, on the other hand, MOF had been defined as just one of many alternative possible semantics corresponding to a flexible UML abstract syntax, then the UML 2 Infrastructure could have been made more useful.

The UML 2 Superstructure expands the original UML sub languages.

The UML Superstructure RFP is primarily about expanding the original UML sub languages, such as state machines, activity graphs, sequence diagrams, and class diagrams. It has taken from 1999 until 2003 to bring the UML 2 definition process to the point where a single proposal has been accepted by the OMG to take forward for adoption. The accepted UML 2 proposal incorporates many ideas from the International Telecommunications Union's SDL definition (see www.sdl-forum.org), which is widely used in the telecommunications industry. Each of the sublanguages in UML 2 is considerably richer and more complex than in UML 1. Unfortunately, like UML 1, UML 2 claims to define precise semantics, but does not. The informal semantics in the definition are written in often impenetrable English, and there are no mechanisms provided to verify conformance with these definitions. The OCL constraints used to define well-formedness in UML 2 are of variable quality, untested, and frequently erroneous. UML 2 permits the definition of a large number of possible "compliance points", which allow the implementation of almost arbitrary subsets of the language. This makes the interchange of UML models between tools even more difficult, unless the tools happen to implement identical subsets.

UML 2 does not cover every aspect of software development.

Even though UML 2 is quite large, it does not cover some important aspects of software development. Data modeling can be simulated using class diagrams, but this is a poor substitute for a well-designed data modeling language. Imperative languages like COBOL are poorly supported, and there are no facilities for user interface modeling.

UML is not an appropriate foundation for defining DSLs.

In its role as the standard notation for documenting and communicating object-oriented concepts, UML 2 represents a useful incremental extension to UML 1. However, it remains poor at representing specific programming languages and platform technologies. In summary, although its notation is and will continue to be a valuable resource for informal communication of object-oriented designs, UML is not an appropriate formal foundation for defining domain specific languages that drive automated software development processes.

Notes

1. Sometimes we refer rather formally to "The UML"; mostly we refer just to UML.
2. MOF classes are often called metaclasses, although this can be misleading because in programming language contexts a metaclass is a class whose instances are classes. A MOF class is a class whose instances are model elements; one kind of model element might be a class.
3. UML 2.0 will permit interfaces to have attributes, helping with the Java mapping problem, but does not address the C# problems.

Bibliography

[2U03] 2U Submitters. Submission to UML 2.0 Infrastructure RFP, http://www. 2uworks.org. 2003.

[Aal99] W. Aalst. Process-Oriented Architectures For Electronic Commerce And Inter-Organizational Work-Flows. Information Systems No. 8, Vol. 24, pp. 639–671. Elsevier, 1999.

[ABM97] I. Aaen, P. Bøttcher, L. Mathiassen. The Software Factory: Contributions and Illusions. Proceedings of the Twentieth Information Systems Research Seminar in Scandinavia, Oslo, 1997.

[ACM01] D. Alur, J. Crupi and D. Malks. *Core J2EE Patterns, Best Practices and Design Strategies*. Sun Microsystems Press, 2001. ISBN 0-13-064884-1.

[AIS77] C Alexander, S. Ishikawa, and M. Silverstein. *A Pattern Language*. Oxford University Press, 1977.

[AK02] D. H. Akehurst, S. Kent. "A Relational Approach to Defining Transformations in a Metamodel." In J.-M. Jézéquel, H. Hussmann, S. Cook (Eds.): UML 2002—The Unified Modeling Language 5th International Conference, Dresden, Germany, September 30–October 4, 2002. Proceedings LNCS 2460, 243-258, 2002.

[Ale79] C. Alexander. *The Timeless Way of Building*. Oxford University Press, 1979.

[Amb02] S. Ambler. *Agile Modeling: Effective Practices for eXtreme Programming and the Unified Process*. Wiley Publishing, Inc., 2002.

[App03] H. Apperly, et al. *Service- and Component-based Development: Using the Select Perspective and UML*. Addison-Wesley, 2003.

[AS96] H. Abelson, G. Sussman, and J. Sussman. *Structure and Interpretation of Computer Programs. 2nd edition*. MIT Press, 1996. ISBN 0-26-201153-0.

[AT93] V. Ambriola and G. Tortora (eds). *Advances in Software Engineering and Knowledge Engineering*. World Scientific Publishing Company, 1993.

[Atk02] C. Atkinson, et al. *Component-based Product Line Engineering with UML*. Addison-Wesley, 2002.

[AW01] K. Aberer and A. Wombacher. A Language For Information Commerce Processes. Third International Workshop on Advanced Issues of E-Commerce and Web-based Information Systems San Jose, California, USA, June 21-22, 2001.

[Bal75] R. Balzer. Imprecise Program Specification. Report ISI/RR-75-36, Information Science Institute, December 1975.

[Bat93] D. Batory, V. Singhal, M. Sirkin, J. Thomas. *Scalable Software Libraries.* ACM SIGSOFT, 1993.

[Bau89] F. Bauer, B. Möller, H. Partsch, P. Pepper. Formal Program Construction By Transformations—Computer Aided, Intuition Guided Programming. IEEE Trans. Soft. Eng., Vol. 15, No. 2, February 1989.

[BCRWxx] D. Batory, G. Chen, E. Robertson, T. Wang. Design Wizards and Visual Languages for Generators. In *IEEE Transactions on Software Engineering,* May 2000, pp. 441–452.

[Bec99] K. Beck. *Extreme Programming Explained: Embrace Change.* Addison-Wesley, 1999. ISBN 0201616416.

[Ber82] H. Berg, W. Boebert, W. Franta, T. Moher. *Formal Methods Of Program Verification And Specification.* Prentice Hall, 1982.

[Ber04] G. Berrisford. Eight Ways to Ossify an Agile Project. Private Communication.

[BJMH01] D. Batory, C. Johnson, B. MacDonald, D. von Heeder. Achieving Extensibility Through Product-Lines and Domain-Specific Languages: A Case Study. In Proceedings of the 25th International Conference On Software Engineering. Portland, Oregon, 2003. pp. 753–754 ISBN: 0270-5257, 0-7695-1877-X.

[Boe81] B. Boehm. *Software Engineering Economics.* Pearson Education, 1981. ISBN: 0138221227.

[Boo94] G. Booch. *Object Oriented Analysis and Design With Applications.* Second Edition. Addison-Wesley, 1994.

[Boo95] G. Booch. *Object Solutions—Managing the Object Oriented Project.* Addison-Wesley, 1995. ISBN 0805305947.

[Bos98] J. Bosch. "Design Patterns as Language Constructs." *Journal of Object Oriented Programming* (JOOP), May 1998.

[Bos00] J. Bosch. *Design and Use of Software Architectures: Adopting and evolving a product-line approach.* Addison- Wesley, 2000.

[Bow03] Bowstreet Factory. Bowstreet Inc. http://www .bowstreet.com.

[Bow53] B. Bowden (ed.) Faster Than Thought: A Symposium on Digital Computing Machines. New York, 1953.

[BPEL] http://www-106.ibm.com/developerworks/webservices/library/ws-bpel/.

[BPSS] ebXML Business Process Specification Schema Version 1.01, http://www.ebxml.org/specs/index .htm#technical_specifications.

[Bre98] E. Brewer. Dictionary of Phrase and Fable. 1898.

[Bro87] F. Brooks. "No Silver Bullet: Essence and Accidents of Software Engineering." *Computer Magazine,* 1987.

[Bus00a] F. Buschmann. Applying Patterns. http://www.cs.wustl.edu/
~schmidt/PDF/applying-patterns.pdf.

[Bus00b] F. Buschmann. Inside Patterns. http://www.cs.wustl.edu/~schmidt/
PDF/inside-patterns.pdf.

[BW01] "America's Future: The Tech Challenge." *Business Week*, August 27, 2001,
pp. 140–144.

[Car04] Carr, Nicholas, "Does IT Matter: Information Technology and the
Corrosion of Competitive Advantage", Harvard Business School Press, 2004.

[CBDi] http://www.cbdiforum.com

[CD94] S. Cook and J. Daniels. *Designing Object Systems: Object-Oriented Modelling
with Syntropy.* Prentice Hall, 1994.

[CE00] K. Czarnecki and U. Eisenecker. *Genererative Programming: Methods, Tools,
and Applications.* Addison-Wesley, 2000.

[CEK02] A. Clark, A. Evans and S. Kent. "A Metamodel for Package Extension
with Renaming." In J.-M. Jézéquel, H. Hussmann, S. Cook (Eds.): UML
2002—The Unified Modeling Language 5th International Conference, Dresden,
Germany, September 30–October 4, 2002. Proceedings LNCS 2460, 305-320,
2002.

[CEK03] A. Clark, A. Evans and S. Kent. "Aspect-Oriented Metamodelling." In
Aspect-Oriented Programming and Separation of Crosscutting Concerns,
Special issue of the Computer Journal, Vol. 46, No. 5, 2003.

[CEK+00] A. Clark, A. Evans, S. Kent, S. Brodsky and S. Cook. A feasibility study
in rearchitecting UML as a family of languages using a precise OO metamodeling approach. Available from www.puml.org, September 2000.

[Chr97] C. Christensen. *The Innovator's Dilemma.* Harvard Business School Press,
1997.

[Civ93]. F. Civello. Roles for composite objects in object-oriented analysis and
design. Proceedings of OOPSLA'93. ACM Sigplan Notices Vol. 28, No. 10.
October 1993.

[CKPW95] S. Cohen, R. Krut, S. Peterson, J. Withey. *Models for Domains and
Architectures: A Prescription for Systematic Software Reuse.* American Institute of
Aeronautics and Astronautics, 1995.

[Cle01] J. Cleaveland. Program Generators with XML and Java. Prentice Hall.,
2001. ASIN: 0130258784.

[CLIPS] Available from a number of sites. See http://www-2.cs.cmu.edu/afs/cs/
project/ai-repository/ai/areas/expert/systems/clips/0.html

[CN01] P. Clements and L. Northrop. Software Product Lines: Practices and
Patterns. Addison-Wesley, 2001. ISBN: 0201703327

[Coc00] A. Cockburn. *Writing Effective Use Cases.* Addison-Wesley, 2000.

[Coc01] A. Cockburn. Agile Software Development. Addison-Wesley, 2001.

[Coe00] F. Coenen. 2CS24—Topics in Information Processing: Declarative
Languages. University of Liverpool, http://www.csc.liv.ac.uk/~frans/
OldLectures/2CS24/declarative.html.

[Con99] J. Conallen. *Building Web Applications with UML.* Addison-Wesley,
1999.

[Coo00] S. Cook. The UML Family: Profiles, Prefaces and Packages. Proceedings of UML2000, edited by A. Evans, S. Kent and B. Selic. 2000, Springer-Verlag LNCS.

[Coo99] A. Cooper. *The Inmates Are Running the Asylum*. Sams Publishing, 1999. ISBN 0-672-31649.

[Cop99] J. Coplien. Multi-paradigm design. In Proceedings of the GCSE '99 (co-hosted with the STJA 99).

[Cox90] B. Cox. "Planning the Software Industrial Revolution." *IEEE Software Magazine*, November 1990.

[Cox95] B. Cox. "No Silver Bullet Revisted." *American Programmer Journal*, November 1995.

[CHE04] K. Czarnecki, S. Helsen, U. Eisenecker. Staged Configuration Using Feature Models. Proceedings Of Software Product Line Conference 2004.

[CW99] *Computer World*, October 11, 1999.

[CY90] P. Coad and E. Yourdon. *Object-Oriented Analysis*. Yourdon Press/Prentice Hall, 1990.

[DF01] B. Dupire and E. Fernandez. The Command Dispatcher Pattern. Proceedings Of PLoP 2001 Conference.

[Dij76] E. Dijkstra. *A Discipline of Programming*, Prentice Hall, 1976.

[DSI] Dynamic Systems Initiative Overview. http://www.microsoft.com/windowsserversystem/dsi/dsioverview.mspx

[DublinCore] http://dublincore.org/resources/faq/.

[Due97] A. Van Duersen and P. Klint. Little Languages: Little Maintenance? Proc. First ACM SIGPLAN Workshop on Domain-Specific Languages, 1997.

[DW98] D. D'Souza and A. Wills. *Objects, Components And Frameworks With UML*. Addison-Wesley, 1998.

[Dso02] D. S'Souza. http://www.catalysis.org/publications/papers/2001-mda-reqs-desmond-6.pdf.

[EBXML] http://www.ebxml.org

[ECOOP94] M. Tokoro, R. Pareschi (eds.). Object Oriented Programming. Proceedings of the 8th European Conference on Object Oriented Programming, Springer-Verlag, 1994.

[EHK02]. P. Eeles, K. Houston and W. Kozaczynski. *Building J2EE Applications with the Rational Unified Process*. Addison-Wesley, 2002. ISBN 0201791668.

[EMF] The Eclipse Modeling Framework. www.eclipse.org/emf.

[EP00] H. Eriksson and M. Penker. Business Modeling with UML. Wiley Publishing, Inc., 2000.

[Fin00] A. Finkelstein (ed.). *The Future of Software Engineering*. ACM Press, 2000. ISBN 1-58113-253-0.

[Flo78] R. Floyd. The Paradigms of Programming. Communications of the ACM. Vol. 22, No. 8, 1978.

[FMW97] G. Florijn, M. Meijers, P. van Winsen. Tool support for object-oriented patterns. Florijn97tool.pdf.

[Foo88] B. Foote. Domain Specific Frameworks Emerge As A System Evolves. Workshop on the Methodologies and Object-Oriented Programming, OOPSLA '88, September 1988.

[Fow99] M. Fowler. *Refactoring, Improving The Design Of Existing Code*. Addison-Wesley, 1999. ISBN 0-201-48567-2.

[Fow03] M. Fowler. Patterns of Enterprise Application Architecture. Addison-Wesley, 2003.

[FRFH+] M. Fowler, D. Rice, M. Foemmel, E. Hieatt, R. Mee, R. Stafford. *Patterns of Enterprise Application Architecture*. Addison Wesley, 2002. ISBN 0321127420.

[Fra00] D. Frankel. UML Profiles and Model-Centric Architecture. Java Report, June 2000, Vol. 5, No. 6, pp. 110–118.

[Fra03] D. Frankel. *Model-Driven Architecture*. OMG Press/Wiley Publishing, Inc., 2003.

[FS97a] M. Fayad and D. Schmidt. Object-Oriented Application Frameworks. Communications of the ACM 40, 10, 1997.

[FS97b] M. Fowler and K. Scott. *UML Distilled: Applying the Standard Object Modeling Language*. Addison-Wesley, 1997.

[FY96] B. Foote and J. Yoder. Evolution, Architecture and Metamorphosis. *See* [PLOPD2].

[FY99] B. Foote and J. Yoder. Big Ball Of Mud. *See* [PLPOD4].

[Gan04] http://www.gantthead.com/default.cfm.

[GAO94] D. Garlan, R. Allen, J. Ockerbloom. Exploiting Style in Architectural Design Environments. Proceedings of the Second ACM SIGSOFT Symposium on Foundations of Software Engineering, Software Engineering Notes, ACM Press, December 1994.

[GAO95] D. Garlan, R. Allen, J. Ockerbloom. Architectural Mismatch: Why Reuse Is So Hard. IEEE Software 12, 6, 1995.

[Gar95] D. Garlan. What Is Style? Proceedings of Dagstuhl Workshop on Software Architecture, February 1995.

[Gar96] D. Garlan. Style-Based Refinement for Software Architecture. Proceedings of the Second International Software Architecture Workshop, 1996.

[Gar00] D. Garlan. Software Architecture: a Roadmap. *See* [Fin00].

[GDB02] T.J. Grose, G.C. Doney and S.A.Brodsky. *Mastering XMI*. OMG Press/Wiley Publishing, Inc., 2002.

[GHJV95] E. Gamma, R. Helm, R. Johnson and J. Vlissides. *Design Patterns, Elements of Reusable Object-Oriented Software*. Addison-Wesley, 1995. ISBN 0-201-63361-2.

[GMW97] D. Garlan, R. Monroe, D. Wile. Acme: An Architecture Description Interchange Language. Proceedings of CASCON'97, 1997.

[GP95] D. Garlan and D. Perry. Introduction to the special issue on software architecture. IEEE Transactions on Software Engineering, 21(4), April 1995.

[Gra92] R. Grady. *Practical Software Metrics for Project Management and Process Improvement*. Prentice Hall, 1992.

[Gra93] I. Graham. *Object Oriented Methods*. Second edition. Addison-Wesley, 1993.

[Gru00] J. Grundy. Multi-Perspective Specification, Design And Implementation Of Software Components Using Aspects. International Journal of Software Engineering and Knowledge Engineering, Vol. 10, No. 6, December 2000, World Scientific Publishing Co.

[GS93] D. Garlan and M. Shaw. An introduction to Software Architecture: Advances in Software Engineering and Knowledge Engineering, Volume I. World Scientific Publishing, 1993.

[GS93] D. Garlan and M. Shaw. An introduction to software architecture. *See* [AT93].

[GS01] A. Gordon and D. Syme. "Typing a multilanguage intermediate code." In Conference Record of POPL 2001: The 28th ACM SIGPLAN-SIGACT Symposium on Principles of Programming Languages, pp. 248–260. ACM Press, 2001.

[Ham02] C. Hamlin. "Formal Platform-based Design Would Tame Risks, Costs of Complexity."*EE Times*, November 25, 2002.

[Ham90] M. Hammer. "Reengineering Work: Don't Automate, Obliterate". Harvard Business Review, July-August 1990.

[HB01] J. Hegel and J.S. Brown. Your Next IT Strategy, Harvard Business Review. October, 2001.

[HW03] G. Hohpe and B. Woolf. *Enterprise Integration Patterns*. Addison-Wesley, 2003.

[Hen02] M Henning. Computing Fallacies or: What is the World Coming To. Presentation to OMG Plenary, OMG document omg/01-07-02.

[Hew77] C. Hewitt. Smalltalk-80: Control Structures as Patterns of Message Passing. Artificial Intelligence, Vol. 8, pp. 323-363. 1977.

[HHG90] R. Helm, I. Holland, D. Gangopadhyay. Contracts: Specifying Behavioral Compositions in Object-Oriented Systems, Proceedings of ECOOP/OOPSLA 1990.

[Hoa85] C. Hoare. *Communicating Sequential Processes.* Prentice Hall, 1985.

[Hoa87] C. Hoare. The Emperor's Old Clothes. 1980 Turing Award Lecture, reprinted in ACM Turing Award Lectures. ACM Press, 1987.

[Hol91] G. Holzmann. *Design and Validation of Computer Protocols.* Prentice Hall, 1991.

[Hor99] I. Horrocks. *Constructing the User Interface with Statecharts.* Addison-Wesley Professional, 1999. ASIN: 0201342782.

[HS00] P. Herzum and O. Sims. *Business Component Factory: A Comprehensive Overview of Component Based Development for the Enterprise.* Wiley Publishing, Inc., 2000. ISBN 0-471-32760-3.

[IEEE 1471] 1471–2000 IEEE Recommended Practice for Architectural Description for Software–Intensive Systems. ISBN 0-7381-2519-9.

[IOTP] http://www.oasis-open.org/cover/otp.html

[Iro03] The Iron Speed Designer. Iron Speed Inc. http://www.ironspeed.com.

[ISO 10746-2] Information Technology—Open Distributed Processing—Reference Model. Part 2: Foundations, ISO/IEC 10746-2:1996[A2] http://www.iso.org.

[ISO/IEC 10165-7] ISO/IEC JTC1/SC21, Information Technology, Open Systems Interconnection— Management Information Services—Structure of Management Information—Part 7: General Relationship Model, 1995. ISO/IEC 10165-7.

[IW01] T. Sullivan. "Web Services." *Info World*, Vol. 23, issue 11, March 12, 2001.

[JBR99] We. Jacobson, G. Booch, and J. Rumbaugh. *The Unified Software Development Process.* Addison-Wesley, 1999. ISBN 0-201-57169-2.

[Jacoo] M. Jackson. *Problem Frames: Analyzing and Structuring Software Development Problems.* Addison-Wesley, 1999.

[Jac04] I. Jacobson. A Resounding Yes to Agile Process–but also to More. http://www.jaczone.com/papers/.

[JCJ+92] I. Jacobson, M. Christerson, P. Jonsson, G. Övergaard. *Object-Oriented Software Engineering: a Use Case Driven Approach.* Addison-Wesley, 1992.

[Jen92] K. Jensen. *Coloured Petri Nets.* Springer, 1992.

[Jen98] M. Jenkins. *Abstract Data Types in Java.* McGraw-Hill, 1998.

[JF88] Ralph E. Johnson and Brian Foote. Designing Reusable Classes. Journal of Object-Oriented Programming, Vol. 1, No. 2, pp. 22-35. June/July 1988.

[JGJ97] I. Jacobson, M. Griss and P. Jonsson. *Software Reuse: Architecture, Process and Organization for Business Success.* ACM Press, 1997.

[Joh92] R. Johnson. Documenting Frameworks Using Patterns. ACM SIGPLAN Notices, Vol. 27, No. 10.

[Joh97] R. Johnson. Frameworks = (Components + Patterns). Communications of the ACM 40, 10 (1997).

[Jon80] C. Jones. *Software Development: A Rigorous Approach.* Prentice Hall, 1980.

[Jon86] C. Jones. *Systematic Software Development Using VDM.* Prentice Hall, 1986.

[JSR26] Java Specification Request 26, Java Community Process, http://jcp.org/jsr/detail/26.jsp.

[JSR40] Java Specification Request 40, Java Community Process, http://jcp.org/jsr/detail/40.jsp.

[KC04] http://www.kc.com/cgi-bin/download.cgi?action=ctn/CTN_27v3_0.pdf.

[KGR99] S. Kent, S. Gaito, and N. Ross. A meta-model semantics for structural constraints in UML. In H. Kilov, B. Rumpe, and I. Simmonds, editors, Behavioral specifications for businesses and systems, chapter 9, pp. 123–141. Kluwer Academic Publishers, September 1999.

[Kie96] R. Kieburtz, et al. A Software Engineering Experiment in Software Component Generation. International Conference on Software Engineering, 1996.

[Kis02] I. Kiselev. *Aspect-Oriented Programming with AspectJ.* Sams Publishing, 2002.

[KLM97] G. Kiczales, J. Lamping, A. Mendhekar, C. Lopes, J. Loingtier, J. Irwin. Aspect Oriented Programming. Proc. European Conf on Object Oriented Programming. M. Aksitand S. Matsuoka (eds.). Spinger-Verlag, 1997.

[KMF] Kent Modeling Framework (KMF). www.cs.kent.ac.uk/kmf

[KR94] H. Kilov and J. Ross. *Information Modeling: An Object-Oriented Approach.* Prentice Hall, 1994.

[Kru00] P. Kruchten. *The Rational Unified Process: An Introduction, 2nd Edition.* Addison-Wesley, 2000.

[KSLB03] Gabor Karsai, Janos Sztipanovits, Akos Ledeczi, and Ted Bapty, "Model-Integrated Development of Embedded Software", Proceedings of the IEEE, Vol 91, No. 1, January 2003.

[Kuh70] T. Kuhn. *The Structure Of Scientific Revolutions*. The University Of Chicago Press, 1970.

[Lar99] C. E. Larson. Intelligent machinery and mathematical discovery. http://www.math. uh.edu/~clarson/, October 1, 1999.

[Lat01] A. Latva-Koivisto, Finding a complexity measure for business process models, Research Report, Helsinki University Of Technology.

[LB94] H. Lee and C. Billington. "Designing Products and Processes for Postponement" in S. Dasu and C. Eastman (eds.) Management of Design: Engineering and Management Perspectives (Kluwer, Boston 1994), pp. 105–122.

[LMB+01] A. Ledeczi, M. Maroti, A. Bakay, G, Karsai, J, Garrett, C. Thomason, G. Nordstrom, J. Sprinkle and P. Volgyesi. The Generic Modeling Environment. Proceedings of IEEE Workshop on Intelligent Signal Processing, Budapest, Hungary, May 2001.

[Lon03] London Transport bus route "spider maps" can be found at http://www. londontransport.co.uk/buses/route_maps.shtml, where one can also compare them to street plans of London.

[Lat01] A. Latva-Koivisto. Finding a complexity measure for business process models. Research Report, Helsinki University of Technology.

[LB94] H. Lee and C. Billington. "Designing Products and Processes for Postponement" in S. Dasu and C. Eastman (eds.) *Management of Design: Engineering and Management Perspectives* , pp. 105-122. Kluwer, 1994.

[LMB+01] A. Ledeczi, M. Maroti, A. Bakay, G, Karsai, J, Garrett, C. Thomason, G. Nordstrom, J. Sprinkle and P. Volgyesi. The Generic Modeling Environment. Proceedings of IEEE Workshop on Intelligent Signal Processing. Budapest, Hungary, May 2001.

[LSOW] K. Lau, L. Shaoying, M. Ornaghi, A. Wills. Interacting Frameworks in Catalysis, Proc. Second IEEE Int Conf on Formal Engineering Methods, pp. 110-119. IEEE Computer Society Press, 1998.

[LRV98] N. Lassing, D. Rijsenbrij, J.C. van Vliet. A View On Components. In Proceedings of International Workshop on Business Process Reengineering And Supporting Technologies For Electronic Commerce, pp. 768–777. IEEE Computer Society Press, Vienna, Austria, 1998.

[Mah90] M. Mahoney. The Roots Of Software Engineering. CWI Quarterly Vol. 3, No. 4 (1990).

[Man 97] http://csweb.cs.bgsu.edu/maner/domains/RAD.htm.

[MB02] S.J. Mellor and M.J.Balcer. *Executable UML: a Foundation for Model-Driven Architecture*. Addison-Wesley, 2002.

[MDA FAQ] http://www.omg.org/mda/faq_mda.htm/.

[MDR] Netbeans Meta-Date Repository (MDR).mdr.netbeans.org

[MEY] B. Meyer. *Object-Oriented Software Construction, Second Edition*. Prentice Hall, 1997.

[Mil99] R. Milner. *Communicating and Mobile systems: the π-calculus*. Cambridge University Press, 1999.

[MO92] J. Martin and J. Odell. *Object-Oriented Analysis and Design*. Prentice Hall, 1992.

[Mon74] R. Montague. "Universal Grammar." In R.H. Thomason (ed). *Formal Philosophy: Selected papers of Richard Montague.* Yale University Press, 1974.

[Moo02] G. Moore. *Crossing the Chasm.* HarperBusiness, 2002. ISBN: 0060517123.

[MR97] N. Medvidovic and D. Rosenblum. Domains of Concern in Software Architectures and Architecture Description Languages. Proceedings of the 1997 USENIX Conference on Domain-Specific Languages.

[MSA EDC] http://www.microsoft.com/resources/documentation/msa/edc/all/solution/en-us/intromsa.mspx.

[MSA IDC] http://www.microsoft.com/resources/documentation/msa/idc/all/solution/en-us/pag/pag.mspx.

[MSDN04] Microsoft Patterns and Practices. Integration Patterns. http://www.msdn.microsoft.com/patterns.

[MSDN UIP] http://msdn.microsoft.com/library/defalt.asp?url=/library/en-us/dnpag/html/uipab.asp.

[MS03] Microsoft Patterns and Practices. Enterprise Solution Patterns Using Microoosft.NET. Microsoft Press, 2003.

[MTAL] S. Mellor, S. Tokey, R. Arthaud and P. LeBlanc. Software-Platform-Independent, Precise Action Specifications for UML. OMG document ad/98-08-03.

[NM01] E. Naiburg and R. Maksimchuk. *UML for Database Design.* Addison-Wesley, 2001.

[NRB76] P. Naur, B. Randell, J.N. Buxton (eds.). *Software Engineering: Concepts and Techniques.* Petrocelli/Charter, 1976.

[OASIS] http://www.oasis-open.org/home/index.php

[OMG ad/01-08-04] UML Action Semantics Revised Final Submission. OMG document ad/01-08-04.

[OMG ad/01-08-19] UML Profile for EDOC Final Submission, OMG document ad/01-08-19.

[OMG ad/01-10-08] UML 2.0 Superstructure Initial Submission, DSTC Pty Ltd., OMG document ad/01-10-08.

[OMG ad/03-04-01] Unified Modeling Language Superstructure, version 2.0, OMG document ad/03-04-01.

[OMG formal/00-04-03] MetaObject Facility (MOF) Specification, v1.4. OMG document formal/00-04-03.

[OMG formal/01-12-45] CORBA 2.6, Chapter 7, "Dynamic Invocation Interface," CORBA Specification. OMG formal/01-12-45.

[OMG formal/01-12-55] CORBA 2.6, Chapter 17, "Interworking Architecture," OMG document formal/01-12-55.

[OMG formal/01-12–56] CORBA 2.6, Chapter 18, "Mapping COM and CORBA," OMG document formal/01-12-56.

[OMG formal/01-12–57] CORBA 2.6, Chapter 19, "Mapping OLE Automation and CORBA," OMG document formal/01-12-57.

[OMG formal/02-01-01] XML Metadata Interchange Specification (XMI) Version 1.2, OMG document formal/02-01-01.

[OMG formal/03-03-01] OMG Unified Modeling Language Specification, v1.5. OMG document formal/03-03-01.

[OMG formal/04-03-26] UML profile for Enterprise Application Integration (EAI), v1.0. OMG document formal/04-03-26.

[OMG orbos/99-07-02] CORBA Component Model, OMG document orbos/99-07-02.

[OMG ptc/01-01-06] UML Profile for CORBA, Version 1.1, OMG document ptc/01-01-06.

[OMG ptc/01-08-22] Meta Object Facility Specification Version 1.4, OMG document ptc/01-08-22.

[OMG ptc/01-09-03] Common Warehouse Metamodel Specification Version 1.1, Part 1, OMG document ptc/01-09-03.

[OMG ptc/01-09-04] Common Warehouse Metamodel Specification Version 1.1, Part 2, OMG document ptc/01-09-04.

[OMG ptc/01-12-03] XMI Production for XML Schema Specification, OMG document ptc/01-12-03.

[OMG ptc/02-05-04] Software Process Engineering Metamodel Specification, OMG document ptc/02-05-04.

[OMG ptc/04-01-10] Human-Usable Text Notation (HUTN) Specification, v1.0. OMG document ptc/04-01-10.

[OMG U2 DIAG] UML 2.0 Diagram Interchange Work In Progress, http://www.omg.org/techprocess/meetings/schedule/UML_2.0_Diagram_Interchange_RFP.html

[OMG U2 INFRA] UML 2.0 Infrastructure Work In Progress, http://www.omg.org/techprocess/meetings/ schedule/UML_2.0_Infrastructure_RFP.html

[OMG U2 OCL] UML 2.0 OCL Work In Progress, http:// www.omg.org/techprocess/meetings/schedule/UML_2.0_OCL_RFP.html

[OMG U2 SUPER] UML 2.0 Superstructure Work In Progress, http://www.omg.org/techprocess/meetings/schedule/UML_2.0_Superstructure_RFP.html

[Par72] D. Parnas. On the Criteria to be Used in Decomposing a System into Modules. Communications of the ACM. ACM Press, December 1972.

[Par76] D. Parnas. On the Design and Development of Program Families. IEEE Transactions on Software Engineering, March 1976.

[Par94] D. Parnas. Software Aging. IEEE Proceedings of the 16th International Conference on Software Engineering, 1994.

[PLOPD2] J. Vlissides, J. Coplien, and N. Kerth (eds.). *Pattern Languages Of Program Design 2*. Addison-Wesley, 1996.

[Por95] M. Porter. "Competitive Advantage". Ch. 1, pp. 11–15. New York: The Free Press, 1985

[POSA1] F. Buschmann, R. Meunier, H. Rohnert, P. Sommerlad, M. Stal. *Pattern-Oriented Software Architecture, Volume 1. A System Of Patterns*. Wiley Publishing, Inc., 1996.

[POSA2] D. Schmidt, M. Stal, H. Rohnert., F. Buschmann. *Pattern-Oriented Software Architecture, Volume 2. Patterns for Concurrent and Networked Objects*. Wiley Publishing, Inc., 2000.

[Pre94] W. Pree. Meta Patterns—A Means For Capturing The Essentials Of Reusable Object-Oriented Design. *See* [ECOOP94]

[Pre96] W. Pree. *Framework Patterns*. Addison-Wesley, 1996.

[PW92] D. Perry and A. Wolf. Foundations for the study of software architecture. ACM SIGSOFT Software Engineering Notes, 17(4), October 1992.

[Rac95] L. Racoon. The Complexity Gap. SIGSOFT Software Engineering Notes, 20(3), July 1995.

[RAS] http://www.rational.com/ras.

[RBP+91] J. Rumbaugh, M. Blaha, W. Premerlani, F. Eddy and W. Lorensen. *Object-Oriented Modeling and Design*. Prentice Hall, 1991.

[Ree96] T. Reenskaug. *Working with Objects*. Manning, 1996.

[RJ96] D. Roberts and R. Johnson. Evolving Frameworks: A Pattern Language for Developing Object-Oriented Frameworks. Proceedings of Pattern Languages of Programs, Allerton Park, Illinois, September 1996.

[ROSETTA] http://www.rosettanet.com.

[RUP02] http://www.rational.com/rup.

[San02] A. Sangiovanni-Vincentelli. Defining platform-based design. EEdesign, http://www.eedesign.com/ story/OEG20020204S0062.

[SARA] R. Kazman, et. al. Report on Software Architecture Review and Assessment. February 5, 2002. http://www.cgl.uwaterloo.ca/~rnkazman/ SARA/

[Sch04] J. Schmitz. Supply Chain Management. http://www-mmd.eng.cam.ac. uk/csp/One_Page_ Summary/Supply-Chain.htm.

[SC00] D. Schmidt and C. Cleeland. Applying a Pattern Language to Develop Extensible ORB Middleware. In Design Patterns In Communications Software. pp. 393–438. Cambridge University Press, 2001.

[SC96] M. Shaw and P. Clements. Toward Boxology: Preliminary Classification of Architectural Styles. Proceedings of the Second International Software Architecture Workshop, 1996.

[SFS02] D. Shukla, S. Fell, C. Sells. "Aspect Oriented Programming Enables Better Code Encapsulation and Reuse." *MSDN Magazine*, March 2002. http://msdn .microsoft.com/msdnmag/issues/02/03/AOP/default.aspx.

[SG96] M. Shaw and D. Garlan. *Software Architecture: Perspectives On An Emerging Discipline*. Prentice Hall, 1996.

[SJF96] D. Schmidt, R. Johnson, M. Fayed. Software Patterns. Communications of the ACM, Special Issue on Patterns and Pattern Languages, Vol. 39, No. 10, October 1996.

[Sim99] C. Simonyi. IP and Disruptive Technologies (1999). http://www. research.microsoft.com/ip/May99/ Disrupt.htm.

[SM88] S. Shlaer and S.J. Mellor. *Object-Oriented Systems Analysis—Modeling the World in Data*. Yourdon Press/Prentice Hall, 1988.

[SM91]. S. Shlaer and S.J. Mellor. *Object-Lifecycles—Modeling the World in States*. Yourdon Press/Prentice Hall, 1991.

[Sma97] Y. Smaragdakis and D. Batory. DiSTiL: a Transformation Library for Data Structures. USENIX Conf. on Domain-Specific Languages, 1997.

[SOPD] Subject Oriented Programming and Design Patterns. IBM Thomas J. Watson Research Center, Yorktown Heights, New York. http://www.research .ibm.com/sop/sopcpats.htm.

[SS02] J. Smith and D. Stotts. Elemental Design Patterns—A Link Between Architecture and Object Semantics. Proceedings of OOPSLA 2002.

[Syz99] C. Szyperski. *Component Software: Beyond Object-oriented Programming.* Addison-Wesley, 1999.

[Tay95] D. Taylor. *Business Engineering with Object Technology.* Wiley Publishing, Inc., 1995. ISBN: 0471045217.

[Tay97] D. Taylor. *Object Technology: A Manager's Guide.* Addison-Wesley, 1997. ISBN: 0201309947.

[Ver99] C. Verhoef. Software Development is a Special Case of Maintenance. http://adam.wins.uva.nl/~x/sea/sea.html.

[Vli93] H. van Vliet. *Software Engineering: Principles And Practice.* Chichester: John Wiley & Sons Ltd., 1993.

[W3C] World Wide Web Consortium. http://www.w3.org/.

[W3C DOM] Document Object Model. http://www.w3.org/DOM/.

[W3C MEP] http://www.w3.org/2002/ws/cg/2/07/meps.html.

[W3C RDF] Resource Description Framework. http://www.w3.org/RDF/.

[W3C SW] Semantic Web. http://www.w3.org/2001/sw/.

[W3C OWL] Web Ontology Language. http://www.w3.org/TR/2004/REC-owl-features-20040210/.

[War] J. Warmer and A. Kleppe. *The Object Constraint Language: Precise Modeling with UML.* Addison Wesley, 1998. ISBN 0-20-137940-6.

[Wat91] D. Watt. *Programming Language Syntax and Semantics.* Prentice Hall, 1991.

[Wat93] D. Watt. *Programming Language Processors.* Prentice Hall, 1993.

[Weg78] P. Wegner. Research Directions In Software Technology. Proceedings Of The 3rd International Conference On Software Engineering. 1978.

[WK99] J. Warmer and A. Kleppe. *The Object Constraint Language: Precise Modeling with UML.* Addison-Wesley, 1999.

[WL99] D.M. Weiss, C.T. Robert Lai. *Software Product-Line Engineering.* Addison-Wesley, 1999.

[WS-I] Web Services Interoperability Organization. http://ws-i.org/.

[Yod97] J. Yoder. A Framework for Financial Modeling. Proceedings of OOPSLA 97.

Index